Quicken® All-in-One Desk Reference For Dummies

Keyboard Shortcuts (For Those Bad Mouse Days)

To Do This	*Type This*
Open the Account List	Ctrl+A
Open the Category List	Ctrl+C
Delete a transaction or a split line	Ctrl+D
Find a transaction	Ctrl+F
Insert a transaction	Ctrl+I
Open the Scheduled Transaction list	Ctrl+J
Memorize a transaction or report	Ctrl+M
Print whatever you're looking at	Ctrl+P
Open the Split Transaction window	Ctrl+S
Copy a field in the register	Ctrl+Ins
Cut a field in the register	Shift+Del
Paste a field in the register	Shift+Ins
Close the Split Transaction window	Ctrl+Enter
Get Help	F1

Quick Tricks for Typing Dates

To Choose This Date	*Type This*
Today	T
The next day	+
The previous day	-
First day of the month	M
Last day of the month	H
First day of the year	Y
Last day of the year	R
The date of your choice	Ctrl+G

For Dummies: Bestselling Book Series for Beginners

Quicken® All-in-One Desk Reference For Dummies®

Cheat Sheet

Using Quicken's Little Calculator

Use your mouse or the numeric keypad to work the calculator.

Quicken's calculator is found on the Tools menu and also as an icon in numeric entry fields. Here are some tips for working with the calculator:

- Click <- to remove one digit at a time from the accumulator.
- Click CE to clear the current entry.
- Click C to clear the entire current calculation.
- Click . to enter a decimal point.
- Click Paste to copy the current number into the numeric field in Quicken.
- Click the X in the corner or press Esc to close the calculator.

Your Daily Bread: Daily Quicken Tasks to Keep your Finances in Order

- Enter all of the checks you wrote today
- Enter all of the debits and charges you made
- Enter all of the money you deposited today
- Enter your ATM transactions
- Update your accounts and portfolio with One Step Update
- Examine your year-to-date budget versus actual comparison report

For Dummies: Bestselling Book Series for Beginners

Quicken® ALL-IN-ONE DESK REFERENCE FOR DUMMIES®

by Gail A. Perry, CPA

WILEY

Wiley Publishing, Inc.

Quicken® All-in-One Desk Reference For Dummies®

Published by
Wiley Publishing, Inc.
111 River Street
Hoboken, NJ 07030-5774

www.wiley.com

Published by Wiley Publishing, Inc., Indianapolis, Indiana

Published simultaneously in Canada

For general information on our other products and services, please contact our Customer Care Department within the U.S. at 800-762-2974, outside the U.S. at 317-572-3993, or fax 317-572-4002.

For technical support, please visit www.wiley.com/techsupport.

Wiley also publishes its books in a variety of electronic formats. Some content that appears in print may not be available in electronic books.

Library of Congress Control Number: 2005931147

ISBN-13: 978-0-471-75466-4

ISBN-10: 0-471-75466-8

Manufactured in the United States of America

10 9 8 7 6 5 4 3 2 1

1O/SX/RS/QV/IN

WILEY

About the Author

Gail A. Perry is a licensed CPA, financial journalist, author, speaker, and instructor. Gail prides herself on her ability to present technical subjects in plain English and often with a touch of humor. Gail is a contributing editor at *Accounting Today* magazine, the premiere business newspaper for the tax and accounting community. Gail is a former senior tax accountant with the Big Four accounting firm, Deloitte, where she provided tax planning services and financial advice to individuals and small businesses. She continues to maintain a tax and financial consulting practice for about 50 clients.

An accomplished freelance writer, Gail is the author of 18 books and coauthor of several more on various aspects of personal finance, taxation, and financial software. Some of her titles include *Surviving Financial Downsizing: A Practical Guide to Living Well on Less Income*, *Show Me QuickBooks*, *TurboTax: The Official Guide*, and *TurboTax For Dummies*. She has also written hundreds of articles for newspapers, magazines, and financial Web sites, and was a weekly tax columnist for five years for the *Indianapolis Star* and *Indianapolis News* daily newspapers.

Gail is a former college accounting instructor and has been teaching adult computer classes (including Quicken) since the mid-1980s. She currently teaches an online personal finance course. She has a bachelor's degree in journalism and English from Indiana University.

Dedication

This book is dedicated to Katherine and Georgia, with all my love.

Author's Acknowledgments

I'm the lucky person whose name goes on the cover of this book, but that doesn't begin to tell the real story. Behind the scenes, many, many people worked as a team to put the *Quicken All-in-One Desk Reference For Dummies* together. Some of the key players, who deserve special recognition, include Bob Woerner, who rode herd over all of us, Linda Morris, for her intelligent and sensitive editing, David Ringstrom, who made sure that everything I describe in this book works as I describe it, and the clever and hardworking people in Composition Services, Graphics, and Indexing who are responsible for designing the finished product.

Publisher's Acknowledgments

We're proud of this book; please send us your comments through our online registration form located at www.dummies.com/register/.

Some of the people who helped bring this book to market include the following:

Acquisitions, Editorial, and Media Development

Project Editor: Linda Morris

Acquisitions Editor: Bob Woerner

Copy Editor: Linda Morris

Technical Editor: David Ringstrom

Editorial Manager: Jodi Jensen

Media Development Supervisor: Richard Graves

Editorial Assistant: Amanda Foxworth

Cartoons: Rich Tennant (www.the5thwave.com)

Composition Services

Project Coordinator: Maridee Ennis

Layout and Graphics: Andrea Dahl, Denny Hager, Joyce Haughey, Lynsey Osborn, Heather Ryan, Erin Zeltner

Proofreaders: David Faust, Carl Pierce, Linda Quigley

Indexer: Steve Rath

Publishing and Editorial for Technology Dummies

Richard Swadley, Vice President and Executive Group Publisher

Andy Cummings, Vice President and Publisher

Mary Bednarek, Executive Acquisitions Director

Mary C. Corder, Editorial Director

Publishing for Consumer Dummies

Diane Graves Steele, Vice President and Publisher

Joyce Pepple, Acquisitions Director

Composition Services

Gerry Fahey, Vice President of Production Services

Debbie Stailey, Director of Composition Services

Contents at a Glance

Table of Contents

Book III: Investments 201

Book VI: Retirement Planning and Other Saving 455

Chapter 1: The Quicken Financial Planner 457

Introduction

I have a few paragraphs here to tell you what makes this book different from other Quicken books and to encourage you to add this book to your library. I've been a devoted Quicken user since the 1980s. Sometimes I wonder how I managed to keep track of my finances at all before Quicken came along. I can't think of a better way to remain totally aware of all aspects of my personal finances than by using this program.

Not only does Quicken provide you with an electronic storage area for all of your bank account transactions — and trust me, saving more than 10 years worth of financial data in one place, with easy access to comparative reports and charts is not something you can re-create out of the boxes of cancelled checks gathering dust in your closet — but the program is so much more than that.

Quicken is an investment tracker, a retirement planner, a home budget minder, a bill payer, a monitor for credit cards, a business organizer, a tax saver, and, oh yeah, a bank account supervisor — all rolled into one neat little package. And using Quicken, you feel like you have a firm grip on all of the numbers that flow through your accounts.

But there's another side to Quicken: financial savvy. Not only do you want to know how much money you have in the bank and in your investment accounts, but you also want to know how you're going to plan for the use of that money 10, 20, or 30 years from now. Maybe you want to send your kids to college, save for your retirement, buy a house, or experiment with the stock market. Or you want to raise your credit rating, take a trip every now and then, keep your bills under control, and still pay your taxes.

With the help of this book, you can look at the big picture. You can stop tracking results of past financial activities and start planning for the results you want to see in your financial future. "A personal finance manifesto" is how my editor and I described this book when we first discussed the vision we had: a book that would transcend the "how-to" and delve into the "why" of financial record-keeping.

I hope you find that this book has lived up to that vision. And I hope you decide to add this book to your library.

About This Book

The *Quicken All-in-One Desk Reference For Dummies* is a reference book, not meant to be read in any particular order. Just as you would pick up a gardening book and look to the Table of Contents and the Index for the particular flowers or shrubs about which you want to know more, I envision you picking up this book and seeking a path to the financial topics you want to study.

You'll notice that, unlike many other Quicken books on the market, this book does not refer to a specific version of the Quicken program. Although I've used the most up-to-date version of the program for my illustrations and examples, I've tried to make the book all-encompassing and useful to owners of any version of Quicken. After all, the rules for basic data entry in Quicken programs over the years have changed very little. I've tried to encompass that continuity and produce a book that can be read by more than the small group who happened to purchase the current model.

When it comes to finding your way around, I hope you'll refer to the Table of Contents and the Index extensively, as they have been constructed with logic and significance in mind. They should lead you directly to the parts of the book that provide you with the information you need.

I strived to avoid redundancy in this book, and yet there are certainly times when one topic requires material from another topic to make an explanation understandable. In these cases, I included cross-references to other parts of the book where you can flip to if you want related or, in some cases, more in-depth information.

Foolish Assumptions

I made only a handful of assumptions about the readers of this book (that means you). I don't make any assumptions at all about the state of your personal finances. And I don't expect you to be financial experts, CPAs, CFOs, AARPs, PETAs, Republicans, Army veterans, or members of any other group. I *do* expect the following:

- You have some finances. Maybe you have a checking account, a savings account, and a retirement plan at work. Maybe you are thinking about buying some stock. Maybe you're worried about being able to afford college or wondering how you'll ever survive when you want to retire. It doesn't matter what kind of financial scenario you have; it only matters that you have some money that you want to keep track of.

- You have a PC with enough memory to run Quicken. An Internet connection is handy but not an absolute necessity.
- You own or are about to acquire a version, any version, of Quicken, and you plan to use that program to keep track of your finances.

That's it.

How This Book Is Organized

The *Quicken All-in-One Desk Reference For Dummies* is a compendium of eight separate books, each covering a completely different aspect of Quicken and personal finances. The minibooks all get along together and freely talk about each other behind their respective backs, but you might find that some books are more to your liking than others, and nobody's going to mind if that happens. Here's a rundown of what you can expect in each of the books.

Book I: Personal Finance Basics

I take back everything I said about your needing to have Quicken. You don't even need Quicken for Book I: This is all about finances and nothing about computers. The idea behind Book I is to get you up to speed on a variety of basic areas of personal finance — areas that can then be translated into Quicken in later books. This personal finance minibook provides you with essential information about earning and spending your money, borrowing money, improving your credit score, budgeting, shopping for insurance, and saving for college and retirement.

Book II: Quicken Basics

It doesn't matter if you've never used Quicken before. Book II provides all the basic how-to information necessary for setting up your finances in Quicken and learning the ropes. You discover how to install Quicken, set up your bank accounts, enter transactions, and reconcile your bank account. You also find out about the world of online banking and how to get your own accounts set up for online services, if that interests you.

Book III: Investments

One of the main reasons people purchase Quicken software is to track their investments. In Book III, you see how to do just this. You can enter all of your investment holdings in Quicken, monitor the performance of your investments, and even use Quicken to keep an eye on investments you're considering for future purchases.

Book IV: Household Finances

Discover how you can use Quicken to help keep your debt to a minimum, stay on top of your credit card spending, reconcile your credit card accounts, save money on your mortgage, and keep track of your personal belongings for insurance purposes. Find out about Quicken's online bill payment services, and see how you can create a budget that really works.

Book V: Taxes

You're going to love owning Quicken when it comes time to prepare your tax return. Book V shows you how to enter information in Quicken that can be readily transferable to your tax return. No more burning the midnight oil in mid-April. Your tax return can be completed in January if you take advantage of the tax features offered in Quicken. See how to produce reports that provide the information you need for your tax return, and, if you like, find out how you can transfer your Quicken data right over to TurboTax to produce your tax return right on your own computer. Tax-planning tips round out this book that is all about individual income taxes.

Book VI: Retirement Planning and Other Saving

In Book VI, you see how to monitor your retirement saving in Quicken and receive some basic planning tools to help determine how much money you need for retirement, and how long it's going to take you to acquire that money. You also get familiar with the rules for withdrawing money from your tax-deferred retirement accounts and find out about receiving Social Security benefits and other joys of retirement. Book VI also presents information about saving for college, including 529 plans and other long-term savings opportunities.

Book VII: Quicken Reports

One of the primary reasons for using Quicken is to assemble all of your financial information in such a way that it can be easily accessed. When you produce reports in Quicken, you provide the tools for real financial planning and analysis. Find out about the standard reports that come with Quicken and how those reports can be useful to you. Then discover how you can customize Quicken's reports so that you get the exact information you need to make informed decisions about your finances.

Book VIII: Small Business Finances

Quicken is the first choice of many small businesses when it comes to tracking business finances. You can create customer invoices in Quicken, prepare estimates and track individual job performance, record and track accounts receivable and accounts payable, generate a payroll for your employees, record fixed assets, and produce reports that show you how your business is doing.

Appendixes

These tips and tools really relate to all of your Quicken use, so I decided to create a series of appendixes on the Web for this information. The Web site for *Quicken All-in-One Desk Reference For Dummies,* which is located at `www.dummies.com/go/quickenaio`, includes the following appendixes:

- **Backing Up Data:** Find out how to back up data on-site and off-site, and about online storage of your backed-up data files.
- **Aggravating Things About Quicken:** I love the program, but that doesn't mean Quicken is perfect. Here are a few of my pet peeves, and an opportunity for you to submit your own.
- **Resources for Personal Finance:** The Internet is full of outstanding resources for personal financial information. Here are a few noteworthy and useful sites.
- **Getting Help with Quicken:** If you're looking for answers to sticky questions, and can't find them here, try the variety of support sources offered by Intuit, the folks who brought you Quicken.

Icons Used in This Book

Watch for these little pictures; they point the way to important information as you go along.

TIP

Tips can help you work smarter and faster. Look for the Tip icon to tell you short cuts and easy ways to make your Quicken experience more fun and more productive.

REMEMBER

This icon saves you the trouble of digging out your yellow highlighter. The Remember points are important little tidbits that I want to make sure you don't overlook.

WARNING!

If you neglect to pay attention to these bits of important information, I get to say, "I told you so!" when things go wrong!

TECHNICAL STUFF

These technical points tell you why Quicken is doing what it's doing, or why certain rules exist. There's not a lot of nerdy technical information in this book, but where it exists, I've tried to set it aside with this icon.

Where to Go from Here

Well, try turning the page. Dig into the Table of Contents and see what looks interesting. But wait! First head back to the very first page and put your name inside the front cover. Take ownership of your book! Feel free to dog-ear pages, scribble in margins, and highlight the daylights out of the points you feel are important. Most of all, enjoy using this book, enjoy using Quicken, and good luck with your future of excellent financial planning!

Book I

Personal Finance Basics

"I'm not sure – I like the mutual funds with rotating dollar signs although the dancing stocks and bonds look good too."

Contents at a Glance

Chapter 1: Earning Income and Investing

In This Chapter

- **Earning income from your job**
- **Getting income from a job you invented**
- **Collecting earnings from your savings and investments**

Fanny Price, the protagonist of Jane Austen's novel *Mansfield Park*, knew a thing or two about income: She said, "A large income is the best recipe for happiness I ever heard of." The information presented in this chapter may not guarantee you happiness or a large income, but you figure out the ins and outs of where income comes from and how to keep track of it all. And that, at least, is a good first step in a recipe for managing your personal finances.

Making Money at Your Job

Work. We spend our childhood merrily going to school, playing in the yards of our youth, practicing scales and etudes, pitching balls on sandlots, making and losing friends, collecting our allowance money, getting tucked in at night, and doing it all over again, day after endless day. When we're really little, the concept of *work* is limited to something our parents do when we're not looking. Later, work gets thrown in our face as an empty threat: "Someday you'll have to work for a living, and then you'll understand . . . ."

Then comes the day when the allowance ends, there are no more exams, the yards all need mowing, the piano keys are dusty, the sandlots have been turned into parking garages, and our friends have moved on. Seemingly overnight, that idyllic youth is replaced with the need to *go out and earn a living*, whatever that is. So we choose a path, master some skills, and get a job, taking our place in a society of worker-bees. We collect our paychecks, and do our jobs all over again, day after endless day, with the goal of amassing enough green stuff so we can enjoy our time off, buy things that make us happy, have a cool place to live, and with luck, have enough left over so we don't starve in our old age.

Not only do you have to fund your lifestyle with the money you get from your job(s), but you have to keep track of it all, make sure there's enough to pay the bills, and figure out how to finance the larger expenses in life. It may seem like a daunting task, but trust me, the task is even more daunting if you leave it to chance. Fortunately, you can follow the paper trail explained in this chapter to keep track of all the money you earn from various sources, and then use the nifty Quicken program, explained throughout the rest of this book, to keep up-to-date financial information only a few clicks away.

Filling out the W-4 form

One of the first tasks you perform whenever you start a new job is the chore of filling out the W-4 form, shown in Figure 1-1. W-4 is another name for Employee's Withholding Allowance Certificate. You use this form to advise your employer, and more particularly the person who writes the checks at your place of employment, of useful details such as

- The correct spelling of your name
- Your real address
- Your date of birth, so they can schedule the appropriate office party (just kidding)
- Your unique Social Security number, so that your paychecks made out to Dolores Schnazeldorf won't get mixed up with the checks for that other Dolores Schnazeldorf down the hall
- Your marital status, so people know whether to invite you to the singles parties
- The number of allowances you are claiming
- Any extra amount above and beyond the regular tax amount that you want your employer to send to Uncle Sam on your behalf

Back up to that one about the allowances because that's the item that usually throws people for a loop. You can use one of four methods to decide what number to put on this line:

- Pick a number that sounds reasonable.
- Calculate the number using the Personal Allowances Worksheet that comes with the W-4 form.
- If you don't like the result you get on the Personal Allowances Worksheet, you can use the Deductions and Adjustments Worksheet.
- If all else fails and you're not yet hopelessly confused, you can use the Two-Earner/Two-Job Worksheet.

All of these worksheets come with the W-4 form, so you don't have to go anywhere to find them. Here's a summary of how each of these methods works.

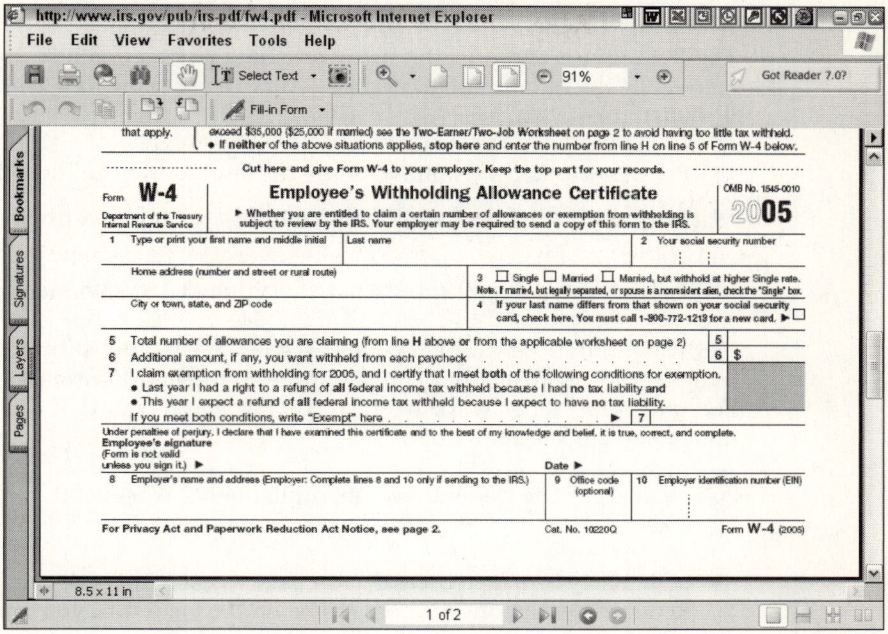

http://www.irs.gov/pub/irs-pdf/fw4.pdf - Microsoft Internet Explorer

File Edit View Favorites Tools Help

that apply. exceed $35,000 ($25,000 if married) see the Two-Earner/Two-Job Worksheet on page 2 to avoid having too little tax withheld.
• If neither of the above situations applies, stop here and enter the number from line H on line 5 of Form W-4 below.

Cut here and give Form W-4 to your employer. Keep the top part for your records.

Form **W-4** Department of the Treasury Internal Revenue Service

Employee's Withholding Allowance Certificate

▶ Whether you are entitled to claim a certain number of allowances or exemption from withholding is subject to review by the IRS. Your employer may be required to send a copy of this form to the IRS.

OMB No. 1545-0010 2005

1 Type or print your first name and middle initial | Last name | 2 Your social security number

Home address (number and street or rural route) | 3 ☐ Single ☐ Married ☐ Married, but withhold at higher Single rate. Note. If married, but legally separated, or spouse is a nonresident alien, check the "Single" box.

City or town, state, and ZIP code | 4 If your last name differs from that shown on your social security card, check here. You must call 1-800-772-1213 for a new card. ▶ ☐

5 Total number of allowances you are claiming (from line H above or from the applicable worksheet on page 2) 5

6 Additional amount, if any, you want withheld from each paycheck 6 $

7 I claim exemption from withholding for 2005, and I certify that I meet both of the following conditions for exemption.
• Last year I had a right to a refund of all federal income tax withheld because I had no tax liability and
• This year I expect a refund of all federal income tax withheld because I expect to have no tax liability.
If you meet both conditions, write "Exempt" here ▶ 7

Under penalties of perjury, I declare that I have examined this certificate and to the best of my knowledge and belief, it is true, correct, and complete.
Employee's signature (Form is not valid unless you sign it.) ▶ Date ▶

8 Employer's name and address (Employer: Complete lines 8 and 10 only if sending to the IRS.) | 9 Office code (optional) | 10 Employer identification number (EIN)

For Privacy Act and Paperwork Reduction Act Notice, see page 2. Cat. No. 10220Q Form W-4 (2005)

8.5 x 11 in 1 of 2

Figure 1-1: A sample W-4 form.

Choosing a reasonable number of allowances

If you've "been there, done that" for a few jobs already, this W-4 form is nothing new to you, so just fill out the number of allowances you always claim, and turn in your form so you can start collecting your paychecks.

Using the Personal Allowances Worksheet

The Personal Allowances Worksheet is an easy fill-in-the-blank worksheet where you answer some simple questions about whether you have children and a spouse, and which options you plan to choose on your tax return this year. Based on your answers in this worksheet and your responses to a quick Rorschach test, you find out if you get the corner office or a damp room in the basement. All kidding aside, you add up the numbers on the right side of this worksheet, and the total is the maximum number of allowances you are supposed to claim on your W-4.

TIP

Keep in mind that this is a maximum number. You don't have to claim all those allowances. If you would rather have more tax withheld, you can go with a smaller number of allowances. Some people like to get a fat refund when they file their tax return in the spring, and, in the spirit of Fanny Price, that's not necessarily a bad thing. So if your worksheet tells you to claim six allowances and you only want to claim three, claim three. The IRS will be happy because they get more of your money to play with during the year.

Using the Deductions and Adjustments Worksheet

The Deductions and Adjustments Worksheet gives a different approach to increasing the number of allowances you can claim on your W-4 form. This is designed for

- ✦ People who take advantage of the tax laws to itemize their deductions
- ✦ People who reduce their income on their tax return with adjustments or credits
- ✦ People who actually know what everything I just said means

Math is required for this worksheet — you have to add, subtract, and divide to figure out the form. And you're supposed to enter information from the Personal Allowances Worksheet, so go back and fill out that worksheet, and then come back here.

Follow along in the Deductions and Adjustments Worksheet, noting these key issues:

- ✦ Step 1 may be a deal-breaker: You have to estimate how much your total itemized deductions are going to be on the tax return you prepare next spring. So, if you're filling out the W-4 form in January 2006, you have to guess what your itemized deductions will be on the tax return that you're going to prepare in April 2007. Go ahead; take a stab. Use an old tax return and round the numbers up or down, depending on what seems right. You only need a ballpark figure here.
- ✦ Do some math, and then you get to step 4, where you have to estimate the adjustments that will be on that tax return you file a year from now. Adjustments include alimony you have to pay, deductible contributions you make to an Individual Retirement Account (see Book VI for more on this), deductible moving expenses (more on this in Book V), health insurance costs, and one-half of your self-employment tax if you're self-employed, interest paid on student loans, and tuition and school fees you may be deducting. The best way to estimate all of this is to repeat what you reported for adjustments on last year's tax return.
- ✦ For step 6, you need to estimate any taxable income you expect to earn this year that is not from your job. This includes the boring income like dividends and interest, as well as the edgier sorts of income such as jury duty fees, fees for sitting on some company's board of directors, income you earn (or amounts you lose) from second guessing (or not) the stock market, income from illegal activities that you plan to report on your tax return, and so on.
- ✦ The rest is math. Do the calculations, and then take the final number and use it for your W-4 allowances. Or not. If you and your spouse both have jobs, or if you have another job, or if you're just a glutton for punishment, move on to the Two-Earner/Two-Job worksheet.

Using the Two-Earner/Two-Job Worksheet

You've made it this far, and you're still trying to figure out what number of allowances to put on that pesky W-4. You're probably rethinking the whole job idea at this point, but hang on — you're nearly finished. Soon you'll start collecting paychecks and amassing great wealth.

Even greater math skills are required to fill out this worksheet because now you get to subtract, divide, *and* multiply, and you get to compare numbers and take the lowest, or the highest, depending on which way the wind is blowing, and you're no doubt thanking your parents for pushing you to take those higher math courses in high school.

If you haven't figured it out yet, the various worksheets that accompany the W-4 form are designed to

(a) confuse the living daylights out of you

(b) persuade you to go to court and change your name to something other than Dolores Schnazeldorf

and

(c) provide a rough estimate of how your tax withholding should be computed in order to come pretty close to the actual amount of tax you will owe for the year.

So do the best you can, and don't fret if your calculation isn't perfect. If you're worried about owing tax on your tax return, do the worksheets, and then subtract 1 from your final number, just to have a little extra withheld so you'll be safe.

TIP

If you start getting paychecks and your personal situation changes in such a way that your answers on those worksheets might be different, ask your employer for another W-4 form and start all over again. You can change your withholding at any time during the year.

Your paycheck

People just starting out in the workforce are always shocked when they see their first paycheck. That large amount of money they were expecting to receive from their job is depleted by income taxes, Social Security taxes, Medicare taxes, "benefits" that the employee has to pay for, and more.

The *pay stub* that comes with your check breaks down all of the various amounts that have been taken from your earnings. The key elements to notice are as follows:

- **Gross pay** (or Total Wages, or Salary, or some similar description — usually the top line on your pay stub): This is the amount you earned from all of your hard work. It's nowhere near the amount you see on your check, but this is what you started with before your employer withheld money to pay for all the other stuff.
- **Federal income tax:** This is the amount that goes to Uncle Sam.
- **Social Security (or FICA):** This is the other amount that goes to Uncle Sam.
- **Medicare:** This is yet another amount that goes to Uncle Sam.
- **State income tax:** This is the amount that goes to Uncle Sam's little helper.
- **Deductions:** This area can include amounts for union dues, health insurance, life insurance, contributions to a flex plan, or pretty much anything else your employer offers that you are allowed to pay for from your paycheck.

Usually your pay stub provides information about your current paycheck and also year-to-date totals, so you can see at a glance how much you've given to the government so far this year and how much you've been allowed to keep.

Benefits you get at work

A job comes with all sorts of benefits. Not only do you get paid real money (after taxes) to do what you love, but, depending on the type of job you have, you may get a fancy uniform to wear, special tools to play with, built-in friends to share coffee and gossip with every day, a free place to park, a big truck to drive, free food, a cubicle to decorate with pictures of your pets, or the occasional trip to faraway places like Des Moines or Pittsburgh to attend free training.

Some benefits are called benefits even though you pay for them. This type of benefit is often billed as a tax-free benefit, which means that you get to pay for the benefit, but the amount you pay gets deducted from your gross pay when it comes to figuring out how much income tax you owe.

Here are some important things to keep in mind regarding the tax-free benefits you get at work:

- The benefits recorded on your pay stub represent amounts paid for certain perks that are offered by your employer. Every employer offers different types of benefits (some employers don't offer anything), so this section of your pay stub varies from job to job.

- ✦ You probably can't take a deduction for the cost of the benefits on your tax return. If you have a certain amount withheld from your paycheck for health insurance, for example, chances are excellent that no tax is being withheld on this amount. When you prepare your tax return next year, you can't deduct the amount you paid for health insurance because the income you report on your tax return (see the section entitled "The W-2 form" later in this chapter) has already been reduced by the amount you paid for health insurance. In effect, you've already deducted the health insurance, and deducting it on your tax return would amount to deducting the health insurance twice.
- ✦ On the other hand, some deductions from your pay are not taken out before taxes and do indeed generate a tax deduction. Contributions to organizations such as United Way are a good example of amounts that appear on your pay stub that you can also deduct on your tax return. Union dues are another.
- ✦ The benefits you see on your pay stub may not appear on your W-2 form at the end of the year. The pay stub may be the only place where you see how much you've spent on the various goodies offered at work. So don't just toss the pay stub in the trash. Use this stub to record and keep track of how much money you have paid for the various benefits. In particular, hang on to the last stub of the year because it shows you the year-end totals of all of your payments.

Bonus time

Some businesses pay bonuses to their employees in addition to the regular pay. The IRS expects you to keep track of the bonus you receive and, of course, share a little bit of it with the federal government.

To make this whole sharing process easier, many employers simply withhold tax on the bonuses they give. It's common for employers to withhold a flat 25 percent income tax from the bonus amount. Trust me, it's kind of a let-down to have the boss tell you your hard work was worth an extra $500 bonus but here's a check for only $375.

Some bonuses are small enough that the IRS is actually willing to let you keep the entire bonus without sharing anything. These bonuses fall under the general heading of, "Turkeys, Hams, and Other Items that are Difficult to Tax." The IRS rules specifically state that employees whose excellent service to their employer resulted in a bonus of a turkey or ham or "other item of small or nominal value" do not have to report the value of such gifts on their tax returns, nor does the employer have to withhold a portion of the gift to send to the government.

You're relieved, I'm sure, to know that you don't have to cut off one of the turkey legs and package it up for delivery to the fine folks at the IRS. However, if instead of a turkey or ham or other item that is difficult to tax, your boss decides to give you cash, or worse yet, a gift certificate or some tickets to an athletic event that you might be able to easily convert to cash, it's your responsibility to report the value of such a gift on your tax return, "regardless of the amount involved."

The W-2 form

Each January, every employer you worked for in the previous year is required to send you a W-2 form. The W-2, or Wage and Tax Statement, summarizes all of the money you earned from that job in the year that just ended, along with all of the taxes you paid and sometimes other information.

Every job, no matter how minimal the pay, is a catalyst for a W-2 form at the end of the year. Even if your entire job consisted of one midnight to 6 a.m. shift as the night waitress at the Hour House Café, and your total wages for the night were only $8.00 (not counting the $.36 in tips you received and not taking into account the cost of the shoes you had to replace when a drunken customer threw up on your feet), you still should expect a W-2 form from the employer. If you move during the year, be sure to contact employers you worked for earlier in the year, even if you never want to speak to them again because they wouldn't pay to replace your shoes, and let them know your new address.

The W-2 form should include the same information that appeared on your last pay stub for the year, so there shouldn't be any surprises.

What to do if the dog eats your W-2 form

You can try your best to hang on to that W-2 form, but sometimes uncontrollable forces are at work, like vacuum cleaners, overzealous housekeepers, children who need to apply their artistic skills, and yes, underfed or drooling dogs.

Fortunately, you can easily circumvent many of life's little mishaps, and in the case of W-2 forms, it's a snap. First of all, if you're only missing one copy of the W-2 form, just photocopy one of the remaining pages. For example, if you lose Copy B of the W-2, the page that's supposed to go with your federal tax return, photocopy Copy C or Copy 2, and attach that to your tax return instead.

If all the copies of your W-2 form are lost or destroyed, call the payroll department at your place of employment and ask that they make you a copy of the W-2 form. There's no magnetic ink on these forms, nor does the color matter, so a photocopy is an easy solution.

If all else fails, copy the income and withholding information from your last pay stub of the year onto a piece of paper, include your name and Social Security number, and attach that to your tax return along with a statement saying the original was lost or destroyed.

The information on your W-2 is used when you prepare your income tax return. In fact, as you probably know if you've ever filed an income tax return, the IRS asks that you attach the W-2 form to your tax return, so don't throw this form away when it comes in the mail.

You're Self-Employed: You've Created Your Own Job!

Just because you don't work as an employee for someone else, doesn't mean for a minute that you don't have to keep track of your income and the amounts you spend for your job. In fact, the record-keeping chore can be rather overwhelming if your work entails getting income from lots of places and buying lots of things for your job.

The advantages of working for yourself and basically creating your own job can sometimes be overshadowed by the paperwork, the sporadic nature of your income, and the sheer personal responsibility for making the job a success. If you've got the bug to work for yourself, here are some points to keep in mind when it comes to tracking your finances.

Getting paid

When you are self-employed, it's up to you to stay on top of how much you earn, where that money is coming from, and how quickly you receive your payments. A record-keeping system is imperative so that you don't lose track of money owed to you. If your business involves customers who don't always pay in a timely fashion, you should develop some sort of collection system so that you not only know who owes you and how late they are, but so that you can successfully recover the money that's owed to you.

You find out more about using Quicken to account for your business receivables in Book VIII. For now, here are some pointers for keeping track of and collecting the money you've earned. (If your business is a cash business where you get paid immediately, you can ignore this list.)

- **Use paper or electronic invoices** to send to your customers, and keep a copy of each invoice yourself.
- **Keep a list of your receivables**, either on your computer or even on paper. Don't rely only on your memory. Record the receivables, along with the date on which the invoices were issued, so none of them slip by unnoticed.
- **Send monthly statements** reminding your customers of unpaid amounts. If you relax the rules and don't send statements, even the best of customers is likely to relax a little too much and send payments late, or not at all.

- **Consider assessing finance charges** for hard-to-collect amounts. If you have customers who regularly pay late, the mere threat of a finance charge may be just what it takes to get those customers on a better schedule.
- **Be aggressive**. It's your money, so don't be afraid to ask for it. *You* wouldn't expect to receive the goods or services you offer and not pay for them promptly, and you have the right to receive the same respect from your customers.
- **Have a serious collection plan in place.** For those times when conventional methods just don't work, you should have a relationship with a collection agency or an attorney to pull out the big guns and go after customers who simply won't pay.

Issuing 1099 forms

Because you are a responsible businessperson, you probably already know the rules for issuing 1099 forms. But if you're new to business, or if this is the first time you made payments that require a 1099 form, you may not be on top of the rules.

Here's the breakdown of who needs to receive a 1099 form from you. Oh, and by the way, don't send a 1099 form whenever you hit the threshold for required forms. Wait until the end of the year and send out your 1099 forms all at once. The IRS requires that the 1099 forms be mailed by January 31 of the year after the payments are made. See the "Sending 1099 forms to your workers" sidebar for the complete rules for preparing and mailing 1099 forms.

- **1099-MISC:** You are required to send a 1099-MISC to any person or partnership to whom your business paid $600 or more for service or for rent (not for stuff you buy) during the entire year. Included in the definition of person or partnership is any attorney, even if the attorney is incorporated. If you paid $599 or less, no form is necessary.
- **1099-INT:** Send a 1099-INT to anyone to whom your business paid $10 or more in interest during the year.
- **1099-DIV:** If your business pays dividends, you must send a 1099-DIV to anyone to whom you paid $10 or more in dividends during the year.
- **1096:** Form 1096 is the cover sheet that needs to accompany all of your various 1099 forms when you send them to the government.

TIP

Filing 1099 forms is serious business. You can be penalized up to $50 per form for each form you neglect to file.

Sending 1099 forms to your workers

If you have a service take care of preparing and sending your 1099 forms, you've succeeded in avoiding a major headache each January. If you prepare and send the 1099 forms yourself, follow these steps in order to avoid raising the ire of the IRS.

1. **Acquire blank 1099 forms.**

   If you don't have any blank forms, contact the IRS at 1-800-TAX-FORM (give them about two weeks' notice) and ask for the blanks, or visit your local IRS office and pick up the forms yourself. Be sure to get a 1096 form while you're at it.

   Although most IRS forms can be downloaded from `www.irs.gov`, forms 1096 and 1099 are exceptions. You must submit *scanable* versions of these documents, so be sure to get these forms directly from the IRS or from an office supply store; otherwise, you might be fined by the IRS.

2. **Prepare the 1099 forms and the 1096 summary form.**

3. **Mail the recipient copies of the 1099 forms to the people whose names appear on the forms by January 31 of the year after the payments were made.**

4. **Send the 1096 and the government copies of the 1099 forms to the IRS by February 28th.**

   (This deadline is March 31st if you're filing the forms electronically.)

TIP: If your business sends out a lot of 1099 forms, you may already have a system in place for processing these forms and may be doing so electronically. If you only need to send out a few forms, poke around the Internet — you can find some great online services that take care of all of this paperwork for a really small fee.

Offsetting income with expenses

In addition to keeping track of how much money your business rakes in, you've got to keep track of how much you spend. There are several reasons why you might want to have this information.

✦ **Taxes:** The more you spend on your business, the more you can write off on your tax return, thus lowering the income on which your tax is calculated (and possibly encouraging a personal visit from the friendly auditors at the IRS). There's really nothing to worry about when it comes to IRS examinations as long as you can (a) justify the expenses you deduct on your tax return as legitimate business expenses, or (b) schedule a lengthy trip out of the country when it's time for your examination. When you start taking deductions for dog food, toys for the kids, and that business (wink, wink) trip to see your old high school buddies at a posh resort, the IRS inevitably starts taking a closer look at your expense deductions.

- **Knowledge:** When you're operating a business, no matter what kind of business it is, you need to know how much money you have. Keeping track of what you earn is one part of the picture. Keeping track of what you spend is another. If you don't monitor your spending (see Book I, Chapter 3 on budgeting for more on how to monitor your spending) and just hope there's money in the bank every morning, you'll probably learn soon enough that you have a lot more to worry about than whether or not the IRS is going to disallow your dog food deductions.
- **Investors and lenders:** At some point, you may want to expand your empire and bring some outside investors into the mix. In order to encourage people to invest in or loan money to your business, you need to show them how well your business is doing, and this means you need to provide detailed and accurate reports (see Book VII for more on reports) of how much you make and how much you spend.
- **Future planning:** Crystal balls may not really exist, but you can get a pretty good prediction of how your business is going to do in the future by looking at how much you earned and how much you spent in the past.

To keep track of your expenses, you should keep a paper trail of what you spent by writing checks or using a charge card instead of paying cash. You'll get bank statements and charge card statements each month itemizing all of your transactions, and then you can have the fun of reconciling those statements to make sure everything was recorded properly.

Fortunately, the days of bank statement reconciliation headaches are a thing of the past thanks to the wonders of Quicken. You'll see in Book II that reconciling bank and credit card statements can actually be fun!

Estimating taxes

Somewhere between the days when you are an employee and the days when you are so wealthy that you can hire someone else to take care of paying your taxes for you, you're going to have to pay your own taxes on your self-employment income. Employees have it easy because their bosses pay the taxes for them. When you're self-employed, you not only have the chore of making the tax payments yourself, but you also get to pay way more tax than employees do thanks to the wonders of our federal stealth tax system.

If you're an employee, you have the regular tax withholdings of federal income tax, Social Security tax, Medicare tax, state income tax, and maybe city income tax too. You may be lucky enough to live in a state or city where there is no income tax, in which case you either pay a higher sales and property tax than the rest of the country, or you have a lot of holes in your roads. The upside of being an employee, from a tax point of view, is that you get to work for an employer who matches your Social Security and Medicare tax payments with equal amounts out of his own pocket.

Self-employed people don't have those employers hanging around to pick up the slack, so they have to pay double the Social Security and Medicare taxes themselves. These Social Security and Medicare taxes, which are called *self-employment taxes* when you're self-employed, get combined with your federal income tax and paid to the government in the form of estimated taxes.

You should pay one-fourth of your estimated tax for the year with each payment. The estimated taxes for self-employed individuals are supposed to be paid quarterly, based on following schedule:

✦ **First quarter payment:** Due April 15

✦ **Second quarter payment:** Due June 15

✦ **Third quarter payment:** Due September 15

✦ **Fourth quarter payment:** Due January 15 after the year ends

For our purposes, *due* means *postmarked by*, and if the 15th falls on a Saturday or Sunday or federal holiday, you get until the next business day to get the postmark.

Note that the rules for making estimated payments are different for corporations. The January payment is due on December 15th.

TIP

Consider making monthly payments. The IRS won't object if you want to make your payments early. Sometimes it's easier to budget tax payments if you pay 1⁄12th of your estimated tax each month instead of paying 1⁄4th of the tax four times a year.

The amount you're supposed to pay for estimated taxes is calculated with one of the following formulas:

✦ Your estimated payments should add up to at least 90 percent of your current year's income tax, or

✦ Your estimated payments should add up to at least 100 percent of your previous year's income tax, keeping in mind that,

✦ If your taxable income is more than $150,000 ($75,000 if you're single or married filing separately), your estimated payments should add up to at least 110 percent of your previous year's income tax.

It probably goes without saying that it's easier to calculate what your estimated tax should be if you keep track of your income and expenses during the year. By keeping good records, you are also prepared for any tax you owe in the spring and won't have any nasty surprises that involve having to go into hock to pay your tax bill.

Keeping Track of Earnings from Your Investments

When you think of investments, you probably think of things like bank savings accounts, money market funds, brokerage accounts, shares of stock, savings bonds, retirement funds, Swiss bank accounts, that stash of cash hidden in your parents' freezer, and so on. These are all called *cash investments* because the only thing you can do with them is turn them into cash (or in the case of Enron stock certificates, make a nice campfire). Other types of investments include stamp and coin collections, artwork, antiques, jewelry, rare books, classic cars, vintage Mr. Potato Head kits, and just about any kind of tangible object you might own that is worth more today than what you paid for it.

It's important to know how much money you are making off of your investments, or by how much your investments are increasing in value, so you can make decisions about whether you want to keep your money tied up in those investments or change your investing strategy.

TIP: Besides knowing how much your investments earn, it's useful to know how much your investments are worth. Although the financial institution holding the money usually insures cash investments, the insurance on tangible objects is your responsibility. Make a list of all of your valuable stuff and how much it's worth, and then pay a visit to your insurance agent. Find out what is covered by your homeowner's or renter's insurance and decide what other type of insurance coverage you might need.

For cash investments, the banks, stockbrokers, and other companies that process and hold your investments send you regular statements showing how your investments are doing. Be sure to hang on to these statements — especially the one you get at the end of the year — so you'll have a record of your progress. If your cash investments aren't making particularly stellar progress, at least you can use the statements for packaging material around your precious (and much more valuable) collection of *Monkees* memorabilia.

In addition to statements, each of these organizations will send a 1099 form to you in January showing your earnings for the previous year. The information on your 1099 forms must be included on your tax return.

WARNING! The IRS gets a copy of your 1099 forms, and they check to make sure there are like amounts on your tax return, so no cheating!

REMEMBER: You don't have to attach the 1099 forms to your tax return — they are for your records. The exception to this rule is that if there is a record of taxes withheld on your 1099 form, you should attach the form to your tax return.

Earning interest on your savings account

Money deposited in a savings account earns interest, which increases the amount of money in the account. The bank gives the depositor interest in exchange for the letting the bank have the use of the money. The bank can lend out the money at a higher rate of interest, and thus make a profit on the use of your savings money. Meanwhile, you are required to pay tax on the interest that the bank gives you.

At the end of the year, your bank statement reflects the amount of interest you earned for the entire year and that amount is also reported to the IRS. (Unless of course you earned less than $10 for the year, in which case the IRS doesn't get a statement, but you're still supposed to abide by the honor system and report the earnings on your tax return.)

If you use a paper passbook and record your interest the old-fashioned way, by writing down the amount of interest every month when your bank statement comes, or if you're more modern and use Quicken to automatically record the interest each month, you already know how much interest you earned and won't have to wait for the bank to summarize the interest for you.

TIP

If you bank online at your bank's Web site, or if you use Quicken's funds transfer features, you can move money into your savings account right from your computer. Saving money doesn't get any easier than that.

Money markets and mutual funds

One of the best ways to get involved in investing is through money markets and mutual funds. These investment vehicles are conduits whereby a group of investors pools their available money and the fund invests all of the money together on behalf of the participants.

Savings, 1950s-style

Back in Leave It To Beaver-land where I grew up, we had a program at my school called Bank Day. On Bank Day, all of us kids would bring the spare change we had collected by mowing lawns (standard rate, 50¢) and taking pop bottles to the corner store for the deposit refund (2¢ per bottle), and we'd give the money to our teacher, who would record our deposit in our savings account passbooks. Somebody from the school would take the money from all the classes to the bank. These nickel and dime deposits would earn a little bit of interest, and in exchange, we learned a little bit about saving.

Meanwhile, our parents belonged to Christmas Clubs at their jobs where they turned in a fixed amount each week. They'd get the money back early in December, plus interest, and that was what they were supposed to spend on presents. It was an easy way of saving so that holiday spending didn't break the budget.

You don't hear much about those programs anymore, and it's kind of a shame. In the 1950s, saving money was a way of life, just another part of going to school or work.

You don't have to know a lot about investing to choose an investment fund, and your risk is minimized because the fund can buy a wide variety of investments instead of putting all of its investment eggs in just one basket.

I've lumped money markets and mutual funds together in this section because the record-keeping for both types of investments is similar. However, there are distinct differences between money market investments and mutual funds.

Money market accounts and money market funds

A *money market account*, also known as a money market deposit account, is an interest-bearing account offered by a financial institution (otherwise known as your friendly neighborhood bank, credit union, or savings and loan). Much like a savings account but with a higher minimum balance, the money market account is insured by the FDIC. Money market accounts pay interest, typically at a rate higher than a savings account.

If you've got plenty of money to invest, you need to know this important info about the FDIC. FDIC insurance only covers the first $100,000 in a covered account, so investments that exceed $100,000 should be spread among multiple institutions to benefit from the FDIC protection.

The banks and other institutions that offer money market accounts limit the number of transactions you can have in the account each month, so you can't use the money market account like an interest-bearing checking account, paying all of your bills from the account while you earn the nice interest rate.

You don't own shares in a money market account — you just put in a certain amount of money and watch it grow. Typically the interest rate on a money market account is stated up front and is non-fluctuating.

You need to keep track of the interest you receive on your money market account because the interest is taxable and must be reported on your income tax returns.

A *money market mutual fund* is sold in shares, with each share costing $1, and usually you must buy a minimum number of shares on your initial investment. The fund purchases short-term debt instruments, such as treasury bills and other government securities, as well as corporate money market securities, and typically the money market investments mature in 13 months or less.

Money market mutual funds are not insured by the FDIC, but don't let that be a deterrent. This is one of the safest investments around.

The interest rate on a money market mutual fund changes depending on the fund's investments, so no interest rate is stated up front.

Money market mutual funds often work like checking accounts in that you can have check-writing privileges and then you have the added joy of reconciling your account each month. But never fear. Reconciliation isn't a dirty word when you use Quicken.

Mutual funds

Mutual funds make the stock market and other types of investing accessible to nearly anyone. One mutual fund might invest in hundreds of stocks or bonds, and with your investment, you own a little piece of each of the fund's holdings. By joining a mutual fund, you don't have to have buckets of money to invest in blue chip stocks, international currency, government bonds, or whatever other type of investment interests you.

The advantage to investing in a mutual fund over investing directly in the stock market is that you get the chance to spread your money over a great variety of investments, thus presumably minimizing your risk. And for a very low fee (which is typically taken out of your earnings, so you don't actually see the cost of participation in the fund), you get to benefit from the expertise of the fund manager, who, with luck, won't take your money and run away to a private island in the Caribbean.

TIP

There is a slim chance that your mutual fund manager actually will take a hike with a bundle of cash from the fund, or, a more likely scenario is that a fund that looked good when you bought into it doesn't do too well and loses money. For these reasons, it's always prudent to spread your investible cash over a variety of investment options.

For a small initial investment, you can open a mutual fund account and continue making regular investments. Over time, if the fund is successful, your investments will continue to increase in value. Many mutual funds require an opening investment of $500 or $1,000 (some high roller funds require much more), but some funds let you open up an account for as little as $50 if you agree to a monthly automatic withdrawal from your bank account for continued investment.

TIP

Rumor has it that even though some funds publicize their opening investment at $1,000 or $2,000, if you call them on the phone and plead your case, you can negotiate a lower initial deposit. The negotiation probably goes more smoothly if you agree to a monthly investment schedule.

Unlike with stock investments, where it's probably more common to take your dividend earnings in checks (see "Playing the stock market" below), most mutual fund participants leave their earnings in the fund to grow and to be reinvested. So instead of receiving little checks in the mail each time a dividend is declared by one of the stocks owned by the mutual fund, your share of the dividend is added to the value of the fund and the value of your investment in the fund increases.

Usually, mutual funds send monthly statements showing how much your shares earned in the last month, how much you invested in the fund (or withdrew from the fund), and how many new shares you now own due to your investment or your reinvested earnings.

Hang on to *all* of your mutual fund statements. You may want to be able to recall all of your investment and reinvestment activity when you take money out of the fund. Taking cash out of a mutual fund has the same effect as selling individual shares of stock, only in this case, you are selling shares of your mutual fund. See Book V for more information on how to report the redemption of mutual fund shares on your tax return.

Playing the stock market

Companies sell stocks, or ownership shares, to raise money for their business. The shareholders of a company actually own the business and have an opportunity to vote on certain business decisions.

If you want to buy stock, you can't just go up and knock on the front door of General Motors and ask to purchase a share of stock. You need to use the services of a stockbroker who makes the purchase for you. You can work with a brokerage company and deal with a real person who helps you make investment decisions, or you can use the Internet to acquire the services of a stock trading service, and make your own trading decisions right at your computer.

When you buy and sell stocks, the most important thing to remember, at least from a record-keeping standpoint, is to keep track of the dates on which you make purchases and sales and the amounts you spent and collected. You are expected to be able to reproduce this information on your tax return.

The purchase information for stocks is also important if you give the stock away, either to another person or as a contribution to an organization.

So find a safe place to keep your stock purchase information because you might have to hold on to this information for many years. In the good old days, everyone had a safe deposit box at the bank, and that is where they kept the deeds to their houses, savings bonds, and stock certificates. Anymore, many people do their banking online or over the phone and purchase stocks through an Internet service such as e-Trade or Ameritrade, so the regular trip to the bank to sequester important documents in a safe deposit box seems to be less of a tradition.

For more information on investing in stocks, pick up a copy of *Stock Investing For Dummies* by Paul Mladjenovic (Wiley).

Bonds and treasury bills

A *bond* is another word for a loan — by purchasing a bond, you in effect loan money to the company or government entity from which you make the purchase. A bond has a fixed life expectancy and when you make the purchase, you expect to have your money returned to you when the term of the bond ends.

Typically, bonds pay interest over the course of the bond's term. Then, when the bond obligation is fulfilled, the bond is retired and you receive your original investment back.

Bonds are rated based on how likely it is you will actually get your money back. The higher the rating, the safer the risk. Likewise, the lower the rating, the riskier the bond. The riskier bonds are usually offered at a higher interest rate, in order to attract investors who are willing to gamble and take the higher risk.

You can purchase bonds in one of several ways:

- Buy bonds at banks. U.S. government savings bonds are available at your bank in increments as small as $25. These bonds are sold at 50 percent of face value, so $25 gets you a $50 savings bond. When the bond matures, you get $50. If you purchase series EE or series I savings bonds and redeem them to pay for higher education costs, there is no tax on the difference on the bond's interest.
- Buy U.S. Treasury bonds and savings bonds online at the Treasury Department's Web site, `www.treasurydirect.gov`.
- Buy bonds from a broker.
- Some employers offer a payroll withdrawal program that allows you to purchase bonds at work.
- Buy bonds by buying shares in a mutual fund that specializes in bonds.

Treasury bills, like government savings bonds, are purchased at a discount. Instead of receiving payments of interest over the course of the bill's life, the bill itself increases in value until it reaches its stated value. At that time, the bill is redeemed and you receive the full face amount of the Treasury bill.

The interest you receive on bonds and treasury bills is taxable, so it's important to keep track of your earnings throughout the year. Some bond interest is taxable on both your federal and state income tax returns, other interest is taxed only on your federal return, and still other interest is only taxable on your state return. Here are the general rules:

- Interest on U.S. savings bonds and other federal government investments is taxable on your federal income tax return but not on state and local income tax returns.

- Interest on corporate bonds is taxable on all of your income tax returns.
- Interest on municipal bonds is tax exempt on your federal income tax return, but may be taxable on your state tax return. If the bond was issued by a municipality or tax exempt organization (such as a school) in your own state, the bond interest is probably not taxable on your state tax return. Check the instructions that accompany your state tax return for more information about municipal bond interest.

Earnings in retirement funds

You've got plenty stashed away for your nest egg, right? Individual Retirement Accounts (IRAs), 401(k)s, 403(b)s, 402(c)s, 609(y)s, whatever. And of course there's that Rumplestiltskin pile of gold called Social Security waiting for all of us. Just knowing you have all this money waiting for you in your waning years should be security enough. But actually knowing how much you can expect to have when you're ready to retire and how much your long-term investments are earning would be pure heavenly bliss, or at least common-sense satisfaction.

Keeping track of earnings in your retirement funds can be a sticky area. Not only is it possible that you own several funds, but the possibility also exists that some of your retirement fund money is tax-free, some of it is tax-deferred, and some of it will be fully taxable. All of those tax rules affect how much money will actually be yours to keep.

It's imperative that you keep track of all of your retirement money, know where it is invested, know how it will be taxed, and maintain some control over the investments, so that you don't jeopardize your financial future. You'll find Book VI on retirement planning to be quite useful in figuring out how you can take advantage of all that Quicken has to offer for helping you stay on top of your retirement investments.

For now, here are some basic descriptions of the various types of retirement funds that may be available to you.

401(k), 403(b) tax-deferred retirement plans

Many employers offer 401(k) plans to their employees. A 401(k) is a long-term savings plan funded by automatic withholdings from your paycheck and often enhanced with matching funds provided by your employer.

If you work for a school or church or government, you may have a 403(b) instead of a 401(k), but the idea is basically the same. These plans are tax-deferred, meaning you can fund them with money on which you pay no income tax, and the earnings in the plans grow, untaxed, until you're ready to take the money out.

When it's time to get your hands on the money in a tax-deferred retirement plan, usually when you turn age 59½ (the minimum age for penalty-free withdrawals), or a bit older if you decide to wait awhile, the amounts you take out of the plan are taxed at your current rate of income tax.

Try not to take the money out of a tax-deferred plan before the plan says you can do so without a penalty. The penalty for taking money out early is 10 percent of the amount you withdraw. This is on top of the income tax you pay.

Typically, participants in a 401(k) or similar plan have a variety of options from which to choose for investing their plan money. The options will be a choice of mutual funds, some riskier than others. You can split your investment if you like so that some of the money goes in safe funds and some in the riskier but potentially higher earning funds.

Monitor your 401(k) money closely and consider changing your mix of investments to take advantage changes in the stock market. Also, as you get closer to your own retirement, you'll want to think about moving your 401(k) money into more conservative investments that may not earn as much but are less risky.

Traditional Individual Retirement Accounts

The traditional IRA ("traditional" is used to differentiate from the IRA's baby brother, the Roth IRA) is a tax-deferred retirement account you can open yourself. Contributions to the IRA of up to $4,000 per year may be tax-deductible if you meet certain picky requirements (see Table 1-1).

The annual IRA contribution limit of $4,000 is good for the years 2005-2007. In 2008 the amount is scheduled to increase to $5,000. Starting in 2009, the amount is scheduled to increase each year based on an annual inflation adjustment. Table 1-1 applies to taxpayers who are covered by a retirement plan at their job.

Table 1-1 Who Can Deduct IRA Contributions?

Filing Status	*Single or Head of Household*	*Married Filing Jointly or Surviving Spouse*	*Married Filing Separately**
Adjusted Gross Income			
$10,000 or less	Full deduction	Full deduction	Partial deduction
$10,000-$45,000	Full deduction	Full deduction	No deduction
$45,000-$55,000	Partial deduction	Full deduction	No deduction
$55,000-$65,000	No deduction	Full deduction	No deduction
$65,000-$75,000	No deduction	Partial deduction	No deduction
Over $75,000	No deduction	No deduction	No deduction

**If you don't live with your spouse at all during the year, you should use the guidelines for Single.*

Table 1-2 applies to taxpayers who are not covered by a retirement plan at their job.

Table 1-2 Who Can Deduct IRA Contributions?

Filing Status	*Single, Head of Household, Surviving Spouse, or Married Filing Jointly with a Spouse Also Not Covered by a Retirement Plan at Work*	*Married Filing Jointly, Spouse Is Covered by a Retirement Plan at Work*	*Married Filing Separately*
Adjusted Gross Income			
$10,000 or less	Full deduction	Full deduction	Partial deduction
$10,000-$150,000	Full deduction	Full deduction	No deduction
$150,000-$160,000	Full deduction	Partial deduction	No deduction
Over $160,000	Full deduction	No deduction	No deduction

**If you don't live with your spouse at all during the year, you should use the guidelines for Single.*

If you're 50 years old or older, you can contribute another $500 each year to your IRA ($1,000 starting in 2006), also deductible if you fit the descriptions above.

No matter what your age or filing status or income level or whether you prefer Original Recipe or Extra Crispy, you can contribute the maximum amount to an IRA each year and *not* take a deduction. So don't use the restrictions from the tables above as an excuse to not sock any money away for retirement. You won't get to take a deduction for your contribution, but the earnings in the account will continue to grow, tax-deferred, until you are ready to retire.

When you retire, you can take the money out of your IRA based on convoluted schedules provided by the IRS that may make the hairs on the back of your neck stand up because they tell you when you're expected to die. Any amounts you withdraw from the IRA are taxed at the time you take the money. The exception to that rule is that if you contributed money to the account but did not take a deduction for your contribution, you've already paid the tax on that amount so you don't have to pay tax again.

Roth Individual Retirement Accounts

Former U.S. Senator William Roth invented the Roth IRA, a hybrid IRA that encourages people to contribute to savings without the benefit of a current tax deduction for their contribution. The pie in the sky with the Roth IRA is that you never pay tax on the money you take out of the account.

So if you invest successfully and your Roth IRA contributions grow astronomically, you can take the money and spend it on yourself, guilt-free, not ever having to share a dime with the IRS.

Setting up a Roth IRA is not quite as easy as it may sound. As with anything touched by the IRS, there are restrictions and hoops to jump through. Table 1-3 shows who gets to contribute to a Roth IRA.

Table 1-3 Who Can Contribute to a Roth IRA?

Filing Status	*Single, Head of Household*	*Married filing Jointly*	*Married Filing Separately*
Adjusted Gross Income			
$10,000 or less	Full deduction	Full deduction	Partial deduction
$10,000-$95,000	Full deduction	Full deduction	No deduction
$95,000-$110,000	Partial deduction	Full deduction	No deduction
$110,000-$150,000	No deduction	Full deduction	No deduction
$150,000-$160,000	No deduction	Partial deduction	No deduction
Over $160,000	No deduction	No deduction	No deduction

**If you don't live with your spouse at all during the year, you should use the guidelines for Single.*

You should note that with both types of IRA, the amount of your annual contribution is limited to lower of the maximum contribution amount or the amount you earn from a job. So if you only made $1,500 at your job during the year, the most you can contribute to an IRA is $1,500, no matter how much more the tables may suggest you can contribute.

If you don't make any money at a job but you are married to someone who does, the spousal IRA rules kick in, and you can "borrow" earned income from your spouse to qualify for your own IRA contribution.

Chapter 2: Paying Bills

In This Chapter

- **Spending money on everyday expenses**
- **Borrowing money**
- **Using credit cards**
- **Monitoring your credit score**

Imagine a life without spending money. You could earn and earn and earn, and never spend a dime. Just think how wealthy you would be! Just think how hungry you would be! Just think how bored you would be! We spend money to keep ourselves fed and housed and to ensure our comfort and to fill our lives with the material possessions and intangible items that give us pleasure. The trick to spending well is to not spend more than you make, pay your bills on time, and still have some money left over. This chapter is about spending, keeping track of your spending, and how that spending affects your economic life.

Spending Money on Required Expenses

The really boring part of spending involves spending money for things that you *have* to buy, like rent and milk. A lot of areas of spending are simply considered requirements of your chosen lifestyle.

Alternatively, the fun choices you make for spending beyond the requirements are personal and differ from one person to the next. Whether you choose to spend your extra money for vacations, books, tickets to sports events, or fancy hats, it's your choice and it's your extra money.

But this chapter is concerned with the necessities: the expenses that you probably pay first, before the fun stuff. Keeping track of those expenses and making sure you have the money to pay them may not be entertaining, but it beats the alternative of not having enough money when the bills come due.

Necessary expenses include the Big Three (food, shelter, and clothing), as well as other important spending like electricity and water, doctor bills, car expenses, and stuff for your kids and pets.

The Big Three: food, shelter, and clothing

Known as the basic necessities of life, or, the expenses that seem to cost way more than they ought to, are taxes, gas for the car, and health insurance. Or at least that's the way it seems.

Seriously, the *traditional* big three expenses, the things we can't live without, are food, shelter, and clothing. And although we each define these items differently, they are a completely necessary part of our ongoing expenses. At first glance it might seem like these expenses cannot be changed. But upon closer examination, you may find many ways that you can cut costs, if that's your desire, even with these necessities.

Keeping records of your spending is the first step to being able to analyze your costs and, perhaps, alter your spending habits so that you have more for the fun things you want to do.

You are what you eat

There are a variety of reasons for keeping track of your spending on food items. Your food costs are manageable and can be controlled to a certain extent. For example, when you add up all of your family's food costs, including groceries, school lunches for the kids, restaurant lunches for the workers in your family, dinners eaten out or carry-outs, midnight taco runs, fancy coffees and teas, and between-meal snacks, the amounts can be staggering. If you're trying to cut costs, try these tips for saving on food:

- Limit your restaurant spending to a fixed amount each month, and keep track of your spending. When you reach your limit, stop going out and stick to food prepared at home.
- Pack lunches for school and work. Make a little more for dinner in the evening and use the leftovers for lunches.
- Choose your favorite type of restaurant and invest in a cookbook that features that type of food. Learn how to make your favorite dishes at home.
- Use coupons. Wait for double or triple coupon days at your local grocery, then stock up on the essentials at great savings.
- Shop at a cooperative or wholesale club. If the 20-pound bag of potatoes is too much for your family to consume, shop with a friend and split the items you buy and the cost.

Save your receipts and keep track of your food expenses (Quicken is great for this!) to see how much you save when you implement some of these ideas.

Your home is your castle

Although your housing expenses may seem fixed, as in a monthly rent or mortgage payment, there are ways you can take control of this necessary expense.

- ✦ Make extra mortgage payments. Book IV on household finances explains in detail how paying even just a little extra in principal or altering the timing of your mortgage payments can have a significant impact on the total amount you owe for your home. In the short run, you're paying more, but in the long run, you save bundles.
- ✦ Ask your landlord if you can do your own repairs and improvements in exchange for a reduction in your rent payment.
- ✦ Refinance your mortgage. Often people refinance their mortgage with the intention of taking equity out of the house. The result is sometimes a new mortgage payment that's even higher than the old payment. Consider refinancing without increasing your equity, just decreasing your interest rate. Your monthly payments will decrease too.
- ✦ Consider moving to a less expensive home.
- ✦ Share living expenses. If the cost of your home has simply gotten out of control, consider living with a friend or other family member and split the costs.

TIP

If you own your home and you don't have a copy of your mortgage interest schedule, otherwise known as a loan amortization schedule, ask your lender. This schedule shows you how much of each payment goes toward interest, how much goes toward the actual cost of your home, and how much is allocated to insurance and taxes. Knowing how much of your payment goes to interest and other expenses will help in any decision you make to refinance or relocate.

The clothes on your back

You might enjoy wearing the latest fashions or trying out a new wardrobe every season. Or you might be the type who mends old clothes until they're threadbare, saving ancient items for sentimental reasons, and only buying new clothes when it's an absolute necessity.

Either way, or some way in between, clothes are a requirement in our society, and the expense can be one to reckon with.

Parents know all about replacing wardrobes every time a child grows an inch. And, alas, children aren't the only ones who change size from time to time. Just take one look at all the diet books in the bookstore and you'll know what I mean.

Keep track of how much you spend on clothes so that you won't be surprised when it's time to make those purchases. It's easy to remember a housing expense because you pay it every month. And food is a constant cost because, well, we eat every day. But clothes can sneak up on you, and they aren't cheap.

The best way to keep track of your clothing expenses is to do a little research. Go back through your checking account and charge card records (this will be a simple process once you get comfortable with Quicken) and summarize a year or two of clothing purchases. See how much you've spent on clothes for yourself and your family members, and use this as a guide for what you can expect to spend in the year ahead.

And while you're contemplating your clothing costs, here are a few tips for saving money in this department:

- Look for sales. Most department stores have frequent sales, clearing the racks of last month's fashions to make room for the newer items.
- Shop off-season. Plan ahead and buy your heavy clothes in the spring when the summer clothes are selling at full price, and look for light-weight items in the winter when everything is faux-fur and wool. You'll find that prices are slashed on the off-season clothes, and nearly every store has a bargain rack where these items can be found.
- Go re-saling. The resale shops have great bargains on gently worn items. If you don't mind secondhand, you'll be pleasantly surprised at the money you can save.

Spending money on utilities

When I was small, the only thing I associated with the word *utilities* was the pair of unpopular properties on the Monopoly board, the electric company and water works. I didn't know much about what those descriptions meant; I just knew that landing on them meant I had to pay a small fee and then I could be on my way.

Real utilities carry the same kind of baggage. They're kind of a nuisance, but unavoidable, and must be paid before you can go on about your business.

Take electricity, for example. You can't say it isn't worth a smidgen of your paycheck each month to be able to have lights come on when you clap your hands. And don't overlook the importance of paying for water. The benefit of not having to walk a mile to the well every time we want a drink is worth way more than the small fee we send to the water company each month. And don't forget the alternative of having to take baths outdoors like the Romans did. It might make for some interesting socializing, but what did those Romans do about bathing outside in January?

Keeping track of your utilities expenses can provide some useful insights. For one thing, if you own a home and ever hope to sell it to someone else, you'll probably be asked to tell how much the utilities cost. Same goes for subletting an apartment.

You'll also find it an interesting exercise to monitor your utilities, making small changes in your lifestyle like turning down the heat while you're huddled under covers at night, or fixing that leaky faucet in the basement. Make a change and watch your utilities expenses for six months, or compare the expenses to the same time period last year, and see if there isn't a difference.

You'll be able to collect this information easily with Quicken when you start recording your expenses and producing analysis reports.

And if you're interested in cutting those utility expenses, here are a few tips:

- Turn off lights when you vacate a room.
- Don't leave water running when you're not using it.
- Have your furnace and ducts cleaned regularly, and replace filters according to the schedule recommended by the manufacturer.
- Take shorter showers (or share a shower with someone you love!).
- Turn off electrical appliances, such as television, stereo, and computer, when they're not in use.
- Enjoy the fresh air and turn off the air conditioner in the summer — ceiling and attic fans are excellent alternatives.
- Switch to florescent light bulbs.
- Check your home for drafts and then have them repaired.

Try some of these suggestions and see if they make a difference in your expenses.

The doctor is in

Sooner or later, everybody needs to spend some money on medical care. If you're the type who goes in for annual checkups, keeps up-to-date with health insurance, and rarely gets sick, your medical expenses are of the more ongoing type. If you ignore the checkups and little signs and wait for the big illnesses, or if you're just prone to getting sick or having accidents, you might be a person who regularly fights with big medical bills. Even if your medical experiences fall somewhere in between, you probably always have an omnipresent concern that medical costs are lurking just over the horizon.

Many types of expenses are lumped into the area of medical expenses. For example:

- ✦ The normal stuff that comes to mind when you think of being sick, like doctors, dentists, nurses, hospitals, medicine, and ambulance
- ✦ Health insurance and amounts for health care that gets paid into flex plans
- ✦ Preventative costs such as vitamins, health club memberships, exercise classes, treadmills, weights, exercise mats, stretchy exercise outfits, and bicycles
- ✦ Elective medical care, including plastic surgery, liposuction, stomach stapling, and teeth bleaching
- ✦ Medical equipment and devices, like glasses, contact lenses, hearing aids, crutches, splints, walkers, wheelchairs, bars in the bathroom, ramps, canes, and so on

Try keeping a handle on medical expenses by knowing the provisions of your health insurance inside and out, lumping elective medical expenses in the same year so that you have an opportunity to take a tax deduction, and not letting money in a company flex plan go unused.

Your taxes and medical expenses

The IRS allows taxpayers who itemize their deductions the opportunity to take a deduction for medical expenses. Sort of. You can deduct any medical expenses (except for non-prescription medicine and the expenses like health club dues, bicycles, aerobics and yoga classes, and the tight outfits that go with those activities), as long as the expenses you deduct exceed 7.5 percent of the adjusted gross income on your tax return.

In layman's terms, this means that if you earned $50,000 last year at your job, and you paid $3,800 in deductible medical expenses during the year, you can take an itemized deduction for a whopping $50 ($50,000 x 7.5% = $3,750; $3,800 – $3,750 = $50). You may think this doesn't seem like much of a return for all of the out-of-pocket money you spent on doctors and crutches, and you'd be right.

If you plan on indulging in some elective medical expenses, like tummy tucking or face lifting or teeth straightening, try lumping all of the expenses in one year. For example, you can probably prepay your doctor for orthodontic work that will span a couple of years. Keep in mind that if you charge the expenses for purposes of calculating a tax deduction, you get to choose whether to include the medical expenses with the year of the charge or the year in which you pay off the charge.

Use-it-or-lose-it flex plans

The flex plan is one of life's little ironies. As an alternative to simply writing a check to pay for your doctor bills that aren't covered by health insurance, the IRS allows employers to entice employees to contribute to a company flex plan for medical expenses.

With a flex plan, you have a predetermined amount of money withdrawn from your paycheck each pay period. The employer hangs on to this money for safe-keeping. Then when you get sick, you either pay the doctor or hospital or buy medicine and ask your employer to pay you back out of your own money in the flex plan, or you hand the bill to your employer and ask him to pay it out of your own money in the flex plan.

Money you put into a flex plan is contributed on a pre-tax basis, meaning you don't have to pay income tax on the money. The catch is that if you don't use all the money in your flex account to pay for medical expenses by the end of the year, you can't have the money back. It's lost to you, and the employer gets to keep it.

The moral of this story is that you must keep excellent records of your spending. Pay careful attention to how much money is in the flex plan and how you plan to utilize the money. As the end of the year approaches, make sure you have receipts for all of your out-of-pocket medical expenses, including prescriptions and any other medical costs that are allowed by the flex plan, so you can get your money back.

TIP

If it looks like you're about to lose some of your flex plan money, go on a medical spending spree. If you wear contact lenses, buy some extra pairs, or get in to see the doctor for your annual checkup, refill all of your prescriptions, get your teeth cleaned, or whatever it takes. There's no point in giving the money away, even if you really like your employer.

TIP

If you had to hustle to use up your flex plan dollars at the end of the year, reconsider your level of participation in the flex plan program for next year. Reduce your contribution or make sure you plan to have enough medical expenses during the year to take advantage of the entire amount you put in the plan.

Planes, trains, and automobiles (and buses, taxis, and trolleys . . .)

A significant part of our spending money goes towards getting ourselves from one place to another. If you live close enough to wherever you need to go each day so that you can walk or ride a bike, you are remarkably fortunate. If you're like most people, you fork over big bucks for some sort of ride to your destination.

You might want to keep track of your transportation expenses because you travel for work and can arrange to get reimbursed for some of your costs. Or maybe you split the cost of transportation with a fellow student or coworker and need to tally up the expenses so you know what to charge your partner.

If your transportation is a tax-deductible expense, you definitely need to keep track of all of your expenses. Here are some situations in which transportation costs are tax-deductible:

- Non-reimbursed work-related travel — other than your commute to and from your workplace.
- Cost of getting to and from tax-deductible classes, such as classes that improve your skills at your job.
- Traveling for medical purposes, such as trips to the doctor or clinic.
- Traveling for charitable purposes, such as transporting Cub Scouts, delivering Girl Scout cookies, carrying supplies for the church picnic, or delivering meals to shut-ins.
- Moving to a new home to take a job that is at least 50 miles farther away from your old home than your old job.

When you keep track of the cost of your travel (using Quicken, of course!), be sure to include not just the cost of your gas and car expenses, or public transportation fares, but also parking, tolls, and any other related expenses. Even if you pay cash for these expenses, you can track them in Quicken and thus have a complete record of your transportation expenses.

Children, pets, parents, and other important people

It's interesting to keep track of all that you spend on the people and animals in your life. Not only does this information make for some entertaining conversation around the dinner table ("I'll bet you can't guess how much little Sally's diapers ran us last month — pass the gravy, please"), but there may actually be some worthwhile reasons why you should know how much it costs to take care of a family member.

- If you're considering adding to the family, you should be aware of how much it costs to raise a child.
- You may be considering taking in an elderly family member; you should have an idea of how much it will cost to add another adult to the family.
- The next time your child says you never do anything for him, you can be prepared to put him in his place (at least until the next time he's feeling shortchanged).
- A four-legged family member costs money too — if there's talk of adding a dog or a cat or some other sort of beast to the family, you should know the costs involved.

If you already have a child or another person or a pet living in your household, it's not too difficult to calculate what it will cost to add another. You can start with the specific costs of a current family member, such as clothing, education, entertainment, medical bills, spending allowance, transportation. Add to this a prorated portion of expenses that you pay for the whole family, such as food, linens, furnishings, and electronic gadgets, and you'll have a pretty good idea of how much more it will cost to increase the family size.

The more difficult costs to allocate to individual family members are expenses like housing, utilities, and insurance, amounts that you spend anyway and would continue to spend at about the same rate, even if you added to the family.

If you are new to the process of adding members to your household, your projections are done with a different approach — guessing. You've got no historical data to determine the cost of formula and baby wipes if you haven't had a child before. Likewise, the cost of frequent carpet cleaning and Frisbees is hard to estimate if you're considering your first pet. At least if you're adding an adult to the household, you can rely somewhat on your own experiences as to what expenses lie ahead.

Of course, no matter what type of add-on you're contemplating, you can estimate all you want, but there's only one certainty you can rely on: diapers (for the very young or the very old), $39.95 in the economy-size box; dog treats, $4.95 for a 20-ounce box; the joy of have a new member of the family, priceless!

Borrowing Money

For better or worse, borrowing money seems to be a permanent part of today's economic landscape. We borrow to purchase big-ticket items like cars, homes, boats, and furniture. We borrow money every time we use our credit cards, whether it's for a new pair of jeans, a stereo system, dinner at a restaurant, or a candy bar.

Some borrowing is *secured* debt, borrowing that is backed up by the item for which the money was borrowed. For example, if you borrow money to purchase a car, the car secures the debt. If you don't make your payments, the company from whom you borrowed the money can take your car.

When you agree to a loan for a specific amount of money, you agree to make payments on that loan for a specified amount of time. Those payments include interest as well as a payback of the amount you borrowed.

Before borrowing money, you need to understand what will be expected from you in return for the loan. Know how much your payments will be and how often they must be paid. Understand the penalties for making late payments, and, for that matter, find out if there are penalties for making early payments.

At times, you may want to pay a loan off early, but the terms of the loan discourage early payment. For example, you might have borrowed money to make some improvements on your house. The loan is at a high rate of interest, and the payment schedule stretches the loan out over five years, but you'd like to pay back the loan in one or two years, thus significantly lowering the effective interest rate. Be sure to check the terms of the loan before you sign on the dotted line to make sure you *can* pay the loan off early. Some loans come with early payment penalties to make sure the lender gets all the interest even if you pay off the debt faster than the agreed-upon payment schedule.

Calculating loan interest

It probably comes as no surprise to you that borrowing money comes with a price tag, and that price tag is known as *interest*. Interest is calculated based on the amount of money you borrow; it's a fee for the privilege of borrowing the cash.

Banks and other financial institution lenders tend to be very up front about the amount of interest they charge, the amount you will pay in periodic payments, and the total amount of the loan plus the interest that you have to pay back. Bankers are capable of telling you with a completely straight face that the $20,000 you borrow will be repayable in 300 easy installments of $100, and that sounds completely reasonable to you, even though they also tell you that comes to a total of $60,000. Hey, that's $60,000 in tomorrow's money, and everyone knows that $20,000 today means a new car in your garage, which easily trumps $60,000 in tomorrow's money. There is stability with a bank loan: You know what the rate of interest is, your payment is always the same, and you know exactly when the loan will be paid off.

Credit card companies get sneaky with interest

Credit card companies are typically a little cagier than bank lenders. They offer low interest rates to lure people to their cards, they have the right to raise the rate, the date when interest starts accruing on your debt may vary from one card to the next, and, rest assured, if you only pay the minimum payment on your credit cards, you'll probably be in debt forever.

The credit card company may tell you they're offering an incredible 0 percent interest, and you have to read really small print to see how short a time this low non-interest rate will be in effect and what the actual rate will jump to once you start making charges on the card.

There's interest, and then there's interest . . .

Two types of interest are most often applied to the amount you owe (and I'm not referring to the descriptions of *merely exorbitant* and *totally outrageous*, even though that might be what the interest seems like). The two most common types of interest are simple interest and compound interest.

Simple interest is interest applied only to the principal of your loan. *Compound interest* is interest that is applied to the principal of the loan plus any interest that has accrued. Bank loans are most often calculated using simple interest. Credit cards use compound interest.

Using Credit Cards

Credit card borrowing is a form of *unsecured* debt. If you charge the cost of a vacation on your credit card and then don't get around to making the credit card payments, the credit company can't come and take away your vacation. Even when you purchase something tangible with your credit card, like car parts or body lotion, the items you purchased are safe from the credit company. That's the good news.

The bad news is that credit card companies make their money by charging interest. And lots of it. Each credit card company determines its own rate and method for applying interest, so it makes sense to shop around for the best deal.

Comparing rates

There are nearly as many credit card interest rates as there are credit card companies. Every company has its own way of computing the interest, so take the time to read the paperwork that comes with a credit card agreement, even if it means getting out your magnifying glass. One credit card's 15 percent interest rate doesn't necessarily mean the same as 15 percent at another company.

Some companies start charging interest the same day you make a purchase on your credit card; others wait a certain number of days after you make a charge before they begin assessing interest. Some companies assess interest on a daily basis, others charge monthly. The worst-case scenario is the credit card that assesses interest the day you make a charge and continues to compound interest on a daily basis.

When shopping for a credit card, or, if you already have several, when deciding which one to use, compare these features to determine which card gives you the best rate:

- ✦ Choose the card that carries the lowest interest rate (and not just for a few months, but the lowest rate overall).
- ✦ Choose the card that has the longest grace period between when you make a charge and when they start assessing interest.
- ✦ Choose the card that assesses the interest on the statement date instead of daily.

Making minimum payments

Your credit card statement includes a tempting offer to make a minimum payment. Beware of the minimum payment! Historically, the minimum payment has been set at 2 percent to 5 percent of the amount you owe. So if your credit card balance is $1,000, your minimum payment might be as low as $20.

If the credit card company assesses 21 percent interest, your payment of $20 may only knock off $2–$3 from the principal balance, and the rest of the payment will be used to pay interest. At that rate, if you only pay the minimum payment, you will never pay off the loan.

Actually, if you pay nothing but the minimum balance, you would eventually pay the credit card off, but, unless there is an incredible medical breakthrough in the next few decades, you would have died long before that happens. Say you pay the minimum balance until the balance gets to $5.00, and then you decide to pay off the remaining balance. You would have been making payments for 164 years and would have paid $6,527 in interest on the $1,000 balance.

For the record, credit card companies have been under pressure to raise the minimum payment amount. Within the next 7 to 10 years, credit card companies are expected to increase the minimum payment to an amount that will ensure the cardholder can make a dent in the principal balance.

Alternatively, say you use that $20 as your regular monthly payment, and you never charge another amount on the card. It will take you 10 years to pay off that $1,000, and your total interest will amount to about $1,400 if compounded monthly, and about $1,450 if compounded daily. Yes, you read that correctly. Paying only the $20 minimum payment each month means your interest alone is about $1,400, not including the $1,000 in charged purchases.

On the surface, 21 percent interest on $1,000 sounds like it ought to be about $210. Instead, the interest totals nearly half again as much as the entire amount you charged.

Another way to think of the 21 percent interest is in terms of earning power. Pay off the credit card that's racking up 21 percent interest, and it's like getting 21 percent return on your investment (actually more, when you take the compounding into consideration). That's right. Save yourself the 21 percent interest and it's like investing your money and earning 21 percent. For this reason, most analysts suggest that if you have extra cash on hand, you should use it to first pay back your credit card balances before you invest it in a savings account that's earning a measly 2 percent or 3 percent interest. It's hard to beat a 21 percent return on investment.

Make late payments on your credit card, and your interest rate increases. Credit card companies can also charge a late fee in addition to the interest that keeps accruing (and that interest then starts accruing on the late fee as well as the rest of the balance in the account).

The bottom line is, credit cards are convenient, no doubt, but don't think that credit card money is cheap. The cost can be astronomical.

Refinancing credit cards

In order to lure new customers, many credit card companies offer especially low rates if you transfer a balance from another credit card. This can be a great way of reducing the interest you pay on your credit card debt. But once again, be sure you read the fine print. Here are some danger signals to watch for:

- Sometimes the credit card company charges a balance transfer fee, a percentage of the amount you transfer. This fee is added to the transferred amount and interest is assessed on the fee.
- The initial interest rate for transferring a balance may be quite attractive, but there may be a time limit on this rate, and then a higher rate kicks in if you haven't yet paid off the balance.
- Although balances transferred from another credit card get assessed a low interest rate, any new charges on the new credit card might get assessed a rate even higher than you were paying on the previous credit card.
- If you begin charging on this new credit card and make monthly payments that are less than the total, read the fine print to see how your payments are applied. Often payments are applied to the transferred balance (the low-interest) balance first, and the new charges remain on the account, getting assessed at the higher interest rate.

If you are considering transferring a balance to a new credit card, do the legwork. Create a spreadsheet that demonstrates how your payments will be applied, how interest will accrue, and how new charges will be treated. Compare these two scenarios over a period of however long you think it will take to pay off the balance:

- **Scenario 1:** Keep your charges on your old card and continue to pay at the same rate you've been paying, estimating new charges based on past performance.
- **Scenario 2:** Transfer the charges to the new card, continue to make the same payments you've been making, and estimate new charges based on past performance.

Make sure you're getting a bargain before making the transfer. Sometimes those transfer deals really are too good to be true.

Mastering Good Credit

There's no trick to having and keeping good credit. All you have to do is borrow a little money or use credit cards from time to time to show you can meet obligations, not take on any more debt than you can handle, and pay your bills on time.

If you apply for a credit card or try to borrow money, the lender or the credit card company will examine your credit history to determine if you are a good credit risk. The better your credit history, the more likely it is you will get the loan, the higher line of credit, or the new credit card.

Continue to maintain good credit, and credit card companies and banks will come knocking on your door, trying to lend you more money.

If you have never borrowed money and never owned a credit card, chances are you don't have a credit history. Even though you might be the best credit risk in the world, it's possible you won't be able to get a loan if you don't have a credit history.

If you're the type of person who prefers to pay in cash, consider getting a charge card just for the purpose of establishing a credit history. Charge a few things, and make the payments on time. That's all it takes to establish yourself in the credit system. Then when the time comes, if you want to borrow money for a house or car, you should be in good shape.

The credit agencies and their reports

If you have had any credit transactions in your own name, including standard credit cards like MasterCard and Visa, department store credit cards, filling station cards, bank loans, and so on, you have a credit history. The stores and businesses report your activity to credit agencies, and then the agencies issue reports about your credit.

You have to authorize the issuance of a credit report. Whenever you apply for credit, you sign a document that gives permission for the lender or company to request your credit report.

The credit report contains plenty of information about you:

- The name of every company that you owe money to, the amounts you owe, and your payment history including information about any late payments and the date of your most recent payment
- Your credit limit with the companies with which you have credit cards
- Your mortgage company, if you own a home, the amount owed, and your payment history

- ✦ Your spouse's name, if you are married, and information about which debts are owned jointly
- ✦ Your real weight (not the weight you put on your driver's license) (just kidding!)
- ✦ Public records of liens, repossessions, foreclosures, and bankruptcies in which you have been involved

There are three primary credit agencies in the U.S., and different lenders rely on the information from any of the three agencies:

Experian
888-397-3742
P.O. Box 2002
Allen, TX 75013
www.experian.com

TransUnion
800-888-4213
Customer Disclosure Center
P.O. Box 1000
Chester, PA 19022
www.transunion.com

Equifax
888-873-5392
P.O. Box 105851
Atlanta, GA 30348
www.equifax.com

You can request a copy of your credit report from any or all of these agencies at any time for a fee. If you have been turned down for credit, ask the lender which credit agency provided the report that resulted in your being turned down, and that credit agency will provide you with a copy of the report at no charge.

Get your credit reports for free

Recent legislation known as the Fair Credit Reporting Act requires that each of the three major credit reporting companies provide you with a free copy of your credit report once each year. You can request your free credit reports online at www.annualcreditreport.com. There you can either obtain online copies of your reports or download request forms that you can mail. You an also get information about making telephone requests for your free credit reports.

It's worth the small fee (usually around $10) to see a copy of your credit report from time to time, so you know what lenders are looking at when they consider you for a loan or as a credit card candidate.

Your FICO score

In addition to the detailed credit reports, potential lenders look at your FICO score. The FICO score is similar to the high score you got on the video game down at your favorite pizza place last week, but not quite the same. And it's a darn shame that we can't improve our credit ratings by practicing up on video games.

FICO stands for Fair Isaac & Company, and this company has a secret mathematical program (probably a lot like a video game) that analyzes the information on your credit report and produces a score. The higher your score, the better risk you are, at least as far as credit card companies and other lenders are concerned.

FICO scores range from 300 to 850. A score of 300 means you'd better start selling stuff on eBay if you need cash because you certainly aren't going to get a loan. A score of 850 means you can charge anything you want: The sky's the limit. Most people fall somewhere in between.

FICO scores are updated continually, just like your credit reports, so anyone who requests your credit report gets a current up-to-the-minute FICO score to go along with the report.

You can find out your FICO score (for a small fee) on the FICO Web site, at `www.myfico.com`, or you can order a copy of your score by phone at 800-342-6726.

FICO scores are not written in stone. If you're disappointed with your FICO scores, you can take steps to improve your score:

- **Don't make late payments.** This rule seems like a no-brainer, but in case it hasn't occurred to you, companies are more likely to lend you money if they think you're going to pay it back on time.
- **Don't charge to the max on your credit cards.** You don't have to pay the whole balance off each month, but leave yourself some wiggle room. This keeps you from looking desperate.
- **Don't take every credit card offer that comes your way.** Too much credit is too much of a good thing, and the FICO people start lowering your score when you have "too many" credit cards. How many is too many? FICO doesn't say, but I'm guessing if you can't fold your wallet because of all the plastic, you probably have too many cards.

- **If you don't have any credit cards, get one or two, use them, and make the payments on time.** This helps establish your reputation as a good credit risk.
- **Give it time.** If you haven't had credit for long, or you're trying to repair bad credit, you need to work at establishing your good credit. Pay your bills and keep your credit cards current, wait a year or two, and try for that loan again.
- **Check for errors and get them corrected.** Credit report companies don't know you — they just report what has been sent to them. A recent study performed by PIRG (Public Interest Research Group) found that 25 percent of credit reports contain errors.

Correcting errors on credit reports

Examine your credit reports for errors and misrepresentations. It's up to you to stay on top of your credit history and make sure the reports contain accurate information. If you find an error on your credit report, here's what you should do:

- **Contact the credit bureau and inform them of the mistake.** The credit bureau will send you a correction form that you need to fill out, explaining the error and giving evidence of the correction. For example, if you paid off an account and the credit bureau shows an amount still owing, make a copy of your statement showing the last payment and send that along with your correction form.
- **Notify the creditor.** If the incorrect information on your credit report was submitted by one of your creditors, get in touch with the creditor and ask that corrected information be sent to the credit agencies.
- **Examine all three of your credit reports.** Chances are good that if there is a mistake on one credit report, there is a mistake on one or both of the other reports too. Correcting the mistake with one credit agency doesn't automatically flow through to the other agencies — you might need to send corrections to the other agencies as well.
- **Follow up.** Give the credit agency (or agencies) two or three months to get your records straightened out after you make a correction request, and then request copies of your credit report(s) again to make sure the corrections have been made.

There is a seven-year statute of limitations on credit information. If an account has been closed or late payments were made or anything else negative about you appears on your credit report (like that thing about the fake weight you put on your driver's license), after seven years, the record must be purged. If unfavorable information on your report is more than seven years old, contact the credit agency and ask them to remove the outdated information. Likewise, if unfavorable information appears on your report and you're coming up on seven years, get ready to celebrate: Your FICO score is about to improve!

TIP

You can add comments on your credit report. If you think the presentation of information on your report is misleading, you are entitled to add a 100-word statement explaining your side of the story.

Chapter 3: Budgeting

In This Chapter

- Setting budget goals
- Creating a budget
- Using a budget
- Altering your budget

Here's a working definition of budget: (ˋbəj•ət) Noun. 1. A plan to show how much money a person or organization will earn and how much they will need or be able to spend. 2. A plan for the coordination of resources and expenditures. 3. The amount of money you have available to spend.

Setting Goals

Everyone knows what a budget is. A budget is the way some people, like parents, for example, try to make you believe you can't have something you really want because there are more important things to buy, like Stove Top Stuffing and car engine repairs.

"Sorry dear, it's just not in the budget," is a common refrain heard throughout childhood, but what kids don't know is that, chances are, there actually is no budget.

Technically, everyone can be said to have a budget in that we all make conscious decisions about whether we can afford to buy something. And, for most people, that's what a budget is — all in the mind.

Budgeting, after all, is a process of knowing what you can afford and spending accordingly. Or not. Many people use budgets as an excuse for not buying boring things they're supposed to buy ("Gee, I wish I could afford to get that noisy squeak in the air conditioner repaired, but it's just not in the budget") when in the next breath, they're busy proposing something fun and much more useful to do with their "extra" money ("Hey, let's go to the riverboat and drop a few hundred bucks at the blackjack table!").

To create and use a budget successfully, a budget should be a formal plan, printed out on paper, designed to help you control spending, monitor income, and plan for future expenses so they don't creep up and bite you. And if your dreams include gambling on the riverboat, replacing the air conditioner, a college education, a comfortable retirement, or even a lifetime supply of Stove Top Stuffing, no problem. Just make your dreams part of the budget and map out a plan for how and when you can afford to realize your goals.

P.S.: If your dreams seem out of reach, all the more reason for a budget. You'll get yourself a dose of financial reality, be able to assess the likelihood of achieving your goals on your current income, and figure out how much more you will have to earn or how much longer you will have to work to have the things you want.

If you live alone, your budget creation is a personal event. But when you live in a family, and the budgeting affects all family members, there should be some planning in which all family members can participate.

WARNING!

Parents should resist the temptation to try to make their children feel guilty about the fact that certain individuals (that is, the grown-ups) go out and work hard and earn a living so that certain other individuals (that is, those who stay home and wear diapers and watch Nickelodeon) get to reap the benefits of that labor. Such discussions end up being battles over the relative merits of television programming like *SpongeBob SquarePants*, and parents always lose these arguments.

Instead of getting trapped in the mire of intellectual discourse with your five-year-old, as parents (and rulers of the family unit), you have the right not to have to share every detail about your finances with the children. However, keep in mind the fact that by allowing children to participate in or at least listen to the financial decision-making process, they learn a valuable lesson to take into their own adult lives (aside from the knowledge that some day they too will get to make the rules). Also, if the kids know up front what the family has agreed upon as necessary as well as luxury expenses, there might be less whining when they start lusting after expensive items.

Budgeting, Family-Style

Few things in life are more fun than sitting around with your family members, cheerfully discussing how to spend a limited amount of money. Getting teeth drilled comes to mind as a pleasant alternative.

In spite of the fact that some people have difficulty discussing money issues, the time spent creating a budget with the other members of your family pays off, so to speak, in an organized and meaningful approach to both short-term and long-term financial goals. Working with your family members to see the big picture means the entire family can take pride when financial goals are achieved.

Goal-setting is most effective when there is some element of realism connected with the goals you choose to strive for. If your family income is limited to $20,000 per year, a plan to live in a Beverly Hills estate with a vacation home on the French Riviera and a Park Avenue condo for those occasional trips to New York City may be a little far-fetched.

But the nicest part about the initial goal-setting family meeting that you're going to schedule is that all wishes can be heard and considered. Gather the family, set out some nice snacks or order everybody's favorite take-out, and start making lists. The first list everyone should make is a wish list. Go ahead: Pull out the stops, list everything you can think of that would truly make you happy. You don't have to go nuts with lists of extravagant items just for the sake of seeing the names of these items in print. Consider what you really dream for, what would truly make your life complete, and put it in writing.

Your family goal-setting meeting should have the following characteristics:

- ✦ Time should be set aside specifically for the meeting
- ✦ All interested family members should attend
- ✦ There should be paper and a writing instrument for each person present
- ✦ Keep an open mind when listening to ideas of other family members

TIP

The one rule you need to follow when making initial budget-session wish lists is that no family member should be made to feel bad about something on his or her list. The first wish lists are for fun, and there's nothing wrong with dreaming a little. Furthermore, you're certain to learn something about your family members. It can be very informative to learn the true desires of your siblings, spouse, or parents.

Prioritizing your goals

After you've created lists of the financial goals each family member hopes to achieve, you need to assign priority values to those goals. Have each person go through his own list and number the goals on the list starting with number one as the most important goal.

Share your ideas with one another, discussing which goals are the most important to each of you and what makes those goals important. Help each other decide which goals belong at the top of each person's list and why.

Pricing your goals

How much do these goals cost? You've got to examine the lists, and estimate how much each goal costs. Don't worry if your estimates are off base. The idea is to get a general sense of how much money is at stake with these goals. That information is helpful when you start thinking about how long it's going to take to actually achieve these goals.

Setting a price on goals can be a difficult task for children, so parents, here's where you have to take charge. Tell your children how much money is involved in order to achieve the goals they have on their lists. This might be extremely eye-opening, especially for children who have a sense of the value of money.

As you discuss each of the goals on your lists, consider how important those goals are to you. Do you really need all these things, or would just some of them suffice? You may be able to cross some of the goals off your lists before you continue to the next step.

Determining the length of time for achieving goals

In addition to assigning priorities to your goals, you must determine how long each goal will take to accomplish. Again, this is just an estimate. Give your best guess in which category each of the goals on all of the lists should fall:

- **1 year:** Goals that need to be achieved within one year. For example, tuition for a family member who is currently in college, a new bicycle for a child who has outgrown her current model, or replacing the furnace that died at the end of last winter.
- **2–5 years:** Goals that you want to achieve within five years. Examples might include orthodontic work for a family member, an expensive vacation like a cruise or a trip overseas, a new car, or elimination of existing debt.
- **6–10 years:** Goals that you hope to achieve within the next ten years. For example, a college education for a child currently in grade school, a move to a new home, new furnishings, an investment in some stocks with an eye toward retirement.

This goal-setting exercise is an important part of budgeting. It's one thing to budget for your current and ongoing living expenses — those items of course are a necessary part of budgeting because they are required expenses. But the real fun in budgeting comes not from having money to pay the electric bill, but in finding the ability to make your dreams come true.

Creating Your Budget

You probably have a pretty accurate idea of how much money you earn on a monthly or yearly basis. You probably also have a fairly good idea of how much you spend, based on how much you have left in the bank at the end of each month. But do you have a clear sense of specifically how you spend your money, month in and month out?

The first part of budgeting involves developing an estimate of your cash inflow and outflow on a monthly basis. After you know how much you make and how your money is spent, you can see clearly where changes can be made, if changes are needed. You can also use your income and expense summary to examine what you have to work with so that you can create a budget that enables you to start planning for your goals.

Your budget starting point

The best starting point for a budget is a recap of past activity. If possible, you should go back a whole year, or even two years, and make a detailed list of your monthly income and expenses for that time frame. As you'll see in Book IV, Chapter 5, if you already use Quicken, you'll find that collecting this information is quite easy. If you are new to Quicken, you'll have to spend some time going back over your paper bank records for the past year or two if you want to get detailed information.

Your goal in this exercise is to create an estimate of your income and expenses for the next 12 months.

An alternative to collecting the detail from the past year or two is to start from scratch, doing the best you can to estimate what you think your monthly income will be going forward, and taking a stab at your monthly expenses.

You may need to spend a couple of months keeping detailed records of your spending in order to get a grasp of how your money is actually spent. Especially if you're the type of person who spends a lot of cash without recording how the money is spent, you may not realize where you spend all your money. Carry a notebook or PDA with you for a month or two and record every expenditure. Then work these expenses into your list of personal expenses.

REMEMBER: Don't hesitate to get picky when recording your cash expenses. You may think that $5 spent on coffee and a newspaper each day is negligible, but when you're trying to figure out where all your money goes, $5 times five days a week times 52 weeks per year is $1,300, and that's an amount worth tracking.

TIP: At this point, you can probably excuse the children from the room. Unless you've raised a son like the Alex P. Keaton character in the old *Family Ties* television show, your children probably won't be terribly interested in the intricacies of budgeting, especially the costs of running a household. Furthermore, you may feel that some of the budget information, like how much you make at your job or how much is spent on the household, is not necessarily relevant to your children.

WARNING! Particularly young children might not be able to exercise discretion regarding private family financial information. And while you may be perfectly willing to share information with your children, you may not want the information shared with the neighbors, parents of your children's friends, or teachers at their school.

Determining average monthly income

When considering your monthly income, include any of the following items that apply to you:

- Income from your job and your spouse's job, net of any taxes that are withheld. If you are self-employed, reduce your net business income by the amount of taxes you expect to owe on this income.
- Interest you earn on bank savings account and other interest-bearing investments.
- Dividends on stocks that you own and earnings on mutual fund investments.
- Tax-deferred amounts earned in your retirement fund. Even though you don't have immediate access to this money, the earnings are yours and should be included with your budgeted earnings.

Determining an average monthly amount of income is easy if you earn the same amount of money each month. But if your income varies from month to month, or is seasonal, or is just completely unreliable, there is some additional work involved in determining a monthly amount of income.

Do your best to estimate. For purposes of this exercise, you can either estimate an annual amount of income and divide by 12 to get a monthly estimate of your income, or you can estimate your income month by month, allowing for the seasonal or other fluctuations that you expect to occur.

Determining average monthly expenses

The other start-up part of creating a budget involves estimating monthly expenses. Again, keep in mind that some expenses do not occur each month. For example, you might pay automobile insurance only once or twice a year. When drawing up a 12-month estimate, you can either average expenses evenly throughout the year, or place the infrequent expenses in the month where they belong.

Everyone's monthly expenses are different, but here is a list of the most common household and personal expenses you might encounter and should consider for your budget:

- Rent or mortgage.
- Utilities: Electricity, gas, water, sewer, trash service.
- Transportation: Gas and oil, public transportation, auto payments, auto repair and maintenance, auto insurance.
- Medical care: Health insurance, doctor and dentist visits, ongoing medications, contact lenses.

- Children: Education fees, day care, diapers, school lunches.
- Clothing.
- Job-related costs: Tools, books, dry cleaning, uniforms, union dues, lunches, parking, professional dues, professional liability insurance.
- Debt service: Loan payments, interest on credit card bills (the actual amounts you charge on your credit card should go in the proper categories such as food, clothes, and so on).
- Insurance: Life insurance, property insurance, any insurance not included elsewhere.
- Pets: Food, boarding, veterinarian, equipment.
- Charity: Religious organizations, other not-for-profit organizations.
- Gifts: Birthdays, other holidays, graduations, anniversaries, showers, weddings.
- Entertainment: Movies, restaurants, sporting events, concerts, CDs, night clubs, vacations, videos, newspapers, magazines, books.
- Personal: Hair care, makeup and other toiletries, fitness.
- Savings: Short-term and long-term savings investments including contributions to retirement funds. Include the amount you recorded in the income section that is being routed to a retirement fund at your job.

The items on the above lists are not meant to appear in any particular order but instead are presented to give you an idea of the kinds of things you want to consider when creating your budget.

TIP

If you're uncertain about how much to enter in your budget for some items, err on the side of overstating expense and understating income. That way you'll be covered if the bills come in higher than expected or your income takes a drop.

Budgeting for unforeseen events

No matter how well you plan, there is always the risk that some unexpected event occurs and completely throws off your financial plans. For that reason, financial analysts recommend keeping an emergency fund on hand, a cash reserve representing three to five months worth of living expenses, designed to get you through rough times and unexpected setbacks.

The emergency fund is discussed in more detail in Chapter 4 of this book. For now, the important thing is to remember your emergency fund when creating your budget. If you already have an emergency fund, you don't need to budget an additional expense to provide for this fund, but if you don't have such a fund, or if you have used up some or all of your emergency fund, you need to add an amount to set aside for your emergency fund into your budget.

Budgeting for your goals

Finally we get to the fun part of creating a budget (unless of course you're a numbers geek, in which case everything you've done budget-wise so far has been fun). The really fun part is getting to incorporate your goals into your budget.

Keep in mind that there has been no discussion yet of making ends meet. That's OK. Right now we're just listing income and expenses as they exist today, without any concern as to whether or not you have enough money to meet your monthly expenses.

For each of your goals that fall into the 1-year category, take the total cost of achieving that goal, divide the cost by 12, and add that item to your budget with $\frac{1}{12}$th of the cost in each month of your monthly budget.

For longer-term goals, such as 5- or 10-year goals, divide the estimated cost by the number of years you anticipate it will take to achieve that goal, divide the resulting number by 12, and add that item to your budget as well.

The idea is that you start now to save for your long-term goals, putting aside a little each month, so that when you're ready to enjoy those goals, the money will be available.

The suggestion that you budget for the entire cost of your goals is based on the assumption that you have not yet begun to save for these goals. If, for example, you already have a college fund in place for your child, or if you expect to receive a quantity of money in the future, perhaps from an inheritance, and plan to use that money to fund your goals, you don't need to budget for those goals currently.

All of this long-range budget planning is being done in today's dollars, without any adjustment for the future value of the money. In truth, if you start saving today for an expenditure that is 10 years away, you can put aside less than $\frac{1}{120}$th of the total cost ($\frac{1}{120}$th = total cost divided by 10 years, divided by 12 months in a year) because you plan to invest your money each month and the earnings on the money add to the total available for the goal.

You may be wondering what you should do with the money you set aside for your savings goals. If your budget works the way you want it to, you'll have additional money to put aside for mid-term and long-term goals. Consider investing the money so that it earns interest or dividends and thus provides even more income toward your goals.

If some of the money you've saved is earmarked for long-term goals, you have the flexibility of investing not just in the liquid investments that can be accessed quickly like mutual funds or savings accounts, but in long-term investments such as bonds, treasury bills, or certificates of deposit.

Balancing your budget

After you've created a breakdown of your anticipated income and expenses for the coming year, look over the entries in your budget and determine how reasonable those amounts are. Look for errors and omissions, keep an eye out for unreasonable amounts, and remember that you're trying to imagine what your financial life is really going to be like for the next year.

Finally, get out the calculator and see how close you come to having enough income to meet all of your expenses and your goals. Add up all of your income for each month, add up all of your expenses for each month, cross your fingers, and subtract. If you're left with a positive number, you can celebrate! If your budgeted expenses are greater than your income, it's time to start figuring out how you're going to make ends meet.

Say that all of your expenses are enough to use up all of your monthly income and there is nothing left for future goal planning. This is frequently the case, as many people adjust their lifestyles so that they can live paycheck to paycheck, leaving nothing or very little left over for saving.

This is where budgeting gets interesting. It's time to analyze your spending and decide what's really important, where you can make changes, and, possibly, what has to go. Here are a few important considerations to remember:

- **Your financial lifestyle is not written in stone.** If you suddenly experienced a drop in pay or a loss of a job, you would have to make changes in your lifestyle. You can make lots of little changes that together have a big effect on the bottom line. See "Living within your means" later in this chapter for tips on making adjustments that really add up.
- **Ease into your budget.** If you're new to saving, you're going to feel like you are making a sacrifice by tucking money away in savings instead of spending the money.
- **Start small.** If you're new to setting money aside for saving, start by trying to put away 5 percent of your income each month for saving. After you get used to making saving a regular part of your lifestyle, you can try to increase this amount. Five percent may not be enough savings to cover your goals. Save 1–2 percent for a few months, and then work up to a higher level of savings.
- **Consider ways to increase your income.** Expenses aren't the only flexible part of your budget. See the section called "Increasing your earnings" later in this chapter.

Using your budget

OK: You finished creating a budget that meets your financial needs, allows enough money to cover your operating expenses and, with luck, leaves some left over for saving. Now what?

The idea is not to stash the budget in your desk drawer, but to actively use the budget by referring to it often, comparing your real performance with the budget plan, making spending decisions based on the information in your budget, and, if necessary, working toward improving the budget so that you can ultimately meet all of your financial goals.

Here are some tips for making use of your budget:

- ✦ Each month, summarize your actual income and expenses, and then compare the real activity to your budgeted activity. Quicken helps you do this effortlessly.
- ✦ When differences arise between actual and budgeted amounts, note the differences and determine what caused them. You don't need to change your budget each month; just know why you aren't in agreement, and save that information for later, when it's actually time to make some changes.

  Sometimes budget differences are simply differences in timing. An expense you thought you would incur next month actually came in this month instead. Or income you were expecting this month is delayed until a later date. There's certainly no reason to amend your budget for simple changes like this. Just take the little timing differences in stride, knowing things will even out in a month or two.
- ✦ Keep track of your spending during the month and try not to let yourself spend more than the budget permits. If you decided to budget $100 a month for eating out, and you've already spent that much three weeks into the month, stay home for the rest of the month and don't eat out. When it comes to discretionary spending, using your budget is just that simple.
- ✦ Remember to keep track of your cash spending as well as checks, credit card spending, and debit cards. All of these spending options need to be tracked and compared to your budget.
- ✦ After a few months have passed, if your budget is not working out, it's time to reassess the amounts you put in your budget to determine if they are reasonable. After you have a bit of a track record to compare your budget to, you can start fine-tuning the budget so that it works with your lifestyle.

The budget can't help you control your spending by itself. If your spending is out of control, don't just change the budget to match your spending. Carefully analyze your spending and determine how you can improve your habits.

- ✦ Spending isn't the only part of a budget. Remember to compare your income to the amounts recorded in the budget and make sure you are earning and bringing home the amounts you budgeted. Analyze any differences and determine where any problems might lie.
- ✦ If income exceeds your budgeted amount, determine how you want to use the additional income, or adjust your savings goals so that perhaps you can speed up the time in which those goals are to be achieved.

Living within your means

Sometimes budgeting means cutting expenses. But cutting expenses doesn't have to translate into changing your lifestyle. Try some of these tips for adjusting your spending without cutting into your way of living.

Cut back on utilities

Go beyond the obvious habits of turning off lights when you leave the room and dialing down the heat while you wear extra layers. Here are some ideas for saving on the cost of utilities:

- Consider upgrading insulation and storm windows and also check for and repair drafts. Some states give tax credits or deductions for this type of expense, so not only do you improve the efficiency of your utilities and the comfort of your home, you can save money on taxes too!
- Try turning down the temperature on your water heater, especially when leaving home for several days at a time.
- Don't go nuts with air conditioning in the summer or heat in the winter. Use these utilities frugally and just when you need them. Consider installing ceiling and attic fans to move the air around instead of relying on the furnace and air conditioner to do all the work.
- Turn off music and television when you're not watching/listening, or when you leave the house.
- Time yourself in the shower and try to beat your previous times. Turn off the water when shampooing or shaving, and then turn it back on again to rinse.
- Check furnace filters and have regular cleaning and maintenance done on the furnace and air conditioner. Consider upgrading to a more energy efficient system if you're still operating on an old system. Call an HVAC service person to get a free estimate of how much a new system costs and the relating savings on utilities. Modern systems can pay for themselves in a very short period of time.
- Switch to cold water in your washing machine.
- Wait until the dishwasher is full to run a load. Wash the big items by hand in the sink so that you can accommodate a greater quantity of smaller items in the dishwasher.
- Close vents and doors in rooms you don't use so that the heat and air conditioning aren't wasted.
- See if your utility companies offer a year-round average cost program. This is a useful budgeting tool to help even out your costs throughout the year. You don't pay any extra under this program, but the exorbitant costs for winter heat and summer air conditioning get spread throughout the year.

- Check out the possibility of installing a timer on your thermostat so that turning down the heat or air conditioning at night or when you're away from home is taken care of automatically.
- Use timers or motion detectors on outside lights so that they're not turned on all the time.
- If you don't make a lot of long distance calls, consider canceling your long distance service and buying phone cards for your long distance. That way, you only pay for the calls you make. Another option for saving on long distance is to take advantage of any available long distance service on your cell phone.
- Read your telephone bills and make sure all of the auxiliary charges are correct and that the long distance calls are to numbers you recognize.

Test the results of your changes. Check your utility meters to determine your usage before implementing some of these changes. Then try one or two adjustments at a time for a month or two and check the meters at the end of each month to see if your utility usage has changed.

Don't operate in the dark (no pun intended). Read your utility bills rather than just paying them, and do the math to determine how much your utility usage actually costs. Then when you notice changes in the usage on your meters, you really know how much you are saving.

Cut back on other expenses too

Utilities aren't the only area where you can trim expenses. Here are some general tips for cutting daily living expenses.

- **Save money on postage and envelopes by paying bills online.** You'll see in Book IV, Chapter 4 that it's easy to pay bills through Quicken. Also, many banks offer their own online bill payment services.
- **Install a smoke detector and a security system.** Not only do these items afford protection, but their usage may enable you to reduce your homeowner's or renter's insurance costs.
- **Buy in bulk.** Shop with a friend; look for bargains often found by buying food, cleaning supplies, and other common items in bulk. Share the savings, and then split the items with your friend if you don't need the entire bulk amount.
- **Make sure you're getting all the savings to which you're entitled on your automobile insurance.** If you have been ticket-free for several years, you should qualify for a rate reduction. Use the same company for homeowner's/renter's insurance, personal health insurance, long-term care insurance, and life insurance as you do for auto insurance, and your overall rates can be reduced because many insurance companies give discounts for multiple policies. Teenage drivers get lower rates for high

grades in school. If you live in a large metropolis, your insurance rates can be reduced if you don't drive into the city for work. Make sure your insurance agent knows how you use your vehicle.

- **Do all of your errands for the week in one trip.** You'll save both time and gas money.
- **If you're paying for your bank checking account, shop around.** Many banks offer free checking, and sometimes you can even get cash incentives to move your money to a different bank.
- **Pay your bills on time!** Avoid late fees! Duh!
- **Increase the deductible amounts on your insurance policies.** The savings on premiums can usually offset the increase in the deductible within a couple of years.
- **If you're paying for daycare so two parents can work, consider switching one parent to a different shift so that there is always one parent at home.** You'll do away with the daycare costs and might even increase the household income if one parent switches to a shift that pays more.
- **Stop eating out.** Eating out can really get expensive, and you can eat more and better food for less at home. Learn some new recipes, or cook and freeze meals for busy nights when there's no time for food preparation. If you enjoy a particular type of restaurant food, invest in a good cookbook for that style of food, and teach yourself how to cook your favorite dishes.
- **Cut the cost of magazine subscriptions.** If you like to have a lot of magazines to read, consider waiting a month or two and buying them cheap at book sales or used book stores. Also look online for bargains on new subscription costs.

These are just a few tips to get you started. See what you and your family can come up with to save additional money, and try to keep track of how much you actually save.

TECHNICAL STUFF

Do you prepare your own income tax returns? If so, you might want to consider meeting with a professional tax preparer to have your previously filed tax returns analyzed. Find out if you're preparing the returns correctly and if there are any cost-saving measures you can employ that will help you cut your taxes. If the advice you receive is beneficial, you might want to have the professional prepare your tax returns in the future.

Increasing your earnings

Cutting expenses is one way to improve on your monthly bottom line. Another way is to increase income. Your first reaction might be that your job pays what it pays, and there's no way to bring more money into the home. If more money is what you want, try experimenting with some of these ideas for adding to the family coffers.

- **Think ahead.** What would it take in terms of effort, time commitment, and skills to advance to a higher paying position at your job? If it's a promotion or raise you want, ask your employer how you can learn the skills you need for the next level of income or advancement.
- **Find out what other employers are offering for the same skills.** Do you like what you're doing but think you could earn more money elsewhere? Shop around discreetly and maybe you'll find a better situation, doing the same work but for higher pay.
- **Look into overtime opportunities at your job.** Alternatively, ask if there are additional responsibilities you can take on that can improve your position and eventually your pay. Maybe switching from days to evenings or nights for awhile can result in a bigger paycheck.
- **Consider taking another job, at least for a short time.** Many retail employers hire part-time workers during the holiday season in November and December. Other employers have different busy seasons and might offer various types of seasonal or shift work.
- **Invest and save.** The more you save, the more your money works for you. Invest your savings from various cost-cutting measures that you implement and watch your income grow.
- **Sell personal possessions you no longer want.** Perhaps you can sell a collection you no longer want, or items you inherited that aren't special to you to bring some income into your home.
- **Pursue continuing education.** You might want to return to school at night or take courses online to improve your skills and make yourself a candidate for a better-paying position.

TIP

There are plenty of opportunities to make money out of your hobbies and interests. If you love gardening, see if you can help others in the neighborhood with their gardens, for a fee. You can even bring your children along and let them help, and give them part of the fee as a reward. Do you love to read? Maybe writing book reviews for the local newspaper can pay off. Are you good with children? Nanny/babysitting services are always in demand. Are you a good cook? Consider catering small parties as an additional source of income. Ask your family members for suggestions. They might recognize skills of yours that you don't even realize you have!

When budgeting fails

Sometimes the budget you made just doesn't do the job. Don't give up on your budget if things aren't working out for the first few months. Give yourself a chance to make the budget work; try various methods of increasing earnings or cutting back on expenses if necessary. By all means, analyze your experiences carefully and make sure you understand why the budget isn't working.

Top ten reasons why a budget fails:

- **Unanticipated costs.** You thought you planned for every contingency, but then there was that car accident and you needed to buy a new car, or the dog bit a neighbor's child and you're stuck with the medical bills, or your daughter gets married and brings the new out-of-work husband home to join the family. You get the picture. (See "Starting an Emergency Fund" in Chapter 4 of Book I.)
- **Unreasonable expectations.** You were certain you could cut your spending by 20 percent, but it's just not happening.
- **Change in lifestyle.** You lose your job, you have a baby, you're ready to retire, there's a death in the family, you get married, you get divorced, you move, you go back to school, you join the armed forces, you have a midlife crisis, or, oh my God!, all of the above!
- **Investments don't work out.** That oil well turned out to be a dry hole.
- **Forgotten items.** Oops! What about birthday gifts for the nieces and nephews? How about those school tuition bills? Or that annual life insurance renewal that sneaks up on you each year? And oh yeah, there's the money you give to charity. Sometimes it's hard to think of everything the first time you make a budget. Don't worry — you'll get the hang of it.
- **Giving up without trying.** Budgeting seemed like a good idea at the time . . . Maybe next month we'll try again, *after* we go on the vacation . . .
- **Failure to keep track of spending.** It's soooooo hard to remember to write down everything. Especially out-of-pocket cash expenses.
- **Cheating.** If you cheat on your budget, there's not much point in having one, is there?
- **Not understanding how a budget works.** A budget is a tool, not a rule. Use the budget to learn more about your spending habits and your income potential. Work with the numbers so they provide a reasonable representation of your financial lifestyle. Then compare real life to the budget and analyze the differences. Use that information to fine-tune your budget so that the budget works for you and provides you with a workable financial plan.

So what do you do when your budget doesn't work? You have three choices:

- Start over, this time with more determination to make the budget plan stick.
- Take some time off, rethink the budget, try again in a few months.
- Fix it.

Notice that "Give up" is not among the options listed above. Yes, you can give up if you really don't think you're cut out for budgeting. But there are better choices. Instead of giving up, try to figure out how to make the budget work for you. A careful analysis of the problem areas should provide you with the information you need to make some useful changes.

Budget time, take two

If at first you don't succeed . . . you can always start over again. If you've never used a budget before, the first few months can be daunting. But if you're confident that the amounts you put in your budget are truly workable, a few months of practice may be all it takes to get you and your family on track.

Remember to really examine your budget each month, comparing your actual income and expenses to those listed on the budget. But don't stop there. Analyze what went wrong (and what went right) and make a concerted effort to correct the problems next month.

Maybe some of the changes you tried to institute were too drastic. Giving up daily trips to Starbucks or Friday night drinks at your favorite watering hole or the latest bestseller in hardback can be a difficult lifestyle adjustment. So ease into the change, and commit to getting yourself on track within a few months instead of all at once.

Consider the possibility that your budget might need adjusting. See "Changing your budget" below for information on how to tweak the budget.

Prepare yourself for the possibility of your income not being enough to cover your expenses. If possible, set aside a bit of extra cash to meet unexpected expenses or deal with emergencies. And don't just prepare yourself monetarily. Understand that budgets aren't perfect and they often need correcting. Don't feel like you've failed if the budget doesn't work out the first time. If you're dedicated to making the budget work, you'll figure out how to get it right.

Maybe all you need is a budget breather. If you're confident that the reason your budget isn't working is a problem with the execution and not with the numbers in the budget, take a break, and then dig in again and see if you can't make it work the next time.

Changing your budget

A budget is a work in progress. Even if your budget works perfectly for you in the beginning, you're going to need to make changes as your income and expenses change over the years.

At least once a year, and more often if you're still working at getting your budget right, take the time to seriously analyze your actual income and spending compared to the budgeted amounts you started with. Reassess goals with your family, and determine the root of any changes in spending and income expectations.

TIP: If you find yourself with more money than you originally budgeted for, don't take that excess as an excuse for extravagance. Instead, consider your list of goals and see where the money can be best utilized. You can chip away at some of those long-term goals, or fund your emergency reserve.

Borrowing and your budget

No matter how well you plan for the future, unexpected events can occur. If your budget won't handle certain expenses, you can work borrowed money into the budget scheme.

Record borrowed money as additional income coming in, and set up a repayment plan as an expense of your budget.

REMEMBER: Charging purchases on your credit cards is a form of borrowing. If you charge expenses on credit cards and don't pay the amounts off in the same month, be sure to increase your budgeted expenses to allow for the repayment of those charges.

If borrowing is out of control, or if the debt repayments including credit card payments are eating away at your ability to put money away and save, consider debt counseling. A professional debt counselor can help you organize your debts, negotiate payment plans, and generally stay out of trouble.

Budgeting for life

Probably the most important benefit that comes from budgeting is that you know how much money you have, where the money is scheduled to go, and you can determine when and how you are going to achieve your goals. Instead of hoping that someday your financial goals will be achieved, you know which ones you're going to reach and when they will be reached.

After you've settled on a budget that works, you have a plan in place that enables you to reach your goals.

Chapter 4: Protecting Yourself

In This Chapter

- **Setting up an emergency fund**
- **Determining what constitutes an emergency**
- **Insuring your vehicles, property, life, and health**

Taking care of yourself and your family involves more than keeping your door locked, letting the dog outside frequently, and setting curfew hours for your children. For some, protection comes in the form of a shotgun or a Rottweiler. But this kind of protection only goes so far. The shotgun, for example, might protect you if you walk in on a robber in the act of cleaning out the silverware drawer, but it won't get you a new heart when your Timex stops ticking (although that gun trick worked pretty well for Denzel Washington in *John Q*). So the point is, no matter what your preferred manner of watching your back, financial protection should be part of the big picture.

Creating an Emergency Fund

There are many types of insurance, and most are purchased through an insurance broker or arranged for by your employer. But the one type of insurance that you can provide for yourself is an *emergency fund*.

Purchased insurance policies cover specific types of emergencies: auto accidents, poor health, damage to property, and even death. With an emergency fund, you name the emergency. The only limit to what your emergency fund can cover is the amount of money you put in the fund. There's no paperwork to fill out, and no one's permission to ask when you want to take the money.

Envisioning the emergency scenario

For most people, life goes on, day after day, with very little change. Especially when it comes to finances, we become accustomed to a routine — paychecks at regular intervals for a predictable amount, the same bills each month, allowances for the kids. Occasionally, an unexpected expense crops up, but we usually find a way to get that paid.

Then an emergency strikes. "Restructuring" at the office means you lose your job, and suddenly that regular paycheck disappears, as does your health insurance, your afternoon trips to Starbucks, and your self-esteem. While you're trying to pull your life back together, who's going to pay the bills? A little rainy day money would come in quite handy.

Determining how much to save

Financial analysts suggest a cash reserve of at least three months worth of living expenses, and a reserve of five months of expenses is recommended, especially for couples. This emergency reserve doesn't have to be enough money to cover all of your monthly expenses, just the necessities. Expenses that are optional, such as tickets to events or dining out, do not have to be covered by your emergency fund.

To determine what constitutes necessary living expenses, go back to the budget you drew up in the previous chapter. When you constructed your budget, you listed your monthly living expenses, costs like rent or mortgage payment, utilities, insurance, food, and so on.

Examine the list, and just write down the expenses that are absolutely necessary. Then add up those amounts. The total represents one month of emergency expenses.

TIP

If you do not already have an emergency fund in place, determine how much you need and how long it will take you to save the money for this fund, and then add a monthly amount to your family budget to start saving for your emergency stash.

WARNING!

Some people intentionally skip creating an emergency fund because they know they have good borrowing power and think they'll just borrow money if they get in a bind. Although this may work for some, sometimes a situation, such as a job loss, negates your borrowing power or your ability to make repayments, and you could be stuck with nothing.

Finding a place to park your emergency fund

Look for these three characteristics when searching for a place to invest the money in your emergency fund:

- Little or no risk
- Easy access to the money
- A chance to earn some money on the investment

The last thing you want to do with your emergency fund money is put it at risk in a speculative investment. The idea behind an emergency fund is that the money is there for you, when you really need it. So find a safe place to put your money, a place where you can get access to the money on short notice.

Because your emergency money might be sitting idle for some time (ideally, you won't have any emergencies and the money can sit idle for a *long* time), the money should be invested so that it earns some interest.

A bank savings account is risk-free and earns a little interest, although *little* is the operative word. A step up from a bank savings account is a money market fund. These funds are still completely safe, usually earn more interest than the bank accounts, and you can find money market funds that have check-writing privileges so that you can get your money right away if necessary.

Other totally safe investments are U.S. Treasury bills and bank certificates of deposit. These investments pay a little more than the bank saving account, but the problem with Treasury bills and CDs is that you lose the ability to get the money whenever you need it. At the very least, you need to sell or cash in the certificate or the bills, and, in some cases, you may face a penalty or a loss if you don't wait until the investment matures.

Other investment choices get progressively riskier. Usually, the higher return an investment pays, the riskier it is, and when it comes to your emergency money, that situation just won't do. So stick to the banks and money markets. You may not earn a lot of interest, but you can always be sure that you have access to your money.

Distinguishing real versus made-up emergencies

When you establish your emergency fund, you should also probably set up some rules regarding how that fund is to be used. If you know you have the emergency money available, it can been quite easy, maybe too easy, to take money out of the fund for situations that may not really qualify as requiring emergency spending.

Only you can decide what constitutes a financial emergency in your life, but if you make the rules in advance, when it comes time to consider drawing money from the emergency fund, it'll be easier to resist using the emergency money for an "emergency" family vacation, or a high-end "emergency" stereo system that just went on sale.

The rules are for yourself and anyone else who has access to the fund. If you are the only person in your family who controls the money, the rules you create are just for you.

Make a list of all the types of situations you can think of that might require use of emergency money. Examples might include

- ✦ Loss of a job, either permanently or temporarily (for example, due to a temporary disability), with not enough money available to pay the required living expenses. Job loss is the leading reason for use of emergency funds.
- ✦ Unanticipated, large, unbudgeted expense, such as the unscheduled need for a new car, a significant home repair, the breakdown of a furnace, or major appliance.

- A relative or *really* close friend gets in financial trouble and needs a *short-term* loan.
- Necessary but uninsured and unanticipated medical costs, such as psychiatric care after a devastating event, or the need for modifications to your home due to a disability.

Dealing with emergency expenses you might not anticipate

When an emergency situation arises, particularly if there is a job loss involved, there can be additional expenses that you didn't count on, expenses that you don't normally have when you're not in a state of emergency.

Examples of emergency expenses related to a job loss include

- **Job-hunting expenses:** You might have to spend money on traveling to interviews, creating a resume, printing, and postage. You might also need to acquire new job-hunting clothes for your interviews.
- **Benefits:** You might have to pay for certain benefits that you were receiving from your employer, in particular health insurance and related medical benefits.
- **Education:** You might need to acquire additional skills in order to obtain a new position.

Restocking the emergency fund cookie jar

Whenever you dip into the emergency fund, whether you deplete the entire fund or just a portion of the money, remember to add an emergency fund item back into your budget so that you begin restocking the fund as soon as the emergency has passed.

At your next family budget-planning meeting (you *are* scheduling these regularly now, right?), be sure to discuss the fact that you are using some of your emergency fund, and after your lifestyle stabilizes, make plans to begin rebuilding the fund.

TIP: If you have a family that includes children, discuss the existence of the emergency and the need to tighten up on expenses in the family meeting. The family meeting setting gives your children an opportunity to ask questions and gives you an opportunity to explain how the emergency is impacting your lives and how you expect the family to work together to get through this rough period.

Purchasing Insurance

You pay money to a third party so that, if you get in an accident, or a tree falls on the house, or you die, the insurance company pays money back to you (or the other guy that you crashed into). But if you're lucky and none of those things happen, the insurance company just keeps the money, eventually paying your money to someone else who's not as lucky as you are.

When you think about it, insurance is kind of weird.

Insuring your car

If you drive, you need insurance. Your state license bureau may require insurance before it issues your driver's license. Your auto insurance agent can tell you what your state requires in terms of the different types of coverage. In addition, your agent can offer advice on what amounts of coverage are reasonable — and that may be more than the state minimum requirements — and what those amounts cost. These are the types of auto insurance that are generally available:

- **Basic liability insurance:** If you look on your auto insurance policy, you'll see something like 25/50/10 as the description of how much liability insurance you carry. Although this may sound like the instructions a quarterback gives in the huddle, the numbers actually refer to an amount of insurance coverage. The first number (25, which stands for $25,000) is the amount your policy covers for injuries and loss of wages for any person hurt by you in an accident. The second number (50, or $50,000) represents the total amount the policy will pay for all the people you hurt. The final number (10, or $10,000) is the total amount your policy pays to the person you hit for property damage.
- **Uninsured motorist insurance:** Maybe it's just me, but it seems to me like there are more and more uninsured drivers out on the roads lately. Maybe that's because auto insurance costs have gotten higher, or maybe it's because drivers can get away with it. In my state, you have to have auto insurance to get your driver's license. As soon as you walk out of the license branch with your license in hand, you can cancel your insurance and seemingly nothing can be done to prevent this from happening. If you carry uninsured motorist insurance, your insurance pays for the injuries, lost wages, and even pain and suffering that would have been paid for if the other guy had been covered.
- **Personal injury insurance:** This may be required by your state as part of your auto insurance. This coverage is like extra medical insurance. It covers some of the costs associated with injuries and ambulance charges if you or your passengers are hurt in a car accident. Other insurance that you carry might provide the same coverage, so ask your agent if there is duplication of your other coverage. Some states require personal injury insurance; others do not.
- **Collision insurance:** This type of insurance covers damage to your own vehicle and is optional. The collision party of your insurance policy is subject to a deductible amount, so you pay the deductible part of the repairs and the insurance pays what's left. You choose the amount of

deductible you want to have in your policy — the higher the deductible, the more risk you take on yourself and the lower the cost of your insurance.

- **Comprehensive insurance:** This covers damage to your car from something other than a crash. This would include damage caused by hail or tree branches that fall on your car, vandalism, flood water damage, and so on. Like with collision insurance, there is a deductible that applies to comprehensive coverage.
- **Extra coverage:** This includes towing, replacement value coverage (nice for vintage cars), high-risk driver coverage for when you or another driver of your car has had previous moving violations (for example, tickets for speeding, running red lights, or other accidents).

TIP

Shop around. Auto insurance rates vary from company to company, so compare rates and don't be hesitant to change insurers if you get a better deal elsewhere.

Insuring your home and other possessions

If you own a home and have a mortgage, the lender requires that you carry homeowner's insurance. This protects the lender's investment in your property. After you've paid off your mortgage, the decision to have homeowner's insurance is not so much one of necessity as it is a common-sense decision.

Homeowner's insurance covers damage to the home, theft, and liability for injuries caused to others in your home or on your property. Often specific types of damage such as damage caused by flood, hurricane, tornado, and so on, are extras on the policy, costing more than the basic rate.

Your possessions inside the home are protected by homeowner's insurance as well, and if you take those possessions outside the home, they can still be covered.

The more valuable the home and the possessions, the more expensive the policy. Sometimes you need a separate add-on, or *rider*, with the homeowner's insurance policy to cover specific items, like expensive jewelry, computers, musical instruments, and so on.

As with auto insurance, there is a deductible with homeowner's insurance that controls how much you have to pay on an insurance claim before the insurance company is required to make a payment. The higher the deductible, the lower your insurance rate.

TIP

Discounts on homeowner's insurance are available if you place fire extinguishers and smoke detectors in the home.

Make a lot of claims against your insurance, and your premium rate increases.

Mortgage companies are picky about wanting to make sure you're homeowner's insurance is up-to-date. To make sure you don't skip town and forget to make payments, mortgage lenders typically include an amount for insurance with your monthly mortgage payment, and take care of making the payment directly to the insurer themselves.

A variation of homeowner's insurance is renter's insurance: It's like homeowner's insurance, only for rented property. The same type of coverage applies.

Insuring your life

OK, it's time to talk about dying. Although this might be an uncomfortable subject for you when you're still very much alive, it's easier to discuss now than it would be, uh, later.

Life insurance stands alone as the most misunderstood type of insurance. Some people view life insurance as a contract that gives another person incentive to have you dead. Others think life insurance is designed to provide gifts to those you leave when you die. Although these may be valid reasons for some people to buy life insurance, they are not the most practical reasons.

The primary reason for buying life insurance should be to provide monetary protection for someone who would suffer financially if you were to die. Most often this refers to children or a non-working spouse. Another common life insurance scenario occurs in the case of certain high-level corporate executives. Their company will insure them, naming the company as a beneficiary in the event of the person's untimely death.

We often hear the phrase "untimely death." I'm not sure I understand what constitutes a "timely" death, but no matter what the timing is, if you have life insurance, there is a payout when you die.

Therefore, single people might not feel the same necessity for life insurance that married people and particularly parents of young children do.

When considering whether or not you need life insurance, and how much to buy, keep in mind this list of suggestions offered by the New York State Insurance Department as the types of expenses your life insurance proceeds should be expected to cover:

- Pay off debts that are in your name, including your mortgage
- Pay for expenses that are incurred as a result of your (untimely or timely) death, such as uninsured health care, funeral expenses, estate taxes, legal fees pertaining to your estate

- Provide for education and living expenses for your surviving children
- Provide income for your surviving spouse or at least some money to help hold over your spouse while he or she is adjusting to a new level of income
- Provide retirement funds for your surviving spouse

There are several types of life insurance. Here's a rundown of the options:

- **Term life insurance:** Term has no cash value while you are alive, so if you stop paying your premiums, the policy lapses. This is the cheapest form of life insurance, although as you get older, the rate increases. There are also higher rates for smokers. Some companies offer a *level premium term insurance policy* that lets you lock in a fixed rate for a lengthy period of time such as 10 or 20 years. Sometimes an insurance company offers you a discount for converting term to a different type of life insurance policy with the same company.

  Keep renewing your term policy each year and don't let the policy lapse until such time as you decide you don't want term insurance at all anymore. Many companies let you continue renewing an existing policy without having to have a physical examination each year. If you start and stop up again, you need to undergo another medical exam.

- **Whole life insurance:** Typically considered an investment you make over the course of your lifetime, a whole life policy offers a fixed amount of insurance for a fixed premium, paid for as long as you live. After you have paid a certain amount of premiums, you have an option of ceasing your own payments and letting the earnings on the previously paid premiums cover the future premiums for you. This policy has a cash value, so if you decide you no longer want to provide for your beneficiaries, you can cash in the policy while you're still alive.
- **Variable life insurance:** A variation on whole life wherein you get to control how the premiums you pay are invested and thus the amount of dividends you earn on the premiums.
- **Universal life insurance:** Yet another variation on whole life insurance. This time you have the ability not only to choose how premiums are invested, but you can increase your premiums to increase the value of the policy. You also have the right to borrow against your universal life insurance policy.
- **Variable universal life insurance:** What will they think of next? Universal whole term insurance? Term variable whole insurance? The names get pretty confusing. This particular type of policy combines all the best features of variable and universal insurance. The policy holder controls how much is paid in premiums, the amount of the face value of the policy, and the way in which the money is invested. And you can borrow against the policy.

And by the way, in case you've lost sight of the purpose of all of these insurance policies, they all pay a benefit when you die. Also, dividends earned by the invested amounts of these insurance policies are tax-deferred until such time as you actually receive the cash.

Insuring your health

Many employees are lucky enough to have health insurance provided by their employer. Even if the employee has to pay for the insurance, the lower rates that are available to groups go a long way toward making the insurance desirable.

The cost of health insurance, if you're not part of a company plan, can be exorbitant. Youngsters get to piggyback on their parents' insurance policies, so it can be a significant financial shock when they finish school and have to start buying their own insurance.

There are three types of health insurance: basic health, major medical, and disability. Here's a brief summary of each type of plan:

- **Basic health insurance:** Includes both hospitalization and medical/surgical. As the name implies, hospitalization covers hospital expenses including the charge for the room, nursing services, the use of the operating room, medications administered by the hospital, x-rays, and lab tests. Medical/surgical insurance takes care of the doctor bills during a hospital stay.
- **Major medical insurance:** Covers the rest of your medical costs, including doctor visits, out-patient surgeries (although sometimes these fall under the basic health plan), prescription drugs, private nurses, therapy, and rehabilitation expenses. Usually there is a co-pay or a specific percentage that the patient is expected to pay. Also, there is a deductible associated with major medical, and usually there is a maximum dollar amount that the policy will cover.
- **Disability insurance:** Replaces lost income when you are forced to refrain from working for medical reasons. Disability policies differ significantly from one provider to another, so if you're purchasing a policy yourself, as opposed to having a policy provided by your employer, determine up front what features you require from the coverage, and read the policy closely before making a decision as to which type of disability plan to purchase.

Don't forget Medicare, the government-provided health care policy we pay for with a portion of our earned income. Medicare is available through the Social Security Administration to citizens over age 65 and some disabled citizens as well.

If you're purchasing your own health insurance, be sure to shop around. The most important thing to consider when looking for a health insurance plan is to decide before you start shopping what it is you're looking for. Make a list of the types of coverage you want to have in your plan, and the amount of deductible you're interested in paying. You may not end up with a plan that is exactly what you think you want, but this gives you an excellent starting point for analyzing and pricing plans.

Here are some other tips to think about when shopping for a health plan:

- Ask about payments options for your insurance premiums. Some companies lower the premium rates if you agree to pay quarterly or yearly instead of monthly.
- Know the COBRA rules (even if you can't remember what it stands for). When you leave a job where you were covered by health insurance, COBRA can be activated and give you the right to continue on the company health plan for 18 months or more. Check with your employer to find out the rules for your company. (COBRA stands for Consolidated Omnibus Budget Reconciliation Act, by the way.)
- Look into the possibility of a group health plan through an organization that you belong to (or that you might be interested in joining). Many professional organizations offer health insurance to members at the reduced group rates.

Insuring your future

Long-term care is the continuous skilled nursing care and custodial care necessary to assist certain people with daily living activities. The people who qualify are those who have a chronic disease, disability, or frailty. Long-term care can last for a few months to a year, several years, or indefinitely. The care can be provided in a nursing home, community setting, or in the home.

Don't shy away from investigating the possibility of investing in long-term care insurance. Analysts estimate the average annual cost to Americans in need of long-term care as $50,000. This amount varies geographically, with care recipients in larger cities paying as much as twice that amount, and care in rural areas not as expensive. By 2020, when the baby boom generation will be among the ranks of the nation's retired, the cost of long-term care is expected to double, not only due to ongoing rising medical costs but also an anticipated shortage of available caregivers.

If you're in your 40s or 50s and expect to have a measurable amount of wealth by the time you retire, long-term care insurance is something you should consider.

The primary alternative to long-term care insurance is Medicaid, a combined federal and state government welfare program designed for people who can't afford their care costs. To qualify for Medicaid, you must first spend down all of your assets and personal savings. This is an unattractive alternative for people who have accumulated assets of at least two or three hundred thousand dollars and would like to live comfortably or leave some of their assets for their heirs.

If one spouse is in need of long-term care, that spouse is required to deplete the family portfolio in order to qualify for Medicaid. This can leave the surviving spouse a pauper when the first spouse dies. The undesirability of this scenario leads many people to look into long-term care insurance.

Long-term care insurance is not prohibitively expensive if you're in your 50s. The problem is that many people don't start thinking about the need for this insurance until they're in their 70s, at which time the cost of a policy might make it unaffordable.

Wondering how much long-term care insurance costs? Use the AICPA LTCI Plan Cost calculator to figure out how much it will cost for you: `https://gltc.prudential.com/gltc/main/Login_preLoginGLTC?EMPLOYER=aicpa`.

Choosing a long-term care policy

There are several factors to consider when choosing an LTCI policy and provider, including

- Rating of the insurance provider.
- Availability of coverage for home care and assisted living situations in addition to nursing home care.
- Ability to select private caregivers.
- Ability to choose non-professional caregivers including family members at home.
- Per diem dollar amount of coverage.
- Cost of the premiums including the ability of the provider to raise rates.
- Duration of the premium period. (Some policies provide for single premium, 10- and 20-year fixed rate plans.)
- Inflation adjustments in coverage.
- Number of years of benefits.
- Length of waiting period before benefits are paid.
- Discount options for group or family participation.
- Right of spousal survivorship.
- Restoration of benefits if part of the policy is used.
- Prorated benefit if policy lapses before being paid in full.
- Waiver of premium after you begin collecting benefits.

Chapter 5: Planning for the Future

In This Chapter

- Saving for college
- Thinking about retirement
- Planning for other large expenses

Doris Day sang "Que sera, sera. Whatever will be, will be," in the Hitchcock movie, *The Man Who Knew Too Much*. It's one thing to throw caution to the wind in a Hollywood movie. But when it comes to your own finances, the better course is to not wait to let "what will be, will be," but to jump in and do your best to try to see the future and make some concrete financial plans that will enable your vision to be a reality.

Planning for College

They say there are two certainties in life: death and taxes. Here's a third: College education costs rise each year. However much college costs today, you can be sure it will cost lots more in five or ten years or whenever you plan to send yourself or a family member off to school. Not only does tuition rise every year, so does the cost of housing, food, books, activity fees (required even for inactive students), sweatshirts, basketball tickets, fraternity paddles, and any other items that are necessary for a complete education.

Some lucky people can just write checks for the costs when it's time to pay for college. For the rest of us, a little advance planning is in order so that we parents don't end up living in a box on the street corner while our kids are living it up on campus.

Saving the 529 way

If you're planning on sending a family member to college any time soon (say, in the next 25 years or so), or if you would like to contribute to someone else's college education, take a look at the 529 college savings plans.

The nifty little 529 programs were introduced in 1996, the year when the members of the baby boom generation looked over their collective shoulders and saw that their little boomlets were about to head for college, *en masse*. Not known for their ability to plan for the future, baby boomers turned to Congress for help and got it, albeit too late for the first wave of baby boomer offspring, but at least in time to help those whose children were still playing Hide and Seek and watching Nickelodeon in 1996.

How 529 plans work

Money is contributed to 529 plans on behalf of a particular beneficiary who, one day, is expected to become a college student. The contributions can come from anyone — parents, grandparents, family friends, or even the student himself.

You don't get a tax deduction for the money contributed to a 529 plan, but the money that is earned in the plan is tax-deferred. As long as the money from the plan is used as intended, for the beneficiary's school expenses (including room and board), the earnings in the plan are not taxed.

If it turns out the beneficiary does not go to college, or does not use all the money in the plan, another member of the beneficiary's family may be named as a beneficiary. Alternatively, the balance in the plan can be returned to the person who made the contributions and the earnings are taxed to that person when they are withdrawn.

WARNING! Earnings in the 529 plan that are withdrawn and not used for education-related costs are hit with a 10 percent penalty. However, if a child receives scholarship money, an equivalent amount of money up to the total amount of the scholarship money can be withdrawn from the plan and returned to the plan contributor, and there is no penalty on that withdrawal.

TIP All 50 states offer 529 programs; each state offers its own version(s) of the tax-deferred savings plan. In most cases, it doesn't matter which state you live in or in which state your student attends or plans to attend school — you can participate in a 529 plan from nearly any state.

Saving for college with a 529

Here are some Web sites where you can find out more about college savings plans and compare options of different plans:

- `www.savingforcollege.com`: Joseph Hurley, author of *The Best Way to Save for College: A Complete Guide to 529 Plans*, operates a Web site that is a great resource for 529 information, definitions, forums, comparative charts, and so on.
- `www.collegesavings.org`: This Web site is sponsored by the College Savings Plans Network, a federal lobbying group affiliated with the National Association of State Treasurers. This site includes a list of all plans available with telephone numbers.
- `http://apps.nasd.com/investor_Information/Smart/529/529_saving.asp`: This Web site for NASD 529 College Savings Plans includes lots of definitions, college savings calculators, and tips for saving.

A small number of states have residency restrictions for 529 plan participants. See the "Saving for college with a 529" sidebar for Web sites where you can find out more about the rules for 529 plans in each state.

Usually the payout from the 529 plan is made directly to the school. You provide the bills you receive from the school to the plan sponsor, who cuts checks payable to the school.

Investing in 529s

Typically, each type of 529 plan offers different options for investing, some riskier than others. Depending on the age of the beneficiary, you may want to choose an investment plan that features long-term growth (for younger beneficiaries who don't need the money in the near future), or you can choose a short-term program that provides less risky and more stable investing.

The 529 plans try not to invest in anything terribly risky: We're talking about money for a college education, not mad money you can afford to put at risk and possibly lose. However, the possibility does exist that the fund you choose for your 529 investment could lose money, so it's important to monitor your investment closely.

REMEMBER

Each state invests its 529 plan money in a different mix of mutual funds. Usually there are three or more funds from which you can choose, and you can move your investment among the funds. Analyze the investment options from all states, and then pick the program(s) you want to sign up for. Compare not just the rate of return on the plans, but the administrative costs as well.

Prepaid tuition plans

Some colleges offer prepaid tuition plans. Similar to the 529 plans that are not associated with specific educational institutions, the college tuition plans are designed to provide an opportunity to spread school payments over a lengthy time period. It's in the schools' interests to hook you early, not only to have the use of your cash but to line up future students. Sometimes these plans lock in a specific tuition rate if you go to that school.

WARNING!

The prepaid tuition plans are only tuition plans. You're still on the hook for room and board and other costs.

If you decide not to go to the school that offers the tuition plan, or if you are not accepted to the school, you can still use your money at another school; you just lose the benefit of the pre-agreed-upon tuition rate. Prepaid tuition plans are transferable to younger siblings.

You should be fairly certain you want to send your child to that school before choosing a prepaid tuition plan. Many plans are designed to penalize you if you use the money for a different school. For example, you might only get your contributions returned to you without any earnings, and you might even have to pay a penalty.

With a prepaid tuition plan, you don't have any choices as to how your money is invested. What you are arranging for is a fixed rate of tuition. After you turn your money over to the school, the school can use or invest the money however it wants.

Coverdell Education Savings Accounts

Formerly known as the Education IRA, until someone in Washington decided that name was way too simple and easy to remember, the Coverdell Education Savings Account provides you with the opportunity to create a savings account with favorable tax treatment, targeted for education costs.

Distinguishing itself from 529 plans, the ESA lets you actually save for high school and grade school education as well as college costs in a tax-deferred/tax-free environment. When you take money out of the ESA for school costs, the earnings portion of the money you withdraw is tax-free. If you don't use the money for qualified school costs, you have to pay tax on the fund earnings when they are withdrawn from the ESA.

Qualified school costs, for purposes of the Coverdell Education Savings Accounts, means the expenses required by the school where the plan beneficiary attends. Such expenses include tuition, fees, books, supplies, equipment, room and board, and expenses for special needs services. High school and grammar school students get to include tutoring fees, uniforms (if required by the school), transportation to and from school, a computer, software (except games and fun stuff), and Internet access, home schooling, and after-school care.

You are allowed to contribute up to $2,000 per year per beneficiary. The Coverdell ESA contribution is not available to married taxpayers who file a joint tax return and whose adjusted gross income on their tax return is over $220,000, or to single taxpayers with adjusted gross income over $110,000.

The money that is contributed to the ESA must be deposited with a bank or other financial institution that administers ESAs. The person making the contributions controls how the money in the account is invested.

If the beneficiary reaches age 30 and hasn't used all the money in the account, the rest of the money must be withdrawn at that time.

Borrowing for college

If you decide to wait until your child is ready to start college to figure out how to finance the college education, all is not lost. There are several types of federal grants and loans available to parents and students who need assistance in meeting college costs.

These financial aid awards are determined based on information provided by students and parents in the annual Free Application for Federal Student Aid (FAFSA) form. All of these programs are funded by the federal government through our tax dollars.

- **Federal Pell grants:** The nicest thing about a Pell grant is that you don't have to pay the money back. Pell grants are awarded based on need, with an upper limit of $4,050 per school year. The maximum Pell grant for the 2004–2005 school year is $4,050.
- **Federal work-study:** Students who participate in the federal work-study program receive wages, just like any employee, for jobs on or near their college campus. The federal government reimburses the employer for 50 percent to 100 percent of the wages (a 75 percent reimbursement is most common).
- **Federal Perkins loan:** Jointly funded between colleges and the federal government, Perkins loans are awarded to qualifying college students who receive a low interest loan of up to $4,000 per year for undergraduate study or $6,000 per year for graduate study.
- **Federal Stafford loan:** These loans have higher interest rates and lower award amounts than the Perkins loans. *Subsidized* Stafford loans, like Perkins loans, accrue interest throughout the college years, but the federal government pays the interest until the student completes the education. *Unsubsidized* Stafford loans accrue interest during the time the student is in school, and the interest is added to the principal after graduation. Perkins and Stafford loans are issued in the student's name.
- **Plus loan:** Plus loans are issued to parents of college students. These loans are unsubsidized, so interest begins accruing immediately.

TIP

These federal programs are the tip of the financial iceberg when it comes to financing college education. There are plenty of state and community scholarship and grant programs available to the industrious student who seeks out available sources of college money and does what it takes to get the money. Many books have been published that provide information on how to get college money, and most high school guidance departments have reams of brochures and information about money that is available.

Using your assets to fund a college education

Many people choose to refinance their home or cash in their Individual Retirement Accounts when it's time to pay for college for the kids. There's certainly no problem with taking either of these steps if it is part of your master financial plan. It makes sense, however, before liquidating assets that you might need later on in retirement, to go ahead and fill out the FAFSA form to see if you qualify for federal aid.

- **Home equity loans:** *Equity* is the difference between how much your house is worth and how much you owe on your mortgage. Banks like to give home equity loans because the money is secured. You can borrow against the unencumbered value of your home, increasing your monthly mortgage payments, and the bank is protected because it holds a lien against your house. Of course, the downside is that if you can't make the payments, the bank can take your house.
- **Home equity line of credit:** An alternative to an outright loan against the equity in the home is a line of credit secured by the equity. You don't have to take all the money at once. You just take what you need and can draw on the balance whenever you want. You only make payments and pay interest on the actual amount you have borrowed, not the entire credit line.
- **Selling the family house is also an option come college time.** Some parents decide that when it's time to send the kids away to college, they can downsize to a smaller home, take out the equity that has built up in their house over the years, and use that money to pay for college.
- **Withdrawing money from an IRA:** Taking money out of an Individual Retirement Account (IRA) before age 59½ is usually a costly way to get money because of the penalties involved, but there is an exception to the penalty rule when it comes to using the money for college. You can take money from an IRA to pay for tuition, books, fees, supplies, and equipment for yourself, your spouse, your child, or your grandchild and incur no penalty. Note that room and board are not included. Keep in mind, however, that you do have to pay income tax on any amounts taken from the IRA that have not been previously taxed.

TIP

Make sure the amount you take out of the IRA corresponds exactly to (or is less than) the amount needed for the tuition and other expenses listed above.

TIP

Grab a copy of *529 & Other College Savings Plans For Dummies* by Margaret Munro (published by Wiley) for more info on saving for college.

Planning for Retirement

It's easy to think of retirement in the abstract. Or for that matter, it's easy not to think of retirement at all. For those of us in the baby boom generation, confronting retirement is not a concept with which we were raised. Our parents aged in a generation where they worked at one company for most of their lives and could count on a company pension to provide them with a regular paycheck throughout retirement. Also, they weren't expected to live as long as we are, so it didn't take as much money to fund retirement as it's going to from now on.

Look at it this way: If you are offered an early retirement package today from the company where you work and are given the opportunity to retire at age 55, there's a possibility you will live more years as a retiree than the number of years you worked.

Do you have enough money to cover your living expenses for the next 20 years or more? It's a scary thought, and one most people ignore.

A more likely scenario is that people will continue to work long into what used to be thought of as retirement years. A number of studies have been done on our country's aging workforce, and most of them have reached the conclusion that complete retirement is not practical.

So, while you're considering what type of work you might want to do when you're not as agile as you are today, think about putting away as much money as you can in all of the attractive retirement savings plans that are available. You might plan on working until you take your last breath, but in case that's not a viable scenario, better get busy and start (or continue) saving.

Investing in 401(k) plans

Today's most popular retirement plan, the 401(k), and its clone, the 403(b), are employer-sponsored plans that enable you to save a percentage of your income in a tax-deferred investment account. As explained in Book I, Chapter 1, 401(k) money is taxed when it is withdrawn.

Many employers offer matching contributions to encourage employees to add to their 401(k) plans. This is like getting free money. When you add to your retirement fund, the employer kicks in a percentage as well.

When trying to make room in your budget for contributions to a 401(k) plan, the best way to proceed is to put as much money as you possibly can in the fund, and have the payments taken right out of your paycheck, so that you don't even notice they're missing. Payroll withdrawals are the most painless way to invest.

REMEMBER

Unlike company pension plans that often require you to work a certain number of years before you are entitled to take the money, the 401(k) money is yours and you can take it with you whenever you leave your job.

Enron employees learned the hard way that putting all of their retirement money in one investment (particular when that investment was Enron stock) can backfire. Spread your investible retirement money over a mix of funds so that if one fund goes bad, it won't take all of your future income with it.

Investing in tax-deferred annuities

A tax-deferred annuity is a type of long-term retirement investment that provides a fixed payment either for a certain amount of time or for the rest of your life. You can customize the annuity plan based on how much and for how long you want to contribute.

An annuity isn't an employer benefit. This is something you choose to purchase on your own.

You can purchase an annuity with a lump sum, or you can arrange for periodic payments, most easily made through payroll withdrawals.

Lump sum annuity purchases are a nice way to tuck away an inheritance or monetary gift that you receive — money that isn't part of your regular budgeted spending so you won't miss it or notice its absence.

TIP

Credit card companies have gotten into the annuity act too. You can purchase an annuity from a credit card company and have monthly contributions charged to your account. Easy peasy retirement planning.

Types of annuities

There are fixed-rate annuities and variable-rate annuities. You get to pick which kind you want when you purchase an annuity.

With a variable rate annuity, you choose the way the money will be invested, and thus have some control over how much will be available to you when you begin withdrawing funds.

If you choose a fixed-rate annuity, where the investments are chosen by the annuity company, and you are guaranteed a particular return on investment, you can shop around for the best deal you can find.

Payout of annuity funds

When it's time to take money out of your annuity, either because you purchased an annuity for a fixed period of time and the annuity has matured, or because you decide you're ready to take the money, there are some tax considerations to remember.

The tax you'll pay on withdrawing funds is the tax on the earnings that have accumulated, not the amount you invested. Prorate the amounts you withdraw to split the amounts between taxable and non-taxable funds.

For example: Say you invested a total of $10,000 in an annuity and it is now worth $15,000. Two-thirds of your money ($10,000) had been previously taxed and is not subject to income tax now. The remaining third is taxable. If you withdraw $300 per month, $200 will be tax-free, and the other $100 is taxed at your current income tax rate.

This is a simplified example, because as you withdraw $300 per month, the rest of the money keeps growing and your proportion of tax-free and taxable money alters a bit each month. Your annuity company will be glad to help you figure out the taxable portion of your payments.

Investing in Individual Retirement Accounts

Individual Retirement Accounts come in two flavors — traditional IRAs and Roth IRAs. Both plan types are self-administered, meaning you get to make all the decisions about how much you invest and how the money is invested.

The most IRA money you can invest in one year is $4,000 as of 2005, plus an additional $500 if you're at least age 50. In 2006, the age 50+ contribution goes to $1,000, and in 2008, the regular IRA contribution amount goes to $5,000. Congress is always futzing with these amounts, so just ask your bank or financial institution (the place where you park your IRA money) to give you the latest scoop on how much you are allowed to contribute.

Like so many other retirement plans, an IRA is a tax-deferred investment, so any earnings that accumulate in the fund do so without having to show up on your tax return — until such time as you take the money out.

Putting money in a traditional IRA

A traditional IRA gives you the option of taking a tax deduction for your contribution. You don't have to take the deduction, but if you want to, it goes on the front page of your federal tax return and reduces your taxable income in the year of the deduction.

You can make an IRA contribution all the way up to the due date of your income tax return. So if it's April 14 and you suddenly realize you owe way more tax than you thought you would, plan a trip to the bank on the 15th and make an IRA contribution. Not only do you get the benefit of tucking away extra money for retirement, you get to reduce your taxable income and thus your tax.

There are some limitations on who gets to take the tax deduction, based on whether you're married, whether you have a retirement plan in place at your job, how much money you earn, and what time zone you live in (skip that last one, unless of course you live in Indiana, where none of us know what time zone we live in and our clocks, not to mention our dairy cows, are in a constant state of confusion). These limitations are listed in Table 1-1 of Book I, Chapter 1.

Putting money in a Roth IRA

No tax deduction is available for contributions to a Roth IRA, yet at the same time, the Roth may be the best investment in town. You control the way in which the money is invested, and when it comes time to withdraw the funds, there is no tax on the earnings. Ever.

Your annual contribution to a Roth IRA, assuming you qualify (see Table 1-2, Book I, Chapter 1), faces the same limit as the traditional IRA annual limits listed above.

WARNING!

Those IRA contribution annual limits apply to all IRA accounts combined. So if you have a traditional IRA and a Roth IRA, you can only contribute a *total* of $4,000 for 2005 (plus an additional $500 if you're older than 50).

Investing in retirement funds designed for the self-employed

Self-employed people whine a lot about all the tax they have to pay, and as a self-employed person myself I can empathize. But say what you will about the extra taxes we face, the self-employed workers have it all over the employees when it comes to making retirement contributions.

A self-employed worker has several options for investing in tax-deferred retirement accounts. Take a look at these examples:

- **IRAs:** Just like the employees, self-employed workers can contribute to IRA accounts up to the annual limits (same limitations as employees).
- **Individual 401(k):** Designed for the self-employed, the individual 401(k) enables a self-employed worker to set up a 401(k) plan and contribute just like the employees do. In addition, the self-employed person can make employer matching contributions to the plan.
- **SEP-IRA:** The self-employed person can contribute a percentage of income up to a maximum of $41,000 annually to this type of pension plan.

Like with anything when the IRS gets involved, the rules for self-employed retirement plans can get kind of confusing, especially in situations where the business person has employees. Be sure to consult with a tax professional to make sure your contributions match the IRS guidelines.

Participating in company pension plans

Company pension plans aren't as prevalent as they used to be, but some companies still offer their employees these benefits. There are two common types of pension plans — defined benefit plans and defined contribution plans. If you're lucky enough to have such plans available at your workplace, you already know that you don't have to do anything to opt into these plans, but there are lots of rules about when you get to claim the money and how much you will be paid.

Participating in a defined benefit plan

As you might imagine, a *defined benefit plan* is a pension plan that spells out exactly how much the employee will receive in monthly payments at the time of retirement.

Typically the benefit is based on the employee's wages and how long the employee worked for the company.

The employer makes contributions to the plan over the course of the employee's years with the company. There's no individual account like there is with a 401(k) plan: Your benefits are part of a large fund that is responsible for paying benefits to all retired employees. It is the employer's responsibility to contribute enough money to the pension plan to meet the plan's commitments to current and future retirees.

In order to qualify to receive the retirement benefits of the pension plan, you must be *vested* in the plan. Vesting is defined by the company you work for, but generally refers to a predetermined number of years that you are required to work.

It's possible to be partially vested in a company pension plan. Many companies vest employees over a number of years so that, if you were to retire from the company before you are fully vested, you would still receive a pension — it would just be smaller than the amount you would receive if you were 100 percent vested.

Participating in a defined contribution plan

The reverse of the defined benefit plan is the *defined contribution plan*. This type of plan includes stock, profit-sharing, and fixed annual contributions made by the employer. Also, you are entitled to contribute to the plan with tax-deferred payroll deductions.

With a defined contribution plan, a separate account is maintained for each employee. The amount you receive when you retire is based on the value of the investments in the account and the value of the company stock you receive.

TIP

As with other contributory retirement plans, it is in your interest to contribute as much as you are allowed to. Years from now, your retired self will thank you.

Planning for Other Big Expenses

Big expenses warrant room in your budget. Just as you wouldn't wait until the last day you work to try to figure out how to fund your retirement, you should give some budget consideration to other big expenses so they won't catch you off guard.

Some of the big expenses work easily into the budget because they come with automatic monthly payments. A house purchase, for example, is typically paid for with a mortgage, and most cars are purchased with the help of a car loan — more monthly payments.

But you're on your own for some big expenses, such as these:

- Weddings
- Travel
- Caring for family member

The list can continue, depending on the types of items that are important to you. Some expenses are just too big to simply write a check for. You can turn to credit cards, but the best way to approach the really big expenses that you know are waiting down the road is to add them to your budget now and start planning.

You'll find information in Book VI about how to use Quicken to create and monitor savings goals. When you get an early start, adding a small amount to your monthly budget, the savings can increase and the large expenses won't seem so insurmountable.

And if it turns out your daughters elope, your parents stay in good health, and you decide you're happy at home and don't want to travel — well, there's no harm in having a little extra stash to add to your retirement savings.

Setting realistic goals

One of the most difficult tasks of planning for events that won't occur for many years is determining how much to save and what those events are really going to cost.

Here are some guidelines that financial analysts suggest using when planning for the big expenses.

✦ **Retirement:** Experts suggest that you can expect your living expenses in retirement to be about 30 percent lower than your living expenses while you're working. Analysts tell us that, on the average, men are expected to live to about age 71, women to age 75. So do the math, figure out how much you spend now, what you can expect to spend at whenever you think you will retire, and determine how much longer you'll live. Compare the result with the amount of retirement money you have saved already, and figure out what that translates to in terms of a monthly contribution starting today.

  P.S.: Don't forget to figure in Social Security with your available retirement income. Or not. Only time will tell if the government's social insurance program will survive the deluge of baby boomers.

  TIP: For retirement planning and planning for other large expenses, Quicken provides little calculators that help you determine how much you need to save. These planners are discussed in Book VI.

✦ **College:** One point to consider as the years go by, is that the more you make, the more you need to save for college costs. (The higher your income, the less financial aid you qualify for.) Another point to consider is whether you plan to send your child to a state school, an out-of-state public school, or a private school. Start early searching for scholarships and positioning yourself or your child so you qualify. Many civic organizations offer scholarship money to children of members who volunteer. And get those college savings into your budget. The more you save, the more comfortable the whole process is.

✦ **Travel:** This type of expense is much easier to determine. Collect travel brochures, contact agencies, write away for information, and determine to the best of your ability the exact cost of your dream vacation. Add in money for souvenirs and some new clothes for the trip, and start saving. The trip you long to take will taste even sweeter if you don't have to pay off the credit card bills for the next ten years.

✦ **Care for elderly relative:** When dad comes to stay with you, he will bring more than his favorite easy chair and a list of complaints. He'll bring Social Security, Medicare, and maybe some savings and pension money too, so the burden won't fall entirely on you. Nevertheless, it's wise to start planning for a new family member. Do some planning and get some savings lined up for the costs you expect to incur.

Paying yourself

The analysts always say, "Pay yourself first." What they mean is, each month when you sit down to pay the bills, start by siphoning off money for your savings. In fact, if you really want to save money based on the out-of-sight-out-of-mind philosophy, set up an automatic payroll deduction, move money into savings before it ever moves through your fingers, and you're much more likely to leave the money where it is.

It's a lot harder to write a check or transfer funds yourself than it is to have your employer take care of the job for you.

So start saving, and the future will seem like less of a financial challenge and more of a chance to pride yourself on how well you take care of your family.

Book II

Quicken Basics

"Great! It comes with Quicken. Now maybe we can figure out where all the money around here is going."

Contents at a Glance

Chapter 1: Setting Up Quicken

In This Chapter

- Installing Quicken
- Converting from earlier versions
- Getting familiar with Quicken
- Setting up categories

If you've never used Quicken, let your family know you're about to install the program so they can prepare for a few weeks of listening to your cries of joy from the computer desk as you figure out all the cool things Quicken can do. They may want to take a trip or at least plan a lot of nights out of the house while you get settled into your new program. If you're upgrading from an earlier version of Quicken, you should still let your family know what to expect: This book should enable you to stretch the boundaries of your program and find out about lots of new ways to have fun watching your money grow.

Getting Quicken Set Up on Your Computer

As a bit of introduction, let me just say that the version of the Quicken program used for the descriptions and images in this book is Quicken 2006 Premier. If you have a different version of Quicken, your screens may look slightly different from those presented here. The logic of the program, however, has not changed over the years, so you should be able to quickly extrapolate the information you need to apply to your own version of the program. This book is not meant to be version-specific, so what you discover should carry across to whatever version of Quicken you have on your computer.

That said, when you place your Quicken CD in the CD-ROM drive of your computer, you should see a screen asking whether you intend to install your Quicken for the very first time or upgrade from an earlier version (Figure 1-1). Choose your option and click Next to proceed.

TIP

If you don't see the installation screen when you load your CD, click the Start⇨Run⇨Browse, and then locate the CD drive letter and click it. The Quicken files appear onscreen. Click the Setup file, and then click OK to close the Browse window. Click OK again to close the Run window.

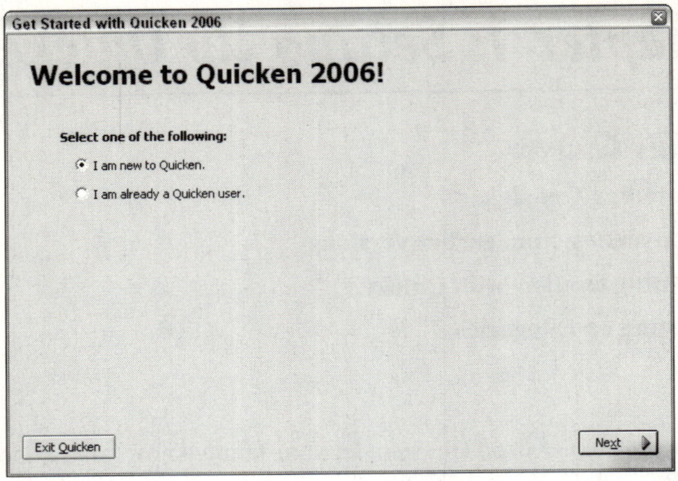

Figure 1-1: Saying hello to Quicken.

Using Quicken for the very first time

Quicken stores your financial information in a file on your computer. Your data file is automatically given a name, QDATA, which is sort of reminiscent of that android guy on *Star Trek*, without the Q.

The data file used for storing your personal financial information is *encrypted,* which means that if someone tries to open the file by himself, without using Quicken, all he sees is weird little hieroglyphics instead of information about how much money you have in your bank account.

Quicken walks you through the initial setup steps so that you can enter some basic information and get ready to use the program. Just follow along, doing what you're told, and nobody will get hurt.

Answering personal questions

When you're new to Quicken, you need to answer some simple questions that identify you to the program. Fill in the blanks with basic stuff like your name, rank, and serial number.

The makers of Quicken know that you're going to be using Quicken to record your most private personal information, like how much you make at your job, how much you paid for your brother's birthday gift, and when you got that face lift. See the sidebar entitled "And the password is . . ." later in this chapter for the lowdown on how to give your program a password so that no one else can sit down at your desk and find out your secrets.

In the next setup screen (Figure 1-2), you're asked to check boxes for what you want to use Quicken to accomplish. I recommend checking everything; that way, the program is ready to go with all its bells and whistles. Just because you check a box doesn't mean you have to use that feature later, but it's easier to have everything in place right from the start.

Gathering the info you need during setup

You can wait for each question, and then run around trying to collect the stuff you need to get yourself set up in Quicken, or you can gather all of these items in advance, and then relax at your desk while you shuffle through your documents and answer the questions. It's your call.

For each type of account you want to set up, click the Add Account button on the setup screen (Figure 1-3), and then enter the information requested. Skip any buttons you don't want to deal with now. You can always set up information later.

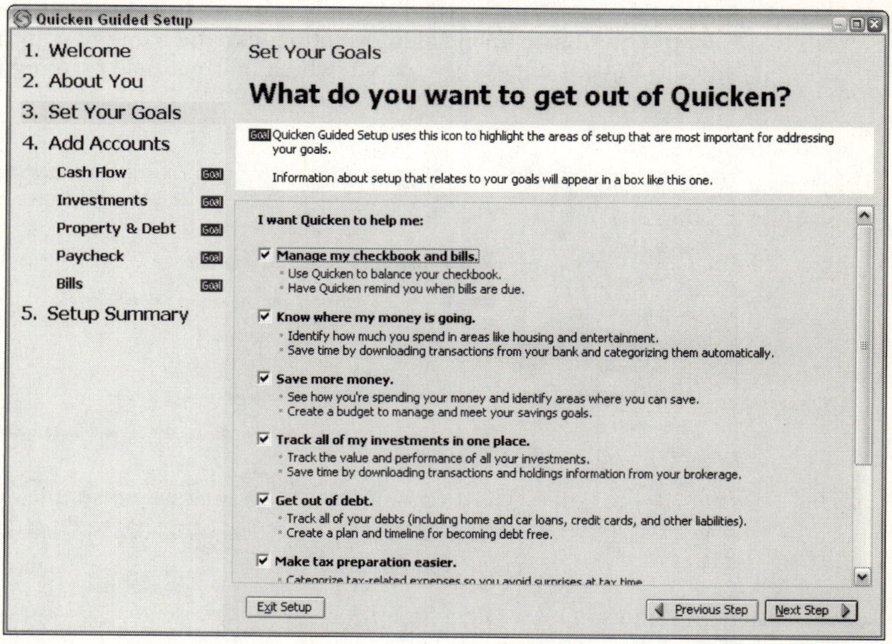

Figure 1-2: Check all of the boxes, and then click Next Step to get on with the show.

Here is a checklist of documents you'll need for Quicken setup (just pick the information you want to set up now):

- Customer ID and PIN number for Quicken online banking services: You need to request this from your bank, and it may take a couple of days. (If you don't want to use the online banking services, choose Manual when asked if this account is Online or Manual.) (See Book I, Chapter 2 for a detailed example of setting up a new bank account.)
- Your most recent bank statement for each account you plan to set up.
- Your bank account number and bank routing number, if you want to sign up for the online Quicken Bill Pay service.
- The names, amounts, and due dates of each regular payment you make.

Entering useful start-up stuff

With Quicken, you can enter as much or as little as you want when you start using the program. The more information you enter up front, the less you have to do later. That's really the only difference. But setup time is a nice time to enter basic financial information, like the name of your bank, how much is in your checking account, which bills get paid on a regular basis, where your savings are invested, and so on.

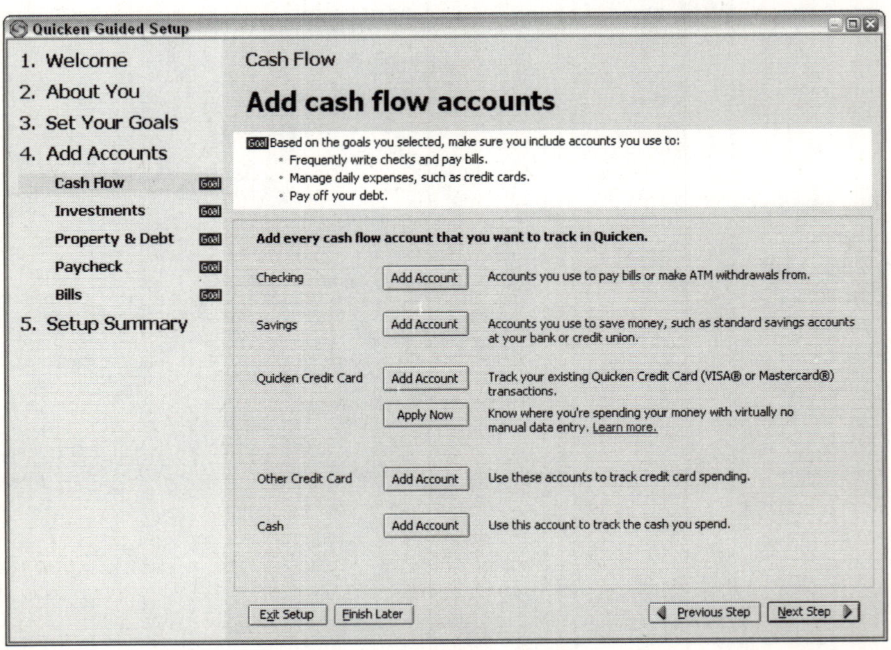

Figure 1-3: Click Add Account to create new accounts.

Click through the introductory screens, entering what information you have available, saving other entries for later on, whenever you're ready.

When you get to the screen for setting up bills, if you choose to pay bills online, you'll be asked to sign up for Quicken's Bill Pay service. The first month is free, so it can't hurt to give it a try and see how you like it. After that, it's $9.95 per month (at least, that was the fee as of this writing). This isn't a bad price if you are used to writing a lot of checks and paying postage for your bill payments.

But if you don't pay a lot of bills, or if your bank gives you an online bill paying service for free or a lesser charge, you may not think the $9.95 is worth it. Give it a try, see what you think, and cancel later if you don't want to pay. Book IV, Chapter 4 covers the online bill payment service in detail.

Entering ongoing bills

If you chose the manual bill payment option instead of the online Bill Pay service, the screen shown in Figure 1-4 pops up, asking you to check off each of the bills you pay on a regular basis. Check all the appropriate boxes, and then indicate how many of each type of bill you pay. Click Next when you've entered everything.

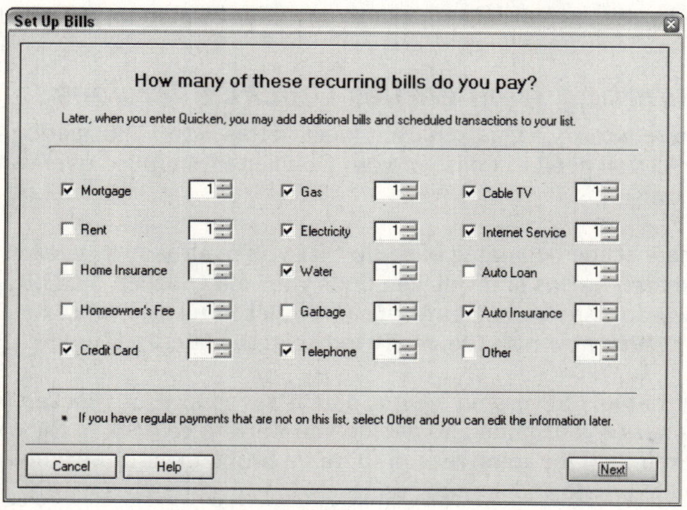

Figure 1-4: Check boxes for each type of bill you pay.

Next you see a list of all the bills you indicated in the check boxes (Figure 1-5). Enter the name of each company that you pay the bills to, and the amount you normally pay.

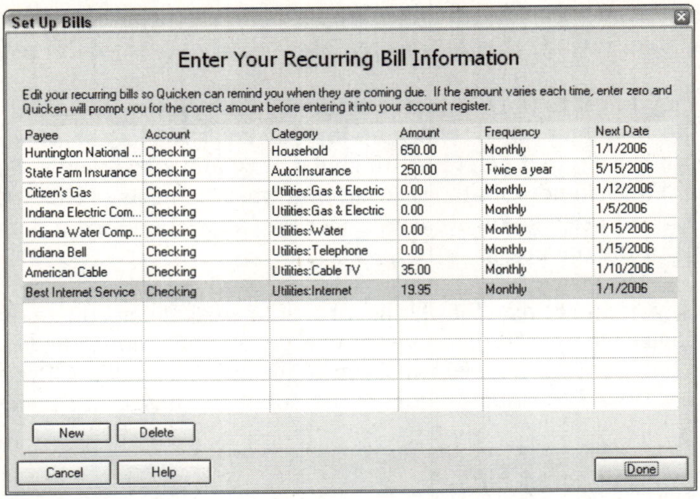

Figure 1-5: Tell Quicken when the bills are due, and Quicken nags you when it's time to pay.

If the amount varies from payment to payment, just leave the amount area blank and you can fill it in each time you pay a bill.

Enter the frequency with which you make these payments, and then enter the due date for the next payment of each bill. From now on, you get a friendly reminder from Quicken to pay your bills on time. Isn't that sweet?

Converting from earlier Quicken versions

If you're already a Quicken user, most of this setup information is wasted on you. All you need to do is get your Quicken files moved over to the new version.

Indicate at the beginning of setup that you're already a Quicken user. Then the search begins and Quicken finds your old Quicken data file. Click OK in the window shown in Figure 1-6, and Quicken turns your rusty old data file into a shiny new data file, ready to use in the latest version of Quicken.

Note that an old version of your data is saved in your Quicken folder, so if you change your mind and decide you want to go back to the old version of Quicken, or if for some reason there's a problem with the conversion, your old data is safe and sound.

Switching between data files

If you need to set up another data file in Quicken, go to the File menu and choose New, and then do all the setup stuff over again for the new file.

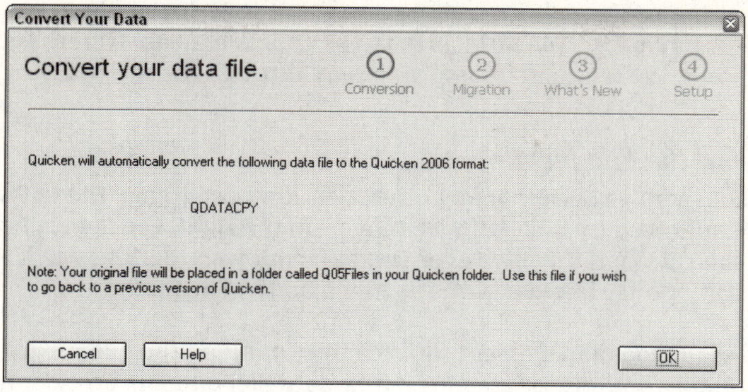

Figure 1-6: One click of the OK button and the conversion is underway.

You don't need to set up a new file for each different account you own. Files most commonly go with people, so if you plan to track finances for another person, like your parents (couples can count as one person in Quicken-land), or a client for whom you do bookkeeping, choose File⇨New and restart the setup process.

After the new file has been created, you can easily switch between files from the File menu. Click File and choose one of these options:

- ✦ If both of your filenames are listed at the bottom of the File menu, click on the name of the file you want to open, and Quicken makes the switch for you.
- ✦ If the name of the file you want to open doesn't appear on the File menu, choose Open, and then click on the filename and click OK.

Finding Your Way Around in Quicken

The easiest way to get frustrated with Quicken is to not know where to find the tasks you want to do. This section is designed to familiarize you with the menus, keyboard shortcuts, Quicken activity centers, and other special features.

This is an overview, highlighting interesting and popular menu features. I give actual examples of the menu options throughout the book when it's appropriate to use these features.

Navigating Quicken's menus

Sometimes the most frustrating thing about understanding how to use a new program is figuring out where all the features are hidden. You may know what the program is capable of doing, but that doesn't help if you can't find the commands. This little intro to the Quicken menu system should help you get over the hump in finding your way through the program.

Using the File menu

Just as you've seen in many other Windows programs, the left-most menu is File, followed by Edit, with Help over on the right. Quicken is no exception to the rule, and if you've ever used a Windows program, you'll find you're already pretty familiar with the items on the File menu.

All of the file management tools can be found on the File menu (Figure 1-7), including options for starting a new data file, opening an existing file, and finding lost files on your computer.

The File Operations choice on the File menu enables you to make copies of your Quicken file for transfer to another computer, delete the file, or change its name. The validation option checks the integrity of your file in case you've been having problems like lost data (very rare). And there is a nifty feature called Year-End Copy that makes a separate data file at the end of the year with just the past year's transactions in it. That's a nice file to save somewhere away from your computer in case of an emergency.

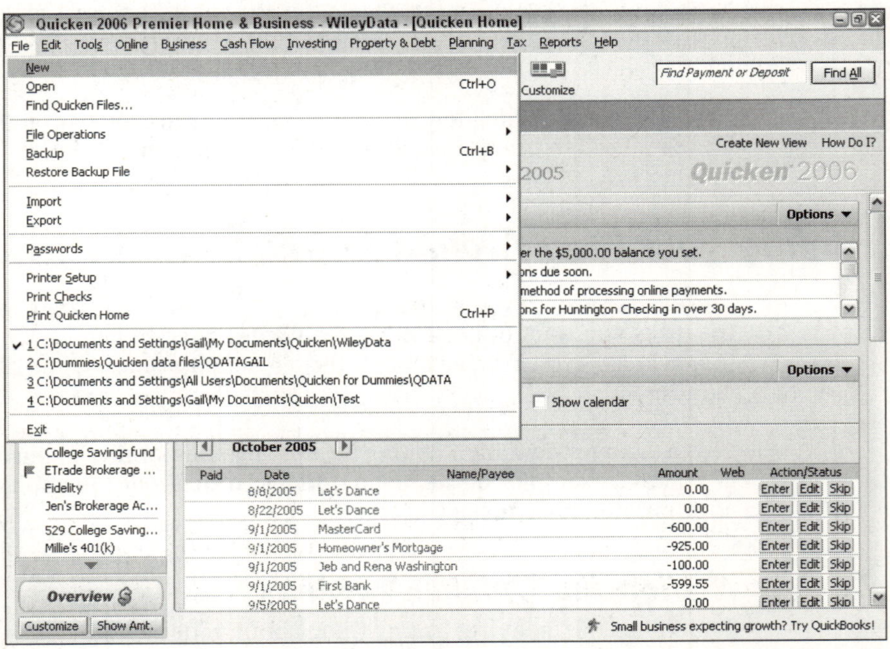

Figure 1-7: The File menu enables you to open, choose, and manipulate files.

And the password is . . .

Passwords aren't a required part of using Quicken, but if you need to prevent prying eyes from seeing your confidential financial data, you can set a password that protects your Quicken file. Here's how:

1. **Choose File⇨Passwords from the Quicken menu.**
2. **Choose File from the side menu.**

   The Quicken File Password window appears.
3. **Enter a password of your choice in the New Password field.**

   You are allowed up to 16 characters for your password, and those characters can include numbers and spaces in addition to letters.
4. **Confirm your password by entering it again in the Confirm Password field.**
5. **Click OK.**

From now on, whenever you open Quicken, you are prompted to enter your password.

You can also use a password to prevent anyone from changing your Quicken data. If you choose Transaction from the side menu in step 2 above, you are prompted to enter a password and a date. No transactions prior to the date you enter can be changed without entering the password.

For Ali Baba, the password was "Open Sesame." You can be as creative as you like within the 16 characters allowed for your password. Passwords are case-sensitive, so a combination of upper- and lowercase letters can lend greater protection. Throwing in a few numerals is helpful too if your goal is to thwart others from figuring out your password. Just be careful that you don't enter a password so confusing that you forget it yourself!

You have a fallback if you do forget your password. For a fee ($9.95 as of this printing), Intuit can remove the password from your file.

The File menu also includes the usual backup and restore features, as well as import and export for transferring information from one program to another.

You can choose the Passwords menu option to set password protection for your Quicken program, or to password-protect an individual transaction.

The Printer Setup command lets you set default features for your printer, and there are familiar commands for printing information from your Quicken file.

TIP

Just like in most Windows programs, you can get to the menu choices with your keyboard if you're tired of playing with the mouse. Press the Alt key on your keyboard and, presto! Little underlines appear under the keyboard shortcut letters in the menu (the "F" in File, the "E" in Edit, the "S" in Tools, and so on). Release the Alt key and type the underlined letter to see the whole menu. Type the underlined letter in the menu choice you want, and you're in business.

Using the Edit menu

There's not much new here — you've seen it all before. Cut, Copy, and Paste appear in every Edit menu known to man.

Also on Quicken's Edit menu (Figure 1-8) are Find options that enable you to dig around in your Quicken program, looking for lost transactions, and customize features that enable you to change the appearance of your screen.

Besides the normal find features that show up in most programs, there's also a useful Recategorize feature on the Find & Replace side menu that enables you to search for all transactions in one category and change the category on all those transactions to something else. You can, well, find more information about the Find feature in Chapter 2 of this book.

The Account bar hangs out on the left side of your screen and shows you all of your various accounts. Choosing Customize the Account Bar enables you to add or remove certain items. The same goes for the Quicken toolbar with its cute little picture icons you can click on to perform certain tasks. Don't just ignore the tool bar and head for the menus — put the tasks you use most frequently on the tool bar and click away. See "Customizing Quicken" later in this chapter for customizing techniques.

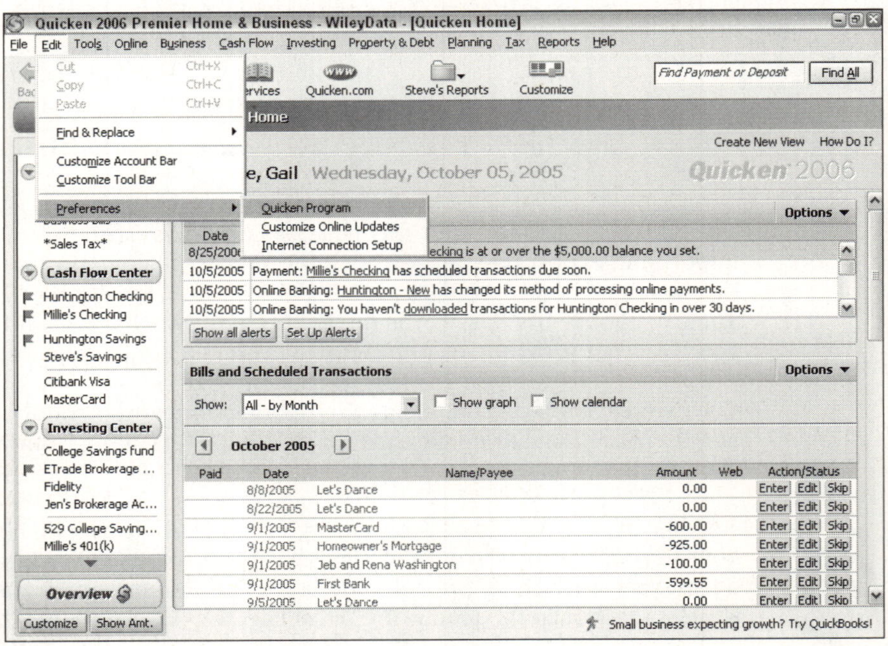

Figure 1-8: Cut, copy, paste, search, and get cozy with setting preferences.

Choose Quicken Program Preferences to adjust the following types of settings in your Quicken display:

✦ Features that appear on your Quicken screen at startup. For example, you can set the program so that your checking account register, your stock portfolio, your credit card account, or any other account or feature you have established in Quicken always appears.

✦ Whether you file your taxes based on the calendar year or a different fiscal year. Most people use the calendar year. Sometimes companies get fancy and decide they want their year to end on something other than December 31. You have to get permission from the IRS to use a different date for your year-end.

✦ QuickFill options (see the sidebar called "Using QuickFill").

✦ Various notifications and warnings regarding events in Quicken, such as entering duplicate check numbers.

✦ Date style. You may like your dates tall and dark or short and blond. Quicken likes them with two digits or four (in the year, that is).

Using QuickFill

If you've used Quicken before or if you're a new user who has started experimenting with the program, you may have noticed that sometimes, when you start typing a word, Quicken steps in and finishes typing the word for you. This is *QuickFill* at work, reading your mind and finishing your thoughts.

As soon as you start typing, QuickFill goes to work, trying to figure out what you're going to type next. As soon as it knows, it finishes the word or words.

For example, maybe you make payments to both the *Chicago Tribune* and the Chicago Transit Authority. As you start typing "C-h-i-c-a-g-o- -T-r-," your computer waits patiently, not knowing which of the two you're going to enter. As soon as you enter an "-i-," the program goes to work, finishing "-bune" on your behalf.

Depending on which QuickFill options you choose, these tasks can be taken care of automatically for you:

- Change the use of the Enter key so that, instead of moving you from one transaction to the next, it moves you from one field to the next within a transaction.
- Have a little drop-down (or sometimes a drop-up) list of choices appear when you start typing an entry.
- Automatically capitalize the first letter of information you type.
- Provide a little button in the fields where QuickFill is available.
- Automatically memorize transactions. With this feature, not only does QuickFill enter the rest of the word that you type, but it fills in the rest of the information from the last transaction you had with the same name. So on that check to the *Chicago Tribune,* the last amount you paid and the payment category automatically appear the next time you enter "Chicago Tribune."

- Special features on checks. Do you like to write messages on your checks — maybe something poetic to go with your rent payment? You can arrange for a message box, and some other odds and ends like having the word "Dollars" printed on your check after the amount.
- Default ranges used in graphs. If you like to use graphs, you can futz with the standard time period that the graphs cover.
- Options for display of reports. Make some choices about how you want your reports to appear, such as adding color, including descriptions, or being able to zoom in for details behind the numbers.

The Customize Online Updates option on the Preferences side menu enables you to make your QuickBooks information available to Quicken online services. You can access information coordinated with Quicken online from any computer that has Internet access.

Using the Tools menu

You can use the Tools menu (Figure 1-9) to get back to the initial setup screens if you want to add something in setup, like a new account or some personal information. Choose Quicken Guided Setup to add or change this information.

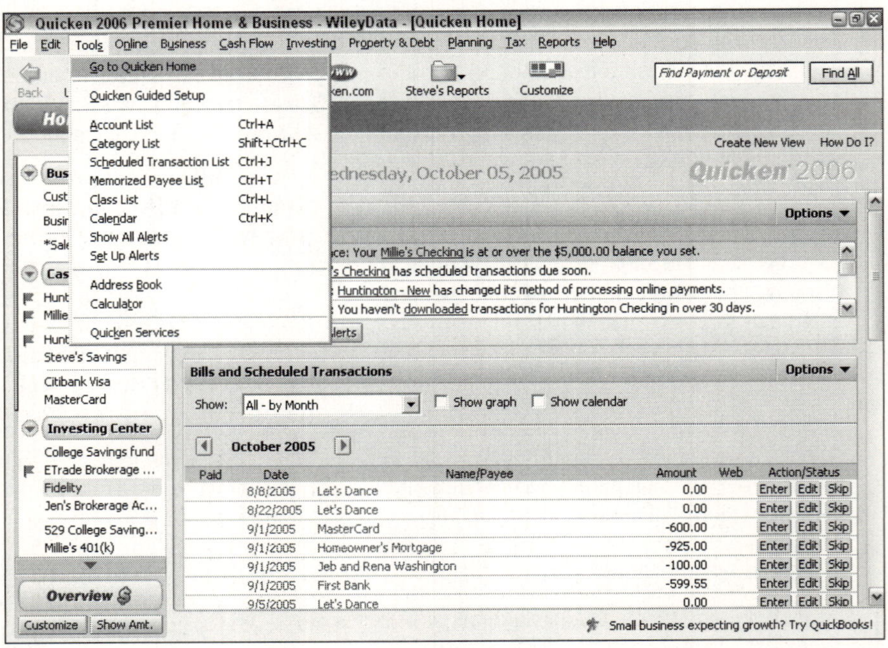

Figure 1-9: The Tools menu contains many popular options.

The Tools menu also gets you to the major lists that you will probably use all the time in Quicken:

- ✦ **Account List:** Includes your bank accounts, your investment accounts, your credit cards, your loans, your assets — just about everything you've entered into Quicken belongs to one of these types of accounts. The master Account List shows everything on one screen, including account balances, so it's a nice place to go to get a good overview of your financial life. Find out more about accounts in Book II, Chapter 3.
- ✦ **Category List:** Whenever you enter a payment or a deposit in Quicken, you're asked to specify in which category the transaction goes. For example, when you pay the landlord each month, the payment is categorized as Rent. The complete category list shows all of the categories you've created as well as those that came with Quicken. If you don't like the categories Quicken gave you, you can open this list and delete the categories you don't want.
- ✦ **Scheduled Transaction List:** When you tell Quicken to start recording payments and deposits automatically, those are *scheduled transactions*. Open this list to see everything you've scheduled, and make changes if necessary. See Book IV, Chapter 4 for more information on this feature.
- ✦ **Memorized Payee List:** Have you ever started typing an entry, only to have the name filled in with a misspelling? If you entered a name in the past and that name contained a misspelling, Quicken remembers the name. The Memorized Payee List is where the QuickFill feature gets its information. All names from the entries you've made are listed here. If you misspelled a name when you first entered it, you can open this list, click on the misspelled name, and click Delete to remove the name from the list. Sorry QuickFill, no more mistakes for you.
- ✦ **Class List:** Classes are ways of tagging certain transactions. Say you enter both your and your spouse's transactions in the same Quicken file, but you want to be able to say, "See, I only spent $50 on clothes last month and you spent $500," you can tag the transactions with a class — his and hers. Or if you run a little business and pay all the business bills from your personal checkbook, set up a class for the business. When it comes time to produce reports, you can request a report that shows only one class or that displays separate columns for each class.

The Tools menu also gets you to the alerts screen where you can ask to be reminded that you're about to hit the maximum on your credit card or a particular stock you've had your eye on is now affordable. You can ask for the alerts to peck at you like a hungry bird by popping up in boxes on your screen, or you can have your alerts placed in a nice little alert list that you look at yourself when you're interested.

Your address book can be found on the Tools menu. If you keep contact information on your computer, the Quicken Address Book can be handy. For example, any companies or people you write checks to can be included in your address book and their address information is then automatically added to the check you write. Many people use other programs like Microsoft Outlook or Act to keep track of names and addresses, so you may think the Quicken address book is a bit of overkill. It really depends on how often you take advantage of address information within your Quicken program.

TIP

This may sweeten the pot if you're considering using the Quicken Address Book. You can import addresses from another program so you don't have to reenter address information. Also, Quicken comes with a nifty little synchronization program called Intellisync that enables you to keep your contact information current across all of your programs that utilize this info.

There's a little calculator on the Tools menu — this is handy for quick calculations, and the result can be easily transferred right into an amount field in Quicken.

Using the Online menu

Not surprisingly, you can take care of all of your online business from the Online menu (Figure 1-10). Update balances, view your online holdings, perform transactions with Quicken's Bill Pay service, record or view information relating to your Quicken credit card, click over to Quicken's Web site, and so on.

The Online Center, found in the middle of the Online menu, is home base for your online business, including downloading information, transferring funds, and creating new transactions. Monitor your online banking, credit cards, and investments from this location, make payments, and stay constantly up-to-date in real time.

TIP

The Online Center creeps up everywhere. You can find it on other menus as well.

Using the Cash Flow menu

For most Quicken users, the Cash Flow menu is like the neighborhood soda fountain — it's where everyone wants to hang out. The Cash Flow menu, shown in Figure 1-11, contains access to the Cash Flow Center, where all of your bank accounts reside. You may not be able to actually sip a soda while lurking at the Cash Flow menu, but look at these other cool things you can do:

- Reconcile your bank and credit card accounts (wheee! Lots of fun!). Find out more about reconciling your accounts in Book II, Chapter 4.

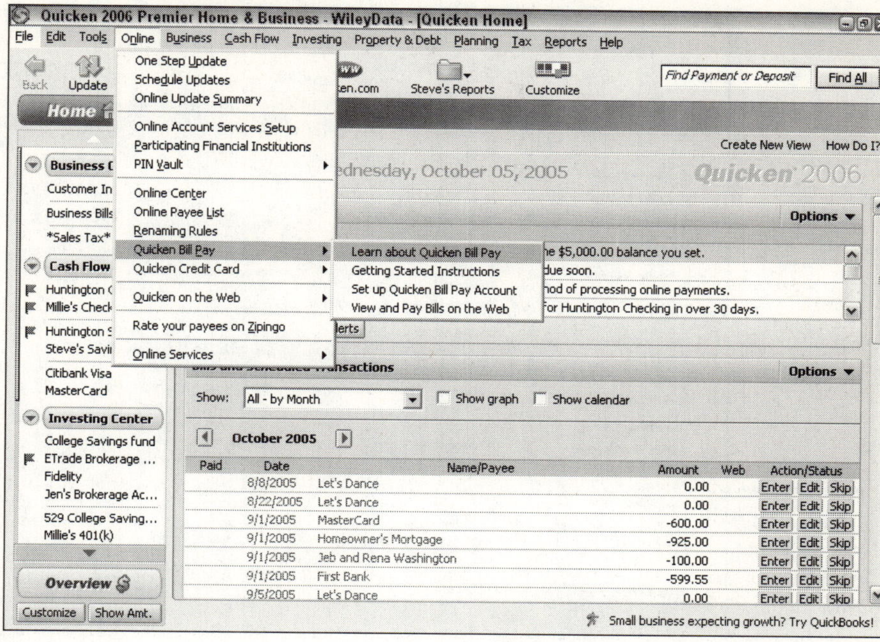

Figure 1-10: Online services are accessible all in one place.

- ✦ Write checks to anybody you please. Find out more about writing checks in Book II, Chapter 2.
- ✦ Work on your budget — make sure you're not writing checks to *too many* people. Find out more about budgeting in Book IV, Chapter 5.
- ✦ Use the Calendar, which enables you to view financial transactions in monthly format.
- ✦ Set up recurring, scheduled transactions — like paying the rent or mortgage each month, student loan payments, car payments, recording your paycheck — the regular stuff that keeps happening over and over again. Find out more about scheduling transactions in Chapter 2 of this book.
- ✦ Get access to the Quicken Bill Pay feature. Find out more about paying bills online in Book IV, Chapter 4.
- ✦ Get with the times — hook up Quicken to your PDA.

Using the Investing menu

You're probably getting the hang of this now. The Investing menu (Figure 1-12) gives you a pass-key to the Investing Center, Quicken's summary page for everything investing.

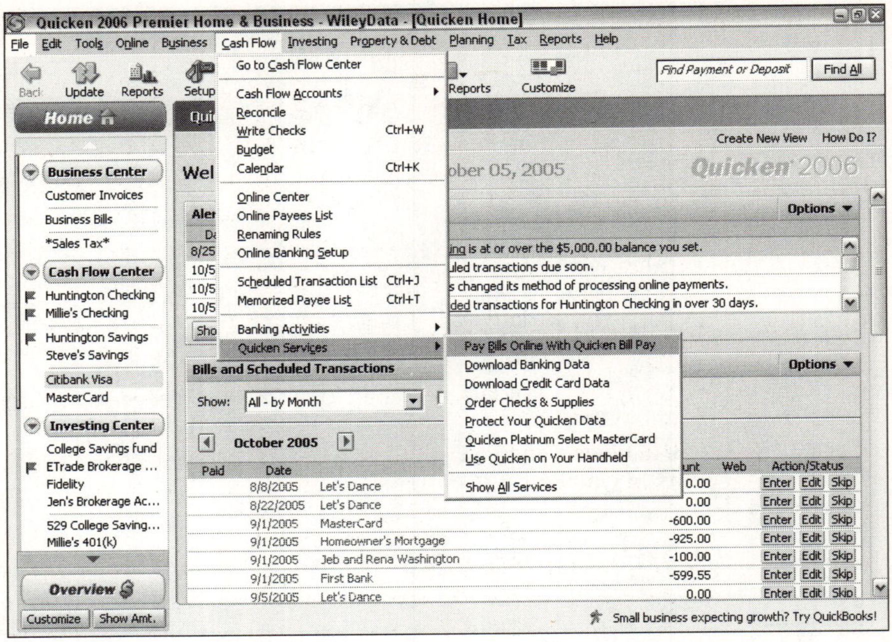

Figure 1-11: Hanging out on the Cash Flow menu.

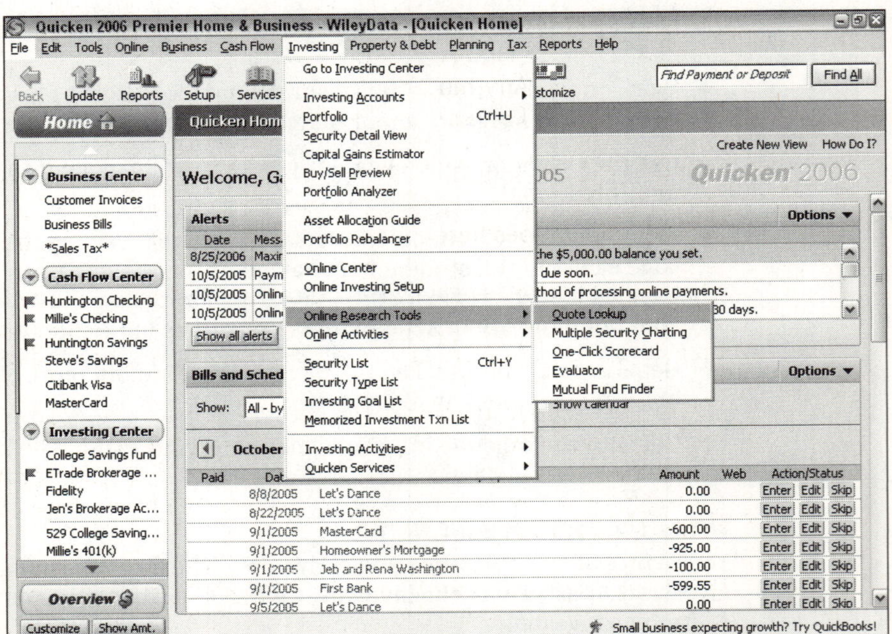

Figure 1-12: Take good care of your investments — someday they'll take good care of you.

- Record all of your stock trading, mutual fund purchasing, bond investing — and let Quicken update the stock market activity while you watch. Set investing goals, and create a Watch List to keep an eye on other investments you're considering.
- Use the Online Research Tools to look up stocks and mutual funds to find out more about them so you can make intelligent decisions about investing.
- If you participate in a 401(k) plan at work, you can track its progress right here along with your other investments.
- Use the Quicken Capital Gains Estimator to figure out the tax ramifications of selling an investment before you make the sale.
- Set investing goals, and then actually turn those goals into action.

Book III gives you lots of guidance and information on tracking your investments in Quicken.

Using the Property & Debt menu

You guessed it — the Property & Debt menu, shown in Figure 1-13, leads you to the Property & Debt Center, where you can keep track of, you guessed it, property and debt. Property is assets you own, like your car, your house, your boat, your Stradivarius, or even your collection of precious aggies. (Not the kind you find in Texas — I'm referring to real aggies, the kind you shoot with your thumb. Otherwise known as marbles for those of you who grew up after the 1950s.) Anything worth keeping track of can be monitored in the Property & Debt Center.

Debt refers to serious debt, like your mortgage, your car loan, or an equity line of credit. Credit card debt appears over on the Cash Flow menu — long-term debt goes here.

The Loans feature in Quicken, found on the Property & Debt menu, enables you to actually set up loan information, and Quicken keeps track of how much of your monthly repayment goes toward principal and interest.

You can use the Quicken Home Inventory feature found on this menu to record a complete inventory of everything in your home. The Home Inventory is an excellent way to make your homeowner's or renter's insurance broker happy. Find out more about keeping track of your home and other belongings in Book 4, Chapter 3.

Quicken also provides an Emergency Records Organizer, a tool for assembling all sorts of vital statistics about you and your family.

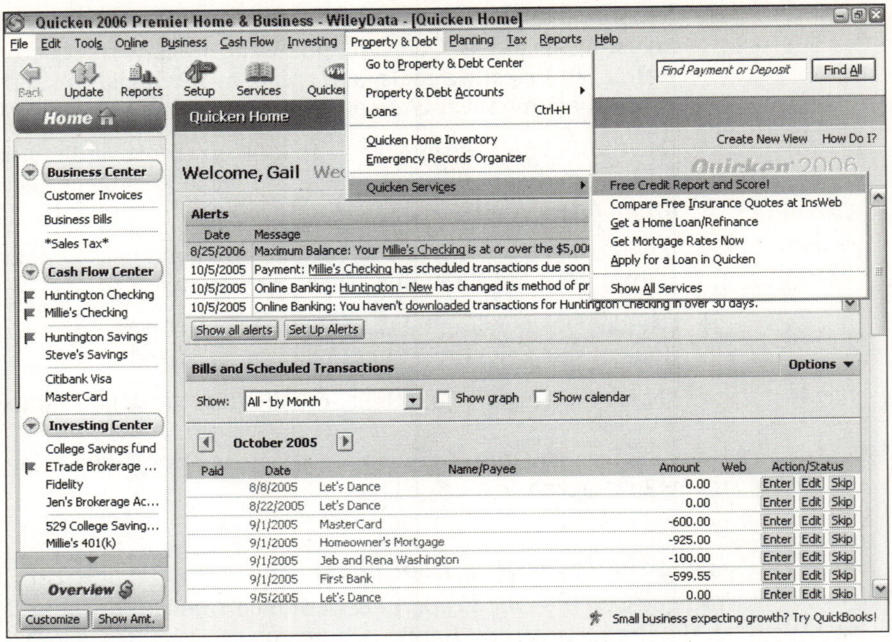

Figure 1-13: Keeping track of what you own and what you owe.

Using the Planning menu

In spite of the fact that Cash Flow gets all the attention, my personal favorite is the Planning menu, shown in Figure 1-14. This menu contains some extremely useful planners and calculators for figuring out how various decisions impact your finances.

For example, you can go to the retirement planner and enter detailed information about how much you earn, how much you owe, your regular expenses, the value of your assets, and any current retirement income you receive or expect to receive, such as Social Security, and the planner shows you how much you need to accumulate for retirement and at what age you'll be able to retire.

In addition to the planners, there are wonderful calculators that calculate how much it will cost you to borrow money, or how much you need to save for college. You can plug in a few numbers and experiment with different scenarios. When you've got the information you want, you can print out a complete payment or saving schedule, showing principal and interest and monthly payments or contributions. I turn to these calculators all the time, even if Quicken wouldn't otherwise be open on my screen because they're so easy to use.

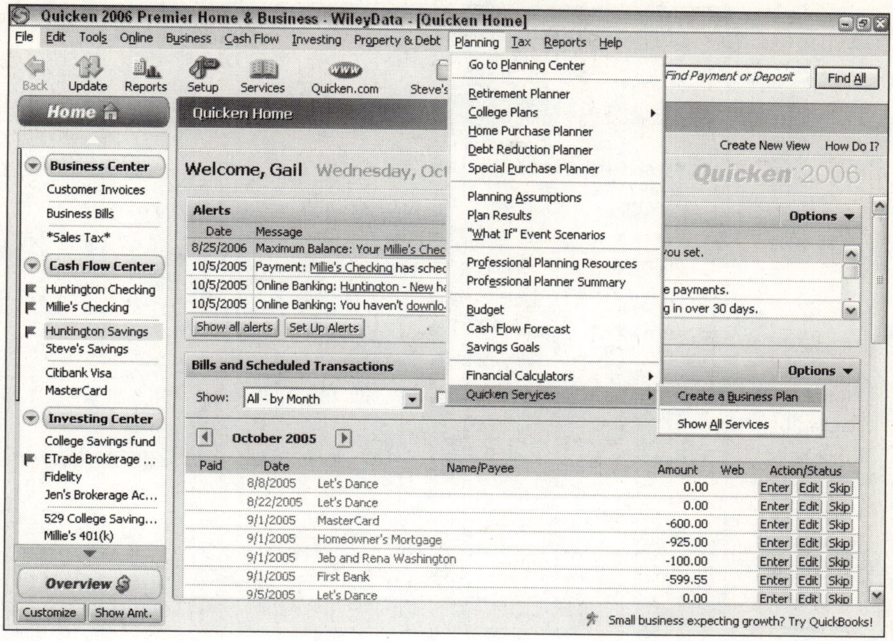

Figure 1-14: Quicken shines when it comes to planners that help you figure out how much money you need for projects.

Go to the Planning menu when you want to set savings goals or to get tips for finding a financial professional to help you out. You can also use the planning tools to forecast future income and to design a plan for getting yourself out of debt.

Using the Tax menu

The Tax menu (Figure 1-15) is your gateway to the Tax Center, where you can play with tax scenarios like whether you should file your tax return with married filing jointly or married filing separately, estimate how much tax you're going to owe, determine if you need to leave the country before April 15, that kind of thing . . .

From the Tax menu, you can set up your Quicken categories so that you have everything you need to prepare your tax return in the spring.

There are direct links to IRS publications in the Online Tax Tools available through the Tax menu (so if you ever have trouble going to sleep at night, you know where to go for mind-numbing reading material). And you can go right from Quicken to TurboTax if you want to take advantage of Intuit's showcase tax preparation software.

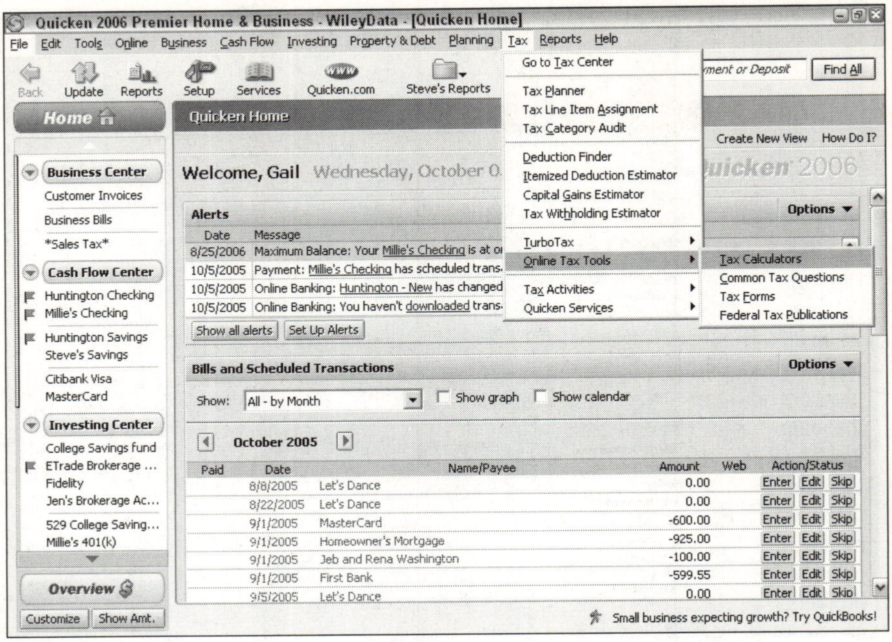

Figure 1-15: Taxes don't have to be intimidating when you keep good records in Quicken.

TurboTax's Deduction Finder is available for your use, as are various estimators and calculators that you can use to stay in touch with the tax side of your finances.

Find out more about Quicken and taxes in Book V.

Using the Reports menu

For many, Quicken is all about reports. It's one thing to enter all of your financial transactions in Quicken, but how about getting some feedback so you can make sense of all those numbers? That's where reports come in. Figure 1-16 shows the Reports menu; each major heading has a side menu with lots of reports from which you can choose.

Quicken is very flexible in letting you design your own reports, but you may be perfectly happy with the reports that come standard with Quicken. There are nearly 40 standard reports to cover nearly all of your needs.

If the standard reports aren't giving you the information you need, you can customize the reports so that you have exactly the data want. Customizing reports is easy, and you can save the reports you customize so that you don't have to re-create them every time you want the same information.

Find out more about Quicken reports in Book VII.

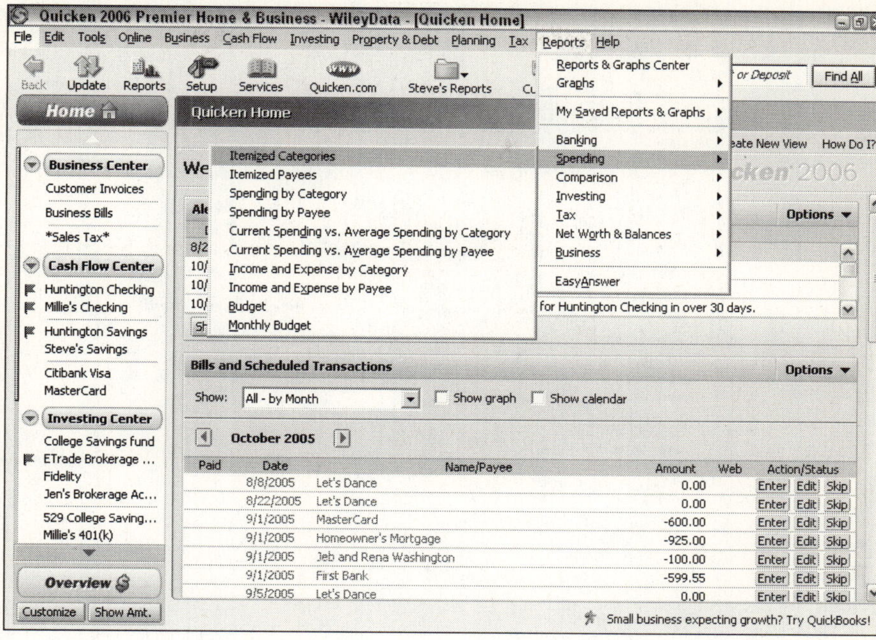

Figure 1-16: Quicken has done the legwork in designing reports for all areas of your finances.

Using the Help menu

Turn to the Help menu, shown in Figure 1-17, for answers to all of your questions. Quicken Help works like other Windows programs, offering a Contents overview, an alphabetical Index, and a keyword Search feature.

Click over to online customer support, or check out the complete program user manual, searchable online, or downloadable if you prefer the print version.

If there's something you don't like about Quicken, or a suggestion you have for improving the program, you can click the Submit Feedback on Quicken option and get your ideas in front of the people who pay attention to user comments.

Keyboard shortcuts

Many keyboard shortcuts are available to you in Quicken: keystrokes you can type when you feel like giving your mouse a break. You'll see many of the shortcuts listed on the menus — for example, look at the Cash Flow menu. Across from Write Checks, you see Ctrl+W. All of the keyboard shortcuts for menu commands appear like this, right on the menu.

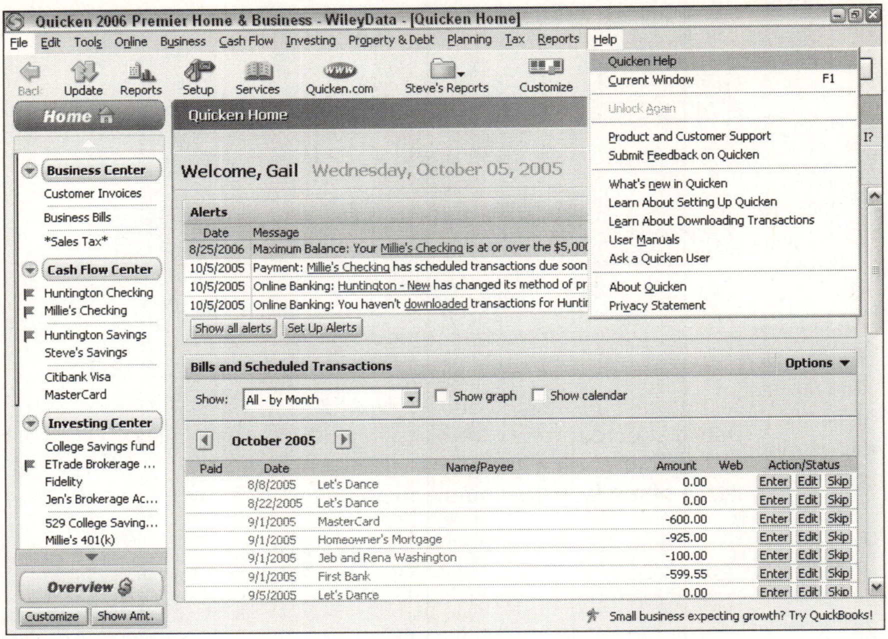

Figure 1-17: Help!

Some of my favorite keyboard commands are the date commands. When you need to change the date that appears in a register, on a check, or in any other date field, you can type the complete date, click the little calendar button that appears in the date field, or use one of the keyboard shortcuts in Table 1-1 to speed up the operation:

Table 1-1 Useful Keyboard Shortcuts for Date Commands

Letter	*Function*
T	Today
M	First day of current month
H	Last day of current month
Y	First day of current year
R	Last day of current year
+	Forward one day
-	Backward one day

For example, press Ctrl+G to open the Go To Date window (Figure 1-18), where you can enter the date you want.

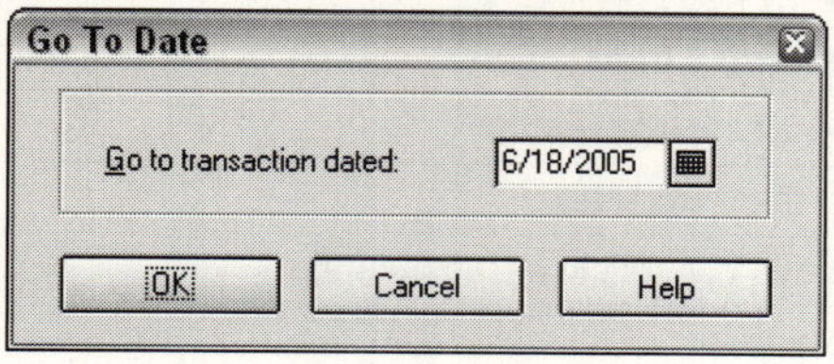

Figure 1-18: Enter the date of your choice and you'll hop right to the first transaction for that date.

Sometimes it's more trouble than it's worth, trying to remember the keyboard shortcut for a command when you could just as easily click the menu or tool bar choice and get there more quickly. Nevertheless, Table 1-2 has some of my favorite commands — the ones I have no trouble remembering:

Table 1-2 Favorite Keyboard Shortcuts

Shortcut	*Function*
Ctrl+W	Write a check
Ctrl+K	Show the calendar
Ctrl+A	Open the Account list
Ctrl+Shift+C	Open the Category list
Ctrl+J	Open the Scheduled Transaction list
Ctrl+M	Open the Memorized Payee list
Ctrl+P	Print
Alt+←	Back one window
Alt+→	Forward one window
Tab	Move from one field to the next
Shift+Tab	Move back one field
Home	Go to beginning of field
Ctrl+Home	First transaction in register
Ctrl+End	Last transaction in register
Ctrl+Ins	Copy selected information
Shift+Ins	Paste selected information
Ctrl+D	Delete a transaction

(continued)

Table 1-2 ***(continued)***

Ctrl+I	Insert a transaction
Ctrl+M	Memorize a transaction
Ctrl+N	Start a new transaction
Ctrl+S	Split the transaction
Alt+X	Remove the split in a transaction
F1	Get help

If you're really zealous about learning shortcuts, you can go to Shortcuts in the Help Index and find more.

Customizing Quicken

Making changes in the appearance of your Quicken program is easier than you might think. You can change the information that appears in the Account Bar at the left side of the Quicken screen, and you customize the icon bar so that you see icons for the tasks you use most frequently.

Customize the contents of the Account Bar by clicking the Customize button on the bottom of the bar. The Account List window appears, showing every account you track in Quicken, followed by a series of check boxes. Check or uncheck the boxes to control the display of the various accounts:

- Checking the Hide In Quicken check box actually hides the account so it no longer appears on the bar and also no longer appears in any of your reports and graphs. The account still exists and can be reactivated.
- Checking the Don't Include In Totals check box leaves the account balance visible on the Account Bar but removes that account's balance from the calculation of totals.
- Checking the Remove from Bar check box removes the account from the Account Bar. The account is still active in your reports and graphs and can be accessed from the Account List, but it no longer appears on the Account Bar.

You can also change the appearance of the Account Bar to not display account totals. Click the Hide Amounts button at the bottom of the bar to remove the display of amounts. The button changes to Show Amt. and can be clicked at any time to reinstate the display of amounts.

Customize your toolbar by clicking the Customize button on the bar itself. The Customize toolbar window appears. Click on any item in the Add to tool bar list, and then click the Add button to move an icon for that item onto your toolbar. Click on any item in the Current tool bar order list, and then click the Remove button to take an icon off of the list. Click OK to enter your changes.

Opening and Closing Quicken

Getting into Quicken is a straightforward affair. You can use the shortcut method and open your program by double-clicking the desktop icon, or you can enter through the front door by using the Start button, and then choosing Programs➪Quicken➪Quicken 2006 (or whatever version you're using).

Getting out of Quicken is pretty simple too, with a couple of exceptions. First, one of the nicest characteristics of Quicken is that the program saves as you work, so you don't need to search around for a way to save your transactions when you're ready to shut down.

Another feature of Quicken is that the program likes to remind you of your duty to back up your files, in case of some sort of computer crisis. The Automatic Backup feature, shown in Figure 1-19, kicks in every third time you close your Quicken program.

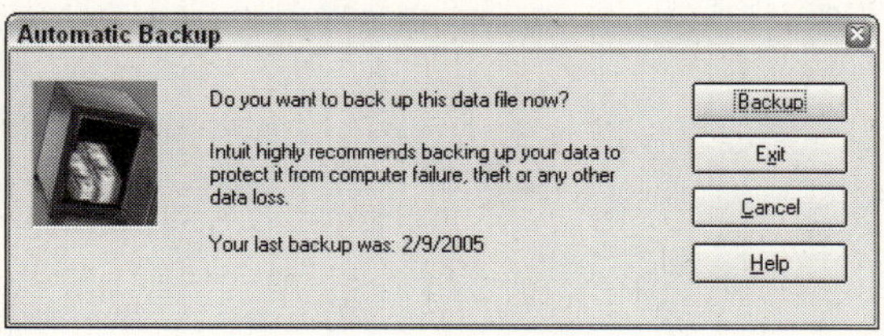

Figure 1-19: You say Exit; Quicken says Backup.

Backing up files always makes sense, no matter what program you use, but with Quicken, backing up is more than merely sensible. Imagine yourself having to re-create all of the financial data stored in your Quicken file. Especially if you've been using Quicken for several years: You don't want to lose all that data.

Make a backup copy and put it on a CD-ROM, Zip disk, or other removable media — somewhere other than on your computer's hard drive.

If you don't like being reminded about backups as frequently as every three times you try to close the program, you can adjust the reminder setting to a more comfortable level of repetition.

Follow these steps to adjust the frequency of your backup reminders:

1. **Choose Edit➪Preferences➪Quicken Program from the menu.**

   The Quicken Preferences window appears (see Figure 1-20).

2. **Click Backup on the left side of the window.**
3. **Change the number in the Remind After Running Quicken field.**
4. **Click OK.**

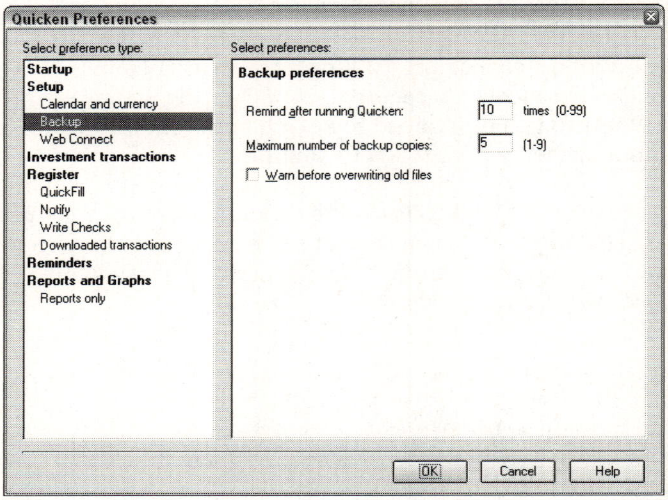

Figure 1-20: You call the shots when it comes to how frequently you want a backup reminder.

Chapter 2: Using the Register

In This Chapter

- Setting up categories
- Setting up your bank account
- Working with checks
- Printing in Quicken
- Scheduling recurring transactions
- Setting up alerts

Probably the single most common use of Quicken is recording checks that you write from your bank account. Whether you write checks yourself and then transcribe the information into Quicken, or write checks directly from Quicken, summarizing that information and then producing reports showing details of spending habits is a frequent Quicken task. This chapter shows you easy ways to get information into Quicken and also demonstrates some more sophisticated techniques for teaching Quicken how to do some of your work for you. After all, using a program that makes your life easier is what makes computers worthwhile (that, and playing cool solitaire games).

Working with Categories

Quicken uses categories to distinguish different types of income and spending. Rather than lumping all of your incoming cash into one category, Income, and all of the checks you write into another category, Expenses, Quicken separates the various types of cash in and cash out so you can see the details of where your money comes from and where it all goes.

Each time you enter a monetary transaction in Quicken, you need to identify which category the amount should be assigned to.

Categories already in place

When you establish your bank accounts, credit card accounts, and other information in Quicken, standard categories are already established for you. Choose Tools⇨Category List from the menu, or press Ctrl+C to view the category list that comes with your Quicken program. (Computer gremlins might change your Category List keyboard command to Shift+Ctrl+C — check the display on the Tools menu to see which keyboard command opens your category list.)

Scroll through the list to familiarize yourself with the categories available to you.

You can edit this standard category list, changing names, deleting, and adding categories until the category list is more conducive to the type of transactions you use.

Removing unwanted categories

Reduce the clutter of categories you don't plan on using by hiding or deleting categories on the list.

Check the Hide boxes next to categories you don't want to totally delete but don't need to use anymore.

Select a category to delete by clicking on the category and then clicking the Delete button. To delete more than one category at a time, hold down the Ctrl button while you click on each category you want to delete, and then click the Delete button.

A warning (see Figure 2-1) appears advising you that you are about to permanently delete categories. Click OK to proceed.

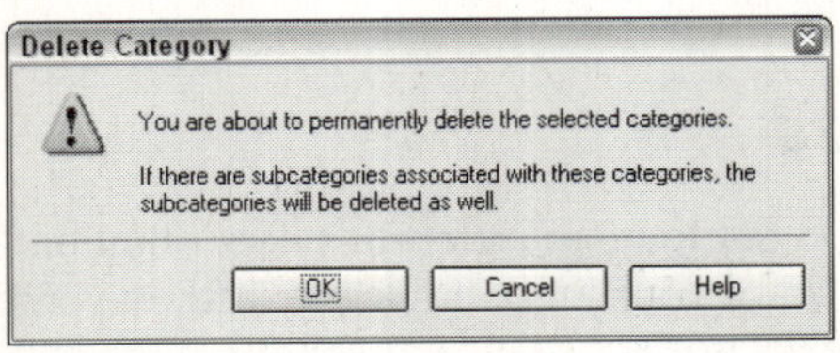

Figure 2-1: Click OK and the unwanted category is history.

Don't be alarmed by the Delete Category warning. If you delete a category and , then later decide you want to use that category, you can always create a new category with the same name.

If you attempt to delete a category that has already been used in some transactions, you have two choices. You can assign the transactions that were previously posted to that category to a new category, or you can leave the transactions marked as "uncategorized." In either case, once you make your decision, the category is deleted.

An alternative to removing categories you don't want is renaming categories to a name you prefer. Click on the category you want to change, click the Edit button, and enter the new name for this category.

Adding new categories

Now that you've cleaned out the categories you no longer want, you can populate the category list with your own choices.

Click the New button. Then enter the name and any other appropriate information in the Set Up Category window that appears (see Figure 2-2). Click OK when you're ready to add this category to your list.

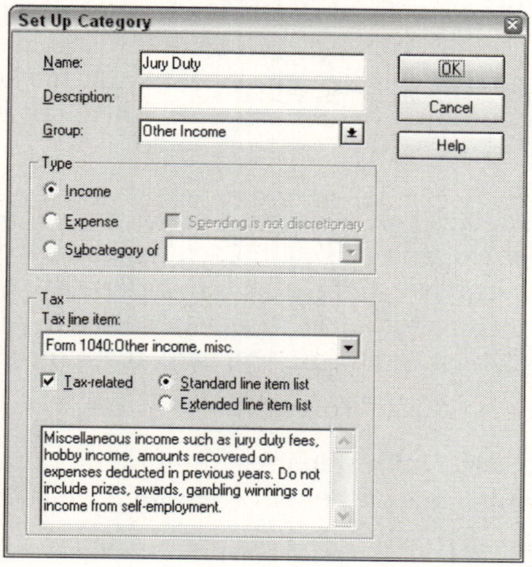

Figure 2-2: Add your own categories to customize the category list.

Add new categories on-the-fly

If you forget to add some categories that you need during this initial setup process, no matter. You can either return to the Category list, click New, and pick up where you left off, or you can add new categories while you enter your Quicken transactions.

To add a new category while entering information in the register (you find out more about that in Chapter 2 of this book), just type the category you want to use. If the category you type isn't recognized by Quicken, the New Category window appears (Figure 2-3).

When you click Yes, the Set Up Category window appears, and you can enter whatever pertinent information you want about your new category.

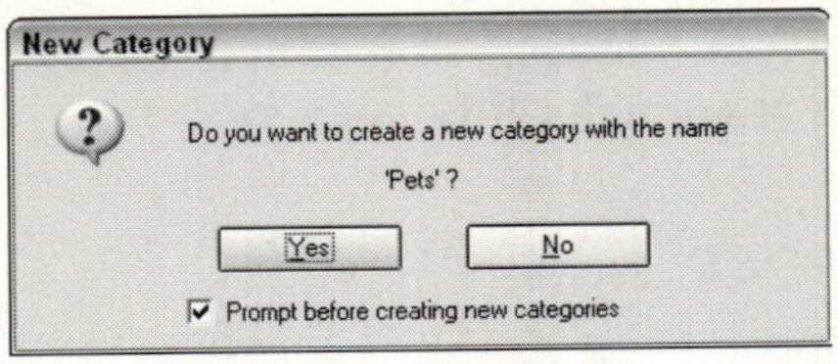

Figure 2-3: Click Yes to create a new category on-the-fly.

Using subcategories, sub-subcategories, sub-sub-sub-sub . . .

When you create a new category, one of the options in the Set Up Category window is the category type. You can choose from Income, Expense, or Subcategory of. The Income and Expense options determine the placement of your category on reports that Quicken produces. Also, Quicken refers to the type of category to determine whether amounts you enter are added to Income or included with Expenses.

The Subcategory option enables you to create a category that is subsidiary to an existing category. For example, if you look on the standard category list, you see Medical as an expense item. Indented underneath Medical are Doctor and Medicine. If you have other medical categories to set up, such as Dentist, Eye care, Orthodontics, and so on, you can create these as subcategories of Medical.

You can create subcategories of subcategories. Continuing with the medical theme, you could create subcategories under Eye Care: Eye Doctor, Glasses and Contacts.

An alternative might be to list each family member's name as subcategories under the main category of Medical, and then include sub-subcategories of Doctor, Dentist, Hospital, and so on under each family member.

Family member–related categories are particularly helpful in situations where parents have divorced and the court requires each parent to keep detailed records of what is spent on each child.

The subcategories you create appear indented under their main category on the category list and also on reports.

Quicken allows you to nest subcategories up to 16 levels deep. You may never have the need to get this detailed in your categories, but it's nice to know you can go there if you want.

Setting Up Your Bank Account

There's a lengthy section in the next chapter on setting up all sorts of accounts, including credit card accounts, 401(k) account, loan accounts, savings accounts, mutual fund accounts, and so on, but that's for Quicken users who have already gotten their feet wet by setting up their first bank account. The bank account is the place to start, and if you haven't yet set up your bank account, you should get it done now. (You might have set up your bank account when you went through the initial setup screens described in Chapter 1, in which case you can take a breather and skip over these steps.)

TIP

Before you start, be sure to have a copy of your most recent bank statement close at hand.

Begin setting up your bank account by following these steps:

1. **Press Ctrl+A or choose Account List from the Tools menu.**

   Either way, the Account List appears on your screen. The Account List displays all the accounts you've set up in Quicken. If you're just getting started, this list is going to be pretty barren, but soon the list will be populated and you'll feel like you're really getting the hang of using your Quicken program.

2. **After the Account list is displayed, click the Add Account button or press Alt+A to open the Quicken Account Setup window.**

   The Quicken Account Setup window appears. In this series of windows, you enter all the start-up information necessary to establish your account in Quicken.

3. **Enter the name of the bank where you have your account, as shown is Figure 2-4.**

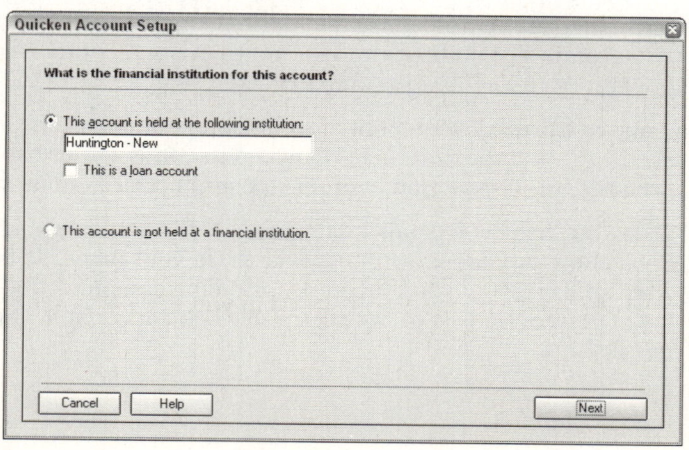

Figure 2-4: Enter the bank where your account resides.

If you're not setting up a bank account but instead a cash account or some other type of account, check the box indicating that the account is not held at a financial institution. Otherwise, choose your bank from the drop-down list provided. Then click Next.

4. **Indicate if you want to use online banking or manual data entry (see Figure 2-5).**

   For this example, I'm using online banking. I've already contacted my bank and have gotten approval to let my bank communicate with my Quicken account. Click Next.

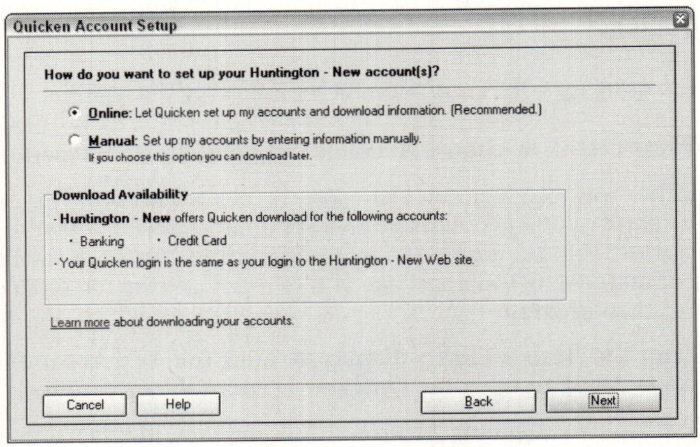

Figure 2-5: Clear it with your bank before you can set up your account for online communication.

5. **Enter your online banking user name and password.**

   This step only applies if you're using the online banking feature. The user name and password is the same access information that you use when signing onto the bank's Web site. Click Next to proceed. At this point, the bank downloads all of your banking transactions for the specified account(s), for about the last month or so. All of these transactions appear in your account register(s) in Quicken.

   If you have firewall protection installed on your computer, you might be asked to give authorization for Quicken to contact your bank. You must authorize this connection in order to use Quicken's online services.

   When your bank starts talking to Quicken, the bank is going to spill the beans about any other accounts that are in your name, so be prepared to set up the rest of your accounts for online communication as well. One of your options is to not set up this bank account in Quicken; it's your choice.

6. **Choose the type of account and then click Next.**

   Select the option that best describes your account, such as Checking, Cash, Brokerage, and so on. Only one choice is allowed.

7. **Enter a name for this account that distinguishes this account from any other account you have set up or plan to set up.**

   For example, if you and your wife each have a checking account, you can distinguish the two accounts by name, such as Clara's Checking and Joe's Checking.

Entering Checks

If you write a lot of checks, entering them in Quicken can get tedious. On the other hand, consider the excellent advantages of recording the checks you write in your Quicken program. For example:

- ✦ You can lose your checkbook and not worry about losing information about what checks you have written.
- ✦ More and more banks are refusing to return paper copies of cancelled checks with monthly statements, so the check register you keep in Quicken replaces the paper checks with a quick, permanent, and easily sortable record of your checks.
- ✦ Is math not your strong suit? You don't have to worry about the numbers not adding up right when you record your checks in Quicken — you'll always have an accurate bank balance.
- ✦ The best part of using Quicken to record your checks is that you can produce reports showing you exactly how your money was spent.

To enter checks in Quicken, you first must set up your bank account. If you haven't done this yet, go back to "Setting Up Your Bank Account" earlier in this chapter and finish the job.

When entering checks in your Quicken bank account register, you follow much the same procedure that you would when entering a check by hand in your checkbook register. Each piece of information that you enter provides information that you can sort by, recall on reports, search for. The more information you provide in the register, the easier it is to extract useful information later.

Here's the information you have the opportunity to enter in your checking account register:

- **Transaction date:** Enter in mm/dd/yy format.
- **Type of transaction (identified as Num):** Choose from Next Check Num, ATM, Deposit, Print Check, Send Online Payment, Online Transfer, Transfer, EFT, Edit List (see the sidebar titled "Editing the type of transaction options" for more info).
- **Name of Payee:** Quicken uses Payee as an all-encompassing term for the name of the party with whom you're doing business. In the case of a deposit, instead of a payee, you might enter the name of a payer.
- **Amount:** Amounts that decrease your account are entered in the Payment column. Amounts that increase your account balance are entered in the Deposit column.
- **Category:** Categories are instrumental in allowing you to review your spending later through the various reports that Quicken offers. Choosing a category for your transaction ensures that the transaction is grouped with other transactions in the same category.

Editing the type of transaction options

When entering a transaction in a Quicken register, you are expected, but not required, to provide some information in the Num area of the register that identifies the type of transaction. If you're entering a check, for example, the check number goes in the Num area. For deposits, the letters DEP go in the Num area.

Quickly enter the next check number in the Num field by pressing either of the plus signs on your keyboard. Alternatively, just enter the letter N (for next), and Quicken automatically fills in the next number.

Other options exist as well, but sometimes you have a transaction to enter that doesn't fit with the choices provided by Quicken. For those cases, you can select the Edit List option and create new transaction identifiers, as shown in the figure.

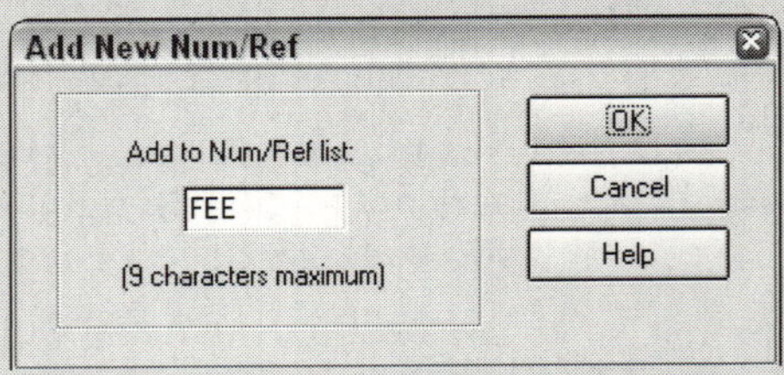

For example, here are some sample descriptions you might want use in the Num area of your register:

FEE: For monthly bank fees, check printing charges, other charges assessed by the bank

DEBIT: For items charged on your debit card

When adding new descriptions, choose Edit List from the drop-down menu that appears in the Num field, and then click the Add button. Enter the name of your description. You're limited to nine characters, including spaces. Then click OK and then Done.

- **Memo:** The memo is optional. And although Quicken doesn't permit you to sort your register by the information in the Memo field, you can include this memo information on reports.
- **Clr:** This column is filled in automatically when you balance your register (see Book II, Chapter 4 for more information), and the information here reflects whether you have reconciled the amount to your financial institution on a preliminary basis ("c") or a permanent, reconciled basis ("R"). You can override the entry (or lack of entry) that appears here by clicking in the top line of the Clr column and then clicking No when asked if you want to use Quicken's Reconcile feature.
- **Balance:** Another automatic column — Quicken keeps a running balance in your register, so you always know how much your account contains.

Voiding checks

It's easy to void a check in Quicken. Click on the register transaction that you want to void, and then press Ctrl+V. Alternatively, you can right-click on the transaction and choose Void Transaction.

Voiding is a one-step process. When you choose Void Transaction from the pop-up menu, or when you press Ctrl+V, the transaction is immediately voided and **VOID** is placed at the front of the Payee name for that transaction.

The amount of the transaction is changed to zero, but the transaction itself stays in the register so later you can recall what happened.

WARNING!

There is no Undo option associated with voided transactions. That said, you can always delete a voided transaction and reenter the transaction in the register.

Splitting categories

How often do you enter a transaction that needs to be assigned to more than one category? For example, you go to the office supply store and purchase office supplies for your business and, at the same time, you purchase school supplies for your children. Part of the transaction amount should be categorized as business expense, and the rest goes with children or household expenses.

When you enter a transaction that needs to be split, press Ctrl+S while entering the transaction. The Split Transaction window appears (see Figure 2-6), providing you with an area where you can list the categories, optional memo information, and amounts for each category that applies to the transaction you're entering.

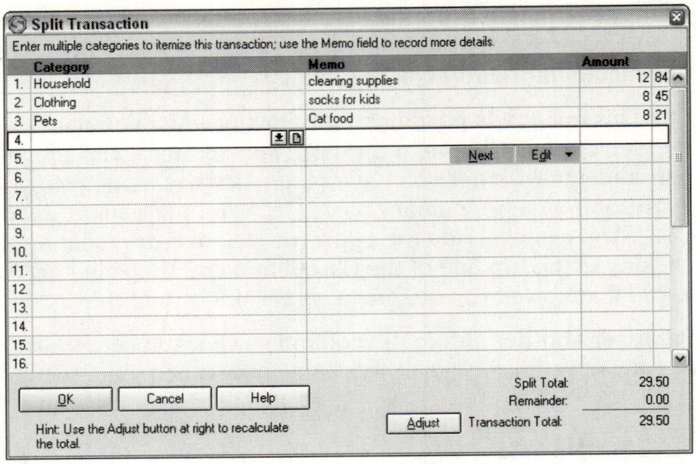

Figure 2-6: Enter the detail from your purchases in the Split Transaction dialog box.

When finished entering split transaction information, click the OK button (or press Ctrl+Enter). You're returned to the register, and in the category information for the current transaction, you see the following notation: –Split–.

To view how a transaction is split, double-click on the term –Split– or press Ctrl+S again on the split transaction, or click the little green check box that appears in the Category field.

Having a bad mouse day? Move from one field to the next in the Split Transaction window using your Tab key. When you're finished making entries, use Ctrl+Enter to close the window and return to your register.

When QuickFill is turned on, the next time you begin a transaction to this payee, the split descriptions automatically appear. To fill in those transaction amounts, press Ctrl+S to open the Split Transaction window. But if you don't want to use the splits, click the little X that appears to the right of the Category field, or press Alt+X on your keyboard, and then choose Yes. Your splits will split.

Entering your paycheck

It's always fun getting paid, and if you really get interested in fastidious record keeping in Quicken, you might find that you want to keep running balances on all of the withholding amounts from your paycheck.

The quick and easy way to enter paycheck deposits is to simply enter your employer's name in the Payee field, enter the net amount of the check in the Amount field, and enter Salary as the category. This won't give you a running balance of any of the taxes or other amounts taken out of your pay, but the data entry is very simple.

The nice thing about entering all of the withholding amounts from your paycheck is that, after you've entered the withholding descriptions in the Split Transaction window, the descriptions return each time you enter a new paycheck, and that saves you a lot of time. If you're salaried and receive the same amount of pay on every paycheck, you're going to save even more time because QuickFill memorizes the entire paycheck, including amounts. Your data entry is limited to entering the name of the employer and your Quicken program will take care of everything else. You can save even more time in entering recurring events like paychecks by telling Quicken to enter the check for you every payday. See "Scheduling Recurring Transactions" later in this chapter for more on this technique.

To enter a paycheck for the first time, with all of the withholding amounts, follow these steps:

1. **In your register for the account where you deposit your paychecks, begin a new transaction with the date on which you deposited your most recent paycheck.**

   Press Tab to move on to the Num column, or click in the Num column.

2. **Enter** D **for deposit in the Num column, and then press Tab again, or click in the Payee field.**

   TIP

   Many people receive their paychecks as direct deposits instead of having a hard copy of a check that needs to be taken to the bank. You can set up your direct deposits in the same way as if you received a check.

3. **Enter your employer's name in the Payee field.**

   By "employer's name" I mean the name of the company where you work, the company that issues your checks, not the actual name of your boss (unless your boss's name is the same name as the company).

4. **In the Deposit column, enter the amount of the check.**

   You've probably noticed that the amount you receive on your paycheck is not the same as the amount of wages you earned. This is one of life's little inequities that really seems to shock people the first time they get a job. Don't worry. You'll get used to it.

5. **OK, here's the fun part. You're going to split the categories for this check.**

   If there is a drop-down list showing in the Category field, great — if not, click the little down arrow in the category field to display the drop-down list. Then click the Split button that appears at the bottom of the list (see Figure 2-7). A shortcut that doesn't require the drop-down list at all is to simply press Ctrl+S to open the Split Transaction dialog box.

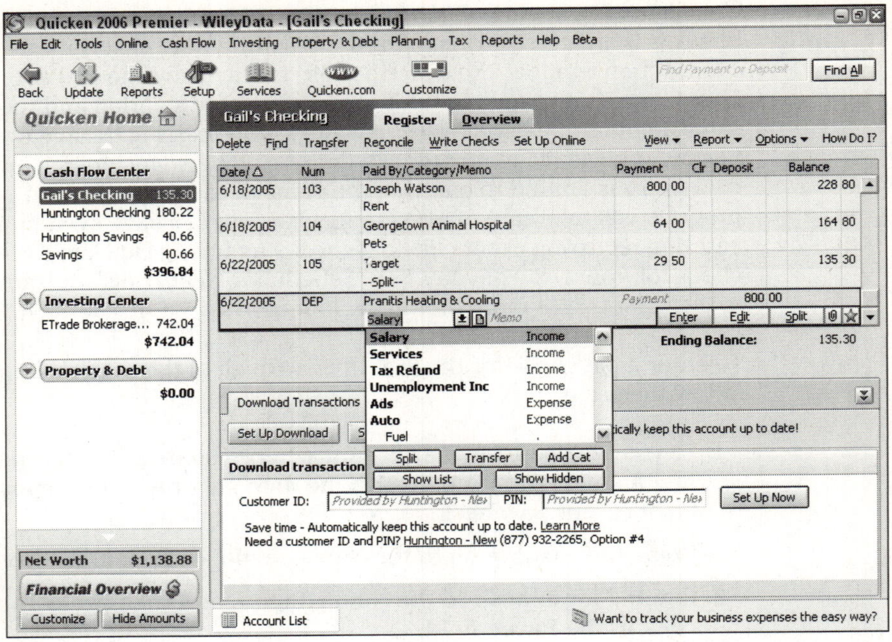

Figure 2-7: Click the Split button at the bottom of this list to display the Split Transaction dialog box.

6. **Enter each of the elements of your paycheck and related withholding. Your gross wages should be recorded in total, and then list each amount of withholding, such as Tax: Fed, Tax: Soc Sec, and so on, as shown in Figure 2-8.**

   Quicken keeps a running balance for you at the bottom of the Split Transaction window, displaying the total you entered in the register for this check and the total detail you've entered in the Split Transaction window.

   TIP: If you enter all of the amounts from your check and the split transaction detail doesn't add up to the total, there will be a remainder showing at the bottom of the Split Transaction window. Double-check your entries to make sure the amounts you entered are correct. If the amounts in the Split Transaction window are correct but the total amount you entered for the check in the register is incorrect, click the Adjust button in the Split Transaction window. The total amount is automatically changed to agree to the detail you've entered.

7. **Press Ctrl+Enter or click OK to close the Split Transaction window, and then press Enter or Alt+T or click the Enter button to complete the entry.**

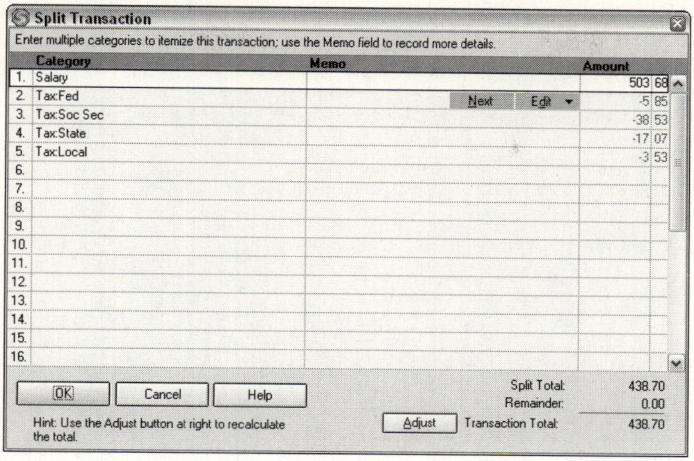

Figure 2-8: Enter multiple categories in the Split Transaction dialog box.

Issuing checks right from Quicken

The traditional method of writing checks by hand is quickly being replaced by electronic alternatives. With Quicken, you can issue and print checks by making some entries on your computer screen. Who wouldn't rather type a check than write one out by hand?

There is one catch. In order to print checks through Quicken, you must acquire paper check forms. These forms are can be purchased from Intuit and can be ordered on the `www.quicken.com` Web site (click Intuit Products in the upper-right corner) or by calling 1-800-548-0289.

Taking check writing one step further, you can issue online payments and do away with paper checks altogether. See Book II, Chapter 5, and also take a look at Book IV, Chapter 4, which addresses Quicken's Bill Pay service.

Even if you don't decide to purchase blank check forms and use Quicken to write your actual checks, you can still use this method of entering information in your Quicken register. For some people, this process is easier than writing directly in the register — it's more like writing a real check and seems more familiar.

Follow these steps to use the Quicken check-writing feature, whether you plan to issue a real check printed from Quicken or you're just entering check information in your Quicken program.

1. **Press Ctrl+W or choose Write Checks from the Cash Flow menu.**

   The Write Checks window, as shown in Figure 2-9, appears. Filling out this window is as familiar a process as, well, writing a check by hand.

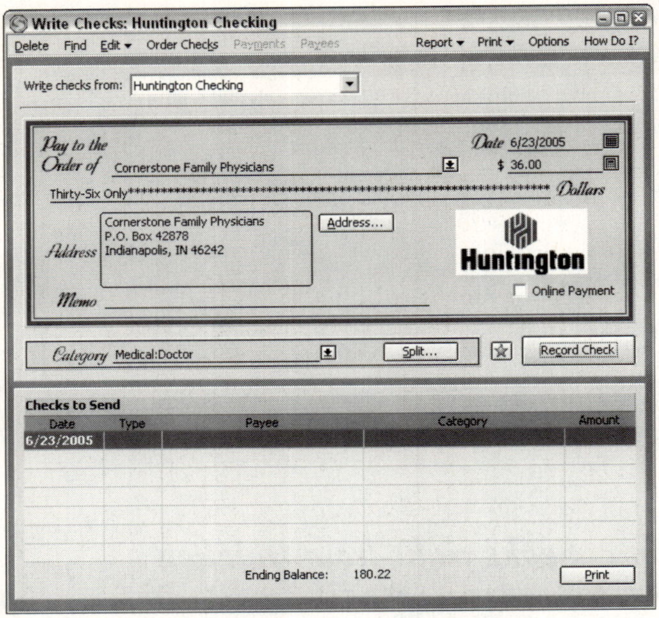

Figure 2-9: It's no coincidence: Quicken's Write Checks window looks just like a real check.

2. **Enter the bank you want to use.**

   Quicken has already decided which bank you're going to use for writing this check. If you've only set up one bank in Quicken, there's no choice to make. But if you have set up more than one bank in Quicken, make sure the correct bank is selected, or click the drop-down arrow in the Write Checks From field at the top of the check screen to select the bank you want.

3. **Enter the name of the payee.**

   When you begin entering the name of the person or company who is to receive this check, Quicken uses its QuickFill feature and fills in the rest of the letters. This assumes, of course, that you've entered this name sometime in the past. Quicken is good at guessing, but not totally clairvoyant, so if you've never entered this payee's name before, you have to type the whole name yourself.

4. **Enter the check date.**

   Not to be confused with today's date (unless of course you plan on dating the check today), the check date should agree to the date on which the check is to be printed.

5. **Enter the amount.**

   You say to-may-toes, I say to-mah-toes; you enter the check amount in numerals, Quicken writes the check amount in text. It's all good.

6. **Enter the address.**

   Quicken may have already taken care of this task for you. If not, and if you want the payee's address to appear on the check, enter the address in the Address field. Addresses are handy to have on the check if you want to mail the check in one of those cool little window envelopes.

   You can jump-start the address by typing the apostrophe key in the address field — do this, and presto! Quicken enters the payee's name in the address field.

   If you want to enter detailed information about this payee, click the Address button. The Edit Address Book Record window shown in Figure 2-10 appears, allowing you to enter several pages of information about this payee.

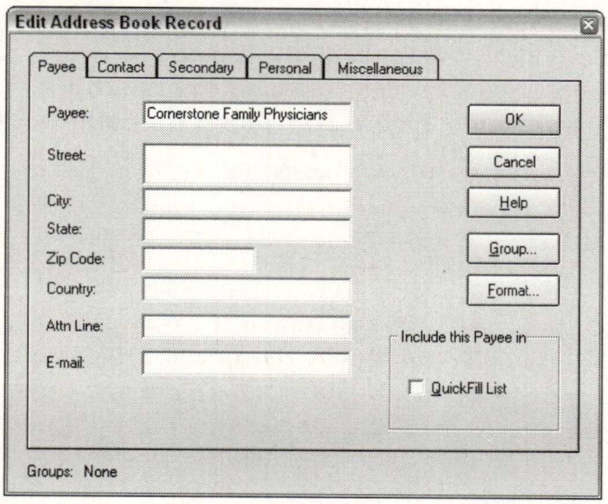

Figure 2-10: Enter all sorts of information about the payee.

7. **Enter a memo. Or not.**

   The memo field, just like it's counterpart on a handwritten check, is optional. Sometimes companies want you to write your account number in the memo field. Sometimes people put personal messages in the field.

8. **Check the box for online payment.**

   If you want this check to be an online payment, make sure the Online Payment box is checked. You can read more about making online payments in Book II, Chapter 5. Note that the Online Payment box does not appear if your account is not set up for online banking.

9. **Choose a category using the Category drop-down list box.**

   You're almost finished, but don't leave the check without choosing a category so the amount can get recorded correctly. If more than one category applies to this check, click the Split button to enter multiple categories.

10. Record the check.

Click the Record Check button to finalize this transaction. The check gets entered in your register, and the paper copy of the check is ready to be printed. Mission accomplished.

Printing in Quicken

Printing operations in Quicken are conducted on the File menu. Click the File menu, and then choose either Print Checks, an option that is always present, or Print Something Else, an option that changes depending on what Something Else is showing on your screen. (For example, if one of the registers is displayed onscreen, the menu choice will read Print Register.) If your portfolio is visible, the menu reads, Print Portfolio, and so on.

When you request a print job, the Print window appears, allowing you to select a printer, determine whether you want your printout portrait (up and down) or landscape (sideways), indicate how many or which pages you want to print, and show how many copies you want to print. Click Print to dispatch the item to your printer. Figure 2-11 shows the Print window.

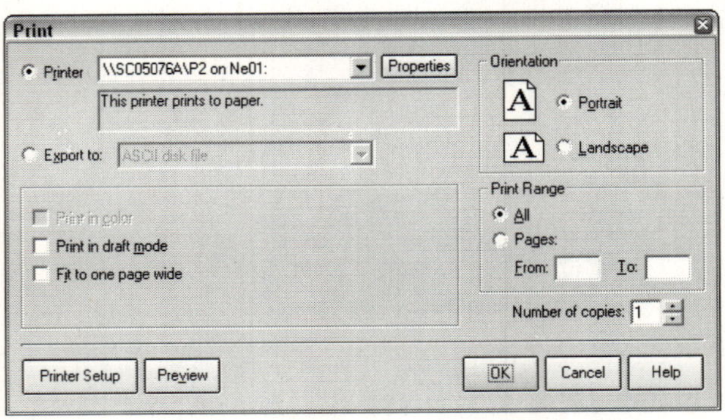

Figure 2-11: Enter the basic information, and then leave the printing to Quicken.

Basic check printing

Printing checks in Quicken involves a little bit of setup time, but after you've jumped through the hoops of setting up your check printing features, your settings are remembered forever by Quicken and never need to be reset until you decide to change the style of your checks.

TIP

When doing the initial setup procedure for printing checks, use blank paper in your printer instead of check stock. That way, you can sample with different alignments until you're satisfied that your print is lining up the way you want it, and you won't waste any precious checks.

Aligning checks

You must let Quicken know what type of checks you are using as well as the type of printer you have. Follow these steps, and your checks will print out perfectly, with all the numbers and text in the correct areas of your check forms.

1. **Open the Check Printer Setup window.**

   Click the File menu, and then choose Printer Setup. Pick For Printing Checks from the side menu. The Check Printer Setup window appears (see Figure 2-12).

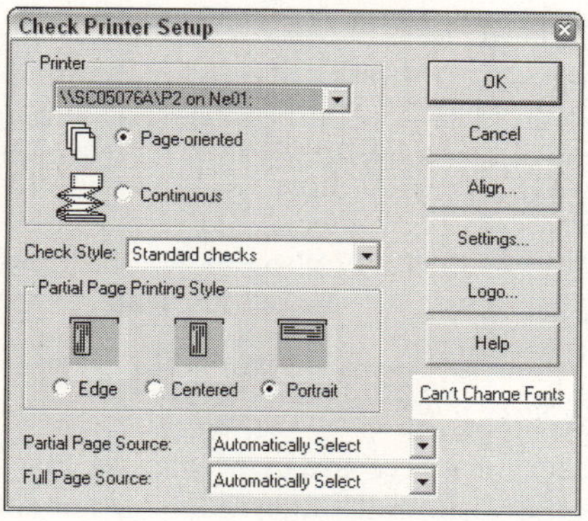

Figure 2-12: Here's where you tell Quicken what type of checks you use.

2. **Choose your printer.**

   You may only have one printer connected to your computer, in which case the choice is simple. But if you have multiple printers, pick the one you want to use in the Printer field.

3. **Identify the type of printer paper.**

   Your choices are Page-Oriented and Continuous. Page-oriented checks are checks on separate pieces of paper, as opposed to the continuous feed checks that are all connected together like a giant accordion.

4. **Choose a check style.**

   Checks come in many different packages. The choices offered here are

   - **Standard checks:** These are no-frills checks — just the check, and nothing but the check. There are three standard checks on a page.
   - **Voucher checks:** These are checks that come with a perforated voucher where you can enter detailed information about the check. The size of the voucher can be anywhere from the same size as the check, all the way up to the voucher and the check combining to fill

an entire 8½ by 11 inch piece of paper. Some voucher checks actually have two vouchers — one gets sent with the check; the other stays with you for your records.

- **Wallet checks:** A wallet check has a small stub on the left side of the check. These checks typically come three to a page. When you issue a wallet check, you send the check and keep the stub.

If you are using the latest version of Quicken, you can scroll down to see an additional option for Wallet checks: Check 21 Image Compatible. This option, scheduled to ultimately replace the plain old Wallet checks option, ensures that the check qualifies for Check 21 processing, the ultra-quick electronic processing that all banks now use.

5. **Choose the placement of your check.**

   The Partial Page Printing Style options are only available if you picked Page-Oriented checks instead of Continuous checks. The options show you in little pictures how your check slides into the printer. Choose the picture that works best with your printer.

   Don't take chances with your check paper. Cut up plain paper into check size and experiment if you're not sure how the printer accepts pages smaller than standard paper size.

6. **Indicate the page source for your paper.**

   Page source options describe where the printer looks for your check paper. Some printers come with multiple orifices for accepting paper, thus the array of options. If your printer has only one place for paper input, you can leave these fields at the default Automatically Select.

7. **Test the check printing.**

   Take your checks for a road test by clicking the Align button. If you are working with checks that come on separate pages ("page-oriented"), choose from full page, two checks, or one check to get to the alignment screen (Figure 2-13) for your check size.

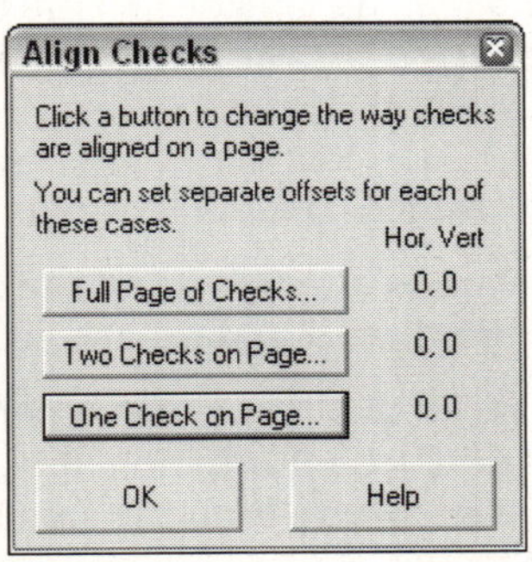

Figure 2-13: Choose the option that describes your checks.

When you make a selection, the little Fine Alignment window appears (see Figure 2-14), allowing you to fine-tune the placement of text on your checks by making vertical and horizontal adjustments to the text location. Start by clicking Print Sample to see a sample of where your text appears.

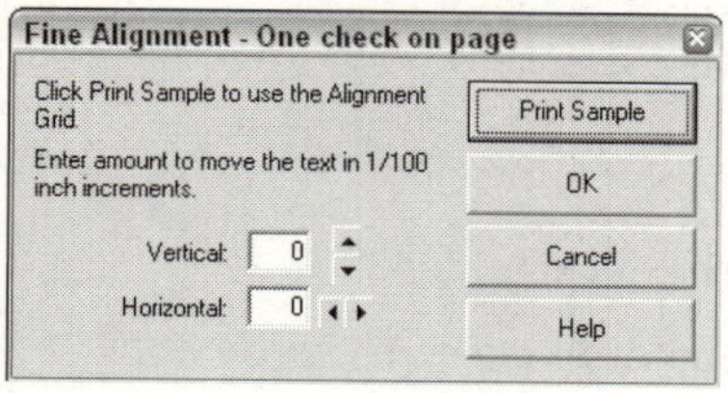

Figure 2-14: Print a sample, and then adjust the placement of your text.

Hold your printed sample up to a real check to see how the text aligns, and then enter small horizontal and vertical adjustments, printing additional samples and holding them up to real checks until you're happy with the placement of the text. Click OK when everything works right, and you're in business.

Alternatively, if you picked continuous feed checks, when you click the Align button, you see adjustment options of Coarse and Fine. Picking either one of these enables you to print a sample that you can hold up to your real checks. Then use Coarse if you need to make a significant vertical adjustment; otherwise, use Fine to make smaller adjustments.

REMEMBER

The nicest thing about these alignment features is that when you've finally got your checks perfectly aligned, Quicken remembers the measurements, and you don't have to go through this exercise again.

Printing reports

Getting ready to print reports in Quicken is much less cumbersome a job than the preparation for printing checks. A few adjustments to customize the report printing so that you're happy with the results, and your reports print just the way you want them.

Follow these steps to quickly set up your report printing options.

1. **Open the setup window for reports and graphs.**

   Open the File menu and choose Printer Setup, and then choose For Reports/Graphs from the side menu. The Printer Setup for Reports and Graphs window appears as shown in Figure 2-15.

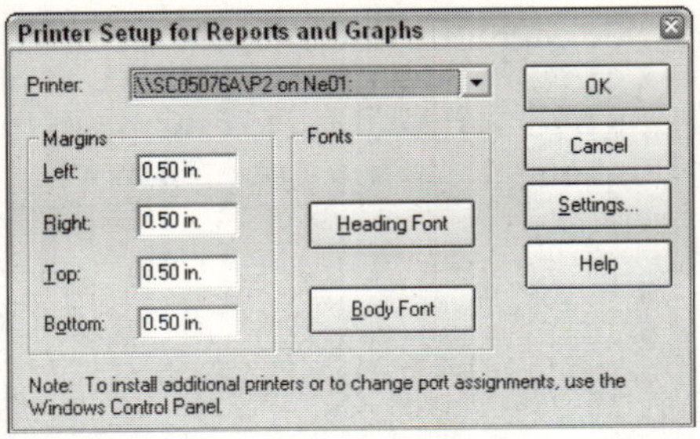

Figure 2-15: You can set margins and select a font for your Quicken reports and graphs.

2. **Make sure the correct printer is selected.**

   Choose your printer from the drop-down list provided.

3. **Set your margins.**

   It might help to print out a sample report in order to see how a report looks with the standard ½ inch margins on each side. Then make some adjustments so that your reports aren't cramped and are evenly spaced on the paper.

4. **Set your fonts.**

   Again, it pays to print out a sample report so you can see what you have to work with. Then click on Heading Font and Body Font to choose the typeface, size, and style you like best. There's no right or wrong answer here — pick any font you want.

   TIP: If you have trouble fitting all of your report information on one page, try changing to a smaller font.

5. **Choose portrait or landscape.**

   Click the Settings button, and then Layout tab to pick between portrait and landscape for your standard reports. Remember, you can always go back and change this setting if you have a report that needs more vertical or horizontal space. While you're here in the settings area, click the Paper/Quality tab to tell Quicken where it should look for the paper you want to use on reports. If your printer only has one paper tray, there's no need to make a change here.

6. **Save your changes.**

   Click OK to get out of the settings area and save those changes, and then give OK another click to lock in your margins and fonts. From here on, your reports will look spiffy with their new fonts and customized margins!

Print a register

When you print a copy of a register, you only see the date, num, payee name, memo, amount, and whether or not the transaction has cleared the bank. You might wonder why you would ever want to print a register. Here are a few reasons that might be useful for you:

✦ **The register for your bank account is a nice cross-reference tool for bank statements.** You can print a copy of the register each month and store it in the same place where you keep your bank statement. Then when reviewing your statement, you can see at a glance the detail behind all the checks and other transactions (listed only by number or, in the case of deposits, by date on the bank statement).

✦ **Think beyond printing the bank account register.** Quicken provides registers for your investments and other assets. Printing a register showing your investment activity for a time period is a great helper when creating your tax return. Print a register for your house showing all the improvements you've made — this is very helpful when you're getting ready to sell the house and want to demonstrate how much money you've put into fixing things up.

✦ **Your Quicken register can actually take the place of a handwritten register in your checkbook.** I've gotten so I make most of my financial transactions online through Quicken, so there's not much need to write out the transactions by hand in my checkbook. And for the checks I do write, I've started making carbons of them with those carbon checks you can order in lieu of the single checks. Instead of writing entries in the checkbook register, I just sit down at the old computer with the carbon checks and enter everything in Quicken. If you can't live without seeing a hard copy of your register, just print one.

To print your register, follow these steps:

1. **Display the register.**

   This may seem like a no-brainer, but you actually have more than one register (one for each account, one for your portfolio, and probably others). Without opening the register that you want to print, Quicken doesn't know which one to choose.

   WARNING!

   The Print command is geared to whatever is onscreen, as opposed to always being associated with a register. When you open the File menu, you are shown two print options: printing checks and printing whatever is onscreen. So, if it's a register you want to print, get that register onscreen.

2. **Choose File⇨Print Register.**

   I gave this step away in the Warning above. Anyway, open the File menu and you see the option to print your register. Click it, and away you go. For a shortcut, skip the File menu and just press Ctrl+P.

3. **Enter a title for your printed register, as shown in Figure 2-16.**

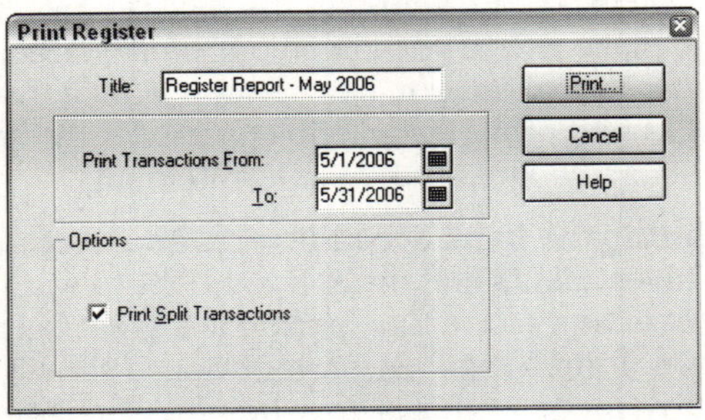

Figure 2-16: Assign a title to this version of your printed register.

   The Print Register window provides you with a field for entering a register name. This name appears as a heading on the printed copy of your register.

   If you leave the Title field blank, your register prints with a generic name. For example, if you are printing the register from a bank account, the report is headed with the title Check Register unless you pick a different name.

4. **Enter a date range.**

   By default, the date range is the complete range of the register, from the opening balance first transaction to today. Override this date range by entering one of your own.

5. **Decide whether you want to display splits.**

   Check the box if you want to display the detail of split transactions. If the box is checked, Quicken displays each of the categories to which the transaction is split. If the box is left unchecked, the word *Split* appears on the report instead of the actual category.

6. **Choose printer options.**

   Click the Print button, and then in the Print window that appears, select from these options:

   - Choose a printer.
   - Choose to export to a file that can be read by another program.
   - Check the box if you want to print in color.

- Check the box if you want to print in draft mode — this lets Quicken choose a font that speeds up printing.
- Check the box if you want to fit to one page wide — this ensures that the report fits within the margins on one page.
- Select between portrait and landscape for the direction of your report.
- Select the pages to print.
- Click Preview to view the report onscreen before printing. Then click OK to print.

Finding Transactions

Quicken's great little Find feature lets you search through your entire register, conducting a financial scavenger hunt for buried transactions. Search for one specific transaction, or find all transactions that meet particular criteria. Quicken produces a report showing the results of your search.

Follow these steps to implement a search throughout your register.

1. **Display a register onscreen. Or not.**

   If the search is to be conducted through one of your registers, bring that register up onscreen. Note: It doesn't matter what appears onscreen if you want to conduct a Quicken-wide search. For example, if you want to see all transactions that occurred on one specific date, Quicken searches through all registers, all entries, not just the register that is displayed onscreen.

2. **Open the Quicken Find window.**

   If you're searching within one register, click the Find button at the top of the register. Keyboard alternatives are Ctrl+F or Alt+I. Perform any of these actions and the Quicken Find window appears as shown in Figure 2-17.

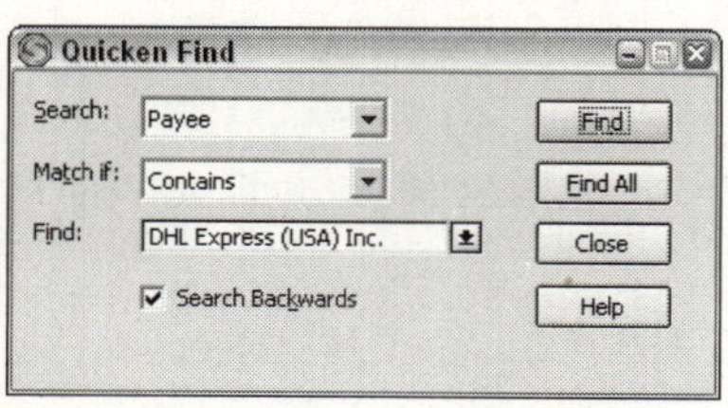

Figure 2-17: Seek and ye shall Find.

3. **Choose the search criteria.**

   You can search for a particular payee, a date, a check number, an amount, a memo, a category, a cleared status, or all of the above.

4. **Select a filter.**

   Indicate if you want the search to retrieve items that match your request based on an exact match, an item that starts or ends with your search example, an amount greater than, less than, greater than or equal to, less than or equal to, or an item that contains your request.

5. **Enter your search request.**

   In the Find field, enter the information for which you want to search. This information can be text or numerical.

6. **Execute the search.**

   Click Find or Find All to begin the search. Find retrieves the next item in your register after the point where your cursor is situated. When your search gets to the end of the register, Quicken asks if it's OK to start at the beginning of the register and continue the search. Each time the Find feature finds a match, that matching transaction is selected for you. Click Find repeatedly to go to each of the register selections that match your criteria.

TIP

Rather than searching one at a time, you can choose Find All and see a report showing all transactions that match your request. Double-click on any transaction that appears on the report to go to the original entry of that transaction.

The universal Find

You can look beyond the register onscreen and search through the depths of your financial data. To do so, choose Edit⇨Find and Replace⇨Find/Replace.

The Find and Replace box appears. You can enter the same type of criteria you entered for the register Find command. The difference is, now Quicken searches throughout the entire program, pulling matching transactions from anywhere they appear. The result is a nice window showing every transaction.

One cool thing about the Find and Replace feature is that, now that you've found all these transactions, you can replace them with something else. For example, maybe you misclassified several transactions to the wrong category. Find the transactions you mislabeled, and then use the Replace feature to change the category.

At the bottom of the Find and Replace window is an option to replace a certain criteria (such as category, date, name, and so on) with something else. Check the items in the list that should be affected by the replace, and then click Done. Your replacements are executed!

Scheduling Recurring Transactions

Having the ability to schedule recurring transactions means you never have to worry again about missing an important payment or completing repetitious tasks like entering your paycheck each pay period. Let Quicken take the responsibility for either sending you reminders of transactions or actually processing the transactions automatically. Use Quicken's scheduling feature and you'll be amazed at how well organized you become! Here's an example of how to schedule a recurring rent payment:

1. **In the register, click on a sample transaction that you would like to automate.**

   The easiest way to create a recurring transaction is to enter the transaction in the register, and then tell Quicken you want to repeat this transaction in the future. For this example, I've entered my rent payment in Figure 2-18. Now I click anywhere on that transaction in the register.

2. **Open the Create Scheduled Transaction dialog box.**

   Right-click on the register transaction, and then click on Schedule Transaction on the pop-up menu that appears.

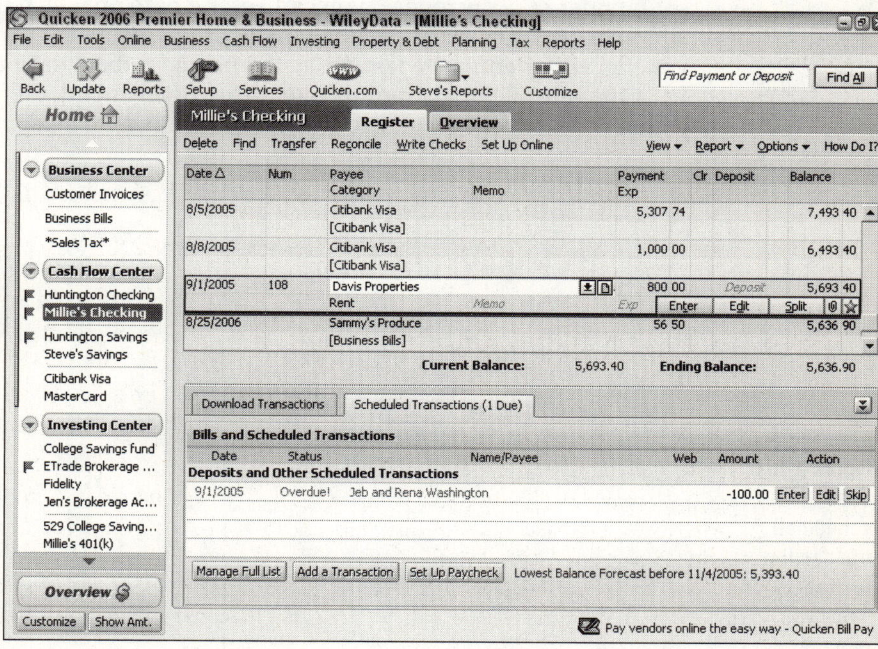

Figure 2-18: Enter the transaction in your register first, and then schedule repeat occurrences.

3. **Verify the amount and other information.**

   Quicken pulls information from your transaction into the Create Scheduled Transaction dialog box, as shown in Figure 2-19. Verify that the amount and payee information is correct.

4. **Enter the start date.**

   In the Scheduling section of the dialog box, enter the date when the next payment is due.

5. **Enter reminder information.**

   Quicken automatically assumes you want a reminder three days in advance of each payment due date. You can change the number of days if necessary so that you'll have enough advance notice so that you won't miss your payment.

6. **Enter the frequency of the payment.**

   Select the frequency (I've chosen monthly), and enter information about which day of the month (or week, quarter, year — whatever you've chosen) the payment should be made.

7. **Enter an end date if necessary.**

   If you're scheduling a loan payment or some other transaction that has a set number of occurrences, you can enter a date on which the last transaction occurs. For example, if you have 12 payments left on your loan, you can either enter the last projected payment date, or you can enter 12 in the After field. My rent payments are open-ended; there is no projected date for rent to end, so I've left the Ending On fields blank.

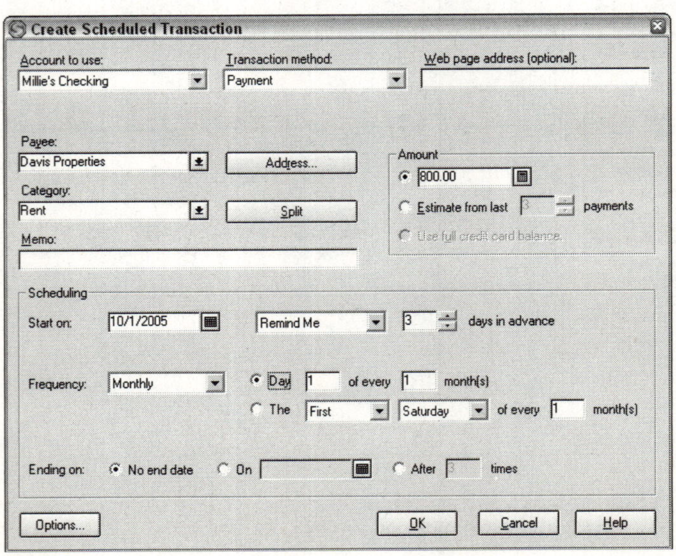

Figure 2-19: The scheduled transaction feature helps you remember future due dates.

8. Click OK to save your transaction.

From now on, you get a reminder each time your payment is due.

TIP

If you're interested in automating your payments so that you don't even have to write the checks, take a look at Book IV, Chapter 4 where I discuss Quicken's Bill Pay service.

Setting Cash Balance Alerts

When it comes to reminders, Quicken is excellent at getting your attention. You can set notices to tell you when a payment is due, remind you of your tax deadlines (especially useful if you file quarterly), let you know the tax implications of selling a particular stock, and much more. In this example, because we're talking about registers, we set an alert to let us know when the balance in our checking account has dropped to a certain level.

1. Open the Alerts Center window.

Choose Set Up Alerts from the Tools menu. The Alerts Center window appears, with several options appearing on the left side of the screen. Click any of the plus signs next to major category headings to see the detail of alerts that are available under that category. Figure 2-20 shows the Setup list in the Alerts Center window.

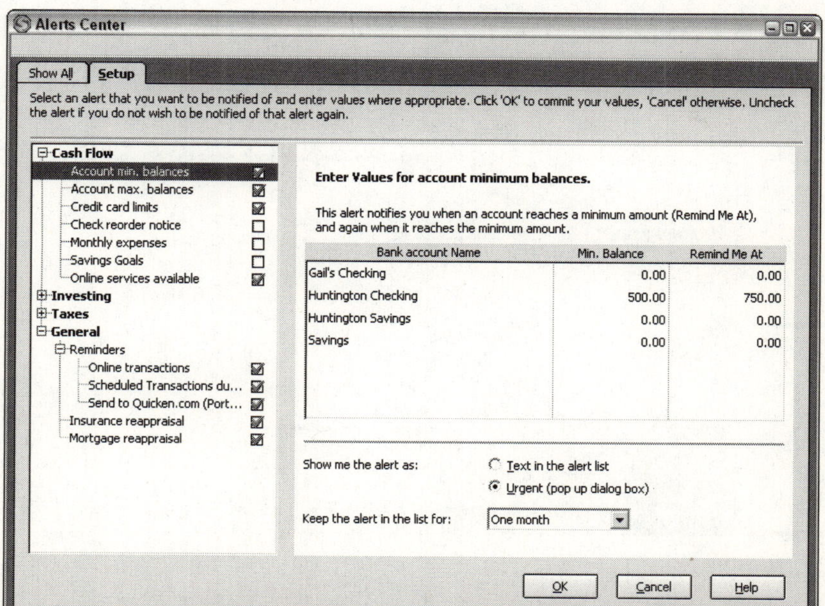

Figure 2-20: Reminder alerts — like tying cyber-string around your finger.

2. **Choose the type of alert you want to set.**

   Look over the list at the left side of the window and click once on the type of alert you want to set. In this case, we want to set a minimum balance reminder on an account. If necessary, click to expand the Cash Flow list, and then click once on Account Min. Balances. All of your accounts appear on the right side of the window.

3. **Select the account and set the alert.**

   Click on any account, and then enter a minimum balance for that account. In the Remind Me At column, you can enter an amount higher than the minimum balance. When the higher amount is reached, the alert is triggered.

4. **Choose your preferred method of notification.**

   Click to receive your alert notice either as text in the alert list or as a pop-up dialog box, as shown in Figure 2-21. I prefer the pop-up box myself. If I use the alert list, I have to open the alert list in order to see my alerts. This seems to defeat the purpose of having the program notify me of important issues.

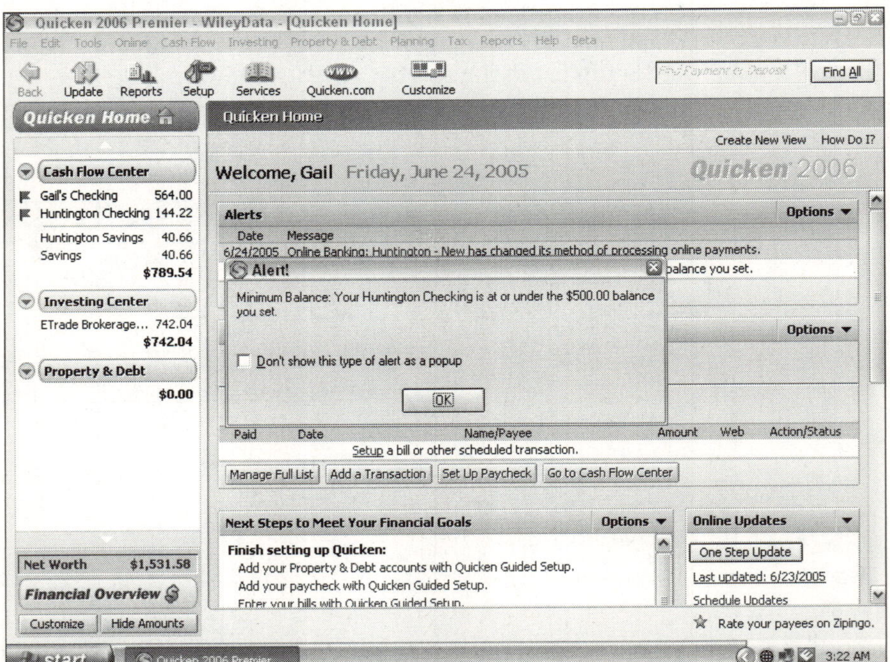

Figure 2-21: Quicken's pop-up alerts really get your attention.

5. **Select the duration of the alert.**

   Choose if you want the alert to be in force for a day, a week, a month, a quarter, or a year. Then you're finished. Click OK.

   If an alert has been triggered, the alert appears in a pop-up box when you start the program. Click OK to close the alert.

If you chose to have the alert appear on your alert list instead of hammering you over the head with a pop-up box, choose Tools➪Show All Alerts to display your current alerts. Make sure you check your alerts window frequently so you'll see all the information that Quicken has been ordered to tell you about.

Chapter 3: Managing Your Accounts

In This Chapter

- **Setting up additional bank accounts**
- **Setting up investment accounts**
- **Setting up asset and liability accounts**
- **Finding your way around Quicken's financial centers**
- **Using the Financial Calendar**

Now that you know how to set up your bank checking account, it's time to venture into deeper waters. Although you might have purchased Quicken in order to track your checking account activity, you can monitor many other types of accounts in Quicken as well. The more accounts you set up in Quicken, the more useful the program becomes to you.

Setting Up a Variety of Accounts in Quicken

You can use the basic setup premise to set up separate Quicken accounts to keep track of your savings account, your retirement account, a mutual fund account, credit card accounts, your house, and your mortgage and car loans. Then you can see how all these accounts work together and are accessible in the Quicken financial centers and the financial calendar.

The initial steps for setting up accounts in Quicken are repetitive. After you create a couple of accounts, the process becomes familiar and you can easily create more accounts whenever you need them.

Setting up a savings account

To set up any account, the first two steps are always the same: Press Ctrl+A to open the Account List window, and then click Add Account to open the Quicken Account Setup window. To continue entering information about your savings account, choose the first option that allows you to enter information about your financial institution (if you were setting up an account not affiliated with a financial institution, you would choose the second option, This Account Is Not Held at a Financial Institution). Follow these steps to set up the account:

1. **Enter the financial institution information.**

   Enter the name of the bank, credit union, savings and loan, piggy bank, bedroom mattress, buried coffee tin, or whatever organization or container holds the money in your savings account. If you choose a financial institution that is on the list of banks that provide online access to Quicken, the name appears when you start typing. When you've got the name entered, click Next.

2. **Choose between online and manual setup.**

   You can have Quicken communicate with your financial institution and download your account information, or you can enter information yourself, without the online access. If you choose to use online services, you need to contact your bank (or credit union, or whatever), and sign up for their online features. For this example, I've chosen manual data entry.

   Sometimes there is a charge to use online banking services. When you contact your bank, be sure to ask about any fees associated with online services, and also ask if there are any free online services available. Sometimes you can qualify for free services if you maintain a certain balance, open a new account, or jump through some other hoops.

3. **Indicate that you are setting up a savings account.**

   On the next screen, you are asked to identify the type of account. As you can see, there are plenty of account types from which to choose. Pick Savings in the Cash Flow group and click Next.

4. **Give the account a name.**

   Enter a name that is easy to remember, in case you add more savings accounts later. You can identify the account by the name of the bank (such as First Bank Savings, or Chase Savings), or by the person who's name is on the bank (Gail's Savings or Minnie's Savings), or by whatever other name makes sense to you.

5. **Enter the ending date and ending balance from your last statement for this account.**

   You can skip over this if you're using online data entry. But for those of us relying on good old bank statements that come in the mail, be sure to have your most recent statement available, and enter the information requested. Click Done when all information has been entered.

A lot of people are going to ask why they should bother setting up their savings account in Quicken. They may make changes to the balance only rarely, and when then do make a deposit or earn a little interest, they can remember how much is in the account, or close enough, without having Quicken tell them about it.

Here are several reasons to keep track of your savings:

- Sooner or later (like around April 15th each year), you need to know the exact amount of interest you earned. If you track the earnings all year in Quicken, you have the information you need at your fingertips when it's time to fill out your tax forms.
- One of the reasons you've decided to use Quicken (I'm guessing) is to provide a complete picture of your finances. Your savings account is part of that picture. Even if you only maintain a modest balance in the account, every little bit should be included in your bottom line.
- If you bank online, you can set up your savings account for online access as well. Not only does this enable you to download your transactions in the account, you can also make online transfers in and out of your savings account through Quicken. Saving money suddenly becomes very easy!
- For some people, adding money to their savings is something that gets forgotten or put aside in favor of other more pressing uses for their money. Keeping your savings account and other investment accounts prominent in Quicken helps keep the idea of saving on the front burner so maybe you'll be more likely to slip a little extra cash into your savings account.

For more information on saving money and setting actual savings goals, take a look at Book VI.

Setting up a 401(k) or similar tax-deferred retirement account

Don't leave it to your employer to keep track of your retirement savings. Your employer's interest is in providing you with a benefit. By making the retirement account available to you, he has accomplished this task. Making the account grow and be profitable is your job.

The best way to monitor your 401(k) (and I'm using 401(k) interchangeably with 403(b) or any other employer-provided retirement savings account) is to set up the account in Quicken and be as attentive to that account as you are to your bank accounts.

Set up your 401(k) by following these steps:

1. **You know the routine — press Ctrl+A to open the Account List, click Add Account to start a new one.**

2. **Choose the Not a Financial Institution option.**

   This time you're not going to set up a bank account, so you need to follow a path that's a bit different from the previous accounts you've set up. Click the This Account Is Not Held at a Financial Institution option, and then click Next to proceed.

3. **Pick the type of investment.**

   For this example, I'm using the 401(k) option. The setup for 403(b) accounts is exactly the same. If you have a Keogh or other type of tax-deferred retirement account, click that instead. The steps you follow will coincide with the steps I show here. Click the correct investment type, and then click Next.

4. **Name that account.**

   Time to give the account a name. Be careful here. If you've changed jobs, you may have more than one retirement account. Be sure to give a name that will distinguish this account from any other similar account you own. Click Next when you're ready to proceed.

5. **Answer questions about the account.**

   As you can see in Figure 3-1, you need to provide some basic information regarding your retirement account. Give the ending date of the most recent statement that you have. Some retirement accounts only provide year-end statements, so your statement may be a bit dated. Indicate whether this account is with your current employer or if it is left over from a previous job. Is this your account or your spouse's? And note whether the statement shows the detail of all of the securities you own. Finally, click Next to continue.

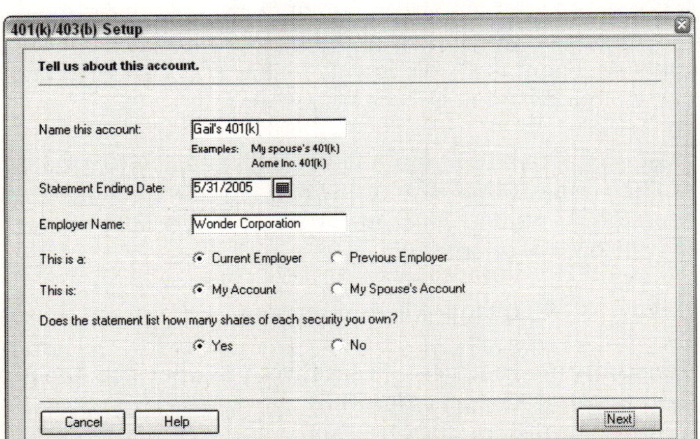

Figure 3-1: Provide nit-picky information about your 401(k) account.

6. **Do you have any loans against your 401(k) account?**

   In case you don't know it, you may be able to borrow against your 401(k) account. If your retirement account is an IRA, it's a different story, but loans against the 401(k) are not particularly rare. For now, I'm assuming there are no loans. I address the issue of 401(k) loans in Book IV, Chapter 1.

7. **Enter the ticker symbols and names of securities in your retirement fund.**

   List all of the investments you hold in your retirement fund. If you don't know a ticker symbol, click the Ticker Symbol Lookup button for help. Click Next when you've entered all of your investments.

   TIP

   The Ticker Symbol Lookup feature, as shown in Figure 3-2, is a service provided by Quicken. Occasionally, I've had some bad luck with this feature for finding the ticker symbols of some mutual funds. Maybe the funds I wanted are too obscure. In any case, another source you can try for online lookup of ticker symbols for both stocks and mutual funds is `http://finance.yahoo.com/l`. (Note: That last letter in the URL is an "L," not a "1.")

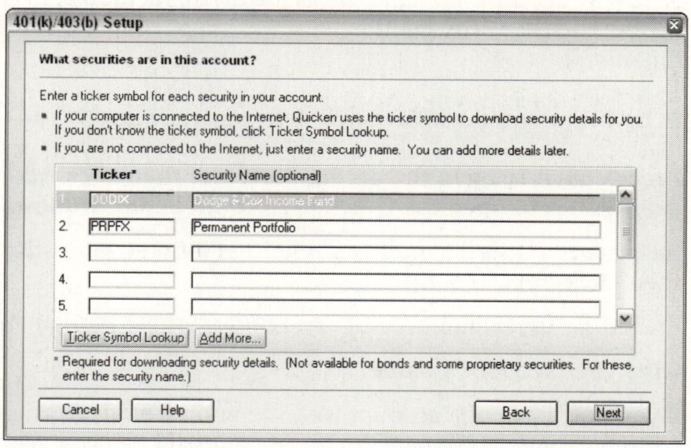

Figure 3-2: You can list up to 10 securities.

8. **Enter the total shares you own and the market value.**

   When you enter your ticker symbols and click Next, Quicken goes online briefly. At this point, you'd think that Quicken is going to get the current market value of your shares so all you have to do is enter the quantity of shares you own and Quicken can do the math. Surprise! Quicken may be looking up the authenticity of the securities you entered, but you still have to enter the market value as well as the number of shares you own. Click Next, and then Quicken gives you a summary of the total value of each investment. Click Done and you're finished.

Nowhere in the 401(k) setup were you asked to provide cost basis information for your investments. When you finish setting up your 401(k) account, a summary screen appears. You can click the Enter hyperlink on this screen, or you can click the Transactions tab, and then click the Enter Cost hyperlink to provide purchase date and cost basis information on these investments.

Entering cost basis information for your 401(k) investments may be more difficult than it sounds. If you're like most people, you contribute to your 401(k) with an amount withheld from each paycheck. Every contribution represents a small purchase of each investment you hold. To track every purchase is a monumental task, especially if you've owned your 401(k) for years. And because there is no need to report the acquisition dates or the costs of each of your investments on your tax return, you really don't need to enter all of this information.

For more information on tracking your 401(k) and how your 401(k) account fits with your retirement planning, see Book VI.

Setting up a mutual fund

You're going to be so proud of yourself for setting up your mutual fund in Quicken. Few tax return–related tasks are as cumbersome, irritating, frustrating, bothersome (you get the picture) as reporting the sales of mutual fund shares.

To set up your mutual fund account, follow these steps:

1. **Press Ctrl+A to open the account list, and then click Add Account or press Alt+A to open the Quicken Account Setup window.**
2. **Indicate that this account is not held at a financial institution, and then click Next.**
3. **Under the Investments category, choose Single Mutual Fund.**
4. **Give your account a name.**

   If you only have one account with the mutual fund, go ahead and enter the fund name as the name of the account. If both you and your spouse own separate shares in the same mutual fund, I guess you're going to have to get personal with the names. Try distinguishing the accounts with His and Hers, Mine and Yours, or simply use your names — Sam's Fidelity Account and Susan's Fidelity Account. (This last example of course works best if your names are actually Sam and Susan . . . feel free to substitute other more appropriate names.) Click Next to continue.

5. **Enter the ticker symbol and the number of shares you own and then click Next.**

   See the tip about looking up ticker symbols earlier in this chapter. For mutual funds with several funds in the same family (for example, there are a mind-boggling 538 different Fidelity mutual funds), make double-sure you get the ticker symbol correct.

Reporting sales of mutual funds on your tax return

Just stop and think about this for a minute. If you own shares in a mutual fund, you probably take advantage of the ability to have your monthly earnings reinvested in more shares instead of receiving a dividend check each month. That sounds like such a good idea, until you consider the tax ramifications. Each time you purchase even a fraction of a share, that constitutes a separate purchase of a security.

Then when you sell shares, you typically sell a block of shares at once. Typically, people sell mutual fund shares in rounded amounts without consideration for the quantity of shares they've sold. Instead, they might sell $200 worth of shares, or $500 or $1,000. That $500 might work out to some strange quantity like 39.382 shares, and together those shares might have been purchased on 40 different dates.

Believe it or not, until not very many years ago, people were required to report each share or group or fraction of shares purchased on their tax return when a sale occurred. Now, the IRS allows you to average the cost of the shares purchased instead of breaking out each individual purchase. Easy? Yes. But does averaging give you the best tax break on the shares? Maybe not.

Your mutual fund statement probably shows you the average cost of your shares for purposes of reporting any sales on your tax return. The alternative to using the average cost is to report the actual cost of shares you sold. If you report the actual cost of shares you sold, you'll probably use the cost of shares in the order in which they were purchased. So, for example, using whole numbers only (which is fairly uncommon for mutual funds but easy for this example), if you own 100 shares of a mutual fund and decide to sell 10 shares, your cost that you show on your tax return is the cost of the first 10 shares you purchased.

There is an alternative to reporting the cost of the first shares you purchased. When you make the sale, you can tell the broker exactly which shares you want to sell. Using the same example, those first 10 shares you purchased may have cost much less than the most recent shares you purchased. If you tell your broker you want to sell the last 10 shares you purchased instead of the first 10, your tax on the sale might be quite a bit less.

You'll never know what the possibilities are for calculating the tax consequences of your mutual fund sales unless you do the math. And Quicken is more than happy to provide you with all the information you need, if you do the initial legwork of entering all of your share purchases. The great part about entering all of your mutual fund info in Quicken is that you only have to enter everything once, and then the information is there forever, for every time you sell any shares and fill out a tax return.

6. **Quicken takes care of finding out the current market value online.**

   Click Done when you're satisfied that all information has been entered correctly.

7. **Enter the cost basis for your shares.**

TIP

If you have lots of transactions to enter, set aside plenty of time to make your entries. If you need to, take a break and return later — you can pick up where you left off.

Now the fun begins. Click the Cost Basis option to go to the Enter Missing Transactions window. Enter an individual purchase like this:

1. **Click the Enter Missing Transaction button.**

   Clicking this button triggers the Buy — Shares Bought window. Here you can enter, one at a time, each purchase transaction, each dividend or capital gain reinvestment, and everything else that has happened in your account since the inception date.

2. **Enter the type of transaction.**

   By default, Quicken has decided that you're entering shares that were purchased (see Buy — Shares Bought in the Enter Transaction drop-down field, as shown in Figure 3-3). If you're entering a purchase, don't change anything. If you're entering a dividend reinvestment, select Reinvest — Income Reinvested from the Enter Transaction drop-down field.

3. **Enter the transaction date.**

   Start at the beginning, and enter the date of the first purchase or acquisition of shares.

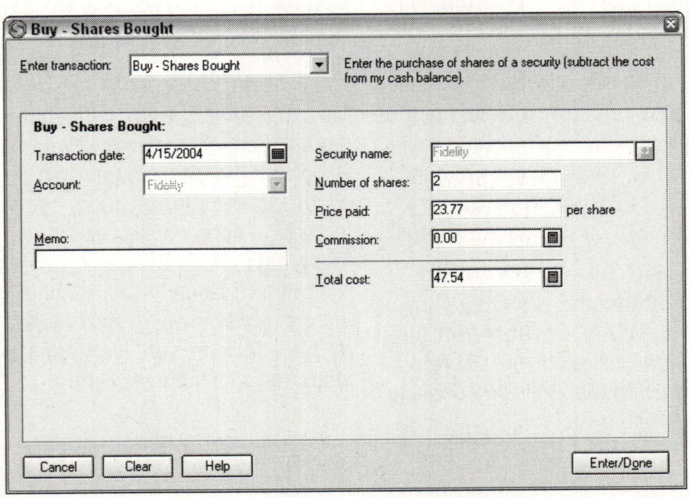

Figure 3-3: Enter all of the details of a mutual fund purchase.

4. **Enter the number of shares acquired.**

   Don't round! If you purchased 32.649 shares, don't enter 33 shares. You need to record the accurate shares, down to the thousandths, as reported on your account statements.

5. **Enter the price per share in the Price Paid box.**

   About now you start to understand why each purchase and dividend reinvestment has to be entered separately. Each time you acquire mutual fund shares, you typically acquire a slightly different quantity of shares and pay a slightly different price. The differences may seem miniscule, but the IRS doesn't care. When it comes time to report your sales transactions on your tax return, you'll need all this stuff.

6. **Enter any commission that you paid.**

   Entries in this field are unlikely when you're talking about a mutual fund, unless you purchase the fund through a broker. Most people just buy mutual funds themselves, directly from the fund, but if you buy through a broker, you may have a commission to add here as well. Quicken takes it from here and calculates the total cost of the shares acquired in this transaction.

7. **Finish the transaction.**

   Click Done or press the Enter key to complete the information. Go back to step 1 and repeat steps 1–6 for each purchase and reinvestment, from the beginning of time to today. Then start all over with any other mutual funds you own and get everything entered in Quicken. And while you're cursing me for having you do all of this setup, give yourself a reminder to send me a thank you note when it's time to prepare your tax return for a year in which you sell some mutual fund shares.

To see how to report the sales of your mutual fund shares on your tax return, see Book V.

Setting up a credit card account

If you're new to keeping track of credit card accounts, you may find this whole process pretty interesting. You could just call your credit card payments a credit card expense without noting any detail of how your credit card funds are disbursed. That would be easy, but not too helpful when trying to set a budget and figure out where all of your money goes.

By tracking credit card spending, allocating the charges to specific spending categories, you get an excellent sense of how you really spend your money, which adds to providing you with a complete picture of your personal finances.

Here's how you can set up a credit card account in Quicken:

1. **As usual, press Ctrl+A to open the Account List, and then Alt+A or click Add Account to open the Quicken Account Setup window.**
2. **Indicate the name of the financial institution.**

   If your credit card is through a bank or other financial institution, enter the name of that organization. Otherwise, choose the option for the account not being held at a financial institution. I've indicated Citibank for the financial institution in this example. Clicking Next takes you to the next step.
3. **Choose between online and manual setup.**

   If your financial institution is on the list of Quicken-compatible financial institutions, you're halfway there in terms of using online setup. Now, look at the list that Quicken provides (see the Download Availability section in Figure 3-4). If credit cards are on the list, you're home-free and have the option of selecting Online setup. If credit cards are not on the list (as is the case in this example), you must opt for Manual setup. Click Next when you've made your choice.

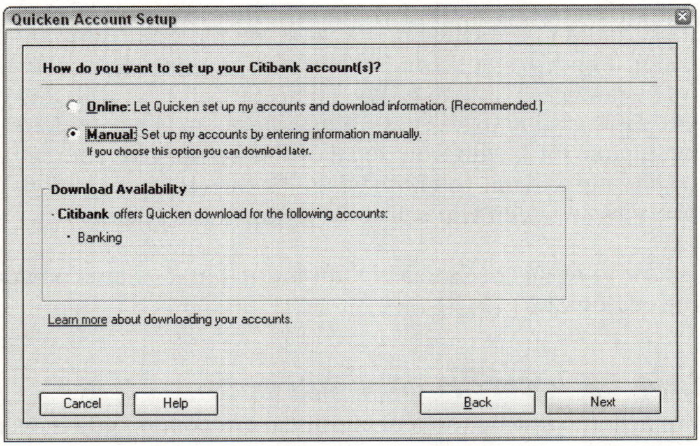

Figure 3-4: Choose Online setup or choose the DIY (do-it-yourself) Manual method.

4. **Click Credit Card as the type of account you want to set up.**

   Your options are many — this time we're setting up a credit card, found in the Cash Flow category. Click Next to move on.
5. **Name your card.**

   Give your credit card a name that distinguishes it from any other credit cards you plan to set up in Quicken. Marcy's Visa won't work if you have more than one Visa card; likewise, simply calling your card MasterCard won't work if you have multiple MasterCards or hope to some day. Just pick a name that easily identifies this card, and then click Next to continue.

6. **Enter the date and balance from your statement.**

   If you've got your most recent credit card statement handy, go ahead and get it (I'll wait until you get back), and then enter the ending date and the ending balance in the fields provided. No statement? No problem. You can skip this part and open the account in Quicken with a zero balance (if only it were that easy to wipe out your credit card balance), and then enter information later. Clicking Next takes you to the next step.

7. **Enter your credit limit. Or not.**

   You have an option of entering the credit limit for your card. This is an interesting dilemma. Those left-brainy types will want to enter every little bit of information about the credit card, including every charge ever made, every separate finance charge, each individual payment, and of course the credit limit too — just because they can't resist getting picky about the details. Others who aren't so concerned about going back in time to make sure they recorded that Amoco gas charge from three years ago, might blow past this step without entering their credit limit (and maybe they don't even know how much the limit is). The upside to entering the credit limit is that Quicken keeps you posted as to how close you're getting to the limit so you won't go crazy and overcharge. The downside is that Quicken keeps you posted as to how close you're getting to the limit, so you might think, "Well, I've got another $2,500 on my credit card limit, so let's go nuts and buy some electronic gadgets." So, do you want to know about the limit or don't you? It's your call.

8. **In any case, click Done and your credit card is officially set up.**

Chapter 2 in Book IV gives you the details on how to actually make this account work for you in Quicken.

Setting up your house in Quicken

Money accounts aren't the only types of accounts you can track in Quicken. And you might be wondering why you should bother setting up your house in Quicken when the tax laws have changed so that most people don't have to pay tax anymore when they sell their homes, nor do they even have to list the sale on their tax return.

Here's why: The home is probably the biggest asset you own. Therefore, the home represents a huge chunk of your net worth (that is, your value to anyone who might want to loan you money). Anyone who wants to know anything about your financial worth is going to require that you provide information about your home, including the purchase price, the cost of major improvements you've made, and the amount of money you owe on the home.

Furthermore, although the IRS allows most people to get off scot-free when it comes to paying tax on the sale of their home, "most" isn't everybody, and some people actually do have to report the sale and pay some tax. For these people, recording the home in Quicken can be an excellent timesaver.

REMEMBER

When I refer to your house, I'm talking about the home that you own. This description can include a condominium, houseboat, trailer, flat, cottage, or any other type of dwelling that you purchased and own.

You can set up your home easily in Quicken by following these steps:

1. **Press Ctrl+A and then Alt+A to open the Quicken Account Setup window.**
2. **Indicate that this account is not held at a financial institution, and then click Next.**
3. **Select House as the type of account you are creating.**

   Under Property & Debt, you see the option House (with or w/o Mortgage). Whether you owe money on your house or not, you can still set up the account. For this example, I assume that a mortgage is owed on the house, and, in the next section, I go over entering mortgage information.
4. **Name the house.**

   Once again, your purpose in selecting a name is to distinguish this account from every other account. If you own two houses, you can call them First House and Second House, Main House and Vacation House, Springfield House and Peoria House, or whatever terms you normally use to tell them apart.

Tax rules associated with selling your home

As with any tax rule known to man, there are plenty of exceptions associated with the requirements for paying tax on the profit from the sale of a home, but for most people, the rule is that you don't have to pay tax on the sale of your personal residence if your profit is no more than $250,000 (or $500,000 if you're married and file a joint return), if you owned the home for at least two of the past five years, and you lived in the home for at least two of the past five years.

For additional information, take a look at IRS Publication 523, "Selling Your Home," where you can find more than 30 pages of rules and exceptions to the rules, worksheets, phone numbers to call where you can hear useful recorded messages, and, buried on page 19, the important words: "Peter and Betty Clark married and bought a home in 1962." Oh wait. I mean the other important words: "Do not report the sale of your home on your main tax return unless . . ." You can find this valuable publication at `www.irs.gov/pub/irs-pdf/p523.pdf`.

5. **Provide cost and value information about your house, as shown in Figure 3-5.**

   Enter the original cost of your house and the date on which you purchased it. Also, you can enter a rough estimate of the value of the house today. If you've had the house appraised recently, you can use the appraisal value, or you can make a guess based on what other houses in your neighborhood have sold for. This figure doesn't have to be accurate. If a lender or someone else wants to know the actual current value, they can request an appraisal.

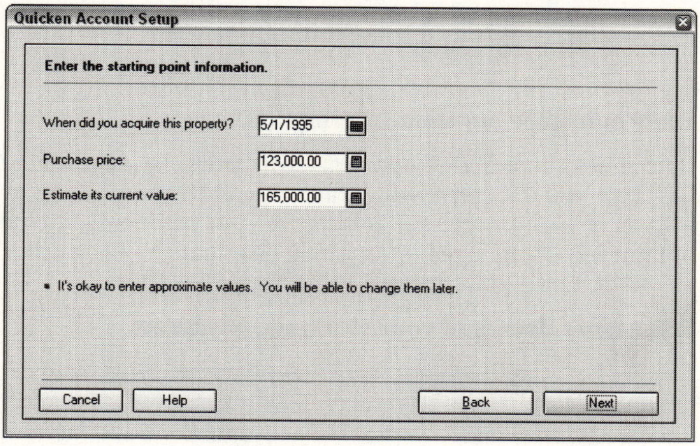

Figure 3-5: Enter information about the value of your house.

6. **Indicate if there is a mortgage.**

   The next screen has three choices. The first choice, the one used for this example, is for houses that have a mortgage. Choose Yes, Create a Liability Account for Me, and the mortgage is created and tracked in Quicken. If you've previously created a mortgage loan in Quicken, the second option is available to you, and you can select the mortgage and link it to your house. The final option is for people who don't owe any money on their house or don't want to track their mortgage in Quicken.

7. **Enter the details of your mortgage loan, as shown in Figure 3-6.**

   Enter the original date of your existing mortgage, the amount you borrowed, the number of years on the loan, and whether interest compounds daily, monthly, or semi-annually. If your memory is a bit hazy on these facts, make the best guess you can. You can always go back and fix any errors later.

   If you make monthly payments, choose that as the payment period. If you pay on a different schedule, select the Other Period radio button and enter the number of payments you normally make each year.

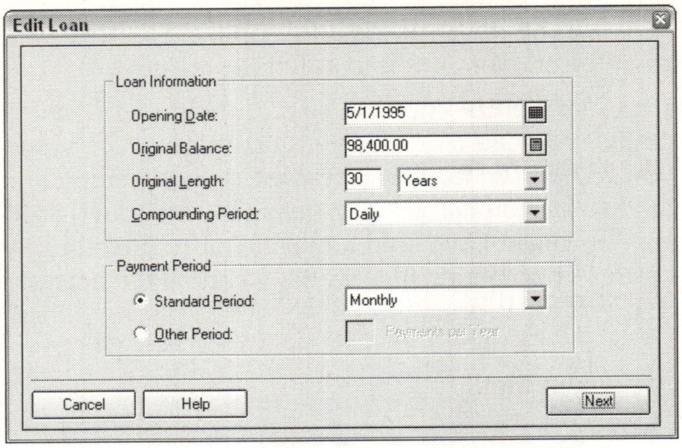

Figure 3-6: Quicken requests information about your mortgage.

8. **Enter mortgage payment information.**

   On the next screen that appears, enter information about any balloon payment you may have with your loan, enter the amount still due on the loan as of today, enter the amount of your payments, including interest, but not including taxes or anything else that the bank adds in with your payment. Enter your interest rate. Then click Done.

9. **Enter more details of your mortgage payments.**

   The Set Up Loan Payment screen appears, and this is where you actually set up your mortgage payments in Quicken. You are asked to provide detailed information about other amounts included in your mortgage payment and also information about how you normally make the payments. In the Payment area of the loan payment screen (see Figure 3-7), click the Edit button to add any other amounts that are included with your monthly payment (such as property tax, homeowner's insurance, and private mortgage insurance).

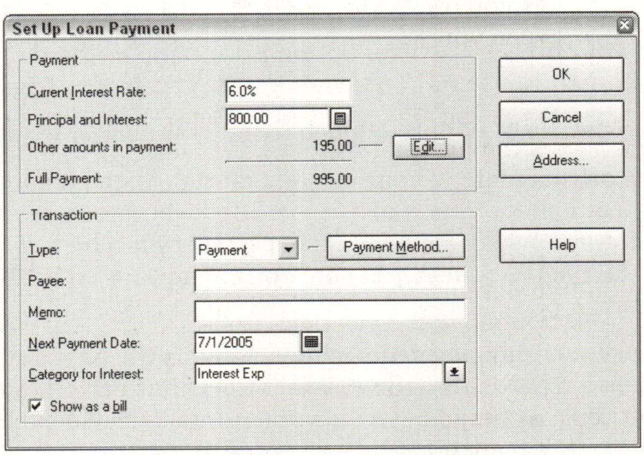

Figure 3-7: Enter the amount you actually pay in your regular mortgage payment.

TIP

Instead of providing the detail of the additional amounts in your loan payment, you can enter one amount and call it Escrow — that's typically how the mortgage companies report the extra amount.

In the Transaction area of the loan payment window, enter the following information:

- Indicate type of payment: Indicate if this is a Payment (that is, you write the check and record the payment yourself), Print Check (a check is generated by Quicken), or Online Pmt (payment is made electronically).
- Click the Payment Method button to set up a scheduled payment for this loan. See Book IV, Chapter 1 for a detailed example of how to schedule recurring loan payments.
- Enter the name of the payee: This is the institution or person who receives your loan payments.
- Enter any memo information (such as account number) that should appear on your checks.
- Enter the date on which the next payment is due.
- Enter the category to which you want Quicken to add the interest portion of the payment.
- Click OK when all payment information has been entered.

In addition to the obvious necessity of making regular mortgage payments and recording those payments in your Quicken accounts, you have other reasons to track your mortgage through Quicken. Here are some examples:

- The mortgage loan represents part of your net worth. When determining how much you are worth (to a banker, at least), the loan balance figures in as a reduction to any assets you have. If you're using Quicken to help provide a complete financial picture of your *assets* (things you own), *liabilities* (things you owe), and *net worth* (generally thought of as the difference between your assets and liabilities), you must include the mortgage loan.
- For better or worse, including the mortgage loan with your other Quicken accounts makes the loan seem more real, and more a part of your entire financial picture.
- If you track your mortgage loan payments in Quicken (which gives you the ability to break out the interest and principal portions as well as taxes and other amounts included in your payment), you have a basis for comparison when you receive your year-end statements from the bank. The year-end mortgage payment summary that your bank provides (Form 1098) is the basis for deductions on your income tax return. Take the time to compare your actual payments to the payments reported by the bank to make sure you are in agreement.

Believe it or not, quite often there are discrepancies between the year-end statements provided by the banks and the actual payments that people make on their mortgages. Because payments are frequently made during the interstice between the end of one year and the beginning of another, people making the payments are fully entitled to rely on their own records of payments being made, even though the recipient institution may not record the receipt of the payment and thus the related deductible interest and tax payments until the next year.

Using the Financial Activity Centers

Quicken organizes your finances into several main groups, each called an Activity Center. You can bring up the lead screen for each Activity Center in Quicken and see a summary of all of the accounts you have within that group, the balances in those accounts, alerts, transactions that are scheduled, graphs, and other forms of analysis. Use these financial Activity Centers to grasp the big picture, and you can initiate transactions within these centers right from the center overview page. Activity Centers also include buttons to set up new accounts and hyperlinks to existing accounts.

Here is a quick summary of each of the Activity Centers, with cross-references to other places in this book where you can find more information about using the features of each center.

You can access the Activity Centers by clicking on the various Quicken menu choices, and choosing the related center from the menu. For example, click the Investing menu, and then choose Investing Center to view that center.

A faster way to move from one Activity Center to another is by clicking on the Account Center names in the Quicken Account Bar. The Account Bar appears on the left side of your screen (see Figure 3-8).

If your Account Bar doesn't show up on the screen, you can make it reappear by choosing Edit⇨Preferences⇨Quicken Program⇨Setup. Uncheck the Never Display Account Bar check box and your bar should return. (Likewise, if you prefer not to have the bar on your screen, put a check in that box, and the Account Bar disappears.)

- **Cash Flow Center:** View balances in your cash accounts and your credit card accounts, and view transactions that are currently scheduled. Here, you can add or edit accounts, schedule online services, pay bills, or sign up for services like a Quicken MasterCard or online banking. Click through to the Financial Calendar from here as well. An Analysis & Reports tab provides you with graphs of your spending and your income, budget analysis, a quick-link list of reports that you use frequently, and a quick summary of your year-to-date income. Read more about how to take advantage of the information in the Cash Flow Center in Book IV.

- **Investing Center:** View a complete portfolio summary, track securities in your Watch List, add or edit accounts, or show the detail of your investments. Here, you can update your stock and mutual fund quotes or schedule updates. Enter ticker symbols to get quick online quotes. Click the Analysis tab to get to graphs and useful reports like a portfolio analyzer, and click the Portfolio tab to see the complete details of your portfolio. Read more about using the information in the Investing Center in Book III.
- **Property & Debt Center:** Here's the summary for all of the assets and liabilities you entered, including your house and home inventory and your car and their related loans. See a quick summary of your automobile expenses, and quickly click over to screens where you can set up a new loan, make a payment on an existing loan, add new assets, or edit existing accounts. Click on planning tools like the Home Purchase Planner and Debt Reduction Planner. Find out more about tracking assets and liabilities in Book IV, Chapters 1 and 3.

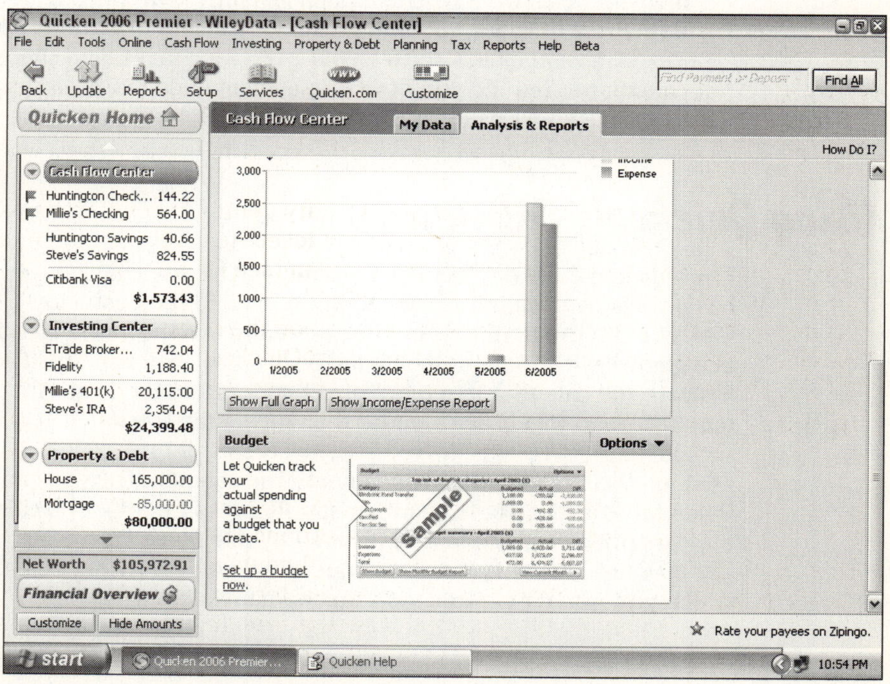

Figure 3-8: The Account Bar on the left side of your screen shows a quick summary of your accounts and provides links to the Activity Centers.

- **Online Center:** Find links to the Online Center on the Online, Cash Flow, and Investing menus. Use the Online Center to see summaries of transactions, payments, transfers, and to request updates to all of your online accounts. Initiate online transactions right from the Online Center. Find out more about the Online Center and online activities in general in Chapter 5 of this book and Book III, Chapter 4.
- **Planning Center:** Access the Planning Center from the Planning menu or by clicking the Financial Overview link on the Account Bar, and then clicking the Planning tab. In the Planning Center, you can see alerts and create your own financial plan, tailored to your financial needs. Also, follow quick links to use Quicken's nifty planners, like the Retirement Planner, the College Planner, the Home Purchase Planner, and more. Click directly to your budget, and to various financial calculators. Find out more about planning with Quicken in Book VI.
- **Tax Center:** Quicken keeps a running balance throughout the year, doing its best to estimate your tax situation based on information you enter in the various parts of the program. Here's just one more reason why you should use Quicken for entering *everything* about your finances. With quick links to the Tax Planner, Capital Gains Estimator, and the Tax Line Assignment tool (so you can advise Quicken of which of your categories and accounts have tax ramifications), you may find you even like working with taxes when you use the information on this page. Also you'll find direct links for uploading your Quicken information right into TurboTax, Quicken's software for preparing taxes, and there's a little tax calendar to remind you of when payments and tax returns are due. Find out more about calculating your taxes in Book V.

Using Quicken's Calendar

The Quicken Calendar has been around since early Quicken versions, and has always been an interesting tool. Go back to the Cash Flow Center, and look over on the right side of your screen to see the little calendar, a month at a glance, with some days shaded in gray. You can use the little arrows beneath the calendar to move from one month to the next. Ah, but there's much more to this little calendar than meets the eye.

Click on the Full Calendar link beneath the calendar (or you can choose Calendar from the Tools menu, or simply press Ctrl+K). The calendar appears in all its glory, in a window all by itself (see Figure 3-9). Your calendar may not look very busy — especially if you're looking at a month in which you haven't entered very much financial activity.

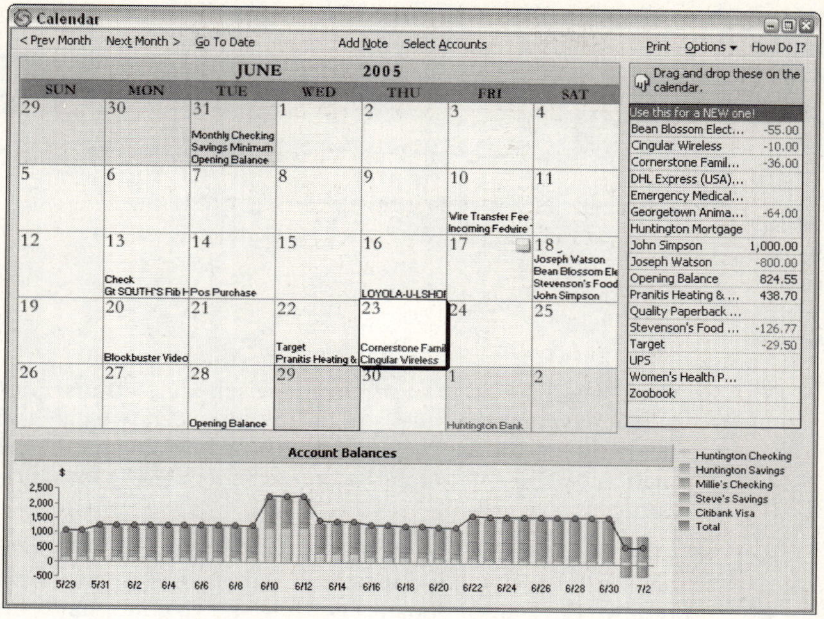

Figure 3-9: The Quicken Calendar makes money management accessible to people who like to visualize their finances.

If you've been using Quicken for awhile, try going back to an earlier month, one where you had a lot of activity. At first glance, you can see on the Financial Calendar an entry for every financial transaction you entered on each day of the month.

TIP

In Figure 3-9, you can see I've got my Memorized Payees list displayed on the right side of my Calendar screen. If you don't see this list on your Calendar screen, click the Options button at the top of the Calendar and choose Show Memorized Payees List.

Clicking around in the Transactions window

Here are some activities you can perform with the Financial Calendar. These activities are available if you double-click on any day in the calendar. You see a Transactions window appear, as shown in Figure 3-10, where you are presented with the detail for each of the transactions entered on that day.

- Click New in the Transactions window to enter a new transaction for that day. The New Transaction window appears. Here you choose an account, enter a transaction type, enter all the particulars about payee, amount, description, and category for your transaction, and enter any schedule information for that transaction. (See also Book IV, Chapter 4 for more examples of scheduling transactions.)

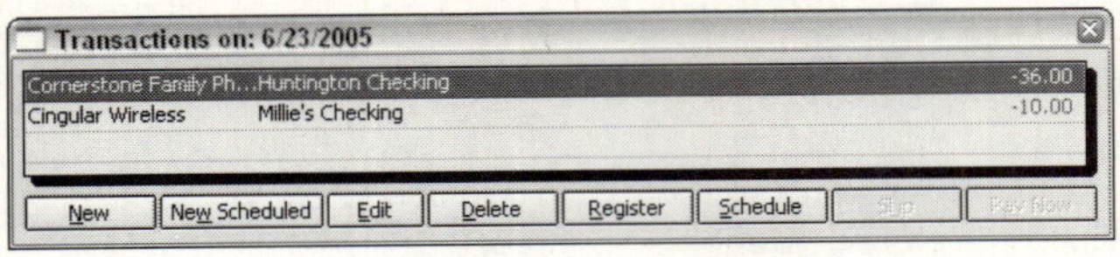

Figure 3-10: The Transactions window is your key to daily transactions in the Financial Calendar.

- Click New Scheduled to set up a new scheduled transaction, for example a loan payment that needs to be split between two categories, and made on the 10th of each month for the next 24 months. All of this information can be entered in the Create Scheduled Transaction window that appears.
- Click on a specific transaction in the Transactions window, and then click Edit to open the transaction and make changes, or click Delete to remove the transaction, or click Register to go to that transaction where it appears in its register. If you click on Schedule, the Create Scheduled Transaction window appears with the details of that selected transaction already filled in for you.

  If you access the Register from the Financial Calendar, the calendar seems to disappear. A Calendar button takes its place at the bottom of your register — just click the button whenever you're ready to return to the Financial Calendar.
- Already scheduled transactions appear on the calendar in Red, and if you click on such a transaction in the Transactions window, you have additional options to either Skip the transaction or Pay Now.

Those are the activities you can perform merely by double-clicking on a calendar day to open the window for that day. There are several other interesting activities you can perform with the Financial Calendar on your screen.

Setting up payments with drag-and-drop

For example, do you want to make a payment? Find the payee in the Memorized Payees list on the right side of the Financial Calendar. Drag that payee over to the calendar and drop it on the date on which you want to make the payment. The New Transaction window appears, already filled in with all of the information available for that payee. Click OK, and the payment is listed on the day you choose. Choose Online Payment in the New Transaction window if you want the payment to be made electronically.

Check your balances

See at-a-glance the balance in your accounts for any day of the month by clicking on the bar graph at the bottom of the Financial Calendar. Each color represents a different account, and the legend appears at the right of the chart.

Remember best friend's birthday

The calendar isn't just for financial activities. You can make this calendar all-purpose by placing notes to yourself on the calendar days, as shown in Figure 3-11.

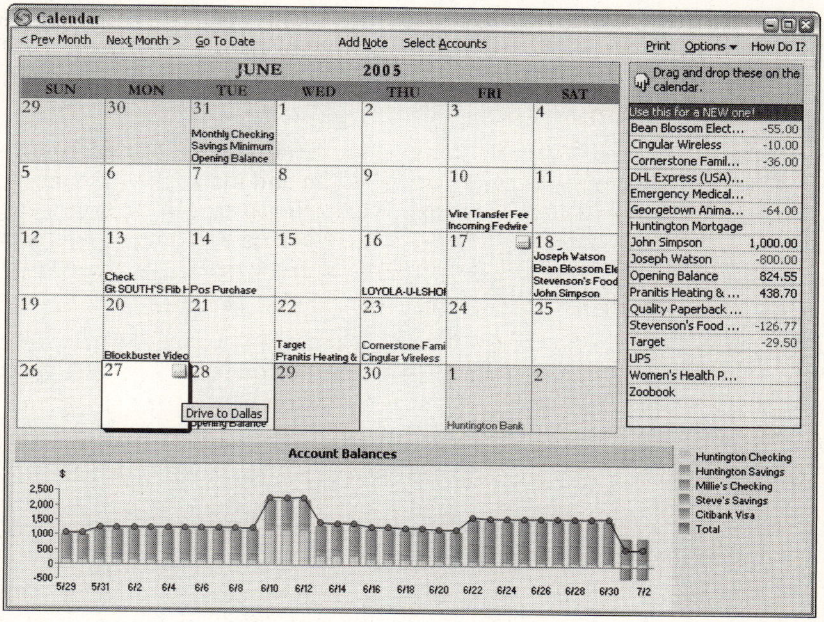

Figure 3-11: Enter personal notes on your calendar, and then stop over with your mouse to see what the note says.

Click on the day when you want a note to appear, and then click the Add Note button at the top of the calendar. Enter your note, and then click Save. A miniature yellow note appears on the day you selected (see Figure 3-11). Read what's in the note by pausing your mouse over the note image or clicking on the note.

Chapter 4: Reconciling an Account

In This Chapter

- **Advantages to balancing your accounts**
- **When to reconcile**
- **The reconciliation process**
- **Fixing mistakes in your Quicken register**

There are people who make sure their checkbook balances to the penny each month. You know who they are. They're often the same people who work at a clean desk, pick up after themselves, fold and put away all their clothes, and match their socks after each load of laundry. Although I can't guarantee Quicken can help you with the socks, I can promise that balancing your checkbook can become a quick and easy task that you might actually enjoy.

What Is Reconciliation, Anyway?

The process of reconciliation is basically a matching game. If it's a checking account that you're reconciling, you try to match the checks you wrote and the deposits you made last month with the checks and deposits that are listed on your bank statement. For credit card accounts, you want to match up the charges you made (assuming you hung on to all of those elusive little slips of paper) with the charges that the credit card company lists on your monthly statement. Unfortunately, the amounts you enter into Quicken during the month don't always match the amounts that appear on the bank statement.

The reasons for the discrepancies are not too surprising, and yet the whole reconciliation process can get very frustrating, very quickly. Here are some of the reasons it's so hard to match your record or memory of transactions with the statements:

- **Timing is a factor.** You wrote some checks in February, but they don't show up on your bank statement until the March statement that you receive in April. Meanwhile, your February statement, the one you're looking at in March, has checks on it that were written in January and even a couple left over from December.

- **Memory plays tricks on you.** Although you might be confident you didn't make any charges on your credit card in January, the credit card statement comes in with all sorts of activity on it. If you don't keep all of your credit card receipts (and who does? OK, I do, but then I play with numbers for a living), you're going to be in for some surprises when you get the credit card statement.
- **Sometimes the bank or creditor makes errors.** Difficult as it is to believe, the bank and the credit card company can make mistakes, and those errors just add to the confusion when it comes time to balance the books.

Especially in this age of identity theft, examining your monthly bank and credit card statements with a fine-tooth comb and making sure you can identify every transaction as something you agreed to is more than common sense — it's a necessity.

Knowing the Best Time to Reconcile

Let me just say that the best time to reconcile your accounts is not when you start bouncing checks or find that you've over-extended yourself on your credit. Also, the best time to reconcile is not when you're in a hurry to get somewhere, when someone is waiting for you, when you're tired and want to go to bed, and so on.

Maybe you're not even reconciling at all — just checking your balance regularly to make sure there's some money in your account or credit available on the credit card — but reconciling regularly really does make sense, to confirm your balances, to verify that there are no errors, and to make sure no unauthorized person is using your account.

The best time to reconcile, if you ask me, is when

- **Your statement arrives, or shortly thereafter:** The longer you wait, the harder it is to remember transactions. If there is an error in your account, the financial institution appreciates hearing about it as soon as possible. And if someone has stolen your identity, you may be liable for amounts taken from your account, and your credit record (see Book I, Chapter 2) may take a beating before you find the problem.
- **You have time on your hands:** If you don't have enough time to devote to balancing your accounts, save the project for later. When rushed, people often make mistakes and just end up spending more time on the project than necessary: time that isn't really available to spare in the first place.

Working Through the Reconciliation Process

The point of reconciling is to make sure all of your deposits were recorded by the bank and posted to your account, and that all of the checks you wrote and other amounts you might have authorized from your account (such as debit card charges) have cleared through your account and agree with the amounts you recorded in your Quicken register. If the bank has stuck you with any fees like a monthly service charge or a stop payment charge, or if the bank has paid interest on the money in your account, the reconciliation process records these amounts. In this way, your Quicken register always shows you exactly how much money you actually have in your account.

REMEMBER

The reconciliation process works for all of your bank accounts, including checking, saving, and money markets. In addition, you can use the same process (with a little twist on the end for making your monthly payment) to reconcile your credit card account.

OK, your bank statement has arrived and you've set aside some time to devote to the reconciliation process, so it's time to get it done. Begin the reconciliation by displaying the register for the account you want to reconcile. Click on the account name as it appears on the Account Bar on the left side of your Quicken screen, or press Ctrl+A to display your complete account list and double-click on the account you plan to reconcile.

Matching the checks you wrote

The first step of reconciling your account involves matching up the checks you wrote and entered in your Quicken register (you *did* enter all your checks in the register, right?) and your ATM withdrawals and debit card transactions with the checks and other transactions listed on your bank statement. Here's the play-by-play for matching your expenditures, including tips for correcting errors and information on what to do if you forgot to enter a transaction:

1. **Open the Statement Summary window (see Figure 4-1) by clicking the Reconcile button at the top of the register.**

   This window shows you the opening balance for your account, which is the ending balance from your last bank statement. In addition, Quicken has taken a guess at the date of your current bank statement.

   TIP

   If you choose to reconcile a bank account that has been set up for online banking, you are presented with an option to reconcile online or from a paper statement. For this example, we are reconciling from a paper statement. Book II, Chapter 5 covers online banking and reconciliations.

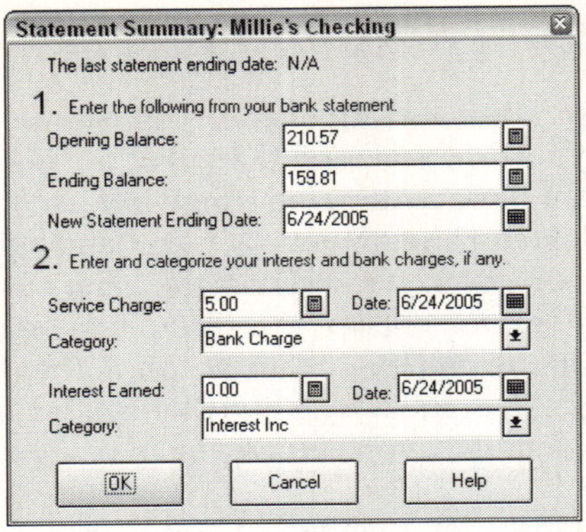

Figure 4-1: Enter details from your bank statement.

2. **Check the beginning balance.**

   Quicken goes back to your reconciliation for last month to find the number that appears for the beginning balance. Make sure the balance agrees with the beginning balance on your bank statement. If there's a difference, you can make a change to the opening balance, and Quicken will enter an adjustment in your register to account for the difference.

   It's likely that the opening balance won't agree with your bank statement if this is the first time you've ever reconciled the account. Go ahead and make an adjustment to the opening balance for this month. In future months, you shouldn't have any problems matching the balances.

   If you haven't reconciled your bank account in six months, the beginning balance number you see in the Statement Summary window is going to be the ending balance from your bank statement of six months ago. No fair starting with the current month's bank statement — you're going to have to go back six months and start reconciling there.

3. **Entering the ending balance from your bank statement.**

   The ending balance you enter in the Statement Summary window should agree exactly with the amount on your bank statement.

   Here's the techie description of how the reconciliation really works. The ending balance provides Quicken with the information it needs to provide a running balance for your reconciliation. Quicken subtracts the beginning balance from the ending balance and the difference is the amount you need to explain in your reconciliation. Here's a simple example. Say your beginning balance on your checking account is $500 and your ending balance is $750. Take $500 from $750 and you're left with $250. When you get to the reconciliation screen, you'll see a running balance of $250. Now say you wrote three checks at $100 each and made one deposit of $400 and one deposit of $150, and all of those transactions cleared your bank. When you compare your actual transactions to those that cleared your bank, you check off each of the checks first. Each check for $100 increases the running (reconcilable) balance by $100, so three $100 checks makes your balance $550. Now you check off your deposits of $400 and $150. Each deposit decreases the reconcilable balance. In this case, when you check off the deposit for $400, your balance is down to $150 ($550 less $400). Then you check off the deposit for $150, your running balance is zero and your account is reconciled to the penny!

4. **Enter the statement date.**

   The date that you enter should agree with the ending statement date on your bank statement.

5. **Enter a service charge.**

   If you pay a monthly fee for your bank account, enter that amount in the Service Charge area, along with the date on which the charge was assessed. Usually this is the same date as the closing date of your bank statement.

6. **Tell Quicken how to categorize the service charge.**

   Quicken automatically adds the service charge to your register, but just like with any other expense, you need to assign the amount to a category. You can use a category like Bank Charge or Bank Fee, or any other name that is appropriate for you.

7. **Enter interest earned.**

   If your account is an interest-bearing account, enter the amount of interest reported on your bank statement. If you already reported this amount in your register, you should skip reporting it here, or Quicken will duplicate the entry. Also enter the date on which the interest is recorded on your statement.

8. **Assign a category for interest income.**

   Interest earned on your account needs to be categorized as income. Be sure to list a category such as Interest Income so your earnings are classified properly.

9. **Proceed to the main reconciliation window.**

   Click OK in the Statement Summary window and you can view a list of all unreconciled items in your register. Now the fun begins. Continuing the example of reconciling a checking account, you see your checks and payments are listed on the left side of the window, and your deposits are on the right. These are all the checks and deposits that you entered in your register that have yet to be marked as cleared. Be sure to also notice the balances in the lower-right corner of the window. Now that you know the lay of the land, you're ready to start the matching game.

10. **Match your payments to those on the bank statement.**

    Examine every check listed on your bank statement and find a matching check in the Payments and Checks column on your reconciliation window (displayed in Figure 4-2). Sound easy? Ha ha! No, I shouldn't laugh. How easy this job is depends on how careful you are when entering your checks in Quicken. If you meticulously enter each check you write, each ATM withdrawal you generate, each debit card payment you make, noting who the money was paid to and getting the amounts exactly right, you're going to breeze through the matching process. If, on the other hand, you neglect to record ATMs and debit card transactions, or if you have all thumbs for fingers and tend to hit the wrong keys when entering amounts, this might be a chore for you.

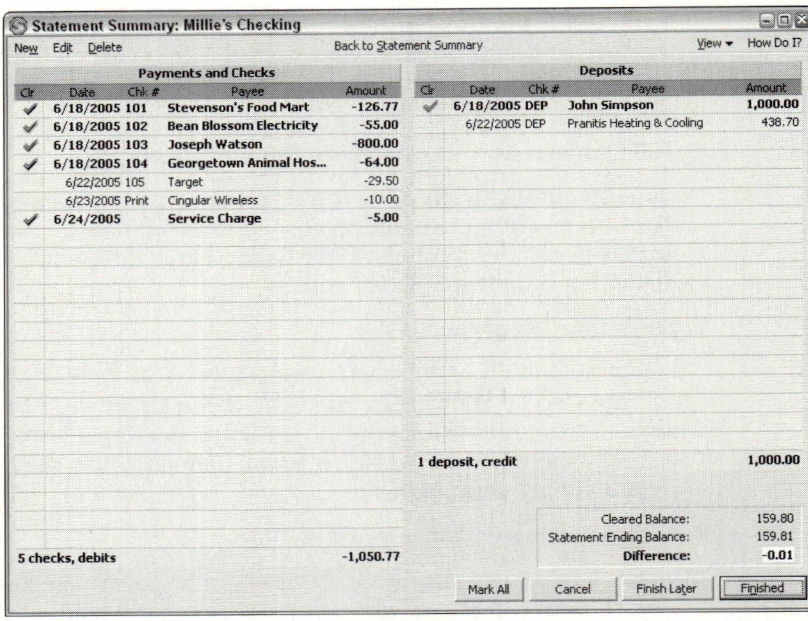

Figure 4-2: Click to check off each item that appears on your bank statement.

TIP: Reconciling an account with only a handful of transactions is a piece of cake. But when your account has dozens of transactions, and lots of mistakes, the chore can get tedious. Don't give up! But it's OK to take a break. Click the Finish Later button at the bottom of the reconciliation window and Quicken remembers which transactions you've already checked off so you can pick up where you left off when you return.

REMEMBER: Before closing up the screen and taking a break, be sure to mark on your bank statement where you left off as well. The paper bank statement doesn't have a "Finish Later" option, so it's up to you to remember where you left off.

Matching your deposits

Money goes out; money comes in. Reconciling involves not just matching the money you took out of your account, but also matching the money that went in. The steps for matching your deposits are almost the same as the check-matching steps.

You're already in the main reconciliation window (unless you closed the window and decided to finish the task later, in which case you need to display your register, click the Reconcile button at the top of the register, and click OK when the statement summary appears). On the right side of the reconciliation window are the deposits you entered in your register. Click on each deposit that matches a deposit on your bank statement.

Here are some tips for matching transactions in your reconciliation window.

✦ To record an exact match, click once on the transaction in the reconciliation window. That places a checkmark to the left of the transaction and changes the type to bold. You can accomplish this same task by pressing Enter or the spacebar if the transaction is highlighted.

✦ Matched the wrong transaction? No problem. Click again (or press Enter or the spacebar again) and the checkmark and the bold type go away.

✦ Numbers don't match. You found the check on your Quicken list, but the amount the bank statement shows for that check is different than the amount you recorded in Quicken. First, figure out which one is right. If you entered the check amount wrong in Quicken, click on the check description, and then click the Edit option at the top of the list. Quicken takes you right to the register where you can make corrections. When finished, click Reconcile again to return to the reconciliation window and then proceed to complete the match.

✦ The bank made an error. If the bank cleared the check for the wrong amount, this is a problem you need to sort out with the bank. Go ahead and edit the transaction and change it to match the bank's amount so that you can complete the match and finish your reconciliation. Be sure to make a note to contact the bank and get things straightened out. Any correction that the bank makes will come through as an adjustment on next month's bank statement and will be part of next month's reconciliation.

✦ Oops! Forgot to enter a transaction in the register! Aside from the possibility that you now have less money in your account than you thought you did, failing to record a transaction in your Quicken register does not create a big problem. Click the New option at the top of the reconciliation window and you are magically transported back to the register. Enter your transaction now, using the date the transaction occurred, not today's date, and click Reconcile to get back to work on this reconciliation. Now the transaction appears on your reconciliation list, ready for you to check off.

Changing the way your reconciliation info is sorted

Your transaction can be sorted in one of four ways. You choose the sort method by clicking the View button on the right side at the top of the reconciliation window (see the figure).

Here are the options you can choose from:

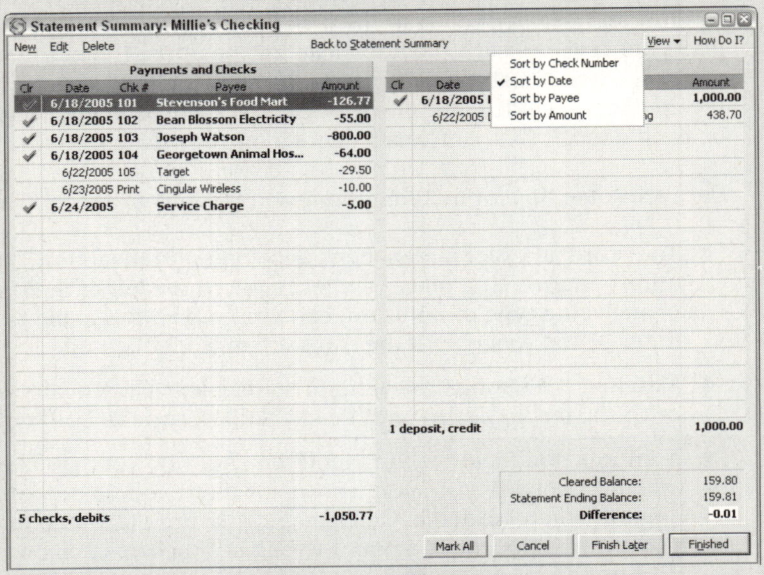

Sort by Check Number: Organize your transactions by check number, and this is the order you get: In your list of checks and other expenses, items without anything entered in the check number field appear first. Next are items with text entries (such as ATM, EFT, VISA, and so on) in the check number field. Finally you see items with check numbers, ordered from smallest to largest number. Meanwhile, over in the deposits column, ordering by check number puts the deposits in order by the date on which they were entered, and then within each date they are ordered from smallest to largest amount.

Sort by Date: All entries in both payments and deposits columns are sorted by date, from earliest to latest. If your payments column includes items charged on your debit card, checks, electronic transfers, ATM withdrawals — these are all sorted by date and intermingled.

Sort by Payee: Looking for a payment made to a particular person? The quickest way is to use this alphabetical sort by payee.

Sort by Amount: This is one of my favorite sort methods. Sometimes I have an amount on my bank statement that I simply can't find on the reconciliation list. Maybe I entered the check number incorrectly or I entered a transaction as a debit card transaction when it was supposed to be entered as a check. In any case, requesting a sort by amount lets me search for the amount that appears on my bank statement, and sometimes that's the easiest way to track a transaction.

✦ There's a duplicate transaction in the reconciliation list. Even with the Quicken warning system that gives you a warning if you enter two transactions with the same check number, it's still possible to get two of the same transactions listed in your register. You might not notice the duplication when you look at your register, but when you see the reconciliation, it's pretty easy to see duplications. When a duplication occurs, click on one of the duplicate entries in the reconciliation window, and then click the Delete option at the top of the window. Click Yes to confirm that you really want to make the deletion, and presto! The transaction disappears.

Reaching the moment of reconciliation

As you match your expenditures and your deposits, the Difference amount in the bottom-right corner of the reconciliation screen changes. For each check and other expense that you check off, the difference decreases. For each deposit that you match, the difference grows. The goal of course is to get that difference down to zero — the moment of reconciliation! — so that your register activity exactly matches the activity recorded on your bank statement.

Unfortunately, sometimes that moment doesn't ever seem to arrive. No matter how hard you try to match every expense and every deposit, you're still out of balance. It's up to you to decide how hard you want to work to balance your account. If the account is out of balance by a couple hundred dollars, it's probably worth your time to figure out where the problem is. If your difference is only a few cents, you might have better things to do with your time.

Determined to balance to the penny

If you are the type who won't quit until everything balances perfectly, here are some pointers that might help you close in on that last penny.

✦ Make sure you entered the ending bank balance correctly in your Statement Summary. The ending balance that you entered appears at the bottom of the reconciliation window. If this amount is incorrect, click the Back to Statement Summary button at the top of the reconciliation window and correct the ending balance to match your bank statement.

✦ Take the difference amount and divide it by nine. If nine divides evenly into the difference, the problem is probably two numbers that have been transposed. For example, say your difference is 18 cents. Probably somewhere along the line you entered a 46 instead of a 64 or a 53 instead of a 35. See how the numbers are transposed? 64–46, 53–35? And the difference between each of these pairs is 18, a multiple of nine. Nine is the magic number for seeking out transpositions. So, if the difference is divisible evenly by nine, you're going to have to go back and examine all of your matched numbers again, looking carefully at the cents.

✦ Figure out whether you're off in your payments or your deposits. It's not hard to do. The reconciliation window shows a balance at the bottom of each column — Total Payments and Total Deposits. When you've finished your matching, those totals should agree to the total payments and total deposits on your bank statement. See which total is off (with luck, only one will be off) and you know which column contains the discrepancy.

✦ Look for a transaction that exactly matches the amount of the discrepancy. If your payments column is off from the bank statement's payments by $43.00, look for a $43.00 payment in the bank statement that you might have missed. Likewise, look for a $43.00 payment in the payments column of the reconciliation that you might not have checked off (or that you duplicated and checked off twice).

✦ Look for a deposit that should have been recorded as a payment, or vice versa. If you're off by the same amount in your payments and your deposits, probably there is a transaction that you recorded as a payment and the bank recorded as a deposit, or the other way around. You've got the amount right but in the wrong column.

You can always give up and find something more fun to do

If finding a needle in a haystack isn't your idea of a fun way to spend an evening at the computer, you might just decide you can live with your account being out of balance by a few nickels or dimes. Face it — if the amount is really small, chances are the bank is right anyway. You can search all night for that check you entered wrong, or you can just let Quicken make an adjustment in the amount of the discrepancy and get on with your life.

If you decide to complete the reconciliation with a balance remaining in the Difference field, go ahead and click the Finished button at the bottom of your screen.

The Adjust Balance window as shown in Figure 4-3 appears, telling you that the total of the transactions you matched is off from the total ending bank balance that you entered.

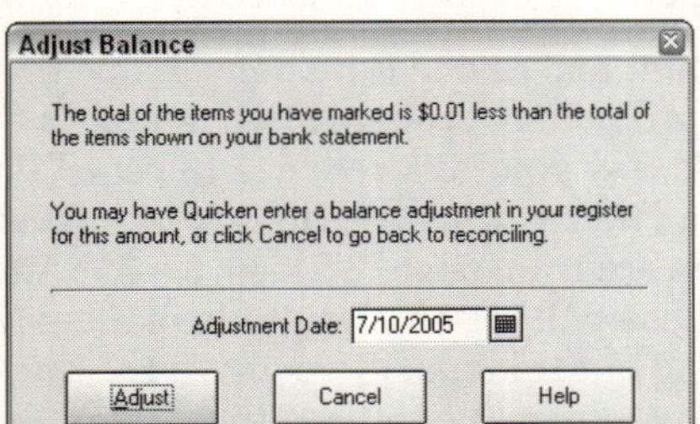

Figure 4-3: As a last resort, you can give up and let Quicken fix your account balance.

Today's date is entered in the window. If you want the reconciliation adjustment created as of some other date (like if you told your wife you already reconciled the account and you want to have the adjustment dated last Saturday), go ahead and change the date.

Click Adjust (or Cancel if you want to go back to the reconciliation and give it one more try), and Quicken enters an adjustment in your register, the account balances with the bank, and all is well.

Reconciliation reports: Who needs them?

Each time you reconcile an account, Quicken gives you the opportunity to print a reconciliation report. Personally I don't have much use for the reconciliation report, but there are some circumstances where it comes in handy:

- The report provides a paper copy of your banking transactions. If you like paper reports, this is a nice one to see at a glance what goes on in your bank account. The bank account statement only shows check numbers and amounts — the All Transactions Detail report gives you complete information. You could print a copy of the report and save it in the same place where you file your bank statement if you want to keep that kind of detailed records.
- If you use Quicken for tracking your business bank account, the reconciliation report provides a good paper trail of banking activity. You might find that printing the reports and filing them in a binder for future reference is a worthwhile activity.

When you complete your reconciliation, if you request a copy of the reconciliation report, you are asked to choose between two types of reports — All Transactions and Summary and Uncleared (see Figure 4-4). The Summary and Uncleared report simply gives totals of the quantity and amount of payments, deposits, service charges, and interest that cleared the account in this reconciliation, and provides a total of how many and how much has been entered in your register that has not yet cleared the bank.

The All Transactions report goes further by including not only the summary information but also a complete detailed listing of all transactions that cleared and did not clear the bank.

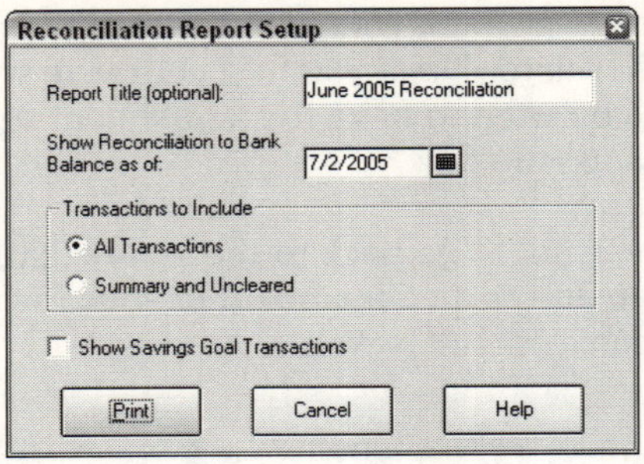

Figure 4-4: Pick your reconciliation report.

QuickBooks saves the last reconciliation report and that's all. If you think you might want to view a reconciliation report in the future, print it now: When you reconcile again next month, your former reconciliation report will be unavailable.

What are these crazy c and R codes?

Back at the register, you might have noticed that some of your transactions have little codes in the column marked Clr. Clr stands for Clear, and the codes refer to whether the transactions have cleared the bank.

Although you actually can enter c's and R's in the Clr column if you want, these codes are actually placed there by Quicken in its effort to keep track of how the whole bank clearing/reconciliation effort is going:

- **c:** Always appears in lowercase. Quicken has received evidence that the item has cleared the bank, either because you checked the item off in the reconciliation window or because you use online banking and in one of its conversations with the bank, Quicken found out about this transaction.
- **R:** Always appears in uppercase. Not only has the item cleared the bank and been awarded a little c, but you have completed your reconciliation. Quicken changes the little c's to big R's when you finish reconciling your account by clicking the Finish button over in the reconciliation window.

Try to delete (Ctrl+D) a transaction in your register that has been reconciled, and Quicken reminds you that you are trying to delete a reconciled transaction (see Figure 4-5). Click Yes if you are certain you want to delete that transaction.

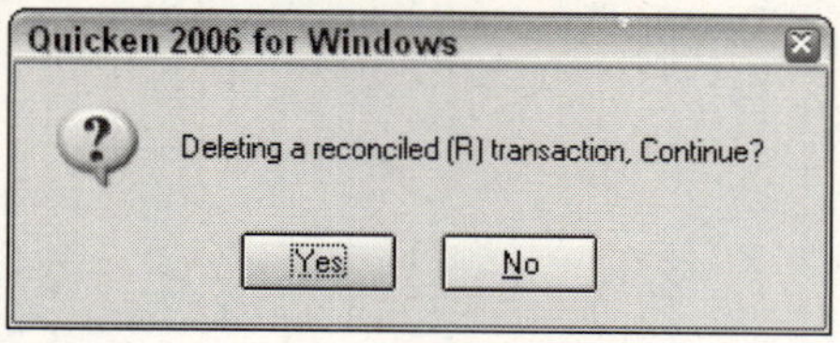

Figure 4-5: Are you sure you want to delete that reconciled transaction?

WARNING! Deleting reconciled transactions can cause problems in future reconciliations. Understand that if you delete a transaction that has already been reconciled, your reconciliation may be out of balance next month (and in future months, until you correct the problem) by the amount of the deleted item.

Chapter 5: Introducing Online Banking Services

In This Chapter

- What is online banking?
- Concerns about online banking
- Setting up online services
- Using online banking services
- Reconciling your online account

Science fiction writers of the last century probably envisioned a superfast electronic worldwide economy that included a Dick Tracy–like command center on your wrist where you could execute payments and transfers of funds and check up on your account balances from any location. Online banking as we know it today isn't a lot different from that made-up world of science fiction.

If you're new to online banking, the whole process might appear mystical and foreign to you, just like all of computing seems to many members of our parents' and grandparents' generations. Trust me, banking on your computer can become just as natural to you as working with e-mail and copy machines. After you get the hang of managing your finances from your desk, the old-fashioned method of banking is going to rank right up there with writing letters by hand and making copies with ditto machines. (Ah, but didn't those ditto copies smell wonderful?)

What's Good (and Bad) about Online Banking?

One man's positive is another man's negative. The things you like might not be the same as the things I like. This section is all about my opinion. You can agree or not, but at least these points should give you some perspective for deciding on the usefulness of banking online.

What I like about online banking:

- **Convenience.** There's no question that being able to do your banking 24/7 is convenient. Whether banking at 3 in the morning is something you would ever do or not, I don't know. But with the schedule I keep, banking on my time instead of on the banker's time is worth the trouble of setting up an online account.
- **No lines.** There never are enough tellers at a bank, but so what? You don't need tellers in cyberspace. Unless there's a line to get to your keyboard, there's nothing to stop you from getting right to the front and conducting your banking transactions right away.
- **You get the whole picture.** When I take care of banking, I like to see which of my checks have cleared and which ones are still out there, floating around. I also like to know what my balance is. I can ask the teller at the bank these questions, but I have to ask them one at a time. It's easier and quicker to pull up my account register onscreen, update the account with the latest information, and see the entire picture of all my activity and my balance.
- **Bank from anywhere.** If there's a computer and an Internet connection, you're ready to access your bank information. When you set your bank up with Quicken, you can also connect with Quicken.com and look at your bank information from any computer, anywhere.
- **You always know your balance.** If you keep a good paper bank account register, never make any arithmetic errors, and always remember to enter every transaction, you always know your balance. If you bank online, you can always see your balance and you don't have to write anything down or add anything up.

What I don't like about online banking:

- **Online banking is impersonal.** I can remember going to the bank with my father when I was a little girl. The bank was a huge marble structure with big pillars outside. The teller would say hello to my father by name and pleasantly offer assistance. Later, when I was much older, I opened my own bank account and I too got to know the people who worked at the bank. I was comfortable asking questions and didn't feel rushed. Small-town banks are still like that, or so I like to believe.
- **Some transactions just don't work online.** The truth is, we still need bricks-and-mortar banks. No matter how cool it is to transfer money and check balances online, there are still limits to what you can do from your desktop. For example, if I need a roll of quarters, I have to go to the bank (or at least somewhere other than my desk) to get them. If I want to pick up a money order, I'm off to the bank. And I have to actually get to the

bank during banking hours and get out of my car and go inside because the drive-up tellers don't like to put rolls of coins in the little canisters and the other cars in line don't like to wait for transactions like money orders.

- **Security is a concern.** Quicken customers have never had a problem with identity theft from online banking, and it's quite possible that condition will remain in force forever. But with all of the paranoia about identity theft these days, some people worry about the security of their financial information when it is available online.
- **You may not be able to use your own bank.** Although most banks have started providing online services for their customers, some still haven't gotten on the bandwagon. If your own bank doesn't communicate with Quicken or offer its own online banking services through its Web site, you're out of luck. If you want those online services, you'll have to pick a new bank.

Online Banking and Security Issues

One of the primary concerns people have about banking online is security. Nobody wants to give their personal financial information to strangers. And banks that provide online services won't be in business for long if they don't offer excellent security.

All banks offering online services use encryption methods that scramble the information you send, so that even if somehow the information were hijacked, it would be indecipherable. Banks make a big deal about how they use the most sophisticated form of security encryption and often compare their level of security to that of the federal government, in case that makes you feel more secure.

Furthermore, protection occurs at your end of the communication with your user name and password or PIN number. If you have any concerns about someone figuring out your password, you always have the right to change your user name and password.

TIP

I recommend keeping track of your user names and passwords if you use the Internet frequently and sign on with different names and passwords at different sites. Different sites have different requirements for usernames and passwords (your password has to contain a numeral, use a certain number of characters, and so on). Although I'm not prepared to publicly share information about where I save my passwords, I do have a secret hideout where I store login information for all the sites I use.

Another method of protection that banks provide their online users is automatic logout. If you are banking online directly at a bank's Web site, and your computer screen remains idle for awhile (usually somewhere in the range of 5–10 minutes), the bank automatically logs you out and you need to sign in again to continue working. The idea is that if you walk away from your computer without logging out of the bank's site and someone else takes your place, that person won't be able to perform any transactions in your bank account.

There are additional steps you can take to ensure your privacy and security when you use online access to your financial records:

- **Don't share your password or PIN number with anyone.** If you suspect someone has discovered this information, change it. These codes should be constantly in your control.
- **Don't let anyone watch you when you sign in to an online banking session.** If you suspect someone was watching when you entered your password information, change it!
- **Don't fall for e-mail messages asking you to update personal information like your login name, password, account number, and so on.** Banks don't ask for this information. You've already provided the bank with the information when you signed up for the service, so any messages you get requesting this info again are probably from someone up to no good. The bank is not going to lose your login information. If you have any questions about an e-mail message purporting to be from your bank, contact the bank by phone or letter to find out how to proceed. Don't ever send personal information in response to e-mail messages.
- **End your Quicken session when you leave your computer.** Whereas banks automatically log you out of online sessions, Quicken provides no such protection. If there is any possibility that someone else might use your computer, end your Quicken session and close the program.

Protecting Quicken data with a password

Perhaps the most famous password ever uttered was the one Ali Baba overheard when the 40 thieves chanted "Open Sesame" and opened the side of the mountain where their treasure was held. You don't have to chant your Quicken password out loud, so there's little chance of others finding out the secret term that opens your precious treasure.

You can choose from two ways to protect your financial data in Quicken. You can protect access to your entire Quicken file, or you can protect your transactions from being changed.

The process is the same for setting either type of password.

1. **Choose Passwords from the File menu.**

   A side menu appears, with options for File and Transaction. With File, you get to prevent anyone who doesn't know your password from opening your Quicken file. Choose Transaction, and you allow access to your file, but no one can make any changes to transactions through a particular date.

2. **Choose File to provide password protection for your Quicken file.**

   The Quicken File Password window appears, as shown in Figure 5-1. You are asked to enter a password. If you have previously set a password for your Quicken file, there is a field for entering your old password. The former password must be entered before you can change your password to something new.

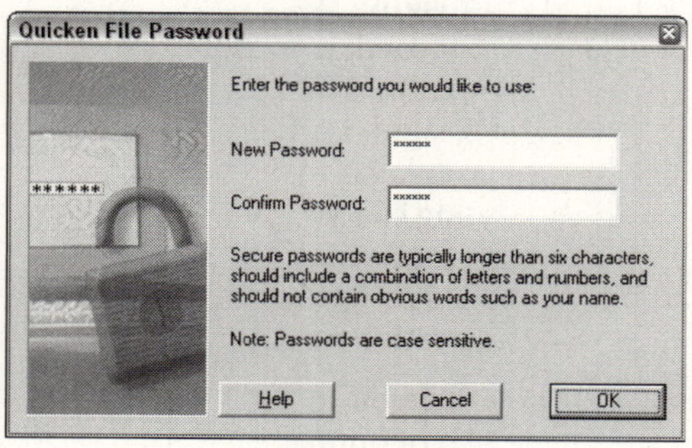

Figure 5-1: If the 40 thieves had typed their password on a computer, Ali Baba wouldn't have heard them say "Open Sesame."

3. **Enter the password you want to use.**

   Quicken recommends that the password be at least six characters and contain a combination of letters and numerals. Quicken, however, accepts any password you give it from 1 to 16 characters. Passwords are case-sensitive, so be sure to remember if you use upper- or lowercase letters. Click OK to save the password. The next time you open Quicken, you must enter your password before you can have access to the program.

   If, instead, you choose to set up a password for transactions instead of the entire Quicken file, the process is nearly the same, except when you choose Transaction from the Passwords side menu, you see the window shown in Figure 5-2. In addition to entering the password that protects your transactions from being changed, you need to enter a date. Only transactions dated earlier than this date are protected by the password.

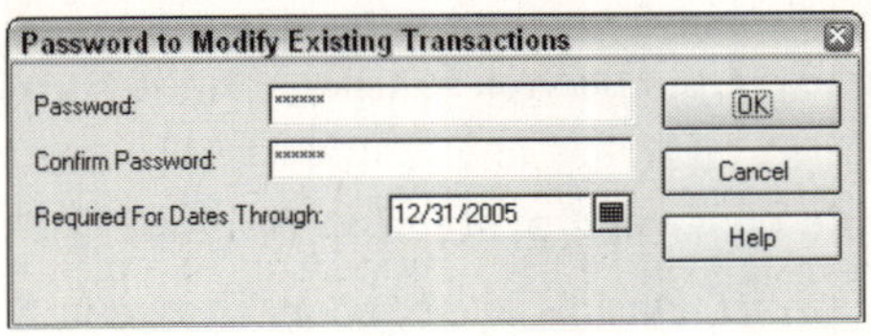

Figure 5-2: You can see but you can't touch with transaction passwords.

From now on, whenever you attempt to change a transaction prior to the date you set in the password window, or if you attempt to create a new transaction with a date earlier than the password date, you are required to enter a password in the window like the one shown in Figure 5-3.

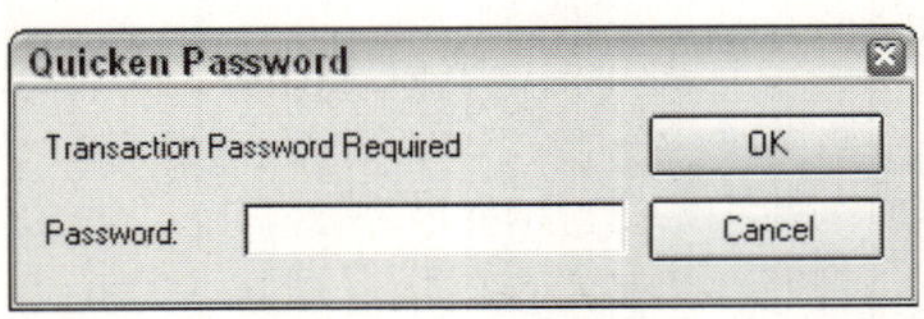

Figure 5-3: No changes or new transactions unless you know the secret word.

Choosing a bank

Every bank is not the same. Before you commit to an online relationship with one bank, find out what online services that bank offers and how much they cost. Here are some factors to consider:

- **Cost:** Many, but not all, banks offer online services free of charge. Find out how much your bank charges for online services before you jump in and start using the services.
- **Perks:** Some banks have great promotions when you open an account or go online. Sometimes there are monetary awards. And some banks give a free copy of Quicken software to customers who want to use the online services.

✦ **Services:** Not all banks offer the same type of online services. With choices ranging from checking balances and viewing banking transactions, to borrowing options, bill paying services, communication with Quicken, and online transfers between accounts, there is a lot to choose from. Think about what you want from a bank, and then find out what the bank you are considering has to offer and how much it costs.

Because this is the age of the Internet, you're not limited to conducting business with a neighborhood bank. A nation of banks is available at your fingertips, waiting to serve you and offering a wide range of online services. What you might have to give up in personalized service from a banker who knows you by name, you have the ability to make up in efficient 24/7 service from a bank that makes all of its services available online.

Setting up your online banking

Book II, Chapter 2 has a detailed example of how to set up a new online bank account. Here's what to do if you have an existing Quicken account that you want to set up for online services.

1. **Click on the Online menu and choose Online Account Services Setup.**

   The window you see in Figure 5-4 appears, listing all of your accounts.

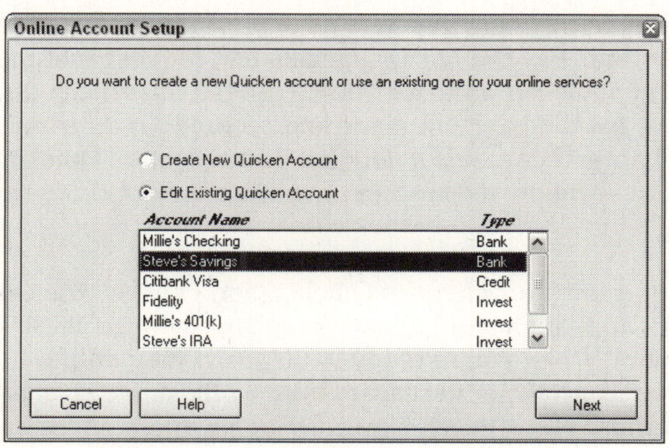

Figure 5-4: Pick the account that is to receive online privileges.

2. **Click on the name of the account you want to set up for online services, click the Edit Existing Quicken Account option, and then click Next.**

3. **Enter your login info.**

   You're asked to enter your customer identification and PIN number. If you've used the bank's online services previously, this is the same login information that you use on the bank's Web site. If you haven't used the bank's online services before now, click the Sign Up Now option or call the phone number that appears in the window to contact your bank and request online privileges. You might have to allow a few days to receive online user information by mail.

4. **Click Next.**

   Quicken hops online to see if it can communicate with your bank. If you've already established an online relationship with the bank, this process should be a snap. If you're waiting to get set up with the bank's online features, you may have to return to this online setup process in a couple of days. Just click Cancel for now, and then repeat the earlier steps when you return and Quicken takes care of the rest.

Paying Bills with Your Online Account

Now that you have online account access, you can choose from several ways to pay bills. There's still the old-fashioned way, where you write a check and send it through the mail. Bor-ing. If you are accustomed to using your bank's online bill payment feature, you can go to the bank's Web site and make a bill payment over there. Nice, but still an extra step or two — you have to get over to the bank's Web site, enter the bill information, and later arrange to transfer information about the bill payment into Quicken.

Here's a fun way to pay bills that gets all of your record-keeping taken care of at the same time. Pay the bill in Quicken, and request that the bill be an online payment. Quicken waits for your go ahead to actually dispatch the bill, but you've got the payment made and recorded right from your Quicken file. Book I, Chapter 2 contains a detailed description of Quicken's check-writing process — follow these steps, choosing the option to use an online check.

After you've entered your check in Quicken and checked the Online payment box, the check appears in your Quicken register with the SEND indicator in the NUM column. When you're ready to dispatch your online checks (and remember, there's no paper necessary here — these are checks you don't print), follow these steps to send your online payment on its way:

1. **Open the Online Center by choosing Online Center from the Online menu.**
2. **Issue the Send order.**

   Click the Update/Send button at the top of the Online Center window. The Online Update window appears (see Figure 5-5).

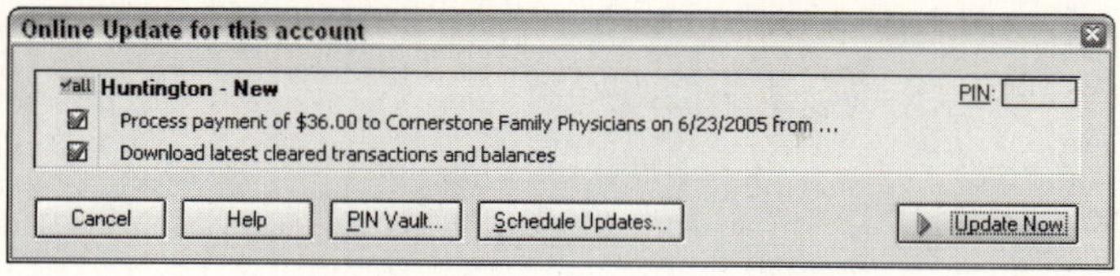

Figure 5-5: Update accounts and send online payments with one easy click.

3. **Enter your PIN.**

   Before you can execute an online transaction, you have to prove that you have the authorization to do so by entering your PIN number/ password in the box provided.

   As an alternative, you can store all of your PIN numbers in Quicken's PIN Vault. Click the PIN Vault button in the Online Update window or the button of the same name at the top of the Online Center. Quicken walks you through the process of entering the PIN number you use for each of your online institutions and asks you to assign a password to the PIN Vault. Later, whenever you initiate online transactions, you are asked only once for your PIN Vault password. Quicken retrieves all of your passwords at once so you don't have to supply a new password each time you conduct a transaction with a different institution.

4. **Make sure the correct boxes are checked.**

   By default, the option to download the latest information from your accounts is selected. Also, the check box to process online payments is checked. Make any changes to the services you want to order before proceeding.

5. **Click Update Now.**

   When you click the Update Now button, QuickBooks communicates with your bank and performs the tasks you requested. When you request an online payment, the payment's processing begins when you click the Update Now button. The accompanying description in your register changes from Send to Sent and a little lightening bolt appears next to the Sent indicator. You can see my payment has been sent in Figure 5-6.

The other online alternative for paying the bills is to use Quicken's Bill Pay service. We talk about this service in Chapter IV, Book 4.

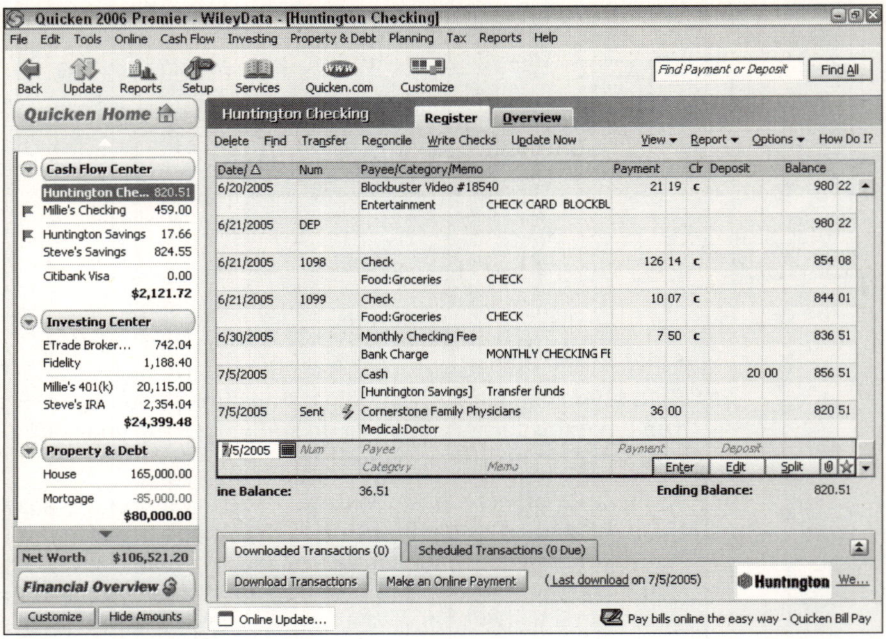

Figure 5-6: Lightening appears in the register, and your payment is sent.

Transferring Funds

You can easily transfer funds between accounts right from your Quicken register using Quicken's online banking features. Move money around from one account to another by following these easy steps:

1. **Open the register for the bank from which you want to transfer the funds.**
2. **Enter today's date.**
3. **Enter a new transaction, using OXFR (online transfer) as the code in the NUM column.**
4. **Enter a description for this transaction.**
5. **Enter the amount of the transfer.**
6. **Choose the account to which you are making the transfer in the Category field.**
7. **Record the transaction.**
8. **Open the Online Center by choosing Online⇨Online Center.**
9. **Click the Update/Send button.**

10. Enter your PIN number for this financial institution.

11. Click the Update Now button.

Quicken contacts the bank and executes the transaction. Unlike online bill payments that usually need a few days to be processed, the funds transfer is instantaneous.

Reconciling Your Online Bank Account

You know how much fun bank reconciliation is because you've already read about the reconciliation process in Chapter 4. There are a few nuances to discover when reconciling an online bank account.

First, note that every time you download your account activity with the Update/Send button in the Online Center, Quicken lists new transactions it has found and asks you to approve those transactions and match them with transactions in your register. Then, each transaction you match is marked with a little c to show that the item has cleared the bank.

Match online transactions pulled into Quicken from your bank account by following these steps:

1. **Go to the register that has online transactions to match.**

   After an online update session, Quicken provides you with an Online Update Summary window. Any registers that have new transactions needing your review include a Go to Register button you can click. Alternatively, you can click the account name in the Account Bar on the left side of your screen.

2. **View the new online transactions.**

   Quicken has listed the new online transactions at the bottom of the register in an area headed Downloaded Transactions. If all of these transactions are the result of online orders you gave in your register (like SEND or OXFR), Quicken has no trouble finding the matching transaction in the register, and you can save yourself some time by clicking the Accept All button at the bottom of the list.

3. **Click on a transaction to match.**

   If you want to make extra sure that Quicken matches these downloaded transactions with the correct transactions in your register, click on one transaction from the list. Quicken highlights the probable matching transaction in the register. If this match is correct, click the Accept button as shown in Figure 5-7.

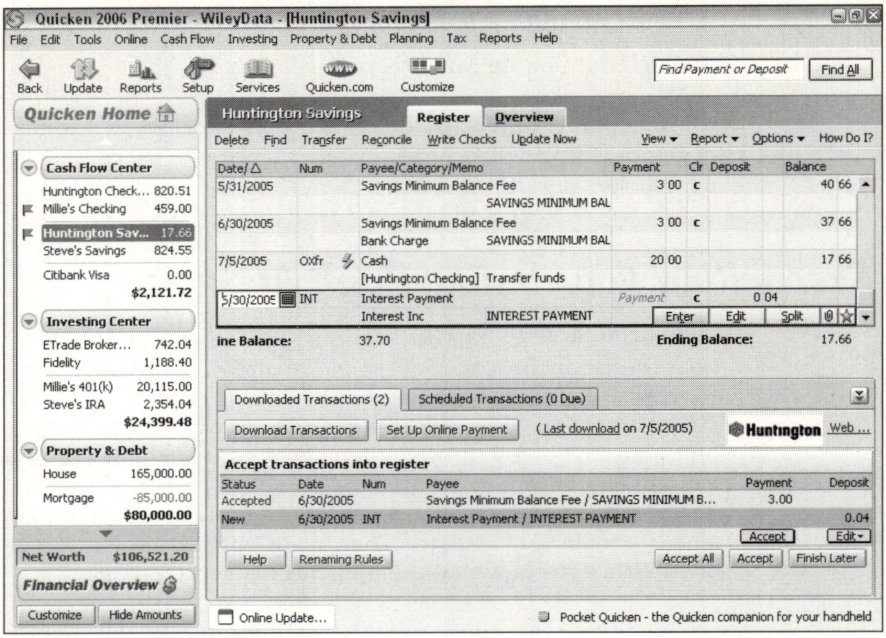

Figure 5-7: Click Accept if you know the match is a good one.

4. **Enter a category (maybe).**

   Sometimes transactions come over from the bank without categories. You may be asked to assign a category to the transaction before Quicken completes the match.

5. **Edit the transaction match if necessary.**

   If Quicken can't find the right transaction to match, click the Edit button, and then click Edit Manually. A list of unreconciled transactions from your account register appears. Check the transaction that goes with this downloaded transaction, and then click Accept.

6. **Enter the transaction if it is not already in the register.**

   When you make transactions at the bank or with your debit card and neglect to enter them in your register, the result is downloaded transactions that don't have any match in the register. If there is no match available and the transaction needs to be added to the register, click the Enter button to update your register by adding this transaction.

Matching transactions that are downloaded from your bank account is not the same as reconciling your account. You still need to reconcile each month when the statement comes. The good news is that all previously matched transactions do not have to be matched again at reconciliation, so the reconciliation process should be quick and easy.

Book III

Investments

The 5th Wave By Rich Tennant

"Oh yeah, he's got alot of money. When he tries to check his balance online, he gets a computer message saying there's 'Insufficient Memory' to complete the task."

Contents at a Glance

Chapter 1: Quicken and Investments

In This Chapter

- Finding your way around the Investing Center
- Entering investments in Quicken
- Tracking your investments
- Recording your investment income
- Selling your investments

Quicken has the capability of tracking all of your investments — from money in the bank to pennies in a jar, from mutual funds in your retirement account to stocks you purchased or received as gifts, and from real estate to vehicles. The more of your financial self that you add to your Quicken file, the more complete a picture you present for your own information as well as your tax returns and even the person who handles your estate. All of Book III concerns itself with tracking your investments. This chapter gives the basic steps for entering investment information in Quicken.

Navigating the Ins and Outs of the Investing Center

Quicken's Investing Center contains four tabbed areas: Today's Data, Performance, Analysis, and Portfolio. Use these areas to find out useful information about your investments, track their performance, and make intelligent trading and investing decisions:

- **Today's Data:** See alerts about your specific investments; click the hot button for automatic online updates to all of your investments; view market value, total gain or loss, and the day's gain or loss on each of your investment accounts; use one-click options for adding new accounts, editing accounts, and viewing a portfolio value report.
- **Performance:** Compare your accounts' performance with that of the major indexes — S&P 500, NASDAQ, Dow Jones Industrials, and Russell 2000; retrieve historic prices for any of your investments going back as much as five years; see a chart comparing your portfolio value to actual cost; see a summary of your investing activity for the year.

- **Analysis:** See a number of graphs and reports illustrating the asset allocation and the Morningstar rating of your mutual funds investments.
- **Portfolio:** See the details of each of your individual investments. Click through on any investment to see a performance chart and your transaction history.

On any of the Investing Center screens, use the Online Quotes field to enter a security symbol and get an instant and timely quote.

Tracking Investments in Quicken

One of the primary reasons people purchase Quicken is to track their investments. If you're not using Quicken for investments and you have any sort of investment, including a company-sponsored retirement plan, it's time to consider beefing up your use of Quicken to include investment tracking.

Setting up investments in Quicken can be quick and easy or tedious and dreary (see Book II, Chapter 3 for details). The mutual funds you've owned forever seem to take forever to set up; that is, if you want to enter all of the detail of monthly dividend reinvestments. But that's all about historical data entry. Entering investment information in Quicken as you acquire the investments is another story. You might find that the setup process is so quick and easy, you'll be encouraged to go out and invest in more stocks and mutual funds, just so you can have the fun of setting them up and then monitoring them in Quicken!

Hey Quicken! I Bought Some Shares of Stock!

You have to record a few basic pieces of information in your Quicken file in order to keep track of your investments. This is all the basic stuff that you ought to know about your investment purchases anyway. You'll need this information someday when you sell the investment — the IRS requires you to keep track of all of this, so you might as well keep it nice and tidy in Quicken.

Here are the facts that you need to know:

- Date of purchase.
- Cost: This is the cost of whatever investment you purchased plus any commission you pay on the purchase.
- Name of investment: This is the name of the company in which you bought stock, the name of the mutual fund in which you bought shares, the name of the organization from which you bought a bond, and so on.

✦ Number of shares.

✦ Source of the money: This is a piece of information that Quicken wants to know that you aren't required to keep for tax records. In Quicken, you're going to record the purchase by showing from which account you took the money.

Entering your investment in Quicken

OK, so you purchased some stock. Now you've got to get the stock into Quicken so that Quicken can keep tabs on your stock's performance and let you know how your investment is doing. But first things first. Here's how you enter your stock purchase in Quicken:

1. **Open a new account.**

   Assuming this is the first stock you've purchased, you're going to need an account for tracking your investment. Go to the Investing Center by clicking Investing Center on the left side of your Quicken window, make sure the Today's Data tab is selected, and then click the Add Account button.

2. **Identify the type of account.**

   In the Account Setup window, click the option that states This Account Is Not Held at a Financial Institution, and then click Next. For this example, I'm choosing Standard Brokerage as the type of account (see Figure 1-1). Use this option for securities you purchase yourself through any type of brokerage, including the online discount brokers. Click Next when you've made your selection.

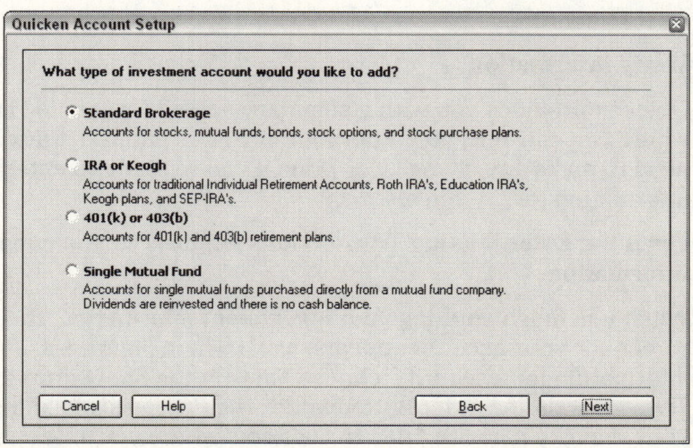

Figure 1-1: Pick Standard Brokerage to identify stocks you purchase through a broker.

3. **Give the account a name.**

   This is to distinguish this account from any other investment account you have or might have in the future. If you and your wife each have an investment account, you might call them Frankie's Stocks and Johnny's Stocks, or if you have accounts with different brokers, you might call them ABC Brokerage and DEF Brokerage. Any name is all right, as long as it makes sense to you.

4. **Enter the cash balance.**

   Sometimes people keep a cash balance at their brokerage firm so that when you get a hot tip on a stock, there is cash on hand, ready to invest right away, and you don't have to wait to transfer funds to the broker. If you have deposited cash with the broker, list that amount and the date of your latest brokerage statement (or today, if you just signed up to trade stocks today) when Quicken asks about your cash. Click Next to continue.

5. **List the securities.**

   Enter the ticker symbol and name of each stock and mutual fund that you bought. If you don't know the ticker symbol, click the Ticker Symbol Lookup button at the bottom of the window and Quicken does the legwork in finding the ticker symbol you need. Click Next to continue.

   REMEMBER

   The ticker symbols are important because that is what Quicken uses to look up your securities and give you information about the latest market value.

6. **Enter the quantity of shares.**

   List the number of shares you own so Quicken can look up your stock on the Internet and give you the current value of your investment. Click Next to continue.

7. **Verify information.**

   Quicken provides you with a summary screen (shown in Figure 1-2) where you can verify the information you've entered. Click Back if you need to make any changes, or Done if you're ready to enter the cost information for your investment.

8. **Open the Enter Missing Transactions window so you can enter cost information.**

   When you finish entering your investment information, the summary screen for your account appears, as shown in Figure 1-3. To enter cost information for a security, choose Value in the Show drop-down list. Then click on the Enter option under the Cost Basis heading across from your security name to open the window where you enter your cost information. The Missing Transaction window appears.

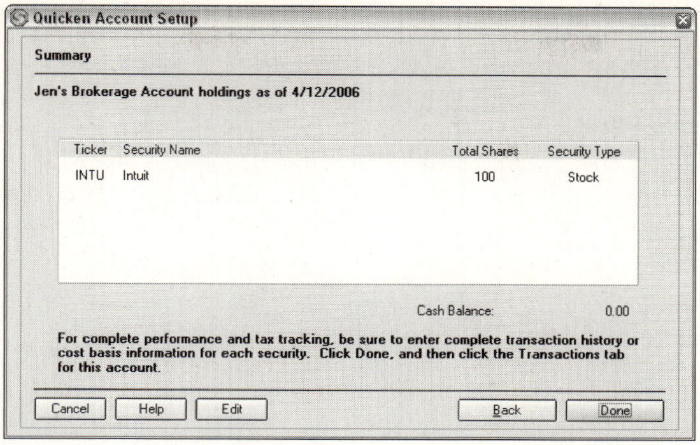

Figure 1-2: Make sure everything is correct on the summary screen.

9. **Enter cost information for your investment.**

   Click the Enter Missing Transaction button and the Buy — Shares Bought screen appears, as shown in Figure 1-4. Make sure that Buy — Shares Bought is selected in the Enter Transaction drop-down box at the top of the window before you begin entering your information. Here you can enter the number of shares you purchased, the price you paid, and the amount of commission you paid. Click Enter/Done to record your entries.

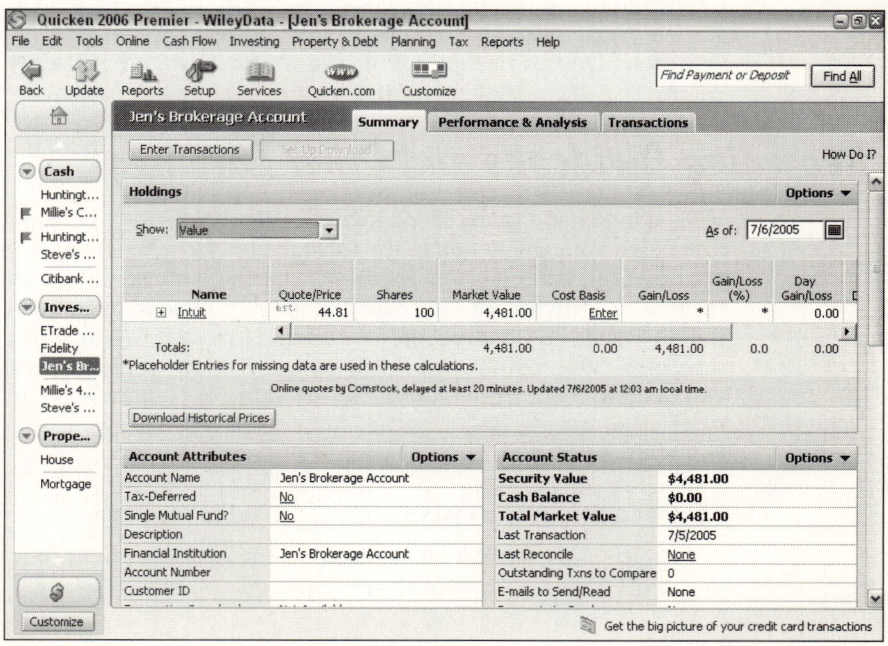

Figure 1-3: Click Enter and you can enter cost information about your security.

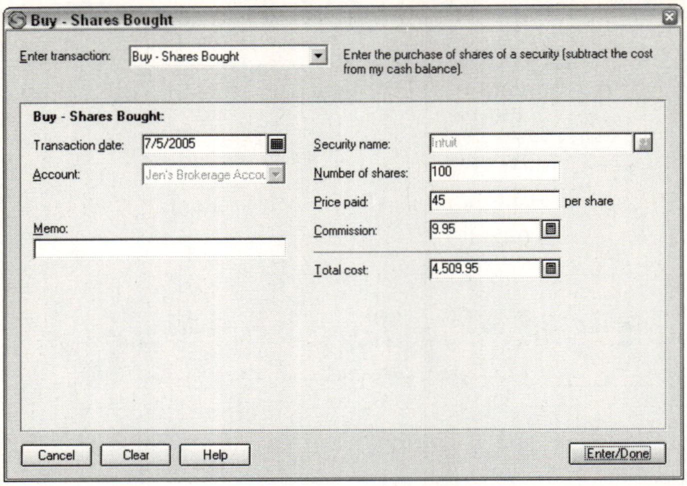

Figure 1-4: Enter cost basis information in the Buy — Shares Bought window.

Tracking investment performance

You've done the hard part in getting your investment entered in Quicken. Now you can sit back and watch your portfolio grow! With live Internet access, Quicken tracks the performance of your investments, giving you current values for each investment you list in your Quicken file.

Quickly update the value of your stock market investments by clicking on the Investing Center on the Quicken Account Bar at the left side of your screen. Next, make sure you're on the Today's Data tab and click the Download Quotes button. All of your investments are instantly updated.

Recording Dividends and Other Earnings

Mutual funds and many stock investments pay dividends. You might choose to receive your dividends in the form of checks in the mail, or you might have your dividends reinvested in more of the same stock and mutual funds. If you receive your dividends as a cash payment, you need to record the deposit of the dividends as Dividend Income and an increase to the cash account where the check is deposited. But if you choose to have your dividends reinvested, you need to record the increase in the value of your investment.

Follow these steps to record your dividends:

1. **Open the account where the dividend is received.**

   On the Account Bar, click on the name of the account that paid the dividend. The account summary appears.

2. **Open the Enter Transactions window.**

   Click the Enter Transactions button at the top of the account page. A window appears with Buy — Shares Bought on view in the Enter Transaction field.

3a. **Indicate the receipt of a cash dividend.**

   Select Inc — Income (Div, Int, etc.) from the Enter Transaction field, as shown in Figure 1-5.

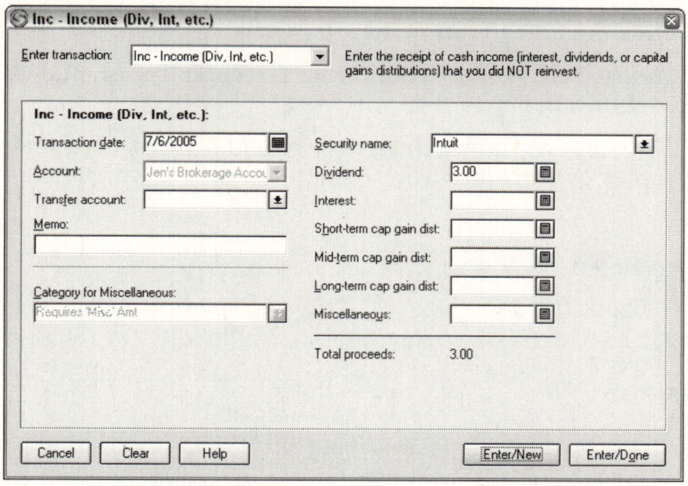

Figure 1-5: Make sure the correct type of transaction appears in the Enter Transaction field.

4a. **Enter pertinent information about your dividend.**

   Enter the date on which the dividend was received, the Transfer Account (the account in which you plan to deposit the money), the name of the security (choose from the drop-down list) and the amount you received, categorized properly as dividend, interest, or one of the capital gain distribution choices. Click Enter/Done to record your transaction and close the window.

3b. **Indicate the receipt of a reinvested dividend.**

   Alternatively, if you choose to have your dividends reinvested in the same security as opposed to taking your money in cash, go back to step 2 and follow instructions 3b and 4b instead of 3a and 4a. Choose Reinvest — Income Reinvested in the Enter Transaction field.

4b. **Enter the date of the dividend, the name of the security, and the amounts and number of shares you earned for each type of income (dividend, interest, or the three capital gain options). Click Enter/Done when you are finished.**

Entering a Sale

Some people buy stock and keep it forever. Others cash out and move on. If the time comes that you decide to sell your stock, you need to remove the investment from your Quicken account; otherwise, Quicken continues to list the investment as one of your assets and part of your net worth.

Enter a stock sale by following these steps:

1. **On the Account Bar, click on the account where the stock is held.**
2. **Click the Enter Transactions button.**
3. **Choose Sell — Shares Sold from the Enter Transaction drop-down list, as shown in Figure 1-6.**

   The window content changes to provide areas where you can enter the details of your sale.

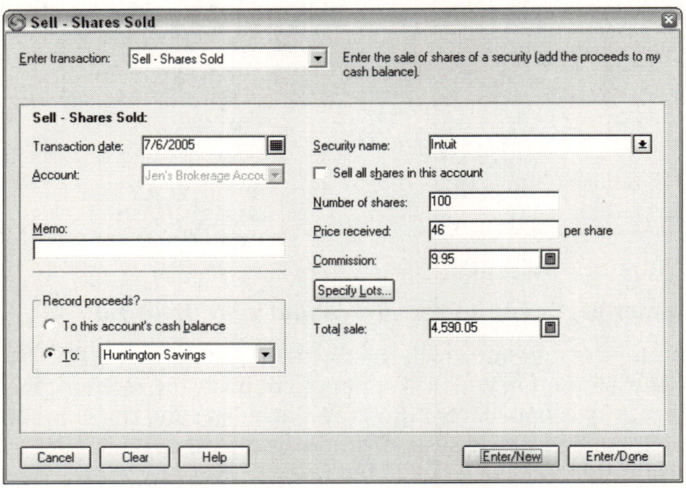

Figure 1-6: Enter the information about your securities sale.

4. **Enter the date of the sale and the name of the security.**

   Quicken automatically fills in the quantity of shares you own.
5. **Enter the number of shares you sold.**

   If you sold all of the shares you own, choose the Sell All Shares in This Account check box that appears in Figure 1-6. Otherwise, enter the exact number (including decimal places if applicable) of shares you sold.
6. **Enter the per share price you received on the sale.**

Selling specific lots of securities

When you sell a security, the assumption is that the shares you are selling are the first shares you purchased. But if you've purchased shares at different times over the years, you might end up paying higher tax by selling the first shares you bought. The earlier shares might have cost less than the more recent shares you bought, and thus the profit (gain) on the sale will be less, as will the tax, if you choose to sell the shares you bought most recently instead of the earlier purchases. (Keep in mind, however, that shares purchased within the past year do not qualify for the favorable long-term capital gain tax rates that are enjoyed by shares from long ago.)

So the bottom line is to be sure to calculate the tax on different shares before you give the Sell order. If you plan to sell shares other than the first ones you purchased, you need to get this information to your broker before the sale is conducted.

Your broker isn't the only one who assumes you want to sell the earliest shares you purchased. Quicken makes the same assumption, so if you decide to pick and choose the shares you're selling, you need to get that information to Quicken as well.

When recording your sale, click the Specify Lots button to bring up a window showing each group of shares that you purchased. You can enter the number of shares from each group that you plan to sell. Your tax accountant is happy that Quicken includes this feature.

7. **Enter the commission you paid on the sale.**
8. **Enter the account where the sales proceeds are to be deposited.**
9. **Close the Enter Transactions window.**

   Click Enter/Done to close the window and record your sale. Quicken records the sale, removing the security from your investment account and adding the sales proceeds to the account you indicated.

Chapter 2: Your Portfolio

In This Chapter

- **Discovering you have a portfolio**
- **Taking a look at your portfolio**
- **Selling investments and preparing for your taxes**
- **Using Quicken.com**

Somewhere along the line, we all make the transition from childhood to adulthood, from *The Breakfast Club* to *Breakfast at Tiffany's*, and from piggy banks to portfolios. It doesn't really matter what type of portfolio you have, or even if your investments are closer to the nonexistent bank account in *I Remember Mama* than they are to the amassed wealth of Warren Buffett. The important thing to remember is that Quicken can help you monitor all of your investments, big and small, and can be useful as a tool that helps your investments grow.

What You See in the Quicken Portfolio

In the last chapter, you discovered how to enter investments in Quicken. Those investments are assembled all in one place for your viewing pleasure — the Quicken Portfolio. Click on the Investing Center over on your Quicken Account Bar, and then on the Portfolio tab, and a summary of your investments appears.

TIP

If all of your investments are not yet listed in the Portfolio (for example, if you forgot to enter all of those shares of Microsoft your grandfather bought for you when you were a baby), head back to Book III, Chapter 1, and finish entering the investments you own.

REMEMBER

To enter additional investments, click on any account name in the Account Bar or in the Investing Center, such as your brokerage account or your 401(k) account, and then click the Enter Transactions button. Note: After clicking on an account name, you must select either the Transactions tab or the Summary tab to see the Enter Transactions button.

Here's a sample of what you can see in your Quicken Portfolio (see Figure 2-1):

- **A list of each of your investment accounts by name.** Each account is hyperlinked so you can click on that account and get right to the detailed screens for that account. The Unclassified category displays the following stock index values: S&P 500, NASDAQ, Dow Jones Industrials, and Russell 2000.

  Standard and Poor's 500 Index is made up of 500 large-company growth stocks. The NASDAQ Composite Index is made up of all common stocks listed on the NASDAQ and is used primarily to track technology stocks. The Dow Jones Industrial Average is the average of 30 blue chip stocks, primarily industrial stocks, chosen by the editors of the *Wall Street Journal*. The Russell 2000 Index tracks smaller company stocks.

- **A column showing the current market value for each account.** Update this market value at any time by clicking the Download Quotes option at the top of the window.
- **A column calculating the percentage that each account represents of your whole portfolio.** This percentage is based on the market value of the investments. The total of this column always adds up to 100 percent.
- **Columns showing the 1-year, 3-year, and 5-year average annual returns on each investment and each index, expressed in percent.**

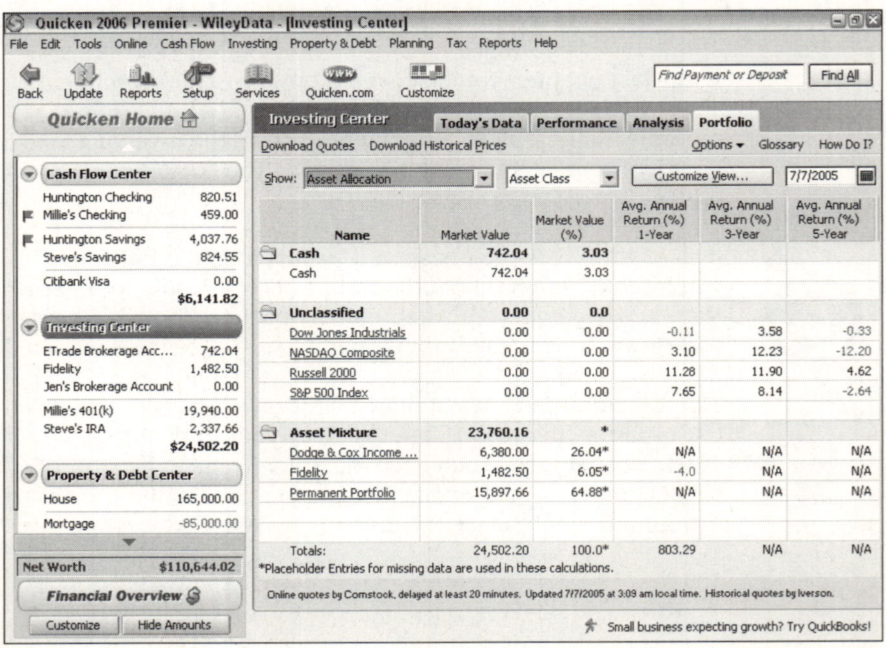

Figure 2-1: Peeking at your portfolio in Quicken.

What you want to see: Changing your portfolio view

Several views of your portfolio are available. Each view provides somewhat different information. However you left your portfolio view when you exited Quicken last is the way the portfolio appears when you return. You can create a customized view so that the portfolio window shows exactly what you want to see.

- ✦ Click on the Show drop-down list to see a plethora of pre-set portfolio views from which to choose. Pick any view and see various elements of your portfolio including gain or loss, historical performance, recent performance, tax information, the change this day, and more.
- ✦ Click the Accounts drop-down list and change how your accounts are sorted.
- ✦ Click the Custom View button and use the Customize Current View window that appears, shown in Figure 2-2, to create your own portfolio window. Type a name for your view in the Name box (as in My Portfolio shown in Figure 2-2), and then pick and choose the types of information and the accounts you want to include in your personal portfolio view.

Changing the portfolio date

By default, Quicken shows you your portfolio as of today. That makes sense, right? Oh, but what if you want a reminder of how things stood a month ago? Or a year ago? Or yesterday?

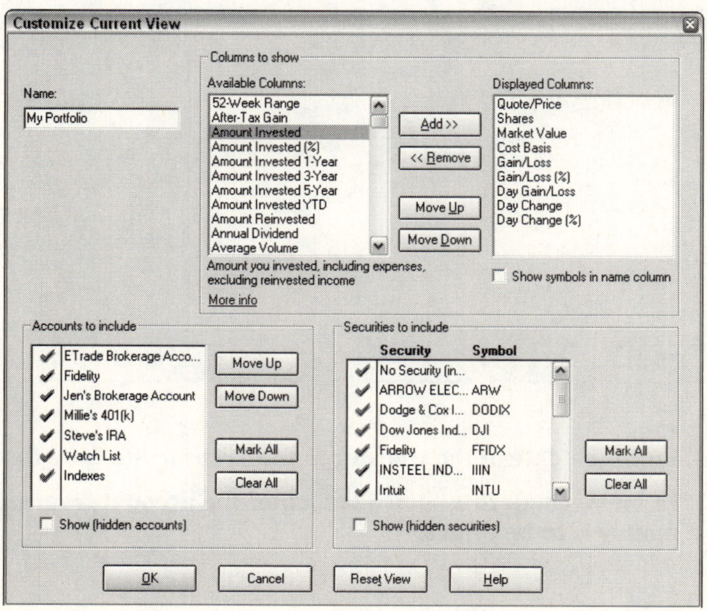

Figure 2-2: Make up your own personalized portfolio view.

Change the date in the date box at the top right side of your portfolio. You can go back as far as the date of the first investment transaction you entered in Quicken and see the historical value of your investments.

Cash transactions in your security account

Many people who actively trade securities keep a cash balance on deposit with their broker, so there is no need to hurriedly transfer cash over to the broker when they decide to make a purchase.

To transfer cash into your security account, follow these steps:

1. **Click on the account name in the Account Bar on the left side of your Quicken screen.**
2. **In the account window, click the Enter Transactions button.**

   The transaction window appears, with the heading Buy — Shares Bought.
3. **Choose a transaction from the Enter Transaction drop-down list.**

   For this example, we want to transfer cash into the account, so select Cash Transferred into Account from the drop-down list, as shown in Figure 2-3.

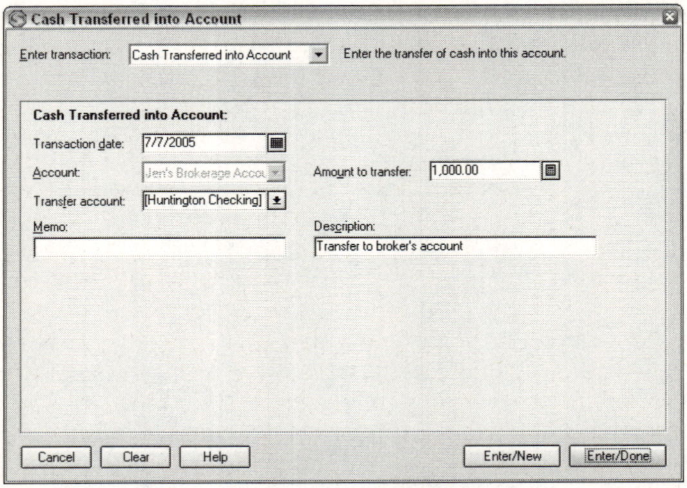

Figure 2-3: Change the Enter Transaction command to Cash Transferred into Account.

4. **Enter the date of the transfer in the Transaction Date field.**
5. **In the Account drop-down list, enter the account from which the money is to be drawn.**

Your bank account is a likely source for funds. Pick the account where the funds that you plan to transfer reside.

6. **Enter the amount you are transferring.**
7. **Enter an optional description.**

   The description is just for your benefit, to remind you of what this transaction is all about.

8. **Click Enter/Done to record the transaction.**

   REMEMBER: Entries such as the transfer of cash to your brokerage account or the actual purchase and sale of stocks are just that — entries. You still have to execute the actual transfer or the purchase or sale yourself. What we're doing here is simply record-keeping.

Marginally interesting: How to record margin interest

People who want to take a greater risk than their cash holdings permit sometimes borrow from their broker. Known as margin trading, this form of investing involves using the stock you purchase as collateral for a loan, and that loan can be as high as 50 percent of the purchase price of the stock.

For example, you might decide to buy 100 shares of a stock that cost $10 per share, or $1,000 worth of stock. With margin trading, you put up $500. Your broker kicks in the other $500 and together you purchase the 100 shares of stock in your name.

When you sell the stock, you get to keep the profits on all 100 shares, and you pay back the broker. Sounds good? It can be a great deal, but there are drawbacks to be sure. First, as long as you have the margin account, you must pay interest on the amount you borrowed. Second, if you sell the stock at a loss, you bear the entire burden of the loss on all 100 shares and still have to pay back the broker the full $500 (plus interest).

WARNING! Some brokers require you to repay part or all of your margin account *before* you sell the stock if it looks like the stock is tanking. Also, the broker has the right to sell the stock bought on margin or even other stock without your permission if it appears that you are in danger of defaulting on your loan. Make sure you read all the fine print that comes with your margin account before making your investments.

When your broker charges you interest on your margin account, you need to record that interest in Quicken. Here's how:

1. **Click on the name of the account where the interest is being charged.**

   For this example, I chose the brokerage account.

2. Click the Enter Transactions button, and the Transactions window appears.

3. Choose the Margin Interest Expense option from the Enter Transaction drop-down list, as shown in Figure 2-4.

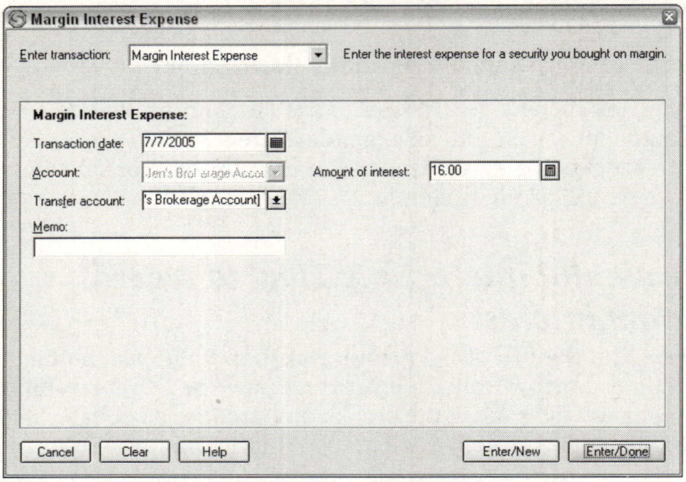

Figure 2-4: Enter your margin interest expense.

4. Enter the pertinent information.

Enter the date the interest was charged, the account that is paying the interest (which may be the same brokerage account to which the interest relates), and the amount of the interest.

5. Click Enter/Done to record the transaction.

Realized versus Unrealized Gains and Losses

In the good old days, investors opened the newspaper each evening to the stock market page, checking to see how their investments did. In today's Internet society, we get an instant update on our computer. The end outcome is the same — either you made a little money (or a lot, if you're lucky) or you lost a little money (or a lot, if you're not so lucky), and you wait until tomorrow and check the results again.

These winnings and losings in the stock market are called gains and losses when you're talking to accountants and your friends at the IRS. But gains and losses on paper, or on your computer screen, although perhaps meaningful to you, don't mean anything to the tax authorities until you actually sell the stock or the mutual fund.

Special tax rates for capital gains

Investments that you own for at least six months qualify for special tax treatment from the IRS. The capital gain tax rate, applicable to long-term (more than six months) capital gains, is 15 percent (or 5 percent if your regular income tax places you in the 10 percent or 15 percent tax bracket).

So, while income taxes soar up to a maximum of 35 percent, your tax on the profit from investments maxes out at 15 percent, a rate that is supposed to give you the incentive to invest and to sell those investments without worrying about paying high taxes.

In order to qualify for this special tax, you must report your investment transactions on your tax return and you must accurately record the dates of your purchases and sales so that you can determine if you meet the six-month holding period.

For this reason, you should look closely at the timing of sales of investments. If you're ready to sell some shares of stock and you are a few days short of owning the stock for six months, consider the impact of the difference in the rate of tax you'll pay on the profit you make.

This is only one of several tax planning considerations to contemplate when selling investments. It's wise to talk with a tax professional when your investments reach a point where they significantly affect your tax return.

And that is the difference between realized and unrealized gains and losses. Unsold equals unrealized; sold equals realized. *Unrealized* means you can talk about how much money you're making in the stock market, but there's nothing in the bank to show for it. *Realized* means that you have to report the sale on your tax return and pay tax on the gain or reduce your taxable income.

Nothing is simple when it comes to dealing with the IRS. Although you are required to pay tax on all of the profit that you make when you sell an investment at a gain, the IRS gets to pull in the reins on your losses and only lets you deduct up to a maximum of $3,000 net loss on sales of investments. Any additional loss gets carried forward to tax returns in future years.

What's in a Date?

You need to keep track of some important dates when buying and selling investments like stocks and bonds and mutual funds. The IRS expects you to report the purchase date and the sales date of each investment so that the *holding period*, the length of time you owned the security, can be determined.

Sometimes there is confusion about the dates. The purchase date is the date you take ownership of the stock. That might not be the same date that you turn your money over to your broker. The broker reports the correct date to you, and even if your Quicken records show you didn't pay on the date of the purchase, it is the official purchase date as stated by the broker that you need to record.

The sales date can be confusing too. The date of the sale is the trade date, otherwise known as the settlement date. This is not the same as the date on which you get your money, and it might not be the same as the date on which you tell your broker to execute the sale.

Check your documentation supporting the sale to make sure you record the purchase and sale date correctly. Because there are different tax rates for capital gain transactions based on how long you owned the asset, it's imperative that you have the correct dates.

Staying in Touch with Your Portfolio on Quicken.com

Hop online and play with your portfolio from any computer, anywhere, by linking your information to Quicken.com. Everything is password-protected and encrypted so you don't have worry about someone else seeing your personal financial information, yet at the same time you can have access to up-to-date information when you're away from home, either by visiting Quicken's Web site while you're at any computer, or even through access on your hand-held PDA.

When you've enabled your accounts for online access (see Book II, Chapter 5), you can view them online by going to `www.quicken.com`, clicking Investing Center — Portfolio, and logging in by entering your Member ID and password. The Member ID and password are established when you register your copy of Quicken. If you can't remember your login information, see the sidebar titled, "I can't remember my @#!^*%$# login information!"

Ten Things You Didn't Know You Could Do on Quicken.com

There are plenty of reasons to take advantage of the online services provided by Intuit for Quicken users. In addition to viewing your own portfolio and having all of your personal information updated, a lot of research and analysis material is available that can keep you informed about the market activity.

REMEMBER

All stock quotes provided by Quicken.com and the other linked information on the Web site are delayed 15–20 minutes.

I can't remember my @#!^*%$# login information!

In this land of constant Internet access, we all have many user names and passwords, all with different letter and number combinations. If you're trying to set up your online access to Quicken.com and getting frustrated because you can't recall the login information you established when you registered your program, don't give up, and don't hurl anything breakable across the room. Instead, follow these quick steps to clear your old registration, register again, and create a login presence:

1. Open your Quicken program.
2. (Hint: Ambidextrousness helps here.) While holding down the Ctrl, Shift, and Alt keys, click on Quicken's Online menu with the left mouse button and choose One Step Update.
3. A little message appears telling you that you have cleared the registration information from your Quicken program. Click OK.
4. Enter your registration information again by choosing Register Quicken from the Help menu and filling in the blanks.
5. After you enter your basic registration info, you get to the Quicken.com registration. Choose a (memorable) member name and password.
6. There might already be a member name stored on your computer. If so, Quicken has entered it for you. For good measure, just click on the option to create a new account, so you can start from scratch with a new member ID and password.
7. Enter the ID name and password you want to use, and then answer the questions that are provided to identify you and give you reminders.
8. Click Submit and then Finished.

Here is a sampling of some of the more interesting things that are available to people who use the Quicken.com Web site:

✦ **Alerts:** Sign up for alerts that tell you if a stock you own or are watching hits a certain price or changes by a certain percent. Also sign up for news alerts regarding your stocks. Click the Customize Alerts option in the Quicken.com Investing Center.

✦ **One-Click Scorecard:** Use Quicken.com for free access to investments analysts, their insights, and recommendations. Click the One-Click Scorecard link in the Investing Center, and then enter a stock symbol to get the analysts' views on the stock or fund you selected. See how the analysts evaluate the stock and receive a scorecard with detailed information that can help you make informed investment decisions.

✦ **Retirement Planner**: The Retirement Planner, found on the Investing Center page, provides you with an interactive tool for determining how much money you need to retire and creating a plan to help you meet your retirement goals.

- **Quotes and Research:** Provided by Yahoo! Finance, you can get instant stock market quotes and tons of research by entering a ticker symbol or looking up a stock name in the Quotes & Research area of the Investing Center. Yahoo! Finance shows you charts, news, and analysis tools. And here's an added plus: Click the Historical Prices link on the Yahoo! Information page and get prices and split information going back to the beginning of time for your chosen stock or mutual fund. This information is indispensable for tax return preparation when you have sold stocks and didn't keep track of the original price information or stock splits over the years.
- **Stock/Mutual Fund Evaluator:** This is another research tool found on the Investing Center page. Click the link to the evaluator, and then enter a stock or mutual fund symbol to see a detailed analysis of the stock or fund performance including historical trends, competitor information, and detailed descriptions of what all the charts and numbers actually mean.
- **Market Overview:** Click the Market Overview button on the Investing Center page to see the Yahoo! Finance summary of the day's activities on Wall Street, what's hot, what's trading, what the trends are, and the day's volume.
- **Price Updates:** When you get to the Quicken.com's portfolio page, your Mini Portfolio appears on the left side. Click the Full Portfolio button to see the details of your investments. Click the Update Prices button at any time and all prices are instantly updated.
- **Synchronization:** You can synchronize your desktop Quicken with your Quicken.com investment information through the One Step Update found on the Online menu in Quicken. Include all of your investments as well as your Quicken reminders, and even click the Schedule Updates button in the One Step Update window to schedule synchronization so that it happens in the background.
- **Quick Links to other Quicken services:** Scroll to the bottom of the Quicken.com Investing Center page to see quick links to the Quicken.com Bills & Banking Center and the Small Business Center.
- **Share information (no, not your financial information — I mean questions and ideas) with other Quicken users:** Click the link to quickenforums.com at the bottom right side of the Investing Center and enter discussions, read and share tips, search for answers to your questions, earn points, win valuable prizes — what fun!

Chapter 3: Monitoring Your Tax-Deferred Retirement Accounts

In This Chapter

- Familiarizing yourself with tax-deferred investing
- Recording tax-deferred investments
- Tracking employer contributions
- Monitoring investment activity
- Making decisions about diversification

Are you saving money for the time in the future when you can't or don't want to work any more? If you have a job now, you probably are saving for retirement, in the form of a 401(k) or similar tax-deferred retirement plan provided by your employer. And if you're like most people, you agree to have a certain amount of money taken out of your paycheck for that retirement plan, you agree to a certain arbitrary mix of investments, and that's as far as your involvement in the retirement planning process goes. You can use Quicken to keep track of your tax-deferred retirement investments, whether your money is invested in a plan at work or if you have your own personal accounts. But tracking your retirement funds is just the beginning. By using Quicken to monitor your long-term investments, you can develop an awareness of how your investments are doing and make intelligent decisions about how your money should be invested. Start being proactive about planning for your retirement!

How Tax-Deferred Retirement Plans Work

Over the years, Congress and the Internal Revenue Service have worked together to create several types of investment opportunities for workers, and the unifying incentive that has been linked to those opportunities is a deferral of income taxes. What that means is that you can take some of your money today and place it in an authorized type of long-term savings plan, and not pay any income tax currently on both the amount you invest and the amount the investments earn. You only pay tax on the money you withdraw from your retirement savings plan when you actually make the withdrawals.

To read more about withdrawing from tax-deferred accounts, see Book VI, Chapter 2.

How 401(k)s work

The most common employer-provided retirement savings plan is the 401(k). Variations include the 403(b) and the 457(b). You are allowed to contribute up to a maximum of $14,000 per year based on 2005 rules, $15,000 in 2006, and the annual amount is indexed for inflation in years after 2006.

The amount you can contribute each year to your 401(k) plan varies with changes in the tax laws, but the amount you actually can contribute is based on a percentage of your annual earnings and also certain limitations at your workplace. Your employer can advise you how much you can actually contribute each year.

If you are age 50 or older, you can take advantage of catch-up provisions that allow you to contribute an additional amount to your 401(k). The catch-up amount is $4,000 for 2005, $5,000 for 2006, and indexed for inflation in years thereafter.

Many employers offer matching plans whereby the employer contributes a percentage of your salary to the plan. For example, say you earn $50,000 a year and your employer has a 3 percent match plan. This means that the employer matches your annual contribution, up to a maximum of 3 percent of your salary or, in this case, $1,500. So if you contribute $1,000 to your plan, your employer contributes $1,000 as well. If you contribute $1,500 or any higher amount to the plan, the employer contributes $1,500. The match can be anywhere from nothing to 100 percent.

According to a 2003 survey conducted by Hewitt Associates, 96 percent of employers provide some sort of matching or other company contribution to employees' 401(k) plans (Hewitt Associates, "2003 Trends and Experience in 401(k) Plans").

When you contribute money to your 401(k), the amount you contribute is withheld from your paycheck and no income tax is withheld on that money. The amount you contribute is not included in your taxable wages on your annual income tax return (however, you do pay Social Security tax and Medicare tax on the amount that you put in your 401(k)).

The amount of tax you can save is significant. For example, if you are in the 25 percent income tax bracket and your state income tax rate is 4 percent, and you stash $10,000 in your 401(k), you just saved yourself $2,500 on federal income tax and $400 on state income tax. That's an excellent instant return on your investment.

Years later, when you start taking money out of your 401(k), the amount you withdraw is included in your taxable income on your income tax return.

Two theories are at play here — the first is that you are given incentive to invest with the tax deferral up front. The second is that, if you play your cards right and don't get particularly wealthy in your old age, your tax rate when you start withdrawing 401(k) money is lower or at least no higher than the rate you were paying when you made the contributions, so you save money on the tax deferral.

How traditional IRAs work

There are similarities between IRAs and 401(k)s, such as tax deferral on contributions and earnings, annual limitations on contribution amounts, and emotional highs from knowing that you're looking out for the future, but there are several differences between the two types of plans as well:

- **You get to pick your investments with an IRA.** With a 401(k), your employer provides you with a selection of some investments from which to choose — maybe 3 or 4 or maybe as many as 15 or 20, but there is a limit. With an IRA, you control the investment choices — you can pick whatever you want to invest it in, be it stocks or mutual funds, and spread your investments over as many or as few different selections as you want.
- **You may not get a tax deferral on your contribution.** Contributions to 401(k) plans are tax-deferred. The tax-deferral opportunities on IRA contributions depend on several factors including how much income you make, whether you participate in a retirement plan at work, and your spouse's income and retirement participation as well.
- **The limit on annual contributions to an IRA can be significantly lower than that of the 401(k).** The IRA contribution is limited to $4,000 in 2005 with a $500 catch-up provision for people age 50 and over. This amount is further limited by the amount of income you earn.
- **It's easier to get your hands on the IRA money.** You can take your IRA money out of its tax-protected environment and spend it whenever you want. Yeah, there's a penalty and some tax involved, but nevertheless, it's your money and you can take it if you need to. The 401(k) money is much more difficult to get at unless you leave your job.
- **There is an option to borrow against your 401(k).** No loans are available with an IRA — either the money stays in the IRA or it doesn't. With a 401(k), you can borrow up to 50 percent of the fund balance without cashing out the fund, and then you make payments back to the fund, reinstating your balance. Loan rules vary from plan to plan — your employer can give you the details of how borrowing works with your 401(k) plan.

- **There's no opportunity for an employer match with an IRA since this isn't a plan created at work.** The annual maximum contribution limit is the maximum and that's final.
- **The IRS permits the creation of a spousal IRA for spouses who don't work.** Even if your spouse has no earned income, a spousal IRA can be created and the maximum contribution can be made to that account each year, as long as the working spouse has earned income at least as high as all IRA contributions for both spouses.

How Roth IRAs work

Like their IRA cousin, the Roth IRAs allow an annual contribution of up to $4,000 for 2005 (with a $500 50-and-over catch-up provision), as long as you earn at least as much as you contribute.

There are, however, some interesting differences between the two types of retirement plans:

- **There is an income threshold on the Roth IRA.** If you make too much money, you can't play the Roth game. You start losing the ability to contribute to a Roth IRA if your income is over $95,000 and you're single, or over $150,000 if you're married and filing a joint tax return.
- **There is no age limit with the Roth IRA.** You can make contributions no matter how old you get. With a regular IRA, you have to stop making contributions in the year in which you hit age 70½.
- **There is no age requirement for mandatory withdrawals of money from the Roth IRA.** You are required to start taking money out of a regular IRA in the year in which you reach age 70½. For the Roth, you never have to take the money out: You can leave the money invested until you die and the investments then get passed on to your beneficiaries. Furthermore, when you do start withdrawing money, you can withdraw as little or as much as you want — there is no required withdrawal formula like there is with the traditional IRA.
- **The money in your Roth IRA grows tax-free as opposed to tax-deferred in the traditional IRA.** As long as you keep your money in a Roth for at least five years and you reach at least age 59½, you can take the money out whenever and however you want, with no tax consequences.

Hey Quicken! How About Keeping Track of My 401(k) Contributions?

Your employer takes your 401(k) contribution out of your paycheck, and you record you paycheck in Quicken. But do you keep track of your 401(k) investment in Quicken? Or do you just record the fact that you made a contribution to the company retirement plan?

Your 401(k) contribution is probably split among a few different funds, based on a percentage you chose when you agreed to make the contribution. It's a simple matter to create those funds in your Quicken portfolio, and then order Quicken to increase each of the funds with each paycheck.

The next obvious step is to have Quicken continuously update your portfolio, including your 401(k) investments, so that you actually know how much money is accumulating in your retirement fund. In this way, you are guaranteed a much clearer picture of your total finances.

Because you already enter your paycheck in Quicken, you know how to create a split transaction for your withholdings. (You do enter your paycheck in Quicken, don't you? If you haven't set up your paycheck yet, head back to Book II, Chapter 2 for a quick refresher.) Before you can update your 401(k) investments with your regular contributions, you need to add those investments to your portfolio. If you haven't done so already, return to Book II, Chapter 3 and set up your 401(k) in Quicken.

OK, so you've got your paycheck set up in Quicken, and you've added your 401(k) investments to your portfolio. The next step is to figure out how much of each paycheck goes to each investment in your 401(k) plan. Start by confirming how your investment contribution is split. You may need to consult with your employer to get this information.

For purposes of this example, say you have your 401(k) investment going into three different mutual funds, one half to one fund, and one quarter to each of the other two funds. I'll cleverly call those funds Fund A (which gets 50 percent), Fund B, and Fund C.

You have two choices for updating your 401(k) activity in Quicken. You can either update your 401(k) contributions manually, or you can arrange for an automatic download.

Updating 401(k) the hard way: Manual updates

As you can see in Figure 3-1, Quicken's standard paycheck setup process allows you to earmark the 401(k) contribution that comes out of your paycheck. However, in this paycheck setup, you don't get to specify the distribution of the money to your various investments. Here's how you can place your 401(k) contributions in the proper funds. Note: You need a copy of your 401(k) account statement in order to complete this task.

1. **Click on the name of your 401(k) account in the Account Bar.**

   The Summary page for your 401(k) account appears.

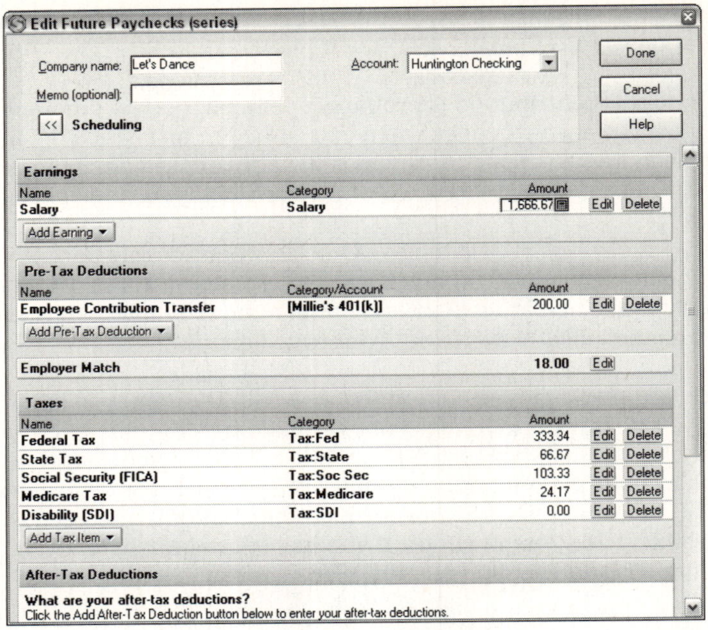

Figure 3-1: How your paycheck is distributed.

2. **Click the Transactions tab.**

   After a paycheck has been entered in your bank account register, you see that your cash balance in your 401(k) has been increased by the amount of your 401(k) payroll deduction. In addition, if you set up an employer matching amount when you set up your paycheck, that matching amount also has been added to your cash balance.

   If you've been entering paychecks in Quicken for quite awhile but haven't been checking in on your 401(k) account in your portfolio, you might find that you have quite a few additions to your cash balance that haven't been transferred over to actual investments.

3. **Enter a "buy" transaction in your register to clear the cash balance and populate your investments.**

   Click the Enter Transactions button, and then choose Buy — Shares Bought to enter a transaction to buy shares. Use the number of shares purchased with your cash transfer according to your 401(k) account statement, and indicate that the cash is to come from the cash balance in this account (see Figure 3-2).

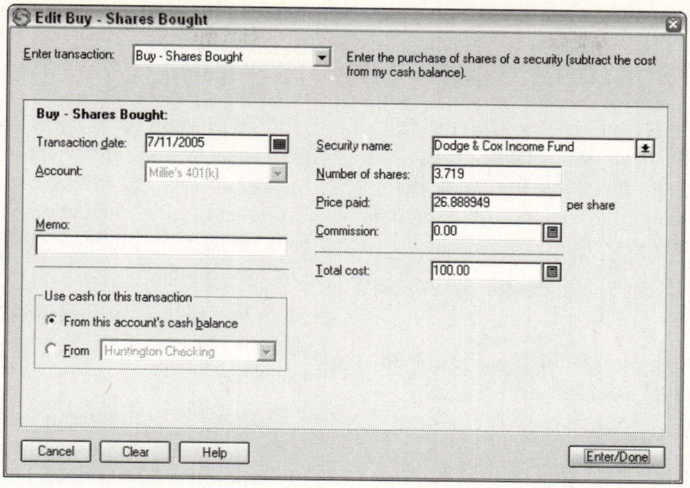

Figure 3-2: Entering a "buy" transaction in your 401(k) account.

There usually is some rounding on mutual fund account statements. The number of shares that you purchase is presented in decimal places (often to the thousandth), but that may not be precise enough to exactly match the dollar amount you invest. Quicken requires precision to six decimal places on the number of shares you purchase, so your share quantity in Quicken may differ minutely from the quantity that appears on your account statement.

Because the value of the shares in a mutual fund constantly fluctuates, you can't set up this transaction as an automatic memorized transaction in Quicken. Each time you make a contribution to your 401(k) account, you need to make an adjustment to the portfolio in Quicken. Otherwise, see the next section for a good argument for using the online update feature in Quicken.

If your employer made a matching contribution, this amount must also be incorporated into your 401(k) account. See "Editing paychecks and entering employer matches" below.

Updating 401(k) the easy way: Entering the statement summary

OK, enough of entering by hand. If you've got several mutual fund accounts floating around in your 401(k), and you make a contribution with every paycheck, you're going to want a quicker way to enter your 401(k) updates.

Editing paychecks and entering employer matches

If you track your paycheck in Quicken and your employer provides you with matching 401(k) contributions, you can track that matching amount along with your other paycheck information. Here's how:

1. **Click the Cash Flow Center on your Account Bar.**
2. **From within the Cash Flow Center, click on one of the paycheck buttons.**

   There is a Set Up Paycheck button on the My Data tab and there is an Add Paycheck button on the Analysis & Reports tab. Both buttons take you to the same place.
3. **Follow the steps to set up your paycheck if you haven't done so already.**

   For detailed information on setting up your paycheck, see Book II, Chapter 2. When you enter your 401(k) deduction information with your paycheck setup, there is an opportunity to enter an employer match amount. If you've already set up your paycheck, a Manage Paychecks window appears when you click the button in step 2. Click on your employer's name and click the Edit button. The Edit Future Paychecks window appears.
4. **Click the Edit button in the Employer Match section in the Edit Future Paychecks window.**
5. **An Edit 401(k) Deduction window appears. Enter your employer's matching amount in the Employer Match field, and then click the OK button.**

   Your paycheck information is now updated to include an employer match.
6. **At any time in the future, you can follow these steps to edit your paycheck, making any necessary changes to your income and deduction amounts.**

Forget about going through the steps listed in the last section. Try this step instead: After you enter your paycheck (or have your paycheck automatically entered as a scheduled transaction), click on the 401(k) account in your Account Bar, and then click the Update 401(k) Holdings button at the top of the window. (Note: the Update button appears in both the Summary and the Transactions tabs.) Quicken uses the Update 401(k) wizard to walk you through entering the latest information from your 401(k) statement.

The wizard asks all the right questions to bring your 401(k) Quicken account in line with the actual 401(k) account (see Figure 3-3).

Combine the Update 401(k) Holdings option with Quicken's One-Step Updates and your 401(k) account will always be completely up-to-date.

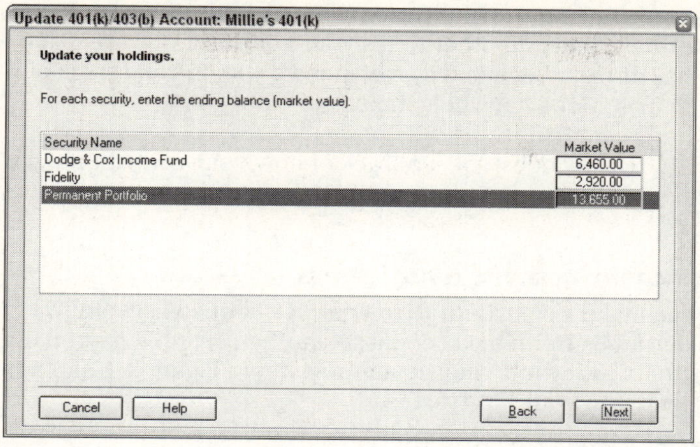

Figure 3-3: Updating your 401(k) information.

Manipulating Your Traditional IRA in Quicken

As important as it is to monitor your company-sponsored 401(k) account, it's even more important to keep tabs on your personal IRA in Quicken. No one is responsible for the performance of the investments in your personal IRA except you. You made the choices regarding how you plan to invest your money, and it's up to you to keep tabs on those investments and make changes when necessary.

If you haven't yet set up your IRA, go back to Book II, Chapter 3 where you can find general information on account setup.

Look, Mom: I'm saving for my retirement!

The simplest way to save money in your IRA is to set up automatic transfers into the account, either from your bank account, or directly from your paycheck. The automatic transfers are a mindless and virtually painless way to save.

WARNING!

Transferring money into an IRA needs to be a one-way street. Don't put money in your IRA that you expect to withdraw and use for everyday expenses. You can use a savings account or a money market for that type of saving. Only transfer money to an IRA when you are committed to leaving the money in there until you can remove it without penalty (typically, this means waiting until you are at least age 59½, although there are exceptions to that rule).

Because of the nature of IRAs (sometimes you can make contributions that are tax-deferred, and other times your contributions are made with money that has already been taxed), you need a way to keep track of whether your IRA contributions have been taxed.

REMEMBER

The IRA trustee doesn't keep track of how your contributions were treated for tax purposes — it's up to you to take care of that.

Entering tax-deferred contributions

You can make a contribution to your IRA in one of several ways. You can transfer funds from one account to another, set up a payroll deduction at work, or, as shown in the account register in Figure 3-4, simply write a check and send it to your IRA trustee.

To make sure Quicken tracks your IRA contributions correctly, ensure that your IRA is set up properly in Quicken. Follow these steps to set up your IRA as a tax-deferred account:

1. **Open the Account List.**

   Press Ctrl+A to open the list of all your Quicken accounts.

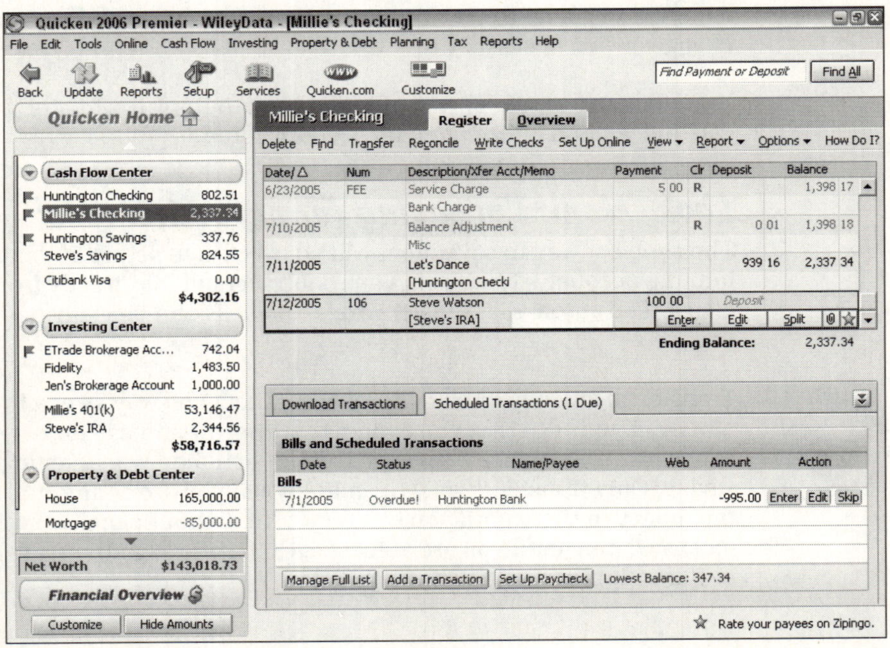

Figure 3-4: One way to make contributions to your IRA is by writing checks.

2. **Choose your IRA account to edit.**

   Click on the IRA account, and then click the Edit button at the top of the list.

3. **Open Tax Schedule information for your account.**

   In the Account Details window that appears, click the Tax Schedule Info button at the bottom.

4. **Enter appropriate tax information to indicate the tax-deferred status of this account.**

   In the Tax Schedule Information window (see Figure 3-5), choose Form 1040, IRA Contribution. Choose from either Self or Spouse, depending on whomever you decide is the self and the spouse in your family. Then click OK, and then OK again to close the windows.

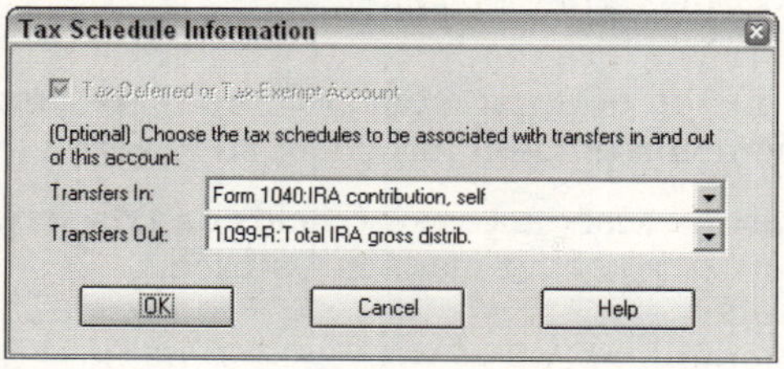

Figure 3-5: Pick the IRA Contribution option.

You can find more information about assigning tax attributes to amounts in Quicken by looking in Book V.

5. **Open the Tax Planner.**

   You can find the Tax Planner on the Tax menu, or click on the Tax Planner link that appears in the Financial Overview window.

6. **Go to the Adjustments screen.**

   Click Adjustments on the left side of the Tax Planner to view the IRA section of your tax information. You'll see that 100 percent of your IRA contribution appears on the first line of the Adjustments to Income section (see Figure 3-6).

The next steps describe how to change this entry so that some or all of the contribution is not allowed as a deduction.

Entering non-tax-deferred contributions

Sometimes IRA contributions are not tax-deductible. Either you don't meet the criteria for having enough income or you participate in a retirement plan at work that, combined with your income level, prevents you from taking a tax deduction. Or maybe you simply prefer to pay tax on your money now and not take a current deduction for your IRA contribution. Whatever the reason, when you make your contribution, as described in the previous section, here's how to tell Quicken *not* to treat this as a deductible contribution.

Continuing from the previous steps:

1. **Click the Allowable IRA Deduction hyperlink.**

   The screen scrolls down, and the Allowable IRA Deduction section appears. So far, all of the contribution is being treated as deductible.

2. **Click the User Entered radio button, and then enter the amount of the IRA contribution that you plan to treat as a tax deduction.**

   For this example, the entire $100 contribution is being treated as non-tax-deductible, so zero is entered in the User Entered field, as shown in Figure 3-7. The amount you enter in the User Entered field remains in place for future contributions.

3. **Scroll back up to the top of the screen, and you'll see that the Allowable IRA Deduction amount has changed to zero.**

   Note: There may be other amounts in the fields on this screen, depending on the other entries you have made in Quicken.

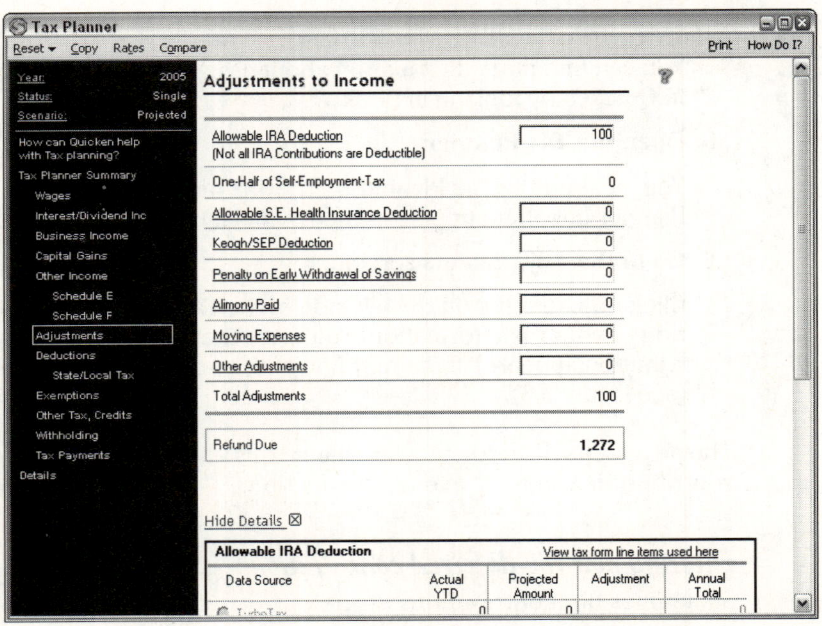

Figure 3-6: The entire $100 IRA contribution is categorized as a deduction from adjusted gross income.

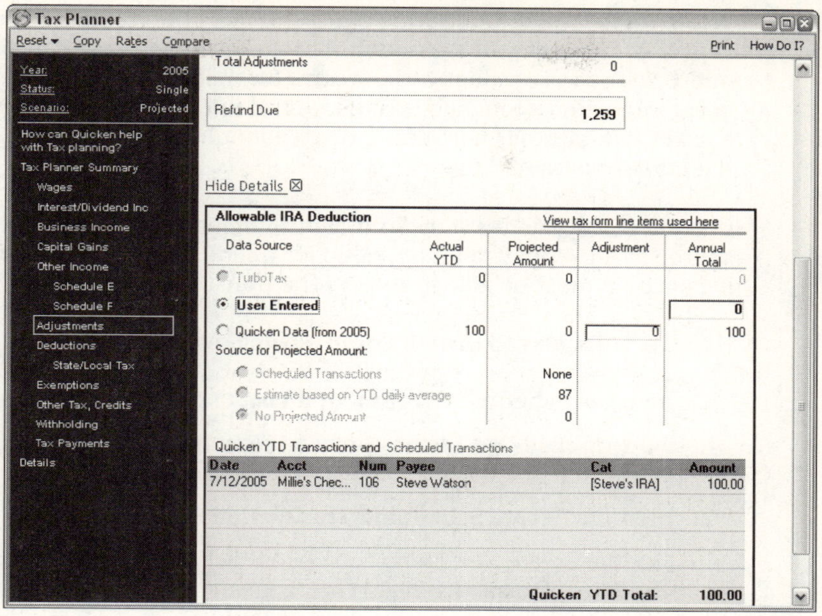

Figure 3-7: Click User Entered to indicate how much of your IRA contribution is to be treated as a tax deduction.

Quicken continues to categorize future IRA contributions in the same way as the one you set up in the Tax Planner. Should you change your treatment of IRA contributions, or find at a later date that contributions previously categorized as non-deductible are indeed deductible, go back to the Tax Planner and change the entry in User Entered. Alternatively, click the Quicken Data button just beneath the User Entered button to switch the contributions to all deductible.

Sometimes you don't know if your IRA contribution is going to be deductible until the end of the year. Make a note, or schedule a reminder to go to the Tax Planner before you prepare your tax return and address the deductibility of your IRA contributions, making any necessary reclassifications.

The IRA tax planning features described here are only available in Quicken Deluxe, Premier, and Home & Business.

IRA contributions are easier when you don't have to think about them

For some people, writing a check and depositing that amount in a savings or retirement account gives them a sense of connection with the money in savings, and a sense of reward. For others, getting around to writing that check just never seems to happen. If you intend to transfer money to your IRA but never seem to get around to it, let Quicken do the job for you.

Set up a scheduled transaction that automates the transfer of money into your IRA. Pick a day of the month, choose an amount you can afford to move out of your bank account without any hardship (remember, this money is going into your untouchable funds — so don't transfer more than you can afford to be without), and don't worry about having to remember to transfer the money yourself.

WARNING!

In order to automate a transfer of funds, the bank account you use as the source of the money must be set up for online transactions, and the receiving account must be able to receive the transfer.

Here's a quick way to turn the job of saving over to Quicken:

1. **Open the Scheduled Transaction List.**

   Choose Scheduled Transaction List from the Cash Flow menu or press Ctrl+I.

2. **Open the Create Scheduled Transaction dialog box.**

   Click the Create New menu and choose Scheduled Transaction. The Create Scheduled Transaction dialog box appears, as shown in Figure 3-8.

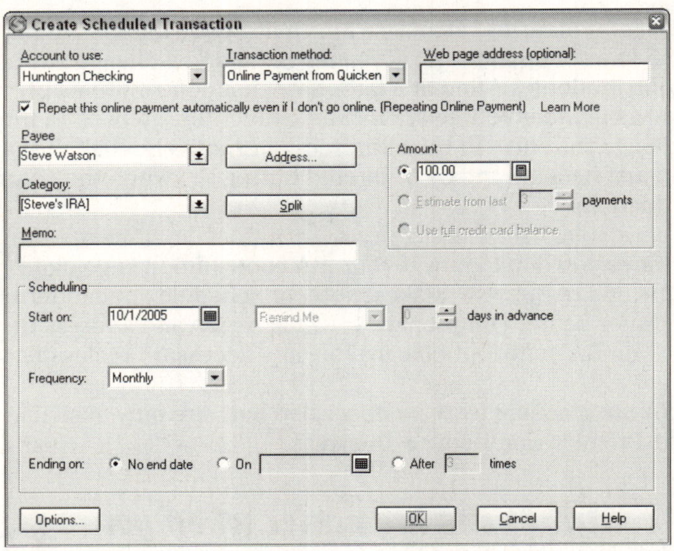

Figure 3-8: Fill in the blanks to schedule your monthly automatic IRA contribution.

3. **In the Account to Use field, enter the account that the money is to be transferred out of.**

   This can be any type of bank account that is set up for online transactions.

4. **Choose Online Payment from Quicken as the transaction method.**

   Because you're going to automate this transaction, you need to pick the online payment method. That way, Quicken can make the transaction even if you're not around. Note: The option for online payment does not appear on the menu if you picked an account that is not set up for online transactions.

5. **Check the box to repeat automatic payments even when you're not online.**

   By checking this box, you authorize Quicken to take the money out of your bank account and make the transfer, even if you don't open your Quicken program.

   Make sure you plan on having money in your account each month to cover the transfer — you've told Quicken to make the transfer without your monthly approval, so the funds need to be in your account.

6. **Enter the name of the payee, and the category (in this case, the category is Steve's IRA, as shown in Figure 3-8).**

   When you enter the payee name, Quicken searches for the address and account information for this payee. If you haven't already entered this information in Quicken, a little box pops up, asking you to fill in the blanks. This information is crucial, so make sure you fill in the blanks accurately. This tells Quicken where to send the payment and to what account number the payment gets credited.

   Here's a timesaver you can use when creating this scheduled transaction. If you've already entered a transaction in your register that is like the one you want to schedule, click on that transaction, and then right-click and choose Schedule Transaction from the pop-up menu that appears. Quicken then automatically fills in information like the amount, the account, and the payee.

7. **In the Scheduling section of the dialog box, enter the next date on which you want a payment to be made. Then, enter the frequency of the payments (Monthly is already selected as the default frequency).**

   Quicken assumes you want to make your payments on the same day each month. So if you enter a payment to be made on the first of the month, as in the example in Figure 3-8, Quicken takes it from there and makes a payment on the first of every month.

8. **Choosing the No End Date option means Quicken continues to make these payments forever.**

   You can set a date when you want the payments to end, or indicate a fixed number of payments by choosing the other options here.

9. **Click OK and your payment is officially scheduled.**

Another easy way to transfer money into your IRA without having to think about it is to set up a payroll deduction at your job. Let your boss take care of getting your money into your IRA and you can think of the transfer as just another payroll deduction.

Wait: I can't spare the money for this month's transfer!

Don't forget that Quicken has been given the green light to transfer funds each month, without waiting you're your approval. But what happens if you want to stop the transfer?

You can intercept a transfer by following these steps:

1. **Open the Scheduled Transactions List (Ctrl+J).**
2. **Click on the Repeating Online tab, where you'll see the next transfer transaction, ready and waiting for the transfer date.**
3. **Double-click on the transaction.**

   The Edit Current Transaction and Enter into Register dialog box appears (Figure 3-9).

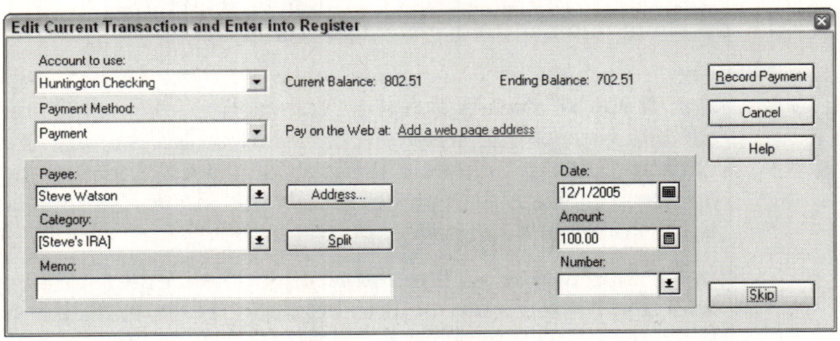

Figure 3-9: The mighty Skip button saves you from making this month's payment.

4. **Click the Skip button.**

   The Edit window disappears, and the transaction listed on the Repeating Online list has now been bumped up to the next scheduled date.

If you don't need to see the details of the scheduled transaction, you can save a couple of steps when skipping a transaction by opening the Scheduled Transactions List (step 1 above), and then clicking the Skip button that appears to the right of each transaction. Click Yes when a box appears asking you to verify that you want to skip one transaction.

WARNING!

If you need to skip a payment, be sure you open up Quicken before the date of the transfer. Otherwise, Quicken will have already sent the money.

TIP

If you decide to remove the automatic payment order completely, go to the Repeating Online tab of the Scheduled Transactions List, click on the transaction, and then click the Delete button at the top of the list.

Having Your IRA the Roth Way

The modern-day alternative to the traditional IRA is the Roth IRA — a tax-free option for those who don't qualify or prefer not to make tax-deductible contributions to a tax-deferred account. The Roth is a totally tax-free investment. The money you contribute is taxed when you earn it, and you get no deduction for your contribution, but the earnings in the Roth are not taxed, not even when you withdraw them.

The details of who gets to contribute to a Roth IRA are covered in Book I, Chapter 1. Here we discuss how to make contributions to the Roth through your Quicken program.

The only difference in the process of making contributions to a Roth IRA and a traditional IRA is that the Roth is set up in Quicken as a tax-free IRA account. Here's how:

1. **Open the Investing Center in Quicken by clicking Investing Center on your Account Bar at the left side of the screen.**
2. **Click the Add Account button.**

   Note that you're adding an investment account. This is different from the type of account you would create if you were to click the Add Account button in the Cash Flow Center, so be sure you're clicking the right button. An alternative is to open the Account list (Ctrl+A) and click the Add Account button at the top of the list. This option also lets you select an IRA.
3. **Indicate whether the account is held at a financial institution, and then click Next.**

   For this example, I choose the option that the account is not at a financial institution.
4. **Choose IRA or Keogh as the type of account, and then click Next.**
5. **Give the account a name that distinguishes this account from every other account you've created.**

You can have more than one IRA account. There's really no limit to how many different IRA accounts you open; the limit is on the annual contribution amount — but that contribution can be made to one account or spread over several accounts.

6. **If you are married, indicate if this account is yours or your spouse's — IRAs cannot be jointly owned.**
7. **Choose Roth IRA for the type of IRA, and then click Next.**
8. **Enter information from your most recent IRA statement.**

   If this is a new IRA, you can leave the amounts set at zero

9. **Enter the securities held in this account, as shown in Figure 3-10. You can just enter the ticker symbol if you want and Quicken will enter the rest of the information. If you don't know the ticker symbol, click the Ticker Symbol Lookup button at the bottom of the screen. Click Next when you've entered all of your investments.**

   It's OK to create your Roth IRA account without any securities. Perhaps you're opening the account with the intention of transferring securities from another account or purchasing securities later. Just leave the securities list shown in Figure 3-10 empty and click Next, and then verify that you don't plan to enter any securities.

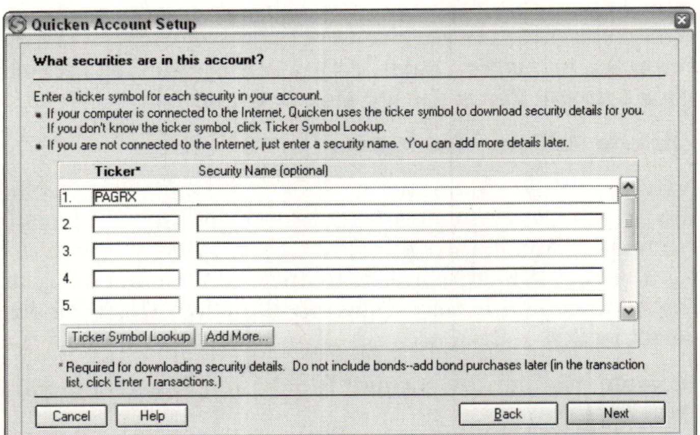

Figure 3-10: Enter the ticker symbols for the securities held in your Roth IRA.

10. **Enter the number of shares you own. Click Next, verify your information, and then click Done.**

Notice that you haven't yet entered any cost information in this account. Click the Enter hyperlink that appears under the title Cost Basis on the summary screen for your Roth IRA, and then you can enter information about when you purchased the shares and how much they cost.

There's no need to monitor mutual fund buy/sell dates in your IRA and your 401(k) like you would in a non-tax-deferred fund — there are no capital gain and loss considerations in the tax-deferred funds because the money is all taxed with your ordinary income.

From Traditional to Roth: Transferring retirement funds

Traditional IRAs have been around since 1974; the Roth IRA was born in 1997, so it stands to reason that a lot more people have money tucked away in traditional IRAs than they do in Roth IRAs. Yet the Roth is a very appealing investment for many people. After you get the money into the Roth, and assuming you follow a few simple rules (you have to keep the money in the Roth for five years and you must be at least age 59 1/2 when you take any money out), there is no more tax to pay — ever.

So what's a person to do if she wants to get that traditional IRA money into a Roth where it can continue to grow, tax-free? Move the money. Period. It's that simple. Well, almost that simple. Truth is, whenever you take money out of a traditional IRA, even if you're moving the money into a Roth IRA, which is another type of IRA, you have to pay income tax on the money. You can transfer the funds from traditional to Roth without the nasty 10 percent penalty that applies to early IRA withdrawals, but you still have to pay the tax.

Many people see this tax situation as a detriment and avoid switching the money because of the tax. That's a fallacy, however: The tax is just a ticking time bomb. The sooner you get the money out of the traditional IRA and into a Roth, the sooner you can lock in the amount of tax and let the rest of the money grow, tax-free.

Converting traditional IRA money to a Roth all at once

Taking all of your IRA money out of your traditional IRA and placing it in a Roth is one option — you'll pay high taxes in the year of the switcheroo, but then you'll be finished with the old IRA and can let your investments grow without a lot of icky rules about taxes and penalties.

Make sure you convert your money from one IRA to another with the help of your IRA trustee. Otherwise, the conversion might be misunderstood by the IRS and you may get hit with a 10 percent penalty on top of the income tax. Your trustee knows what paperwork needs to be filed to get the conversion done properly.

Converting traditional IRA money to a Roth at a leisurely pace

Moving your money over to a Roth a little bit each year, paying the tax when the extra money fits into your budget is another very attractive option.

There's no limit to how much or how little money you transfer to the Roth or when you make the transfer. The only catch is that your income has to be under the Roth threshold. In other words, in any year in which you transfer money from a traditional IRA to a Roth IRA, you must qualify to make a Roth contribution (see Book I, Chapter 1 for the Roth contribution rules).

The possibility exists that you thought your income was going to be low enough that you would qualify for a traditional-to-Roth IRA conversion, but it turned out that you got a big bonus in December and your income catapulted over the Roth threshold. Call your IRA trustee as soon as you know this and arrange to have the conversion undone — this is called *recharacterization.* There's no tax or penalty on recharacterizing the conversion, as long as you get it done by October 15 of the year following the year of the conversion.

Diversification: The Great Investment Elixir

Most analysts tell you that the best advice for safe investing is diversification — otherwise known as not putting all your eggs in one basket. By diversifying, you ensure that if one investment goes sour, you don't spoil all of your savings. Most former Enron employees would probably agree with that advice today, and you might agree with it as well.

One of the main principals of investment diversification is to divide your money among investments with varying degrees of risk. Some money should be placed in low-risk funds that might not have a great return in terms of interest rates or dividend payout, but that are most likely to keep your money safe and secure. Money that you hope will grow but that, if worse came to worse, you could actually live without, can go into the riskier investments, investments that pay a higher return but that could just as easily go belly-up at a moment's notice.

Most people strive for lower risk in their investments as they age, switching their invested money from items like speculative stocks to the more reliable investments such as bonds and bank CDs. Today, however, investment advisors are taking a second look at that advice in light of the fact that life expectancy continues to lengthen and cutting your investments back to the least risky bonds and CDs can lessen your revenue to the point where you won't have enough money to grow old on.

The most important consideration when planning on your retirement investment mix is to constantly monitor your investments, making sure that they perform the way you want, and also regularly review your retirement plan so that you can be secure in your old age. Book VI covers retirement planning and various savings plans in much more depth.

Chapter 4: Watch Lists and News You Can Use

In This Chapter

- Getting investment news through Quicken
- Setting up reminder alerts
- Taking advantage of investment news
- Creating and using Watch Lists

Do you feel like you're operating in the dark when it comes to choosing which investments to buy and allocating your money between your various investments? If you do, you're certainly not alone. Esteemed financial analysts agree that at least 93.7 percent of people who invest money in stocks and mutual funds are completely clueless as to how they should make investment decisions. OK, I'm making that percentage up, but I'm sure that there are lots and lots of you out there who invest based on a tip from a trusted friend or family member, choose investments because your employer made them available to you, and buy shares of some stock you never heard of because you overheard a tip on the bus or train on the way home from work. Am I right? Your approach can and should be more businesslike, and in this chapter, I show you how.

Start by Reading the News

Every major city has a newspaper that contains a business section. In addition to the business section in major city newspapers, *USA Today* has a business section, and there is always the *Wall Street Journal*, a national newspaper that is nothing but a business section. If you really want business news, it's not difficult to find.

In addition to the sources just mentioned, specialized newspapers and magazines about business abound, and entire newspapers and magazines are devoted to educating people who are really serious about learning how to invest. And that's just the print media.

Because you're reading this book about Quicken, one can presume that you have a computer at your disposal, and thus one can further presume that you have Internet access, and there's very little to read about any subject that can't be found somewhere on the Internet.

The trick to educating yourself about investing is not so much finding the news as it is sifting through the news and deciding which news to read. The best way to start is to just pick something and start reading. As you get familiar with one source of business and investment information, you can find what interests you and what you want to find out more about. At that point, you can start seeking more specialized information.

What to look for when you read the investment news

Because each person has different tastes in investing (which goes a long way toward explaining why there are actually more than 10,000 mutual funds in existence), I can't tell you what to read about, but I can tell you some points to remember when you start reading about businesses and investments:

- **Read more than one source of information about a particular company.** Each article you read presents an opinion of someone who is supposedly educated about analyzing investments choices and about the company or mutual fund in question. So seek out a second opinion. And a third. When you start hearing the same things over and over again, you can start believing what you read.
- **Look for some background information on the companies in which you consider investing.** Don't buy stock in a company because the name sounds good. If you're considering investing in a manufacturing company, find out what the company makes and why it makes that, how long it's been making that, who buys it, how the item is used, and how long into future we can expect people to want that item. Who else is making the same thing, and which company makes the better item, which company charges more and why, how long the people making decisions have been around at that company? In other words, know what you're buying.
- **Find out how to read stock market reports.** Plenty of Web sites, books, and articles explain how to understand all of the mumbo-jumbo (highly technical financial term) that appears on the stock pages in the newspapers. Do an Internet search or pick up a copy of *Investing For Dummies,* 3rd edition, by Eric Tyson (Wiley) if you need a primer on what the numbers mean.

Reading news in Quicken

Lo and behold! You can read investment news right in your very own Quicken program! Click on the Investing Center over on the Account Bar in Quicken. At the top of the Investing Center window, you see Investment Alerts. Quicken mines news from highly regarded sources including BusinessWire and PRNewswire, Morningstar, Zacks.com, and Briefing.com to provide you with the latest news and analysts' opinions about the investments you have chosen.

Click on any of the hyperlinks in your investment alerts (see Figure 4-1) to see what's happening with the companies and mutual funds that interest you.

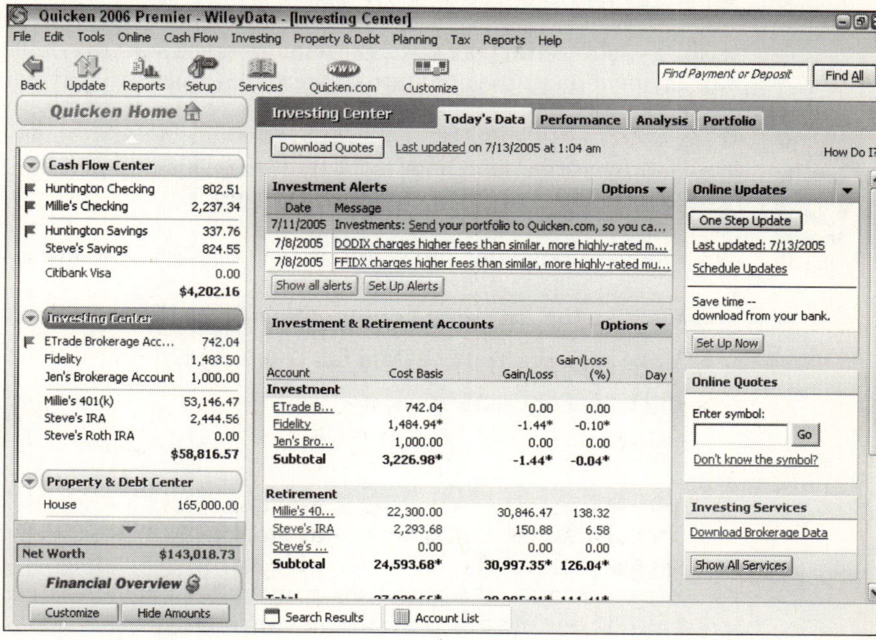

Figure 4-1: Quicken found some news while you were sleeping.

Hey, Don't Forget This Important Investment News!

The Alerts section of your Investing Center is not just for the alerts that Quicken provides. This section is customizable: You can ask Quicken to add your own alerts, reminding you of specific events, transactions, or anything else financial.

For example, you can set alerts to tell you when a stock hits a certain price, or you can ask to be reminded that you get an extra paycheck in June, so that is a good time to give your investments a boost. Remind yourself a month before annual or semi-annual payments like life insurance or property tax are due so that you won't be caught off-guard when the bills arrive.

Consider setting reminders for more esoteric events, such as scheduling an appointment with your homeowner's insurance agent to make sure you're getting the best price and covering your home and your possessions properly.

If you're one of those people who pays quarterly estimated tax payments, set a reminder so that you won't miss your filing date. Keep in mind that whenever the 15th of the month falls on a Saturday, Sunday, or post office holiday, your tax payment is not due until the next business day.

Also, if you're setting tax payment reminders, be sure to double-check the tax payment dates in your state. Some states' quarterly payment dates do not coincide with the federal dates.

TIP

Find more information about estimated taxes, including a complete chart of federal estimated tax filing due dates, in Book V.

Set yourself a reminder about a particular account by following these steps:

1. **Click on the Investing Center option in the Account Bar.**
2. **Make sure the Today's Data tab is selected.**
3. **Click the Set Up Alerts button.**

   The Alerts Center window shown in Figure 4-2 appears.
4. **On the left side of the window, select one of the alert types.**

   Note that the headings are not types. You must select one of the types, such as Price and Volume under the Investing heading, or Monthly Expenses under the Cash Flow heading (see Figure 4-2). For this example, I do one of each of these two reminder types.

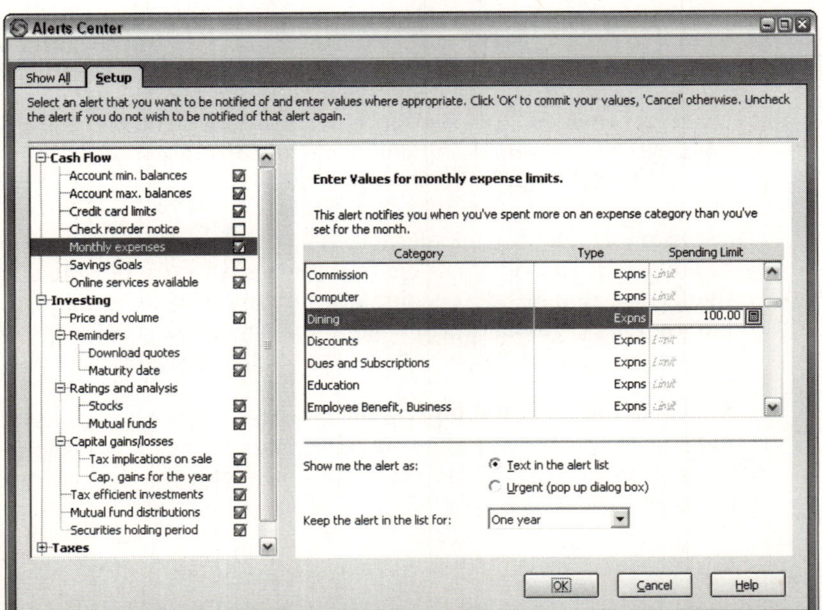

Figure 4-2: Pick the topic for which you want to set an alert.

5. **Click on Monthly Expenses under the Cash Flow heading.**
6. **Click on one of the expenses in the category list that appears on the right.**

   A little box appears to the right of the expense category. Enter a spending limit. Click on as many expenses as you want, entering spending limits for each one.

7. **Indicate how you want the alert to appear.**

   If you exceed your spending limit, the alert can either appear in your financial alert list, or you can ask that Quicken get your attention with a pop-up box. Choose either Text or Urgent at the bottom of the expense list.

8. **Indicate how long you want this limit to stick around.**

   You can have the spending limit stay in the reminders list for a day, a week, a month, a quarter, or a year. Choose your time limit from the drop-down list that appears at the bottom of the window.

Now set up an investing alert:

1. **Click on Price and Volume under the Investing heading.**
2. **Click on the Go to Quicken.com to Customize Price and Volume Alerts option.**

   Quicken takes a moment to update your portfolio, and then it takes you to Quicken.com, where you can enter price and volume limits.

3. **Enter the price and volume percentages by which any one of the securities must change to trigger an alert (see Figure 4-3).**
4. **To enter alert values for individual securities, click the Select % by Symbol button.**

   A list of your securities appears, and you can enter either specific dollar amounts or percentages for each security individually.

   TIP: While you're visiting the alert setup screen at Quicken.com, check the Announcements/Industry Buzz area to indicate which types of alerts you want to receive, and then scroll down to Section Three, where you can set alerts for account balances that drop below or rise above a particular amount.

5. **Click the Finished button to save your requests.**

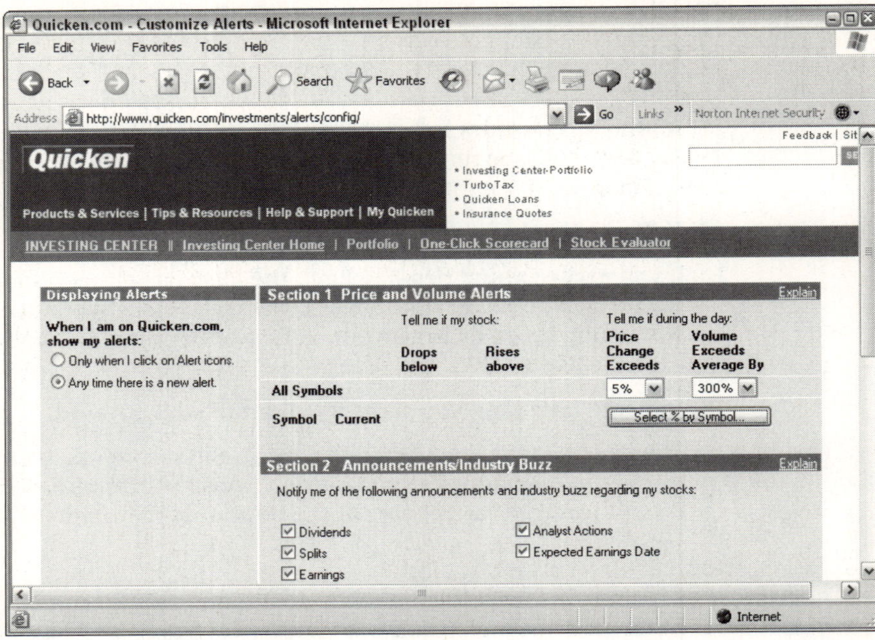

Figure 4-3: Enter the percentages that will trigger alerts.

Quicken Watch Lists

For those Quicken users who prefer a more vicarious approach to tracking the stock market, the Quicken Watch List fits the bill. You can add stocks and other investments to your Watch List and, well, watch them, just as you would watch a stock you own, but without the need for prescription drugs when your stocks take a nose-dive.

I recommend that beginning investors work with play money for awhile before they commit to the real thing. Pick a nice round amount, say $5,000, and pretend you're going to invest that money in the stock market. Choose the stocks or funds or bonds that you would buy, if you were going to do this for real, and place those investments on your Watch List. Then watch. Read the news alerts every day. See how your investments improve (or don't). Wait 30 or 60 days, or however long it takes until you feel like you're comfortable enough with these investments to talk intelligently about them and maybe even make some reasonable predictions as to what they're going to do next. (This is not to say that investments are ever predictable. The only think I've ever been able to predict about investments is that as soon as I buy them, the price goes down, and as soon as I give up on them and sell, the price shoots right up.)

TIP

If your investments soared sky-high, use what you learned about picking those investments to choose again, this time for real.

TIP

If you lost your shirt during your watching period, take solace in three important pieces of information. First, you didn't lose any real money. Second, somebody else did. Third and most important, the investments that interested you at the beginning of the watch period now cost less than they did when you started watching. If you're still convinced they are good investments, now might be the time to buy. Look at all the money you earned, just by not investing until the price went down.

Creating your Watch List is easy

When you set up a Watch List, you can list securities that you own, securities that you want to own, securities that are similar to ones that interest you, stock indexes, any type of investment that you want to monitor.

Here's how to set up a Watch List in Quicken:

1. **Open the Investing Center by clicking the Investing Center in the Account Bar.**

   Make sure that the Today's Data tab is selected.

2. **Scroll down until the Watch List (Figure 4-4) appears at the bottom of the screen.**

   Even if you have no securities in your Watch List, the list appears, ready for you to populate.

3. **Click the Add a Security button.**

4. **In the window that appears, enter the ticker symbol for the security you want to track.**

   If you don't know the ticker symbol, enter the name of the security (or your best guess) and click the Look Up button. Quicken whisks you over to Quicken.com, where a search for your security begins. If for some reason (like you misspelled the name of the company or the company is remarkably obscure) Quicken doesn't find the security, go ahead and search for the ticker symbol through other sources while you're hanging around on the Internet. A good place to look for ticker symbols beyond Quicken is `http://finance.yahoo.com/l` (note that the last letter is a lower case "L" and not a numeral "1").

5. **When you've got the ticker symbol, click Next.**

   Quicken hops online and finds out the name of your security and what type of security it is. A little box appears, showing you what Quicken found (see Figure 4-5).

6. **Click Next to accept the security.**

   Make sure that the security Quicken found is the one you're interested in tracking. If the security that appears in the Add Security to Quicken window is the wrong security, click Cancel and try again. If the correct security appears, click Next and Quicken adds the security to your Watch List. A window appears asking if you want to do this again — choose Yes or No, and then click Done.

When Quicken adds securities to your Watch List, the most recently available price quote is added as well. To get additional information, like an updated price quote or the day's price change and percentage change, click your Download Quotes button at the top of the Investing Center.

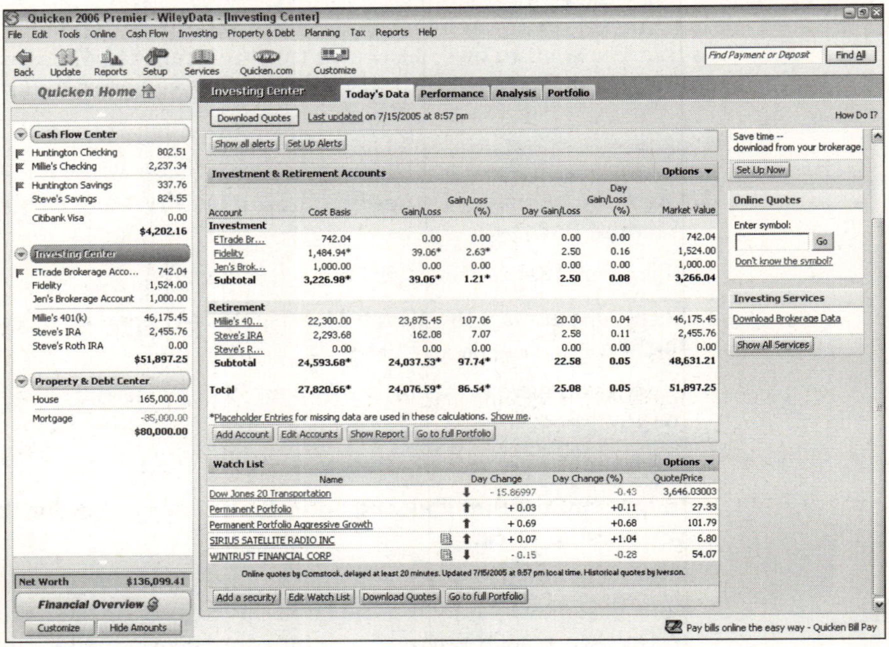

Figure 4-4: The Quicken Watch List.

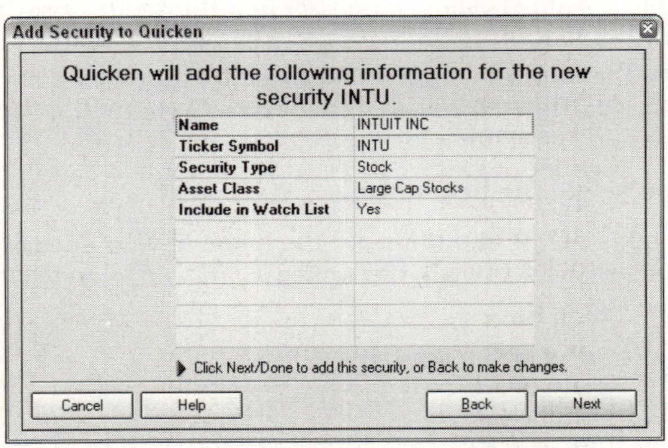

Figure 4-5: Quicken has found the security you sought.

Quick trick for adding securities to Watch List

If you have ever owned a security and recorded that security in Quicken, the name of the security resides on the Quicken security list, a compendium of all the securities you have ever taught Quicken to play with.

Open the security list by choosing Security List from the Investing menu or press Ctrl+Y (see the following figure):

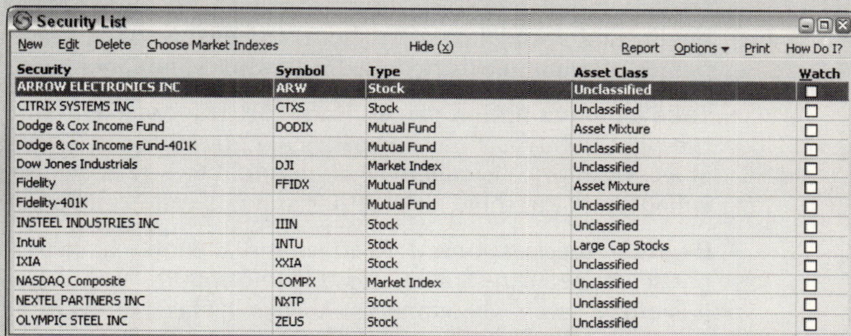

Security List

New Edit Delete Choose Market Indexes Hide (x) Report Options Print How Do I?

Security	Symbol	Type	Asset Class	Watch
ARROW ELECTRONICS INC	ARW	Stock	Unclassified	☐
CITRIX SYSTEMS INC	CTXS	Stock	Unclassified	☐
Dodge & Cox Income Fund	DODIX	Mutual Fund	Asset Mixture	☐
Dodge & Cox Income Fund-401K		Mutual Fund	Unclassified	☐
Dow Jones Industrials	DJI	Market Index	Unclassified	☐
Fidelity	FFIDX	Mutual Fund	Asset Mixture	☐
Fidelity-401K		Mutual Fund	Unclassified	☐
INSTEEL INDUSTRIES INC	IIIN	Stock	Unclassified	☐
Intuit	INTU	Stock	Large Cap Stocks	☐
IXIA	XXIA	Stock	Unclassified	☐
NASDAQ Composite	COMPX	Market Index	Unclassified	☐
NEXTEL PARTNERS INC	NXTP	Stock	Unclassified	☐
OLYMPIC STEEL INC	ZEUS	Stock	Unclassified	☐

Click the box in the Watch column for any security that you want to add to your Watch List.

You can also quickly add any of the market indexes to your Watch List by clicking the Choose Market Indexes at the top of the window, checking the index(es) you want to view, clicking Done, and then checking the Watch box next to the index.

So you've got a Watch List: Now What?

It's time to dig around in your Watch List and see what kind of information you can find about the securities that interest you:

- ✦ **For starters, click on any security in your Watch List.** All the securities are hyperlinked. Even clicking is a task with options. A quick click on one of the securities opens a new window that displays securities details such as the ticker symbol, the stock exchange where the security can be found, the number of shares you own, if any, complete quote information including highs, lows, trading volume, and all the technical information that appears in the newspaper stock market quotes, as well as a chart of the stock's price and trading activity.
- ✦ **Before you click on a watch-listed security, let your mouse hover over the security for a sec, and you see that you have a clicker's choice of asking for Quote or Chart.** Pick Quote, and you see not only the quote and trading volume info, but also the latest news headlines and links to reports you can purchase, analyst's opinions, company profile, and information about the industry as a whole. Pick Chart, and you see a

nice big chart that can be redrawn for various periods of time, as well as the quote information that appeared over on the quote screen.

If you click on either the Chart or Quote selection, you get the full array of clickable options provided by Yahoo! Finance. Along the left side of the window that appears are hyperlinks that can display many different types investment information for you, including

- **Check out real-time quotes provided by Electronic Communication Network, also known as ECN.** ECN quotes are cherished by day-traders, those investors who sit panting at the computer all day, buying and selling hour after hour, and ensuring the success of companies that manufacture coffee and other stimulants.
- **Take a look at option prices.** Hard-core traders like to buy and sell the right to buy and sell securities at certain prices. The right to buy at a certain price is called a *call;* the right to buy at a certain price is called a *put*. Put them all together and it is called an *option*.
- **Read the message board.** Read what real people have to say about a particular security. Sometimes this information is worthwhile; often it is crazy personal comments. Always it's fascinating or at last an interesting way to pass some time. You can post your own messages here, including inquiries. Warning: Don't take the answers you get too seriously.
- **Look over SEC filings.** Back to serious issues — get direct links to actual reports that companies file with the Securities & Exchange Commission.
- **See what the competitors to your stock are doing.** Find out who the competition is for a particular company and how their stock is doing. You might find some companies to add to your Watch List by checking out the competition.
- **Find out the analysts' opinions.** Read what the professional market-watchers have to say about the securities.
- **Research the owners.** Find out who the primary stockholders are in a particular company, how much stock they own, who has been buying and selling, and how much.
- **Review financial statements.** See the most recent balance sheet, income statement, and statement of cash flow for a particular security.

Tired of watching? Remove an item from the Watch List

It's easy to take securities off of your Watch List. Simply click the Edit Watch List button beneath the Watch List, and the entire list of your securities appears. All securities you're watching are marked with a little green checkmark in the Watch column, as shown in Figure 4-6.

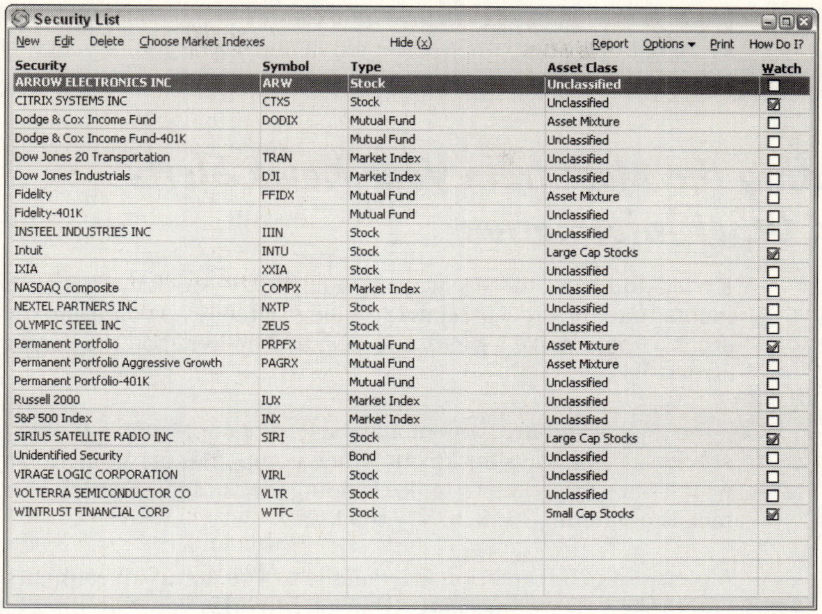

Security	Symbol	Type	Asset Class	Watch
ARROW ELECTRONICS INC	ARW	Stock	Unclassified	☐
CITRIX SYSTEMS INC	CTXS	Stock	Unclassified	☑
Dodge & Cox Income Fund	DODIX	Mutual Fund	Asset Mixture	☐
Dodge & Cox Income Fund-401K		Mutual Fund	Unclassified	☐
Dow Jones 20 Transportation	TRAN	Market Index	Unclassified	☐
Dow Jones Industrials	DJI	Market Index	Unclassified	☐
Fidelity	FFIDX	Mutual Fund	Asset Mixture	☐
Fidelity-401K		Mutual Fund	Unclassified	☐
INSTEEL INDUSTRIES INC	IIIN	Stock	Unclassified	☐
Intuit	INTU	Stock	Large Cap Stocks	☑
IXIA	XXIA	Stock	Unclassified	☐
NASDAQ Composite	COMPX	Market Index	Unclassified	☐
NEXTEL PARTNERS INC	NXTP	Stock	Unclassified	☐
OLYMPIC STEEL INC	ZEUS	Stock	Unclassified	☐
Permanent Portfolio	PRPFX	Mutual Fund	Asset Mixture	☑
Permanent Portfolio Aggressive Growth	PAGRX	Mutual Fund	Asset Mixture	☐
Permanent Portfolio-401K		Mutual Fund	Unclassified	☐
Russell 2000	IUX	Market Index	Unclassified	☐
S&P 500 Index	INX	Market Index	Unclassified	☐
SIRIUS SATELLITE RADIO INC	SIRI	Stock	Large Cap Stocks	☑
Unidentified Security		Bond	Unclassified	☐
VIRAGE LOGIC CORPORATION	VIRL	Stock	Unclassified	☐
VOLTERRA SEMICONDUCTOR CO	VLTR	Stock	Unclassified	☐
WINTRUST FINANCIAL CORP	WTFC	Stock	Small Cap Stocks	☑

Figure 4-6: Checkmarks tell you which securities are on your Watch List.

Uncheck any security that you want to remove from the Watch List. Click the X in the upper-right corner of the window to close the window, automatically saving your changes. Your Watch List is revised immediately to no longer display the securities you removed.

News Alerts and More at Quicken.com

Quicken Investing Center (not the one on your Quicken program but the one on the Quicken.com Web site) is all about providing you with as much information as you can absorb about all of the investments you care about. Not only can you get the latest news from more than 20 highly regarded financial publications, stock quotes from all the U.S. and international exchanges; investment information about stocks, bonds, currencies, mutual funds, commodities (like pork belly futures), and options; mergers and acquisitions; initial public offerings; the stock indexes; and so on. But you can also find exciting fodder for cocktail chatter such as "The Five Dumbest Things on Wall Street This Week" with its Dumb-o-Meter ranking system and daily financial cartoons.

The list of available information is virtually endless. Start clicking around the Quicken.com Investing Center home page and you'll be taken to all sorts of interesting financial sites, many courtesy of Quicken's association with Yahoo! Finance, a gateway for scads of information.

Back on the Quicken.com Investing Center home page, you can see your personal list of stocks you've invested in and those you're watching on the left side of the screen.

Getting the Most from Your News Alerts and Other Information

If tried-and-true, surefire ways to analyze the stock market and make investments that are successful every time existed, everyone who invested in stocks would make a bundle of cash and be living on the proverbial easy street.

If the Wall Street investment analysts, the people who get paid to analyze stocks, can't always figure out which companies are going to skyrocket and which ones are going to tank, deciding for ourselves which investments to pick is a daunting task, to say the least.

A plethora of information is available to you about investments that you own and those you are watching. Quicken provides you with direct links to a huge variety of information sources, and a quick Internet search will unearth even more information. So what do you do with all this information?

Here's my advice:

- Read as much as you can so that you can speak knowledgeably about the companies you invest in and those you're considering investing in.
- Follow the ups and downs of the stocks and funds that interest you, trying to determine what conditions exist that have effects on the share prices.
- Watch. Use your Watch List to monitor your investments carefully and constantly. Don't just watch the stocks and funds you're considering purchasing; watch the ones you have already invested in. Don't be afraid to change your investment mix if it's not working.
- Wait. A stock or mutual worth investing in will continue to be worth investing in as time goes by.

In my opinion, a lot of money is lost in the stock market by people trying to jump in and invest as soon as they think an investment looks good, before they take the time to watch and analyze. Time spent studying pays off with sound investments based on knowledge, not whims.

Book IV

Household Finances

The 5th Wave By Rich Tennant

"Oh, that's Jack's area for his paper crafts. He's made some wonderful US Treasury Bonds, Certificates of Deposit, $20's, $50's, $100's, that sort of thing."

Contents at a Glance

Chapter 1: Borrowing Money

In This Chapter

- **Determining the cost of borrowing**
- **Borrowing online**
- **Entering loan information in Quicken**
- **Automating loan payments**
- **Using Quicken's loan calculator**

In fiction, when people borrow money, a limb or a first-born child is often on the line if the money isn't paid back on time. Borrowing money in real life isn't nearly so scary. In fact, it's the rare person in today's society who doesn't borrow money. Automobile loans and home mortgages and college loans seem like a way of life, and why shouldn't they? Interest rates are extremely low (at least compared to the late 70s and early 80s when mortgage interest rates hovered just under 20 percent), and Uncle Sam does his best to make the interest on home mortgages and college loans an attractive way of reducing federal income tax.

It Costs HOW MUCH to Borrow That Money?

The downside of borrowing money, aside from the fact that you have to pay it back, is that you have to pay interest as well. The interest is a fee for the privilege of borrowing the money.

Shopping around for the best loan deal

Interest rates vary based on several factors, some of which are in your control. Here are the different features that influence interest rates:

- **National economic factors.** The U.S. Federal Reserve interest rate (the rate that banks charge each other for overnight loans), and other factors that are completely out of your control, including the rate of inflation, the stock market, the strength of the U.S. dollar against other international currencies, the demand for money, the size of Abraham Lincoln's face on the $5 bill, and so on.

- **Loan fees, or points, that you pay to the lender up front.** The more points you pay, the lower the interest rate on the loan. Points are frequently offered on mortgage loans, and the IRS is often nice about letting you deduct your points on your tax return.
- **Other banking relationships you have with your lender.** If you have accounts on deposit and other loans with your lender, you may be able to negotiate a lower interest rate on a new loan.
- **Amount borrowed.** Borrow less, and you might have more wiggle room on the interest rate.
- **Loan term.** Offer to shave a little time off your repayment schedule, and you might be able to negotiate a lower interest rate. You might also have a higher monthly payment, so be sure to weigh the pros and cons of shortening your loan term.
- **Automatic payments.** Some lenders will negotiate on the rate of interest if you allow them to deduct payments automatically from your bank account.
- **Your overall credit risk.** This includes your level of income, your credit history, your credit score, and your employment history, all of which can affect the interest you pay.

TIP

If any of the above factors change during the life of your loan, you may be able to refinance at a lower rate. For example, if you take steps to improve your credit rating, or if you put money on deposit with the lender, check to see if there is a possibility of restructuring your loan with lower interest.

There's interest, and then there's interest

Interest comes in many shapes and sizes. The way in which interest is computed greatly affects the total amount you ultimately pay. Knowing the type of interest you're paying and how the interest is computed can impact decisions about how you pay back your loan.

With simple interest, interest is calculated as a fixed amount, based on a percentage of the loan amount, and the amount of interest is adjustable only by the duration of the loan. So, for example, if you borrow $10,000 at 10 percent interest for two years, the interest is 10 percent of $10,000, or $1,000, per year, or $2,000 total. Pay the loan back a year early, and your interest is cut to $1,000.

With compounding interest, the interest rate is recalculated after each payment, based on the remaining principal owing on the loan. Make extra payments directly against principal and you can reduce the amount of interest you owe on the loan and thus reduce the total amount you are required to pay.

When you create loans in Quicken, as demonstrated later in this chapter, your interest is recorded as well as your principal payments. If you decide to make early payments or other adjustments, be sure to adjust your records in Quicken as well so that your payments are recorded properly.

Some loans don't permit extra payments, otherwise known as prepayments, of principal. If you think you might want to make extra payments in order to reduce the amount of your interest, make sure your loan plan allows for such payments. Some loans have a lock-out period in the early years, preventing prepayments of principal, but then allowing such payments after a certain amount of time has passed.

Borrowing money on the Internet

Not too many years ago, the idea of borrowing money via the Internet would have seemed as surreal as communicating with aliens on a UFO. Now, people borrow money online frequently and easily. Many Web sites enable you to compare rates from different lenders, not just in your area, but all across the country. Many of the lenders even allow you to fill out an application right from your computer.

Quicken offers mortgage and refinancing loan services at `www.quickenloans.com`. Although Quicken.com doesn't provide auto loans, the site recommends the following for online automobile financing:

```
www.autobytel.com
www.carpoint.msn.com
www.carfinance.com
www.autoweb.com
```

When considering taking advantage of the opportunity to borrow money from an online source, keep in mind the following points:

- **Borrowing online is quick:** You don't have to go anywhere to meet with a lender. The lending institution checks your credit reports instantly and determines your creditworthiness right away.
- **Major banks are represented online:** Familiar bank institutions have an online presence and are available to loan money to new customers via the Internet.
- **Security is crucial to conducting confidential business online:** Bankers and other lenders are aware of this and employ strict rules of encryption. Check the privacy notice of a potential lender for more information.

Encryption means that when you enter personal information on a Web page and click Send, all of your letters and numbers are scrambled so that hackers and other nefarious types can't read them.

Using Quicken to Track Your Loans

Quicken has the ability to keep track of all of your loans — not just how much you owe, but how much you pay each month, how much of that payment is interest, and how much of that payment reduces the amount you owe. (And how much of that payment should have been spent on useful things like stale movie popcorn that comes slathered in something you would never mistake for butter.)

You can use Quicken's loan tracking features to prepare schedules of deductible interest for your income tax return. You can also make extra payments of principal and recalculate your loan in Quicken.

Accountants use a fancy term, *amortization*, to signify the dispersion of loan payments over the term of the loan. Breaking your big loan into little payments and spreading those payments over a period of time is called amortizing your loan.

Meet the Quicken Property & Debt Center

You might think we don't care a lot about the property portion of the Property & Debt Center in this chapter because we're talking about borrowing (debt). But actually, property often goes hand-in-hand with debt. You take on debt so that you can acquire property. You get a mortgage so you can have a home. You get a loan for your car. So it's sensible to place information about both the property you own and the debt you carry all in the same place.

In the next section, you discover how to set up a loan in Quicken. Setting up your loans is the first part of loan tracking in Quicken. The second part is setting up your loan payments. By doing all of this setting-up stuff, your loan payments get assigned to the correct loan, and you can always see how much you have left to pay off on your loans.

You also find out how to link loans to property so that your Quicken account provides a complete picture of not only what you owe but also what you own.

Adding a loan

You can either set up an existing loan or a new loan in Quicken. When you're ready to set up a loan in Quicken, follow these steps:

You don't get a leave-and-come-back option with Quicken's loan setup wizard. If you have to cut and run before you've entered all of your loan information, click Cancel and plan on starting over later.

1. **Click on Property & Debt Center on your Account Bar, and then click Add Loan near the bottom of the page.**

   Alternatively, you can choose Loans from the Property & Debt menu, or press Ctrl+H, and then when the View Loans window appears, click the New option at the top of the window. Either way, a Loan Setup wizard pops up onscreen (see Figure 1-1).

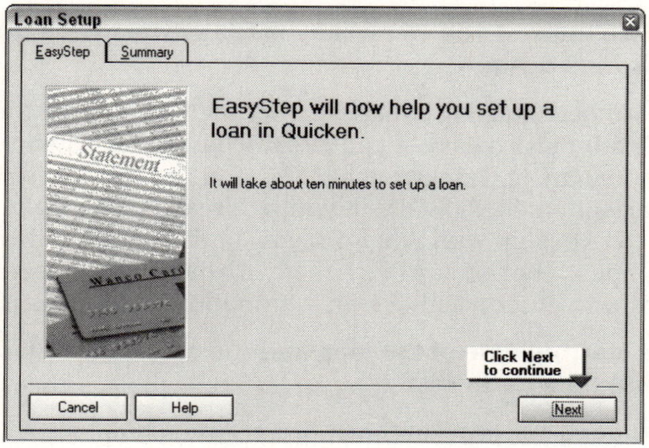

Figure 1-1: Quicken's Loan Setup wizard.

2. **With the EasyStep tab selected, click Next to get into the heart of the Loan Setup wizard.**

   Quicken asks a bunch of questions in the wizard, designed to get you to give up all the information you can find or remember about your loan. If you don't have the loan documentation at your fingertips and can't remember all the particulars, no worries. You can go back and change your information later (see "Making changes in your loan" later in this chapter).

   TIP: If you're comfortable with loan lingo and want to cut to the chase, click the Summary tab in the Loan Setup wizard. Here you can fill in the blanks with your loan information and save yourself time and clicking effort.

3. **Indicate if you are borrowing money or lending money in this particular loan, and then click Next.**

   Loans work two ways. Depending on which road you choose, Quicken sets up loan accounts and classifies them property, treating a loan you make as a *receivable* (an amount you'll ultimately get back, someday, you hope, that is if you can find your brother who was last seen driving west toward Omaha), and treating a loan you borrow as a *payable*, an amount you have to return. For this example you're borrowing money.

4. **Give this loan a name and click the ubiquitous Next button.**

   Pet names like Muffy, Fluffy, and Rin Tin Tin don't necessarily capture the essence of the loan (unless of course you're borrowing money on behalf of your pet), so think of something a bit more succinct, such as Auto Loan or Mortgage or Loan to Sister. I'm using Auto Loan for this example. If you prefer, you can click Existing Account and then choose from the accounts listed. If this is the first time you've entered loan information, you'll probably use the New Account option.

5. **Let Quicken know if you've already made payments on this loan and then click Next again.**

   If you coordinate starting a loan with setting up Quicken, the setup process is a bit less messy. If you already had a loan when you decided to set the loan up in Quicken, that's OK. You just need to be ready to enter information like how much you've already paid on the loan so that Quicken can keep up with you from now until the payoff day. For this example, I pick Yes and say I've already made some payments, so you can see how to enter existing loan information into Quicken.

6. **Enter the starting date of the loan and the original amount you borrowed, and then click Next.**

   Now it's time to start racking your brain. Again, don't forget that you can change loan information later if you don't quite remember everything now. Enter the starting date, or a close approximation of when you borrowed the money, as I've done in Figure 1-2, and then enter the initial amount of the loan.

7. **Answer the Balloon Payment question, and then click Next.**

   Some loans come with an option called the *balloon* payment. This doesn't mean your money drifts up into the stratosphere, although it may feel that way. Actually, what happens is you get lower monthly payments up front with a guarantee that you'll pay a big payment at the end. Often these loans are structured so that you pay only interest for your monthly loan payments, and then pay the entire principal at the end of the loan. Many people take out these types of loans with a plan to refinance the principal when the balloon payment is due.

8. **Enter the length of the loan.**

   Your options here are years, months, weeks, and payments. Payments? Sometimes loans are set up based on the number of payments you're going to make, instead of a fixed time period. For this example, I've selected a four-year loan.

   If your loan is a 4-year loan, payable in 48 monthly payments, it doesn't matter if you select 4 years or 48 months for the length of the loan. You get to specify that your payments are monthly for either entry.

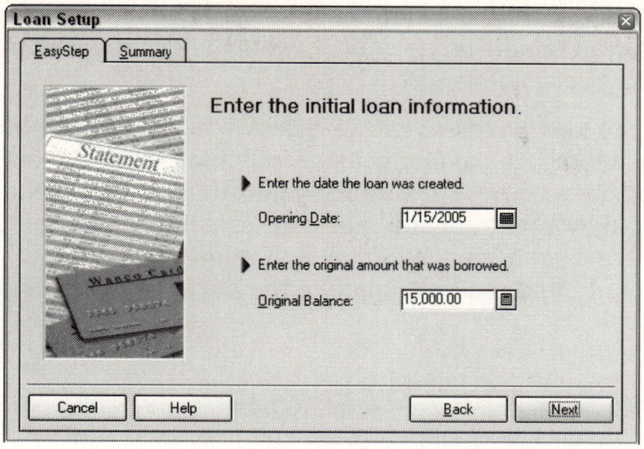

Figure 1-2: Fill in the blanks about your loan.

9. **Enter the payment period.**

   Here's where you specify how frequently the payments are going to be made. Even if you plan to make extra payments in order to get this over with quickly, or even if, heaven forbid, you end up missing payments, just enter the frequency that the lender expects for your payments.

10. **Enter the compounding period.**

    You must tell Quicken about the compounding period for your loan so that Quicken can accurately calculate the interest. Your loan document should specify the compounding period, and your lender should certainly be able to tell you. For this example, I've entered a monthly compounding period.

    Interest that is calculated on not just the principal of the loan but on unpaid and accrued interest as well is called *compound interest*.

11. **Enter the current balance of the loan.**

    If you know the current balance of your loan, answer Yes when asked about this, and then enter the balance as of today's date. You can call your lender to find out this amount. You can also decide not to worry about entering the current balance and just answer No when Quicken asks if you know your loan balance. If you don't enter the balance, Quicken does the calculations and tells you what your balance is. Quicken's calculation may be off a few pennies due to some rounding, but you can make changes later.

12. **Enter the date of your next payment and the amount.**

    Enter the date your next payment is *due*, even if that date might not agree with the date on which you actually plan to make the payment. Enter the amount of your payment as shown in Figure 1-3. If you're not sure of the amount, just look back in your checkbook or at your cancelled checks or bank statement to see how much you're paid previously. If haven't made any payments yet, you can find the payment amount on your loan papers.

Entering the loan payment can get tricky when you are setting up a mortgage. Mortgage payments usually include odds and ends like real estate tax, homeowner's insurance, and private mortgage insurance. Quicken only wants to hear about your principal and interest — the rest of those items get added later. You might have to get out some of your loan papers to find out how much of the payment is just loan principal and interest.

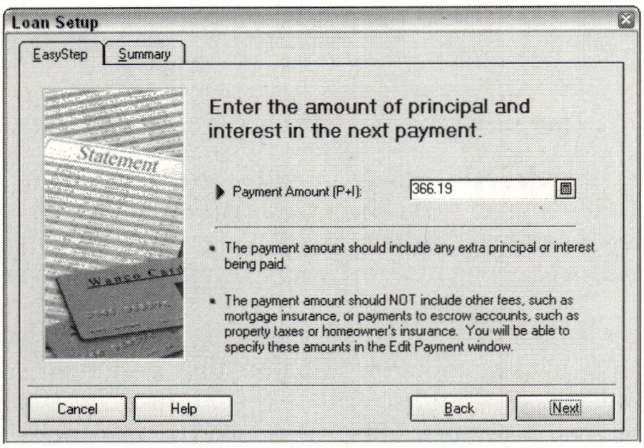

Figure 1-3: Enter only the amount you pay for principal and interest.

Entering principal and interest for your loan payment means entering *all* principal and interest. If you are the type of person that typically pays extra principal with your loan payment, enter that extra amount in addition to the requirement payment amount in the window shown at Figure 1-3. Quicken can then calculate accurately how early your loan is going to be paid off due to your extra payments.

13. **Enter your interest rate.**

    Back to the loan papers, or call your lender. Either one can tell you what rate of interest you are paying on this loan.

    Sometimes the loan papers for loans with compounding interest show not only the basic interest rate but also the compounded interest rate. Make sure you enter only the basic interest rate in Quicken.

14. **Review the summary and click Done when you are finished.**

    Clicking Next after you enter your interest rate takes you to the Summary tab, where you can review all of the information you just entered. Click Next a couple of times to get through the summary screens. Make any changes that might be necessary if you entered information incorrectly, and then click Done to save your loan information. The Set Up Loan Payment window appears. In the "Looking at your loans," sidebar, I discuss your options for setting up your loan payment in Quicken.

Setting up your loan payments in Quicken

Immediately after you set up a loan in Quicken, the Set Up Loan Payment window appears. You don't have to set up your loan payment in Quicken, but if you want Quicken to keep track of your loan balance, you should set up the payment. Otherwise, why did you go through all of the steps to set up your loan?

Looking at your loans

Care to take a quick look at the details of the loans you set up in Quicken? Hop over to the View Loans window, where all at once you can see the principal, payment amount, interest rate, and term for every loan you have, make changes in the loan information, edit the payment details, order up a payment, and see and print a complete payment schedule. Talk about full service!

To open the View Loans window, choose Loans from the Property & Debt menu, or press Ctrl+H.

When you click Loans (or do a Ctrl+H), the View Loans window appears. If you've already set up a loan in Quicken, the information about that loan is accessible in this window. If you have not set up any loans yet, don't bother with this because there's nothing to see in this window.

Choose the loan whose details you want to view by clicking the Choose Loan drop-down list at the top of the window and clicking on the appropriate loan.

The Loan Summary tab shows the date you entered for the start of the loan, the loan's opening balance, your payment amount, the term, and the interest rate.

Click the Payment Schedule tab to see your complete payment schedule, otherwise known as your *amortization schedule*. This schedule shows all of your payments, the due dates, and the breakdown of principal and interest.

The payment amount on the loan payment schedule only reflects principal and interest. If your loan payment includes other amounts, such as property tax or homeowner's insurance, those amounts are not reflected in the table.

Click the Payment Graph if you are interested in seeing a line graph representing the amount of principal and interest you have paid and will pay on the loan.

Use the buttons on the right side of the window to make changes in the loan or payment information, make a payment, or change the interest rate. These features are described in the section later in this chapter called, "Making changes in your loan."

When the Set Up Loan Payment window materializes, follow these steps to set up your loan payment.

1. **Make sure the interest rate and the loan payment amount are correct.**

   If necessary, you can edit the interest and loan payment amounts while you're hanging around in the loan payment setup window. But these amounts come from the loan setup information, so they are probably correct.

2. **Enter other amounts that are part of your loan payment.**

   Here's where you get to enter the homeowner's insurance, private mortgage insurance (PMI), and real estate tax, and any other payments that you make with your regular loan payment. Click the little Edit button if you need to add additional payment information. A Split Transaction window appears. You can list each additional expense that is part of your loan payment, and then click OK to close the window and return to the setup window.

   Private Mortgage Insurance, known to its friends as PMI, is an insurance payment that your lender tacks on to your mortgage payments when your down payment is less than 20 percent of the purchase price or appraised value of your home. The lender's concern is that if you default on your loan, the lender may not be able to sell the house for enough to recoup the entire loan. Thus, the insurance is there to protect the lender. As soon as you've paid enough so that your remaining mortgage balance is under the 20 percent of value threshold, you can request that the PMI payments be terminated.

3. **Select the payment type.**

   In the Type field (see Figure 1-4), choose between Payment (you write the check, and then enter it in Quicken), Print Check (issue and print a check within Quicken), and Online Pmt (online payment).

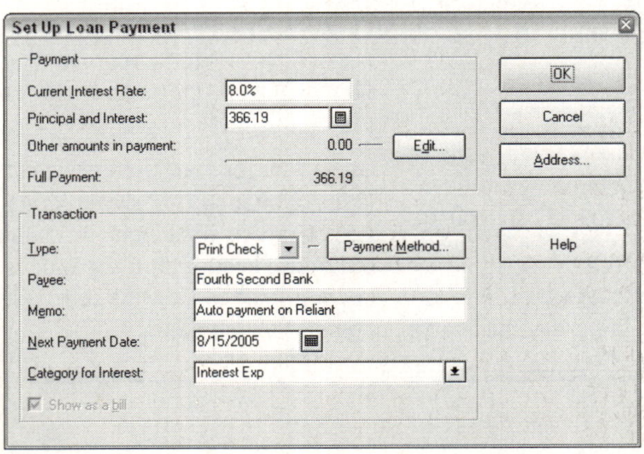

Figure 1-4: Enter information about your loan payments.

4. **Set up a scheduled payment (optional).**

   If you are interested in automating the payment process, now's your chance. (If you are not going to use the scheduled payment feature, skip to step 5.) Click on the Payment Method button. The Select Payment Method window appears.

   - Click on Scheduled Transaction.
   - In the Register Entry field, identify when or how you want Quicken to enter this transaction in your register. Prompt Before Entering means you receive an alert telling you Quicken is ready to enter this transaction. Automatically Enter means you don't have to take any action at all to have Quicken automatically enter the transaction in your register.
   - Choose the account from which the payment is to be made.
   - Indicate how many days before the due date you want Quicken to prompt you or to enter this transaction. Then click OK.

5. **Enter the name of the payee.**
6. **Enter an optional memo.**
7. **Enter the date of the next payment.**
8. **Enter the category where you want Quicken to enter your interest expense.**
9. **Enter an address for automatic payments.**

   If Quicken is to issue a check for this payment, click the Address button and verify the name and enter the address of the payee.

   You can click the Pay Now button if you're anxious to get a payment made right away. Otherwise, click the OK button and the Set Up Loan Payment window closes.

You now have an opportunity to enter asset information to go with this loan. Remember? This is the property part of the Property & Debt center. Clicking Yes in the box shown in Figure 1-5 takes you to the Account Setup window, where you enter the name of the asset, the date you acquired the asset, and the cost.

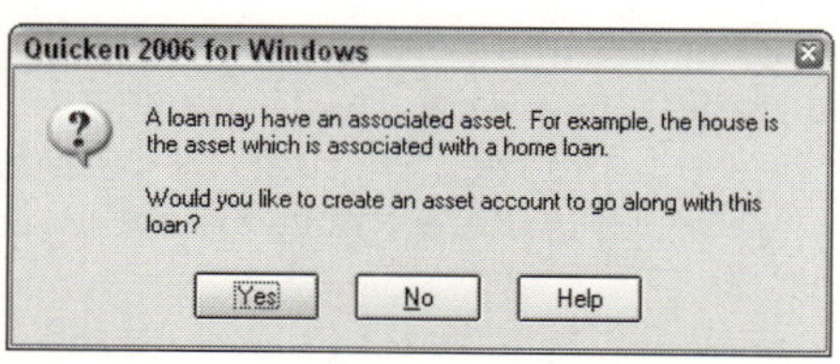

Figure 1-5: Click Yes to enter an asset and link that asset to this loan.

Personally, I prefer not to associate an asset with a loan *at the time I'm setting up the loan*. Here's why. When you agree to associate an asset with the loan, you get to enter the name of the asset, the date acquired, and the cost. If instead, you wait and click Add Account in the Property & Debt Center, you get to add more detailed information. For example, if you're setting up a car in Quicken, you get to enter information like the make and model and year. And you still get to associate the car with the loan. Maybe it doesn't matter which way you enter the asset; it's just my personal preference to set up the asset separately.

Making changes in your loan

Here are a few reasons why you might want to make changes to your loan:

- You made a mistake with the original information you entered.
- The interest rate has changed.
- The loan was sold or turned over to a new financial institution, so you need to change the name of the payee.
- You decide to make a change in the way in which you've been paying the loan. For example, maybe you want more notice before the payment is posted to your Quicken register, or maybe you want to switch from writing checks to automatic payments.

It's easy to change your loan information:

1. **Click on the Property & Debt Center.**
2. **Scroll down to the Loan Accounts Summary section so that you can see the loan you want to edit.**
3. **Right-click on the loan and choose Edit This Loan from the pop-up menu.**

   Be sure to right-click on the loan as it appears in the Loan Accounts Summary and not the loan that appears in your Debt (Liabilities) summary. Even though the two items represent the same loan, you don't get to edit as many facets of the loan if you choose the loan account in the Debt section.
4. **On the screen that appears, you can change any of the information about the loan.**

   If you need to change the current balance of the loan, click on the loan's hyperlink in the Property & Debt center. The loan register appears. You can click on the Overview tab and then click on the Current Balance. A window appears (see Figure 1-6), where you can make an adjustment to the current balance.

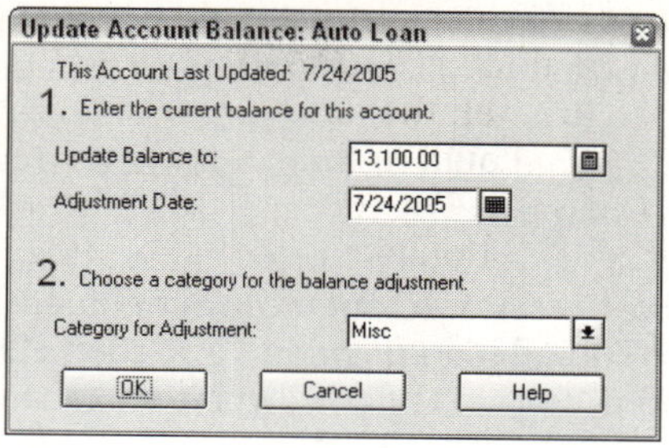

Figure 1-6: Enter the corrected amount for the loan balance.

If you're changing the loan's current balance, enter the new amount as a positive number, even though the loan amount actually appears on the Overview tab as a negative number.

The last payment: Removing a loan from Quicken

It's not unusual for the last payment of a loan to be slightly different from the rest of the payments you've made. Either there is a slight rounding difference on the last payment, or perhaps you want to consolidate the last couple of payments and get the loan over with.

You can change the amount of your loan payment by clicking on the Make a Payment button in the Loan Accounts Summary section of the Property & Debt Center. When the View Loans window appears, click the Edit Payment button.

When the Edit Loan Payment window appears (Figure 1-7), enter the amount of your payment. If you're ready to make the payment now, click Pay Now. Verify the amount and the bank account you are using, and then click OK to record the payment.

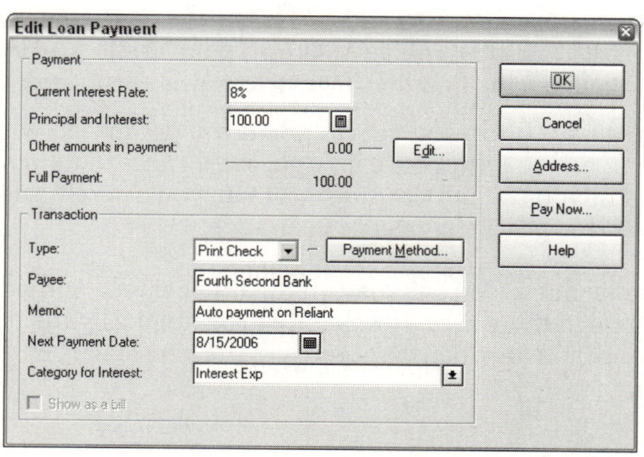

Figure 1-7: Never mind what Quicken wants you to pay. Enter the amount you want to pay in the Principal and Interest field.

If you want to pay later instead, click OK in the Edit Loan Payment window and the amount you entered takes the place of your next scheduled payment.

There's no need to remove the paid-off loan from your account list. Quicken takes care of zeroing out the loan balance.

After you've paid off your loan, be sure to open the Scheduled Transactions List (Ctrl+J), click on the scheduled loan payment, and then click the Delete button at the top of the screen, so that Quicken won't make any more payments on your behalf!

More loan fun: Refinancing your loan

It's not uncommon for people to refinance their loans. Usually it's mortgages that are refinanced. Often the reason for refinancing is the opportunity to lock in a lower interest rate and produce lower monthly payments. Here are some other reasons for refinancing:

- When you have accumulated equity in your home, you can refinance to increase your loan and borrow some of the home's equity as cash.
- If you have an adjustable interest rate on your home and want to lock in a fixed rate, you can refinance at a fixed interest rate.
- Some people refinance their home loan as a means of consolidating debt. They borrow more against their home and use that money to pay off other debts.
- Although you can usually make extra payments on a loan in order to pay the loan off sooner, you can also refinance and restructure the loan so that it is payable in a shorter time period. Lenders sometimes offer a reduced interest rate if you reduce the term of the loan when you refinance.
- If your credit wasn't stellar when you first borrowed money, you probably had to agree to a higher interest rate than you might have with better credit. But after you've built up a good credit history, you can look into refinancing in order to get a lower interest rate.
- You might have borrowed heavily when you purchased your home and as a result had to pay private mortgage insurance. If now you have more money that you can put down with a loan, you can refinance and do away with the private mortgage insurance.

When you refinance a loan, you pay off the original loan and borrow a new loan. Even though there are two separate loans, typically the transaction is all done at once; the old loan is retired and the new loan is entered into in one session.

In Quicken, you need to transfer the balance of the old loan into the new loan in order to record the refinancing property. Here's how it's done:

1. **Choose Loans from the Property & Debt menu, or press Ctrl+H.**

   The View Loans window appears.

2. **Click the New button.**

   The Loan Setup wizard appears onscreen, ready for you to enter the information about your new loan. Be sure to have all of your loan documentation with you so you can fill in the blanks properly.

3. **Enter the information about your new loan, just as you did in the section, "Adding a loan," earlier in this chapter.**

   Don't bother trying to attach your asset to this new loan at this time. For example, if you are refinancing a mortgage loan, your house is already tied to the previous mortgage loan and, in this screen, Quicken won't let you tie the same asset to two loans. Be patient. You link the loan and the house together in a few more steps.

4. **After your loan is added, go to the Property & Debt center and click on the new loan.**

   The register for that loan appears.

5. **Go to the split screen for the new loan's opening balance.**

   Click on the opening balance transaction in the new loan's register (the first transaction). If you see the Split button, click it. If you've turned off the use of these buttons, press Ctrl+S to open the Split Transaction window.

   TIP: If those Enter/Edit/Split buttons bug you (or if you wonder where they went), control their appearance by choosing Preferences from the Edit menu, and then choosing Quicken Program. Click the Register option on the left side of the Quicken Preferences window, and then either check or uncheck the box for Show Transaction Toolbar.

6. **Enter the breakdown of how the new loan money is distributed, as shown in Figure 1-8.**

   Enter the payoff amount for the old loan and enter any other expenses you paid at the refinancing meeting, such as loan interest or other fees. If you received cash, enter the amount you received and the account where it was deposited. When all amounts have been added (you'll see that the Remainder amount at the bottom of the window has turned to zero), click OK to close the Split Transaction window.

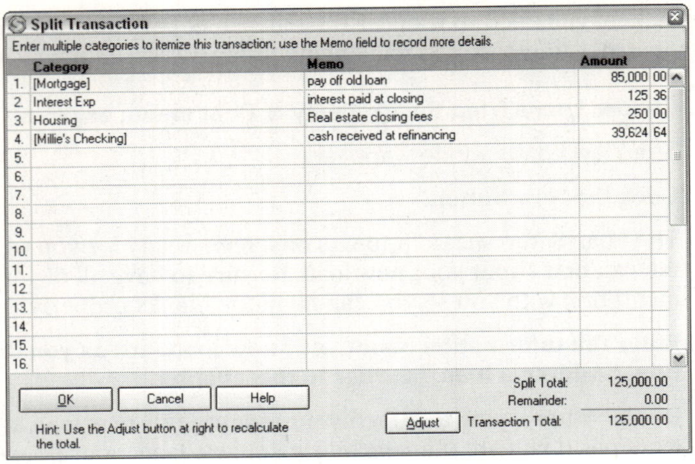

Figure 1-8: Enter the detail of how your new loan money was disbursed.

Don't forget to record the transaction by pressing or clicking Enter. Until you record the transaction, none of the amounts get disbursed to the appropriate categories.

7. **Return to the Property & Debt Center.**

   Now you can see that the old mortgage balance has been replaced with a zero. You could delete this mortgage, but because there are transactions associated with the old mortgage, I recommend keeping it around. By leaving the zero-ed out mortgage on the list of loans, you can always click on that old mortgage and see the detail of all of your previous transactions. You never know when you'll need to look up an old transaction.

8. **Attach your asset to the new loan.**

   Because the example I'm using here is a mortgage refinancing, we need to attach the house to the new mortgage. Here's how:

   1. Open the Account List by pressing Ctrl+A.
   2. Click on your new loan.
   3. Click the Edit button at the top of the Account List.
   4. Click the drop-down arrow next to the Linked Asset Account field (see Figure 1-9).
   5. Choose the house that should be attached to this loan.
   6. Click OK.

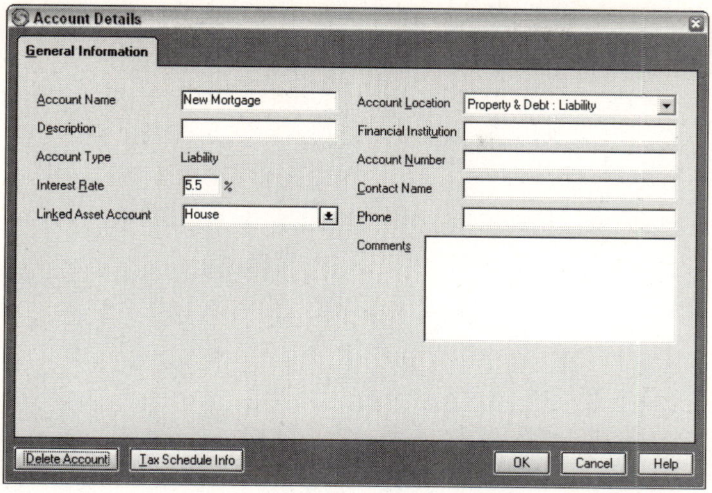

Figure 1-9: Link your house to your new mortgage loan.

Using Quicken's Loan Calculator

I love the loan calculator. I use it any time I'm thinking about borrowing money for any reason. Sometimes I just use it for fun. You can enter any type of loan scenario and Quicken tells you how much your payments are going to be, how long it is going to take you to pay off a loan, and how much interest you are going to pay. You can print out an amortization schedule showing the detail of all of your payments. This is a wonderful tool and it's really easy to use.

Here's how the loan calculator works:

1. **Go to the Planning menu and choose Financial Calculators⇨Loan Calculator.**
2. **Decide if you want Quicken to tell you how much you can afford to borrow (Loan Amount) or how much your payments will be (Payment Per Period).**

   Click the appropriate option in the Calculate For area of the Loan Calculator window (see Figure 1-10). For this example, I've indicated that I want Quicken to calculate the payment for me.
3. **Fill in the blanks, entering the amount you want to borrow, the interest rate, the number of years and number of payments per year, and how interest is to be compounded.**

   For this example, I've indicated that I want to borrow $5,000 and pay it back monthly over four years, with monthly compounding. Quicken tells me I can expect to pay $122.06 per month.

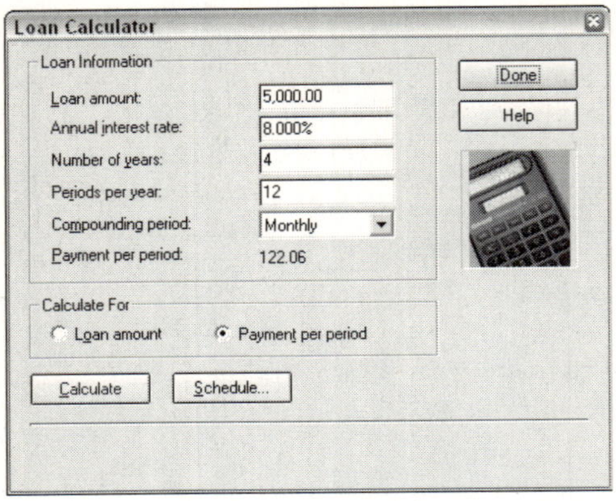

Figure 1-10: Click on one of the Calculate For options, and then fill in the blanks to have Quicken tell you what to expect from the money you borrow.

Click the Calculate button to have Quicken recalculate the loan when you make a change in one of the fields. Actually, all you have to do is make your change, and click in any other field, and Quicken automatically recalculates the loan information.

4. **View the details of your loan by clicking on the Schedule button.**

   A payment schedule appears as shown in Figure 1-11, displaying the breakdown of the payments you would make to pay back this hypothetical loan.

5. **When the payment schedule is displayed, click Print in the top-left corner of the schedule to print a paper copy of the required payments.**

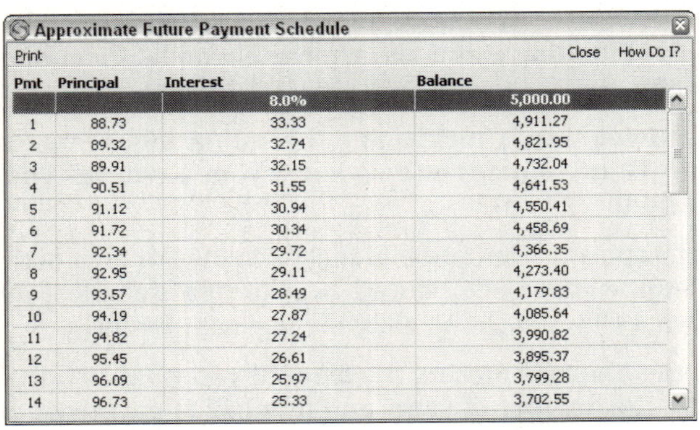

Pmt	Principal	Interest	Balance
		8.0%	5,000.00
1	88.73	33.33	4,911.27
2	89.32	32.74	4,821.95
3	89.91	32.15	4,732.04
4	90.51	31.55	4,641.53
5	91.12	30.94	4,550.41
6	91.72	30.34	4,458.69
7	92.34	29.72	4,366.35
8	92.95	29.11	4,273.40
9	93.57	28.49	4,179.83
10	94.19	27.87	4,085.64
11	94.82	27.24	3,990.82
12	95.45	26.61	3,895.37
13	96.09	25.97	3,799.28
14	96.73	25.33	3,702.55

Figure 1-11: Quicken calculates the principal and interest portion of each payment for the entire term of the loan.

TIP: Quicken's little payment schedule doesn't include totals. But it's an easy task to determine how much the total interest burden is going to be on the loan. For this example, Quicken already told us we're to pay back $122.06 per month for 48 months. Multiply that payback amount by 48 and you get $5,858.88. Subtract the principal, $5,000, and you're left with $858.88. That's how much interest you'll pay on this particular loan.

Now, switch the scenario. This time, say you know you can afford to pay $200 per month for four years, and you'd like to know how much you can afford to borrow at 8 percent. Change the Calculate For field to Loan Amount, and fill in the blanks, as shown in Figure 1-12. The calculated amount you can borrow is $8,192.38.

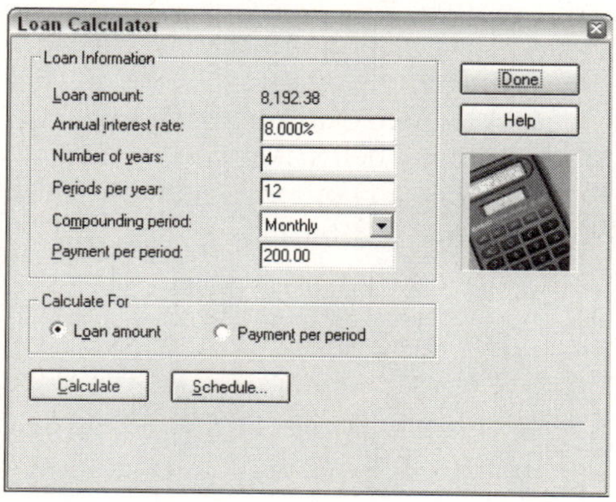

Figure 1-12: Quicken says you can afford to borrow $8,192.38.

Pull up the loan calculator any time you're contemplating borrowing money. Quicken can help you figure out what you can borrow and what you have to pay, so you won't have any surprises when you visit the lender.

TIP: The Loan Calculator works both ways. Not only can you use this tool to help figure out your own borrowing needs, but you can also use the calculator to determine the correct payback amount if you're contemplating loaning money to someone else. You can then print the payment schedule so your borrower has the detail supporting all of the payments.

Chapter 2: Using a Credit Card Account

In This Chapter

- ✔ **Recording credit card activity**
- ✔ **Reconciling your credit card account**
- ✔ **Making credit card payments**
- ✔ **Setting credit alerts**

It's the rare wallet that doesn't contain a credit card, and we find it difficult to imagine life without credit. But credit cards have only been in existence for a short while. The first credit card was created in 1950 — a Diners Club card. Prior to that time, people still bought furniture and took trips and ate meals in restaurants and rented cars and did all the other things they can do today with credit cards (except maybe open locked doors), and somehow everyone seemed to manage. Today, credit cards are a part of your personal financial picture and should be accounted for just like your bank accounts. In this chapter, you find out how easy it is to keep track of your credit card charges in Quicken.

Setting Up Your Credit Card

Before you can start monitoring your credit card charges in Quicken, you must first set up the credit card account. With the account in place, you can then track all of your transactions, thus helping you keep track of your charge expenditures and also making your reports more complete and accurate. When your credit card statement comes in the mail, it's easy to balance the statement and compare your statement activity with the activity you've recorded in Quicken.

See Book II, Chapter 3 for step-by-step instructions for setting up any credit card in Quicken.

You might choose to acquire a Quicken credit card, a card issued by Citibank for Intuit customers. See "Applying for a Quicken credit card" below for more information on this option.

Applying for a Quicken credit card

Some credit card companies cooperate with Quicken and allow you access to your statement online. Or, you can just get your credit card from Quicken and ensure that all of the online access is in place.

Quicken credit card users enjoy the ability to pay their credit card bills online, view their credit card statements including transactions that have not yet been billed, confirm their balance, and download their credit card information directly into Quicken.

As an incentive, Quicken offers a zero annual percentage rate for the first six months on new Quicken credit cards.

The application process is easy and can be initiated right from Quicken. You get an instant response. To apply for a Quicken credit card, choose Online⇨Quicken Credit Card⇨Apply Online Now. Quicken connects to the Internet and opens a window that displays the terms of their credit card. Fill out the form and submit it online.

Tracking Your Credit Card Charges in Quicken

Tracking the charges you make on your credit card is easy and fun! At least, it's pretty easy as long as you hold on to your credit card receipts, and it's even fun if you're the sort of person who rolls your socks together in matching pairs instead of just tossing them all into the sock drawer without mates.

To enter your credit card charges in Quicken as you make the charges, you need a method for transferring information from your charge receipts to your Quicken account. This is an easy task if you have a manageable number of charge receipts. Here are some suggestions for simplifying the task of entering charge receipts in Quicken:

- As you collect charge receipts, save them all in the same place, such as your billfold, a box or basket on your desk, a manila folder or envelope. Try to avoid using the vast array of less organized places such as car glove compartments, pockets in jackets and other clothing, purses, backpacks, and so on. It's easier to retrieve receipts if you have a specific credit card receipt place.
- At the end of each day, or once a week, or whenever it works best in your schedule (schedule is the operative word), enter all of your receipts in your Quicken credit card register. In the best of all worlds, you should then hold on to your receipts until the statement arrives in case there are any discrepancies. Discrepancies might not happen often, but it's not impossible that the restaurant cashier misread the handwritten tip you wrote on a restaurant receipt. It's also possible you might need to return an item, and receipts always come in handy in those situations.

✦ At the very least, before you toss a credit card receipt or before you forget that you made a charge, enter the charge in Quicken so you'll have a record of the charge.

✦ Or, none of the above. If you prefer, you can just wait until your credit card statement arrives and enter all the charges right off your statement into Quicken without double-checking the charges against the actual receipts. I don't recommend this method, but it does work. Note that I'm not advocating the method of simply recording your credit card payments as credit card expenses without breaking out the expenses to their appropriate categories. It's impossible to budget properly or monitor your spending in any of your spending categories if you simply account for the credit card expense as a miscellaneous expense.

When you enter your charge receipts in Quicken, the amounts you enter are immediately incorporated into any reports that you produce, if those reports include your credit card expenses. So, if you enter charges when they occur, even if you haven't gotten your credit card bill yet, when you produce a report of your restaurant expenses for the month or your automobile gas expenses, your information is completely current including all the latest charges.

Enter your current charge receipts in Quicken by following these steps:

1. **Open the register for your credit card.**

   Press Ctrl+A to display the Account List. Then double-click on the credit card name (or click once on the account name and click the Go To option at the top of the Account List) to display the register. Note: This step assumes you have already set up your credit card account in Quicken.

2. **Enter the date of your first charge.**

   Either type the date in mmddyy format (Quicken automatically inserts slashes), or click the little calendar to the right of the date field and then click on a date to select it. You can also use the keyboard shortcuts (described in Book II, Chapter 1) to speed up the date entry. Press Tab to move to the next field.

   It doesn't matter if you enter your credit card charges out of order. Quicken automatically re-sorts the register in date order as you make your entries.

3. **Enter an optional reference.**

   In the field marked Ref, you can enter a reference of your choice, up to twelve characters, letters or numbers accepted. Or you can leave the field blank.

4. **Enter the Payee in the Payee field.**

   Payee is the name of the business that accepted your charge. Usually the name is printed somewhere on the charge receipt.

   Sometimes the name of the payee has nothing to do with the name of the place where you thought you were making the charge, which can make it difficult to reconcile your account when you get a statement that shows you made a purchase at Senator Sam's Exports and you actually bought tickets to the Celtics game. Keeping your receipts at least until your statement arrives is one way to make sure the amounts you charged are the same amounts that appear on your statement.

5. **Enter the charge amount.**

   As you can see in Figure 2-1, there are two amount columns in your credit card register: Charge and Payment. The Charge column is where you enter amounts you've charged on your card. If you receive a credit or refund on your credit card, that amount goes in the Payment column, as do any payments you make.

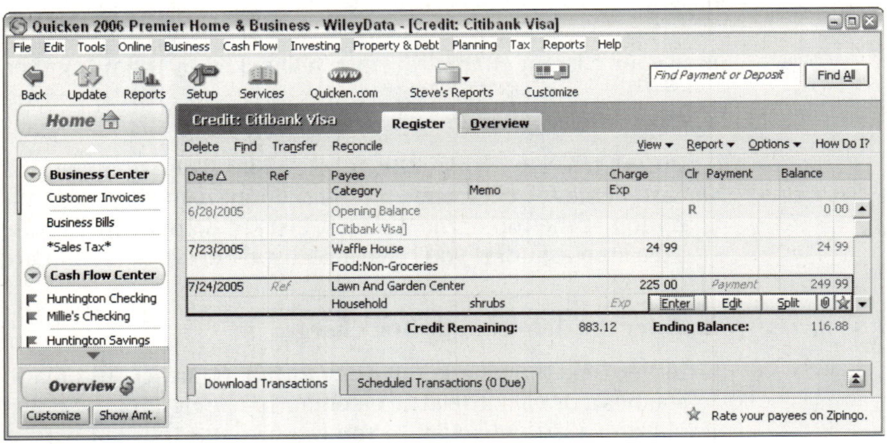

Figure 2-1: Enter amounts in the Charge column.

6. **Enter the category.**

   Each charge needs to be associated with a category. That way, Quicken knows where to classify the amount when preparing reports. Choose the category that is most appropriate, and create a new category if you can't find a category that describes this charge (see in Book II, Chapter 1 for more on how). If your charge is for amounts that should be recorded in multiple categories, use the Split Category feature (Ctrl+S) to list each of the charge amounts and their respective categories.

TIP: The categories you set up in one account are accessible by all of your Quicken accounts, so when you display your category list or begin typing a category name, you see that a category you've used before is available to you now as well. The same goes for payees — the QuickFill feature fills in the name of a payee you've encountered in a different account as soon as you begin typing the payee name.

7. **Enter a description.**

   Some expenses are obvious and a description isn't necessary. But for certain expenses, such as those where the reason for the charge isn't obvious, or for tax-related charges where you want to record information that will be useful in your tax return preparation, you can enter a short memo description with information about the charge.

8. **Click or press Enter to record the transaction.**

   Note: Your credit card account carries a negative balance because this is an amount you owe instead of an amount you own, so don't be alarmed when you see the red number in the balance column.

TIP: If you're the type of person who likes to keep your receipts for longer than just the current billing cycle, consider setting up a place where you can store an envelope or file folder for each month's receipts, or staple the receipts for one month on a piece of paper, and then file the paper or envelope with the credit card statement for that month.

Tracking your debit card charges in Quicken

Debit cards look just like credit cards, and most of the time they are used just like credit cards. The big difference between debit cards and credit cards is that amounts charged on your debit card are applied immediately to the balance in your bank account, and you don't have to pay against an invoice from the credit card company each month.

Instead of getting a separate statement from a credit card company, your debit card charges are recorded on your regular bank statement, ready to be reconciled each month along with the rest of your bank account activity.

If you use a debit card and if you are the type of person who is very detail-oriented, you probably like to enter in Quicken each debit card charge you make, as soon as you make it. By entering your transactions in a timely manner, your checking account balance in Quicken is always accurate.

Debit charges reduce your bank account balance as soon as you make the charge, so while you might use the card in a fashion similar to the way in which you use your credit card, the debit card is actually an extension of your checking account. When you reconcile your checking account, you must include your debit card activity.

You must save the receipts that support expenses you plan to deduct on your income tax return. Be sure to write pertinent information on the back of the receipt or on the paper to which the receipt is stapled. Information such as explanation of the charge, business purpose, and the name of the person you were with will help you justify the deduction should a tax authority examine your tax return.

Balancing Your Credit Card Account

Each month, you receive a statement from the credit card company showing you all of the charges you made during the month, any payments you made within the last month, and the amount of finance charge that the credit card company has assessed against you.

It is your job to balance this credit card statement, comparing your actual charges to the credit card charges and entering the information in Quicken.

When you get your statement in the mail, you should begin the reconciliation process by first making sure that you have entered all of the credit card charges that you made in the past month into your credit card register, as described earlier in this chapter. Having all of your charge information already entered in your Quicken register speeds up the reconciliation process considerably.

To balance (reconcile) your credit card account when your statement arrives, follow these steps:

1. **Open your credit card register in Quicken and open the reconciliation window.**

   Go to the Account List by pressing Ctrl+A, and then double-click on the credit card account for which you have received a statement. The account register appears. Click the Reconcile button at the top, and the Statement Summary window appears (see Figure 2-2).

2. **Fill in the blanks, entering the amounts from your credit card statement.**

   Notice that you are required to enter amounts in all of the fields — Quicken won't let you leave blanks. If your statement doesn't reflect any charges or if you didn't make a payment last month, those amounts are zero on your statement and you should enter corresponding zeros in the reconciliation window.

3. **Click OK to proceed to the main reconciliation window.**

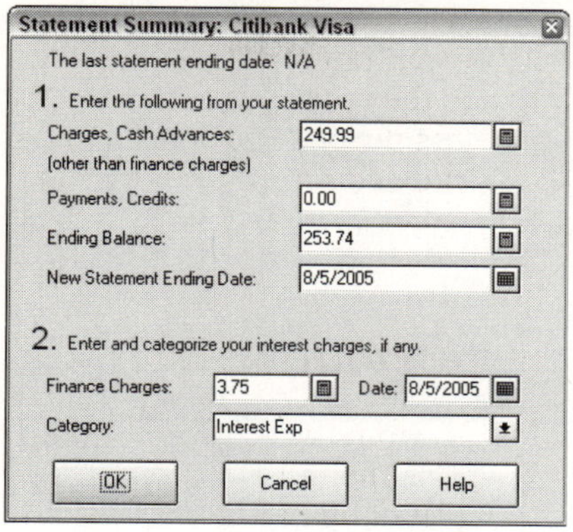

Figure 2-2: Enter information from your credit card statement.

4. **Check off all charges that match the charges on your statement.**

   The charges listed on the main reconciliation window are the charges you listed in your Quicken register. If you haven't listed any charges in your register, nothing is listed in this window. Click on a charge to indicate a match. A checkmark appears in the Clr column. You can also arrow to the charge and press Enter to check off the item.

5. **Correct any discrepancies.**

   The charge you listed in your Quicken register might not agree with the charge that appears on the statement. If the amounts differ, first determine which amount is correct. Don't automatically assume the statement is right — here's where it's really useful to go back to your charge receipt and verify the amount that you authorized. If you entered an amount in your register incorrectly, you can easily change your amount by clicking on the item in the register and then clicking the Edit option at the top of the reconciliation window.

6. **Edit a transaction.**

   When you get back to the register, enter the correct amount. If you use the transaction toolbar in the register, you can click the Return to Reconcile option, as you can see in Figure 2-3. Click Yes when asked if you want to save the transaction. If you have turned off the transaction toolbar, press Enter to save your changes, and then you can click the Statement Summary button at the bottom of your register window, or the Reconcile button at the top. Either one gets you back to the business of reconciling.

TIP

You might have entered a charge transaction twice in your register. If you see a duplicate entry when you're reconciling, click on one of the duplicate entries, and then click the Delete button at the top of the reconciliation window. Click Yes in the window that appears to confirm that you want to delete the transaction. Bye-bye, duplicate transaction.

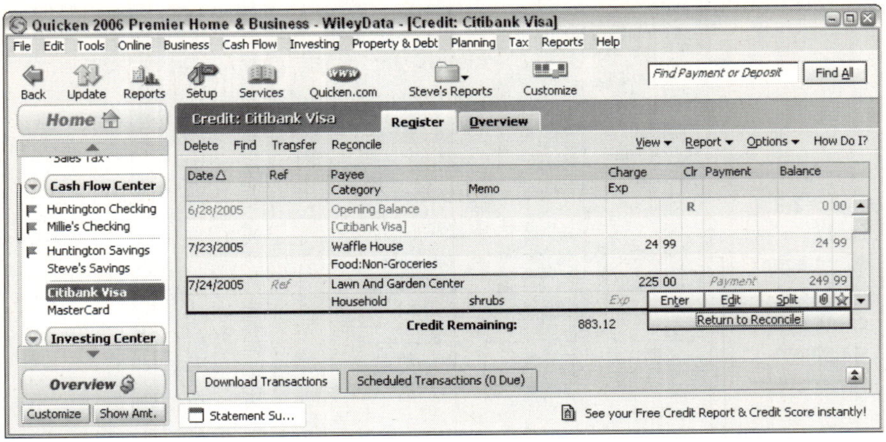

Figure 2-3: Quicken gives you a button for a quick return to the reconciliation.

7. **Continue matching your recorded activity to the statement.**

   Match the rest of your charges and any payments you made or credits you received, until everything on the statement has been checked off. If some items on the statement weren't recorded in your Quicken register, click the New option to return to the register to enter additional transactions. Your goal is to get to a difference of zero at the bottom-right corner of the reconciliation window (see Figure 2-4).

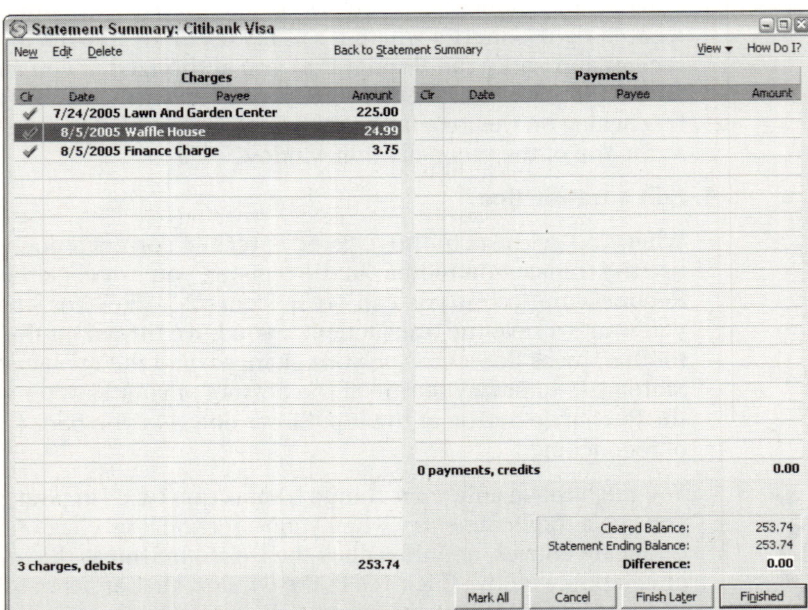

Figure 2-4: A zero difference means you've finished the reconciliation.

8. **Complete the reconciliation.**

   Click Finished when you're done matching all the items in your reconciliation. Click Finish Later if you're not done but you have to cut out. Click Cancel if you want to close the reconciliation and not save any of the checkmarks you entered. When you return, you have to start over again.

9. **Indicate if you want to make a credit card payment.**

   When the credit card reconciliation is complete, a window appears (Figure 2-5) giving you the opportunity to make or record a payment. Click No if you're not interested. If you're ready to make a payment, first indicate from which account the money is to be drawn. Then choose whether you plan to print a check in Quicken, write a check by hand, or make an online payment (the online option only works if your account is set up for online activity). Click Yes when you've entered your choices.

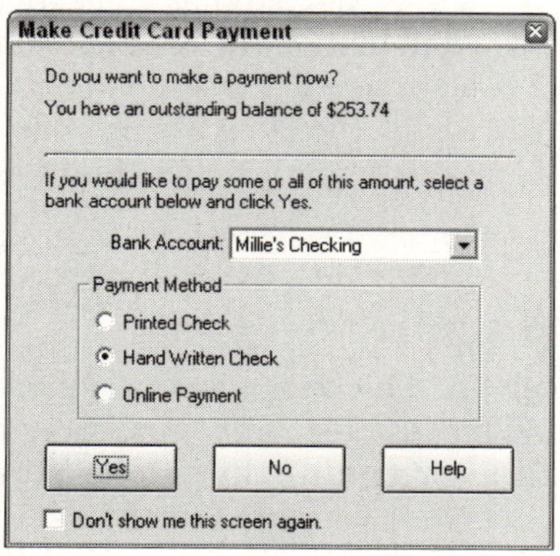

Figure 2-5: Time to pay the piper.

10. **Fix the payment amount.**

    Quicken automatically assumes you're going to pay the entire amount. So when your register appears showing the amount of the check you're going to write by hand, or when a check window appears showing the amount of the check you're going to write in Quicken, or when an online payment window appears showing the amount you're going to transfer from your bank account, *double-check the amount* and make any necessary corrections. When you're certain the amount is correct, record the transaction.

WARNING!

Be careful when recording credit card payments, especially where electronic payments are concerned. If you click mindlessly, you might find yourself paying off the entire balance of your credit card even though you only meant to make a minimum payment.

Borrowing money from your credit card

Credit card companies are not just in the business of fronting the money for your charges. Often these companies send loan offers in the mail, in the form of blank checks that you can write as if they are your own personal checks — except that you don't have to worry about having the money. (No, seriously, you *do* have to worry about having the money to cover the credit card checks — just not today.)

Writing a check from your credit card is like making another charge. The amount should be recorded in the charge column of your register, just as if you were paying for a bucket of chicken or a car rental.

TIP

And speaking of car rentals, sometimes when you make certain types of charges, you are required to record a deposit. For example, you might rent a car and the car rental company charges your credit card for a $150 deposit. Be sure to set up a category to track deposits, so that you can monitor them and make sure the money is returned to you. In the case of a car rental, the deposit should be credited back to your account when you return the car, or applied as a price reduction to the rental. By categorizing your deposits in a separate account, you're more likely to remember them and follow up on any deposits not reimbursed.

Changing your credit limit

The better a customer you are (defined by credit card companies as someone who carries lots of credit and makes at least the minimum payment but not much more than that on time each month), the more likely it is that the credit card company is going to increase your credit limit.

You can, of course, choose to use this new higher credit limit, or you can continue operating as if the old credit limit is still in force. If you decide to tell Quicken about the new limit, and thus avoid getting disturbing little messages telling you you've overspent your limit, you can enter the new limit in your Quicken program by following these easy steps:

1. **Open the account list (Ctrl+A) and click once on your credit card account to select the account.**
2. **Click the Edit button at the top of the window, and the Account Details window appears (see Figure 2-6).**

   Alternatively, you can click the Edit Account button.

Credit cards and finance charges

Some credit card companies offer lower interest rates if you transfer balances from another credit card to a new account. And if you write a check to borrow cash against your credit card, that amount can often be borrowed at a rate different — and usually higher — from the interest assessed on your regular charge activity.

Trying to figure out the calculation of your finance charge on your monthly statement can turn into a regular nightmare when two or three interest rates are in use.

And here are some other finance charge issues to keep in mind. Each credit card company has different terms, so get out the magnifying glass and read the fine print. Here are some details you might see:

- **Penalties for late payments:** Don't miss the due date or your credit card company might assess another finance charge in addition to the regular interest you pay on unpaid balances. And it's not just your credit card payment that you have to make on time. If you make a late payment on your mortgage, your car loan, or any other debt that appears on your credit report, that can trigger an increase in your finance charge rate by your credit card company.
- **Minimum charge:** Some credit cards assess a minimum finance charge even if you pay your balance on time every month.
- **Extra fees for exceeding credit limit:** The credit limit is your ceiling. Go up on the roof with your charges and you might get hit with additional finance charges.
- **How your payment is applied:** If you have different interest rates in force for different amounts owing on your credit card, the credit card company will probably apply your payments to the amounts with the lowest interest rate first, keeping the higher rate compounding longer on the other charges. One way to avoid this lack of control over how your payments are applied is to use different credit cards for different types of credit; that way, if you want to make extra payments, you can target the card with the highest interest rate.
- **Increasing rates:** Credit card companies have the right to raise your rate if you don't behave the way they want you to. If you make a late payment, exceed the credit limit, don't pay the minimum amount, or get caught serving red wine with fish, they might increase the rate of your finance charge.
- **Your credit report comes into play:** Credit card companies can periodically check your credit report to see how well you do with other forms of credit. Events that can lower your overall credit score, such as liens and garnishments, bankruptcy, excess or unpaid debt, can also trigger an increase in your credit card finance charge rate.
- **Bad check:** Sending a bad check in payment for your credit card bill can result in a higher interest rate for you.
- **Acquiring a new credit card or loan:** That's right — the simple act of acquiring a new credit card or a mortgage or car loan can give your existing credit card company enough of a reason to raise your finance charge rate. Indeed, even inquiring about new debt can have a ripple effect and raise your finance charges on your existing credit cards.
- **Annual fees:** Don't forget the annual fee. Some credit cards charge you a fee just for the right to carry their card.

But wait! Don't let any of this keep you from determining that the correct finance charge has been assessed. You have the right to contact the credit card company and ask for the details of how the charge is assessed.

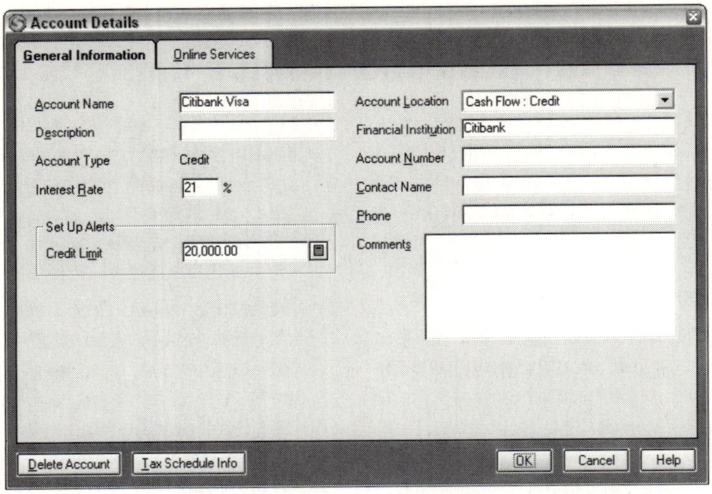

Figure 2-6: Enter a new credit limit.

Enter the new credit limit in the Credit Limit field. While you're here, you can enter your card's interest rate too (assuming you can figure out the rate — see the "Credit cards and finance charges" sidebar earlier in this chapter for an introduction into the dark world of computing finance charges).

3. **Click OK to close the window and return to the account list.**

Quicken Can Help You Put a Leash on Your Spending

OK, so the credit card company has generously upped your credit limit to $20,000. Does that mean you have to run up charges of $20,000? Of course not! You can keep track of your spending yourself, or you can get some assistance from Quicken.

First, you can simply enter a lower credit limit in Quicken instead of entering the full $20,000. This is done by editing the account and is described earlier in this chapter under "Changing your credit limit." Quicken sends you a message when you exceed your credit limit.

But why lie to Quicken? Go ahead and enter your real credit limit, but get Quicken to remind you when you reach your self-imposed limit. Ask for a credit card alert by following these steps:

1. **Open the Alerts Center by choosing Set Up Alerts from the Tools menu.**
2. **Click on the plus sign next to Cash Flow to expand the Cash Flow menu.**

3. **Click on Credit card limits.**
4. **Enter your own limit for your credit cards.**

   For each card you own, you see the name of the card, the card's credit limit, and an option to enter another amount in the column called Remind Me At (see Figure 2-7). Enter your own limit in the Remind Me At column.
5. **Choose how you want to be notified.**

   Your choices are to see an urgent alert box pop up on your screen, or to have an alert appear in your alert list.
6. **Indicate how long you want the alert to be in effect.**

   Pick from various time limit options up to one year. After a year, you need to set the alert again.
7. **Save your alert information by clicking OK.**

   Setting a spending alert doesn't prevent you from spending — you can still say "Thanks, but no thanks" to the alert (by clicking OK and closing the window shown in Figure 2-8) and go about your business of charging amounts on your credit card. The alert is just there as a reminder, so at least you're aware of the fact that you're getting in deep.

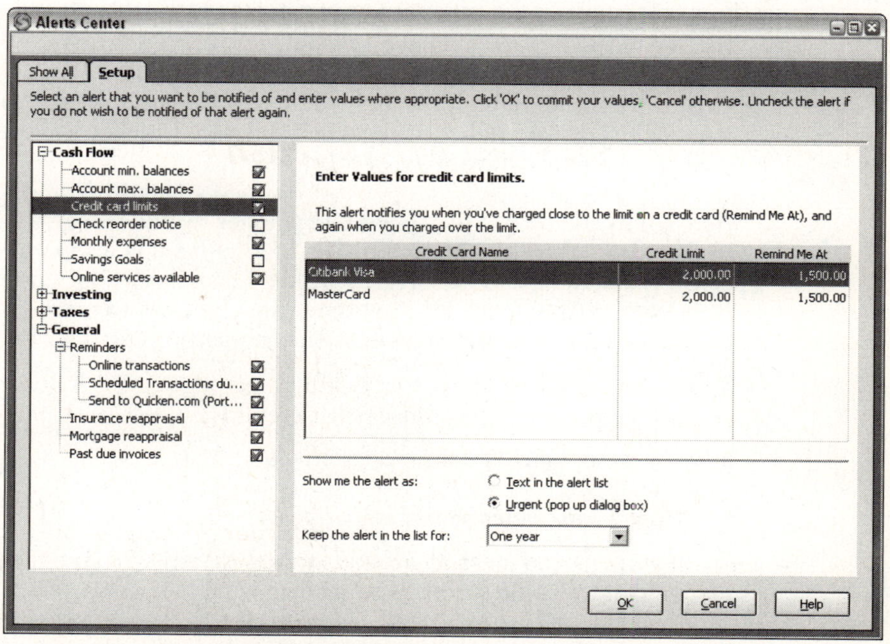

Figure 2-7: Set your own credit limits with alerts.

Figure 2-8: Quicken's reminder that you have reached your credit limit.

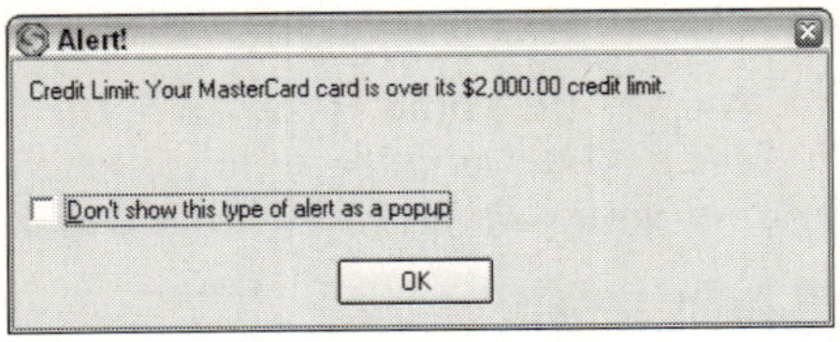

You can also monitor your spending by using budget alerts. Chapter 5 in this book shows you how to create and use a budget in Quicken and also how to set up budget-based alerts.

Quicken's Debt Reduction Planner

One of the most valuable tools in your Quicken program is the Debt Reduction Planner (DRP). The DRP can help you get control of and actually retire your debt, and at the same time, make sure you pay the least amount of interest. Use the DRP to design a plan that improves your debt situation by evaluating your debts and organizing them in such a way as to maximize the use of the money you have available for retiring debt.

Alas, the Debt Reduction Planner is not available in Quicken Basic. You must have Quicken Deluxe, Quicken Premier, or Quicken Premier Home & Business to take advantage of this feature.

Here's how the DRP works. Open the planner by choosing Debt Reduction Planner from the Planning menu. The DRP appears in a separate window. If you've used the DRP before, the window displays a chart and information from your existing plan. For first-time users, you get to make your way through a wizard, answering questions and settings up your debt reduction plan.

When the welcome screen appears (Figure 2-9), follow these steps to create your own customized debt reduction plan.

1. **Oops — no welcome screen appears.**

   If you've been messing around in the DRP already, you might not see the official welcome screen. That screen is just for new users. Click the New Plan button to begin a new plan (and get to the welcome screen).

Figure 2-9: Hello! Welcome to the Debt Reduction Planner!

2. **Pop some popcorn and watch a movie (optional step).**

   For a video presentation of how the DRP works, make sure your Quicken CD is inserted in your CD-ROM drive and click Next on the welcome screen. If you prefer to bypass the movie, click Next without the CD inserted in the CD-ROM drive, and you can get right down to business.

   P.S.: If you went the movie route, click Next when the movie ends to get on with the DRP.

3. **Review your debts.**

   Figure 2-10 shows an example of a debts list. The list of your debts appears under the heading, "How much do I owe?" Make sure all of your debts are listed, even that hundred bucks you owe your brother. All of your credit cards and loan amounts should appear here. If you've left off any debts, click the Add button to bring the list up-to-date.

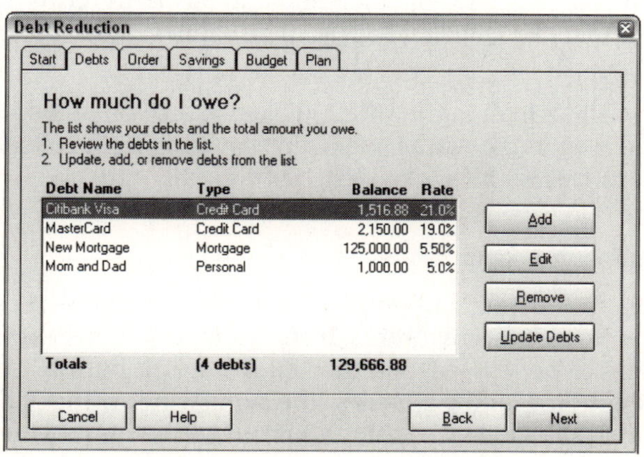

Figure 2-10: Quicken displays a summary of all of your debts.

4. **Add a debt.**

   When you click the Add button, the Edit Debt Reduction window appears (see Figure 2-11). Enter all the pertinent information about your loan, including the amount of the loan, the amount of your payments, and the interest rate. Click OK when you are finished.

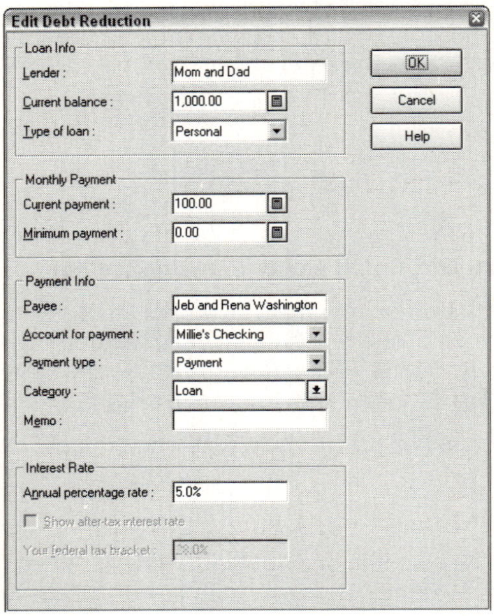

Figure 2-11: Entering information about your new loan.

Quicken requires that you enter amounts in every monetary field. You can't leave the payment and minimum payment fields empty, even if this is a casual loan with no specific minimum payment terms. Enter something, just to make Quicken happy, or you'll never get to close the window.

When you add a loan in the DRP, Quicken gives you an opportunity to set up the loan in the main Quicken program as well. Following the loan setup steps creates a Quicken loan without disrupting your progress in the DRP.

5. **Verify and revise your debts.**

   Make sure the correct amounts you owe appear on the debt list, along with their correct interest rates. If any changes are necessary, click on the debt to be revised, and then click the Edit button. The Edit Debt Reduction window appears (the same window that's displayed in Figure 2-11), showing everything Quicken knows about your loan. Enter any necessary corrections in the current payment amount, the annual interest rate, and make adjustments to payment information including the name of the payee, the account from which your payments are made, and how payments are made. For example:

- Payment: You write the check
- Write Check: Quicken writes the check
- Online Payment: Electronic transfer

Also, enter the category to which the payments are charged. Click OK when all the information is complete.

6. **Remove debts from DRP.**

   There might be old debts listed that you forgot were lurking around in Quicken, debts that were long ago paid off and not recorded in Quicken. Or there might be debts you want to exclude from the DRP because you plan to schedule those payments at your own pace. Click on a debt you want to remove, and then click the Remove button. The debt disappears from the DRP list, but never fear! The debt still exists within Quicken.

   If you need to remove a debt completely from Quicken, when you're no longer in the DRP, open Quicken's Account List, click on the debt you want to remove, and click the Delete button.

7. **Review your debt status.**

   Quicken gives you a mini-review of your current debt, your current minimum payments, and the year when your current debt will be liquidated. Click Next to continue.

8. **Adjust payment order.**

   Click Next in the DRP to get to the Order tab. Your debts are presented in the order of the most expensive debt first, the least expensive debt last. Expensive doesn't refer to the debt with the highest outstanding balance. Expensive in this case means the debt with the highest interest rate.

   Now you see why it's important to include the interest rate with each debt! If you skipped over step 4 earlier, click the Back button to return to the Debts tab and edit the debts that need an adjustment to the interest rate. Then click Next to continue.

   The order list is designed to expedite the payoff of debt in the order listed. A logical payoff method is to eliminate the most expensive debt first. However, this approach might not be appropriate for you. There might be loans you're committed to paying off first, or some debt you want to keep for a long time, even though the interest is higher than the interest on other debts. Click the Change Payment Order box, and then click Next if you want to change the order in which the debts are paid off.

9. **Examine optimized payment plan.**

   Quicken offers a payment plan that allows you to pay off the most expensive debt first, thus minimizing interest. Then you are to roll the payment from the debt you retired into the next debt, thus increasing your minimum payment on the next debt, and so on. In this way, you can speed up the extinguishment of all of your debt. Click Next after examining the plan.

10. **Apply savings to your debt.**

    If you have money in savings accounts, Quicken suggests you make a one-time payment out of savings to lower your debt. The accompanying video explains that saving money at a lower interest rate while paying debt at a higher rate isn't the most advantageous use of your money. If you choose to direct a one-time payment from savings toward your debt reduction, enter the amount in the field provided (see Figure 2-12).

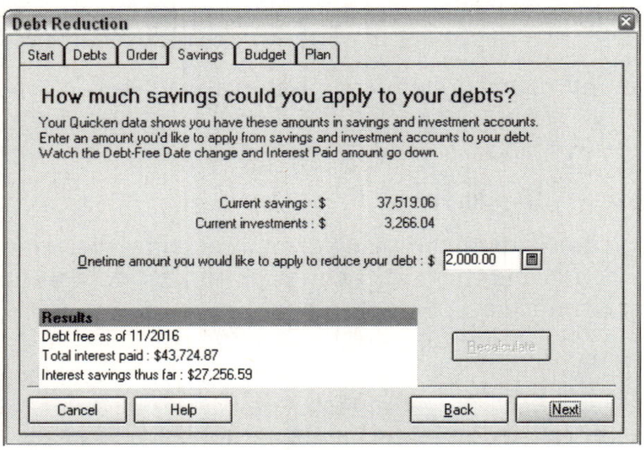

Figure 2-12: Shoot over some money from savings to help extinguish your debt.

11. **Consider trimming your budget.**

    Some of your budgeted expenses are displayed, with the encouragement to cut back and apply some of the money from those expenses toward your debt. We talk more about budgeting in Chapter 5 of this book. You can make some budget adjustments now if you want. You can also return to your DRP later and fine-tune the plan, making budget adjustments or increasing your minimum payments if you want to increase the amount you target for your debt.

    TIP: Any changes you make should automatically adjust your debt scenario at the bottom of the DRP window, but in case no change appears, you can click the Recalculate button to update your debt plan.

12. **Review the final plan.**

Quicken presents you with the final debt reduction plan, and you can print the plan by clicking the Print button right in the DRP window. This plan details how your money will be used for extinguishing various debts, how much the plan is projected to save you, the schedule of extinguishment, the use of a one-time payment from savings, and adjustments to your other spending. Print the plan, refer to it often, and monitor your progress.

TIP: If you add additional debt, or find yourself with a cash windfall that can be applied to your debt, go back to the plan and make changes.

13. **Automate your plan.**

    When you click Next after reviewing your plan, the DRP gives you options to receive alerts if you fall behind on your plan, and also options to produce a complete payment schedule to accompany your plan. Choose either or both of these options if you like, by checking the appropriate boxes and then clicking Next. If you choose to be alerted if you fall behind in your plan, Quicken sends you an alert whenever you miss a plan-related payment. If you choose the schedule, you see a detailed schedule of all payments due from now until the plan ends. You have the option to print this schedule.

14. **Update your plan.**

    After you've created a plan, returning to the DRP window produces a graph. Change existing debt information by clicking the Update Debt Balances option at the top of the graph. Each of your debts appears in an update window (Figure 2-13) where you can make changes to balance and payment information, or you can click on a debt and click the Edit button to make more detailed changes to the loan (such as a change in interest rate on your credit card). Click Done to close the update window.

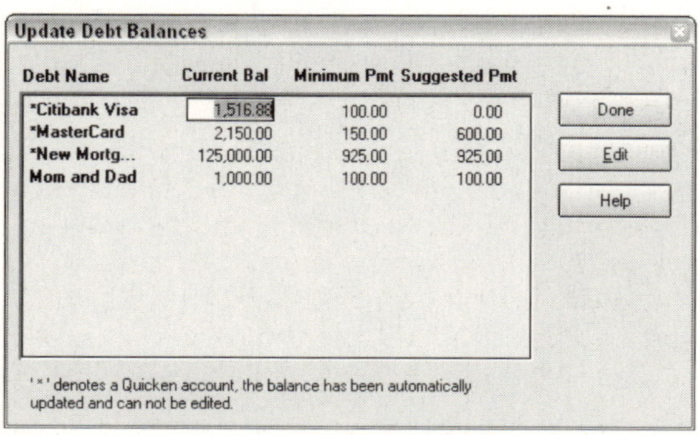

Figure 2-13: Click on an amount to make changes to your debt payment information.

WARNING! Choosing the New Plan option that appears at the top of the DRP graph results in replacing your current plan with a new plan.

Chapter 3: Your Home

In This Chapter

- Buying a home
- Understanding your mortgage
- Making home improvements
- Tracking your home inventory
- Valuing collectibles
- Making insurance claims

For many people, the home is the most valuable asset they own. So it only makes sense that you should want to have a record of the cost of the home as well as the improvements you added to it. In addition to your home, you probably own other items that have value to you, such as your vintage Barbie dolls, a coin collection (not just the jar of loose change from your pocket, but serious collector coins like Indian head pennies, Mercury dimes, and gold double eagles), musical instruments, silver serving dishes, and so on. There are insurance reasons, tax reasons, and personal reasons for keeping track of information on these items. This is a job for Quicken!

Quicken's Home Purchase Planner: Don't Buy a Home Without It!

Don't wait until you get to the bank only to have a mortgage lender tell you the home you want is out of reach. Use Quicken's Home Purchase Planner before you start house hunting, and you'll have a good grip on how much you can afford to spend on your new home. Not only can you avoid surprises at the bank, but you can also focus your search on homes that are within your price range.

Choose Home Purchase Planner from Quicken's Planning menu. Then follow these steps to take advantage of this planning tool:

1. **Click Next on the Welcome screen.**

   When you select the Home Purchase Planner from the Planning menu, the Can I Afford That House? window appears with the Welcome screen displayed. Click Next to move to the next step.

2. **Enter calculator amounts.**

   On the How Much House Can I Afford? screen (Figure 3-1), enter information about your personal financial status. You can estimate these amounts, but the amounts you enter should approximate amounts you would provide a potential lender. You can leave the Maximum Monthly Payment field blank.

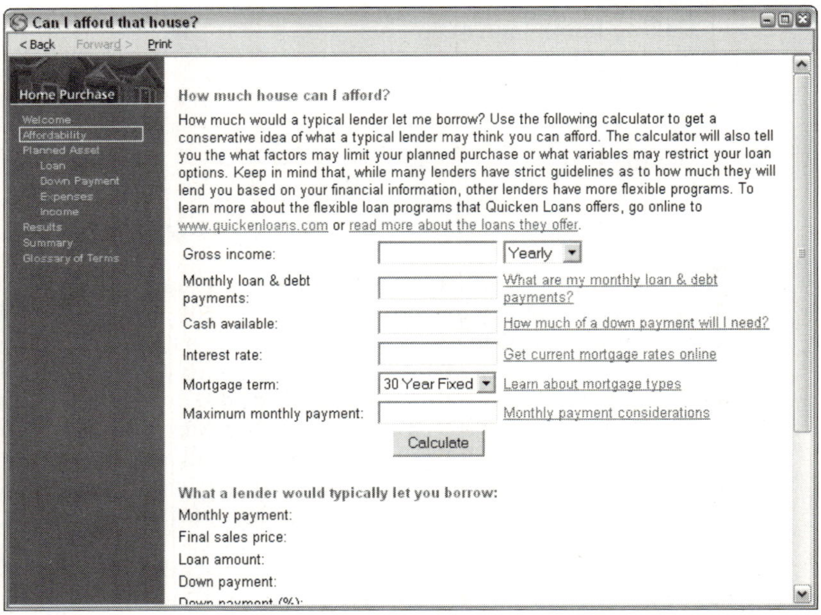

Figure 3-1: Enter financial information so the Home Purchase Planner can help you determine how much you can afford to borrow.

3. **Click the Calculate button.**

   Click Calculate and, in the same window, Quicken provides you with a little statement showing how much you can afford to borrow and what your monthly payment will be if you borrow that amount.

4. **Continue clicking through the Planner.**

   You can proceed through the rest of the Home Purchase Planner, clicking Next on the bottom of each page. On other screens in the Planner, you find a link to QuickenLoans.com, where you can explore loan programs offered by Quicken, enter information about an actual home you're contemplating purchasing, and see the results of having Quicken enter your projected home purchase information into your personal financial plan.

5. **Close the Planner.**

   Click the X in the upper-right corner to close the planner at any time.

Mortgage Basics

A mortgage is a loan secured by a personal residence, like a house, a condominium, a trailer, or a houseboat. The residence is used as *collateral* against the loan, meaning that if the loan doesn't get paid, the lender gets the residence.

The amount you borrow is called the *principal*; the payment you make is increased by interest, and sometimes an extra amount, which goes into an *escrow* account, to cover expenses that the lender pays on your behalf, including property taxes, fire and hazard insurance, and mortgage insurance.

Types of mortgage loans

The most common mortgage is a 30-year fixed-rate mortgage. But you might be surprised to learn that there are lots of different types of mortgages available. Just look at some of the options:

- **Fixed rate mortgages:** A fixed rate mortgage is a mortgage with a set interest rate that doesn't change over the term of the loan. Fixed rate mortgages can be arranged for 15 years, 20 years, 30 years, or another term agreed upon with the lender. Sometimes a lender offers a lower interest rate with a shorter-term loan.
- **Adjustable rate mortgage:** The interest rate on this type of loan is determined by using the rate on one-year U.S. Treasury bills, bank certificates of deposit, or the Federal Reserve interest rate. The rate is typically recalculated once a year, meaning the amount of your mortgage payment varies from one year to the next. There is risk involved with this type of loan because no one can really predict what the interest rate will be from year to year.
- **Balloon mortgage:** A low interest rate tied to a short-term loan (typically five to seven years) with a large payment at the end describes this type of mortgage. This loan is ideal for people who either expect to have a lot of cash available to pay off the loan at the end of the term, who plan on refinancing the loan within five to seven years, or who expect to sell the house before the balloon payment is due.
- **Interest-only mortgage:** With this type of loan, the borrower's payment only covers the interest on the loan, not the principal. The borrower accumulates no equity in the home, but the trade-off is lower monthly payments. This type of mortgage is designed for people who own homes that are expected to increase in value, or who don't plan to be in a home long enough to build equity.
- **Reverse mortgage:** Designed for senior citizens with little or no balance remaining on their existing mortgage, this type of mortgage results in the homeowner receiving money from the lender who holds a lien on the home. This is a way for older people to increase their monthly income without having to sell their home.

Mortgage loans are typically written as 15-year or 30-year loans, although it's possible to arrange for a loan over a different length of time.

Find out everything you ever wanted to know about mortgages in *Mortgages For Dummies*, 2nd Edition, by Eric Tyson and Ray Brown (Wiley Publishing).

Recording a mortgage

When you're ready to set up your mortgage in Quicken, it's helpful to have all the facts and figures ready and waiting. Here's a checklist of the information you need to have on hand before you begin the setup process:

- The original principal of your mortgage
- The rate of interest you're paying
- The total principal and interest included in each monthly payment
- The amount you're paying into escrow each month
- The cost of the home
- The date you purchased the home
- The amount of principal you owe on the home today

When you've gathered all of the above information, you're ready to begin the setup. Follow these steps to enter your home and your mortgage in Quicken:

1. **Open the Loan Setup window, and then click Next.**

   There are a couple of methods for getting to the Loan Setup window. For example, you can open the View Loans window by pressing Ctrl+H and then click the New option. Or you can click on the Property & Debt center over on your Account Bar, and then click the Add Loan button.
2. **Choose the Borrow Money option, and then click Next.**
3. **Enter a name for the account, such as Mortgage, and then click Next.**
4. **Indicate if you have previously made payments on this loan. For this example, I've chosen Yes (Figure 3-2).**
5. **Enter the original date of your loan, and the original principal amount, as shown in Figure 3-3.**
6. **Answer the balloon payment question, Yes or No.**

   If you answer Yes, a question appears in a couple of screens asking you for the *amortized length of the loan*. In other words, you need to enter the number of years you expect to make payments on the loan. The balloon payment is due at the end of this amortized length. For this example, I'm entering No as the answer to the balloon payment question, so that issue of the amortized length of the loan won't even come up.

A balloon payment doesn't mean you get clowns and surprises and helium-filled balloons delivered to your door when you make a payment, although it's nice to think that perhaps the first person who made a balloon payment, back when someone came up with the name, received just such a celebration. Instead, the balloon payment is a monumental event of a financial nature — a large payment made at the end of the loan term, paying off the entire balance.

7. **Enter the length, or term of the loan.**

   The term is the number of years this loan is scheduled to be in existence. I've entered 30 years in this example, as shown in Figure 3-4.

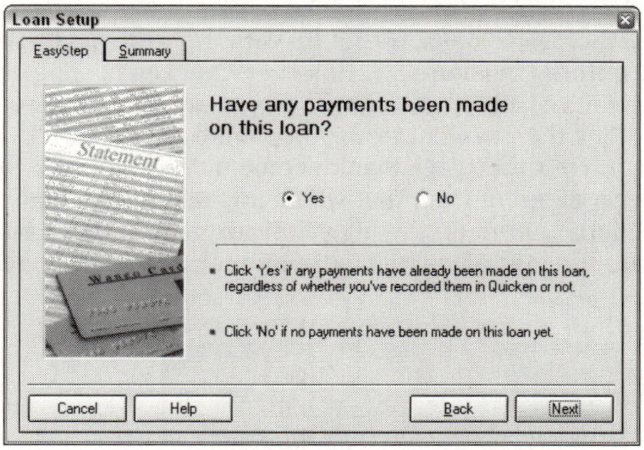

Figure 3-2: Yep, we've already made some payments.

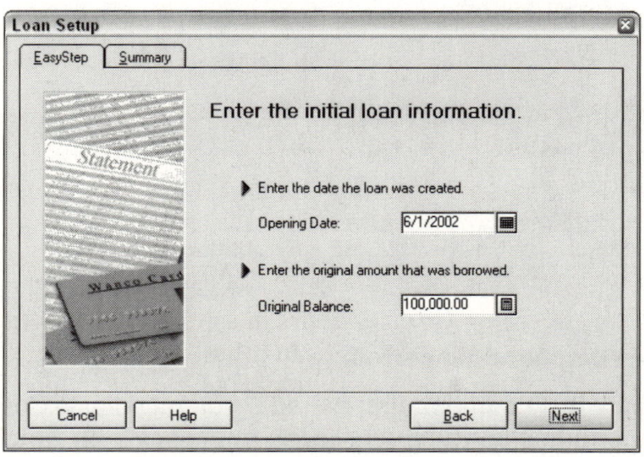

Figure 3-3: Refer to your checklist items, and enter the date and amount of the loan.

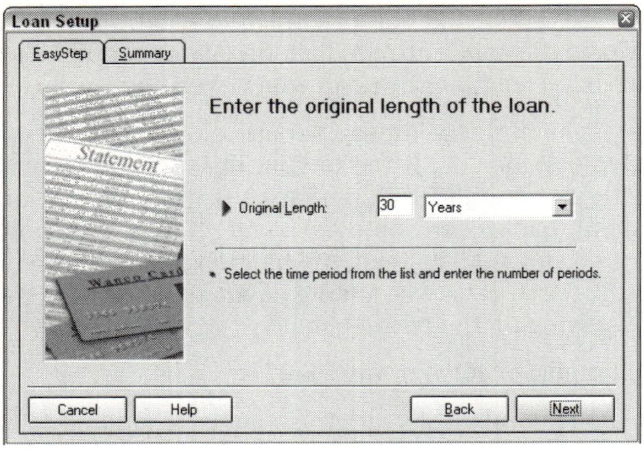

Figure 3-4: Thirty years: Think how old you'll be when this loan is finally paid off!

8. **Next, you are asked to enter the payment period.**

   Generally, mortgage loans are set up with monthly payments, so that is what I've entered in Figure 3-5. However, Quicken is equipped to deal with payments of all types, from weekly to annually and everything in between. Pick the payment term you plan to use, even if that differs from the term on your mortgage loan document. Why, you ask, would you enter a term different from that which appears on the loan document? See the sidebar entitled, "Paying your mortgage early," for an interesting insight into the joys of making more frequent mortgage payments.

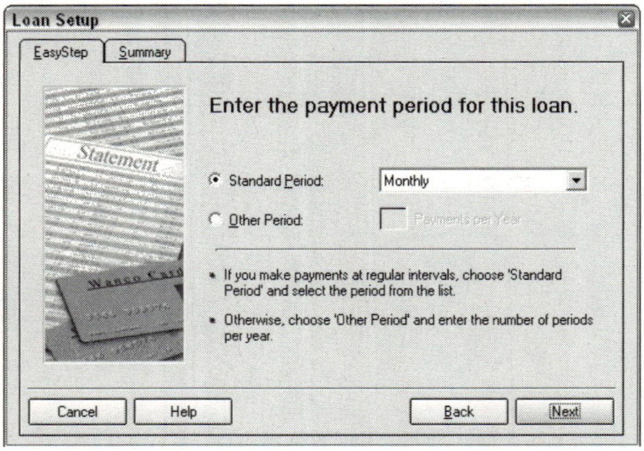

Figure 3-5: Choose the frequency of your payment.

9. **Enter the compounding period.**

   "Hey, what's this compounding period?" you might ask. Good question. The compounding period refers to the frequency with which your interest is calculated. Most mortgages come with a daily compounding period. Quicken gives you choices of daily, monthly, or semi-annually.

Here's an example that might shed some light on how the interest is compounded. Say you have a $100,000 loan at 6 percent interest. If your interest is compounded annually, you'd multiply the principal $100,000 times the interest rate of 6 percent, and the result would be $6,000 interest for the year. One calculation, one amount. For monthly compounding, the calculation is a bit more complex — 12 times more complex, to be exact. The first month is easy. You multiply the $100,000 by 6 percent, get $6,000, and divide that by 12 (representing 1 month), for a total of $500 interest for the month. In month two, you reduce the principal by the amount of principal you paid last month (I'll use $100, which leaves $99,900 in principal), multiply the remaining principal by 6 percent ($5,994), and divide by 12 to get $499.50. And so on. Each month, you reduce your loan balance by the amount you've paid against that balance, and then calculate the interest on the remaining loan balance. Daily compounding results in a new computation each day instead of once a month. Daily compounding also results in a slightly higher amount of interest paid than monthly.

10. **Enter the current loan balance. Or not.**

    If you know the amount you owe on your mortgage as of your last mortgage payment, go ahead and answer the question Yes on Figure 3-6 and, on the next window, you get to enter the balance. If you're not sure of the balance, enter No and Quicken computes the loan balance for you.

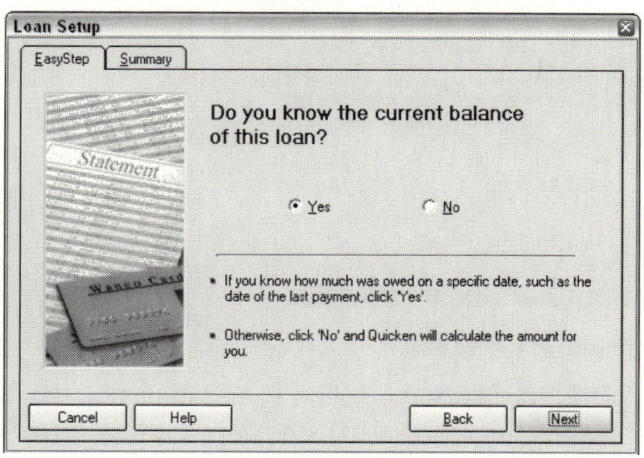

Figure 3-6: Do you know how much your current mortgage balance is?

11. **Enter the date and amount of the loan.**

    If you told Quicken you know the amount of your loan balance, here's your chance to enter that information. Enter the most recent date for which you know the loan balance (this might be the date of your last mortgage payment), and the balance on that date. Otherwise, go on to the next step.

12. **Enter the date of your next payment.**

    This one's easy. Enter the due date for your next mortgage payment.

13. **Enter the amount of your next payment.**

    Ha! You probably think you know the amount that you owe on your next mortgage payment, but don't be so quick to answer. See the warning below. You can let Quicken calculate the amount if you're not sure.

    When Quicken asks for the mortgage payment amount, this is a trick question. Be sure to enter just the loan principal and interest. Many people have additional payments included in their mortgage, like taxes and insurance. The question in step 13 and shown in Figure 3-7 is referring only to principal and interest. The information about your supplemental payments gets entered later.

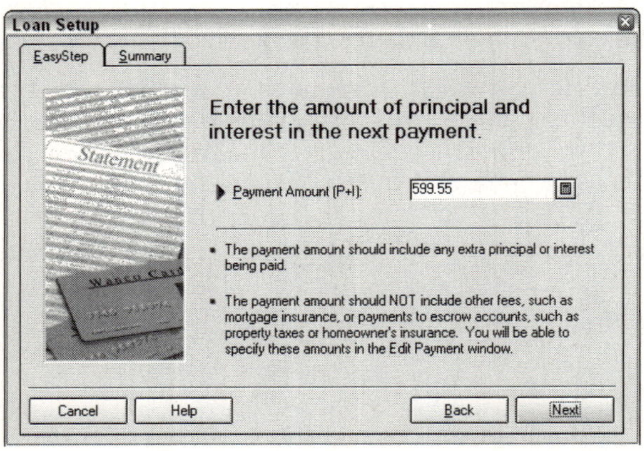

Figure 3-7: Be careful when entering the amount of your mortgage payment — Quicken only wants to hear about principal and interest at this point.

14. **Enter the interest rate for the loan.**

15. **Review summary screens.**

    As you click Next, Quicken displays some summary screens showing you the detail of the information you entered. Review these screens and make sure everything agrees with your loan documents.

16. **Done — but not quite.**

    When you click Done to exit out of the Loan Setup wizard, the Set Up Loan Payment window appears, giving you an opportunity to automate your loan payment in Quicken. And why not? Your loan payment is the same each month, so it makes sense to set up the payment so that it appears or is paid automatically.

Paying your mortgage early

One of the topics you should discuss with your mortgage lender is the treatment of early payments of principal. Some lenders include a penalty clause in the mortgage if you make extra principal payments. In particular, if your credit isn't the best and as a result you have a mortgage loan with a higher-than-average interest rate, you may be penalized if you try to make extra or early principal payments on the loan.

If your lender allows you make extra payments, take a look at the amazing amount of money you can save by simply making one extra payment a year, or by altering the pace at which you make your payments.

For example, a 30-year mortgage for $80,000 at 8 percent interest results in 360 payments of $479.64 over the 30-year period, or $172,670.40, representing $80,000 in principal and $92,670.40 in interest. Make 13 payments per year instead of the standard 12 payments, and the 30-year loan becomes a 24.75-year loan, with 297 total payments equaling approximately $153,758. You've managed to knock nearly $19,000 off in interest. Just think what you could do with an extra $19,000! And the amount of time and money you can save increases if your loan amount or your interest rate is higher.

One of the easiest ways to squeeze in an extra payment during the year is to make your mortgage payment every two weeks instead of once a month. This works especially well if you get paid weekly or bi-weekly. You can arrange for automatic payments to coincide with the receipt of your paycheck. Instead of squeezing out a 13th payment at the end of the year, the extra payment just becomes part of your regular monthly cycle.

When the Set Up Loan Payment window appears, you can refer back to Chapter 1 of Book IV for information on how to fill out this section.

REMEMBER

When entering information in the Set Up Loan Payment window, you can click the Edit button that appears in this window to enter information about miscellaneous payments that are included with your loan, including real estate tax and homeowner's insurance.

Associating your home asset with your mortgage

As soon as you finish with the instructions for setting up your loan payment, you are asked if you want to associate an asset with this loan (see Figure 3-8). Click Yes because you do want to set up your home in Quicken and have the home associated with the loan. That way, you can produce a report showing the true value of the home, offset by the loan. You can follow these instructions to set up your home in your Quicken file.

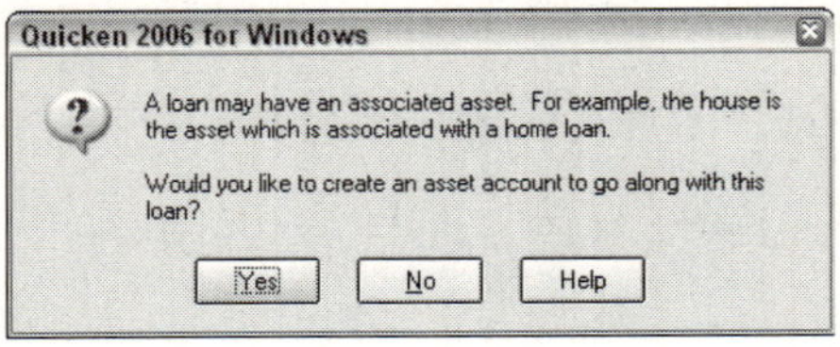

Figure 3-8: Click Yes to set up your home in Quicken.

1. **After answering Yes to the question about setting up the asset, it's time to give the asset a name.**

   You can use "House," or "Home," or the street address of the home, or a nickname that you use for your home. You are limited to 40 characters, including spaces, for the name.

2. **Enter a date and value for the home, as shown in Figure 3-9. This is where the asset setup gets a bit tricky.**

   If you need to track the cost of your home for tax purposes, you should enter the purchase date of the home and the original cost. Alternatively, if you simply want to keep track of the home at its current value, you can enter today's date, or the date of your last appraisal, and the market value of the home. See the information in the "Tax rules for home sales" sidebar to help determine if you should track the cost of your home.

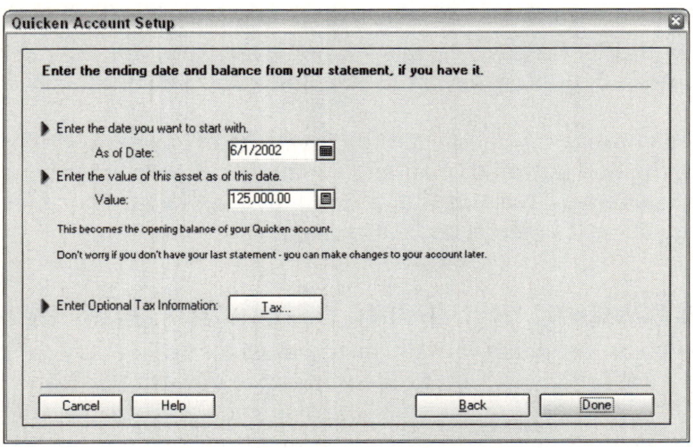

Figure 3-9: Enter the date and value of your home.

3. **You can skip the Tax button in the Account Setup window.**

   This button is for accounts where cash is transferred in or out, so that won't apply to your home.

4. **Click Done to save the information about your home.**

   TIP: If you choose to enter the cost of your home and its related improvements (see the section titled "Home Improvements," later in this chapter), be sure to include the miscellaneous settlement fees you paid when you purchased the home. These get added to the cost of the home and become part of the home's *basis*.

TIP: If you set up your home separately in Quicken, before you set up your mortgage, you can easily associate an existing home with a new mortgage. First set up the mortgage, and then, in the Property & Debt Center, click on the home account, click on the Overview tab, and then click the Edit Account Details button. In the Mortgage Account field, select the mortgage that relates to this home. Then click OK to save the information.

Tax rules for home sales

Until ten years ago, if you purchased a home, you were required to keep track of the original cost and the cost of improvements to the home for tax purposes. Then, when you sold the home, if you made a profit on the sale (which most people do), you had to either pay tax on the profit, or roll the profit forward into your next home, and next home, and next home, until someday, when you stopped buying homes, you might have to pay tax on the accumulated profits on all your homes. Unless of course you were over age 55 when you sold the final home, in which case you were exonerated from at least some of the tax bite.

But times change, and so do tax laws. Keep in mind that, as with any tax law, there are exceptions to the rules and special rules for special cases, and it always makes sense to speak with a tax professional before making decisions that affect your tax return. That said, here are the basic rules you need to know when buying and selling your personal residence:

- If you own the home for at least five years and live in the home as your primary residence for at least two of those five years, and sell the home for a profit of not more than $250,000 (or $500,000 if you are married and filing a joint tax return), you don't have to pay tax on the profit, nor do you have to report the sale of the home on your income tax return.
- If you don't meet the above requirements, you might have to pay tax on the profit from your house.
- If you use part of the home for business purposes, you do need to keep track of all of the costs associated with your home, so that you can take a tax deduction for the business portion of your home.

Home Improvements

Sooner or later, your home is going to need some work. You might need to make some repairs, or you might have to replace windows. Hail might have damaged the roof. And improvements do not always mean bad news. Maybe you want to upgrade your kitchen to include fancy cabinets and state-of-the-art appliances. Or maybe you decide to build a deck out back, redo the shelving in your closets, or cover a wall with built-in bookcases.

If the changes you make improve or add to the value of the home, prolong the life of the home, or adapt the home to a new use, they are considered improvements. If they simply maintain the status quo (like painting the walls that are covered with fingerprints, or replacing a malfunctioning hot water heater), they are considered repairs.

Because improvements add to the value of the home, you should keep track of the cost of improvements, just as you keep track of the cost of your home. Not only is there the possibility that you might have to report a future sale of the home on your tax return (see the "Tax rules for home sales" sidebar), in which case the cost of the improvements you made is a crucial part of calculating the profit on the home, but there are other reasons why you might want to keep track of your improvements. Just look:

- **Insurance:** Your homeowner's insurance covers the value of your home, right? So it stands to reason that if you make changes that increase the value of your home, your insurance agent needs to hear about those changes and what they cost. Keep a detailed list (oh wait! Quicken can do that for you!) and provide a copy of that list to your insurance agent.
- **New owner:** If you plan on selling the home, even if there are no tax ramifications applicable to the sale, the new owner might want to know about all of the changes and improvements you've made. Your real estate agent probably wants to know too.
- **Taxable sale:** I can't emphasize enough the possibility that the sale might be taxable. You can add a new wing this year and maybe five years from now you decide to make that wing into a home office. Suddenly all of the costs of the new wing become part of your tax return, and the IRS doesn't like it when you don't have records and receipts.

The best advice is to keep track of your home improvements, the cost and the date acquired, and save the receipts too. Stash all the information in a file, just in case you need it.

What qualifies as home improvement

The IRS sets out examples of what types of expenditures qualify as home improvements for purposes of adding to the basis of your home. Here are some samples of what can be considered home improvements:

- Upgrading windows with storms, triple-tracks, thermal glass, or other options better than what you had previously
- Upgrading or adding heating, cooling, and ventilation systems and insulation
- Outdoor improvements, including adding a garage or carport; paving a previously unpaved driveway; adding a tennis court, in-ground pool, deck, porch, patio, permanent landscaping (including trees, shrubs, and perennials), walkways, ponds, and so on
- Remodeling a kitchen or bathroom or other room, improving the room or its use over what it was before the remodeling
- Improving plumbing or wiring
- Adding built-in appliances or storage units
- Erecting a fence or retaining wall
- Installing a satellite dish
- Installing a central vacuum system
- Finishing an unfinished basement, attic, or crawlspace
- Putting on a new roof
- Installing an underground sprinkler system
- Replacing a septic system or water well
- Installing new flooring or wall-to-wall carpets
- Adding a security system

Be sure to keep track of the original cost, including delivery and installation charges, of any of the improvements you make on your home.

Recording home improvements in Quicken

Quicken allows you to adjust the value of your home with just a few clicks. Here's how you can add the cost of your home improvements to your home basis.

1. **Open the Property & Debt Center.**

   Click on the Property & Debt Center heading on the Account Bar.

2. **Go to the asset account for your home.**

   In the Property section of the Property & Debt Center, click on the hyperlink that is the name you gave your home. The asset detail appears.

3. **Go to the Overview tab.**

   If the asset register appeared when you clicked on the asset hyperlink, click now on the Overview tab that appears at the top of the register (see Figure 3-10).

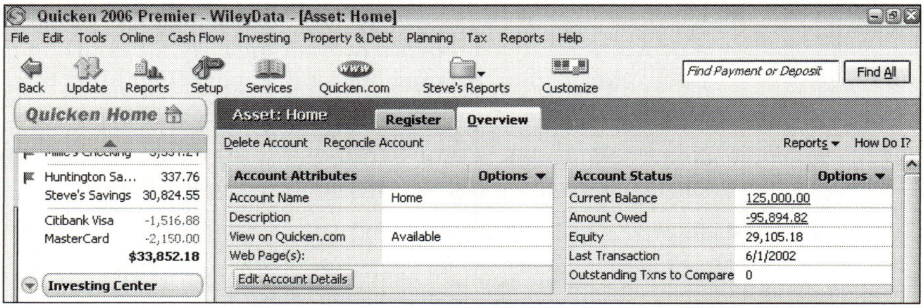

Figure 3-10: Click the Overview tab.

4. **Click the number that represents the Current Balance — this number is hyperlinked — to open the Update Account Balance dialog box (see Figure 3-11).**

   The hyperlinked amount for this asset's Current Balance appears under the Account Status heading.

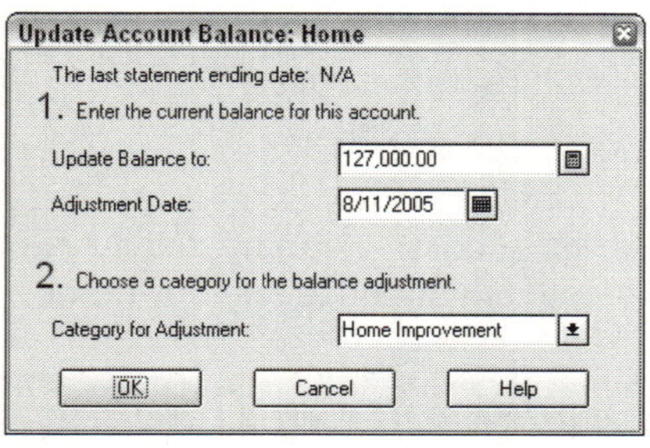

Figure 3-11: Update your home's balance by adding the cost of improvements.

5. **Update the home's balance.**

   Click in the Update Balance To field, and then enter the new value of the home. This new value is the value you clicked on in the asset screen plus the cost of the improvements you've added.

TIP

If you need to use the computer to do some math, click the little calculator button to the right of the data field.

6. **Verify or change the date.**

   Quicken has selected today's date as the date on which you made the improvement. You should change this date to coincide with the date on which the improvement was purchased or the work was completed, whichever is later.

7. **Choose a category.**

   You might have already established a category where this improvement should be tracked. That would have happened when you entered the expense for the improvement. Choose that category now, or, if you haven't yet set up your improvements category, do so now by entering a new category name in the field, and then setting up the category on-the-fly. Click OK to save your adjustment to the home's basis.

TIP

You can read about setting up categories on-the-fly in Book II, Chapter 1.

Working with the Quicken Home Inventory

Quicken's Home Inventory feature is a nifty little tool that works in conjunction with your Quicken program, sharing information with your Quicken accounts, and at the same time, providing a little service that is different from the mainstream Quicken features. The Home Inventory is a program that insurance agents love — it's a method for listing and valuing basically everything you own, or at least everything you own that you want to have a record of.

With the Home Inventory program, you can keep track of your furnishings, your books, your home accessories such as antiques and appliances, clothing, toys, tools, you name it. The inventory program is also nice for keeping track of collectible items, not just for insurance purposes, but also for tax and inheritance purposes.

You can go nuts with this program, entering every little item you own, down to the latest issue of *TV Guide* and the new alligator-shaped corn-on-the-cob holders (corn-igators!) you bought last week. Or you can be a bit more reserved with the program, and use it as a listing both for homeowner's or renter's insurance purposes as well as a useful and interesting listing of your possessions.

When you open the Home Inventory program, a separate screen appears. You work in the inventory program, entering and updating information about your personal possessions, and then you update the information in your main Quicken program. After that update is accomplished, you can close the inventory program. Your home inventory assets are now added to the total assets reported in your Quicken program and are a part of your net worth calculations.

Follow these steps to record home inventory items and update Quicken:

1. **Open the Home Inventory program.**

   Choose Quicken Home Inventory from the Property & Debt menu. The Home Inventory program opens in a separate window.

2. **Familiarize yourself with the Home Inventory program.**

   Click around a bit — you won't hurt anything. Here's a sample of what you see:

   - At the top of the inventory list there is a View By Location field, as you can see in Figure 3-12. Clicking the drop-down arrow displays all of the possible rooms Quicken can think of that might be in your home. There's even an option for your Safe Deposit Box, and another for Unassigned, in case the location where some assets are stored isn't on the list. For example, you might own some items that a friend is borrowing, or maybe you own some items that you are trying to sell and they are on consignment at a store.

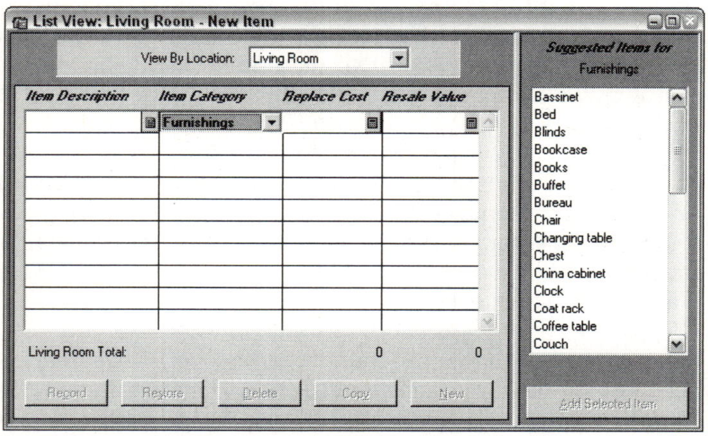

Figure 3-12: Learning the ropes in the Home Inventory program.

   - At the right is a list of suggested items that you might own. These are just suggestions, but the list can give you ideas of items you might have forgotten. Also this list can serve as a timesaver — if you select an item from the list, Quicken adds the item to the room or other location that is currently active, and assigns a suggested replacement and resale value for the item.

- No matter which room or location you choose, at the top of the item list, the item category column displays the category of Furnishings. Click the down-arrow next to Furnishings, and you see other options, including clothing, electronics, jewelry and valuables, and so on. Clicking on one of these categories changes the detail of the suggested items list on the right.
- Click the Locations button and you see the list of all of your locations (Figure 3-13). Each location displays the number of items, the total replacement cost, and the total resale cost for items in that location. Add, edit, or delete locations with the buttons at the top of the window.

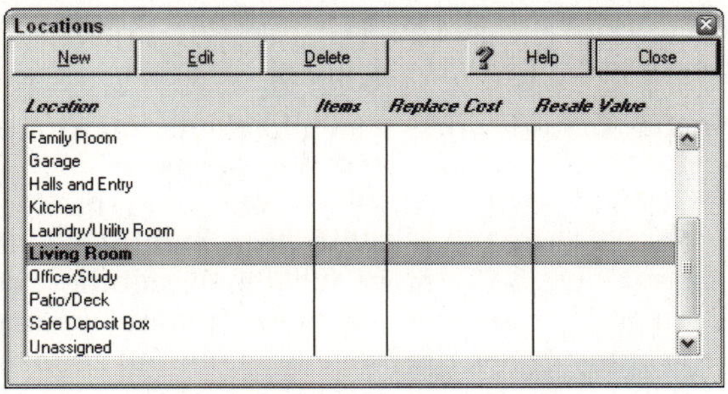

Figure 3-13: A summary of your possessions, accumulated by location (blank, because I haven't added anything yet).

- Click the Categories button to see the complete list of categories in editable form. You can remove categories you don't need with the Delete button, edit the names of existing categories with the Edit button, and add categories that aren't already listed here with the New button. For example, I've added Musical Instruments as a category on my list (Figure 3-14).

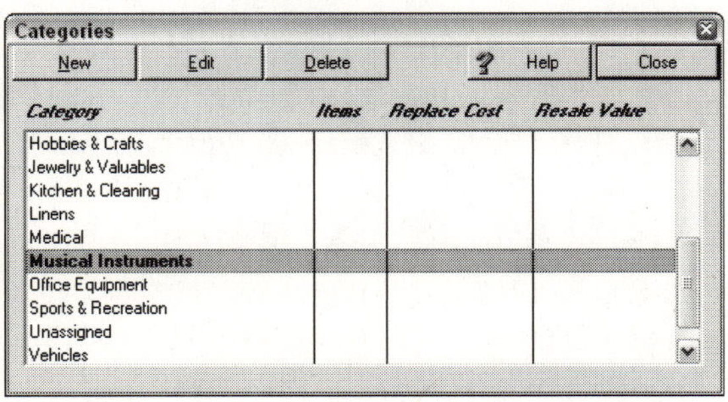

Figure 3-14: Musical Instruments has been added to the category list.

- The Policies button gives you a window with a place for listing each of your insurance policies, and how much the actual coverage is. Quicken calculates the replacement cost of all covered items, and then informs you of the difference between the two amounts.
- The Claims button gives you a place to list insurance claims and related proceeds. This is important information to save should you sell any of the insured items. If you receive insurance proceeds for a damaged item, the amount of insurance you receive affects your basis for the item.
- I love the Find button! This button enables you to perform a search throughout the home inventory archives. Those of us who are starting to get forgetful can really take advantage of this tool. Seriously, spend a day or two and list everything you own in the inventory, in the room where it belongs. Then when you lose something (where did I put that crystal vase I got last year for Christmas?), you can run a search, and voilà! The vase is found!
- The Move Item feature works well in conjunction with the Find feature. Say you decide to move that crystal vase from the living room to the den. Don't just move the vase. Move it in the Home Inventory program too! Click the Move Item button, and then, in the window that appears (Figure 3-15), move the item to another room. Here's an example: I'm going to relocate my violin from the bedroom to its new home in the study. I click the Move Item button, choose Bedroom for the Current Location, and the program displays a list of the items I've entered for the bedroom. Then I click on the violin, click on the Office/Study as the new location, and then click the Move button.

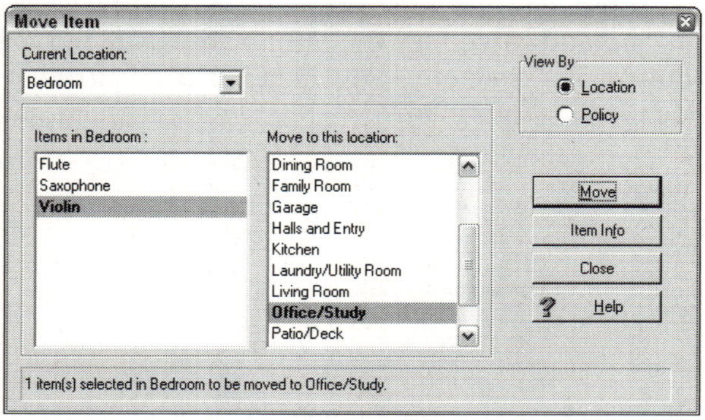

Figure 3-15: Tell the Home Inventory program where you're moving items, and you'll never lose anything again!

* Update Quicken with your additions to the Home Inventory by clicking the Update button. In the little window that appears (Figure 3-16), click Yes to send the updated information to your main Quicken program. The next time you're in Quicken, click on the Property & Debt center. Under Property (Assets), you see an entry for Home Inventory with the total that you entered as resale value for all of your Home Inventory assets.

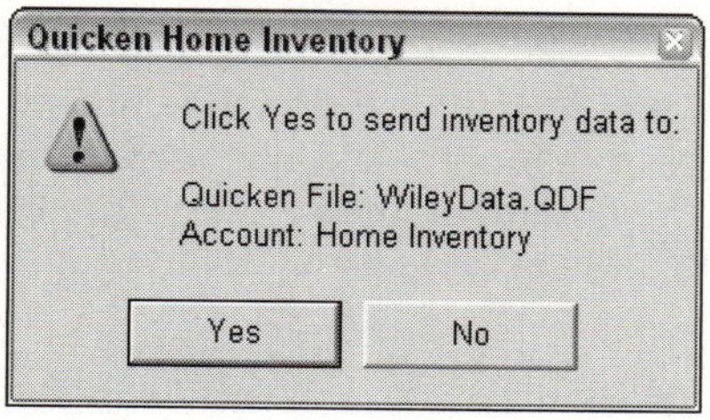

Figure 3-16: Update your assets in Quicken.

* If you want to go back to Quicken and leave the Home Inventory program open, click the Goto Qkn button. Alternatively, if you're ready to close the Home Inventory program, just close the program by clicking the little X in the upper-right corner.

Valuing Collectibles

You can use the Home Inventory feature to record your collections. You probably won't want to list all of the individual stamps or coins you own, but you can list the entire collection, with one value, and then make changes in the value as the need arises. If you have a collection of a manageable size, you can enter each item in the collection in the Home Inventory program.

Notice that when you enter an item with a replacement cost, Quicken immediately assumes the resale cost (the cost at which you could actually sell the item) is one-half of the replacement cost. This is an automatic entry and probably has little to do with the actual resale cost.

REMEMBER

Be sure you check the resale values carefully — you know better than Quicken how much your possessions are really worth. And, because it's the resale value that Quicken uses when valuing your possessions in your Quicken reports, you should take care to make sure the amount that appears as resale value is as close as possible to the actual resale value and not just an arbitrary estimate.

There are several reasons why you might want to record the value of your collectible items. Here are some of them:

- **Taxes:** Ah, the ubiquitous tax issue. Should you sell a collectible item, the IRS certainly wants to hear about the sale. You need to record your original cost and any additional costs you've incurred for that item, as well as the sales price of the item. Unfortunately, the Quicken Home Inventory program doesn't give you an opportunity to enter acquisition dates — you have to keep that information stored somewhere else, or enter the items as separate assets within the main Quicken program.
- **Gifts:** We've heard that it's bad form to ask someone how much a gift costs. But sometimes the recipient of the gift needs that information. The person who receives the gift might need to know the original cost information in order to calculate taxable gain should that person ultimately sell the gifted item.
- **Insurance:** We're back to insurance again. Collectible items might need to be listed separately on your insurance policy. Check with your insurance agent to find out how much of your personal possessions is covered by your homeowner's or renter's insurance. For items that need to be insured separately, you need to decide first if you're going to insure the replacement value or the resale value. Then, in either case, you need to give that information to the insurance agent.

Chapter 4: Quicken Billminder and Bill Pay

In This Chapter

- Enrolling and paying for the service
- Setting up payees
- Paying bills
- Scheduling payments
- Stopping online payments

I've taught Quicken classes for several years, and for the longest time, when the topic of online bill payment would come up in the classroom, I'd have to explain how the service was supposed to work, without first-hand experience. Fortunately, somebody in my class would have actually used an online bill payment service, and in addition to sharing firsthand insights, this person would invariably say, "Once you try online bill-paying, you'll never go back to writing checks by hand." I finally got around to signing up for online bill-paying service a few years ago, and you know what? Those students of mine were right.

What's the Difference? Billminder versus Bill Pay

Billminder is an old standby feature of Quicken that has been around almost ever since I can remember. This little program operates independently of your Quicken program in that it pops up each time you start your computer and reminds you of scheduled transactions that are due, even while Quicken isn't running. The Billminder program is completely optional, so if you don't want to use it, you don't have to. There is no fee for the use of Billminder (as opposed to Bill Pay).

Bill Pay is a fee-based service offered by Intuit. For $9.95 per month (as of this writing), you can pay bills online, schedule payments up to a year in advance (for people who *really* like to be organized about paying their bills), receive notification when bills arrive, set up repeat payments, transfer money among accounts (my personal favorite feature), and automatically transfer all the bill-paying activity into your Quicken register.

TIP

When you sign up for Bill Pay, Intuit gives you the first month for free. So, you can fool around with the program for 30 days and decide if you like it without having to purchase the service. After you sign on, you can cancel at anytime.

How do these services work?

Billminder is a reminder program that works when you enable the program (as described in "Getting Friendly with Billminder," later in this chapter). Billminder tells you that you need to pay a bill, print some checks, buy your best friend a birthday present, clip your toenails, or whatever else you want it to tell you. The important thing to remember is that Billminder doesn't have a mind of its own. The alerts that you receive from Billminder are the alerts that you set up in your Quicken program. If you forgot to mention to Quicken that your mortgage is due on the 5th of every month, Billminder isn't going to know about that payment either.

Bill Pay, on the other hand, is a completely different breed of software. Bill Pay is the 4-H Grand Champion of interactive bill paying programs (forgive me — it's State Fair time in my home state and I've got giant zucchinis and blue ribbon Holsteins on my mind). Bill Pay doesn't come as a part of your Quicken program; instead, you have to go to the Quicken Web site and sign up for the service. Then it is your choice to use Bill Pay, or not, whenever you want.

So, do I really need all this bill-related stuff?

The bill features are extras, and you can get by just fine without these services. The Billminder is just a little alerts program that hovers around on your computer screen, happy to remind you of impending payment deadlines and other events, and just as happy if you choose ignore the reminders. The Bill Pay program is 21st century–style automation. If you're happy writing checks by hand and then entering those checks in Quicken, don't feel any pressure to use the Bill Pay service that Quicken provides. In fact, you might already have an online bill paying relationship with your bank and in many ways the Quicken program would be redundant. You might not need two online bill-payment services.

The Bill Pay service offers extra advantages, however, that your bank might not be able to provide. For example, Bill Pay interacts completely with Quicken so you don't have to enter your bills in your Quicken register after you've paid them. You can also set up ongoing scheduled payments in Bill Pay so you don't have to return each month or each quarter to make sure the payment is sent. And, you can use Bill Pay to transfer money easily from one account another, even if the accounts are not at the same bank. See a complete list of Bill Pay features later in this chapter in the sidebar titled, "What's so cool about Quicken Bill Pay?"

Getting Friendly with Billminder

Because Billminder works outside of Quicken, you don't need to be working in Quicken to turn on the Billminder program. In fact, you actually have to close your Quicken program before you can open the Billminder program. You'd think these two would be friendlier than that with each other . . .

Explore how the Billminder program works by opening the Billminder program and checking out the options. Follow these steps and you'll be there:

1. **From your taskbar, click Start⇨All Programs⇨Quicken⇨Billminder (see Figure 4-1).**

   TIP: I put Billminder on my desktop by right-clicking on the Billminder option that appears on the Start/All Programs menu, and then choosing Send To, and then Desktop (Create Shortcut). Now I can see my Quicken alerts anytime I want by just clicking the Billminder icon.

2. **When the Billminder window appears (see Figure 4-2), catch up on what you've been ignoring in Quicken.**

   For example, see the scheduled transactions that are ready to occur (or that you've missed), and get a quick glimpse of account balances that have exceeded the ceiling you designated or spending limits you've gone over. (Tsk. Tsk.)

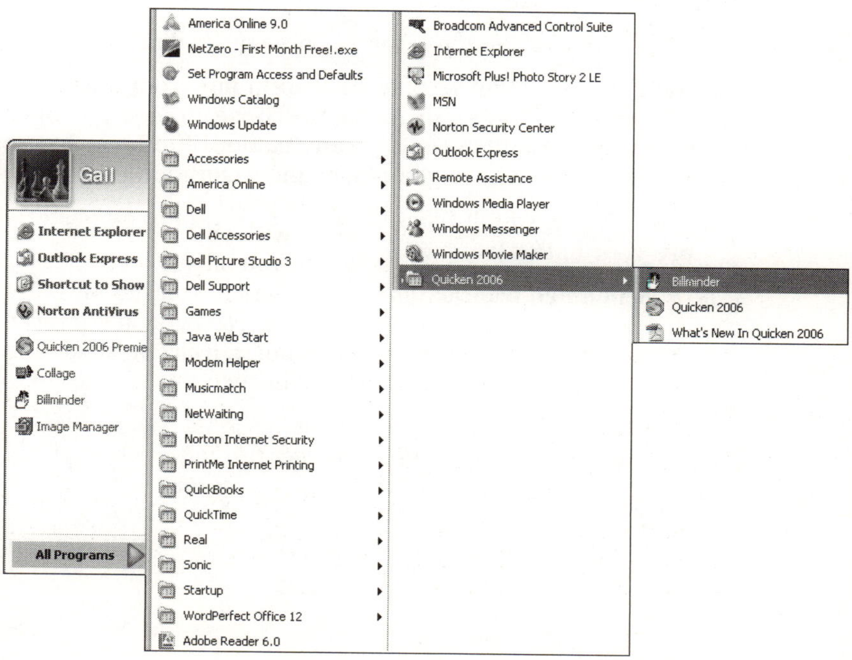

Figure 4-1: Finding Billminder.

3. **By default, Billminder is not turned on when you install Quicken, so click the Options menu choice in Billminder.**

   The Billminder Options window appears (Figure 4-3).

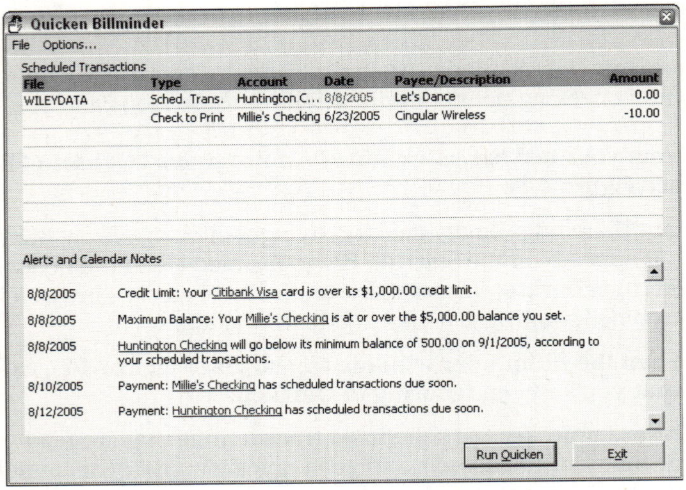

Figure 4-2: Billminder is ready and waiting.

4. **Turn on Billminder by checking the box to Enable Billminder on Windows Startup.**

   The list of alert options that was previously dim comes alive!

5. **Next, decide if you want to have Billminder popping up all the time, like a feisty little puppy (leave the first indented box unchecked), or if you only want to see Billminder when Billminder has something worthwhile to say to you (check the first indented box).**

6. **Now, choose which types of alerts you want to be pestered with. Here are your options:**

   - **Scheduled transactions:** This refers to transactions that you've already scheduled in Quicken. You can schedule transactions for any date or frequency — Billminder gives you advance notice when it's time for the transactions to occur.
   - **Checks to print:** You've scheduled some checks to be printed in Quicken but the checks don't get printed by themselves. Checks waiting in the print queue trigger a message in Billminder. Billminder gives you advance notice of checks that are due to be printed in the future, and also reminds you of checks that you were supposed to print but did not.

- **Online payments:** You've arranged for some online payments, but the payments have yet to be dispatched. Billminder lets you know that you've got online business to take care of.
- **Investment reminders:** Any reminders you set for yourself in the investment transactions window flow through to Billminder.
- **Calendar notes:** Remember the financial calendar? We discussed this in Book II, Chapter 3. You can create a reminder entry on the calendar for anything you want, including both financial and non-financial matters. Your financial calendar reminders flow through to the Billminder so you won't forget that money you promised to send your brother, your best friend's birthday gift, lunch with the boss, or the school PTA meeting.

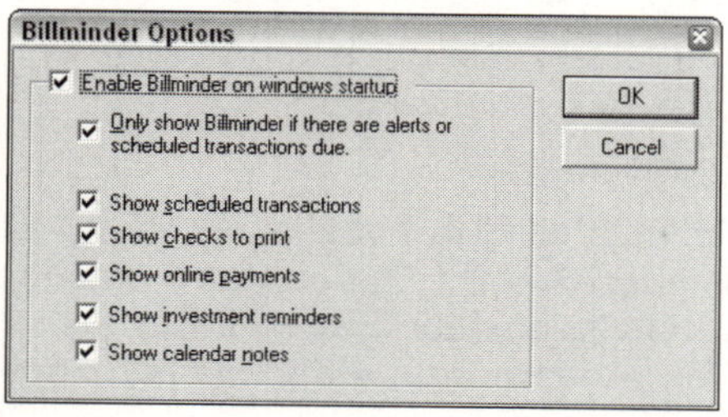

Figure 4-3: Enable Billminder and select your options.

OK, I've got an alert that needs action: Now what?

Billminder has done its job, appearing onscreen and telling you to get busy and finalize your Quicken transactions. Now it's time to actually get things done in Quicken: Click the Run Quicken button at the bottom of the Billminder window. Poof! As quickly as you can say, "Hey! What was that alert about the tax payment I was supposed to make?" Billminder has closed, taking its alerts out of sight and opening Quicken in its place.

TIP

Not interested in running Quicken at this time? Just click the Exit button in Billminder, and the program leaves you alone until the next time you start your computer.

Don't forget that you can see all of your alerts in Quicken too, so you can get back to reading about that tax payment and other alerts as well. Depending on how your Quicken program opens, you might see your alerts right at the top of the screen from the get-go.

If Quicken opens with the Home page displayed, alerts appear at the top. Any of the other centers (Cash Flow, Investing, and so on) also start with an alerts section at the top of the window. You can always click the Show All Alerts button beneath the alerts list to see alerts in all categories.

TIP: Don't let your Quicken program push you around: You get to control how Quicken appears when the program opens. Choose Edit➪Preferences➪Quicken Program to open the Quicken Preferences window. Click on Startup, and then choose from all the options in the drop-down list to decide what screen you want to see each time you open Quicken.

TIP: If you open a window that doesn't show any alerts, you can pull up your alerts list quickly by going to the Tools menu and picking Show All Alerts. An Alerts Center opens in a separate window that you can close by clicking on the X in the upper-right corner.

TIP: For faster service, or at least a different way to get back to Quicken from Billminder, you can double-click on one of the scheduled transactions listed in Billminder. You get the same routine as if you clicked on the Run Quicken button: Billminder closes, Quicken opens, and all's well with the world.

Bye-bye, Billminder

Each time you boot up, Billminder kicks in and lets you know what's pending. If you're sick of seeing Billminder, click the Options button again and uncheck the Enable Billminder box. Billminder slinks away, playing solitaire and keeping itself idle until you decide you miss your old friend and want to see the alerts again.

Let's Sign Up to Pay Bills Online!

If you decide to use the Quicken Bill Pay service, you have to jump through some sign-up hoops before you can use the service. Sign up for Bill Pay, and you get the service free for 30 days.

TIP: This 30-day free offer for Bill Pay was in place when this book went to press. I can't guarantee it's still in place, but if they give you a hard time, try telling them the folks at *Quicken All-in-One Desk Reference For Dummies* all agree that they should give you the first month free and see how far that gets you . . .

To sign up for Bill Pay, open Quicken, choose Online➪Quicken Bill Pay➪Set up Quicken Bill Pay Account from the menu. Click the Sign Up Now button.

Alternatively, you can go to `www.quicken.com`, click on the Bills & Banking Center hyperlink, and then click on Quicken Bill Pay and click Enroll Now.

REMEMBER

You need your bank account number and routing number and your Social Security number to sign up for the Bill Pay service.

What's so cool about Quicken Bill Pay?

You might still be wondering why you should use Quicken Bill Pay when you already have the ability to make online payments, and your bank lets you pay bills from its Web site. If you've explored other bill payment services, some of Bill Pay's features probably look familiar, but some are unique to Quicken's program, and they are what sets this program aside from other online services.

- Pay bills from any computer, anywhere, 24/7.
- All necessary information about your payees is stored the first time you enter it, so you never have to enter addresses and account numbers again.
- Payments can be made to any person or company anywhere in the United States — the recipient of your payment does not have to be able to receive electronic payments. If an electronic payment cannot be made, Quicken sends a check to the recipient.
- Schedule payments up to one year in advance, reducing the chance that you'll miss an important payment.
- Set up recurring payments once and forget about them — Quicken makes sure they continue to get paid on the schedule you picked.
- Save money when you use Bill Pay by doing away with the need for envelopes, postage stamps, and paper checks.
- Save time with Bill Pay by entering payment amounts and authorizing payments right on your computer instead of having to handwrite checks.
- Your Bill Pay transactions automatically get entered into Quicken every time you initiate an online update from within Quicken. That way, you don't have to worry about making an online payment and forgetting to enter it in your register. As an added bonus, this ensures that your register balance stays current and correct.
- Set up your bills so that the companies send the bill directly to Bill Pay — then all you have to do is approve the bill for payment.
- Make payments from up to 10 different accounts.
- Stop worrying about late payments. You can schedule payments in advance to make sure the money arrives when it's due.
- Transfer funds from any of your accounts to another account. This includes transfers between bank accounts and investment accounts as well as bank to bank transfers.
- Payments are guaranteed to be accurate and received on time or Quicken takes the heat and pays any late fees you incur.
- You can receive e-mail notification when bill payments are actually made.
- Bill Pay's technical support is available 24/7.
- Bill Pay's service provides safe encryption of your sensitive financial data.

Reading the fine print

Paying bills online is mega-fun if you enjoy efficiency and time-saving tools. And the process is easy and completely intuitive. Before you jump in with both feet, here are the little warnings that are hidden in the fine print:

- **Cost:** Don't forget that this program costs money to use. The fee is $9.95 per month. That might be small change to you, or maybe not. If you only pay two or three bills per month, it might not be worth it to you to sign on for this type of service. (Intuit reserves the right to raise the price at some point in the future.) On the other hand, if you pay tons of bills per month — see the next point.
- **More cost:** The $9.95 fee covers 20 payments per month. If you go over the limit, your price increases at a rate of $2.49 for each additional five transactions. So 21–25 transactions per month generate a $12.44 price tag, 26–30 transactions means you pay $14.93, and so on.
- **Timeliness, sort of:** Quicken recommends that if you're making a tax payment or any type of court-ordered payment, the type of payment that absolutely positively has to be paid on time, you best not use Bill Pay. Hmmm. That doesn't evoke a lot of confidence in the program. I think the main message here is that you shouldn't wait until the last minute to send a payment using this program. Leave yourself some time, a bit of a cushion between the date Bill Pay says the bill will be paid and the actual due date. The guarantee that Intuit makes for on-time payments does not apply to tax payments and court-ordered payments. I'm sure the reasoning is that with these types of payments, a late payment can result in more than just a slap on the wrist and a late fee, and Intuit doesn't want to assume the responsibility for problems that might ensue from paying these important payments late.

Enter the requested information, including

- Name
- Address
- Date of birth
- E-mail address
- Home phone number
- A user ID and password of your choice
- Choose one of the secret questions (secret word, pet's name, or mother's maiden name), and then enter the corresponding answer. Note: I used to think I was clever and would make up answers to these questions. I had a heck of a time trying to remember my made-up answers in order to get back into various sites. Now I just bite the bullet and tell the truth. I guess there are worse things that could happen than some hacker somewhere finding out the name of the pet I had when I was five years old.

- Bank name
- Name you use to refer to this bank account
- Type of account
- Account number
- Bank routing number
- E-mail format preference (text or HTML)
- Version of Quicken that you use

When everything has been entered, you can click the Sign Me Up button to complete the application process.

Setting up accounts in Bill Pay

If you haven't yet done so, you must establish at least one bank account as your bill-paying account. Doing so enables you to pay bills through Bill Pay and access your funds in your bank account.

You can set up your account right in Quicken, or you can set up the account through the Bill Pay Web site.

Set up a bank account from your Quicken program

Before you can activate an account for use with Quicken Bill Pay, the account must have been activated for online transactions in general. If you need to set up online access for your account, refer to Book II, Chapter 5, and then come back here to set up the account for Bill Pay.

Oops, wait just a minute! Before you can activate a bank account for Quicken Bill Pay, you must clear any transactions that you downloaded but have not yet accepted into your register. Any downloaded transactions awaiting your approval are sitting patiently at the bottom of your register screen. Clear those transactions by accepting them (and editing if necessary). Click Done when you're finished, and then you're ready to proceed with making your account available to Quicken Bill Pay.

Here's how to connect a bank account with Bill Pay from within the Quicken program.

1. **Display the bank account you want to use for online payments**

   Your accounts might be listed on the left side of your Quicken screen, in the Account Bar. If so, click on the account you want to use. If your accounts aren't visible, press Ctrl+A to display the account list, and then double-click on the account you want to view.

2. **Click on the Overview tab that appears at the top of the account display.**
3. **Click on the Activate Quicken Bill Pay option.**

   The Quicken Account Setup window appears (Figure 4-4).

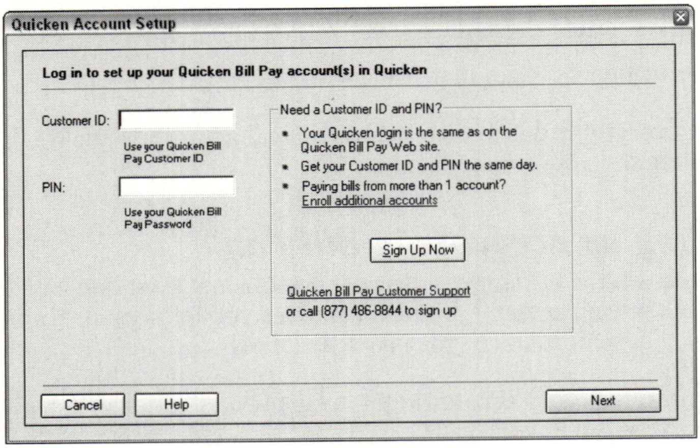

Figure 4-4: Enter your login information.

4. **Enter your login information, which is the same login name and password you use on the Quicken Bill Pay Web site. Click Next when you're ready to proceed.**

After the account is activated, the Online Center opens, ready to accept your transactions.

Set up a bank account from the Bill Pay window

You can set up an account from your Quicken Bill Pay screen on the Internet — you don't have to be at your own computer to accomplish this.

1. **After logging in to Quicken Bill Pay, click the Payment Accounts option.**

   A list of the accounts you have already activated appears. A green dot next to the account indicates that the account has been approved for use in Bill Pay. A yellow dot indicates that approval is still pending — you might have to contact your financial institution or Quicken Bill Pay to determine why the account has not been approved.
2. **Click the Add Payment Account hyperlink.**

   A Funding Account Information worksheet appears (Figure 4-5).

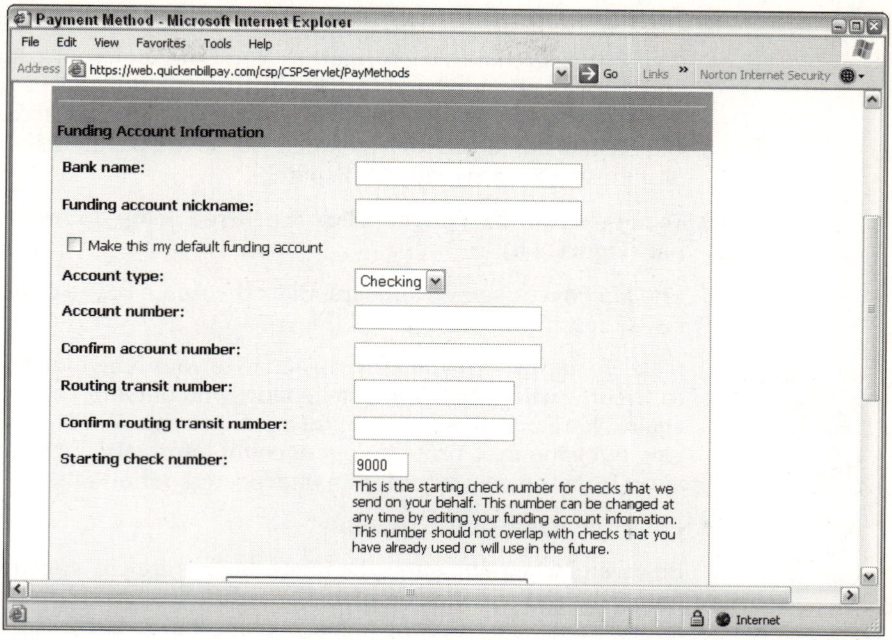

Figure 4-5: Enter account information.

3. **Enter the information necessary for setting up your account.**

   You need to provide the name of your bank, a name you use to refer to this account, the account number, the bank routing number, and a starting check number that doesn't duplicate check numbers you use in your register.

4. **Check the box that gives authorization to initiate debit entries at your request.**

   At the bottom of the Funding Account Information window, check the authorization check box to give Quicken authorization to take money from your account when you make a Bill Pay request. Check this box, and then click Continue. The account is added to your funding accounts list.

Setting up payees in Bill Pay

You've already established your account (or accounts) within Quicken Bill Pay. Now it's time to pay some bills! Before you can make a payment using this service, you have to identify to whom each payment should be sent. Follow along to see how this works.

1. **Choose Online⇨Quicken Bill Pay⇨View and Pay Bills on the Web from the Quicken menu.**

   The Bill Pay login window appears.

2. **Enter your username and password, and then click the Login button.**

   If you've forgotten this information, you can enter your e-mail address in the space provided and Quicken will e-mail the information to you. When you log in, you are taken directly to the My Bills screen. Any bills Quicken has received for you are listed, as are payments you entered previously that are ready to dispatch.

3. **To set up your first payee, click the Payee Setup option on the menu bar (Figure 4-6).**

   The My Payees screen appears. Click the Add a Payee option. The Add a Payee setup window appears (Figure 4-7).

   TIP

   Make it snappy — if you lollygag and take your time moving from window to window within Bill Pay, Quicken logs you out and you have to log in again. Not a problem; just a bit of an inconvenience. This process of logging out is done to protect your account information in case you step away from the computer for an unexpected period of time.

4. **Enter the name of the payee.**

   Be careful when you enter the name. Make sure you spell the name correctly, and use the complete name, not an abbreviation (unless an abbreviation is part of the name, such as Inc. or Ltd.). The name you enter here is the name that appears on any payments that you instruct Bill Pay to make.

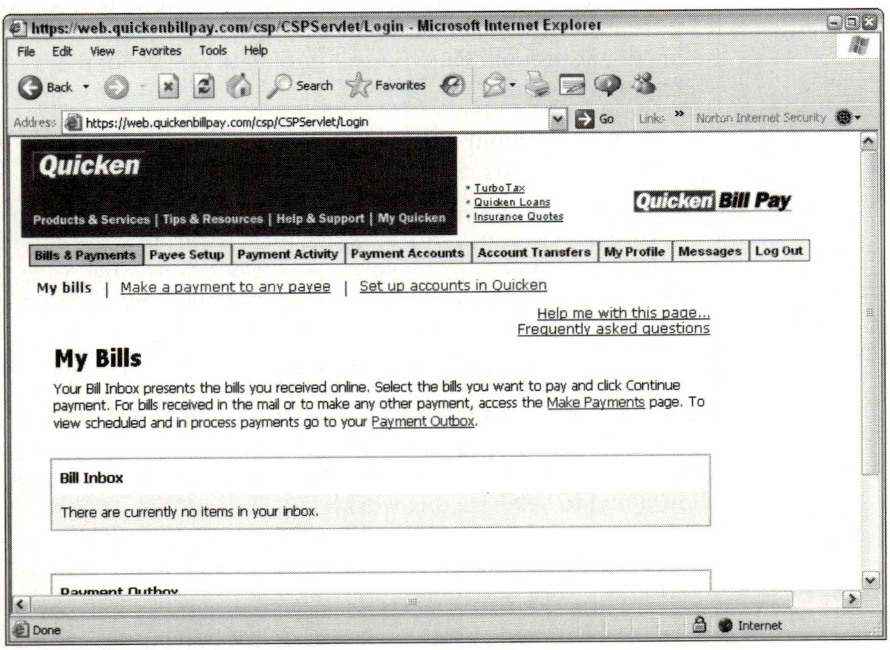

Figure 4-6: Click Payee Setup on the menu bar.

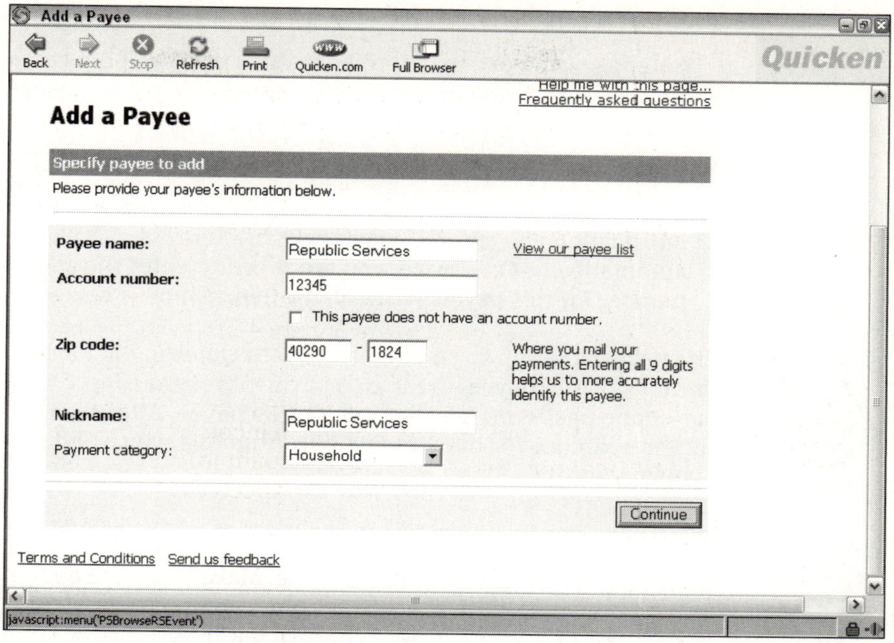

Figure 4-7: Enter info about your payee.

5. Enter an account number.

When you write a check by hand, you probably don't think about writing an account number on the check because you're attaching the check to the bill stub or a copy of the bill that is being paid. But when Bill Pay sends a payment on your behalf, there's no bill stub to attach to the check, so the only way to identify the payment and get it to the right account is to include the account number. Make sure you enter this number accurately. You are limited to 22 characters including spaces.

TIP

If there is no account number (for example, if you're setting up an individual as a payee instead of a business), just enter your last name in the account number field. There's a check box where you can indicate that there is no account number, but I think it makes more sense to just enter your last name.

6. Enter the ZIP code.

Quicken requests that you enter the extended nine-digit ZIP code if this information is available.

7. Enter a nickname.

What? A nickname for your payee? You can leave the name of the payee in this field (the name fills in automatically), or you can enter a shortened name if you prefer.

8. **Select a category.**

   Enter the category that applies to this expense. If the category you want to use doesn't appear on the list, choose Add a New Category and enter your new category.

9. **Click Continue.**

   If Quicken is able to match the payee information you entered with other information you entered previously, the address and phone number fill in automatically. Otherwise, you are asked to enter the address and phone number for this payee. When all the information is correct, click Continue.

If the payee is set up to communicate with Quicken Bill Pay, Quicken detects this and sets the payee up for an e-payment relationship. Quicken requests your online password information for this payee. After that is provided, Quicken searches for outstanding bills from this payee and presents them to you in your Bills Inbox.

Most companies include a telephone number on their invoices, so you can enter this number when Bill Pay requests information about the payee. But what should you do if there is no phone number? I've only had this happen once, and I just entered my own number. I figured that if someone at Bill Pay has a problem with making this payment, they can just call me about it. I don't know if this is proper or not, but it got me through the data entry window.

At this point, you can continue setting up payees, or move on to the next section if you're ready to make a payment.

Time to pay your bills

If you have exited from Bill Pay, you need to get back into Bill Pay the same way you did in steps one and two in the last section. You see a screen like the one in Figure 4-6. This time, instead of setting up a payee, you're going to make a payment.

1. **Click the Bills & Payments option on the toolbar, and then click Make a Payment to Any Payee.**

   I'm assuming you've set up your payees already. If you haven't yet set up the person or company you're going to pay, go back to the section "Setting up payees in Bill Pay" and get your payee information entered, and then come back — I'll wait. After you've set up payees, your list of payees appears when you execute step 1.

2. **Enter the amount you want to pay next to the appropriate payee.**

   You can pay multiple bills at once — just enter the amount next to each payee you want to pay (see Figure 4-8).

3. **Verify the date. You can change the delivery date to any date later than the date shown.**

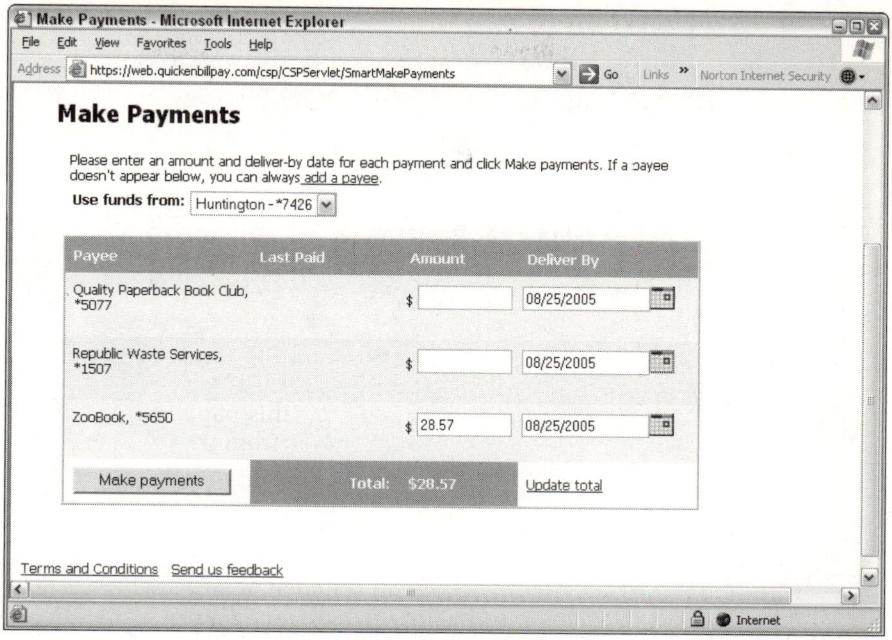

Figure 4-8: Enter payment amounts.

4. **Click Make Payments to dispatch your payment(s).**

A payment confirmation notice appears, indicating that your payments have been moved to your Payment Outbox.

Important: The next time you download transactions for your bank, these Bill Pay payments will be included with the batch of transactions.

Confirming your payments

It's easy to make sure your payments have been made. Here are a couple of different ways you can find out about your payment activity.

- **Click on the Bills & Payments option at the top of the Bill Pay screen.** The list of current payments appears in your Payment Outbox. Click on the Payment Detail for any payment in the Outbox. Payment information appears, showing you the date the payment was initiated, and the delivery date.
- **Click on Payee Setup.** Then click on Payee Details for any payment you want to track. Click on E-Mail Notifications at the top of the Payee Details screen. Check the box to request an e-mail notification of when the payment is actually made (see Figure 4-9). Click Submit and then just watch for the mail.

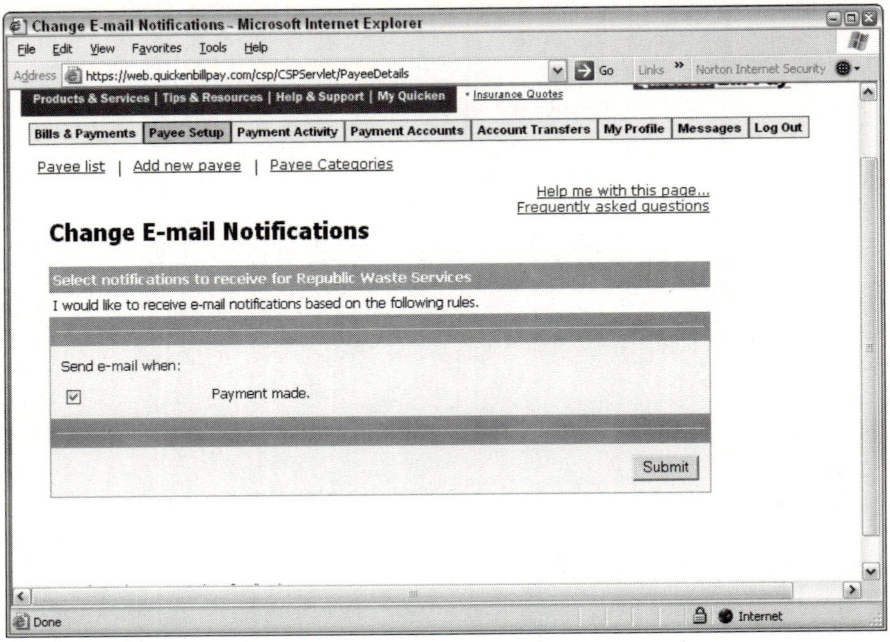

Figure 4-9: You've got mail! (Or, at least you'll have some mail soon . . . .)

Intercepting online payments

When you make a payment in Quicken's Bill Pay, you receive a notice that your payments have been moved to the Outbox. You can click the hyperlink on the Payment Outbox to see your pending payments.

Payments in the Outbox are waiting for their next destination. Either they get dispatched to the intended payees, or, if you change your mind, you can intercept the payments and prevent them from being sent.

In the Outbox, you can click on the Payment detail option (see Figure 4-10) to see when the payment is scheduled to be sent. That gives you an idea of how long the payment will be held in the Outbox. After a payment is sent, you can't intercept it.

As long as a payment appears in the Outbox, you can click the Edit option to make changes in the payment, or the Stop option to prevent the payment from occurring.

TIP

There is also a Notes option in the Payment Outbox. Clicking this option opens a little window where you can enter personal notes about this payment. These notes are for your information only and are not sent with the payment.

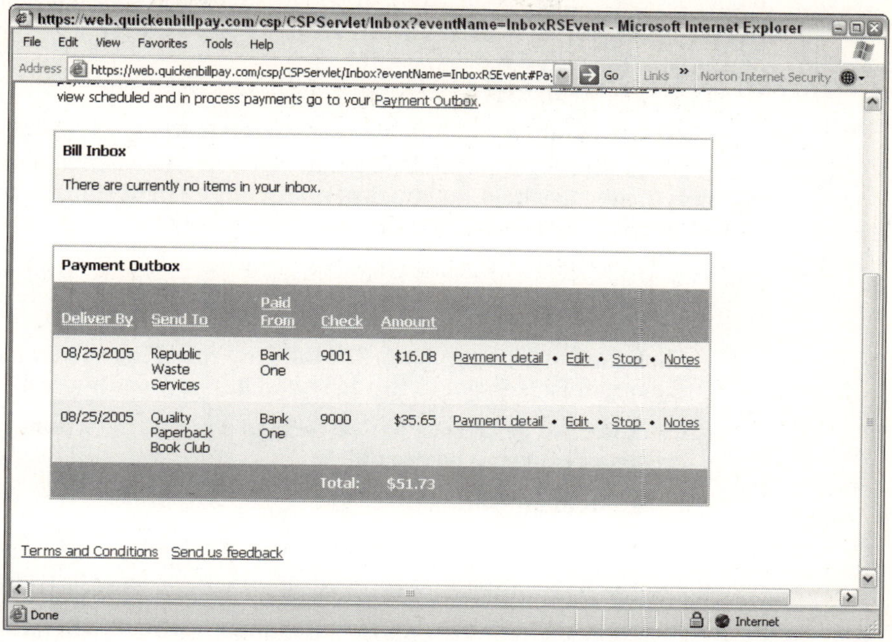

Figure 4-10: The Outbox = Payment Purgatory.

Getting fan mail from Intuit

You might have messages that need attention. At the very least, you should have received a welcome message from Quicken Bill Pay. That's very chummy of them. Follow these steps to read your mail:

1. **Click the Messages option on the Bill Pay tool bar.**

   Your Message Inbox appears (Figure 4-11).

2. **Click the View hyperlink to read a message.**

   When the message appears, press Ctrl+P if you want to print the message. Otherwise, scroll down to the bottom of the message for other options.

3. **Choose your next action.**

   Pick from Back to My Messages if you want to go back to the main message list, Delete message if you no longer need to save this message, or Create New Message if you want to send a message to Bill Pay's client services.

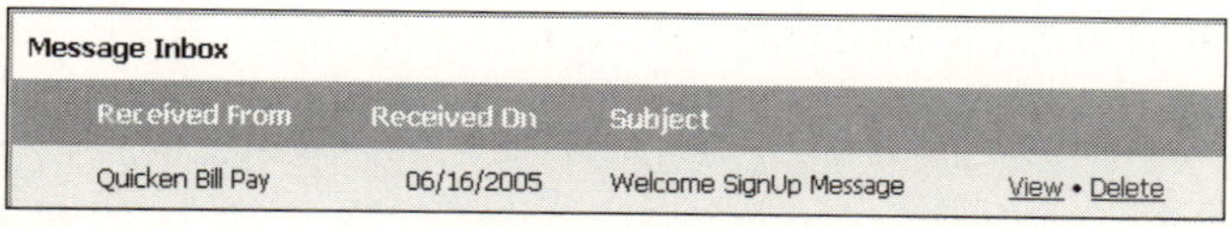

Figure 4-11: Communicating with the mothership.

Scheduling (and Unscheduling) Recurring Payments in Bill Pay

In Book II, Chapter 2, you found out about scheduling payments in Quicken. But guess what: You can also schedule recurring payments in Bill Pay. Bill Pay actually pays bills, so you dispense with the middle-man (Quicken), and get the bill paid directly from Bill Pay. Here's how to set up a recurring payment in Bill Pay.

1. **Open your payees list in Bill Pay.**

   Click the Payee Setup button in Bill Pay. Your Payee list appears. (There are other ways to get to this list as well — any method will do.)

2. **Click the Payee Details option next to a payee for whom you want to create a recurring payment.**

3. **Click Payment Options.**

   The Change Payment Options window appears.

4. **Choose a funding account.**

   First you are asked to choose a funding account. If you have set up more than one online account in Bill Pay, and you plan on creating a recurring payment, you need to indicate to which account the payments for this payee are to be made.

5. **Choose the Recurring payment option.**

   By default, the payment option is set to Manual, meaning the payee is available for online payments through Bill Pay, but each payment is to be authorized individually by you. Now you're going to change that by choosing the Recurring payment option (see Figure 4-12).

6. **Enter the payment details.**

   Enter the amount of the recurring payment, the frequency with which the payment is to be made, the date of the next payment, and the number of payments. For a loan repayment or a mortgage, there will be a set number of payments. For an ongoing service or recurring fee, there isn't a fixed number of payments, so you can leave the No. of Instances field blank.

7. **Save your recurring payment information.**

   Click the Save Payment Options button to authorize the recurring payment.

REMEMBER

After you set up recurring payments in Bill Pay, the payments are going to be made automatically, without your approval. Double-check to make sure all of the information is correct.

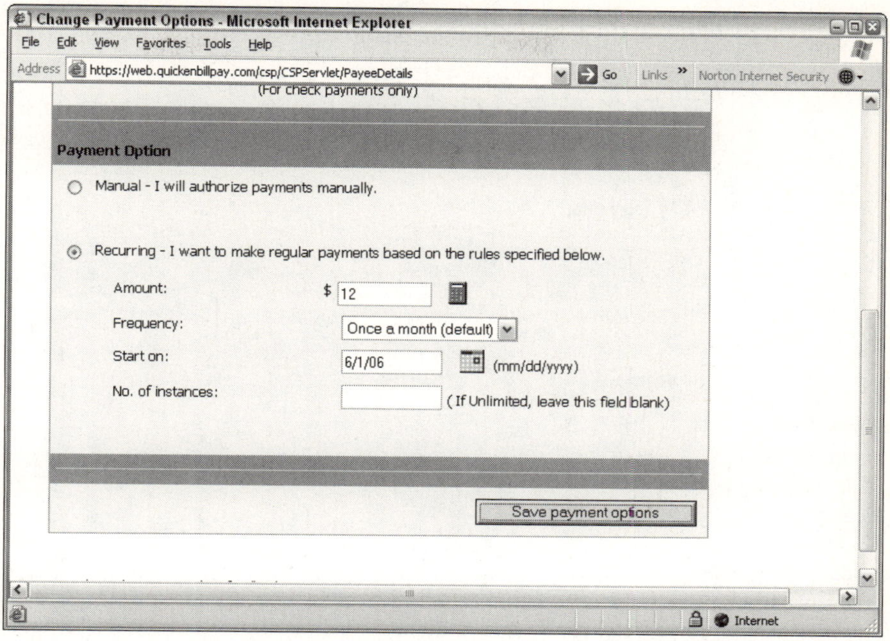

Figure 4-12: Setting up a recurring payment.

From now on, the recurring payment option, along with the amount of the payment, appears in your payee list, as a constant reminder of the fact that you've already taken care of having this payment made.

Maybe you've decided you really prefer writing checks the old-fashioned way. Or maybe you've moved and no longer have that monthly rent payment. No matter what the reason, if you've got a recurring payment going in Bill Pay, especially one with an open-ended payment schedule, someday you might need to cancel the payment. Here's how:

1. **Open up Quicken Bill Pay, and click on the Payee Setup option.**

   The goal here is to display your Payee List. When the list appears, you can see at a glance where you have recurring payments.

2. **Click on the recurring payment you want to terminate.**

   The recurring payments are hyperlinked, so you can click right on the payment description (see Figure 4-13).

3. **Switch the payment from Recurring to Manual.**

   The Change Payment Options window appears. All you really need to do is click on Manual instead of Recurring. Me, I like to be extra sure I've got all bases covered, so I go ahead and remove the amount that appears in the Recurring section of the Payment Option window as well.

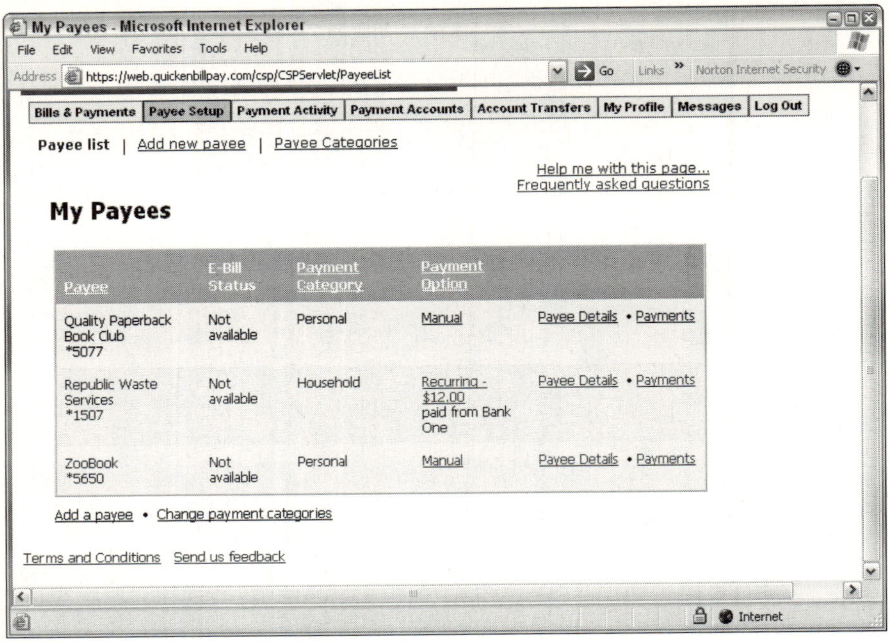

Figure 4-13: Click where it says Recurring along with the amount.

4. **Save your changes.**

   Click on Save Payment Options. The recurring payment is history. If you want to make extra sure, you can follow the previous steps to click back to those Payment Options, only to see that your recurring payment information is completely obliterated.

Don't forget about your recurring payments! My fear is that I'll set up a recurring payment in Bill Pay, and then just keep paying my Bill Pay fee each month (Quicken automatically charges my credit card for this fee), and forget all about the fact that I set up a recurring payment awhile back. I might be 80 years old and still sending in payments for my Wave Rider if I'm not careful.

Double-check amounts and decimal places when you enter bill payment instructions in Bill Pay. Before you dispatch a payment request, make sure you've entered the amount correctly. It's easy to make a typographical error that, left uncorrected, would result in your sending more (or less) money than you intended to the recipient.

Transferring Funds

With Quicken's Bill Pay service, you can arrange for a transfer of funds between accounts. No big deal, you say? I can do this on my own bank's Web site, you say? Hah! I say. Maybe you can transfer funds between accounts on your bank's Web site, but can you transfer funds to *another bank's account* on your bank's Web site? Probably not.

I have accounts at two different banks, and I love being able to move funds between the banks right from my desktop. And when a friend needed a loan last year, I was able to transfer the funds from my account to his, across the country, without ever leaving my office.

Each of the accounts — the sending account and the receiving account — must be set up in Quicken Bill Pay before you execute the transfer. So refer back to "Setting up accounts in Bill Pay," earlier in this chapter, if you need to set up an account, and then follow these steps:

1. **Click Account Transfers at the top of the Bill Pay window.**

   The Transfer Funds window appears, displaying a From field, a To field, and an Amount field. Each of your authorized accounts is listed in the From and To drop-down lists (Figure 4-14).

2. **Choose the appropriate to and from accounts for the transfer.**
3. **Enter the amount of the transfer.**
4. **Click Continue.**

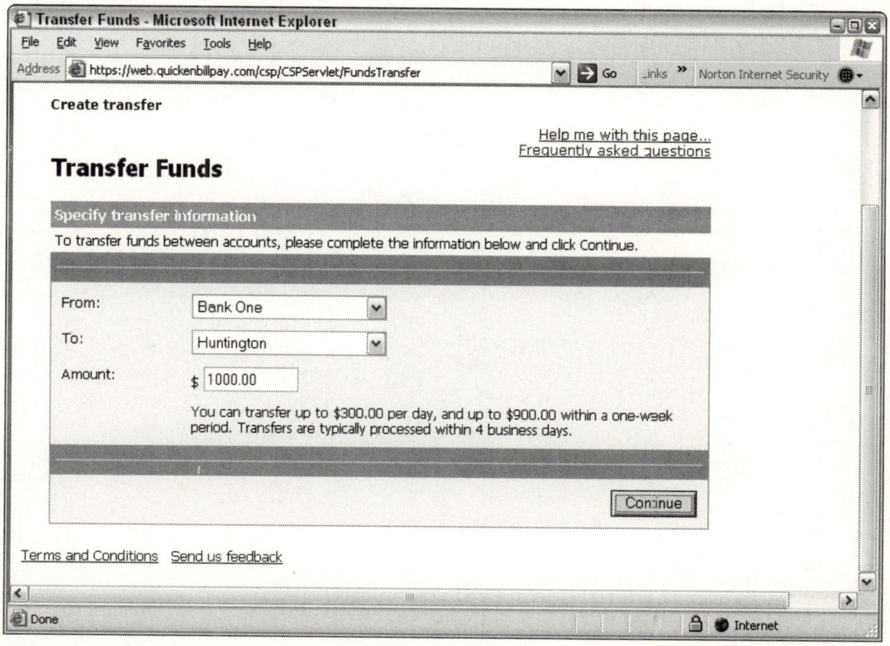

Figure 4-14: Transferring funds is easy as pie.

5. **Verify the transfer information, making sure the correct accounts have been chosen and the amount is correct.**

6. **Click the Transfer button.**

   The transfer process is initiated. Unlike with bill payments, you can't intercept a transfer-in-progress (although you can transfer money back in the other direction if you want to undo the transaction).

Bill Pay tells you that the transfer takes as many as four business days. I've had luck with transfers going through more quickly than that.

Transfers are not automatically downloaded into Quicken like the bill payments are. You need to make an entry in your Quicken register yourself to record any transfers you make through Bill Pay.

Chapter 5: Budgeting in Quicken

In This Chapter

- Creating a budget
- Revising a budget
- Using a budget

You probably think that using a budget to predict and control your spending is a lot like that movie where alien creatures drop in from outer space and hypnotize the children and the rats by playing a sweet tune . . . wait, sorry. What I meant to say is that you probably think budgeting is a combination of science fiction and children's stories — and you're absolutely right. The science fiction part is that you're actually expected to be able to figure out what you're going to earn and spend in the next year — or the next *five years* if you really go crazy with budgeting. The children's story part is that there's a sweet innocence tied to the concept of setting a budget, getting up the determination to stick to it, and congratulating yourself when you accomplish your task.

Before you go any further in this chapter, I recommend you flip back to Book I, Chapter 3, a chapter that explains what a budget is and gives recommendations about how you and your family members can actually create a budget. Why? Although Quicken is a great place to store your budget numbers and gives your budget an excellent starting point by showing you how much you earned and spent in the past, the true future budget planning goes on outside of Quicken: in your thoughts, conversations across the dinner table, in bed at night, or wherever else you are when you think about money.

Creating an Automatic Budget with Quicken

So, now that you've read up on budgeting and have had some time to think about what amounts you actually might want to put in your budget, it's time to dig in and start making a budget! You can fine-tune the process later, after you've got the basics down pat. Start by choosing Budget from the Planning menu. If you've played with this feature before, your existing budget information appears. For you first-timers, Figure 5-1 is the screen you see when you initially request the budget command.

Right off the bat, you have two choices. Choosing Automatic enables Quicken to start you off on a budget using your actual income and expense items that already exist based on all the entries you've entered in Quicken. Picking

Manual starts your budget with a blank screen. That's right. You get no help if you pick Manual. Guess which one I'm going to pick for this example? You guessed it: Choose Automatic.

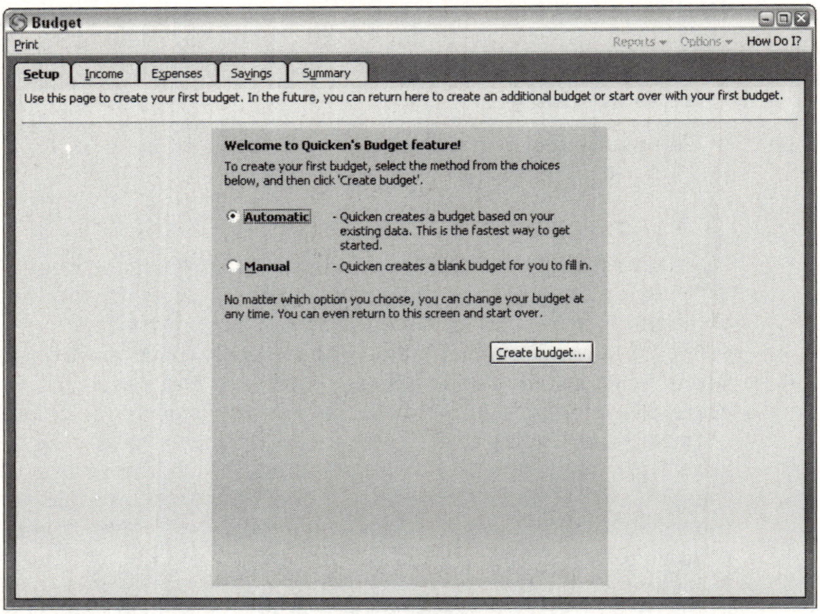

Figure 5-1: Welcome to your first day of Quicken's Budget!

Seriously, choosing Manual isn't just for those who like to do things the hard way. If you earn income irregularly, or your expenses vary *greatly* from month to month, setting up an automatic budget might not be for you. You might find it easier to simply set up your budget manually, rather than making extensive changes to the budget that Quicken creates automatically. If you fall into this category, flip ahead to the section entitled, "Using the Manual Method for Creating Your Budget."

TIP

If you open the Budget window and your existing budget appears, click the Setup tab, and then choose Automatic for your new budget. Because a budget already exists, you are required to give this new budget a name to distinguish it from the old budget before you can continue.

Now that you've chosen the Automatic route for creating your budget, click the Create Budget button and away we go.

TIP

Keep in mind the fact that the budget Quicken prepares is going to be for an entire year. The information you provide is going to be spread over the upcoming year as your preliminary budget, based on the method and dates you select.

Choosing your date range

After clicking the Create Budget button in the window shown in Figure 5-1, the Create Budget window appears. You are expected to enter a range of dates for your budget, as I've done in Figure 5-2. Quicken uses the amounts that fall in that date range to establish your preliminary budget amounts. Allow me to elaborate on a few of these phrases.

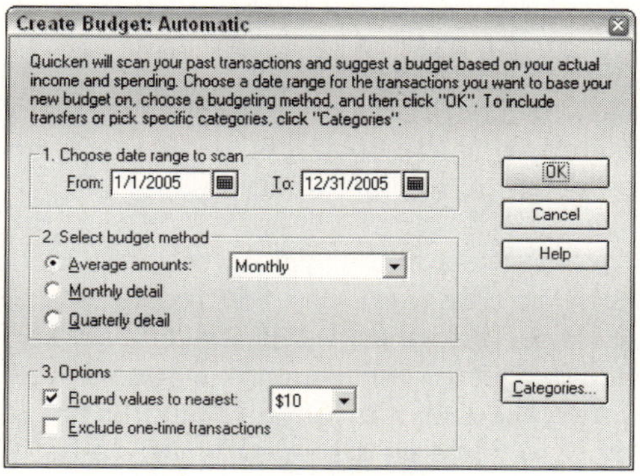

Figure 5-2: Enter some introductory budget setup information.

First, *range of dates* means a beginning and end date, and all the dates in between. If you choose March 1 to March 31 as your range, Quicken is going to mimic everything you entered for the month of March, and make up a whole budget for the year based on what you earned and what you spent in March. If you pick dates that span five years, Quicken averages your income and expense activity for the entire five-year period and makes up a budget based on those averages. The idea is to try to pick a range of dates that represent a typical period of time for analyzing your income and expenses.

Next, *amounts that fall in that date range* refers to everything, monetarily-speaking, that you already entered in your Quicken register for the range of dates that you select. Even though Quicken is made by a company called Intuit, and you might therefore think that this program ought to be intuitive, Quicken is just plain incapable of rummaging around in your desk drawer and getting out your checkbook or your old bank statements, and basing your budget on information in those records. You have to have actually entered the information in your Quicken register for your past financial activity to be considered in the creation of the budget.

Finally, the phrase *preliminary budget amounts* means that Quicken is going to come up with a budget for you, and that budget is preliminary, meaning the budget is just a dry run and you can change the numbers to amounts that seem more reasonable after you take a look at them. Here's a good example of something you might want to change. Perhaps you bought a lottery ticket and won $5,000 in July of last year. If you base your budget on the activity from last year, that lottery income is going to show up as a budgeted amount for next year. In other words, you're telling yourself that you have to win $5,000 from the lottery next year. Although winning from the lottery perhaps is a worthy goal, it probably shouldn't be a budgeted amount because, correct me if I'm wrong, the odds of winning $5,000 from the lottery are not as great as, say, the odds of spending $5,000 on lottery tickets in hopes of winning another $5,000. So as you can see, the budget might need some fine-tuning once you see the preliminary numbers.

Choose a budget method

You get to pick — would you like Quicken to take the average of the amounts from your date range for creating a new budget, or do you want to use exact amounts? Here's a comparison of the methods:

- **Average:** Your budget is based on the average of all the income and expenses that fall into the date range you selected. If you entered just one month in your date range, that month's financial activity serves as the basis for your annual budget for every month. If you selected an entire year in your date range, the amounts for all 12 months are added together, and then divided by 12 to come up with monthly budgeted amounts for the coming year. But wait! You're not limited to averaging a month or a year. You can request a daily average, bi-weekly, quarterly, semi-annually, and so on. Click the drop-down arrow to determine the time frame of income and expenses that you want to average for your budget.
- **Monthly:** Quicken uses the actual amounts from the corresponding months in your date range to complete your budget.
- **Quarterly:** Again, Quicken uses actual amounts instead of averages for completing your budget. In this case, the amounts are chosen from each quarter instead of each month in the date range you provide. If you only specify one quarter in the date range, that quarter is repeated for each quarter of the year you are budgeting.

Pick some budget options

Before you proceed, you need to make a couple of selections from the Budget Options setup category. You get to pick how you want your numbers to be rounded, and whether to include one-time transactions.

- **Rounding:** Quicken lets you select a method of rounding — you can have your budget numbers rounded to the nearest dollar, the nearest $10, or the nearest $100. For example, if it works out that last year you spent $3,943.44 on groceries, that results in an average of $328.62 per month for grocery spending.

  If you're using a monthly average for your budget computation, and you choose to round your budgeted items to the nearest dollar, Quicken assigns a monthly budgeted amount of $329 for groceries. If you choose to round to the nearest $10, your monthly budgeted amount for groceries is $330. And if you round to the nearest $100, you get $300 as your monthly budget for groceries.

Or, you cannot round at all, and use the exact amount of your prior year spending as your budgeted amount for the next year.

If you want to choose a rounding option, check the Rounding box in the Options section that appears in Figure 5-2, and then choose from the options in the drop-down list.

- **One-time transactions:** When you base your budget on last year's financial activity, Quicken goes back over the past year and computes averages to use in this year's budget. But what if you wrote a check last year for a down payment on a new car? This is probably an expense that you're not going to need in next year's budget. For items like this, it's handy to have the option to exclude one-time transactions from the budget computation.

  On the other hand, maybe you pay for life insurance or auto insurance with one payment, once a year. Even though the payment is made only once a year, that's a recurring event; every year, you need to pay for insurance again. For this type of one-time transaction, it might make sense to budget for the amount all year long, setting aside money each month instead of having to come up with a large amount of cash all at once for the annual payment. So if this is the type of one-time transaction you have, you may want to include these transactions in your budget.

  To have Quicken omit one-time transactions from your budget, check the Exclude One-Time Transactions box in the Options section shown in Figure 5-2. Leave the box unchecked if you want to include your one-time transactions in next year's budget.

  TIP: Just because you don't want Quicken to average your one-time transactions and spread the amount through each month of your budget doesn't mean you can't include these transactions in your budget. Check the Exclude One-Time Transactions box to have Quicken exclude the transactions, and then when you get your hands on the actual budget (see "Fine-tuning your budget" later in this chapter), you can add the one-time transactions in the actual months when they should occur.

You've finished entering your options choices, but don't click OK yet — you've got to take one more step before you're ready to proceed.

Choose categories for your budget

Before you leave the Create Budget: Automatic window, click the Categories button. The Choose Categories window appears (Figure 5-3). Scroll through the list, clicking to uncheck any of the categories that you don't need to use in your budget computation.

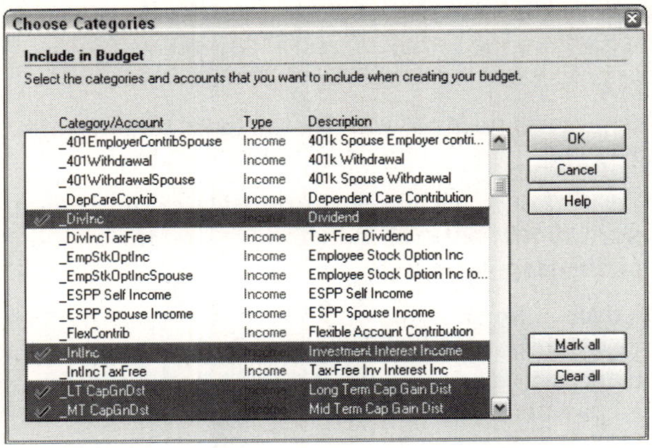

Figure 5-3: Pick and choose from the category list.

If you find there are more categories you don't need than the ones that you do need, try clicking the Clear All button to uncheck everything, and then just check the categories you want.

When you see lots of categories that you don't need, that's an indication that you should probably clean out your category list, getting rid of categories that were on the original list Quicken gave you, but that you never use. Check back to Book II, Chapter 1 for advice on cleaning out the rubbish in your category list.

You might have categories on your list that you used in the past, but no longer need. These aren't categories that are slated for removal; they're just categories you don't need to include in your budget going forward. Just because you spent money on landscaping last year doesn't mean you're going to spend that money next year. Just pick the categories you plan to use in the coming year.

You can quickly exclude all categories that have zero for their amount. In the Choose Categories window (Figure 5-4), click the Clear 0 Amounts button to remove categories that have a zero balance. Remember, however, that even if there is a zero balance in the month of the budget you're viewing onscreen, there might not be a zero in another month during the year. This month's zeros (a good name for a rock band) might be next month's insurance payments — the Clear 0 option won't remove a category if there is an actual balance somewhere down the line.

When you finish choosing the categories you want to include in your budget, click OK to close the Choose Categories window, and then click OK in the Create Budget: Automatic window. Quicken sifts through your transactions for the date range you provided and comes up with a preliminary budget for the next year.

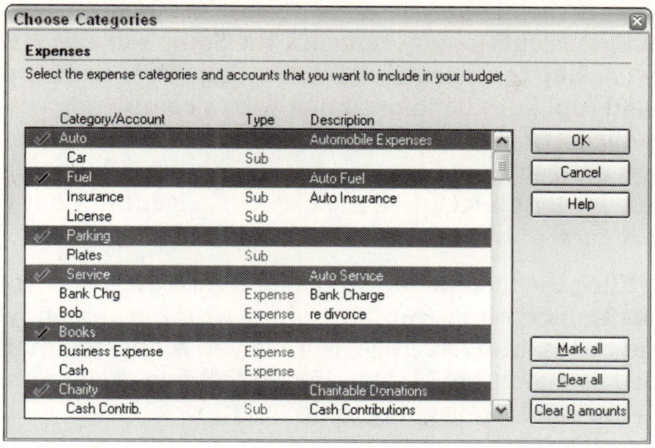

Figure 5-4: Click Clear 0 Amounts.

Fine-tuning your budget

Now that you have a preliminary budget to work with, you can start examining your budget up close, making adjustments in individual categories and months, so that the final budget is as close to true expectations as possible. The budget window has five tabs across the top, as shown in Figure 5-5. Click through the various budget tabs to explore the budgeted amounts Quicken has provided for you.

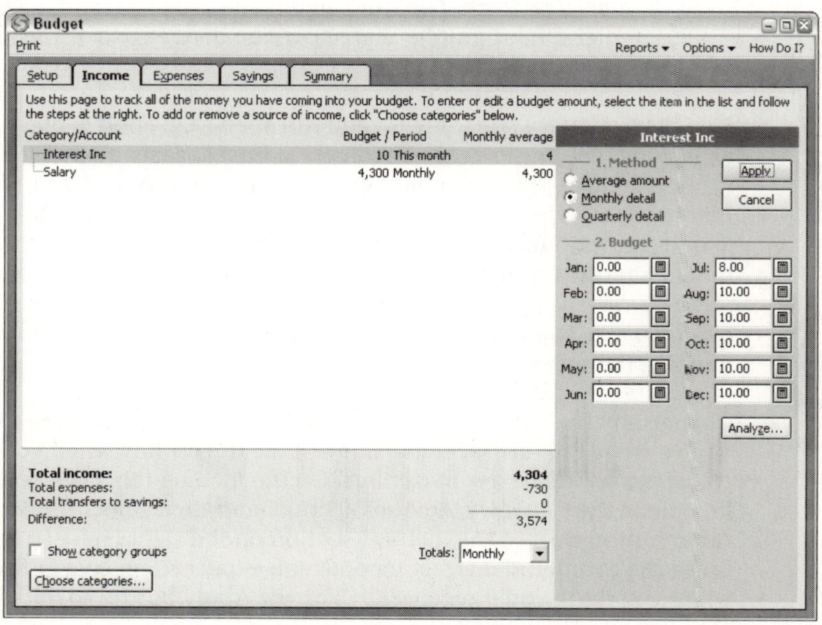

Figure 5-5: Click the various tabs to explore your new Quicken budget.

- **Setup:** This is the back-to-the-drawing-board tab. If you want to try a different budget scenario, you can click the Setup tab and start all over again by clicking the Start Over button. Start Over erases your current budget and replaces the information with a completely new budget. You can also click Rename to give your budget a different name, you can open a different budget, or make a copy of your current budget as a starting point for another budget. Use the Create Budget button if you want to keep your current budget and create another budget.
- **Income:** Click the Income tab, and any of the categories you budgeted that relate to income appear here, along with the amount you've budgeted and the monthly average. Note: If you requested that your budget be created as a monthly budget, the budget and the monthly average amounts are most likely going to be the same.
- **Expenses:** The Expenses tab displays all of the expenses you selected in your budget setup. Budgeted amounts are displayed as negative numbers.
- **Savings:** If part of your budget includes transferring money to any of your savings categories, the budget for those transfers appears on this tab.
- **Summary:** See a total of everything you budgeted, one year's worth compiled by month. Click on a particular month, and then click the Details button to see the complete budget of income and expenses and transfers to savings for that month. In addition, there is a graph feature on the Summary page that provides a visual representation of how your income and expenses are budgeted. Click the drop-down list in the graph section to choose from an income-related graph, an expense-related graph, or graphs that show non-discretionary spending and discretionary spending.

REMEMBER

Non-discretionary spending is required spending. Food is non-discretionary, as is your rent or mortgage, medical expenses, basic clothing, and any other expenses you've committed to such as college costs or pet care. Discretionary spending is money you don't *have to* spend. Although food is non-discretionary, restaurant food is discretionary. Rent or mortgage is non-discretionary, but the cost of a vacation home is discretionary.

TIP

Discretionary spending is the spending you can limit if you're having trouble meeting the non-discretionary expenses in your budget.

Change any budgeted amounts. Changes are easy to make. Say you know you're going to start receiving interest income in July when you expect to transfer a windfall over to savings. On the Income tab, click on Interest Income in the Category/Amount section, and then select the Monthly Detail radio button over in the method section on the right (refer to Figure 5-5). Enter the estimated interest income you expect to receive in the months when you think you'll receive it. Click the Apply button to inject your changes into the budget.

The Apply button isn't available unless you make a change in at least one of the monthly slots.

Perhaps you pay your auto insurance quarterly instead of monthly and you want to record the insurance that way. Click on the Expenses tab, and then click Auto: Insurance. Change the payment amount to one-fourth of the total in the four months when you plan to make a payment, change the rest of the months to zero, and then click Apply.

Adding missing categories

If, while choosing your categories for your budget, you find that the category you want to use doesn't appear on the list, click the Options button at the top of the Budget window, and then choose Go to Category List. The budget is minimized, and the category list appears. You can add any categories you need, and then click the X in the upper-right corner to close the category list. The budget window can be restored by clicking the Budget icon that appears at the bottom of your Quicken screen.

Your budget list might show categories with plus or minus signs next to the title. These are the standard expand and collapse buttons. Click all the plus signs to hide the detail and display only the main categories on your budget. Click the minuses, and you see the detail beneath the main category headings.

Printing your budget

At any time, and from any tab, you can print a copy of your budget by following these steps:

1. **Click the Print button that appears above the tabs.**

   The Print window appears (Figure 5-6).

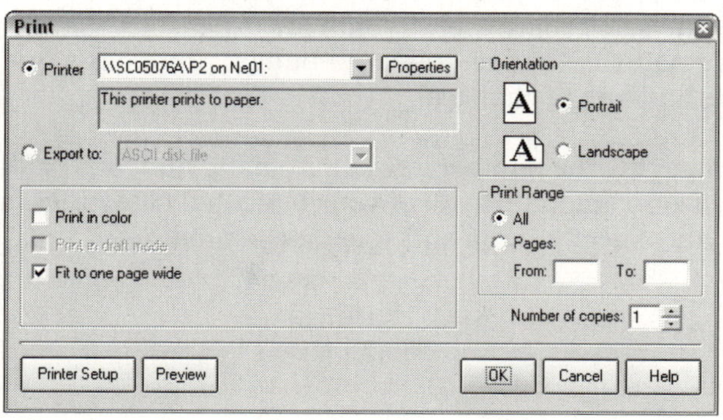

Figure 5-6: Make any necessary print modifications before printing your budget.

2. **Click Preview to see how your budget appears.**

   In the Print Preview window that appears, you can page through your budget, zoom in or out, and Print by clicking the Print button at the top of the Preview screen.

3. **If you close the Preview window without printing, you need to reopen the Print window.**

4. **Make any print modifications, such as changing from portrait to landscape, making your budget fit in one page wide, or printing to an Excel-compatible file so that you can work with your budget in a spreadsheet.**

   If you choose to print to an Excel-compatible file, choose Export To, and then ASCII Disk File.

5. **Click OK when you're ready to print.**

Important: The budget prints out with a separate column for each month. This is a great format, especially if income or expense amounts vary from month to month. You can make notations on the pages for use in family budget meetings or just for your own information so you know what caused you to veer from your budget.

Saving your budget

Just as with any information you enter in your Quicken program, your budget is automatically saved as you work on it. You don't need to take any special steps to save your budget.

Using the Manual Method for Creating Your Budget

The automatic method for creating a budget works really well if your income and expenses stay pretty much the same, month in and month out. But what about the person whose income is earned sporadically, or someone who doesn't pay the same thing every month for expenses? That person finds that the automatic method of creating a budget produces a budget that requires lots and lots of changes.

Instead of changing the numbers in an automatic budget, try starting from scratch, with zero amounts in all of your budgeted categories, and filling in how much you expect to earn and spend each month.

TIP

Students might prefer the manual method of creating a budget, especially that first year out of school. An FOC (Fresh Outta College) has tuition and housing and job-hunting expenses the first five or six months, perhaps followed by some time off living at home or traveling, and then maybe by job income and new types of expenses related to a new job.

On the budget start-up screen, choose Manual instead of Automatic. Quicken takes you right into the main budget window, with the tabs for Setup (not necessary because you're using Manual setup), Income, Expenses, Savings, and Summary, just like you saw before. The big difference, however, is that there are no amounts in any of the windows. There aren't even any categories listed. This is total start-from-scratch budgeting.

When you begin your manual budget, you might be asked to give this budget a name and description. This step enables Quicken to distinguish this budget from any other budget you've already worked on.

TIP

It helps to have a written budget prepared on paper, or at least some notes where you've contemplated what you expect to earn and what types of expenses you think you'll encounter in the year ahead. You can use this information to help get yourself started.

Here are the steps to follow when creating a budget manually:

1. **When you're in the budget window, click the Income tab, and then click the Choose Categories button at the bottom of the window.**

   The list of all your Quicken categories appears.

2. **Check off the categories you want to include in your budget.**

   Remember: The Mark All and Clear All buttons are available to make the job easier.

3. **Click OK when you have selected all of your categories.**

   TIP

   You need to choose categories on each tab separately. When you select the Income tab and click Choose Categories, only income categories appear. From the Expenses tab, only expense categories appear. Likewise, on the Savings tab, you only see your bank accounts, asset accounts, and other investment accounts.

4. **Quicken populates the tabs with the categories you choose, but all the amounts are zero (Figure 5-7).**

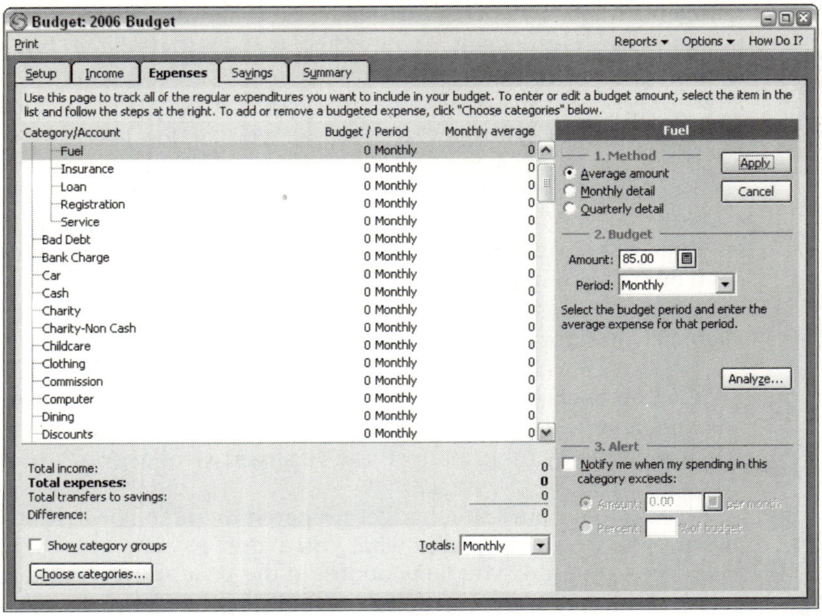

Figure 5-7: Manual budgeting means you start with all zeros.

Click a category, and then use the boxes at the right of the budget list to enter an amount, and choose a frequency for that amount (anywhere from daily to yearly or any frequency in between). In the example in Figure 5-7, I've entered $85 per month as my Auto–Fuel cost. Click the Apply button to enter the amount, and then repeat this step for each budget item you want to create.

Use the Analyze button to help you set up your budget. Click the Analyze button to display a graph and summary of any previous activity you've entered in Quicken.

While you're busy creating your budget, don't overlook the budget alert feature. Nestled at the bottom-right corner of the expense tab of the budget window is the Alert area. For any budgeted amount, including amounts you leave at zero, you can set an alert to have Quicken tell you when your spending exceeds the budget by whatever amount you designate.

In Figure 5-8, I've set an alert to have Quicken give me a little nudge when my automobile fuel costs go over $100 per month. Just check the box in the Alert area of the window, and enter the amount. If you prefer, you can enter a percentage in lieu of an amount.

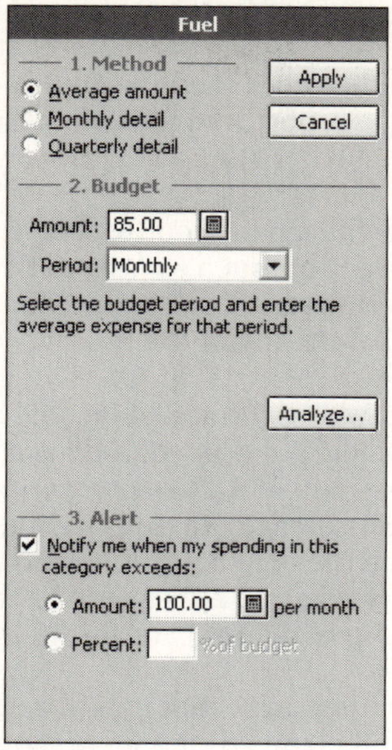

Figure 5-8: Set an alert to monitor your spending.

How to Use a Budget in Everyday Life

I'm going to refer you back to Book I, Chapter 3 to read about how budgets are actually used. Rather than being redundant about all the ways you can use a budget, I'm going to give you something a little different in this section. I give you some information here on how to use Quicken to see the budget you created and your budget progress, and I've got some un-tips for what not to do with your budget. I also offer just a few concluding remarks about how cool budgets really are once you get the hang of them.

Producing budget reports

What good is a budget if you can't tell whether or not you're meeting your budget goals? Use the budget reports that come with Quicken to monitor your progress and then, if necessary, either make changes in your financial activities or make changes in your budget.

Quicken provides two reporting tools — the Budget Report and the Monthly Budget Report. The reports are similar, except that the Budget Report shows your year-to-date activity, and the monthly report gives you a separate set of columns for each month.

From the Budget window, click the Reports option at the top, and then choose Budget Report. If you prefer to use the menus, click the Reports menu and go to the Reports and Graphs Center, and then click the How Am I Spending My Money? option. Next click on the Budget Report, and then click the Show Report button.

If you don't like the dates Quicken has chosen for your report, you can change them to a more appropriate selection, such as Year to Date, Quarter to Date, or Last Month. There are several available date options, accessible from the Date Range drop-down menu at the top of the report.

The report includes an Actual column, where the actual income and expenses that you have reported to Quicken are listed. Next is a Budget column that displays your budgeted amounts for the same period of time as you have chosen for your actual amounts. Finally there is a column that displays the amount of difference between the actual amounts and the budgeted amounts. Negative differences (where you either didn't earn as much as you budgeted or spent more than you budgeted) are shown in red.

WARNING! One problem with the standard Budget Report is that non-budgeted categories do not appear. For example, maybe you spent a lot of money in a category that you neglected to include on your budget. I think this happens most often when you copy a budget from a prior year to use as a starting point for a new budget. You might have added categories during the year without realizing that they need to be added to your budget. You can circumvent this problem by clicking the Customize button on your budget report, and then clicking the Advanced tab. There is an option under Categories to choose Include All instead of the default, Budgeted Only.

TIP When examining your budget reports, be sure to analyze them from a logical point of view as well as an analytical point of view. If an amount looks out of line, or if something seems to be missing from the report, don't automatically assume the report is right. Dig a little, find out where the numbers originated, and make sure you've got accurate information in your report. For example, you might have posted one or more transactions to the wrong category.

Customizing your budget report

Customize the Budget Report if you want to by changing the date range at the top of the report. Instead of year-to-date, maybe you only want to see quarter-to-date or month-to-date or some other selection of dates. Click the Customize button and the Customize Budget window appears (Figure 5-9).

The Display tab of the Customize window gives you the option to assign a different name to your budget. You can check the box to show cents instead of rounding to the nearest dollar. You can also control column headings, select a different budget to use for comparison purposes, and choose from three different types of report organization. Report organization options include Cash Flow, which organizes your budget items by cash inflows and outflows; Income and Expense, which organizes by income categories and expense categories; or Category Group, which organizes your report by discretionary and non-discretionary spending categories.

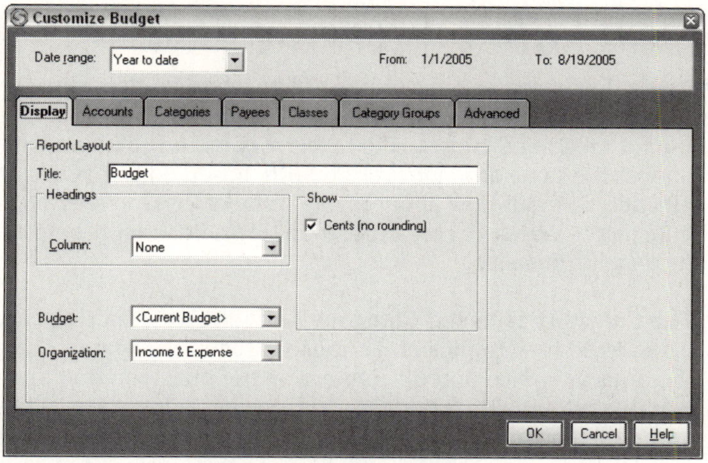

Figure 5-9: Customize your budget report.

TIP

Discretionary and non-discretionary designations can be assigned to a category when you create a new category. For existing categories, you can designate whether the category is discretionary by selecting an expense category on the category list (found on the Tools menu or by pressing Ctrl+C) and then editing that category. There is a check box for discretionary categories on the Setup and Edit page for each expense.

You can click other tabs in the Customize window to choose which accounts, categories, classes, and category groups to include in your report. For more about customizing reports, see Chapter 3 of Book VII.

Viewing the Monthly Budget Report

Much like the Budget Report, only with more detail, the Monthly Budget Report presents you with a set of three columns for each month. This is a massive report, especially if it's close to the end of the year and you're looking at 12 or so months worth of data, meaning 39 or so columns of numbers. Unless you've got a *really* big monitor, you probably need to use the scroll bar at the bottom to see all the columns in the report.

For each month, you get a column of your actual income and expenses, a column for the budgeted amount, and a column showing the difference. Then at the far right side of the report, there are the three columns summarizing the year-to-date activity.

Just like with the other Budget Report, you can customize the monthly report by requesting a particular date range, or clicking the Customize button and choosing exactly which accounts and categories you want to analyze and which budget you want to use for comparison purposes.

Thinking About Different Types of Budgets

Quicken is flexible and allows you to create a budget that is just what you need. When you start using the budget feature, the obvious and easiest method for creating a budget is to take every income item and every expense, and budget the same amount every month, based on last year's activity. That's all well and good, but how about trying some of these scenarios instead? They might be just what the doctor ordered in terms of actually helping you get a handle on your finances.

- **The Carefully Selected Category Budget:** Earlier in this chapter, you discovered how to pick and choose categories for your budget, adding the ones you need and disconnecting the ones you don't need. When you're working with a budget of all of your income and expenses, you may well have had some expenses last year that won't occur again next year. Maybe you bought a dog, or had some cosmetic surgery, landscaped the yard, took a vacation, or attended a seminar. By picking and choosing your categories carefully, you can weed out the ones that don't belong in your new budget.
- **The Business Budget:** Do you own your own business? Do you have a hobby that is about to turn profitable? Or are you thinking about starting a business next year? Create a budget where the only categories are those that relate to your business. Don't hesitate to create new categories for income and expense areas that you haven't used in the past. Your business budget is of particular interest to anyone who is considering investing in or loaning money for the business.
- **The Classy Budget:** Use classes (described in Book VIII) to separate financial transactions by members of the family, to distinguish between different family business ventures, to track income and expenses that relate to different jobs, or any other creative way you can imagine to analyze your financial activity. You can click the Customize button on your budget reports and click the tab labeled Classes to indicate which classes you want to report in your budget. In this way, you can produce a report that only displays the budget items for the class you choose.
- **The Specific Category Budget:** Who says you have to create a budget that shows all of your income and expenses when what you really want is a budget for just your medical expenses? In the Budget Setup window, choose only the categories that relate to medical expenses (or whatever other type of category you want to report on), excluding everything else.

Seven Ways Not to Use a Budget

You can benefit from using a budget in lots of ways, but here are some budget techniques that are not recommended:

✦ **Don't rely on the budget alone to get the job done.** A budget is a tool for helping you monitor your income and spending. Earning the income and keeping the spending in line is still your responsibility.

✦ **Don't try to pass your budget off as a financial statement.** If you're applying for a loan, your financial institution is going to ask you for financial statements. Although a budget can be included with the entire package you give to your potential lender, the lender is really looking for your actual income and spending activity. The income/expense statement and net worth statement are more interesting and useful to your banker than a budget.

✦ **Know that your budget isn't the law.** Sometimes unbudgeted events occur. Live with it. You can do your best to predict your financial circumstances, but you can't always control life. Understand that your budget needs to be flexible and that you might need to make budgetary changes during the course of the year.

✦ **Don't change the budget to meet every whim.** In spite of what I just said in the previous statement, your budget isn't going to be very useful if you change it *every* time your income or expenses don't agree with the budgeted amounts. Analyze the differences, make sure you understand what caused them, but try to get back on track. Remember: You can use future months to make up for problems in months gone by.

✦ **Don't get mad at your budget.** Remember, the budget is an inanimate object. Hurling squishy vegetables at the computer screen or shouting obscenities at your budget won't improve the situation. Try to remember that you need to figure out the problem of why the budget isn't working and find a way to get back on track.

✦ **Don't think of your budget as an albatross, dragging you down, preventing you from spending money on items you want or need.** In truth, the budget should have the opposite effect. Keep tabs on your budgeted categories, and see when the money is available for spending. By following your budget, you know when it's OK to spend.

✦ **Don't use the budget to start family feuds.** Especially because you're getting this information from me. The last thing I want to hear is that families are arguing because "Gail Perry said we should follow our budget and not buy theatre tickets when the bills haven't been paid." C'mon! Make budgeting a positive experience!

Book V

Taxes

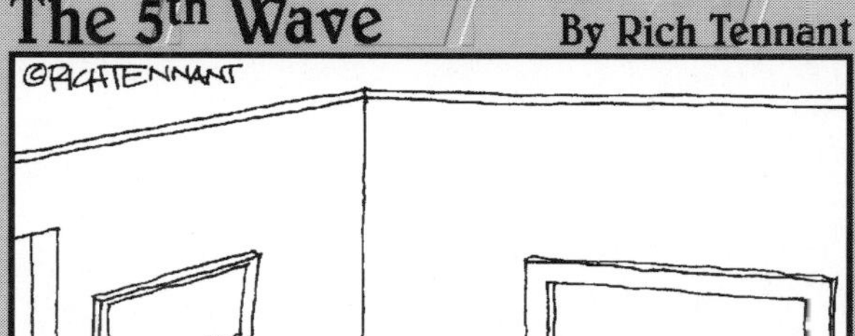

"I bought a software program that should help us monitor and control our spending habits, and while I was there, I picked up a few new games, a couple of screen savers, 4 new mousepads, this nifty pull out keyboard cradle..."

Contents at a Glance

Chapter 1: The Quicken Tax Center

In This Chapter

- Exploring the Tax Center
- Tracking your tax-related income and deductions
- Projecting your income tax
- Relying on the tax calendar
- Setting tax alerts

I'm sure some psychologists somewhere have run tests where they say words such as "tax" and "IRS" to see what kind of brain patterns appear on computer scanners — the results are probably too scary to publish. For most people, taxes are at least a source of concern, if not downright fear and loathing. Allow Quicken to make it easier for you to get a grip on your taxes, and leave the scary stuff to people like Stephen King and Roger Corman.

Poking Around in the Quicken Tax Center

To open the Tax Center, choose Tax⇨Go To Tax Center. Welcome to the Tax Center! Quicken opens up the Financial Overview page with the Tax tab selected (Figure 1-1). Here's a selection of what you can find in the Tax Center.

- **Tax Alerts:** You can ask Quicken to give you a nudge when a major tax event is about to occur. You might not have any trouble remembering that the federal tax return is due on April 15, but what about those pesky quarterly payments? You can also ask Quicken to monitor your tax withholding on your paycheck and let you know if the withholding looks like it's going to be too much or too little. Quicken can give you alerts about tax deductions you might not have thought about. See "Alert! Alert! Incoming Tax Payments!" later in this chapter for information on how to set tax alerts in Quicken.

  TIP: Having too much tax withheld doesn't get you into trouble, at least not with the tax authorities. On the other hand, having too little tax withheld can spell big trouble because you can run the risk of having to pay penalties.

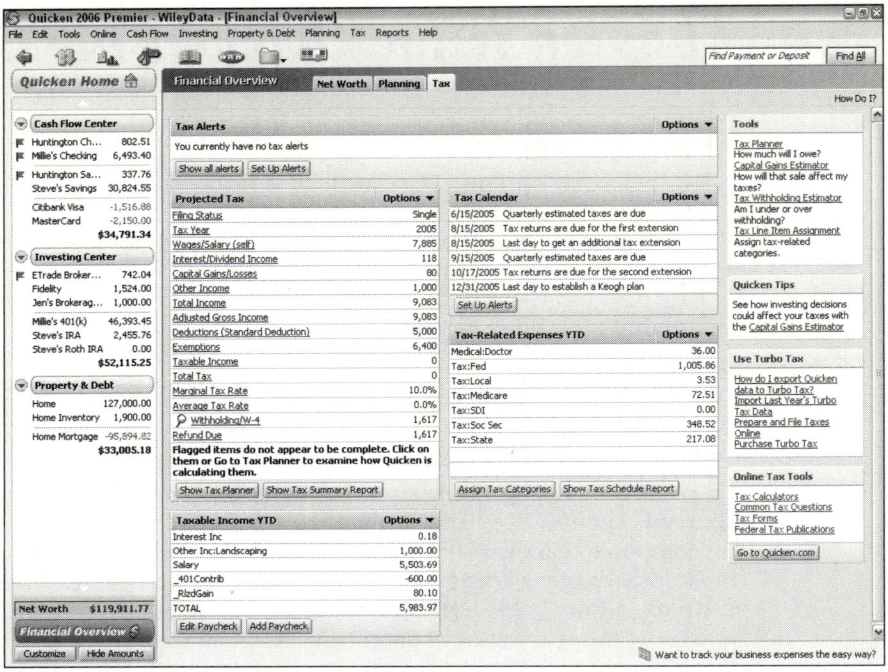

Figure 1-1: Mmmmm! Taxes! What fun!

- **Tax Planner:** Without your even having to ask, Quicken has created a little tax planner for you, rifling through your expense accounts and coming up with a guess of how much tax you're going to owe or how much of a refund you can expect in the spring. More information about the tax planner is coming up in Chapter 5 of this book.
- **Tax Calendar:** The IRS doesn't mess around when it comes to due dates for tax returns and tax payments. In addition to the alerts you can create in Quicken, keep an eye on the tax calendar so you won't forget to keep your nice old Uncle Sam happy.

WARNING! The tax alerts available in Quicken are pre-set, meaning you can't add your own tax-related alerts to the tax alerts list. If you have made arrangements to make tax payments on dates different from the regular quarterly payment dates, or if you have state tax payments due on a date different from the federal quarterly payments, you can create a calendar alert or a Billminder reminder, but you can't add a tax alert to cover these situations.

- **Tax-Related Expenses YTD:** Quicken keeps a little list for you of the expenses that might generate tax deductions, summarizing how much you've spent in each of these categories thus far in the current year. See "Adding categories to the Tax-Related Expenses list" later in this chapter for instructions for expanding this list.

- **Taxable Income YTD:** The counterpart to the list of taxable expenses is the list of taxable income items. This list displays the detail that makes up your taxable income. Make additions (or deletions) to this list as necessary and as described later in this chapter, so that the list provides a clear summary of all of your taxable income.
- **Tools, Reports, Tips, TurboTax:** On the right side of your Tax Center screen are hyperlinks to a variety of tax tools, reports, and help items. Sift through these at your leisure, when you're interested in reading more about taxes (and aren't we all interested in reading about taxes all the time?). I cover them in this chapter as well.

What's Taxable, What's Not

If only I had about 5,000 extra pages in this book, I could include the U.S. Tax Code, but trust me, even with the entire code in hand, most people still don't know what's taxable and what's not. That's because for every rule, there are exceptions, gyrations, emanations, explanations, right ways and wrong ways, tried and true ways, black and blue ways, ways and means, tangos and hustles, and more new tax laws coming our way every year.

But the limited size of this book won't stop me from trying. Herewith, my capsule analysis of what you need to know about the tax laws.

Sharing the fruits of your labors with your dear old Uncle Sam

Quicken displays your taxable income year-to-date in the Tax Center section appropriately called Taxable Income YTD. If it doesn't look like all of your income is showing up in this section, that doesn't mean you get to exclude the missing income from your income tax return; it just means that Quicken hasn't found out about all of your sources of income yet. Chapter 2 of this book goes into more detail about how to set up your categories so that they appear properly in the Tax Center.

The easiest way to explain how to tax income is that, if you think it might be taxable, it probably is. Most of the money you receive is taxable. That includes the obvious stuff like income from jobs, interest on your savings account, and dividends on stock investments. In the next section, I've listed some other examples of common types of taxable income and not-so-taxable income.

Keep track of the following types of income in Quicken because chances are, you're going to see them again when you fill out your tax return. I'm going to go right down the front page of the federal income tax return with a quick explanation of the most familiar forms of income.

- Income you earn at work, which is reported to you by your employer on a W-2 form.
- Interest on savings accounts and interest you receive from money you loaned — most of this interest (but not all) is reported to you on a 1099-INT form.
- Dividends on stocks you own and investments in money market funds and mutual funds. Most of the dividends are reported on 1099-DIV forms, or on the year-end report you receive from the fund in which you own shares.
- Income you earn at a business or farm you own. Expenses that are directly related to the business offset this income.
- Profit on the sale of items you own, including tangible items like stamps and coins and vintage cars as well as shares of stocks and mutual funds.
- Amounts you receive from a pension, IRA, Social Security, or other source of retirement income. Sometimes these amounts aren't taxable. Sometimes they are.
- Unemployment compensation.
- The odds and ends of income like jury duty, director's fees, insurance proceeds (sometimes these amounts aren't taxable), certain grants and fellowships, and so on (that's technical accountant language for, "I'm not ruling out anything until I check my 5,000 page tax code to find out if it's taxable or not").

Like I said, tax laws give new meaning to the term confusing. Check with a tax professional before making any final decisions on what amounts to put on your tax return. Meanwhile, use Quicken to store and report all of your income.

Money you receive as a loan isn't really your money, so you don't have to pay tax on it. Tax on money you receive as a gift or inheritance presumably was already paid by its former owner, and you don't have to pay tax on it either. But remember the golden rule of taxation — there's always a catch. There are times when you do have to pay tax on these sorts of monies, so be sure to check in with your friendly tax professional.

I spent it, so it must be deductible, right?

I'm afraid that calculating tax deductions is a bit more complicated than simply adding up everything you spent and writing that on the tax return. Although the tax code allows you to reduce your income by certain expenditures before tax is calculated, those expenditures must fall into particular categories, and even those categories come with rules and limitations.

Once again, remember that this is just a generalization, but here is a list of common tax deductions that you might be able to use to lower the income on which tax is calculated. You have to be able to itemize your deductions on Schedule A of the federal income tax return in order to take advantage of these methods to reduce your taxable income.

- **Medical expenses:** Most things medical qualify as a tax deduction, including doctor and dentist expenses, hospital costs, health insurance (as long as it hasn't already been paid with before-tax money), lab fees, ambulance rides, stop-smoking programs, and so on. Unfortunately, the amount you deduct is first reduced by 7.5 percent of your adjusted gross income.

  Adjusted gross income = all the money you received during the past year, reduced by certain special adjustments like money invested in tax-deferred retirement funds, moving expenses, interest paid on student loans, alimony you paid, one-half of your self-employment tax, and 100 percent of your health insurance if you're self-employed.

- **Tax expenses:** You get to deduct amounts you paid for state and local income tax, such as the amounts that were withheld from your paycheck during the year. Also if you paid real estate tax or any other type of property tax, that counts as a deduction.
- **Interest expenses:** You can deduct the amount of interest paid on your home mortgage.
- **Charitable contributions:** Give money to charity, take a deduction. Give stuff to charity, you also get to take a deduction, but look for Congress to limit the stuff-giving deduction in the near future.
- **Miscellaneous deductions:** The IRS allows you to deduct a variety of odd and ends, but first you have to reduce the amount of your miscellaneous expenses by 2 percent of your adjusted gross income. If there's anything left over, you get the deduction. Miscellaneous deductions include unreimbursed business-related employee expenses, tax preparation fees, job search costs, and education costs that relate to your job.
- **Casualty losses:** If you are the victim of a theft, or if you suffer a casualty such as damage from a flood or an earthquake or an alien attack from outer space, and if your insurance doesn't reimburse you for your damages, you might get to deduct some of the amount you lost. First, you have to have lost more than $100 worth of cash or stuff, or else the IRS doesn't want to hear about it. Second, the amount you deduct has to be reduced by 10 percent of your adjusted gross income. Anything left over?

Adding categories to the Tax-Related Expenses list

In the Tax Center, Quicken assembles your tax deductions in the area labeled Tax-Related Expenses YTD. You can monitor your year-to-date deductible spending in this section. You can also add or remove categories to this list by designating your categories as being tax-related.

This category assignment is covered in more detail in Chapter 2 of this book, but for now, if you want to add a tax category to the Tax-Related Expenses list, click the Assign Tax Categories button beneath the list, find the category you want to add in the category list that appears, and put a check in the Tax column to the right of that category. When you close the category list, that category gets added to the Tax-Related Expenses list.

Cut your taxes in other ways

You can reduce your taxes in other ways, the most famous of which is to earn less money. Having children is another good way to cut taxes, although there are other expenses like diapers and college education (in that order, one hopes) that take the place of all the tax money you save.

Want to read more about how to figure out what's taxable and what's not? You can pick up a copy of the U.S. Tax Code in a nice coffee-table edition, or you can get a copy of *Taxes 2006 For Dummies* by Eric Tyson, Margaret A. Munro, and David J. Silverman (Wiley Publishing). And by the way, the purchase of either of these books is a tax-deductible expense.

OK, So What's the Bottom Line?

The Projected Tax section of the Tax Center attempts to display for you a running estimate of your income tax for the current year. Income and deduction categories are updated each time you make an entry or perform an automatic update in Quicken.

The amounts you see are annual projections, not actual amounts. In other words, if you have earned $40,000 this year and today is September 30, Quicken projects that amount to be $53,333 for the entire year, and it's that larger amount that goes into the tax projection.

Projections are calculated mathematically. If you earned $40,000 in the first nine months of the year, divide that amount by nine to come up with $4,444.44 in average earnings each month. Now multiply that result by 12 to get $53,333 estimated earnings for the entire 12 months. This is by no means an exact science, but it is a reasonable method for estimating your tax. As you discover in Chapter 5 of this book, the IRS approves of this method for calculating quarterly estimated taxes due.

The only amounts that appear in the Project Tax section are amounts that come from Quicken categories that have been assigned to tax lines. Some of your categories might not appear in this section, so there's a chance this projection is flawed. For more on assigning tax lines, see Chapter 2 of this book.

Good news or bad news

The bottom line in the Projected Tax section either shows a Refund Due (good news) or Remaining Tax Due (bad news). Remember, this is only an estimate and is perhaps based on incomplete information, so don't start celebrating (or selling the silver) just yet.

Dig in a little deeper if you want to see the source of this good or bad news.

Notice that every item in the Projected Tax section is hyperlinked. These hyperlinks lead to Quicken's Tax Planner, an area of Quicken that lets you see the detail of how each line in the Tax Center summary is calculated.

For example, in Figure 1-2 you can see that the taxpayer has $118 in Interest/Dividend Income. To examine the source of this amount, click on the hyperlink for Interest/Dividend Income. The Tax Planner opens, showing the summary that appears in Figure 1-3.

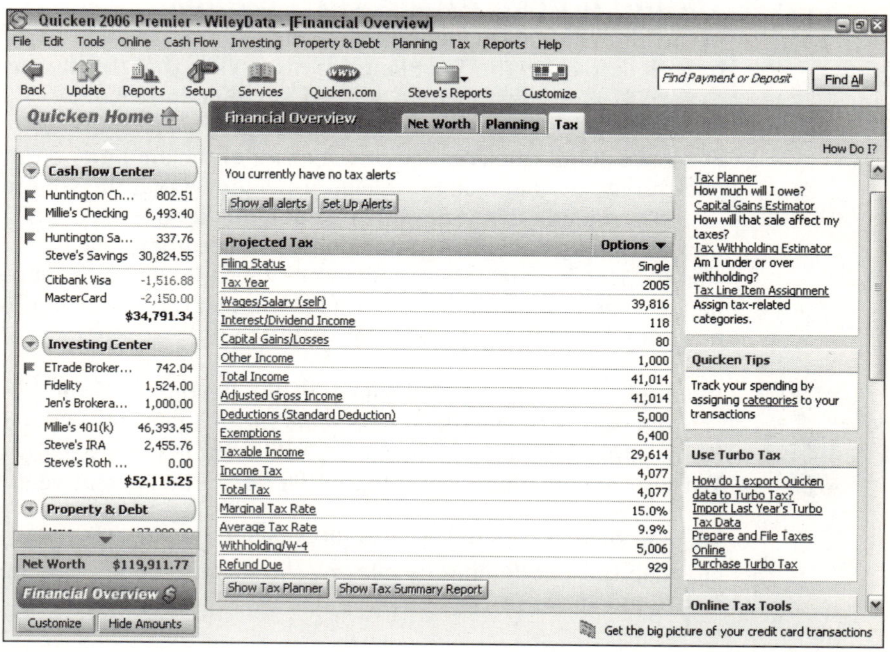

Figure 1-2: Drilling down in the Projected Tax area.

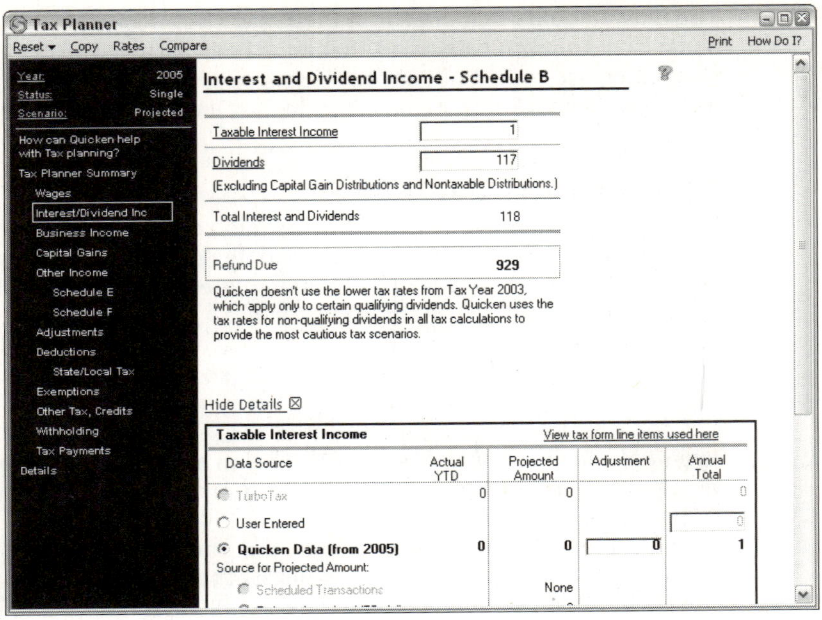

Figure 1-3: Picking apart the Tax Planner.

Taking a peek at the Tax Planner

In the Interest and Dividend Income display that appears when you click the hyperlink to open the Tax Planner, you can see that this taxpayer is expected to earn $1 in interest income and $117 in dividend income.

For more detail, click on one or the other of the amounts; for this example, click on the dividend amount. Figure 1-4 shows that the source for the projected dividends this year comes from a dividend and capital gain distribution earned from a Fidelity investment in December of last year. That amount was $113.90. Because the taxpayer still owns the Fidelity shares, Quicken has assumed another dividend (slightly larger) will be paid this year and has added that amount to the tax estimate.

REMEMBER

What this means is that Quicken is not just taking existing amounts you've entered during the year and averaging those amounts across all the remaining months. Quicken is doing some intelligent tax planning by going back to last year and making assumptions that affect the current year.

You can read more about the Tax Planner in Chapter 5 of this book. For now, close up the Tax Planner by clicking the X in the upper-right corner, and return to Quicken's Tax Center.

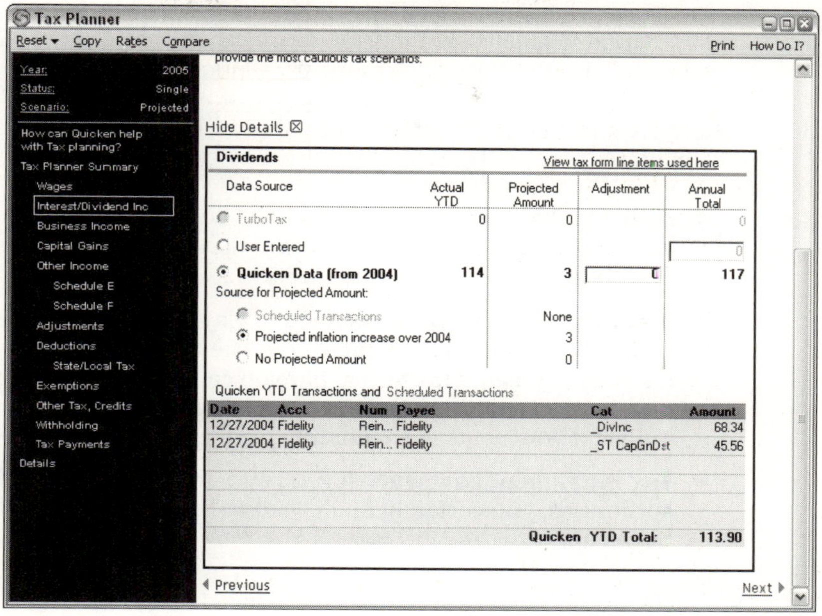

Figure 1-4: Detail of dividends earned.

Tax Due Dates and Other Dates Worth Noting

Over on the right side of the Tax Center window, or right beneath the Project Tax area, depending on the screen resolution you use, you can find the Tax Calendar (Figure 1-5). Quicken populates the calendar with dates provided by the IRS, such as the ever-popular April 15th, estimated tax due dates, due dates for tax return extension forms, and due dates for extended tax returns.

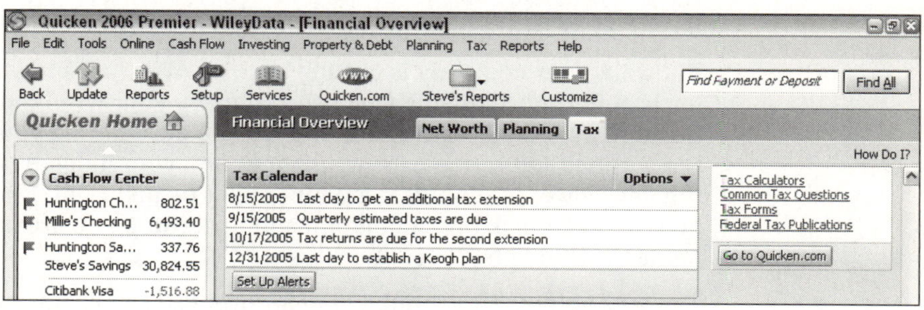

Figure 1-5: The calendar according to the IRS.

But what if you want to set up alerts for other dates? The Tax Calendar has particular dates that it is geared to warn you about. For other dates, you need to set up reminders that appear on your main alerts list and in Billminder. You can create reminders in the Financial Calendar (choose Tools➪Calendar➪Add Note button to create a reminder), or you can set up your tax payments as scheduled payments that automatically generate alerts.

Here are some of the other tax dates about which you might want to receive reminders:

✦ **State tax due dates:** Some states have due dates for income tax returns, extensions, and estimated payments that are different from the federal due dates.

✦ **Non-quarterly estimated payments:** Maybe you pay your estimated payments monthly instead of quarterly. The IRS doesn't specifically provide monthly estimated tax forms, but you can use the quarterly forms for payments of any frequency. For a lot of people, it's really much easier to budget if you just make a monthly payment.

✦ **Tax installment payments:** If you're on an installment plan with the tax authorities, you certainly don't want to forget to make the installment payments.

Alert! Alert! Incoming Tax Payments!

Other items that appear in the Tax Calendar are alerts that relate to taxes. Click the Set Up Alerts button beneath the Tax Calendar, and then click Taxes to set any of the following alerts. Just check the box to turn on any of the alerts (see Figure 1-6), or uncheck the boxes if you're not interested.

✦ **Withholding threshold:** Get an alert when Quicken projects that your tax withholding is going to be either above or below the threshold you set. For example, say you want to make sure your federal income tax withholding is at least $6,000 for the year and you set a threshold of $300. Based on the withholding from your current job, you're right on track.

But wait. Your company is cutting back on overtime and your withholding is suffering. Suddenly Quicken estimates your withholding is going to be more like $5,500. Quicken sends you an alert letting you know that the withholding is down. Now, chances are, your income is down too, so the new, lower withholding amount might be just right. But it doesn't hurt to do a quick tax calculation and make sure you are having enough money withheld to cover your taxes.

The withholding threshold works in reverse as well. Say you received a bonus along with some extra withholding, throwing your projected withholding up to about $6,500. Quicken notifies you of this excess withholding with an alert. Again, because your income is up, the additional withholding might be right on target, but you should check out your tax computation and make sure you're covered.

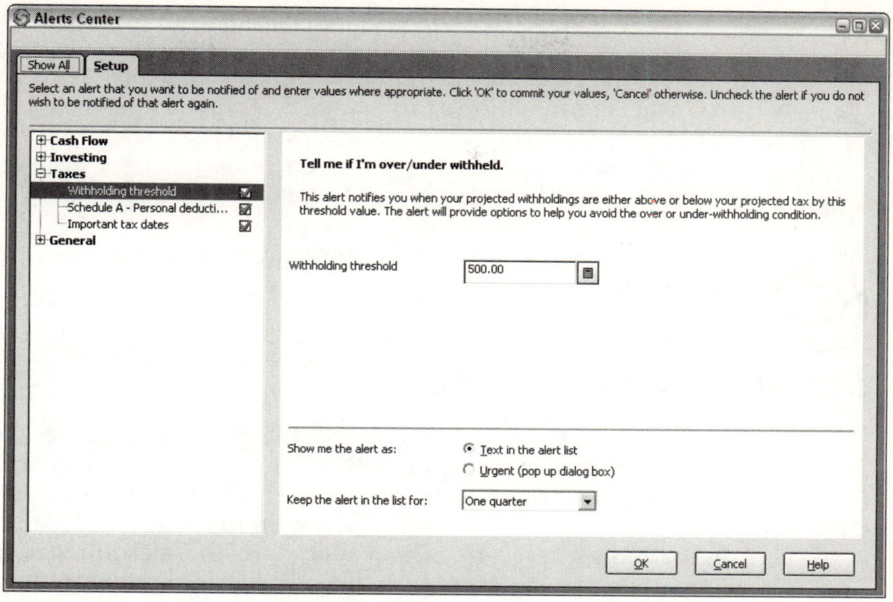

Figure 1-6: Check or uncheck boxes to display or hide tax alerts.

TIP

You can change the withholding threshold whenever you need to by going back into the Alerts Center and entering a new amount.

Important: If it looks like your withholding is not corresponding with your estimated tax, you can fill out a new W-4 form and have your employer adjust your withholding. Find out more about Form W-4 in Book I, Chapter 1. You can also simply wait until next April 15th and hope that the IRS doesn't notice that your withholding is nowhere near the amount of tax you owe and send you scare-tactic letters with invoices for penalties and threats of dismemberment. Or you can look into changing that W-4.

- **Personal deduction alert:** Quicken promises to provide you with "insightful information" about personal deductions you might be able to claim. The program is a little cagey (translated as — provides no explanation whatsoever) about what qualifies as a personal deduction type of tax alert, but hey, it can't hurt to turn this on and see if you get a useful hint every now and then. I have the personal deduction alerts turned on in my Quicken program, and I see I have a reminder on my tax alerts list reminding me to think about signing up for a Keogh plan before December 31.

TECHNICAL STUFF

A Keogh plan is a tax-deferred retirement plan for self-employed people. The plans have suffered a loss of popularity in recent years due to the influx of easier-to-establish plans like SIMPLE plans, SEP-IRAs, and the new kid on the block, the individual 401(k).

- **Important tax dates:** This is the option that adds the tax filing dates to your tax calendar. Interestingly, I unchecked this option, but the important tax dates stayed right where they were in my tax calendar. Once again, it can't hurt to turn on this feature.

For each alert, there is an option at the bottom to have the alert appear as a text entry on the regular alert list, or as an urgent message in a pop-up box.

Tax alerts are only available in Quicken Deluxe, Premier, and Premier Home & Business.

Tax Tools You Can Use

In addition to the lists that appear in the Tax Center, you see, along the right side of the screen, plenty of tools for those of you who just can't get enough of their taxes.

In the Tools box (Figure 1-7) are quick links to Quicken's four tax tools. These four features help you estimate your taxes and plan for your upcoming tax return as well as prepare your Quicken information for use in tax reports and in the TurboTax tax preparation software.

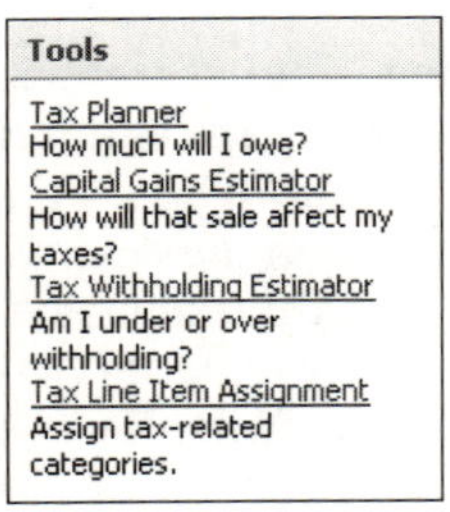

Figure 1-7: Quicken's tax toolbox.

- **Tax Planner:** We've peeked at the Tax Planner already in this chapter, and in Chapter 5 of this book, you get a heavier dose of this tool. Basically, the Tax Planner helps you zero in on a tax projection for the year. You can experiment with different scenarios and different filing statuses to try to ensure you pay the least amount of tax possible.
- **Capital Gains Estimator:** Use this tool to determine how a sale of an investment will affect your tax before you actually make the sale. Quicken helps you take advantage of the special tax rules for capital gains to maximize your income and minimize your tax. The Capital Gains Estimator helps you choose the best time to make the sale and reminds you of ways you can reduce tax by offsetting gains with losses. Also, the Estimator helps you determine how much of a stock or mutual fund investment you need to sell in order to have enough cash to pay the tax on the sale.

In the Capital Gains Estimator, you are asked to identify your anticipated rate of federal and state income tax, then Quicken displays your investment holdings. You select the investments you are considering selling, and the estimator shows you the tax impact of those sales as well as the net amount of cash you can expect to receive.

✦ **Tax Withholding Estimator:** This estimator helps you determine how much withholding you need to have in order to meet your tax obligation. The Welcome window appears with a basic summary of your tax projections for the year. Click one of the worksheet options shown on the left side of the window if you need to add or correct information.

  For example, in Figure 1-8, the Adjust Basic Information worksheet has been selected. Here you can change the filing status, the number of dependents, or you can make adjustments to the projected income and itemized deductions. Each of your changes is entered in the Tax Projection Data at the right side of the window.

  Use the Experiment with W-4 Allowances worksheet to plug in different W-4 allowances and see what effect they have on your withholding. That way, you can easily tell if you need to revise your W-4 form with your employer.

✦ **Tax Line Item Assignment:** We're going to assign tax lines in Chapter 2, so be patient for just another couple of pages and you can read all about this tool.

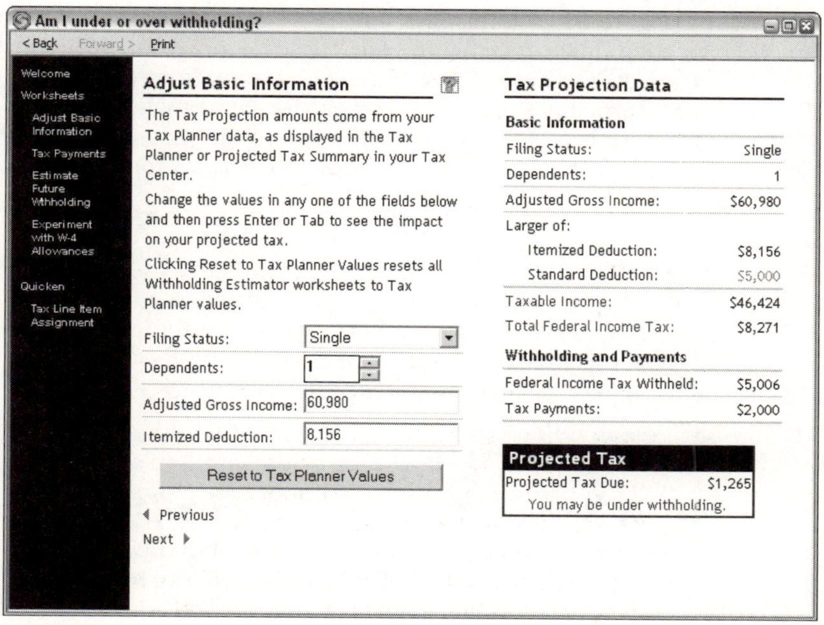

Figure 1-8: Experiment with tax withholding.

Quicken's rotating (and redundant) tips

Look for a little box in the Tax Center, beneath the tools, called Quicken Tips. Every time you open the Tax Center window, the information in this box changes. You'll see a brief description accompanying a hyperlink to the particular tool that Quicken wants to tell you about. Sometimes the tips are tax-related, but sometimes they aren't. For example, in Figure 1-9, you are reminded to assign categories to your transactions.

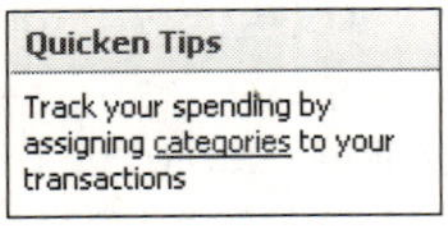

Figure 1-9: Quicken has tips for you.

WARNING!

These tips are a bit redundant — often they direct you to a tool or link that appears elsewhere on the Tax Center screen.

TurboTax links

We are in the Tax Center, after all, and Intuit, the maker of Quicken, does make TurboTax too. So it stands to reason that sooner or later you were going to get a sales pitch for TurboTax.

Over on the right side near the bottom of the Tax Center is a Use TurboTax box (Figure 1-10). In this box, you find a link to Help menu information about exporting Quicken data into your TurboTax program, the Import Last Year's TurboTax Data hyperlink to bring information from TurboTax into Quicken; a link to TurboTax's online tax preparation center, where you can prepare and file your return online; and another link to the same tax preparation center, where you can also purchase a copy of TurboTax for your personal computer.

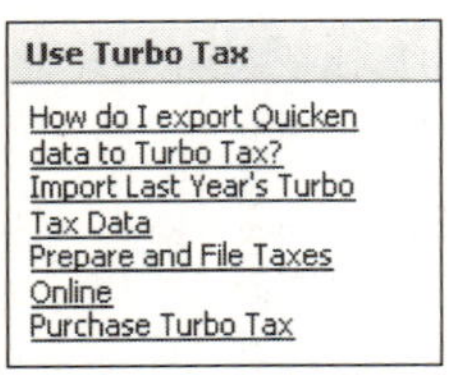

Figure 1-10: Quicken's little sister — TurboTax.

Tax tools that live beyond the walls of Quicken

The final box, down in the lower-right corner of the Tax Center screen, is the Online Tax Tools box, shown in Figure 1-11. These tools ostensibly send you to places outside of Quicken where you can find additional help about your taxes. Actually, they take you over to some of Intuit's Web sites.

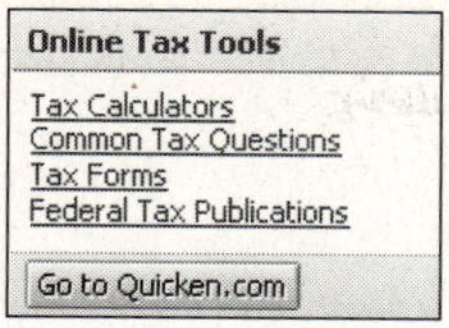

Figure 1-11: Tax tools = links to Intuit online.

The Tax Calculators hyperlink takes you right to the TurboTax Web site. Once there, if you click the Tax Tips & Resources tab and do some digging, you can find some tax calculators that help you estimate how much money your home mortgage is saving you, whether you're taking all the deductions to which you're entitled, and a tax estimator that helps you estimate how much tax you should expect to owe, or how much of a refund you will receive. The tax estimator is especially nice because it includes the dreaded Alternative Minimum Tax, originally a tax on the rich that is now creeping into mainstream America.

Chapter 2: Entering Tax-Friendly Information

In This Chapter

- Assigning tax lines
- Figuring out what is relevant to your taxes
- Looking for mistakes in your tax category assignments
- Changing tax categories

Tax lines are the cords that connect your Quicken categories with the tax reports you can produce in Quicken and the tax returns you prepare or have prepared for you.

In the last chapter, we discussed the Quicken Tax Center and all of the resources that appear there for you. Many of those resources are made much more functional when you take the time to assign tax lines to your Quicken categories.

In this chapter, we see how to assign tax lines to your Quicken categories. You find out how to determine which categories receive tax lines and which categories don't need tax lines because they don't affect your taxes.

What's a Tax Line?

A *tax line* is an attribute that you assign to your categories, linking them to particular lines on the federal income tax return. Then when you produce a tax report, you can see, line-for-line, where the totals for the year belong on your tax return. The tax lines in Quicken actually correspond directly with the IRS tax forms. To see what I mean, take a look at the 1040 U.S. Individual Income Tax Return forms reproduced in this chapter.

When to assign tax lines

You can assign tax lines when you first establish a category, or later. Remember the categories that came with your program, that were provided by Quicken? Some of these categories came with tax line assignments; others did not. Take the time to examine your existing list of categories to see which ones are assigned.

Here's the best approach: Set aside some time to go through the entire category list, assigning tax lines where necessary, remembering that all categories do not need line assignments (see "Determining Which Categories Don't Need Tax Lines" later in this chapter).

How to assign tax lines

You can assign tax lines to your categories in a couple of different ways. You can edit the categories, one-by-one, adding tax lines where they're necessary. Or you can view the entire category list, including the tax line assignments, and add your additional tax line assignments right on that list.

In the next two sections, I discuss the two methods — pick the one you like best.

Here's how to assign tax lines one category at a time:

1. **Open the category list (Ctrl+C or Shift+Ctrl+C) and make sure tax information is showing by checking the Display Tax Information box at the top of the list.**
2. **Scroll to a category that needs a tax line assignment and click once on that category.**

   For this example, I've chosen Home Insurance. Because I have a home office, some of my home insurance qualifies for a tax deduction.
3. **Click the Edit button.**

   The Edit Category window appears (Figure 2-1). You can make any entries or changes to the information for this category while this window is open. For this example, we're just going to add a tax line.

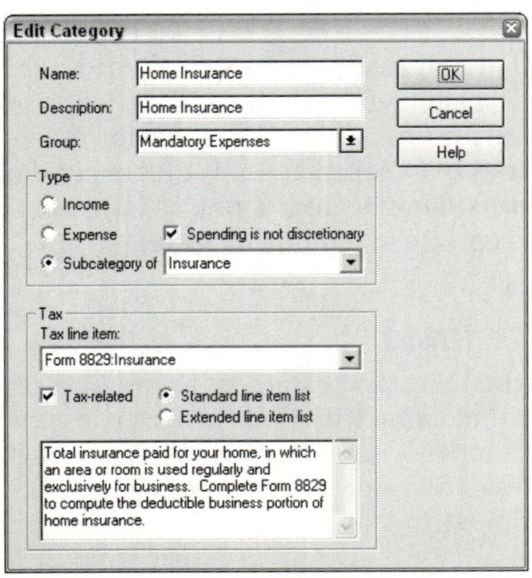

Figure 2-1: Adding a tax line to your category description.

4. **Click the Tax Line Item drop-down list and scroll to the appropriate tax line.**

   For this example, I've chosen Form 8829: Insurance. Form 8829 is the Home Office Deduction form.

5. **Click OK.**

   Your tax line has been assigned.

TIP

You can also assign tax lines when you create a category on-the-fly. For example, if you're making an entry in a register and need to create a new category, the tax line assignment option appears in the Set Up Category window.

TIP

The Category List is sorted by category, not by tax categories. There are many categories on the list that do not have, nor do they need, tax line assignments. You can display a category list of just categories that have tax line assignments. In the Show drop-down list at the top of the category list, choose Tax-Related Categories, and your list is displayed with only the tax-related categories.

Here's how to assign tax to several categories at once:

1. **Open the Category List by pressing Ctrl+C (or Shift+Ctrl+C).**
2. **Scroll to the first category that requires a tax line and click on that category.**
3. **Make sure the Display Tax Information box at the top of the window is checked.**
4. **On the right side of the screen is an area labeled Tax Line Item Assignments (see Figure 2-2). Scroll down the Tax Item list until you find the appropriate tax item, and then click on that item.**

   For this example, I've selected Property Tax as my category, and Schedule A: Real Estate Taxes as the tax line. When you click on the tax line, the tax box is checked for the selected category, and the tax line assignment is entered on the category list.

5. **Click on the next category that you want to assign, and repeat step 4. Continue with as many categories as you need to assign.**

   TECHNICAL STUFF

   Quicken has an annoying habit of returning you to the top of the category list after each tax line assignment. It drives me buggy, having to scroll down the list again every time I want to make a tax line assignment. For this reason alone, I actually prefer Method 1 for assigning tax lines.

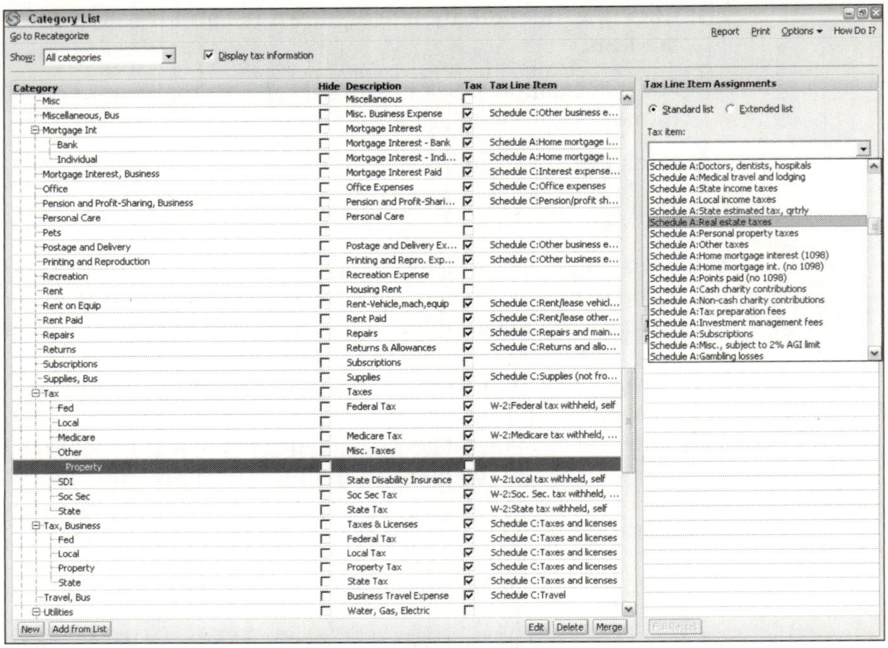

Figure 2-2: The complete tax item list is available on the upper right side of the category list.

Don't worry if you make a mistake on the tax line assignment — you can always fix it later (see "Changing Your Tax Lines" later in this chapter).

Tax Form Cross-Reference Key

In order to assign tax lines, you need a basic understanding of what types of income and expenses go on the lines of your tax return. If you've never prepared your own income tax return, this might seem extraordinarily foreign to you. Maybe you plan on continuing having someone else prepare your tax return, but with the information presented here, you can prepare your information for that person (or for yourself) so that your tax return preparation goes smoothly. Figure 2-3 and Figure 2-4 illustrate the 1040 and Schedule A tax forms, two forms you may be familiar with.

The best way to determine on what tax return lines your income and expenses should appear is to use last year's income tax return as a reference.

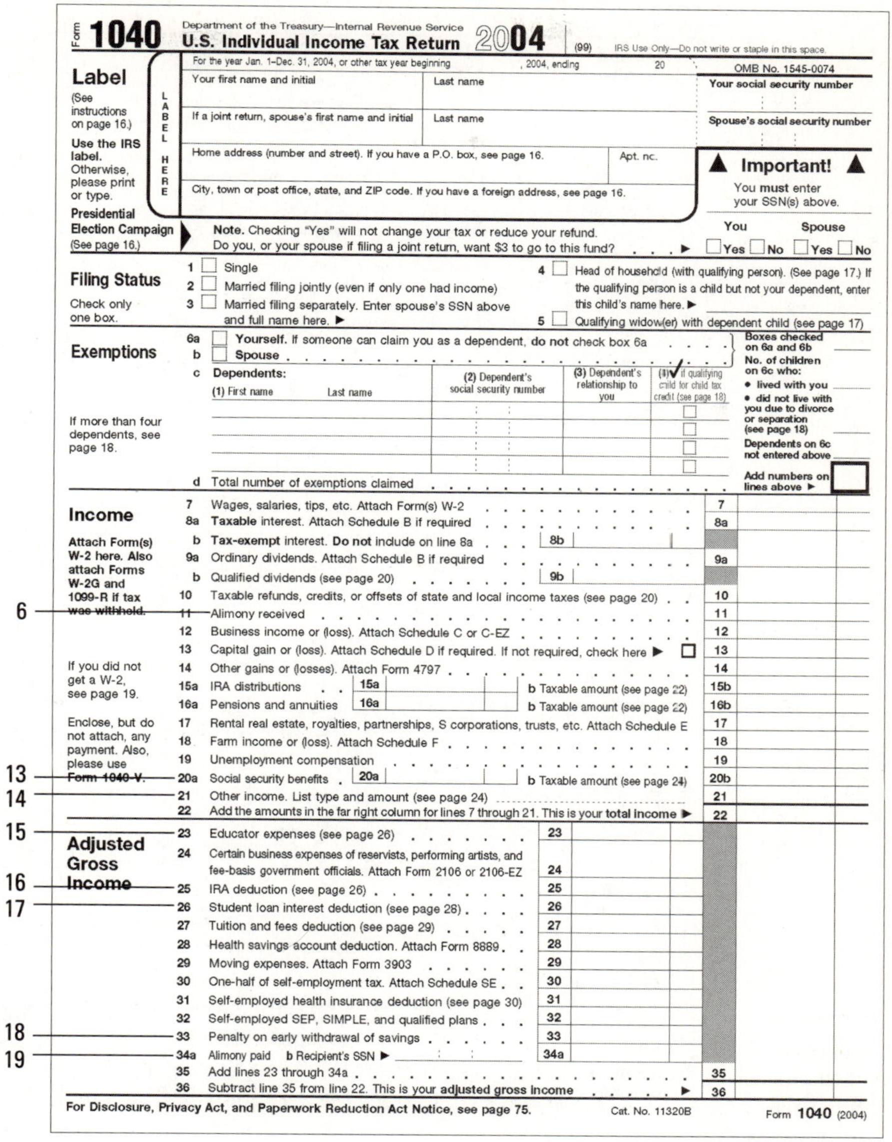

Form **1040** Department of the Treasury—Internal Revenue Service **U.S. Individual Income Tax Return** 2004 (99) IRS Use Only—Do not write or staple in this space.

For the year Jan. 1–Dec. 31, 2004, or other tax year beginning , 2004, ending 20 OMB No. 1545-0074

Label (See instructions on page 16.) **Use the IRS label.** Otherwise, please print or type. LABEL HERE

Your first name and initial | Last name | **Your social security number**

If a joint return, spouse's first name and initial | Last name | **Spouse's social security number**

Home address (number and street). If you have a P.O. box, see page 16. | Apt. no.

City, town or post office, state, and ZIP code. If you have a foreign address, see page 16.

▲ **Important!** ▲ You **must** enter your SSN(s) above.

Presidential Election Campaign (See page 16.) **Note.** Checking "Yes" will not change your tax or reduce your refund. Do you, or your spouse if filing a joint return, want $3 to go to this fund? ▶ You ☐ Yes ☐ No Spouse ☐ Yes ☐ No

Filing Status Check only one box.

1 ☐ Single
2 ☐ Married filing jointly (even if only one had income)
3 ☐ Married filing separately. Enter spouse's SSN above and full name here. ▶
4 ☐ Head of household (with qualifying person). (See page 17.) If the qualifying person is a child but not your dependent, enter this child's name here. ▶
5 ☐ Qualifying widow(er) with dependent child (see page 17)

Exemptions

6a ☐ **Yourself.** If someone can claim you as a dependent, **do not** check box 6a
b ☐ **Spouse**
c **Dependents:** (1) First name Last name | (2) Dependent's social security number | (3) Dependent's relationship to you | (4) ✓ if qualifying child for child tax credit (see page 18)

If more than four dependents, see page 18.

d Total number of exemptions claimed

Boxes checked on 6a and 6b. No. of children on 6c who: • lived with you • did not live with you due to divorce or separation (see page 18). Dependents on 6c not entered above. Add numbers on lines above ▶

Income

Attach Form(s) W-2 here. Also attach Forms W-2G and 1099-R if tax was withheld.

If you did not get a W-2, see page 19.

Enclose, but do not attach, any payment. Also, please use Form 1040-V.

7 Wages, salaries, tips, etc. Attach Form(s) W-2 — 7
8a **Taxable** interest. Attach Schedule B if required — 8a
b **Tax-exempt** interest. **Do not** include on line 8a — 8b
9a Ordinary dividends. Attach Schedule B if required — 9a
b Qualified dividends (see page 20) — 9b
10 Taxable refunds, credits, or offsets of state and local income taxes (see page 20) — 10
6 — 11 Alimony received — 11
12 Business income or (loss). Attach Schedule C or C-EZ — 12
13 Capital gain or (loss). Attach Schedule D if required. If not required, check here ▶ ☐ — 13
14 Other gains or (losses). Attach Form 4797 — 14
15a IRA distributions 15a — b Taxable amount (see page 22) — 15b
16a Pensions and annuities 16a — b Taxable amount (see page 22) — 16b
17 Rental real estate, royalties, partnerships, S corporations, trusts, etc. Attach Schedule E — 17
18 Farm income or (loss). Attach Schedule F — 18
19 Unemployment compensation — 19
13 — 20a Social security benefits 20a — b Taxable amount (see page 24) — 20b
14 — 21 Other income. List type and amount (see page 24) — 21
22 Add the amounts in the far right column for lines 7 through 21. This is your **total income** ▶ — 22

Adjusted Gross Income

15 — 23 Educator expenses (see page 26) — 23
24 Certain business expenses of reservists, performing artists, and fee-basis government officials. Attach Form 2106 or 2106-EZ — 24
16 — 25 IRA deduction (see page 26) — 25
17 — 26 Student loan interest deduction (see page 28) — 26
27 Tuition and fees deduction (see page 29) — 27
28 Health savings account deduction. Attach Form 8889 — 28
29 Moving expenses. Attach Form 3903 — 29
30 One-half of self-employment tax. Attach Schedule SE — 30
31 Self-employed health insurance deduction (see page 30) — 31
32 Self-employed SEP, SIMPLE, and qualified plans — 32
18 — 33 Penalty on early withdrawal of savings — 33
19 — 34a Alimony paid b Recipient's SSN ▶ — 34a
35 Add lines 23 through 34a — 35
36 Subtract line 35 from line 22. This is your **adjusted gross income** ▶ — 36

For Disclosure, Privacy Act, and Paperwork Reduction Act Notice, see page 75. Cat. No. 11320B Form **1040** (2004)

Figure 2-3: Federal tax form 1040.

Form 1040 (2004) Page 2

Tax and Credits

37 Amount from line 36 (adjusted gross income) 37

38a Check if: { ☐ **You** were born before January 2, 1940, ☐ Blind. } { ☐ **Spouse** was born before January 2, 1940, ☐ Blind. } **Total boxes checked ▶ 38a** ☐

b If your spouse itemizes on a separate return or you were a dual-status alien, see page 31 and check here ▶ 38b ☐

Standard Deduction for—

- People who checked any box on line 38a or 38b **or** who can be claimed as a dependent, see page 31.
- All others:

Single or Married filing separately, $4,850

Married filing jointly or Qualifying widow(er), $9,700

Head of household, $7,150

39 **Itemized deductions** (from Schedule A) **or** your **standard deduction** (see left margin) . . 39

40 Subtract line 39 from line 37 40

41 If line 37 is $107,025 or less, multiply $3,100 by the total number of exemptions claimed on line 6d. If line 37 is over $107,025, see the worksheet on page 33 41

42 **Taxable income.** Subtract line 41 from line 40. If line 41 is more than line 40, enter -0- . 42

43 **Tax** (see page 33). Check if any tax is from: a ☐ Form(s) 8814 b ☐ Form 4972 . . . 43

44 **Alternative minimum tax** (see page 35). Attach Form 6251 44

45 Add lines 43 and 44 . . . . ▶ 45

46 Foreign tax credit. Attach Form 1116 if required 46

47 Credit for child and dependent care expenses. Attach Form 2441 47

48 Credit for the elderly or the disabled. Attach Schedule R . . 48

49 Education credits. Attach Form 8863 49

50 Retirement savings contributions credit. Attach Form 8880. . 50

51 Child tax credit (see page 37) 51

52 Adoption credit. Attach Form 8839 52

53 Credits from: a ☐ Form 8396 b ☐ Form 8859 . . . 53

54 Other credits. Check applicable box(es): a ☐ Form 3800 b ☐ Form 8801 c ☐ Specify ________ . . 54

55 Add lines 46 through 54. These are your **total credits** 55

56 Subtract line 55 from line 45. If line 55 is more than line 45, enter -0- . . . . ▶ 56

Other Taxes

57 Self-employment tax. Attach Schedule SE 57

58 Social security and Medicare tax on tip income not reported to employer. Attach Form 4137 . . 58

59 Additional tax on IRAs, other qualified retirement plans, etc. Attach Form 5329 if required . 59

60 Advance earned income credit payments from Form(s) W-2 60

61 Household employment taxes. Attach Schedule H 61

62 Add lines 56 through 61. This is your **total tax** . . . . ▶ 62

Payments

20 — 63 Federal income tax withheld from Forms W-2 and 1099 . . 63

21 — 64 2004 estimated tax payments and amount applied from 2003 return 64

If you have a qualifying child, attach Schedule EIC.

65a **Earned income credit (EIC)** 65a

b Nontaxable combat pay election ▶ 65b

66 Excess social security and tier 1 RRTA tax withheld (see page 54) 66

67 Additional child tax credit. Attach Form 8812 67

68 Amount paid with request for extension to file (see page 54) 68

69 Other payments from: a ☐ Form 2439 b ☐ Form 4136 c ☐ Form 8885 . 69

70 Add lines 63, 64, 65a, and 66 through 69. These are your **total payments** . . . . ▶ 70

Refund

Direct deposit? See page 54 and fill in 72b, 72c, and 72d.

71 If line 70 is more than line 62, subtract line 62 from line 70. This is the amount you **overpaid** 71

72a Amount of line 71 you want **refunded to you** . . . . ▶ 72a

▶ b Routing number ☐☐☐☐☐☐☐☐☐ ▶ c Type: ☐ Checking ☐ Savings

▶ d Account number ☐☐☐☐☐☐☐☐☐☐☐☐☐☐☐☐☐

73 Amount of line 71 you want **applied to your 2005 estimated tax** ▶ 73

Amount You Owe

74 **Amount you owe.** Subtract line 70 from line 62. For details on how to pay, see page 55 ▶ 74

75 Estimated tax penalty (see page 55) 75

Third Party Designee

Do you want to allow another person to discuss this return with the IRS (see page 56)? ☐ **Yes.** Complete the following. ☐ **No**

Designee's name ▶ Phone no. ▶ ( ) Personal identification number (PIN) ▶ ☐☐☐☐☐

Sign Here

Joint return? See page 17. Keep a copy for your records.

Under penalties of perjury, I declare that I have examined this return and accompanying schedules and statements, and to the best of my knowledge and belief, they are true, correct, and complete. Declaration of preparer (other than taxpayer) is based on all information of which preparer has any knowledge.

Your signature	Date	Your occupation	Daytime phone number ( )
Spouse's signature. If a joint return, **both** must sign.	Date	Spouse's occupation	

Paid Preparer's Use Only

Preparer's signature ▶	Date	Check if self-employed ☐	Preparer's SSN or PTIN
Firm's name (or yours if self-employed), address, and ZIP code ▶		EIN	
		Phone no. ( )	

Form **1040** (2004)

Figure 2-3: Page 2 of form 1040.

SCHEDULES A&B (Form 1040) Department of the Treasury Internal Revenue Service (99)

Schedule A—Itemized Deductions

(Schedule B is on back)

► Attach to Form 1040. ► See Instructions for Schedules A and B (Form 1040).

OMB No. 1545-0074 2004 Attachment Sequence No. 07

Name(s) shown on Form 1040 | Your social security number

Key	Section	Line	Description	Box
	Medical and Dental Expenses		Caution. Do not include expenses reimbursed or paid by others.	
		1	Medical and dental expenses (see page A-2) . . .	1
		2	Enter amount from Form 1040, line 37 [2]	
		3	Multiply line 2 by 7.5% (.075).	3
		4	Subtract line 3 from line 1. If line 3 is more than line 1, enter -0-	4
	Taxes You Paid (See page A-2.)	5	State and local **(check only one box)**: a ☐ Income taxes, **or** b ☐ General sales taxes (see page A-2) . . .	5
24		6	Real estate taxes (see page A-3).	6
25		7	Personal property taxes	7
		8	Other taxes. List type and amount ►	8
		9	Add lines 5 through 8	9
26	Interest You Paid (See page A-3.)	10	Home mortgage interest and points reported to you on Form 1098	10
	Note. Personal interest is not deductible.	11	Home mortgage interest not reported to you on Form 1098. If paid to the person from whom you bought the home, see page A-4 and show that person's name, identifying no., and address ►	11
		12	Points not reported to you on Form 1098. See page A-4 for special rules	12
		13	Investment interest. Attach Form 4952 if required. (See page A-4.)	13
		14	Add lines 10 through 13	14
27	Gifts to Charity	15	Gifts by cash or check. If you made any gift of $250 or more, see page A-4	15
	If you made a gift and got a benefit for it, see page A-4.	16	Other than by cash or check. If any gift of $250 or more, see page A-4. You **must** attach Form 8283 if over $500	16
		17	Carryover from prior year	17
		18	Add lines 15 through 17	18
	Casualty and Theft Losses	19	Casualty or theft loss(es). Attach Form 4684. (See page A-5.)	19
	Job Expenses and Most Other Miscellaneous Deductions	20	Unreimbursed employee expenses—job travel, union dues, job education, etc. Attach Form 2106 or 2106-EZ if required. (See page A-6.) ►	20
28		21	Tax preparation fees.	21
	(See page A-5.)	22	Other expenses—investment, safe deposit box, etc. List type and amount ►	22
		23	Add lines 20 through 22	23
		24	Enter amount from Form 1040, line 37 [24]	
		25	Multiply line 24 by 2% (.02)	25
		26	Subtract line 25 from line 23. If line 25 is more than line 23, enter -0-	26
	Other Miscellaneous Deductions	27	Other—from list on page A-6. List type and amount ►	27
	Total Itemized Deductions	28	Is Form 1040, line 37, over $142,700 (over $71,350 if married filing separately)? ☐ **No.** Your deduction is not limited. Add the amounts in the far right column for lines 4 through 27. Also, enter this amount on Form 1040, line 39. ☐ **Yes.** Your deduction may be limited. See page A-6 for the amount to enter. ►	28

For Paperwork Reduction Act Notice, see Form 1040 instructions. Cat. No. 11330X Schedule A (Form 1040) 2004

Figure 2-4: Federal tax form Schedule A.

Table 2-1 displays some sample Quicken tax line descriptions that correlate to the numbered items in the tax form reproductions presented here. This list is not meant to be all-inclusive, nor are all tax form lines defined by a single Quicken tax line assignment. But this at least gives you a starting point for matching tax lines with tax line assignments.

Table 2-1	Form 1040 Cross-Reference with Quicken Tax Lines
Line Number	*Quicken's Tax Line Description*
1	W-2: Salary or wages
2	Schedule B: Interest income
3	Schedule B: Dividend income
4	Schedule B: Qualified dividend
5	1099-G: State and local tax refunds (found on the Extended list)
6	Form 1040: Alimony received
7	Choose from the various Schedule C options
8	Schedule D: short-term gain/loss — security Schedule D: long-term gain/loss — security
9	1099-R: Total IRA gross distrib.
10	1099-R: Total pension gross distrib.
11	Choose from the various Schedule F options on the Extended list.
12	1099-G: Unemployment compensation
13	Form 1040: Social Security income
14	Form 1040: Other income, misc.
15	Form 1040: Educator expense
16	Form 1040: IRA deduction
17	Form 1040: Student loan interest
18	Form 1040: Early withdrawal penalty
19	Form 1040: Alimony paid
20	W-2: Federal tax withheld
21	Form 1040: Federal estimated tax, qtrly
22	Choose from — Schedule A: Medicine and drugs; Doctors, dentists, hospitals; Medical travel and lodging
23	Choose from: Schedule A: State income taxes; Local income taxes; State estimated tax, qtrly
24	Schedule A: Real estate taxes
25	Schedule A: Personal property taxes
26	Schedule A: Home mortgage interest (1098)
27	Schedule A: Cash charity contributions
28	Schedule A: Tax preparation fees

Tax Forms That Quicken Recognizes

Depending on how complicated your tax return is, you might use some tax forms for which Quicken doesn't provide tax lines. Table 2-2, reproduced from Quicken's Help screen, is a complete list of the tax forms recognized by Quicken:

Table 2-2 Tax Forms Recognized by Quicken

Form or Schedule	*What It's For*
1099-G	Used to report certain government payments from federal, state, or local governments.
1099-Misc	Used to report miscellaneous income received and direct sales of consumer goods for resale.
1099-R	Used to report taxable and non-taxable retirement distributions from retirement, pension, profit-sharing, or annuity plans. Use a separate Form 1099-R for each payer.
1099-MSA	Used to report medical savings account distributions.
Form 1040	The main form of your tax return.
Form 2106	Used to deduct unreimbursed employee business expenses. You must file this form if you were not reimbursed by your employer for job-related travel, transportation, meal, or entertainment expenses. Use a separate Form 2106 for your spouse's expenses.
Form 2441	Used to claim a credit for child and dependent care expenses.
Form 3903	Used to claim moving expenses.
Form 4137	Used to compute Social Security and Medicare tax owed on tips you did not report to your employer.
Form 4684	Used to report gains and losses from casualties and theft.
Form 4835	Used to report farm rental income received as a share of crops or livestock produced by your tenant if you did not materially participate in the operation or management of the farm. Use a different copy of Form 4835 for each farm rented.
Form 4952	Used to compute the amount of investment interest expense deductible for the current year and the amount, if any, to carry forward to future years.
Form 6252	Used to report income from an installment sale (in other words, casual sales of real or personal property when you will receive any payments in a tax year after the year of sale).
Form 8815	Used to compute the amount of interest you may exclude if you cashed series EE U.S. savings bonds this year that were issued after 1989 to pay for qualified higher education costs.
Form 8829	Used only if you file a Schedule C, Profit or Loss from Business, and you meet specific requirements to deduct expenses for the business use of your home. IRS rules are stringent for this deduction. Refer to IRS Publication 587.
Form 8839	Used to report qualified adoption expenses.

(continued)

Table 2-2 *(continued)*

Form or Schedule	*What It's For*
Form 8863	Used to compute the Hope and Lifetime Learning education credits. IRS rules are stringent for these credits. Refer to IRS Publication 970 for more information.
Schedule A	Used to report your itemized deductions.
Schedule B	Used to report your interest and dividend income.
Schedule C	Used to report income from self-employment. Use a separate Schedule C to report income and expenses from different businesses.
Schedule D	Used to report gains and losses from the sale of capital assets. If you received capital gain dividends, use the capital gain dividend category found on Schedule B.
Schedule E	Used to report income or loss from rental real estate, royalties, and residual interest in REMICs. Use a different copy for each rental or royalty. Use the Schedule K-1 categories for partnership rental income and loss amounts.
Schedule F	Used to report farm income and expense. Use a different copy of Schedule F for each farm you own.
Schedule H	Used to report federal employment taxes on cash wages paid this year to household employees. Federal employment taxes include Social Security, Medicare, withheld federal income, and federal unemployment (FUTA) taxes.
Schedule K-1	Used to report your share of a partnership's income, credits, deductions, and so on. Use a separate copy of Schedule K-1 for each partnership.
W-2	Used by your employer to report the amount of wages and other compensation you earned as an employee, and the amount of federal and state taxes withheld and fringe benefits received. You should use a separate copy of Form W-2 for each employer.
W-2G	Used to report certain gambling winnings.

Determining Which Categories Don't Need Tax Lines

Some Quicken categories relate to your income tax return, but you don't want to assign tax lines to them. These are categories where the amounts don't carry dollar for dollar onto the main 1040 tax form, or where there is not a clear method of determining on which tax form line the amount should appear. Here are some examples of categories that might be better off left unassigned, even though ultimately the amount in the category is going to find its way onto your tax return:

- **Home mortgage expense:** If you don't distinguish in your Quicken register between home mortgage principal and interest, you don't want to assign a tax line to the home mortgage expense, because only the interest represents a tax deduction.
- **Home mortgage interest and real estate tax:** If you own your home and run a business from your home, a portion of your home mortgage interest and your real estate tax count as business expense for your home office; the rest counts as itemized deductions.
- **Itemized deductions in general:** There's no point in taking the time to identify tax lines for itemized deductions that you can't deduct on your tax return. For example, if you don't qualify to take the medical deduction (medical expenses have to exceed 7.5 percent of your adjusted gross income before you can take the deduction), why bother assigning tax lines to these expenses? Likewise, if you don't have enough itemized deductions overall to itemize on your tax return, you don't need to assign tax categories to any of the deductible items.
- **Education:** Here's a tricky one. You can reduce your taxes with education expenses in several ways. You might qualify for the Hope Scholarship Credit, or the Lifetime Learning Credit. Maybe your education expenses belong with your itemized deductions as business-related expenses. Or perhaps your best tax advantage comes from claiming the education expenses on page one of your tax return as part of the tuition and fees deduction.
- **Income from a hobby:** If you have a hobby that has started producing income, you might have to include Schedule C with your tax return, the form where business income is reported. The income and expenses from the activity are all reported on Schedule C.

  TIP

  Sometimes hobby income and expenses get reported on Schedule C as described above. Sometimes the hobby income is reported on page one of your tax return as Other Income and the related expenses are required to be treated as miscellaneous itemized deductions and reported on Schedule A. Sometimes no deduction is allowed at all for your hobby expenses. Contact your tax advisor if you have questions about how to report income and expenses from your hobby.
- **State income tax refunds:** These are taxable, but only to the extent that you got some benefit from deducting the state income tax on the previous year's federal income tax return. So the refund might or might not be taxable.
- **Sales tax:** Sales tax is a deduction on your Schedule A, but only as an alternative to deducting state and local income tax. You're supposed to figure out which one gives you the better deduction, sales tax or state and local income tax, and then deduct just one or the other.

✦ **Cost of gambling:** These costs, including buying lottery tickets, playing games of chance, betting on horses, or any other type of gambling, is deductible as an itemized deduction, but only to the extent of the amount of gambling winnings you report as income. So until you get to the end of the year and find out how much you've won for the entire year, you don't know how much, if any, of your gambling costs are deductible.

✦ **IRA contributions:** These can be deductible, or not, depending on how much income you earn, whether you or your spouse are covered by pension plans at work, or even just depending on whether you choose to take the deduction.

TIP

When making tax line assignments, you can choose the alternative of checking off the Tax check box for a category without assigning a specific tax line. That way, the category gets included in the Tax Summary report and is available for analysis when preparing your income tax return (see Chapter 3 in this book for more information on the Tax Summary report). This is especially useful for the situations described above, where transactions belong on your tax return, but it's not clear exactly what tax line they'll go on or exactly what amount of the transaction is going to qualify for a deduction.

Income limitations affect the tax treatment of many expenses, including various education expenses, childcare expenses, and even your itemized deductions as a whole. As you can see, it's very difficult to identify which expenses are going to generate income tax deductions for you.

Hunting for mistakes: Searching through your tax line assignments

You might find it helpful to examine tax reports (see next chapter) and look at the details to see what kind of transactions are showing up in each tax line. You might have miscoded categories to the wrong tax line, or some tax line assignments might be correct but the transaction was coded to the wrong category. A careful analysis of the transactions being directed to each tax line can ensure accuracy when you get ready to prepare your income tax return.

It's very important to make sure you get your tax line assignments right. The IRS doesn't like mistakes.

Changing Your Tax Lines

If you've assigned tax lines to your tax categories, and then decide you made a mistake and want to make a change, you'll find that it's an easy task to switch from one tax line assignment to another, or to remove a tax line assignment altogether.

Removing tax lines

Just follow these steps to remove the tax line assigned to a particular category:

1. **Open the category list by pressing Ctrl+C (or Shift+Ctrl+C).**
2. **Click on the category whose tax line assignment you want to change.**

   For this example, I've selected IRA Contrib. I've decided I no longer want to make tax deductible contributions to my IRA. Future contributions will not be deducted on my income tax return, so I want to change the tax line assignment for this category.
3. **Uncheck the box in the Tax column next to the IRA category (see Figure 2-5).**

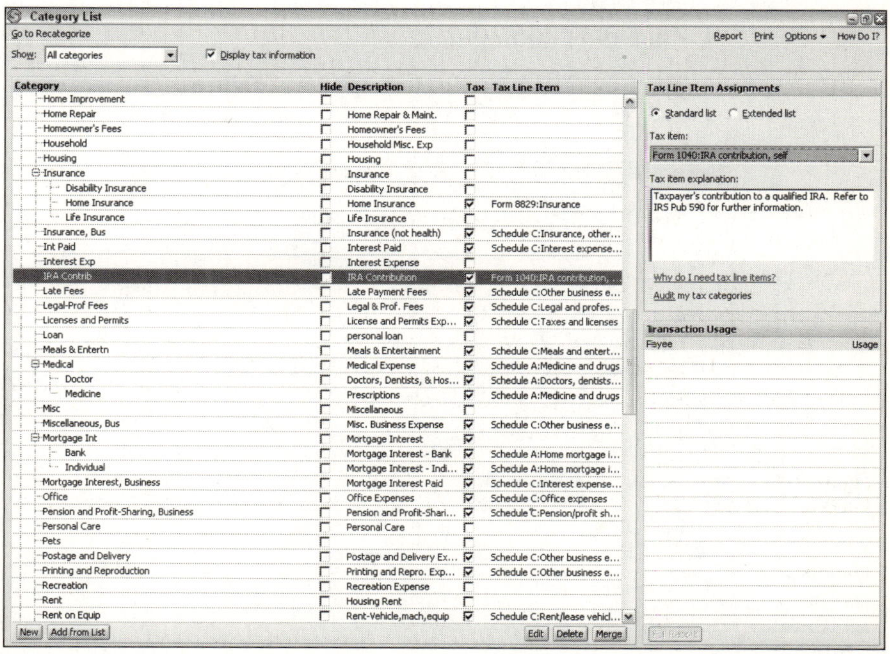

Figure 2-5: Uncheck the little tax box to turn off the tax line assignment.

A window appears, asking if you're sure you want to remove the tax line assigned to this category (Figure 2-6).

4. **Click Yes to remove the tax line assignment.**

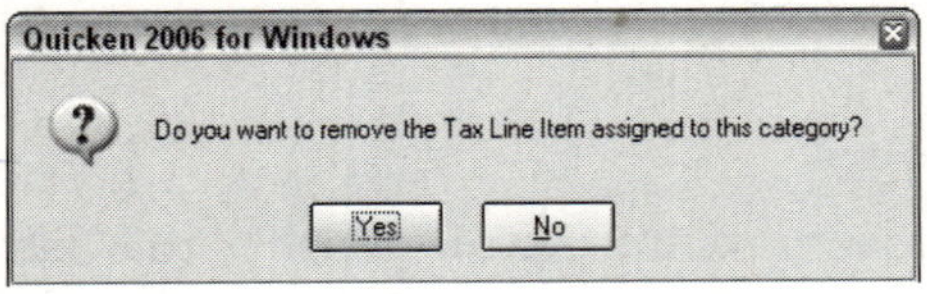

Figure 2-6: Click Yes to give the green light.

Picking a new tax line

Say that instead of removing a tax line, you want to change an existing tax line to something different. For this example, I'm changing my hobby into a real business that I plan to report on Schedule C of my tax return. I need to change the tax line on my Subscriptions category from Schedule A: Subscriptions to Schedule C: Other Business Expenses. Here's how to make the change:

1. **Open the category list (Ctrl+C or Shift+Ctrl+C)).**
2. **Click on the category that you want to change (in this case, Subscriptions).**
3. **Click the Edit button.**

   The Edit Category window appears (Figure 2-7).

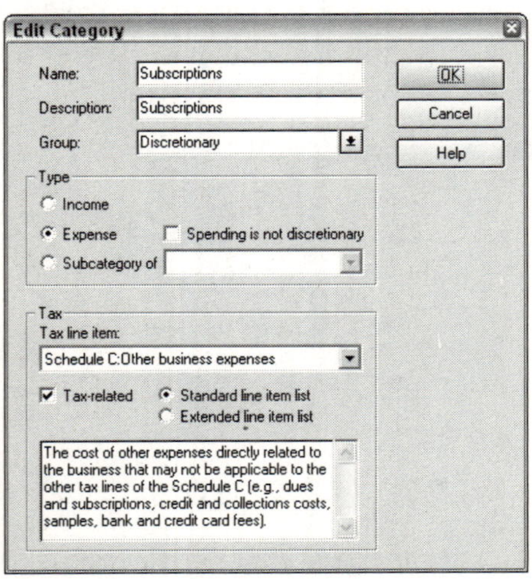

Figure 2-7: Edit the category to change a tax line.

4. **Make the appropriate change in the Tax Line Item drop-down list.**
5. **Click the OK button.**

   The Edit Category window closes, and your tax line assignment has been changed. You can view and verify the change in the category list.

When you make a category change, from that point forward, all reports showing that category are coded to the new tax line. Even reports from a previous year, when the category was coded as a different tax line, now show the new tax assignment. If you're concerned that this change might alter previous tax records that you might need to show to the IRS some day, you might want to print out hard copies of your old tax reports before you start changing tax categories.

Working with an Accountant or Tax Professional

You might be a do-it-yourself kind of person who really enjoys putting together your income tax returns. And that's great. Or maybe you're the type of person who prefers to hire a pro to make sure you've got it right.

You can hire a tax preparer, or you can hire a tax helper. A preparer is going to use your tax reports and put together your entire tax return. Alternatively, you can prepare your tax return yourself, but consider hiring an experienced tax preparer to at least look over your tax return and make suggestions.

Several types of professional tax preparers are out there. Here's a quick look at the credentials you may see mentioned when you start leafing through the yellow pages.

- **CPAs:** A Certified Public Accountant is someone who has been educated as an accountant, who has passed a rigorous test and who has worked for awhile in the accounting profession. CPAs maintain their licenses by attending relevant continuing education courses each year. Be aware of the fact that just because someone is a CPA, that person might not be a tax professional. Make sure you find out a little about the background and the area of specialization of the person you're considering hiring before you commit to the relationship.
- **PAs and accountants:** The difference between a public accountant and a CPA is that the public accountant has never passed the CPA exam, or has passed the exam but hasn't worked long enough in the profession to receive the CPA license. Or, a PA can be a CPA who has chosen not to maintain the CPA license. PAs are licensed accountants and they attend continuing education classes each year, just like the CPAs, in order to maintain their licenses. An accountant is anyone who claims to be one,

but usually only persons educated in the area of accounting attempt to make this claim. Fees for PAs and accountants are usually less than those that CPAs charge.

- **Enrolled Agents (EAs):** An EA is a tax preparer who has passed an examination administered by the IRS and who has received a license from the IRS to prepare tax returns.
- **Tax preparers:** Be aware of the fact that *anyone* can call himself or herself a tax preparer. Just because a person calls himself a lion trainer doesn't mean the lion isn't going to have him for dinner if he flinches at the wrong time. There is no training necessary for someone to use the designation *Tax Preparer*, so be careful when choosing someone with no credentials.

Chapter 3: Tax Reports You Can Use

In This Chapter

- Using the Tax Summary report
- Making sense of the Tax Schedule report
- Specialized tax reports
- Preparing information for your tax advisor

Before you actually have to prepare a tax return, you can cozy up to Quicken's tax reports, analyze your spending and income, make sure everything you've coded for tax lines is in the right place, and make sure any transactions you haven't coded for tax lines get coded properly. And how are going to do all this? Just let me show you how!

The Tax Summary Report: Your Starting Point for Tax Return Preparation

The Tax Summary report is the first place I look when I'm getting ready to assemble information for my income tax return. I enjoy examining the Tax Summary report because I'm a tax nerd and these numbers all make sense to me. I also enjoy examining the Tax Summary report because it's easy to spot any errors in my tax line assignments when I look at this report. Transactions that don't belong in certain tax-related categories stick out like the proverbial sore thumb when you see them on the Tax Summary report.

The Tax Summary report is a nit-picker's dream. The report displays all of the tax categories that are tagged for inclusion in your tax records, subtotaled by category, and with the complete detail of every transaction that has been posted in those categories for the selected time period.

One feature of the Tax Summary report that I particularly like is that all of your categories that have been marked as being tax-related appear on this report, even if the categories have not been assigned to a tax line.

REMEMBER

You can designate a category as being tax-related without assigning the category to a specific tax line. Just check the Tax check box when editing information about the category, as described in Chapter 2 of this book.

Working with the Tax Summary report

You can view the Tax Summary report, as displayed in Figure 3-1, by clicking on the Reports⇨Tax⇨Tax Summary. The first time you view the report, you might want to customize the report in certain ways so that the data you see is useful to you:

- ✦ Set the Date Range to reflect the current year, current quarter, or whatever time period is best suited to your needs.
- ✦ Remove unwanted columns: For example, you might not need to see the check numbers, account names, or account clearance (Clr) columns. Remove a column from view by clicking on the double bar to the right of the unwanted column heading, and then dragging the bar over to the left until it overlaps the bar for the previous column. When you release your mouse button, the column disappears.
- ✦ Resize remaining columns: Because you have more room after removing columns, you can expand remaining columns by dragging the double bar on the right side of a column header over to the right. Make a column smaller by dragging the double bar over to the left (but not all the way over to the next column, unless you want this column to disappear too!).
- ✦ Bring back lost columns: Did you remove a column by accident? Click Customize in the top-right corner. On the opening customization screen is a box labeled Show Columns. Select the little check boxes for each column you want to display.
- ✦ Save your revised report: Click the Save Report button on the Report toolbar to give a unique name to this report and make it available for future viewing, without having to re-create the entire report. Call the report "My Tax Summary Report," or "Info I Need for My Tax Return," or whatever name seems most appropriate to you.

TIP

Turn your Tax Summary into a Tax Schedule report instantly by changing the Subtotal By option to Tax Schedule.

When you examine the information that appears in your Tax Summary report, look for transactions that seem misplaced — items that got coded to the wrong tax category, or transactions that don't seem to fit with the other transactions in a group.

If you need to change the category on a transaction so that it fits into a different tax group, double-click on the transaction as it appears in the Tax Summary report. The actual transaction appears. You can change the category if necessary, and then click Enter to record the transaction. Return to the Tax Summary report by clicking the Tax Summary Report button at the bottom of the register.

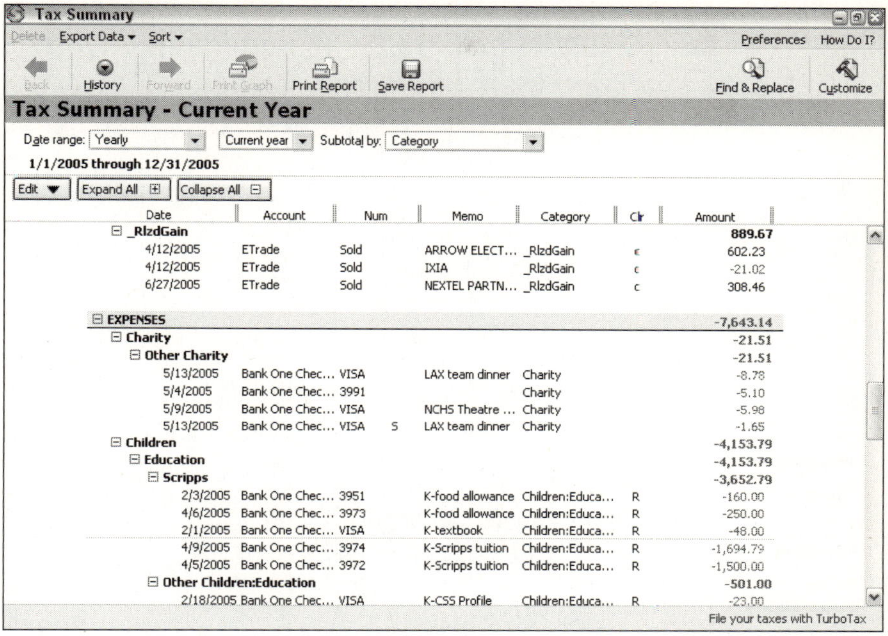

Figure 3-1: The Tax Summary report.

Using the Tax Schedule report

The Tax Schedule report, also found on the Reports menu and then on the Tax side menu, is a report you'll need when preparing your income tax return. This report (see Figure 3-2) is organized by tax schedule, and then by tax line within each tax schedule. Only categories to which you assigned tax lines appear on this report.

Like its Tax Summary report buddy, the Tax Schedule report provides the complete detail for all transactions in each category that appears on the report. You can examine the report to make sure the information in each tax line is coded correctly.

Although Quicken's customization features enable you to change the appearance of the reports to fit specific needs, you might find that you can save time if you're interested in using the specialized tax reports that are new to the 2006 version of Quicken.

Quicken's tax reports can only display information that you've entered in Quicken. To make sure your tax reports are thorough and provide all the information you need for the preparation of your income tax return, you must enter all of your financial transactions for the entire year in your Quicken program and assign tax lines where necessary to your categories.

Medical and Dental Expenses		**Caution.** Do not include expenses reimbursed or paid by others.		
	1	Medical and dental expenses (see page A-2) . . .	1	
	2	Enter amount from Form 1040, line 37 [2]		
	3	Multiply line 2 by 7.5% (.075)	3	
	4	Subtract line 3 from line 1. If line 3 is more than line 1, enter -0-		4

Figure 3-2: The Tax Schedule report.

When to use the tax reports

Some important steps are necessary for the preparation of your income tax returns (beyond getting your hair done so you'll look nice for the tax preparer, renting a condo in the Cayman Islands for that quick escape when the tax examiner calls . . .). Examining the information on your tax reports to make sure everything has been accounted for correctly can help you complete many of those steps.

Here are some tips for when and how to use the Quicken tax reports:

- ✦ Do a preliminary analysis. Before you start preparing your tax return or before you get ready to meet with your tax advisor, examine the Tax Summary report carefully. Look at the detail that appears in each section of the report and make sure that those transactions appear in the correct section. Double-click on any transaction that needs to be revised, and you are taken to the original transaction, where you can correct the category if necessary.
- ✦ Compare your Tax Summary report to the Tax Schedule report to make sure that all amounts that need to go on your tax return are properly coded with the correct tax line. (If you're not sure of which tax lines you need to use on your tax return, your tax professional can help you with this.)

- Print copies of your tax reports to store with your tax records for the year.
- Print more copies of your tax reports to give to your tax preparer if you don't prepare your tax return yourself.

Quicken's new specialized tax reports

These reports give you additional insight into the information required for preparation of your income tax return, and enable you to isolate and examine the information for specific areas of your tax return. Find them by choosing Tax on the Reports menu.

- **Schedule A: Itemized Deductions:** Only the categories that have been assigned to tax lines for itemized deductions appear on this report. This includes medical expenses, deductible interest and taxes, charitable contributions, casualty losses, and miscellaneous deductions such as job costs, tax preparer fees, gambling losses, and investment-related expenses (see the following figure).

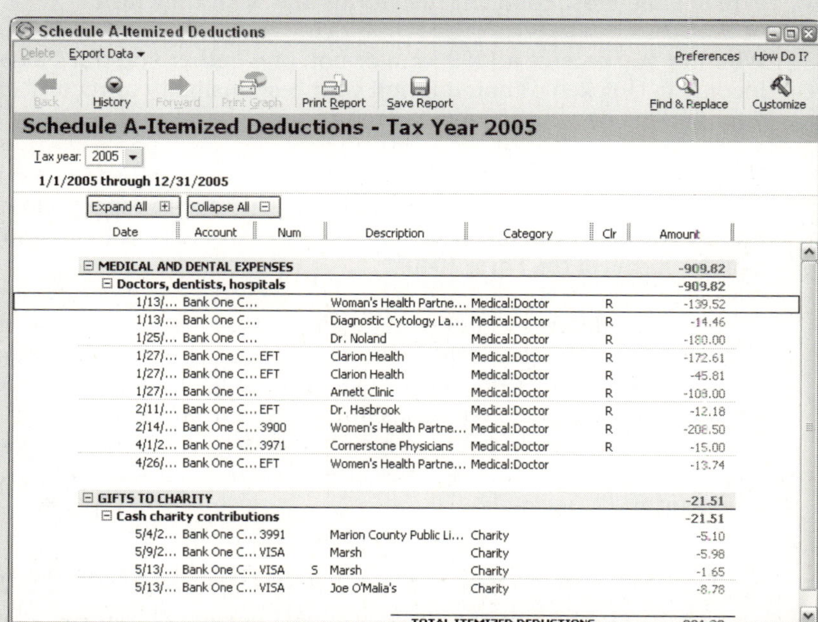

- **Schedule B: Interest and Dividend Income:** Schedule B categories include interest income and dividend income.
- **Schedule D: Capital Gains and Losses:** The categories included on this report are short-term and long-term gains and losses from sales of investments.

Analyzing Your Income

When you think of income and your taxes, you need to think beyond the obvious income you earn at your job. The IRS expects you to report several types of income on your income tax return. If you track all of your income in Quicken, you have ready access to the information you need for your tax return.

For some reason, most people use Quicken to track their job income and their expenses, but they don't always get around to including *all* of their income in Quicken. Income can arrive in the form of interest on your savings accounts, dividends on investments, and other miscellaneous payments you receive during the year.

Many of the people or companies that pay you income during the year send you little reminders in January in the form of information returns, or 1099 forms. The sidebar entitled, "Annual information returns you might receive," explains the most common 1099 forms and what they mean.

Whether you receive a 1099 form or not, or whether you track all your income in Quicken or not, it is still your responsibility to record all of your income on your income tax return.

The 1040 is the standard federal income tax return. Depending on how many different types of income and deductions you have to report and how much money you earn, you might be able to use a Form 1040A or a Form 1040EZ, simpler forms of the Form 1040.

Payers of dividends and interest are not required to provide you with 1099 forms if your earnings for the year are less than $10. Payers of miscellaneous income reported on a 1099-MISC don't have to give you a form unless your income is at least $600. This does not free you from the obligation to report such income on your tax return. It's up to you to keep track of your earnings and report the amount you earned even if you don't receive a 1099 form.

Agreeing your income to your information return

As I detailed in the sidebar titled, "Annual information returns you might receive," you might receive any of several types of information returns after the first of each year. One of the most common mistakes people make on their income tax returns is assuming the amounts on these information returns are accurate and reporting those amounts as income on their tax returns.

Annual information returns you might receive

Every January, you can count on receiving forms in the mail that tell you how much money you earned in the previous year. You are expected to account for the amounts on these forms on your tax return (see the following figure). Here's a sample of the most common income-reporting forms:

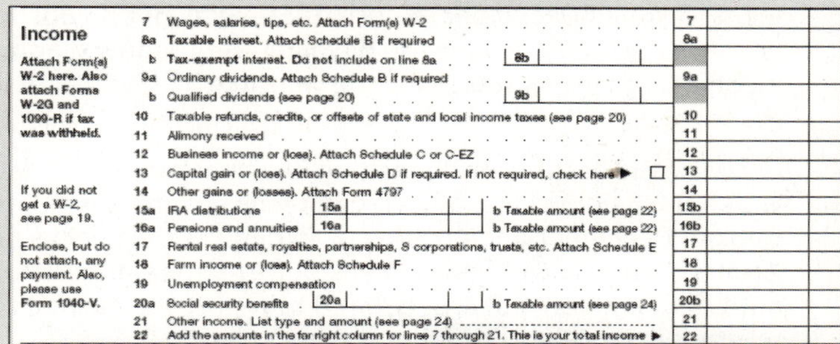

Income				
Attach Form(s) W-2 here. Also attach Forms W-2G and 1099-R if tax was withheld.	7	Wages, salaries, tips, etc. Attach Form(s) W-2		7
	8a	**Taxable interest.** Attach Schedule B if required		8a
	b	**Tax-exempt interest. Do not include on line 8a**	8b	
	9a	Ordinary dividends. Attach Schedule B if required		9a
	b	Qualified dividends (see page 20)	9b	
	10	Taxable refunds, credits, or offsets of state and local income taxes (see page 20)		10
	11	Alimony received		11
	12	Business income or (loss). Attach Schedule C or C-EZ		12
	13	Capital gain or (loss). Attach Schedule D if required. If not required, check here ▶ ☐		13
If you did not get a W-2, see page 19.	14	Other gains or (losses). Attach Form 4797		14
	15a	IRA distributions	15a	b Taxable amount (see page 22) 15b
	16a	Pensions and annuities	16a	b Taxable amount (see page 22) 16b
Enclose, but do not attach, any payment. Also, please use **Form 1040-V.**	17	Rental real estate, royalties, partnerships, S corporations, trusts, etc. Attach Schedule E		17
	18	Farm income or (loss). Attach Schedule F		18
	19	Unemployment compensation		19
	20a	Social security benefits	20a	b Taxable amount (see page 24) 20b
	21	Other income. List type and amount (see page 24)		21
	22	Add the amounts in the far right column for lines 7 through 21. This is your **total income** ▶		22

- **W-2:** Every employer you worked for sends you a W-2 form showing how much money you earned, how much tax was withheld, and how much money you contributed to an employer-sponsored retirement fund. This form might also include information about amounts you contributed to health insurance, union dues, flex plan, and other company-sponsored funds.
- **1099-DIV:** You should receive a 1099-DIV from any company that paid you dividends on stock you owned, any mutual fund in which you own shares, and any credit union of which you are a member. These forms come in many different styles and sizes, and often, especially in the case of the mutual funds and credit unions, the 1099-DIV information is incorporated into the monthly statement for December.
- **1099-INT:** If you have money tied up in a savings account, certificate of deposit, or bond and you receive interest related to these investments, you should receive a 1099-INT form after the end of the year.
- **1099-MISC:** Money you receive for services you provide is supposed to be reported to you on a 1099-MISC form. For example, if you're a wage-earner by day and a free-lance personal trainer for a gym by night, the gym should give you a 1099-MISC showing your share of the fees for your training services. (Note: Typically, individuals don't prepare 1099 forms, so if you hire yourself out to give private personal training sessions, you probably won't receive any 1099-MISC forms from your customers — however, you of course must still report the income on your tax return.)

So what should you do if you compare your information return income with the actual income you receive during the year and you think the amount on your 1099 form is incorrect? Here are some points to keep in mind when dealing with the discrepancies:

- If you're a shareholder in a company that declares dividends in late December but mails the dividend checks so that they aren't received until January, you don't have to report the dividend income until the year in which you receive the income. Your 1099-DIV form is going to include the amount of the December dividend. You have the right to match the dividend income to the year in which the income is actually received and pay tax on the income in the proper year.
- The same goes for miscellaneous income if a company authorizes a payment to you in December, reports that payment on your 1099-MISC, but you don't actually receive the payment until January. You can report the income on your tax return for the year in which you actually receive the income.

Delaying the cashing or depositing of a check does not delay the year in which the income is taxable. If you receive some payments in the last week of December and decide not to deposit the checks until January, or if you're out of town the last week of December and don't get your mail until January, you still are required to report the income on the tax return for the year in which it was received.

If the amount reported on your 1099 form is not the same amount you received during the tax year, you should report the actual amount you received on your tax return. The IRS receives copies of the same 1099 forms that you receive, so it is helpful, when making such a change, to attach a statement to your tax return explaining the discrepancy between the 1099 form and the amount you report. Here's a sample statement:

> Name: Barney Rubble
>
> Social Security number: 222-333-4444
>
> I received a 1099-DIV from XYZ Corporation reporting $200.00 in dividend income for the year 2006. I actually received $150 in dividend income from XYZ Corporation in 2006. The remaining $50 dividend was declared payable in December 2006 but not received by me until January 10th, 2007.
>
> Therefore I am reporting $150 in dividend income from XYZ Corporation on my 2006 income tax return. I will add the remaining $50 to the dividend income reported on my 2007 form 1099-DIV and report that on my 2007 income tax return.

If you report an amount on your tax return that is less than the amount reported on the 1099 form due to the fact that you received the money in the year after the year in which the money was paid, be sure to make a note to yourself that on next year's tax return, you are going to have to increase the 1099 amount from that payer to reflect the extra amount from the prior year.

Reporting your W-2 income

Income from the job or jobs where you worked as an employee is reported to you on a W-2 form. You can count on receiving this form from your employer sometime in January. If the amount on the W-2 form does not agree with your records, you should take up the problem with your employer and not alter the amount on your tax return. You might have to request your employer to issue a revised W-2 form if there is an error.

REMEMBER

The IRS expects you to report the full amount of income and tax withholding from your W-2 form on your tax return.

Tax-deferred income

If you receive income on which tax has been deferred, such as income from an IRA or 401(k) plan, that income is reported on a 1099-R form and you are required to pay income tax on the income in the year in which you receive the money.

For more information about receiving income from your retirement plans, see Book VI, Chapter 2.

Analyzing Your Deductions

Deductions are amounts that you spend that reduce the income on which your tax is computed. In other words, you can subtract the amount you spend on deductible items from your income before you calculate your income tax on your tax return.

Not all of the money you spend during the year qualifies as a deduction on your tax return, but you might be surprised just how much of your spending does generate a deduction.

The main categories of deductions are itemized deductions, deductions and credits for childcare and education costs (including education for the parents or adults in the family), and other miscellaneous deductions and adjustments. A brief summary of these types of deductions follows, with suggestions for how to analyze these categories when they appear on your tax reports.

Itemized deductions

These are the deductions that appear on your Schedule A. Your deductions have to surpass the standard deduction that is allowed to all taxpayers (except dependent children) before you are allowed to use these deductions to reduce your taxable income. The standard deduction increases every year. For 2006, when this book went to press, the standard deductions were as follows:

Married filing jointly and surviving spouse taxpayers	$10,000
Married filing separately taxpayers	$ 5,000
Head of household taxpayers	$ 7.300
Single taxpayers	$ 5,000

Itemized deductions fall into six main categories. These categories are described below, along with pointers for analyzing your expenses that have been coded to these categories.

Medical deductions

The medical expenses you've coded to tax lines in Quicken will be transferred to the Medical and Dental Expenses section of your Schedule A (Figure 3-3). These expenses should be organized in Quicken as follows:

- **Medicine and Drugs:** This category on your Tax Schedule report should include only medicine that is prescribed by a doctor. Over-the-counter medications, such as aspirins and cold medicine, do not qualify for a tax deduction. In Quicken, you need to break out prescription and non-prescription medicine in two categories, so that the prescription medicine can be assigned to the Medicine and drugs tax line. The IRS permits you to include insulin with prescription medicine.
- **Doctors, Dentists, and Hospitals:** This is really the catch-all medical tax line in Quicken. Because Quicken only provides the four medical tax lines described here, you need to expand the definition of the tax lines in order to account for all medical expenses. When I code Quicken medical categories to tax lines, I include all deductible medical expenses in this category except items that are specifically prescription medicine or mileage, travel, and lodging. Therefore, in my Doctors, Dentists, and Hospitals category, you'll find eyeglasses and contact lenses, lab fees and x-rays, health insurance that is not paid by my employer, crutches, oxygen, nursing services, psychiatric care, special education costs, fees for a stop-smoking program, telephone equipment for hearing-impaired, seeing-eye and hearing-ear dogs, the cost of close captioning equipment on the television for the hard-of-hearing, and so on. OK, so I lied a little bit. I don't really have all these things going on. But if I did, this is the tax line I'd use to categorize all of these expenses properly so they will show up on my Quicken tax reports.
- **Medical Travel and Lodging:** In this category you should include any transportation and lodging that are expressly related to medical care. You can include ambulance fees, or taxis taken to see the doctor or to get to a medical facility. Include the cost of attending a medical conference.

Figure 3-3: Medical expenses get entered in the top section on Schedule A.

Medical and Dental Expenses				
		Caution. Do not include expenses reimbursed or paid by others.		
	1	Medical and dental expenses (see page A-2) . . .	1	
	2	Enter amount from Form 1040, line 37 | 2 |		
	3	Multiply line 2 by 7.5% (.075)	3	
	4	Subtract line 3 from line 1. If line 3 is more than line 1, enter -0-	4	

✦ **Medical Mileage:** You also are entitled to a deduction for mileage when driving to medical facilities. It's difficult to break out the medical mileage when you pay for gas and enter your auto expenses in Quicken, so make a note to yourself that you need to include on your tax return or provide your tax preparer with the information about how many miles you drive for medical care. If you specifically pay for a tank of gas that is used exclusively for medical purposes, you can code that gas purchase as medical mileage, but you still have to perform a calculation of the number of miles you drove for medical purposes for the entire year. This particular tax line really isn't going to do you much good in Quicken.

Plenty of medical expenses don't qualify for tax deductions. Here are some examples of expenses that should be categorized in Quicken as medical expenses, but not included in the tax line assignments described above: non-prescription drugs; health insurance paid at the office and deducted from your pay before taxes are withheld; cosmetic surgery (although some surgical procedures are deductible — check with your tax advisor); maternity clothes; health club dues; teeth whitening treatments; weight loss programs; and nutritional supplements.

Tax expenses

The IRS allows you to deduct certain types of taxes in the Taxes You Paid section of your Schedule A (see Figure 3-4). Here are the tax-related tax lines and what you should look for when analyzing expenses in these categories:

✦ **State income taxes:** Because there is a separate tax line for state income tax withheld from your wages, the amounts assigned to the State Income Taxes tax line should only include state tax amounts other than your withholding. Expect to see a state tax refund in this category if you received a refund last year. And if you paid any state income taxes for a prior year, that amount should appear here too. The state tax refund is potential taxable income to you, and the extra amounts you paid for earlier tax years represent an itemized deduction.

✦ **Local income taxes:** The rules are the same as for state taxes. W-2 amounts get coded to the W-2 withholding tax line, so for this local tax line, you should only see refunds or back taxes paid.

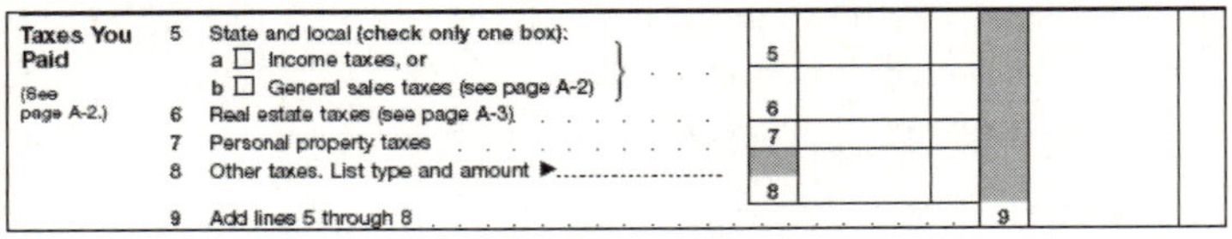
Taxes You Paid (See page A-2.)
5 State and local (check only one box):
a ☐ Income taxes, or
b ☐ General sales taxes (see page A-2) 5
6 Real estate taxes (see page A-3) 6
7 Personal property taxes 7
8 Other taxes. List type and amount ▶.................... 8
9 Add lines 5 through 8 9

Figure 3-4: Tax expenses get entered in the second section on Schedule A.

- **State estimated tax, qtrly:** This is the tax line you use when you make payments of quarterly state and local estimated taxes. The amount you paid during the year gets added to the state tax withheld, and any back taxes you paid to arrive at your state income tax deduction.
- **Real estate taxes:** In this tax line, you should see the tax you pay on any real estate that you own. Real estate tax that you pay with your mortgage payment might need to be recoded so that it appears on this tax line. Real estate tax on other real property investments that you own, including the tax portion of condominium fees, should also be assigned to this group.
- **Personal property taxes:** The personal property tax line is a little tricky. Not all states charge personal property taxes, so many people don't have any amount here. If you live in a state where you pay personal property tax along with your vehicle license plate fees, you need to split out the personal property tax portion of the fee when you enter the payment in Quicken and make sure you assign this tax line to the category containing the tax amount. Other types of personal property tax include property tax on large vehicles such as recreational vehicles, trailers, and boats.
- **Other taxes:** Are there any other taxes left for this tax line? Foreign tax comes to my mind. If you have investments in companies with overseas operations, you might have foreign tax withheld from your dividend income. You have a choice whether you want to deduct the tax or claim a credit for the tax. In either case, the tax should be placed in a category that is coded as Other Taxes, and then when you prepare your tax return, you can decide on the best way to treat the tax.
- **Sales tax paid:** The IRS has reinstated the sales tax deduction (effective with 2004 tax returns), but you can only take a deduction for either your sales tax or your state and local income tax. The sales tax deduction was reinstated after lobbyists from states without a state sales tax complained, and the deduction was designed to benefit residents of those states. But sometimes even if you pay state and local income tax, the sales tax you pay is higher. You can pick which deduction you want to take, so if

you want to really take advantage of Quicken, throughout the year, split every one of your purchase transactions so that you break out sales tax into a separate category, and give that category a tax line of Other Taxes. Then at the end of the year it should be a simple matter to see whether you paid enough sales tax to make the deduction worthwhile.

Quicken reports alone aren't enough to support your deduction for sales tax, or, for that matter, for anything. You are responsible for saving receipts that support your tax return deductions.

Interest expenses

You can take a deduction for certain types of interest expense on Schedule A in the Interest You Paid section, as shown in Figure 3-5. When recording interest payments, make sure you've coded all entries properly so that only the interest appears in the tax category and not the principal portion of your payment. For example, when you pay your mortgage or a car loan, only the interest portion of your payment is a deductible expense.

The tax lines available for reporting interest expenses include the following:

- **Home mortgage interest (1098):** The amount you pay in home mortgage interest (including points) should agree with the amount reported on the 1098 form you receive from your lender. However, refer back to the section titled "Agreeing your income to your information return" earlier in this chapter. Those rules apply to your mortgage 1098 form as well. If the form you receive from your lender doesn't jibe with the amount you know you paid, record the actual amount you paid on your tax return and attach a statement to the tax return explaining the difference.

  Don't be afraid to call attention to your tax return by attaching a statement. There's nothing wrong with calling attention to the fact that there is an error on your information return. All you're doing is pointing out the fact that you keep excellent records and that you are entering the correct amounts on your tax return.

Interest You Paid (See page A-3.)	10	Home mortgage interest and points reported to you on Form 1098	10		
	11	Home mortgage interest not reported to you on Form 1098. If paid to the person from whom you bought the home, see page A-4 and show that person's name, identifying no., and address ▶	11		
Note. Personal interest is not deductible.	12	Points not reported to you on Form 1098. See page A-4 for special rules	12		
	13	Investment interest. Attach Form 4952 if required. (See page A-4.)	13		
	14	Add lines 10 through 13		14	

Figure 3-5: Interest expenses get entered in the Interest You Paid section on Schedule A.

- **Home mortgage int, (no 1098):** So you didn't receive a 1098 form from your lender? If you paid mortgage interest and have no 1098 to show for it, this is the tax line you should have assigned to your mortgage interest payments. Make sure when analyzing your tax reports that you got your mortgage interest on the correct tax line. You *do* call attention to your return when you have interest that was not reported on a 1098. The IRS wants to know who received the interest and wants to make sure that person is reporting the interest income properly. You will be expected to provide the name, address, and Social Security number or federal ID number for the person or company to whom you paid your interest.
- **Points paid (no 1098):** If you didn't receive a 1098 form that specified how much you paid in points, but you did pay points, you should code the points to this line. Sometimes points are a deductible expense, and sometimes they are not. If you have an amount in this category showing up on your tax report, be sure to call attention to this amount to your tax preparer and determine the rules for reporting the points that you paid.

There is no tax line available for interest paid on money that was used for investments, even though this amount can qualify for a tax deduction. Make a note of any interest you paid on money used for investments (you can code it to a tax-related category without giving it a specific tax line) and check the tax rules or ask your tax professional for advice on how to handle this interest.

Charity expenses

Amounts you give to charity result in a tax deduction on Schedule A in the Gifts to Charity section (Figure 3-6). Examine the amounts that appear in the following categories to make sure an actual deduction is allowed.

- **Cash charity contributions:** Amounts paid to charities appear on your tax reports with this tax line assignment. But make sure that the charities are the kinds of charities that qualify for a tax deduction. Some non-profit groups might be good causes but they don't count for a tax deduction. For example, political groups and public action committees don't qualify for tax deductions. Contributions to individuals don't qualify for a tax deduction, nor do raffle tickets (even when sold by charities). The cost of keeping a foreign student in your home is partially deductible, so include those expenses too. Look through your list of charitable expenses and make sure only the viable deductions are included.
- **Non-cash charity contributions:** I doubt many people use this tax line because most of the non-cash contributions that people make are in the form of old clothes, books, and household items that were purchased many years ago and those purchases don't show up as current expenses in Quicken. But if you purchased something during the year that was donated to a charity, such as food that you gave to the food bank, baking

supplies for the brownies you made for the school bake sale, or other items that you purchased and immediately donated, those amounts should appear in this tax group.

✦ **Charity mileage:** Here's a tax line that seems unnecessary. Much like the tax line for medical mileage, unless you have specific automobile costs that you can attribute exclusively to charity, you probably won't use this tax line. The charity mileage deduction is based on the actually number of miles you drove for charitable purposes during the entire year.

Gifts to Charity				
If you made a gift and got a benefit for it, see page A-4.	15	Gifts by cash or check. If you made any gift of $250 or more, see page A-4	15	
	16	Other than by cash or check. If any gift of $250 or more, see page A-4. You must attach Form 8283 if over $500	16	
	17	Carryover from prior year	17	
	18	Add lines 15 through 17	18	

Figure 3-6: Charity contributions get entered in the Gifts to Charity section on Schedule A.

Miscellaneous expenses

There is a handful of other types of expenses that should appear on your tax return and thus should be assigned to particular tax lines. These expenses are included as Job Expenses and Most Other Miscellaneous Deductions on your Schedule A (see Figure 3-7). Here are the remaining tax lines with a description of what you should see and what you should look for when these tax lines appear on your tax reports.

✦ **Tax preparation fees:** If you pay someone to prepare your taxes, that cost should be categorized as a tax preparation fee and should appear on your tax reports. Included in the category of tax preparation fees is the cost of tax preparation software, books you bought to help you understand taxes, and the cost of filing your tax return electronically.

✦ **Investment management fees:** Costs of getting investment advice and maintaining your investments (including the cost of Quicken if maintaining investment information is its primary use), and fees paid to brokers qualify as tax-deductible expenses.

✦ **Subscriptions:** Before you get excited about taking a deduction for your subscription to your favorite recipe magazine, note that the only subscriptions that are tax deductible are subscriptions to publications that help you earn or maintain your income. Investment publications qualify, as do publications relating to your profession. Beyond that, you're going to have a tough time proving your personal fun reading qualifies for a tax deduction.

Figure 3-7: Other deductible expenses go in the sections for Casualty and Theft Losses, Job Expenses, and Miscellaneous Deductions.

Casualty and Theft Losses	19	Casualty or theft loss(es). Attach Form 4684. (See page A-5.)		19
Job Expenses and Most Other Miscellaneous Deductions	20	Unreimbursed employee expenses—job travel, union dues, job education, etc. Attach Form 2106 or 2106-EZ if required. (See page A-6.) ▶	20	
	21	Tax preparation fees	21	
(See page A-5.)	22	Other expenses—investment, safe deposit box, etc. List type and amount ▶	22	
	23	Add lines 20 through 22	23	
	24	Enter amount from Form 1040, line 37 [24]		
	25	Multiply line 24 by 2% (.02)	25	
	26	Subtract line 25 from line 23. If line 25 is more than line 23, enter -0-		26
Other Miscellaneous Deductions	27	Other—from list on page A-6. List type and amount ▶		27

- **Misc., subject to 2 percent AGI limit:** Plenty of other expenses count as miscellaneous deductions. If you have any of these expenses and they don't show up on your tax reports, you should go back through your register, try to find which categories these expenses have been assigned to, and give those categories the proper tax lines. Isolated occurrences of these expenses can be listed on your tax return Schedule A and coded to the Schedule A tax lines. If you have several of these expenses, or if they are ongoing throughout the year, use the Form 2106 as described in "Other job expenses" below and code your expenses to those tax lines. Here are the types of expenses you should be looking for on the Miscellaneous deductions line of your tax reports:

  - **Job search expense:** You don't have to be out of work to take a tax deduction for the cost of looking for a new job. Included in this description are printing, postage, cost of traveling to interviews, and resume service.

    You can only take a deduction for job search expenses if you already have or have had a job in the same profession. If you're looking for your first job, if you've been out of the workforce for an extended period of time, or if you're making a career change, you're on your own — no help from the IRS with your expenses.

  - **Education:** If you are employed and take classes that maintain your skill in your profession or improve your skills within the same profession, or if the classes are required by your employer, you have an option of taking a deduction for the cost of those classes. But see the section later in this chapter called "Tax deductions and credits relating to children and education." You might qualify for a tax credit for your tuition costs, and that can be more lucrative than the miscellaneous deduction. If you do decide to claim your expenses as a miscellaneous itemized deduction, you can deduct the tuition, books, fees associated with your class, and travel expenses to and from the classes.

- **Uniforms:** If you purchase clothing or shoes exclusively for work and those items cannot be mistaken for clothes you would wear outside of work, the cost of purchasing and caring for the items is a tax-deductible expense. Care of the uniform includes dry cleaning and laundering and repairs. If you wear a business suit to work and only to work, that doesn't qualify as a uniform because you could wear the suit outside of work without the suit being mistaken for a uniform.
- **Tools:** The cost of tools purchased for use at your job qualifies as a deductible expense. The items that qualify as tools vary from job to job. Be sure you can justify the need for your tools as being necessary to the accomplishment of your job.

  It is presumed that you have not received a reimbursement from your employer for any of these tax-deductible items that you purchase. If you are reimbursed, there is no deduction allowed.
- **Other job expenses:** Some people have lots of job-related expenses, including travel and meals, equipment they have to purchase, home office expenses, and more. Those expenses get summarized on Form 2106 and there are a dozen related tax lines for reporting employee business expenses (see Figure 3-8). Partially reimbursed expenses can be reported on Form 2106 as well, and then your deduction is reduced by the amount of your reimbursement.

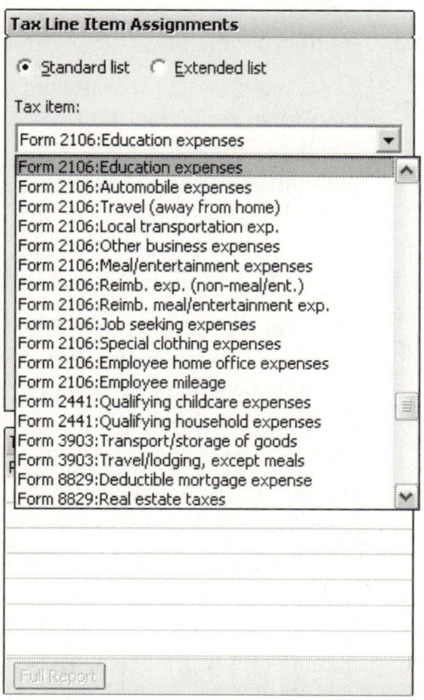

Figure 3-8: Use the Form 2106 tax lines for expenses relating to your job, including expenses for which you get reimbursed.

TIP

Most of the deductions that fall in the miscellaneous categories are subject to a pesky little rule that states that only the amount of the expenses that surpasses 2 percent of your adjusted gross income can be included with your itemized deductions.

- **Gambling losses:** You are allowed to take a deduction for gambling losses, but only to the extent of any gambling winnings that you report in income. When examining transactions that appear on this tax line, make sure you have included the cost of lottery tickets, raffle tickets, slot machines, and any betting that you did during the year. You should also have a place in Quicken where you record gambling winnings, and those amounts should be coded with a tax line of Other Income, Misc..
- **No 2 percent AGI limit:** The most common expense that should appear in this tax line on your tax reports is the cost you incurred that relates to casualties such as storm damage repair. Be aware, however, that the deduction calculation for casualty losses can get complicated, and you should consider consulting with a tax professional if you have expenses of this nature.

Tax deductions versus tax credits

Tax deductions and tax credits are two different species, both designed to reduce your income tax but in different ways. You'll find that when given a choice, the tax credit is usually more attractive than the tax deduction (although there are exceptions to this rule).

Tax deductions reduce the amount of income on which your tax is calculated. For example, if your total income is $40,000 and you have $5,000 in tax deductions, you get to subtract the deductions from your income and calculate your tax on $35,000 instead of $40,000. If the tax rate you pay is 15 percent, your tax on $40,000 would have been $6,000 ($40,000 x 15 percent). When you cut your income to $35,000, your tax goes down to $5,250 ($35,000 x 15 percent). In effect, you cut your tax by 15 percent of your deductions or $750 ($5,000 x 15 percent). Another way to look at this is that for every dollar of tax deduction you can come up with, you save 15¢ on your taxes.

Sounds good, right? But get a load of this:

Tax credits reduce the amount of tax that you pay, dollar for dollar. So if you have $40,000 in income and you pay tax at a rate of 15 percent, you start with owing $6,000. But if you have $5,000 in tax credits, you reduce the actual tax by $5,000 instead of reducing the income by $5,000, so your tax goes from $6,000 to $1,000. Cool, huh?!

The catch is that some tax credits aren't available to you if your income is too high (or too low), and in some situations, you could take a deduction for the full cost of something but you only can take a credit for a percentage of the cost, so it might work out the same or even better if you take the deduction instead of the credit.

The bottom line is that deductions and credits and basically everything about taxes provide tons of confusion for taxpayers and a lucrative income for tax professionals.

Tax deductions and credits relating to children and education

When you consider the amounts on your tax reports, you should look closely at any amounts you spent during the year for childcare and education costs. Many of these costs can result in either tax deductions or tax credits and can reduce your income tax substantially.

Dependent care

Costs that you pay to have someone take care of your child (or your disabled spouse or an elderly or disabled person if that person is your dependent) can qualify for the dependent care credit. Here are the rules to keep in mind. If you qualify for this tax credit, be sure to code all of the amounts you pay to the caregiver to a category assigned to one of these tax lines:

- Form 2441: Qualifying childcare expenses
- Form 2441: Qualifying household expenses

The types of expenses that qualify for this credit include the following:

- Caregiver, including babysitter, housekeeper, cook, maid, governess, any person who is providing care for the dependent or spouse — the caregiver can come to your home or you can take the dependent to the caregiver.
- Food, if food is part of the care provided.
- Schooling, if schooling is part of the care provided and is inseparable from the cost of the caregiver. Schooling can include preschool and kindergarten costs, but beware that kindergarten costs don't qualify for the credit if you live in a state that requires kindergarten.

In order to qualify for the dependent care credit, the following stipulations must be met:

- The expenses must be incurred in order for you to work, and must be incurred during hours while you work.
- If the dependent is your child, she must be younger than 13 years old.
- If you are married, both you and your spouse must work during the time the care is given.
- You must live in the same home as the dependent receiving the care.
- The person providing the care is not your spouse, nor is it another dependent of yours. If the person providing the care is another child of yours, that child must be at least age 19.

- You must include the name, address, and Social Security number or federal ID number of the person or organization providing the care on your income tax return.

The amount of the credit is a percentage of the total amount you spent, and that percentage decreases from a maximum of 35 percent to a minimum of 20 percent of your actual expenses as your income increases. The total amount of expenses you can use when applying for this dependent care credit cannot exceed $3,000 per year for one dependent or $6,000 per year for more than one dependent.

So, for example, if you have two children who are receiving care, and your income places you in the 30 percent bracket for calculating the dependent care credit, the most you can claim for the credit is $1,800 or $6,000 x 30 percent. If your expenses were less than $6,000, the credit amount decreases accordingly.

Higher education costs

Most taxpayers are entitled to take tax benefits for the higher education costs they incur. Such costs include the tuition and any course-related fees paid directly to the educational institution, such as lab fees. Costs associated with room and board and books and supplies do not qualify for the various tax benefits available.

Depending on your level of income and the actual amount you spent, you might qualify for one or more of these tax benefits. I strongly advise you to speak with a tax professional when considering these benefits, as you might have a choice to make between various benefits and certainly want to claim the benefit that saves you the most money.

The tax lines available for these expenses include the following:

- Form 8863: Hope qual. higher ed. exp
- Form 8863: Lifetime qual. higher ed. exp
- Form 1040: Tuition and fees deduction
- Form 1040: Student loan interest

Personally I think these tax lines are misleading (except the last one for student loan interest): Until you actually prepare your income tax return, you probably won't know which of the education tax credits (Hope Scholarship Credit or Lifetime Learning Credit) or the tuition and fees deduction or even the education deduction available under itemized deductions on Schedule A will give you the better tax break.

I think it's wiser to not assign a tax line at all to education expenses, but instead create an education expense category and tag that category as being tax-related. Then when you see the amounts on your Tax Summary report, you can consider those amounts when preparing your income tax return, or make the information available to your tax professional, and determine the best course of action for taking either a tax deduction or a tax credit.

Here are the options that might be available to you. Some of these options are limited based on your taxable income. In general, the more you earn, the less likely it is you are going to be eligible to take full advantage of the tax credits or deductions available to you.

- **Hope Scholarship Credit:** Available to offset tuition paid for students in their first two years of a post-secondary education. The student must be enrolled as at least a half-time student in a program that leads to a degree, certificate, or other recognized educational credential. The student must be you, your spouse, or your dependent. If the student is your dependent, he or she must be claimed as your dependent on your income tax return. The credit is 100 percent of the first $1,000 paid for tuition, and 50 percent of the second $1,000 paid for tuition, for a total of $1,500 for one tax year.
- **Lifetime Learning Credit:** Available to offset tuition paid for students attending courses at any qualified education institution. The courses do not have to be part of a degree or certificate program and the student (you, yourself, or your dependent child), does not have to be enrolled full-time or half-time, but instead can be taking as few or as many courses as he or she likes. The credit is 20 percent of the first $10,000 spent on education over the student's lifetime, with a maximum of $2,000 credit per year.
- **Tuition and fees deduction:** If you don't take a credit for education expenses, you might qualify for the tuition and fees deduction for yourself, your spouse, or your dependent. This isn't an itemized deduction, so you don't need to file Schedule A with your tax return to take advantage of this. Depending on how much income you earned you might be able to deduct as much as $4,000 of tuition and course-related fees. Like the Lifetime Learning Credit, the student does not have to be enrolled in a degree or certificate program.
- **Student loan interest:** Where tuition is being paid, there often are student loans, and where there are student loans, there is interest. Again, depending on your income, you might be able to deduct as much as $2,500 in student loan interest paid during the year. The loan must be for higher education costs for yourself, your spouse, or your dependent. Unlike the other education-related tax benefits described above, the student loan interest can be interest on a loan for not just tuition but also room and board, books, and supplies.

The IRS instructions that accompany Form 1040 contain worksheets for calculating how much of a deduction you can take for tuition and fees and student loan interest. Here's a Web address where those instructions and worksheets reside: `www.irs.gov/pub/irs-pdf/i1040gi.pdf`.

Chapter 4: Interfacing with TurboTax

In This Chapter

- **Sharing Quicken information with TurboTax**
- **Preparing your tax return with TurboTax**
- **Sending Quicken information to TurboTax on the Web**

In 1984, while the Baltimore Colts were sneaking out of their locker rooms in the middle of the night and moving to their new home in Indianapolis's Hoosier Dome, two gentlemen in San Diego, Scott Cook and Tom Proulx, founded the company called Intuit and introduced the world to the first version of Quicken. Remarkably, in the same year and the same southern California town, a man named Mike Chipman created a little program he called TurboTax. Years passed and eventually these financial software wizards pooled their talents. Today, Quicken and TurboTax are both produced by Intuit, where they happily work together, ready to provide you with the tools you need to create your income tax returns and survive April 15th.

Telling TurboTax about Your Quicken Information

Whoa! Before you send your Quicken information over to TurboTax, you have to take care of a couple of housekeeping tasks. You want to make sure that the data in Quicken is complete and ready to go to your tax return, don't you?

Take a few minutes to make sure these steps have been completed in Quicken. This ensures that the information that travels over from Quicken to TurboTax is exactly the information you want to include on your income tax return:

✦ Open the category list (Ctrl+C or Shift+Ctrl+C) and examine the tax line assignments you have made. If the tax lines aren't displayed, check the Display Tax Information box at the top of the list. Scroll through the list, taking the time to read each category and assigning all of the tax-related categories to the appropriate tax line.

TIP: It wouldn't hurt to print a copy of your category list and show your tax line assignments to a tax professional. It will only take a short amount of the tax pro's time to review the list and make sure you have your tax line assignments completed correctly.

- ✦ View or print a copy of the Tax Schedule report and examine this report closely. This is the information that you're going to send to TurboTax. Look for amounts that seem inconsistent with what you know you earned or spent during the year. Look for omissions of categories that ought to appear here. For example, if you know you donated to charity last year and you want to take a deduction for your donations on your tax return, make sure that the Cash Charity Contributions line appears on your report.
- ✦ Make a backup file of your Quicken data. I don't expect you to have any problems, but just to be extra extra sure, back up your data in Quicken so that you can always re-create your data if there is an emergency. See Appendix A for details on how the backup process works.

If you haven't gotten around to assigning tax lines to your various categories in Quicken, you can't move forward with the import information in this chapter. TurboTax is good, but not that good. You have to give the program a little guidance as to how the various categories relate to your income tax return.

So what's so cool about TurboTax?

If you are new to using tax software, you're in for a treat. It's easy to prepare your income tax return with the help of TurboTax, and the end result is quite professional-looking. One of my favorite features is the fact that if you decide you need to change a number on the return, the program goes through and re-adds everything, so all of the forms and schedules reflect the change. Here are some other reasons that make TurboTax appealing:

- The easy Q&A format is designed to cover all the information you need to prepare a complete income tax return.
- You can prepare both federal and state tax returns in TurboTax, and, if you moved during the year, you can produce state returns for each state you lived in, and TurboTax makes it easy to divide your income properly between the states.
- TurboTax extracts the information you entered all year in Quicken, so you don't have to reassemble information you've already collected.
- You can prepare your entire tax return from start to finish in this ready-to-file product.
- Tips to help you better understand taxes and to help you find all the deductions you deserve are scattered throughout the program.
- The basic information you enter in TurboTax one year rolls over into the next year's return, making the setup process for future tax returns much easier.
- You'll save an enormous amount of time preparing your tax return when you use TurboTax.
- No math errors!
- Planning tools that come with the program teach you how you can lower your taxes.

When assigning tax lines, you might have noticed that Quicken automatically assigns a lot of the tax lines for you — at least in the most recent versions of the program. So a lot of the guesswork has been removed regarding which tax lines go with which categories.

As of press time, I resorted to using TurboTax 2004 in order to accomplish the steps shown in this chapter. It's possible that the screens and commands for future years of TurboTax software will change and that the steps described here will not match with your experience. I can say, however, that TurboTax has traditionally been an intuitive program. If you read the TurboTax screens carefully, you should be able to figure out how to work the import process.

Getting started in TurboTax

When you're ready to experiment with importing your data to TurboTax, and your Quicken file is all backed up and safe, these are the steps you're going to follow:

1. **Open TurboTax and choose Start Return to get started using TurboTax.**
2. **Decide whether you want to transfer information from your prior tax return.**

   If you used TurboTax the year before to prepare your tax return, you are given an option to transfer some of the information from last year's tax return into this year's tax return. Transferring makes great sense. It's the busy-work part of the return that transfers — information like your name and address and the names of your kids, the names of the jobs you had last year, and so on. Numbers don't transfer, so you don't have to worry about getting last year's income and expenses all jumbled up with this year's transactions. If you didn't use TurboTax last year, transferring is not an option. To begin your tax return without transferring data from last year, click Continue Without Transferring.
3. **Choose your filing status.**

   Transferred returns skip over the filing status question at first, proceeding with the assumption that you will use the same filing status as last year. Non-transfers see the filing status options (Figure 4-1). Pick the status that applies to you (click the Guide Me button if you're not sure which status is correct), and then click Continue to move to the next step.

   Occasionally you are prompted to save your file in the TurboTax program. These prompts don't come frequently enough for my taste. At any time you can save the information you've entered by choosing File➪Save from the TurboTax menu. The first time you try to save your return, you need to give the file a name. TurboTax offers a name for you such as "2005*LastnameFirstinitial*TaxReturn.tax." I highly recommend you take the name that is offered — using the standard TurboTax filename makes finding your file a lot easier for next year's TurboTax program.

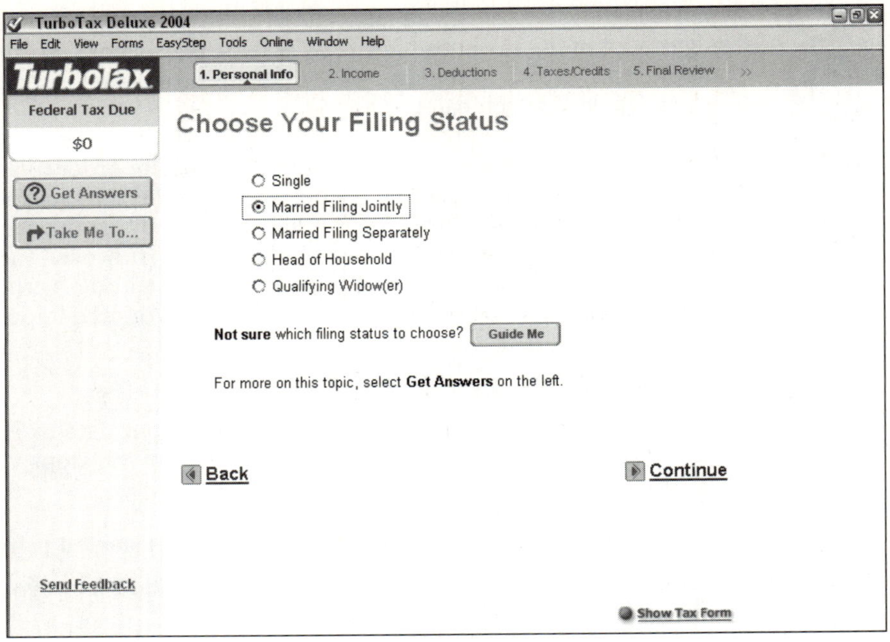

Figure 4-1: Choose your filing status, and then click Continue.

4. **Enter name and address, Social Security number, and occupation.**

   Verify the information that transferred from the prior year return and make changes as necessary. If you didn't transfer from a prior year, fill in blanks when prompted to enter name and address, Social Security number, and occupation.

   Because this is a book about Quicken and not a book about TurboTax (and alas, my *TurboTax For Dummies* is out of print), I'm going to skip pretty quickly over the technical aspects of the TurboTax program, so that I can focus on importing Quicken information into your tax return. Do not rely on the TurboTax material presented here as being a complete description of how to prepare your tax return.

5. **Answer a few questions by checking or leaving the various boxes blank (see Figure 4-2). If you are filing a joint tax return, there is a check box for both you and your spouse.**

   - Can the taxpayer be claimed as a dependent on someone else's tax return?
   - Did the taxpayer serve in the armed forces last year?
   - Is the taxpayer legally blind?
   - Did the taxpayer die before the year ended?

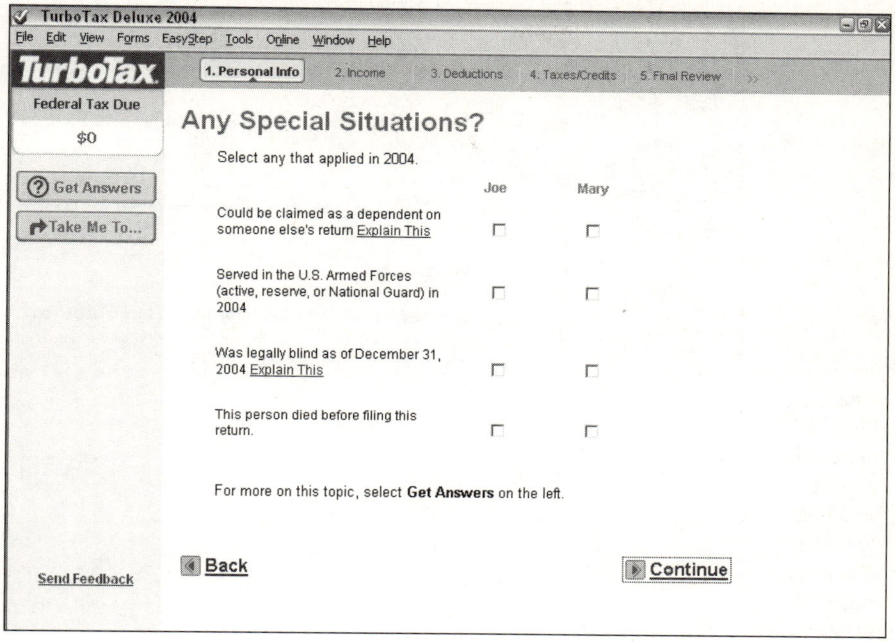

Figure 4-2: Clearing up some tax return housework with a brief Q&A.

6. **Enter information about dependents.**

   Confirm the dependent information transferring from last year's tax return, or enter the name, relationship, date of birth, type of dependent (child that lived with you, child that didn't live with you, teenager that eats at your house but doesn't speak to you, and so on), and Social Security number of each of your dependents.

7. **Here's a key question: Answer Yes when asked if you want to import info from Quicken.**

   When the screen shown in Figure 4-3 appears, click Yes to initiate the import process. On the next screen you are asked to identify which program you use that contains your financial information. Click the check box to choose Quicken, and then click Continue to proceed to the next screen.

   If you use a password to protect your Quicken data, you are asked to supply that password when TurboTax accesses your Quicken file.

   Don't worry about the fact that you've got more than one year of data stored in your Quicken file. All of your Quicken transactions are dated, and TurboTax knows what year it is. Only the information from the correct year is imported into your tax return.

8. **Continue using the TurboTax program, answering questions, moving from screen to screen.**

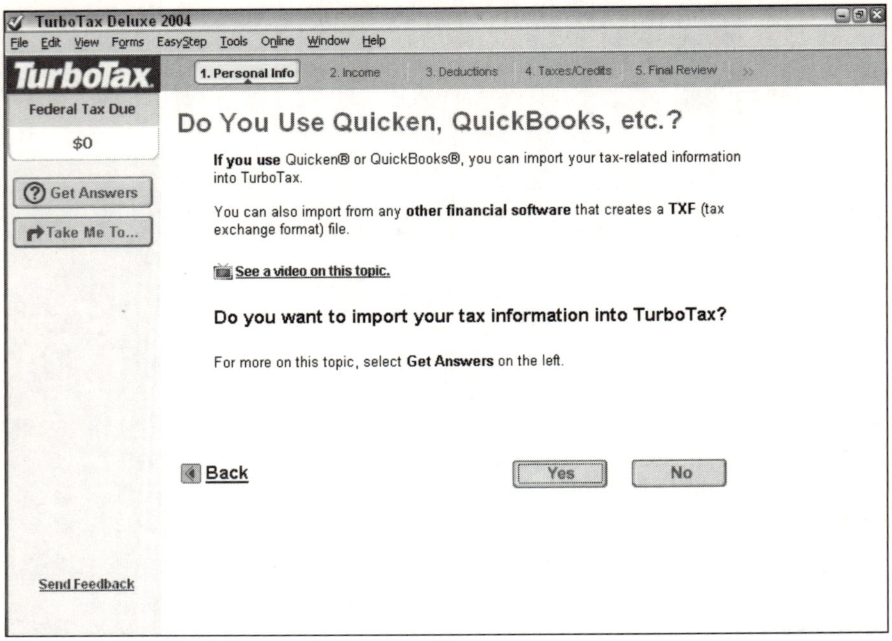

Figure 4-3: Click Yes to begin the process of sending data from Quicken to TurboTax.

9. **Indicate if you want to import specific financial data.**

   The first opportunity you have to import information from Quicken is when you are asked if you want to import a variety of types of income, including pension income, Social Security, income tax refunds, income reported on 1099-MISC forms, and so on. If you want to import the kind of financial information shown in Figure 4-4, click Yes. Otherwise click No, and Quicken proceeds without performing an import at this time.

10. **Confirm the import of specific amounts.**

    Just like a kitty bringing home a mouse for your approval, when TurboTax imports data from your Quicken program, it shows you what it found, as displayed in Figure 4-5. Only then do you have to commit to actually importing the specific amount into your tax return. If you see an amount that belongs in your tax return, check the box next to that item. If you don't want to transfer an imported item, uncheck the box. After checking and unchecking boxes, click Import Now if there are checked boxes for items that need to be imported. Click Skip Import if there is nothing you want to import at this time.

WARNING!

Be careful with the timing of your tax return preparation. If you upgrade your Quicken to a new version (typically Quicken upgrades occur in the fall) and you haven't yet prepared your tax return for the previous year, your TurboTax and your Quicken programs might not talk to each other.

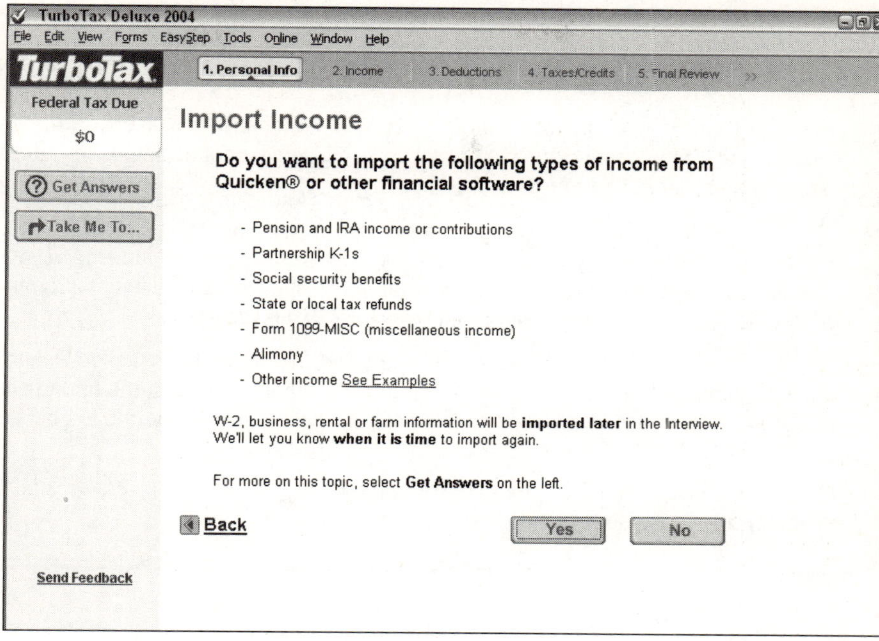

Figure 4-4: Here's your first chance to import data into Quicken.

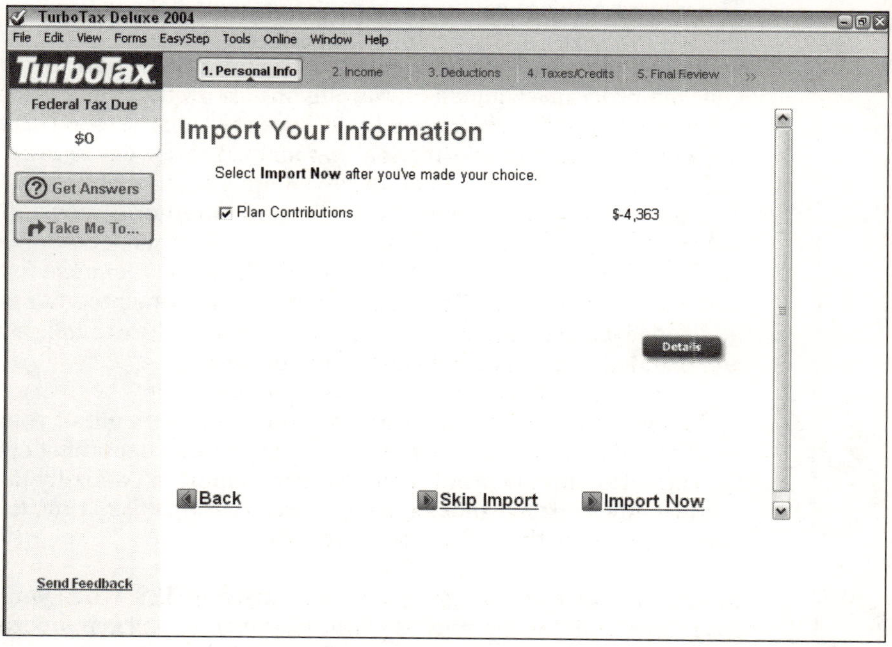

Figure 4-5: Check an item you want to import, and then click Import Now. Click Skip Import if you don't want to import at this time.

Importing is not an all-or-nothing process

Importing from Quicken is not an all-at-once process, and it's not an all-or-nothing process. Here are some points about how the import process works:

- The import process goes step by step as you prepare your return; you can see what is imported as you go and make changes as necessary.
- Each time you get to a new topic in TurboTax, you are asked if you want to import data on that topic.
- TurboTax presents a list of what has been imported — you can review the list and uncheck check boxes for any item you don't want to include in your tax return.
- And it might be the case that even though you want to include that item in your tax return, you want to enter it yourself instead of using the amount brought over from Quicken.
- When you are satisfied with the data on an import list, click the Import Now button to actually incorporate the data into your tax return.

Importing information from your tax lines

The import process will become routine as you make your way through TurboTax. As you continue the preparation of your tax return, periodically you'll see screens that ask if you want to import information from your Quicken program (Figure 4-6). Nothing is imported automatically, and this is the way it should be. You need to give your permission for TurboTax to go and get the pieces of information that make up your tax return.

To agree to the import, click the Yes button. Another screen appears (Figure 4-7), showing you exactly what TurboTax found when it scrounged around in your Quicken program. You can check the boxes and choose to accept these amounts in which case TurboTax incorporates them into your tax return, or you can leave the boxes unchecked and tell TurboTax to take a hike, as it were, at least regarding these bits of information.

TIP

In case you were wondering, when you take numbers out of your Quicken program to incorporate in your TurboTax tax return, nothing changes in Quicken. The import process from TurboTax doesn't actually take these numbers away from Quicken, it just borrows the information, leaving your Quicken file exactly the way you left it.

REMEMBER

Quicken alone isn't enough support to satisfy the IRS. When you prepare your tax return based on numbers that appear in your Quicken program, you still need to keep receipts that support those numbers. I recommend printing a copy of your Tax Schedule report and saving it in a file along with a copy of your tax return and copies of all of the receipts that relate to that tax return.

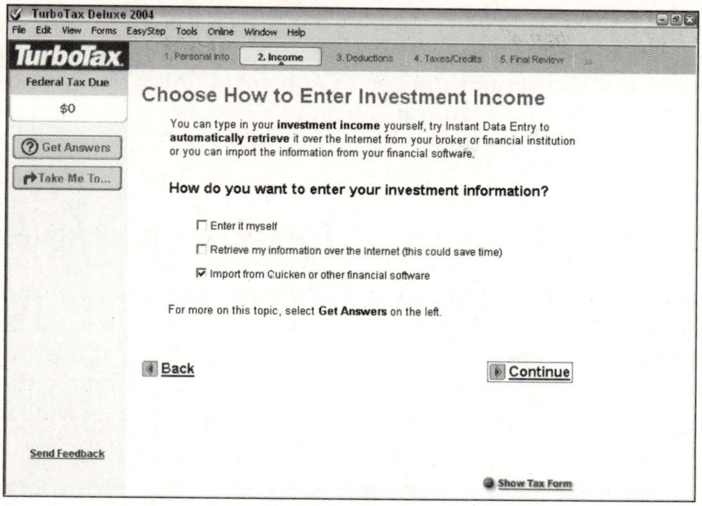

Figure 4-6: Check the third box if you want to import from Quicken, and then click Continue.

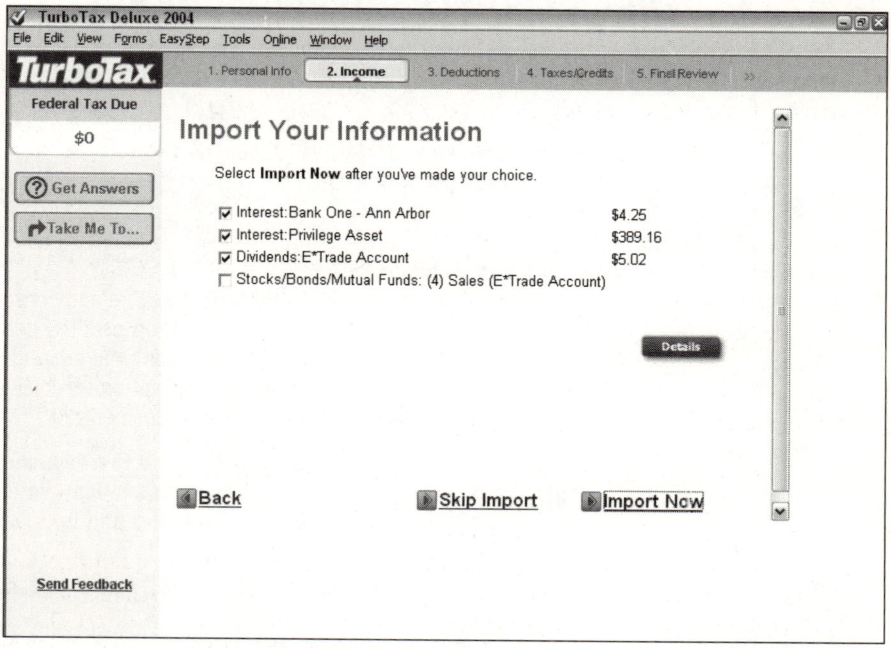

Figure 4-7: Check the boxes for any amounts you want to import, leave other boxes unchecked, and the amounts are entered on your tax return.

TIP

The IRS requires that you save your receipts for at least three years. After three years, it's OK to discard the miscellaneous receipts that support your tax data, but you should still keep a copy of your tax return and a copy of your W-2 forms. The W-2 forms are your evidence of tax that you paid (had withheld) during the year.

Sending Your Information to TurboTax on the Web

If you like using the Internet, you might really enjoy using TurboTax's Web-based program. The online version of TurboTax operates just like the store-bought version, only you prepare your return entirely at the TurboTax Web site instead of on your hard drive. You don't have to prepare the return all at once — you can start the return and come back at a later time to finish.

Types of federal income tax returns

There are three types of federal income tax returns. See the requirements below to decide which return is right for you:

The simplest federal income tax return around, the 1040EZ is only available for certain taxpayers. You must meet the following requirements to file a 1040EZ. (Note, these are the requirements for 2005. The limitation amounts might vary for future years.)

- Taxable income for the year is less than $100,000.
- Your filing status is either Single or Married Filing Jointly.
- You do not claim any dependents.
- You do not claim any adjustments to income (such as IRA contribution, moving expense, student loan interest, higher education costs, or educator expenses).
- You are under the age of 65.
- Your interest income does not exceed $1,500.

The 1040A is more complex than the 1040EZ, but not as complex as the standard 1040. This is the mama bear of tax returns. You can file on a 1040A form if you meet these requirements.

- Taxable income for the year is less than $100,000.
- You have no capital gains or losses except capital gain distributions, such as from a mutual fund.
- You claim only certain tax credits: child tax credit, education credits, earned income credit, credit for child and dependent care expenses, adoption credit, elderly and retirement savings credits.
- You claim only certain deductions: IRA contributions, student loan interest, higher education tuition and fees, and educator expenses.
- You do not claim itemized deductions.

If you don't qualify for either the 1040EZ or the 1040A, you are required to use Form 1040 for your federal income tax return. You can use the 1040 to report all types of income and deductions and credits. In fact, if you like, you can use the 1040 even if you qualify for the 1040EZ or the 1040A.

Agreeing to TurboTax's terms

TurboTax's user agreement basically states that if you enter false information on your tax return and you get caught, any penalties or prosecution that befall you are your own problem and not TurboTax's fault.

The agreement also states that if you choose to file your tax return electronically through the TurboTax Web site, it's up to you to come back and make sure the IRS and any state taxing authority to which you submit your tax return actually accept the return.

If you did something wrong that prevented your return from being successfully filed electronically (like enter the wrong birth date when asked for this identifying information), it's not TurboTax's fault if you failed to check back and straighten out the problem.

This is a key issue if you're filing your tax return really close to the deadline, which is a common occurrence with the online filing process. You *must* remember to go back and check to make sure everything went through OK. To help you with this step, TurboTax is willing to send you an e-mail message to remind you of the need to check back.

One really nice feature of using TurboTax on the Web is that you can prepare the return without any up-front payment. This is a great way to experiment with TurboTax and see if you like the program before you either (a) complete your tax return online and file the return electronically from the TurboTax Web site, or (b) decide to purchase the software and use it on your own computer.

Follow these steps to get started using TurboTax on the Web:

1. **Go to `www.turbotax.com` and follow the links to get to the online TurboTax program.**

   From the TurboTax home page, click either 1040EZ, Basic, or Premier to begin the tax preparation process (see Figure 4-8). If you are certain you will file a 1040EZ form (see the "Types of federal income tax returns" sidebar) you can click this option. If you have a business and know you want the extra advice that comes with the business program, you can click the third option. Most taxpayers probably choose the Basic option.

   TIP: If you're not sure whether you qualify to file the 1040EZ return or not, go ahead and click the 1040EZ option. You have to answer a series of questions before you proceed, and from your answers, TurboTax determines whether you qualify for the return. If you don't qualify, you're sent back to pick another return, and then you can choose the Basic return.

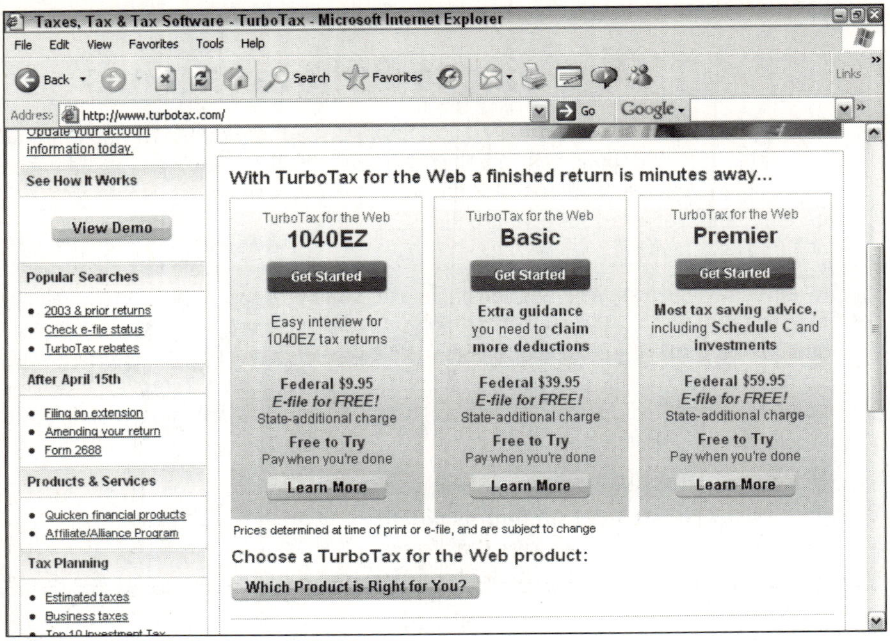

Figure 4-8: Click Start Return under one of the three tax return options to use the 1040EZ, Basic, or Premier service.

2. **Get started.**

   Indicate if you're new to TurboTax or if you've been there, done that. If you are a returning user, you'll avoid having to enter some of the repetitive information like your name, rank, and serial number. I'll assume you're new to TurboTax for the Web and proceed accordingly.

   Choose whether you want to establish a user ID now or just play around for a bit without saving anything. Choosing an ID lets you save your data for later use. In either case, you have to agree to the user agreement (see the "Agreeing to TurboTax's terms") before you can continue.

   Click the Start a New Return option.

   Before you go any farther — go find your copy of last year's tax return. That is the most important tool to have around when preparing a new return.

   It's not a bad idea to create a User ID for your online tax return. If you have to get up and leave the computer for awhile, your session is at risk of being automatically terminated (TurboTax lets your screen sit idle for 20 minutes, and then cuts you off). If you've got a User ID, you can get right back to where you left off. If you have no ID, you have to start over again from the beginning. You can create a User ID at any time by clicking the Create User ID button at the top of your TurboTax for the Web screen.

3. **Choose your filing status.**

   You need to pick your filing status (Figure 4-9) from the options provided. You'd think this would be easy, but even this can be a complicated decision. You can look at your last year's tax return for a hint, or you can get help from TurboTax. There's a little Guide Me button to click if you're not sure which status to choose. Click this button and you are asked some more questions that help you zero in on which status is the right one for you.

   After you've chosen the filing status, and from now on, after each step, click the Continue option to proceed.

4. **Enter the personal information that TurboTax requests.**

   You are required to fill in all the blanks. Notice in Figure 4-10 that there is a field for your birth date in addition to the name, address, and Social Security number fields. The birth date information doesn't appear anywhere on your tax return. Nevertheless, you shouldn't fudge on the date, even if you're temped to shave a few years off your age. The birth date is one of the things that is used to identify you to the IRS. In order to file your tax return electronically, you must provide the correct birth date.

   TIP: Don't sweat the small stuff — in this case, the slashes and the dashes. You can enter your birth date without slashes and your Social Security number without dashes — TurboTax fills in these missing pieces for you.

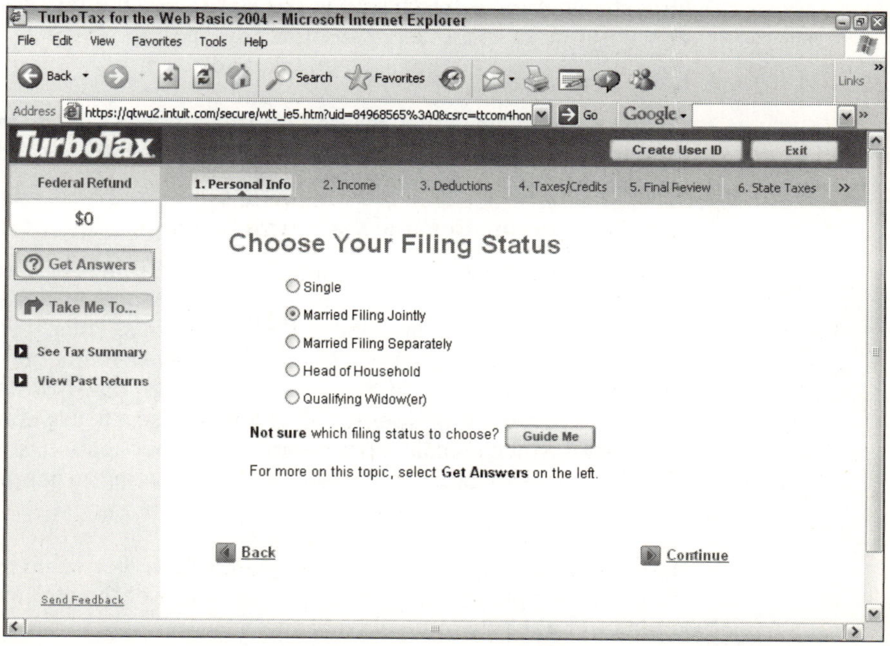

Figure 4-9: Click Guide Me if you're not sure which filing status you qualify for.

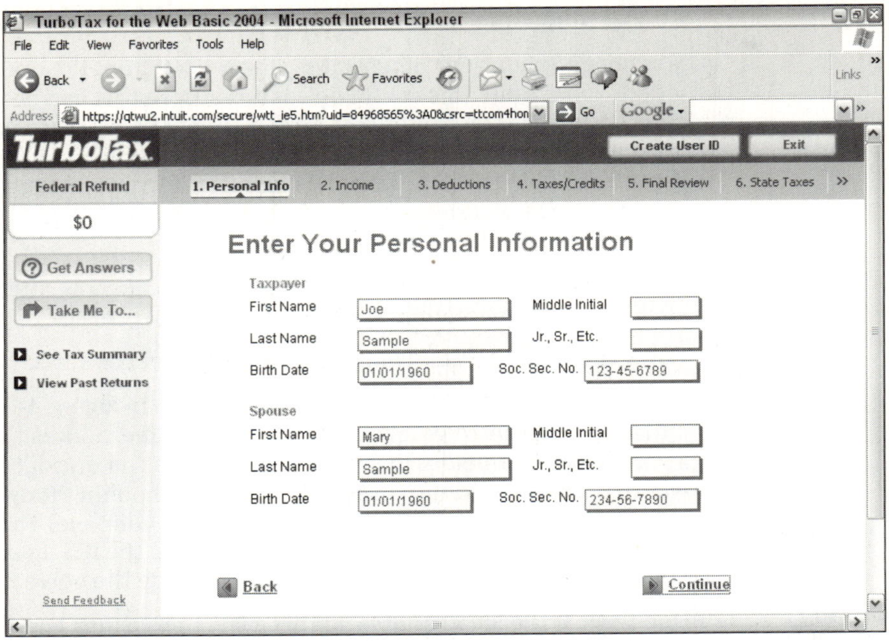

Figure 4-10: Enter your birth date in addition to other vital statistics. Who knows, maybe the IRS will send you a cake on your birthday?

5. **Pick a location.**

   Indicate whether you're based in the States, at a military base, in a foreign country, or in a U.S. possession.

6. **Enter your mailing address.**

7. **Pick the state where you resided on December 31 of the tax year, and then indicate if you lived in that state (even if you moved to a different address within the state) all year.**

8. **Enter your occupation and your daytime phone number.**

   There's really no right or wrong answer when it comes to entering your occupation. The IRS likes to try to pigeonhole people in certain occupations and see if they claim appropriate deductions. Thus, if you enter that you are a teacher, no one is surprised if you take a deduction for teaching supplies. But if you say you're a teacher and then take deductions for traveling salesman-related expenses, that might raise a few eyebrows. On the other hand, you can make up a name for your occupation, such as Rising Star or Fly in the Ointment, and nothing bad is going to happen to you.

9. **Answer the questions.**

   Here we are again — we saw these questions earlier when discussing TurboTax the program. Check the boxes if any of the circumstances in Figure 4-11 apply to you.

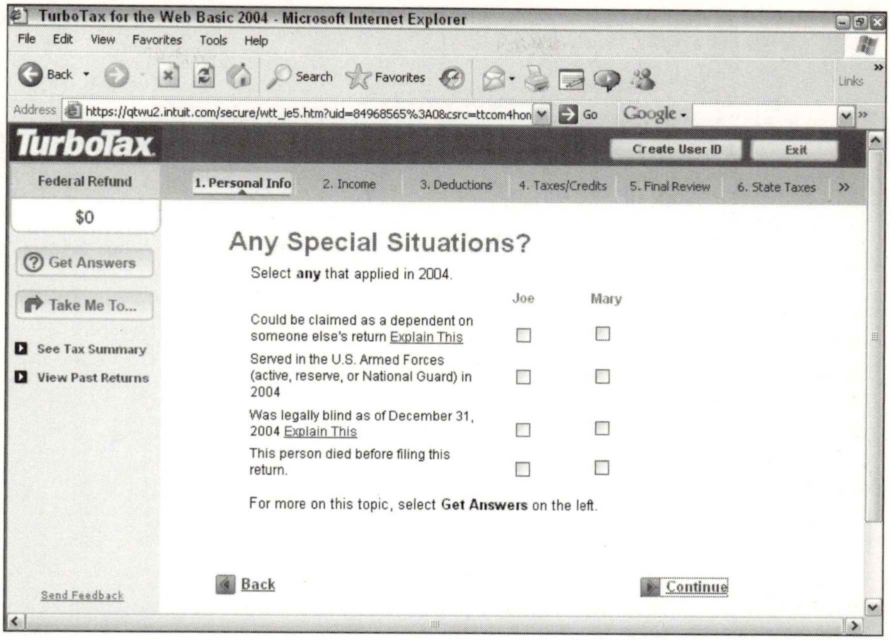

Figure 4-11: Sometimes it seems like the questions will never end.

10. Enter dependent info.

If you've got kids or other people you take care of, you might be able to claim them as your dependents. If you know for sure you can claim the dependents on your tax return, go ahead and click Yes and enter the requested information about each dependent. If you're not sure if someone qualifies as a dependent or not, click the Guide Me button, and you'll get some more questions that will help you determine how to proceed.

11. Finally! Time to import from Quicken.

Click Yes when asked if you're ready to import your information from Quicken. You have to click the Yes button shown in Figure 4-12 in order to have access to Quicken for the rest of your tax return.

12. Choose between Entire Interview and Customized Interview.

You're going to get a question about whether you want your interview to be Entire or Customized. If you pick the Entire interview, this means that, for this section (income) of your tax return, you have the pleasure of seeing every question that TurboTax can think of to ask you about your income from every source imaginable. If you already know what types of income you have to report on your tax return, you can choose the Customized option. With Customized, you see a list of the various types of income and you just check off the income types that apply to you. The only questions you see in your TurboTax interview are the questions that relate to your types of income.

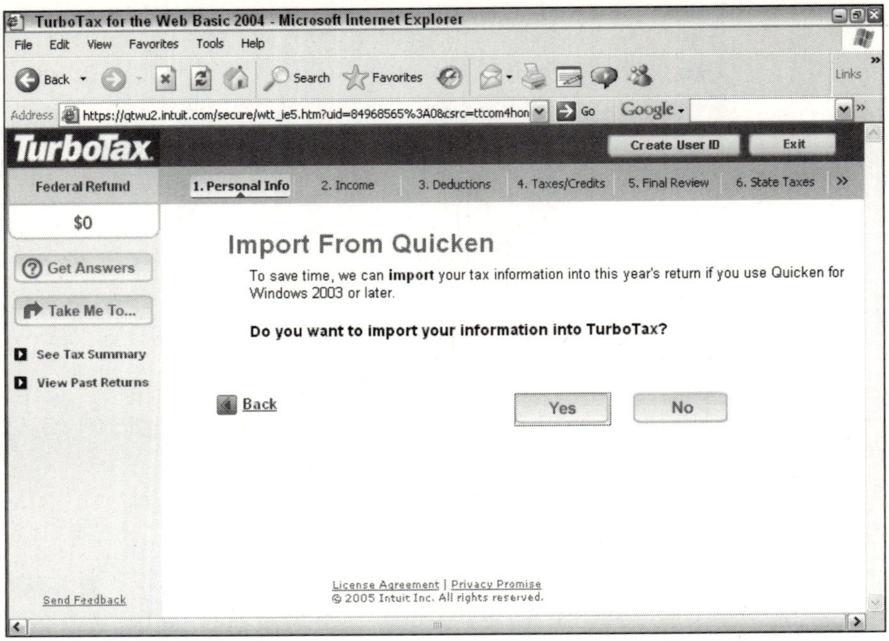

Figure 4-12: Click Yes if you want to transfer any of your Quicken information over to your tax return.

13. **Pick Income items.**

    If you went with the Customized interview, as I did, you're going to see a list of the various types of income that you might have to report on your tax return. Check off each income type that applies to you.

14. **Indicate your willingness to import from Quicken.**

    When asked if you're ready to import from Quicken, answer Yes. You might be directed to log off from the TurboTax program you're using (be sure to establish a User ID before doing so) and reenter the TurboTax program from within Quicken. These step-by-step instructions appear on the TurboTax screen.

15. **Return to TurboTax and proceed with the import.**

    If you left TurboTax in the last step, follow the onscreen steps to return to the program, and then respond by clicking Yes to any import questions (see Figure 4-13).

16. Choose the items to import.

Whenever TurboTax gets information from Quicken that fits with an area of your tax return, a list of the found information appears. Just as you saw back in Figure 4-7, you can place a checkmark next to any item you want to import from Quicken, and uncheck any amount that you don't want to import. Click Import Now and the rest is magic. TurboTax takes the numbers provided by Quicken and places them in exactly the right places on your tax return.

17. Continue until your tax return is completed.

Continue working through the TurboTax screens, clicking Continue to move from one screen to the next (or Back if you want to return to a previous screen), responding to questions, and entering or importing the information necessary for the completion of your tax return.

TIP

To print any of the forms you create in TurboTax for the Web, you must pay the fee for the Web service. The type of tax service you chose when you began using the program (1040EZ, Basic, or Premier) determines the amount of fee you are required to pay. After you've paid the fee, you can print any or all of the forms you've created at any time. Click the Filing button at the top of the TurboTax for the Web page to print copies of forms suitable for filing with the tax authorities. Click the Finish button to print forms for your records. The forms you print for your records include supporting worksheets that don't get submitted to the tax authorities.

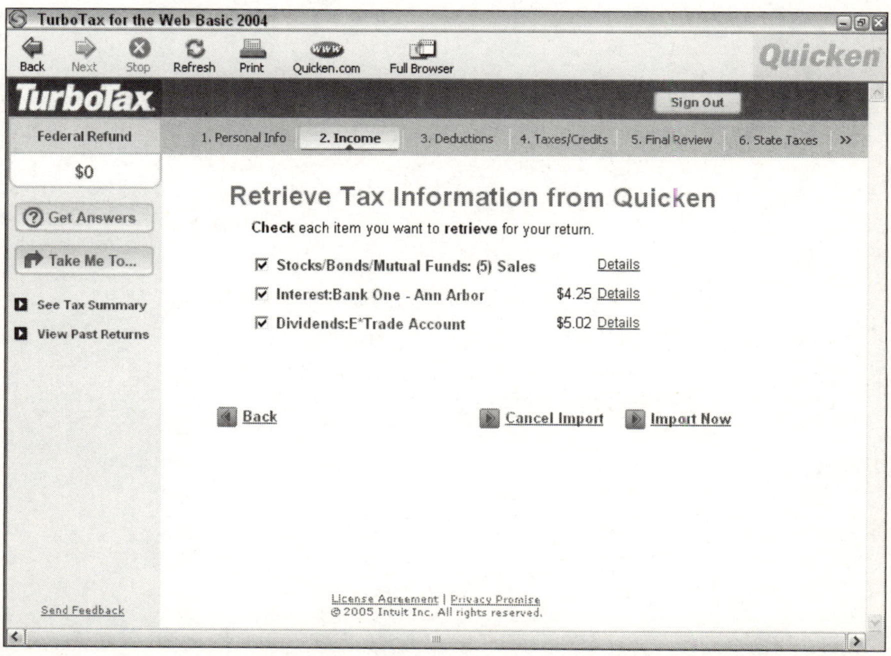

Figure 4-13: Click Yes, and TurboTax chats with Quicken to find out what info can be imported into your tax return.

You can leave your TurboTax for the Web tax return at any time by clicking the Sign Out button. When you return to `www.turbotax.com`, you just need to click the Sign In button and enter your User ID information to get back to where you left off on your tax return.

You might want to flip ahead to the next chapter to find out how to incorporate tax information from TurboTax into the Tax Planner. You'd be surprised how useful it can be to reverse the import procedure and put your TurboTax material into Quicken instead of the other way around.

Chapter 5: Tax Planning with Quicken

In This Chapter

- Calculating your estimated income taxes
- Estimating taxes on capital gains
- Using the Tax Planner to estimate taxes
- Keeping track of your year-to-date taxes paid
- Making estimated tax payments

The Beatles warned us in *Tax Man*: "That's one for you, nineteen for me." Estimated taxes are nature's way of reminding you that the IRS is watching. Just when you think you've got plenty of money in the bank, bam! It's time to zero-out your balance and send it all to Uncle Sam.

Understanding Estimated Taxes

Many people can handle their federal tax liability by having income taxes withheld from their paycheck. Are they lucky? Maybe. Some people who swear by estimated taxes would say the wage earners are dupes, letting the government take their money without asking (and you can choose for yourself who you think I'm referring to with the pronoun, "their"). Others, who are burdened by estimated taxes, yearn for the simple lifestyle of wage-earners, where you don't have to calculate how much your tax is going to be; instead, you just let your employer take tax out of your check and you hope for a fat refund in the spring.

No matter how you feel about paying taxes, the bottom line is that you have to find a way to come up with the bottom line. You calculate the tax on your tax return each spring, but you are required to have paid that tax throughout the previous year or else you can be assessed penalties and interest for late payment. In order to avoid the extra fees, you might be faced with having to estimate taxes.

If your only income is the income you earn from your employer, you can count on your employer to use the information you provided on your W-4 form (see Book I, Chapter 1) to calculate and withhold enough tax so that you won't owe any penalties in the spring. But for many people, the income from one job isn't the only income that appears on their tax return.

Excuses that help you avoid the penalty for late payment of taxes

If you owe more than $1,000 on your federal income tax return, you also owe a penalty for late payment, unless you can show that one of these situations exists:

- **You didn't have an income tax liability for the preceding tax year.** This isn't the same as saying you had enough tax withheld in the preceding year so that you got a refund on last year's tax return. What this excuse means is that you actually didn't owe any tax in the preceding year. If you look on that tax return from a year ago and the "Total Tax" amount is a big fat zero, this excuse will fly. If there was any tax, even a dollar, you had a tax liability for the preceding year and you can't use this excuse.
- **The tax you paid for the current year in withholding or estimated taxes is at least equal to 100 percent of the tax on last year's tax return.** The tax you paid for this year has to at least equal whatever amount appears on last year's tax return on the "Total Tax" line. So, say it's April of 2007 and you wonder if you're going to have to pay a penalty because you owe $1,200 in tax on your 2006 tax return. Look back at the "Total Tax" on the 2005 tax return and see how much that is. If your withholding and other tax payments for 2006 equal at least as much as that total tax amount on the 2005 tax return, you're penalty-free. (Note: If your adjusted gross income on that 2005 tax return was higher than $150,000, you have to have paid in 110 percent of the tax on that return in order to avoid the penalty for 2006.)
- **You paid at least 90 percent of this year's income tax throughout the year in withholding or estimated taxes.** Here's where the guesswork comes in. You have to estimate your taxes throughout the year and make sure your tax payments come up to at least 90 percent of the amount that appears on your tax return in the spring. The information in this chapter will help you come up with that estimate.

Some people have two jobs; with some married couples, each person has one or more jobs. Or you may have interest and dividend income on investments, odd-job money, and money from a variety of other sources, all of which needs to be reported on your tax return. Then there are the deductions. As you saw in earlier chapters of this book, many different methods are available for reducing your taxes with deductions and credits. Calculating the actual amount of tax you owe in advance is truly an art.

The rules state that if you don't have enough tax withheld at your job(s), you need to make up the difference by paying estimated taxes quarterly, or four times a year. Now there's a little cushion allowed — you can owe as much as $1,000 beyond your withholding and pay that amount with your tax return, and the IRS isn't going to hit you with penalties. But owe more than $1,000, and watch out. The IRS expects you to either pay a penalty for paying your taxes late or have a darn good excuse for not paying enough tax throughout the year.

Calculating Estimated Taxes

The estimated payments are supposed to be a reflection of what you think you're going to owe on your tax return in the coming year. Somehow you have to come up with a total amount that you expect to owe, subtract the amount of tax you expect to have withheld at your job(s), and pay the rest in estimated taxes. If you happen to have a functioning crystal ball, you can just look inside, read what it says you're going to owe, divide it by four, and pay one-fourth of the total with each quarterly payment.

To make life a little easier, the IRS has devised methods you can use to estimate your taxes. And to make life easier still, Quicken has its tax planner that you can use as well. But first, some basic information.

If you have to make quarterly tax payments, the IRS expects you to split the total amount you owe into fourths and pay the same amount each quarter. Leaving the total amount until the fourth quarter and paying it all at once negates the effect of the estimated payment program and, worse yet, can still result in an underpayment penalty and interest.

You can choose from three methods for estimating taxes, and these methods are derived from the three excuses you can use to get out of paying taxes described in the sidebar, "Excuses that help you avoid the penalty for late payment of taxes," earlier in this chapter. We use Quicken's Tax Planner to come up with the actual amount of your estimate for the current year taxes. For now, just worry about getting the methods down.

FYI, the first method, the one based on last year's taxes, is the most common method used, and for that you don't need any estimating: You just need a copy of last year's tax return.

TIP: If you like to work out your tax estimates on paper, you can use the worksheet provided with the IRS instructions for estimated taxes. Here's the URL for the instructions and the worksheet if you want to grab this from the Internet: `www.irs.gov/pub/irs-pdf/f1040es.pdf`.

Estimated taxes Method #1: Using last year's tax return

Probably the safest way to estimate your taxes for the purpose of making quarterly payments (and avoiding penalties and keeping the IRS off your back) is to start with your previous year's federal income tax return.

TIP: These estimated tax rules are probably similar to the rules you need to consider for your state income taxes. That's right! Don't forget to pay tax to your state! Check the tax laws for your own state to see how to do the estimated taxes, but you're probably going to see much similarity between the way you compute estimated taxes federally and the way you do it, uh, stately . . .

So that I won't keep getting caught up in confusing statements about this year, next year, and last year, I'm going to refer to the year 2005 as last year, 2006 as this year, and 2007 as next year. So if you're reading this book in the spring of 2006 when you're preparing your 2005 income tax return, you're going to be right with me. If it's a later year, add a year or two to each of my sample years and go from there.

OK, so back to Method #1. It's the spring of 2006, and you're trying to figure out how much to pay during 2006 for estimated taxes.

For Method #1, you want to get out your 2005 income tax return (if you haven't prepared your 2005 tax return yet, get busy with that, and then come back when you've got the return completed). Look on the line that says "This is your total tax." Figure 5-1 shows the tax section of the 2005 Form 1040 — I'm looking at Line 63.

Other Taxes					
	58	Self-employment tax. Attach Schedule SE	58		
	59	Social security and Medicare tax on tip income not reported to employer. Attach Form 4137	59		
	60	Additional tax on IRAs, other qualified retirement plans, etc. Attach Form 5329 if required	60		
	61	Advance earned income credit payments from Form(s) W-2	61		
	62	Household employment taxes. Attach Schedule H	62		
	63	Add lines 57 through 62. This is your total tax ▶	63		

Figure 5-1: The tax section of Form 1040.

That total tax number is the number you want to match with your 2006 tax payments. Now, if you think your tax withholding is going to be high enough to cover that amount, you don't have to worry about estimates. If you aren't going to have enough tax withheld, get busy with some estimated payments to make up the difference.

Say for example that your total tax on the 2005 income tax return is $6,000. You expect your tax withholding to be about $4,000 in 2006. Therefore, using Method #1, your estimated payments should be $2,000, or $500 each quarter.

REMEMBER

If your adjusted gross income (see line 37 of the 2005 Form 1040) is more than $150,000, the tax you pay in during the coming year should be 110 percent of the 2005 tax instead of 100 percent.

TIP

If your income fluctuates during the year, you might not have to make equal quarterly estimates. In fact, you might even be able to skip an estimated payment and not pay in every quarter. See the section on annualizing your income for more information on dealing with fluctuating income.

REMEMBER

Your total tax paid during the year should be within $1,000 of the total amount of tax still owing on your tax return. That doesn't mean you should short your estimates by $1,000. The $1,000 is a cushion so that if your estimated payments, based on your calculations, come up short, you still have some playing room before any penalties kick in.

I'm giving you line numbers for Form 1040. Some people have tax returns that are uncomplicated enough that they can get away with filing the simpler tax returns, 1040A or 1040EZ. In that case, the line numbers are going to be different. But the descriptions are the same. Just look for the line that points out your total tax — it's on each return; it just may be on a different line.

Estimated taxes Method #2: Using this year's tax return

Now we get into the fun part of estimating. Using Method #2, you can choose to pay 90 percent of the current year's tax (that is, if you can figure out what the current year's tax is going to be). (See the section "Estimating Taxes with Quicken's Tax Planner" later in this chapter.)

When you figure out your current year's tax, you take 90 percent of that amount, and then deduct what you think your income tax withholding is going to be. The remaining amount represents the amount you should pay in estimated payments, so divide that by four and there you go.

For example, suppose you estimate your 2006 tax to be $8,000 and, based on your current paychecks, you think your withholding for the year is going to be $5,000. Therefore you have a $3,000 shortfall to make up. The IRS expects you to pay 90 percent of this shortfall in estimated payments, so 90 percent of $3,000 is $2,700. Divide that amount by four and you get $675 for each quarterly payment.

If your income situation changes during the year, so should your tax payments. If you get a raise at work, your withholding increases, but so does your total income and therefore so does your tax. Whenever there's a measurable change in your income or expenses, redo your estimates to make sure you are covered.

Estimated taxes Method #3: Annualizing your income

The third method of figuring out payments of estimated tax is called *annualizing* your income. In order to use this method, you have to monitor your income and expenses during the year and base your estimated payments on actual income rather than on estimates. This method is particularly useful for people whose income fluctuates during the year. Here are some examples of people who can really benefit from the annualization method of determining estimated payments:

- Seasonal workers
- People who change jobs during the year

- Self-employed people who don't have a lot of control over when their income is received
- People who incur a sizeable deductible expense during the year

With the annualization method, taxpayers can pay more tax at the times when they are earning more money, and less tax when their receipts are down or their expenses are up.

The goal when annualizing your income is to determine what your full year's earnings would be if you continued to earn at the same pace at which you have earned income thus far during the year. To annualize your income for a particular estimated payment, you should follow these steps:

1. **Figure out your actual income for all the months of the year prior to the month in which the quarterly payment is due.**
2. **Divide the amount from step 1 by the number of months represented, and then multiply that amount by 12.**

   This gives you the amount of total income you would earn if everything stayed the same for the rest of the year.
3. **Perform steps 1 and 2 on your itemized deductions so that you have an estimate of the total amount of your itemized deductions for the entire year.**
4. **Compare your itemized deductions that you calculated in step 3 to the Standard Deduction (the Standard Deductions are listed back in Chapter 3). Take the greater amount and deduct that amount from your income that you calculated in step 2.**
5. **Deduct your exemptions from the amount calculated in step 4. Exemptions for 2006 are expected to be $3,300 a head, which means that you're going to deduct $3,300 for yourself, another $3,300 if you have a spouse and file a joint tax return, and another $3,300 for each of your dependents. The result is your annualized taxable income.**

   Personal exemption amounts increase each year, generally about $100 with each increase. The exemption amount for 2006 is an estimate, but a pretty close one. Check with your friendly tax advisor, or try searching for "Personal Exemption Amount" on the Internet to find the exemption amount for the year that interests you.
6. **Figure out the tax on the taxable income computed in step 5. (See the section "Estimating Taxes with Quicken's Tax Planner" later in this chapter.)**

7. **Multiply the tax you calculated in step 6 by 90 percent, and then divide by four.**

   This is the amount you should pay in estimated tax for the current quarter.

8. **Next quarter, do this exercise all over again.**

TIP

You'll be so grateful that you use Quicken when it comes to trying to annualize your income. All of those itemized deductions, income from a variety of sources — it's all right there, just a Tax Summary report away.

Estimating Taxes with Quicken's Tax Planner

Ooooo, I love the Quicken Tax Planner! I can play with different tax scenarios all day long and never get tired of it! I can still remember the days when I used to have to calculate taxes without the aid of a computer (and in the really dark ages, I used to calculate taxes without a calculator, if you can imagine that . . .).

The Tax Planner is designed to give you a quick estimate of the taxes you owe based on the entries you have made in Quicken. The transactions you enter get culled and collected in the Tax Planner, and then Quicken shows you how much you can expect to owe the IRS.

WARNING!

Keep in mind what I've mentioned previously when discussing tax reports: Quicken can't completely read your mind. You have to actually enter transactions and also assign tax lines to the appropriate categories in order to get a good estimate from the Tax Planner.

In addition to utilizing the information you've already entered in Quicken, you can use the Tax Planner as a staging area for your own calculations. Create your own scenarios, entering the information you've estimated or calculated, and Quicken spits out a tax estimate for you.

For example, you can gather information from tax reports and from your own receipts and documents to come up with the numbers you need for the annualization method of calculating your estimated taxes, and then plug those numbers into the Tax Planner and presto! Quicken calculates the tax you owe!

Using the Tax Planner's default method of calculating tax

Without your having to enter any information at all, Quicken gathers all the information it can find and creates a tax projection for the current year (see Figure 5-2). The Tax Planner Summary screen shows your anticipated income, deductions, and the tax calculation.

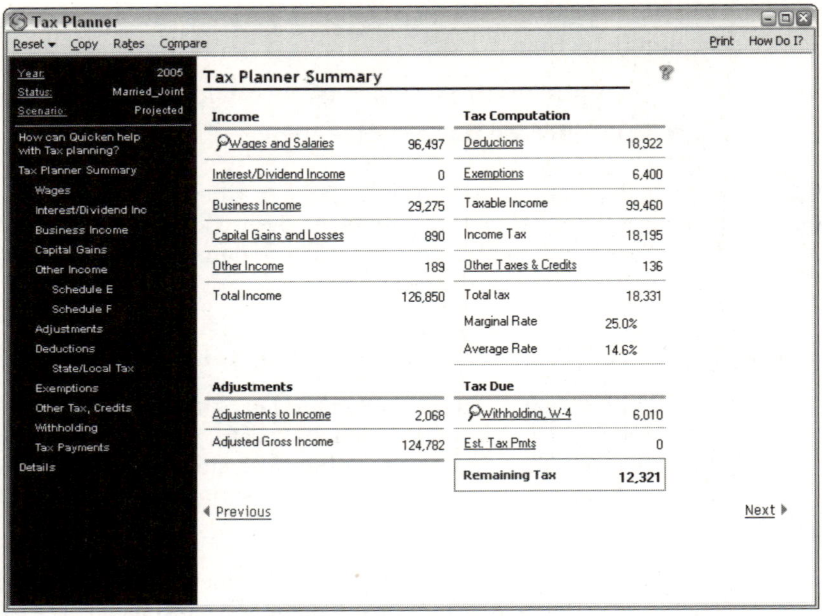

Figure 5-2: Quicken's Tax Planner Summary gives you an overview of your tax projection.

When poking around in the Tax Planner, you can always return to the summary screen by clicking on the Tax Planner Summary link over on the left side of the Tax Planner window.

The numbers that appear in the Tax Planner Summary are projections, based on amounts you've already entered in Quicken for the current year. The numbers are enhanced with information from TurboTax (if you choose to import this information), as described in "Incorporating tax information from TurboTax into the Tax Planner" below.

You can examine the detail of any of these numbers (and make changes if you like) by clicking on one of the hyperlinks in the Summary window, or by clicking the title of the item you want to examine over on the left side of the window.

When you click any hyperlink, the detail appears, displaying where the information came from, and giving you an opportunity to make any changes that are necessary.

For example, say you want to know what that Other Income amount is that the Tax Planner is displaying. Click the Other Income link, and the detail of that income appears (Figure 5-3). I see! Quicken has assumed I'll have a taxable state income tax refund of $189.

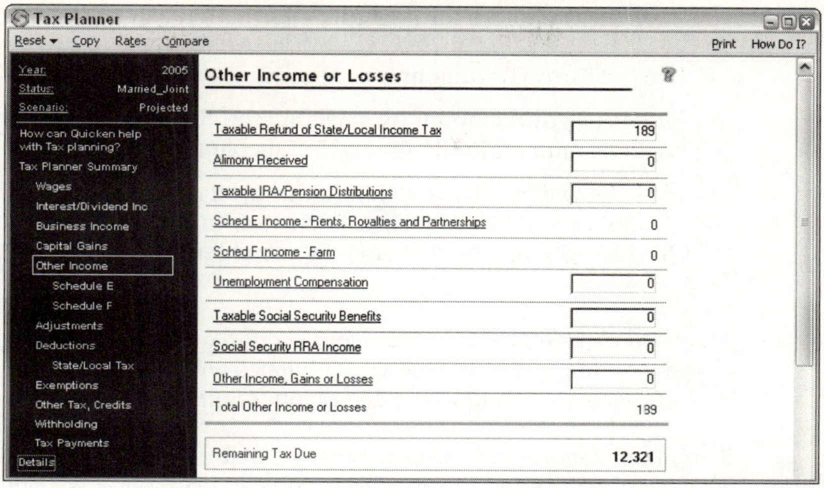

Figure 5-3: Clicking any item on the Tax Summary displays the detail behind that item.

For more detail, scroll down to the bottom of the window and you see (as shown in Figure 5-4) that this assumption about the state tax refund is based on information that came from the TurboTax import.

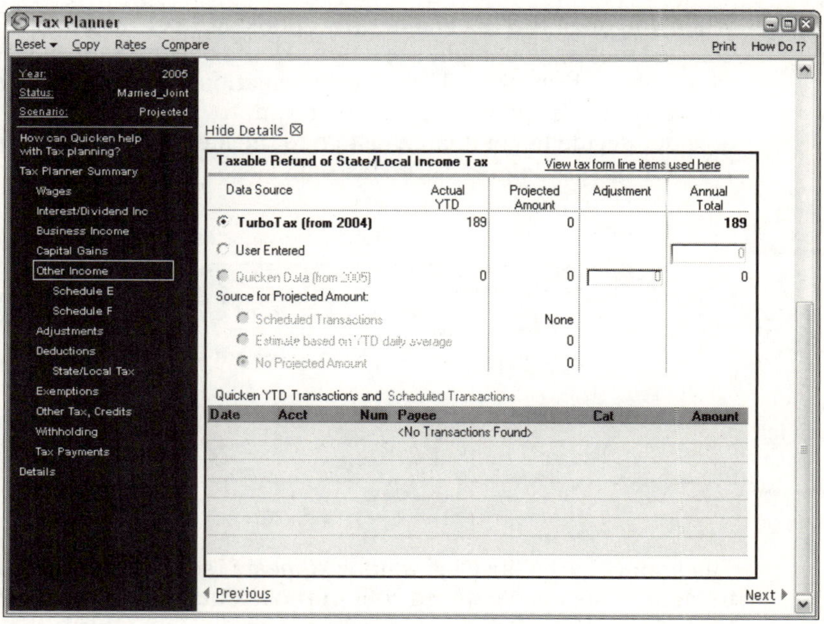

Figure 5-4: Scroll down to see the source of the data.

You have three choices for how this information can be determined:

- Use the TurboTax amount, as shown.
- Enter your own amount by selecting the "User Entered" option and filling in an amount in the Annual Total column.
- Click the Quicken Data option (if this option is available to you) and use the amount that Quicken has calculated based on data already entered in Quicken, or override that amount and enter your own in the Adjustment column.

After you make changes in the lower section of the Tax Planner window, click or tab to a different field, and your changes will be reflected in the upper part of the window and in the Tax Planner Summary.

TIP

If you have tagged various categories as being tax-related, but haven't assigned tax lines to the categories, you can print out a Tax Summary report to use as a guide while entering and checking the information in the Tax Planner.

Incorporating tax information from TurboTax into the Tax Planner

When you open the Tax Planner (by choosing Tax⇨Tax Planner from the Quicken menu), you might see a box like the one in Figure 5-5, asking if you would like to bring your TurboTax information into Quicken's Tax Planner. You can click Yes now, or if you don't want to use the TurboTax information now but decide to get it later, just go to the menu at any time and choose Tax⇨TurboTax⇨Import TurboTax Data File.

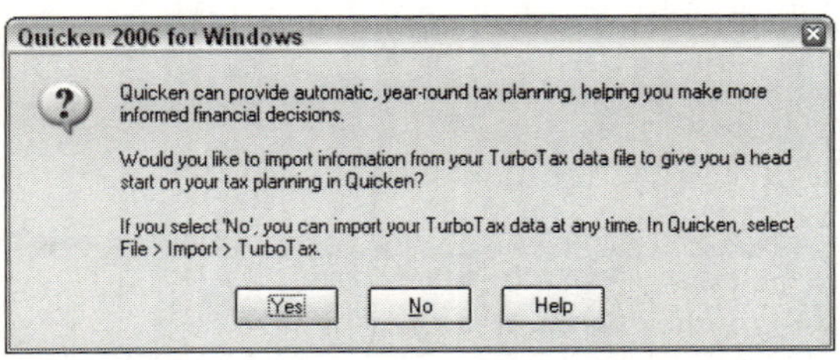

Figure 5-5: Click Yes to bring your TurboTax info into the Quicken Tax Planner.

The Import TurboTax Files window appears (see Figure 5-6), where you are to identify the tax file where your TurboTax tax return is saved, then click OK to import the data. You are asked to confirm that this is the file you want to import, and then Quicken displays the name(s) that are saved with that data file. Confirm those names, and the import is completed.

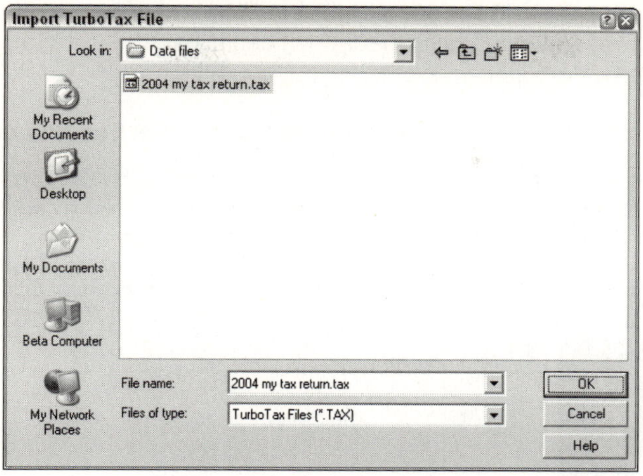

Figure 5-6: Identify the location of your TurboTax data file.

The Tax Planner opens up as soon as the import is completed, and is populated with information from the TurboTax file. When you bring your TurboTax information into the Tax Planner, Quicken cleverly incorporates last year's tax data with the information that it found in your current year Quicken registers to come up with a very sophisticated tax projection.

Just in case you are worried, importing your TurboTax information into your Quicken Tax Planner doesn't have any effect on the rest of your Quicken program. It's not like your checking register is going to be filled up with transactions that come from your tax return — the only place where the TurboTax information goes is into the Tax Planner.

This might seem like a "Duh" comment to you, but just for the record, you can't import TurboTax information into Quicken if you didn't use TurboTax for your tax preparation.

Creating tax scenarios

You can create more than one projection with the Tax Planner. Start another projection from scratch, or use the existing data in the Tax Planner to begin with, and play around with alternatives. For example, if you want to experiment with the effects of changing from filing as Married Filing Jointly to filing as Married Filing Separately, you can create a scenario based on the same information you used in your main project, but change the filing status. Or try using a scenario with different withholding amounts. The possibilities are endless.

You can create up to three scenarios in addition to your main projection (and of course you can change existing scenarios, thus providing endless possibilities). Here's how:

1. **Click the Scenario option on the left side of the Tax Planner.**

   The screen changes to reflect Tax Planner Options. On the Tax Planner Options screen (Figure 5-7) are three fields you need to address.

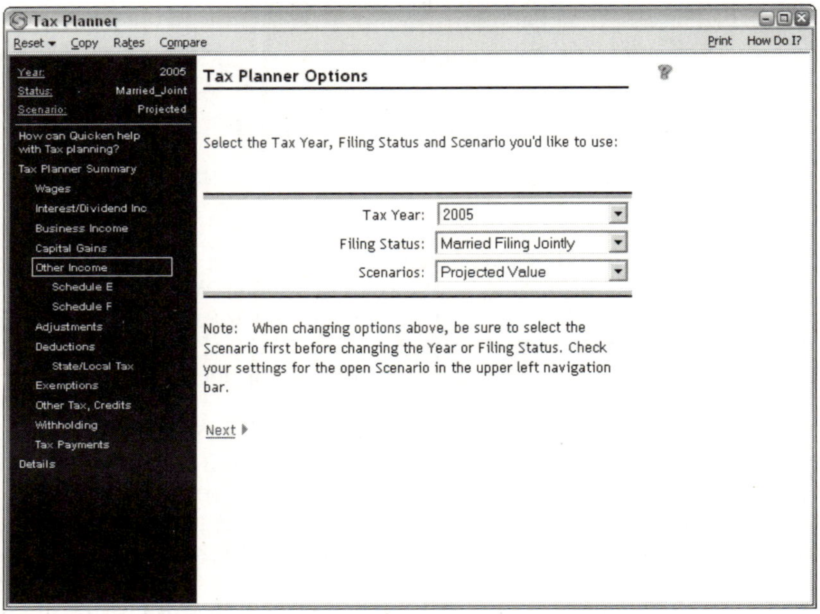

Figure 5-7: Choose your scenario options.

2. **Choose the tax year for your scenario.**

   Your choices are the current year and next year. Note that if you attempt to choose next year while the Scenarios choice is pointing to Projected Value, you get a little message telling you that you can't do that. You have to select a numbered scenario (see step 4) in order to experiment with taxes for next year.

   Interestingly, there is a note beneath the scenarios telling you that you need to choose the scenario first. Why Quicken doesn't just put the scenario selection at the top of the list is one of life's little unanswered questions.

3. **Choose a filing status.**

   Choose from the usual suspects: Single, Married Filing Jointly, Married Filing Separately, Head of Household, and Qualifying Widow (also referred to as Surviving Spouse).

4. **Select your scenario (if you haven't already done so — see step 2).**

   Choose from Projected Value, or Scenario 1, 2, or 3.

5. **Click Next.**

6. **Enter the information you want to use in your scenario.**

7. **Copy scenario information from one scenario to another.**

   If you would like to take the numbers from your Projected Value, or from another scenario, for use in this scenario, go back and display the scenario with the numbers you want to copy (click the Scenario option on the left, and then choose the scenario you want). Then click the Copy menu choice. The Copy Scenario window appears (Figure 5-8). Click the scenario that is to receive the copied information, and then click OK.

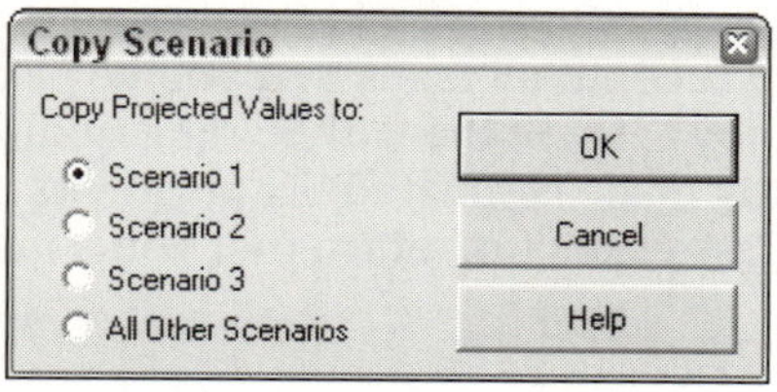

Figure 5-8: Pick which scenario (or all three) is to receive the copied information.

Switch back and forth between your scenarios by clicking the Scenario option on the left side of the Tax Planner window, and then entering your choice of scenario in the Scenarios field.

You can compare the results of your scenarios by clicking the Compare menu choice at the top of the Tax Planner.

Determining the amount of tax you owe

After you've verified the accuracy, or at least the reasonableness of the amounts in the Tax Planner Summary, view the Remaining Tax amount on the Summary screen. That is the amount that you are working with for your estimated tax payments.

The amount of tax that appears in the Remaining Tax field is the total amount of tax still owing for the year, based on the information you entered or the information Quicken extrapolated in your tax projection. (Of course, if the box at the bottom of the Planner says Refund Due, you have no tax currently owing).

Creating a tax payments report

Here's a quick little report you can make to help find all the income taxes you've already paid this year.

1. Choose Reports➪Tax➪Tax Summary from the menu.
2. Set the Date Range for Current year.
3. Click the Customize button.
4. Click the Categories tab.
5. Click the Clear All button.
6. Type Fed to get to the Fed category that appears as a subcategory of Tax. If you want to see the state income tax you paid, in case you're preparing state estimates as well, click the State (and, if applicable, Local) tax options as well.
7. Click OK to display the report.

TIP: Make sure you have taken into account all taxes that you've paid when calculating your estimates. Not only is there the withholding from your jobs, but also you might have already made estimated tax payments this year, or there might be a refund from last year's tax return that you chose to apply to this year's tax liability.

To determine the amount of estimated tax you owe, divide the Remaining Tax amount, not by four, but by the number of quarters remaining in the year (see "When your estimated payments are due," later in this chapter, to determine how many payment due dates are remaining).

It's possible that the amount reflected in the Tax Planner is not the amount that you actually will owe on your tax return. Here are some factors that can affect the calculation:

- You expect your income to substantially decrease. You know better than Quicken how much money you can expect to earn between now and the end of the year. If your income is expected to take a dive before year-end, go back and adjust the income amounts to reflect the anticipated reduction in income.
- You anticipate large expenses between now and the end of the year, expenses that may result in deductions that will have a measurable effect on your income tax calculation. Perhaps you are going to start your child in orthodontics, or you need to purchase some equipment for your business. Whatever the expense, if something large is due before year-end and you expect to be able to deduct that amount, make some adjustments to the projection for your expenses.

- You plan on adjusting your withholding before the end of the year. Many people set their withholding at a low rate early in the year, and then boost the withholding at the end of the year by filing a new W-4 form requesting fewer allowances (see Book I, Chapter 1 for more information on altering your W-4 form). If you expect to increase your withholding, you can decrease the amount you need to pay in estimated payments. Adjust the projection accordingly.
- You plan on selling some stocks before the end of the year, and that sale is going to generate a taxable loss. A loss on the sale of investments can lower the amount of tax you owe, just as a gain can raise the tax. Determine how much of an effect the sale will have on your taxes by entering amounts in the Capital Gains and Losses section of the Tax Planner. And see the next section for more information on how capital gains and losses are taxed.

Estimating Capital Gains Taxes

The IRS allows taxpayers a special tax rate on profits made in the stock market or from selling other types of investments. And there are special rules for losses on the sale of investments as well. In a nutshell, here's how these transactions are seen in the eyes of Uncle Sam.

A capital gain is a profit on the sale of an investment item. A profit is determined as follows:

- **Purchase price.** Start with the amount you paid for the investment. Add any purchase costs, such as broker fees, shipping costs, or any other costs you paid as part of the purchase price. The total of all of these costs is your purchase price.
- **Selling price.** Determine the amount you receive for the investment. Subtract any costs of the sale from the amount you receive. The difference is the selling price.
- **Gain or loss.** Subtract the purchase price from the selling price. If the difference is a positive number, you have a gain on the sale. If the difference is a negative number, you have a loss.

Short-term gains and losses

The IRS defines the short-term holding period as one year or less. If you owned the investment that you sold for 365 or fewer days, your gain or loss is considered a short-term gain or loss.

Short-term gains are reduced by short-term losses to produce a net short-term gain or loss.

Long-term gains and losses

If you owned the investment you sold for more than 365 days, your gain or loss is considered a long-term gain or loss.

Long-term gains are reduced by long-term losses to produce a net long-term gain or loss.

Putting the two together

On your tax return, you report all of the sales of your investments on Schedule D, Capital Gains and Losses.

Here are the options for the way in which these gains and losses are taxed:

- **Your short-term sales and your long-term sales are both net gains.** The short-term net gain is taxed just like your other income, at your regular income tax rates (income tax rates are displayed in Figure 5-9). The long-term net gain is taxed at a special lower capital gains tax rate. That rate is 15 percent for most taxpayers, and 5 percent for taxpayers who pay regular income tax at no more than the 15 percent tax rate.
- **Your short-term sales and your long-term sales are both net losses.** You are entitled to reduce your regular taxable income by the amount of your capital loss, up to a maximum of $3,000. If your loss exceeds $3,000, the remaining loss is carried over to next year's tax return.
- **Your short-term sales are a gain and your long-term sales are a loss (or there are no long-term sales).** The gain on your short-term sales is reduced by the amount of the long-term loss, if applicable. Any remaining gain is taxed at your regular income tax rate.
- **Your long-term sales are a gain and your short-term sales are a loss (or there are no short-term sales).** The gain on your long-term sales is reduced by the amount of the short-term loss, if applicable. Any remaining gain is taxed at the special capital gains tax rates described in the first option, above.

WARNING!

This is a really bare-bones description of how capital gains taxes work and how long- and short-term sales are treated. As with any tax rules, there are plenty of exceptions and special rules. If you sell investments, it's a wise move to discuss the tax ramifications with a tax professional.

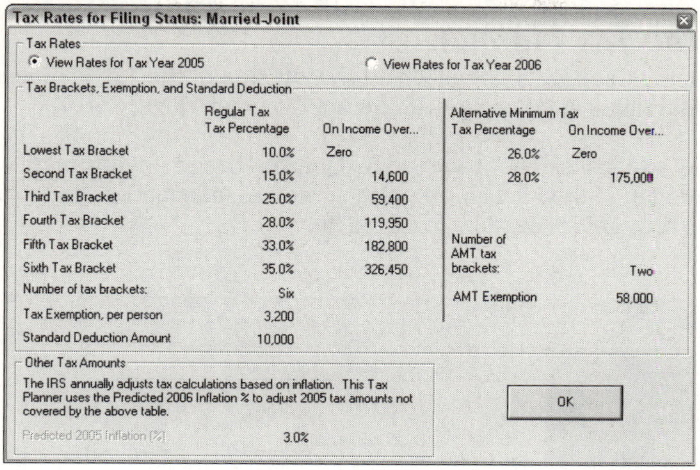

Figure 5-9: Click the Rates menu choice at the top of the Tax Planner to see the federal marginal income tax rates and the corresponding income brackets.

Five important tax things to know about selling stocks and other investments

- Timing is extremely important. Know how many days it's been since you purchased an investment before you sell the investment. The tax can be double or more if you sell an investment before you've owned it for at least 365 days.
- Consider the amount of tax you're going to owe on the sale of your investment before you make the sale. That knowledge might affect whether or not you want to sell the investment. For example, you might want to sell some stock that you've owned for a few months because you've made $100 on the increase in the stock's value. But if it costs you $20 in broker's fees to sell the stock, and if your regular income tax rate is 35 percent resulting in $35 in federal income tax, not to mention what you might owe in state income tax, that $100 profit is cut to less than $50. Do you still want to sell?
- Sell a stock at a loss, and then repurchase shares of the same stock before 30 days have passed, and do you know what you've got? A wash sale, according to the IRS. When you have a wash sale, you lose the opportunity to take advantage of the loss on the stock on your tax return. Wait 30 days before purchasing the same stock and you get the tax benefit of the loss.
- Selling an investment that you received as a gift causes some strange ripples in the tax laws. Your basis in the investment, or the purchase price, if you will, actually changes depending on whether you're going to make a profit or have a loss on the sale. Check with your tax advisor before selling gifted items.
- Inherited items come with a stepped-up basis. The basis, or purchase price of an inherited item is the value of the item on the date of the previous owner's death.

Entering capital gain and loss information in the Tax Planner

Click the Capital Gains option on the left side of the Tax Planner to open the Capital Gains and Losses — Schedule D screen (Figure 5-10).

Gains and losses are projected by Quicken based on information already entered in your Quicken program as well as information that might have been brought forward from TurboTax.

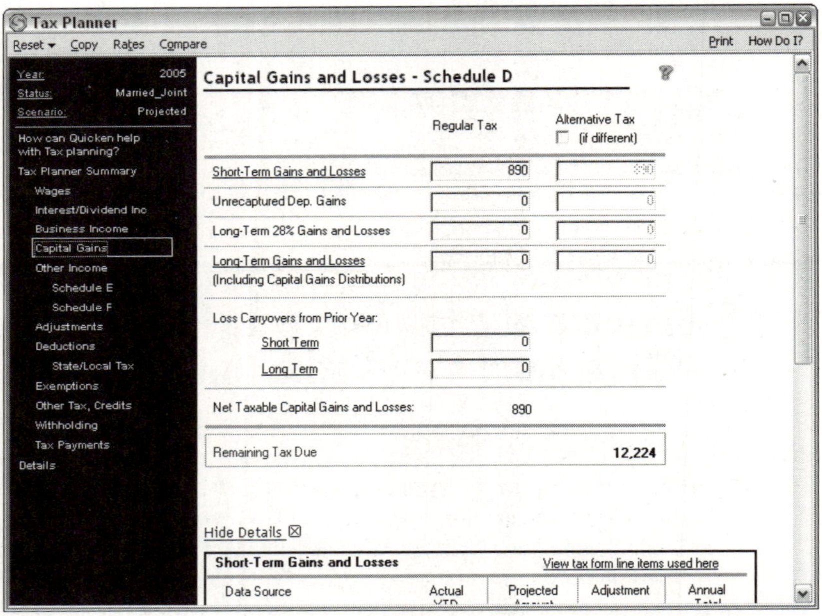

Figure 5-10: Enter information about the sales of your investments.

Click on either Short-Term Gains and Losses or Long-Term Gains and Losses to open the corresponding worksheets at the bottom of the screen.

You can also enter carryover capital loss information from your prior-year tax return. If you imported information from TurboTax, it won't be necessary for you to enter the carryover information.

Exploring New Deduction Frontiers

Quicken comes with a Deduction Finder that can help you identify tax deductions that you might not have considered. This is a significant tool because, as I've pointed out before, Quicken can only incorporate deductions into your tax reports if you've tagged the categories as being tax-related. If you don't know something is deductible, you probably missed out on tagging the category, and the deduction slips by unnoticed.

Answer easy questions in the Deduction Finder and Quicken can help you find some deductions to help reduce your income taxes. Follow these steps to new forms of tax saving:

1. **Access the Deduction Finder by clicking the Tax menu, and then choosing Deduction Finder.**
2. **Click OK in the little introductory window that appears (Figure 5-11).**

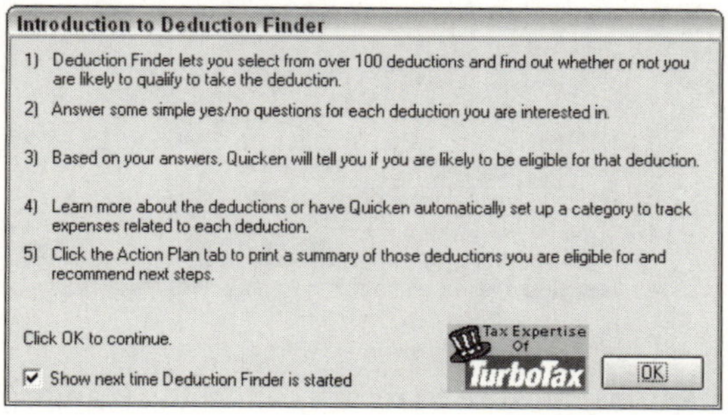

Figure 5-11: Read the introductory info, and then click OK.

3. **Choose a type of deduction.**

   Click the little drop-down menu that appears in the upper-left corner of the Deduction Finder. Choose from Employee, Homeowner, Individual, Investor, Medical, and Self-Employed. With each choice, a different list of deduction categories appears.

4. **Pick a deduction category.**

   Click on one of the choices under the Choose a Deduction heading on the left side of the Deduction Finder (Figure 5-12). The questions change depending on the deduction you choose.

5. **Click Y or N for each question that appears.**

   Go through the list, answering each question. Be sure to check an answer for each question. Based on your answers, Quicken advises you at the bottom of the Q&A list as to whether you qualify for a deduction.

6. **Click More Information to read up on the potential deduction you might have missed.**
7. **Click Create a Category if you need to establish a new category for deductions of this type.**
8. **Continue going through the deduction list, responding to questions, to find more deductions.**

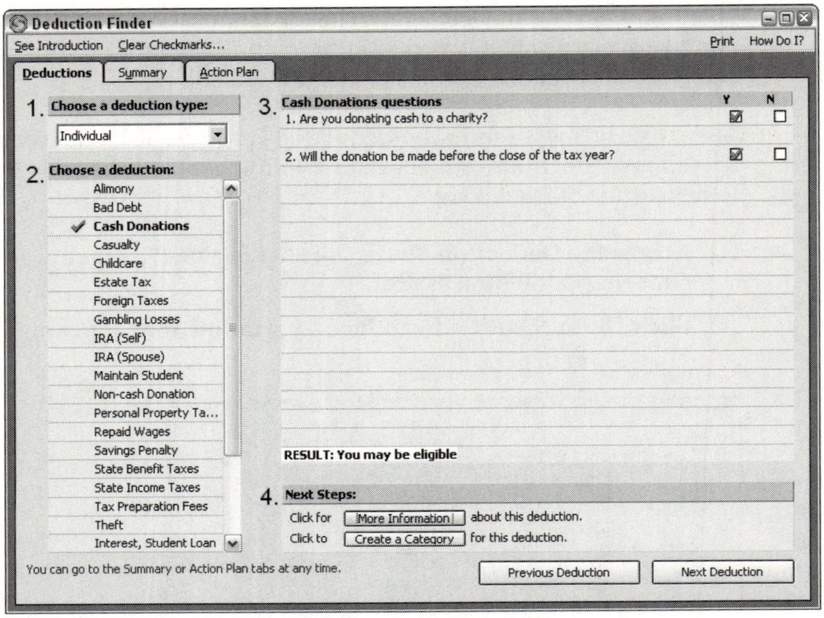

Figure 5-12: Answer all the questions to see if you win a prize.

If you find new deductions, be sure to return to the Tax Planner to incorporate your deductions into your tax projection.

Paying Estimated Payments

Say you've determined that you owe estimated payments. The estimates are paid with Form 1040-ES, Estimated Tax for Individuals (see Figure 5-13).

The only information you need to enter on the Form 1040-ES is your name and your Social Security number (and the same for your spouse if you're filing a joint tax return), your address, and the amount of estimated tax you're including with this payment.

Include a check, payable to U.S. Treasury (or IRS, or Uncle Sam, or just about any variation on the government that you want — don't worry — they'll cash it). Put your Social Security number on the check, just in case it gets detached from the little voucher form.

Although it's quick and easy to write IRS as the payee on your check, Frank Abagnale, consumer fraud specialist, subject of the Stephen Spielberg movie *Catch Me If You Can*, and author of the consumer protection guide, *The Art of the Steal*, suggests that writing IRS on a check is an open invitation for a criminal to change the letters to MRS, fill in another name after the MRS, and cash the check. So be warned — stick with using actual words in the Payee area of your check.

Now what? You have to know when to make the payments, where to make the payments, and how the payments should be made. I won't leave you hanging — here are the particulars for getting those payments made.

When your estimated payments are due

Although these estimated payments are called *quarterly payments*, the IRS's definition of a quarter might not quite agree with what you and I think when we consider splitting the year into four equal parts. Here's the breakdown for how the IRS expects you to calculate and pay your "quarterly" payments.

- **1st Quarter:** Payment is due April 15. If you annualize your income, use the net income from January through March.
- **2nd Quarter:** Payment is due June 15. If you annualize your income, use the net income from January through May.
- **3rd Quarter:** Payment is due September 15. If you annualize your income, use the net income from January through August.
- **4th Quarter:** Payment is due January 15. If you annualize your income, use the net income from the entire tax year, January through December.

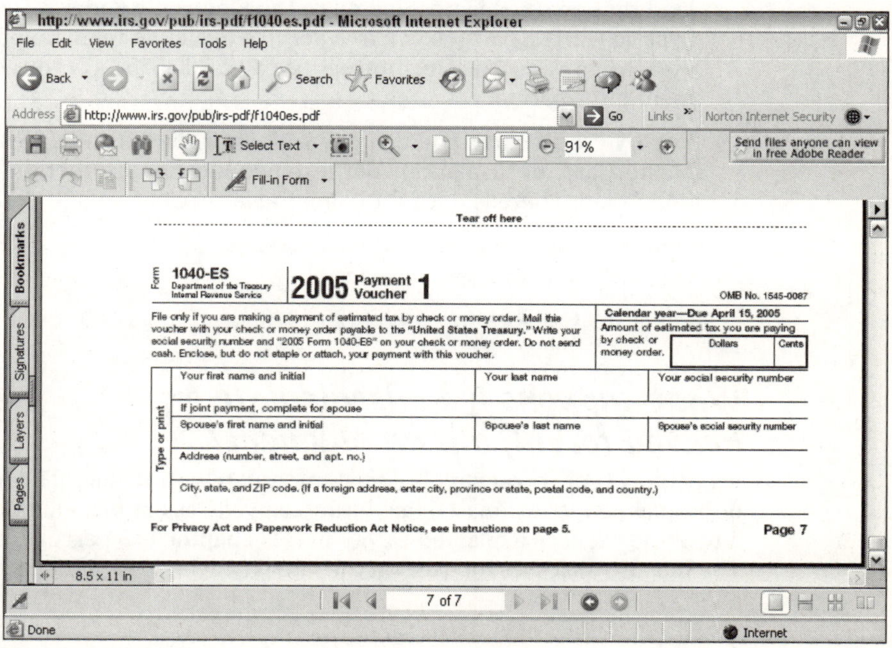

Figure 5-13: Fill in the blanks, and then pop it in the mail with your check.

If the 15th of the month ever falls on a Saturday, Sunday, or a holiday that results in the post offices being closed in your state, the tax payment is due on the business day *following* the 15th.

Where to send your estimated payments

Pay close attention here. The estimated tax payments *do not* get sent to the same address as your tax return. Furthermore, the IRS has a tendency to change the addresses frequently, just to make sure everyone is paying attention. Rather than give you addresses that might turn out to be incorrect, you should look at the instructions for the 1040-ES, the estimated tax form, for the mailing address.

You can find the 1040-ES instructions, along with a copy of the 1040-ES form at this URL:

`www.irs.gov/pub/irs-pdf/f1040es.pdf`

You can also ask the IRS to mail you a copy of the 1040-ES with instructions by calling 1-800-TAX-FORM.

Paying estimates online or by telephone

You can also pay your estimated tax payments online or by phone.

- **Pay online.** If you want to pay online, be sure to give yourself some lead time to set this up. Sign on to the Electronic Federal Tax Payment System (EFTPS), which is a free service available to all taxpayers. Go to `www.eftps.gov` on the Internet or call 1-800-555-4477 to receive enrollment information.
- **Pay by credit card.** You can pay with your American Express, Discover, MasterCard, or Visa at one of these two locations, either online or by telephone. There is a fee for using these services:

  Official Payments Corporation, 1-800-272-9829, `www.officialpayments.com`

  Link2Gov Corporation, 1-888-729-1040, `www.pay1040.com`

What happens if I miscalculate or, heaven forbid, miss a payment?

It's penalty time if you pay those estimates late or not at all. The penalty for underpayment of estimated tax during the year, assuming you don't qualify for any of the excuses explained earlier in this chapter, is 5 percent (annual rate). The IRS also assesses interest on the late payments (the interest rates vary).

TIP

Here's a tip that might help you budget for estimated payments. Instead of trying to come up with the cash quarterly, go ahead and pay your estimates monthly. You can make estimated payments as frequently as you like. Just fill out the estimated tax form (Form 1040-ES), choosing a voucher that applies to the current quarter. Vouchers are numbered 1, 2, 3, and 4, so if you're making a payment in July, that's considered the third quarter, so use Voucher #3. Monthly payments can be a lot easier on the bank balance.

Using a last-minute alternative to paying estimates

So, it's late fall and you do a little tax projection and suddenly realize that you're going to owe a whopping amount of tax in the spring. You can wait to bite the bullet, pay the tax, and chomp on the underpayment penalty too, or you can employ a sweet little trick that can save you the penalty money, assuming you can afford to pay the tax right away.

Remember that W-4 form you gave your employer? Fill out a new W-4, altering the number of allowances you claim, and thus changing your withholding. The fewer allowances you claim, the more tax is withheld. You can even request that extra tax be withheld.

What's the advantage in that? The IRS doesn't look at the dates on which your tax is withheld. Instead, the IRS assumes your withholding is performed evenly, throughout the course of the entire year. Therefore, you can make a large tax payment in December by arranging to have extra tax withheld from your paycheck. If you were to make the payment as an estimated payment, you might be assessed a penalty for the payment not being made on time.

Book VI

Retirement Planning and Other Saving

The 5th Wave By Rich Tennant

"Oh, look! Mr. Peepers just picked the very same mutual funds your investment software did!"

Contents at a Glance

Chapter 1: The Quicken Financial Planner

In This Chapter

- **Finding your way around the Planning Center**
- **Setting planning alerts**
- **Creating a financial plan**
- **Using Quicken's other planners and planning resources**

Hey, how about looking ahead a bit when thinking about our finances? Having a personal financial plan is more than just a good idea. A financial plan is just like any other plan for your future. You can either move through life, one day at a time, without striving for any goals, or you can set a course and try to follow through. You might not achieve all that you plan for, or you might achieve more than you could have hoped for. But going through life without at least the bare bones of a financial plan is like jumping in the river and starting to swim, without even knowing in which direction you're traveling or what awaits you if you reach the shore.

Getting Familiar with Quicken's Planning Center

When you open the Quicken Planning Center by choosing Planning⇨Go to Planning Center, you see an overview screen that is ready to receive your financial plan. In addition to the main Plan: Results area, you also see sections for alerts, plan assumptions, Quicken's various planners, miscellaneous tools, the most commonly used calculators, a link for signing up to receive the Quicken newsletter, and a link to Quicken's business planning feature. All of this is displayed in Figure 1-1.

TIP: You can also get to the Planning Center quickly by clicking the Financial Overview option on the Account Bar on the left side of the screen, and then clicking the Planning tab.

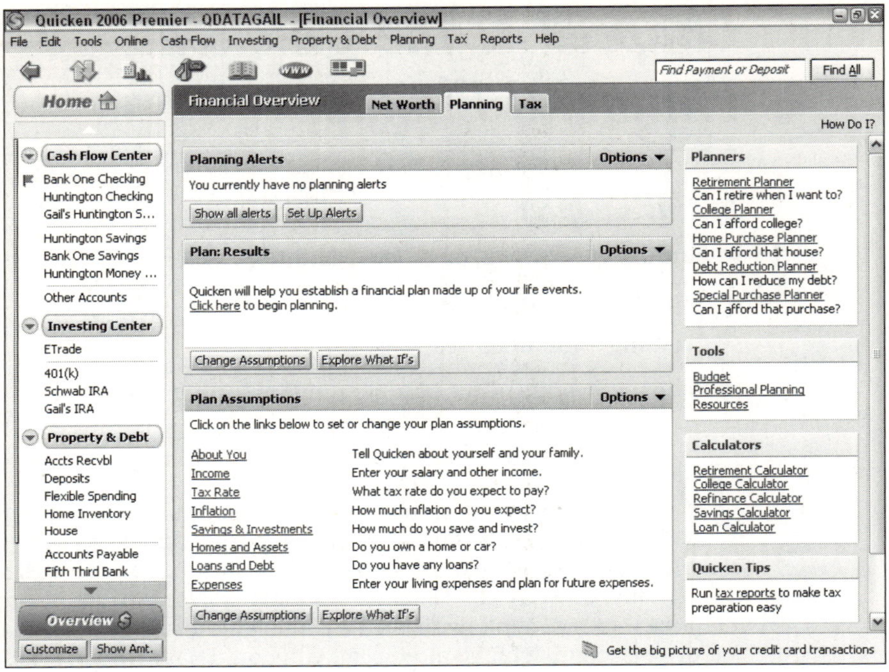

Figure 1-1: An aerial view of the Planning Center.

Here's a shortcut for getting to the Planning Center window in a hurry. You can set the Financial Overview to be your start-up screen every time you open Quicken. If the Planning tab was the last tab you used when you last closed Quicken, the Planning Center appears the next time you open Quicken. Even if you were using the Net Worth or the Tax tab in the Financial Center when last you closed Quicken, one quick click on the Planning tab, and you're right at the Planning Center.

Set the Planning Center as your Quicken home page by following these steps:

1. **Choose Edit⇨Preferences⇨Quicken Program from the menu.**

   The Quicken Preferences window appears, with Startup selected.

2. **Click the drop-down arrow in the Startup Preferences window.**
3. **Choose Financial Overview, as shown in Figure 1-2.**
4. **Click OK.**

   From now on, each time you open Quicken, the Financial Overview is your start-up screen.

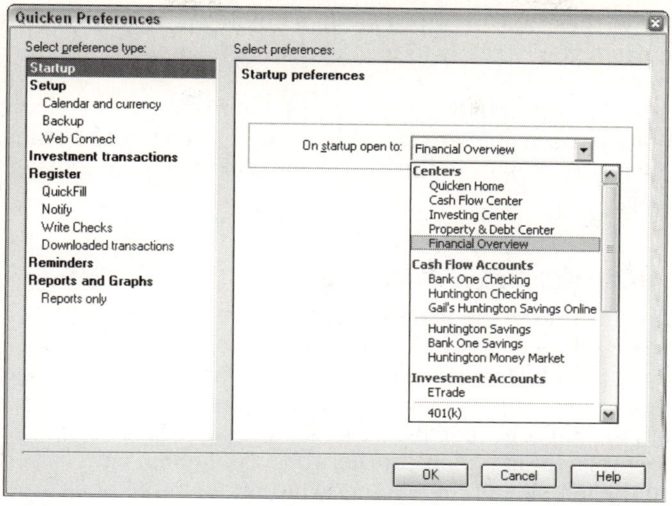

Figure 1-2: Make Financial Planning a part of your everyday Quicken life by setting the Financial Overview to be your start-up screen.

Using the planning alerts

You've seen these alerts before — they're your reminder-buddies that tell you when you're about to go over the spending limits you've set for yourself or when your favorite stock hits an attractive buying price.

Click the little Show All Alerts button if you want to see a display of all the alerts that are currently in play. A separate Alerts Center window appears, listing the alerts accompanied by hyperlinks that rush you over to the exact spot where you can take care of whatever action is required.

Click the little Set Up Alerts button if you want to establish some new alerts for yourself. Flip back to the index and look up Alerts to find various places throughout this book where different types of alerts are addressed.

Peering at the plan results

Hmmm, the Plan Results section of the Planning Center looks pretty barren when you first drop by for a visit. This is all going to change quickly when we dig in and actually make our financial plan. When you're ready, page over to "Creating Your Own Financial Plan" later in this chapter for the nitty-gritty on plan set up. For now, just enjoy the scenery because this screen is going to get quite busy in just a couple of pages.

Our plan is based on assumptions

Continuing down the main stage of the Planning Center, you get to the Plan Assumptions arena. Here are the basic building blocks of your financial plan.

Right now, these assumptions are in a holding pattern, waiting to hop into action when you're ready to begin your financial plan.

You can read through the assumptions, familiarize yourself with the types of questions you are going to be asked so that you won't be stumped when the time comes to step up to the proverbial plate and take a swing at your financial plan.

The planners have arrived

On the right side of the Planning Center screen is a little box called Planners (Figure 1-3). These guys are ready to scramble into action as soon as you give them a click. If your overall financial plan is Uncle Scrooge, these little planners are the Huey, Duey, and Luey nephews who can help you work through the kinks in specific areas of your financial life. These planners look and operate a lot like their brother the Tax Planner, with hyperlinked headings on the left side of the Planner window, fill-in-the-blank options on the right, and useful calculations on the bottom line. Here's a rundown of the Planning team:

- **Retirement Planner:** You're going to hear more about actual retirement plans and various types of tax-deferred savings in the next chapter, which is all about retirement plans and the money they produce. Meanwhile, you should know that the Retirement Planner is the same thing as the Quicken Financial Plan — and no matter what you call this plan, this is the means to planning your financial future. With the Retirement/Financial Planner, you can determine how much money you really need to have on hand if you want to retire and not end up on the street. Later in this chapter, we use this planner to help zero in on the year when you actually can pull the plug on your job.
- **College Planner:** Head over to Chapter 4 of this book to experience the College Planner firsthand and find out if you're really going to be able to send your children to college or if they're going to have to get busy and start applying for scholarships. This is a good dry run for those delightful experiences with the FAFSA form, the form all parents of college students know and love — it's almost as much fun as filling out a tax return.

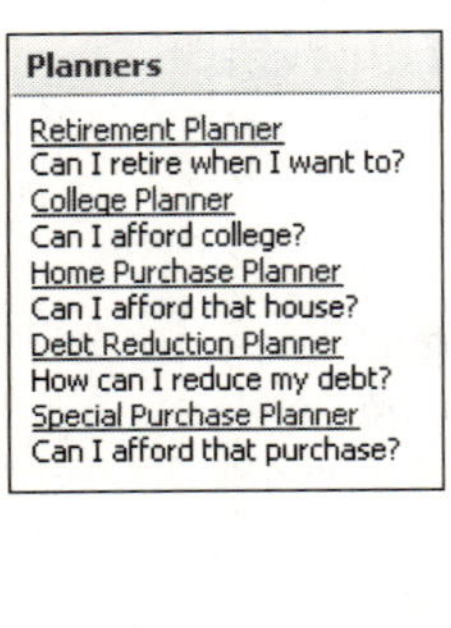

Figure 1-3: Quicken and Planning go together.

✦ **Home Purchase Planner:** Described back in Book IV, Chapter 3, the Home Purchase Planner is designed to help you determine whether you can actually afford the home you want to buy. Quicken looks at all of your income and existing debt and helps you determine the amount you can place as a down payment and the amount of monthly mortgage payments you can afford. Then, the planner goes on to help you with filling out a loan application, and even directs you to Internet loan sites where, if you like, you can apply for a loan from the comfort of your laptop.

✦ **Debt Reduction Planner:** How much is too much debt? Quicken helps you get a handle on the answer to that question with the Debt Reduction planner, a tool for measuring your debt against your ability to repay the amounts you owe. This planner is explained in detail in Book IV, Chapter 2, where the concept of maximizing the value of the money you use to reduce your debt is discussed.

✦ **Special Purchase Planner:** You can use this planner to help you organize your finances in order to help make room for a measurably large purchase such as a wedding, an addition to your home, a boat, a ride to the International Space Station, or whatever strikes your fancy. See Chapter 3 in this book for examples of how to use this planner in conjunction with setting savings goals.

Tools you can use

Quicken offers lots of tools — you could say the entire program is one great mass of tools. But here are some tools that specifically appear on the Planning Center screen. Click any of these tools in the box shown in Figure 1-4 to be transported to a land of financial bliss (honestly, I haven't been drinking . . .). Anyway, here they are, the tools offered to people who are busy working on their financial plan:

✦ **Budget:** We've heard all about the budget before. Book I, Chapter 3 tells you about what a budget is, how to create a budget with the help of your family, and somehow manage to remain civil while living under the same roof. Book IV, Chapter 5 tells you how to automate that budget in Quicken. That's what this Budget tool in the Planning Center is all about — a link to Quicken's budget feature.

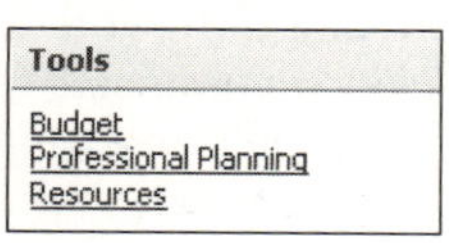

Figure 1-4: Quicken's little toolbox for financial planning customers.

- **Professional Planning:** Whoa — this sounds like something beyond what we bargained for when we purchased our Quicken program. Sure enough, this is a little training session on picking a financial pro to help you with all of these monetary mysteries. You'll be pleasantly surprised to learn that this link doesn't offer you sales pitches or links to any kind of professional planner network organized through Intuit. Instead, there are useful tips for determining when you need to call in the pros, what to look for in a financial professional, and what information you want to pull together from your Quicken file so that you don't look like a complete idiot when you meet the planner face to face.
- **Resources:** In the Planning Center toolbox is a link to Resources. The Resources link is a fooler. That link isn't a link to Resources. It's a continuation of the line above — which should have read Professional Planning Resources. I guess it's back to Google for me if I want some other resources. But wait! You can flip to Appendix C at the back of this book and find plenty of financial resources. Thank goodness!

Calculators for every occasion

Finding calculators in a financial program is no surprise. Although, just as a side note, I find it interesting that *the* calculator, the 10-key type that you use to perform math functions like adding and subtracting, is nowhere to be found in the Calculators box. (Hint: Look on the Tools menu.) There are, however, some interesting calculators here in the Calculators box shown in Figure 1-5, and I think you'll find these to be quite useful, even if you never get around to trying out the rest of the financial planning tools that Quicken has to offer.

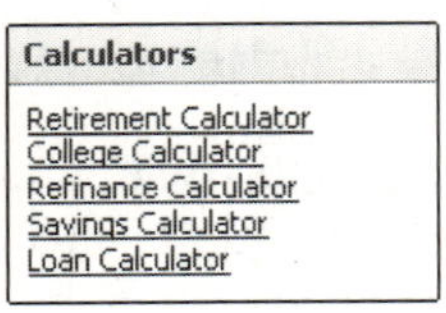

Figure 1-5: Quicken's calculators help pass the time on a rainy afternoon.

The calculators are simple little pop-up boxes that allow you to enter numbers in a quick setting, and spit out even quicker responses. Play around with these calculators anytime you're contemplating borrowing money, saving for one of those rainy days, contemplating a college education, or mulling over your retirement options.

One of the nice features of these calculators is that they allow you the opportunity to print out a schedule of payments or savings amounts that you can use to follow along and check your progress on a monthly and yearly basis.

- **Retirement Calculator:** More on this in the next chapter. This is the quick tool for determining how much money you're going to have to live on when you retire based on your current rate of savings, or how much you need to save in order to have what you want to live on when you retire.
- **College Calculator:** Experiment with various scenarios to determine how much you can afford to pay for college, or how much you need to save in order to meet your anticipated needs. Start with your current savings, enter either the total amount you expect college to cost or the total amount you are able to sock away each month, and let Quicken tell you whether you're going to end up in the poor house. For more on college saving and other college payment options, refer to Chapter 4 of this book.
- **Refinance Calculator:** Are you thinking about borrowing money against your house? Here's a little calculator that takes the guesswork out of how much you can borrow and how much you can afford to repay. Read more about the refinancing process in Chapter 3 of Book IV.
- **Savings Calculator:** The savings calculator helps you design a savings plan for whatever savings goals you are contemplating. Chapter 3 of this book goes into detail about how to create and manage your savings goals. This little calculator helps you determine how much you need to save in order to meet certain goals, or how much money you will have if you save a certain amount each week, month, quarter, or year. Enter the interest rate that you earn and Quicken computes the earnings on your savings as well.
- **Loan Calculator:** My personal favorite of the calculator family, the little loan calculator is never far from my reach. Any time you want, you can use this calculator to contemplate how much you can afford to borrow, or how long it will take you to pay back a loan. Determine the difference in payments based on a change in the interest rate. See examples of the Loan Calculator in use in Chapter 1 of Book IV. A couple of quick entries, a click or two, and you've got yourself a complete loan schedule, showing all of your payments along with the interest portion of each payment. Easy, peasy.

Li'l tips from your friends at Quicken

If you like receiving e-mail that is a little more highbrow than spam offers to expand certain parts of your anatomy or opportunities to purchase drugs from Canada, consider subscribing to Quicken's e-mail newsletters. You can choose from *Money Matters*, a personal financial planning newsletter, *Small Business*, for small business owners, and *TurboTax*, filled with tax news and tips.

These newsletters are written by financial professionals and really do contain useful information. For example, I recently learned that you can click the little paperclip button on the Transaction tool bar in your register to attach a scanned copy of a cancelled check or a receipt. Maybe I can operate in a paperless office after all!

Go to `http://preferencecenter.intuit.com/optin/quicken/`, a sign-up Web page where you enter your name and e-mail address and check the box for each newsletter that you want to receive. See the sign-up page in Figure 1-6.

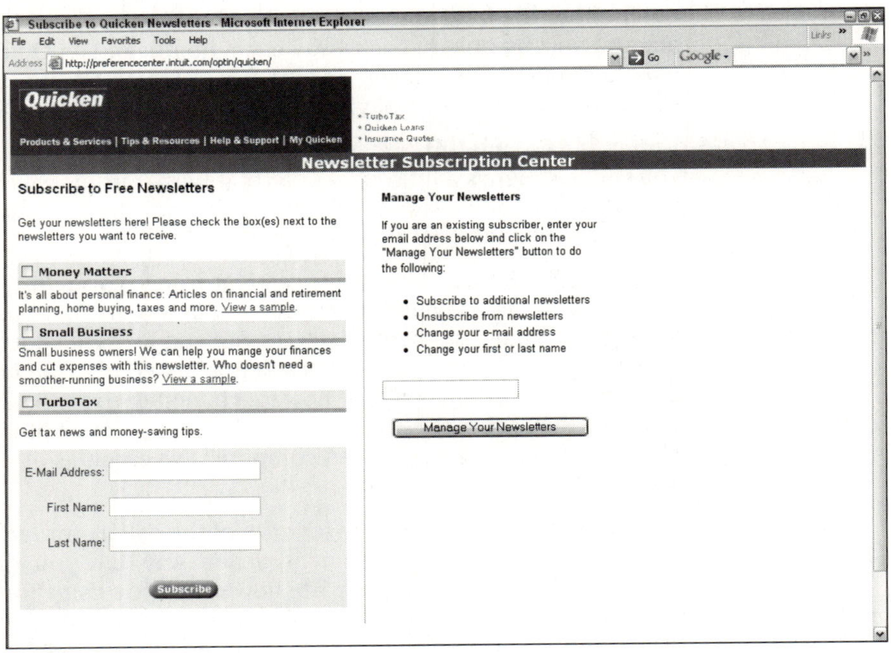

Figure 1-6: Quicken's tip-filled newsletters are just a free subscription away.

Gettin' jiggy with Quicken's business plan

The last tool in the financial planning shed, so to speak, is the little link at the bottom of the page (Figure 1-7) to Quicken's offer to Create a Business Plan. This one is a partial sales pitch. When you take the bait, you're given a cash flow calculator to play with. Enter some numbers, slide around on some slider bars, watch the bars in a graph move up and down, and see how your cash flow is affected by different circumstances.

Figure 1-7: Click to create a business plan.

Then you're given an opportunity to buy some software that can help you organize your business ideas into a formal business plan.

We're going to talk about business plans and using Quicken to keep track of your business in Book VIII, so sit tight.

Creating Your Own Financial Plan

As I stated earlier in this chapter, Quicken's Financial Plan is the same thing as the Retirement Plan. Now we're going to experiment with this Planner and find out just what it can do for us. To avoid confusion, I'm going to refer to this plan as the Financial Plan — you can call it whatever you like.

All of the Plan Assumptions that appear on the main Planning Center screen are covered in the actual Financial Plan. After you create your first plan, you can click on any of the assumptions to make a change. For now, go right into the Planner, where you answer the questions and enter the information that enables Quicken to produce a workable plan.

Getting started with the financial plan

It's easy as pie to start the process of creating your own financial plan in Quicken — open the Planning Center, and then click the Click Here link in the Plan: Results section of the screen. If you've already fooled around with the Financial Plan before, the Click Here link might not appear. As an alternative, you can click the Retirement Planner link in the Planners section on the right side of the screen. Either way, it's one click, and away we go!

The Planner appears in a separate window with the Introduction screen displayed (Figure 1-8). Some basic tips for making your way through the Planner are covered here. This Planner is supposed to take about a half an hour to complete; however, Quicken saves everything you enter, as you enter it, so if you have to quit the Planner and come back later, no problemo. Just get back in and pick up where you left off.

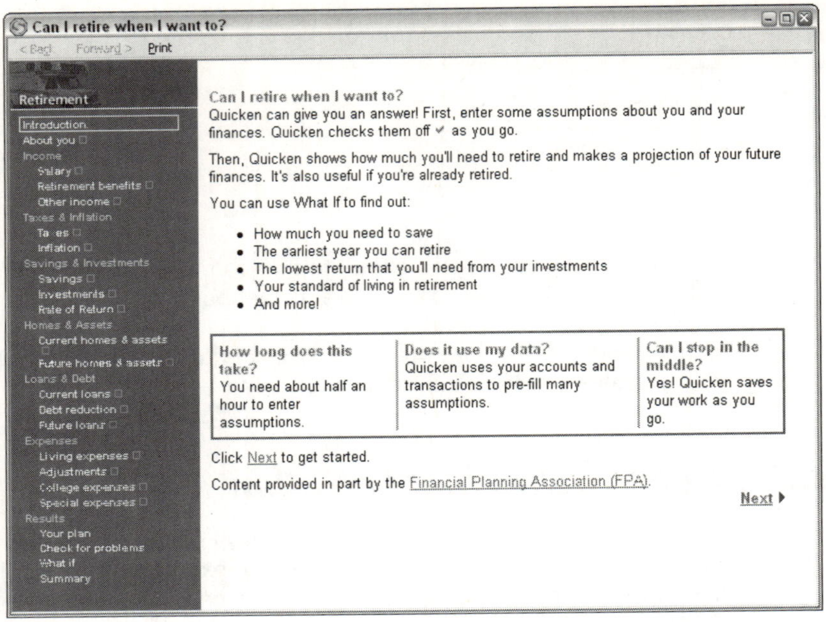

Figure 1-8: Financial Planner/ Retirement Planner — it's all the same.

After you get started, you may notice that there are little check boxes along the left side of the Planner window. Each area you've completed gets a check, so jumping back into the Planner after a brief hiatus just means that you need to click on the Retirement Planner over on right side of the screen in the Planner box, and then click on the first unchecked menu item in the planner. Presto! You're ready to pick up where you left off.

After you've read the Introduction screen, and from here on whenever you're ready to continue, click the Next option to proceed.

For each of the Planner screens, there is a Click Here link that opens a separate input window. A Done button returns you to the planner window. The Next button always takes you to the next item in the Planner menu. After you've entered information on the Planner screens, an Edit option appears that you can use to get back in and change your information.

It's all about you

Right after the Financial Planner's introduction, it's time to answer some simple questions about who you are and who else is in your family. Click the Click Here option on the About You page to open the Quicken Planner: About You window (Figure 1-9).

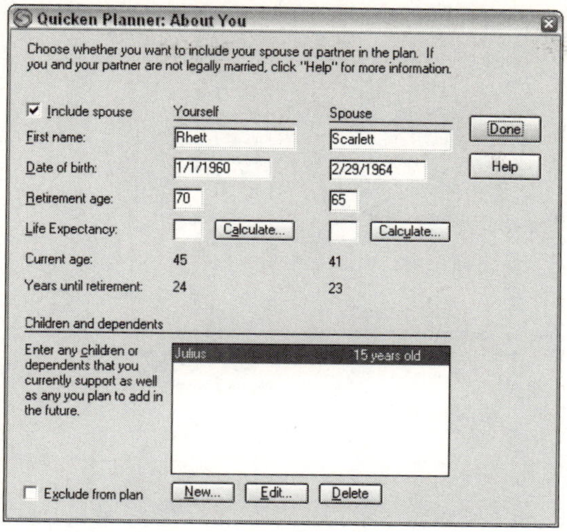

Figure 1-9: Time for some vital statistics.

Enter your name, birth date, expected age of retirement, and the same information for your spouse. If you support any children, or other dependents, click the New button and enter name and birth date for each dependent.

To determine life expectancy, click the Calculate button after you've entered your age, and the Calculate Life Expectancy window appears (Figure 1-10). Enter your gender and information about your health. Quicken uses an actuarial table to calculate your expected lifespan, and then asks you if you want to add some years to that calculated amount. Well, who wouldn't? You are "allowed" to give yourself up to 10 extra years beyond the age the tables say you are expected to reach. Enter your own guess at your life expectancy age in order to continue. Good news — if you come back in 10 years and run the age expectancy calculation again, you'll find out you're going to live even longer than the original prediction.

Click the appropriate OK and Done buttons to close up these windows, and you're back to the Planner and ready to proceed. From now on, when you open the Planner and look at the About You screen, the personal data you entered will appear. From now on, there is an Edit button you can click if you need to make any changes in this information.

Your salary information

Next screen, next question — how much do you earn in a year? Click the Click Here link to enter salary information. A Salary Income window appears. You can't make any entries directly in this window. Click the New button to open the Add Salary window (Figure 1-11), and then fill in the blanks to enter salary information, one salary at a time.

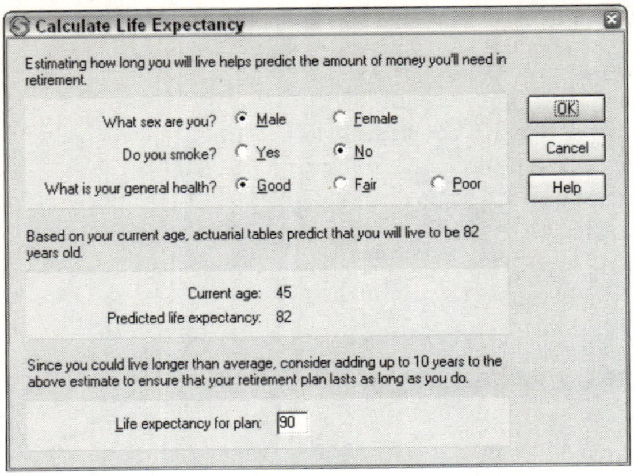

Figure 1-10: Enter information about your health into the Calculate Life Expectancy window.

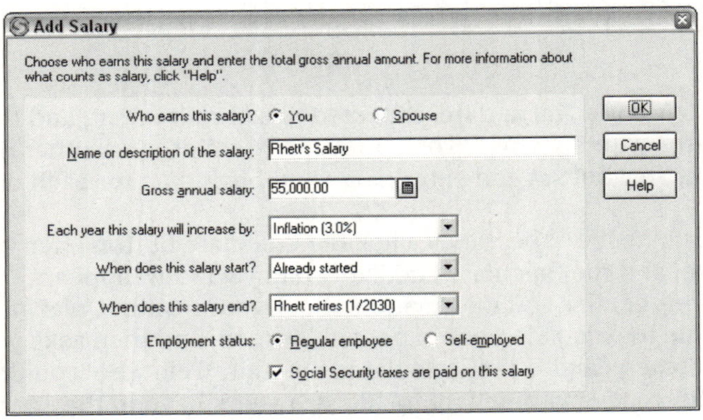

Figure 1-11: Enter your salary information, one salary at a time.

Enter the date when this salary is expected to begin, or choose Already Started if this is the salary you already receive.

Quicken assumes your salary increases by a modest 3 percent per year — you can adjust that percentage up or down depending on your history. And of course you can keep returning to the salary screen and adding new salary amounts or new jobs as your life events change.

Answer the rest of the questions about your salary, and then click OK to get back to the Planner. Keep clicking that New button in the Salary Income window over and over again until each salary is entered for you and, if you are married, your spouse.

Entering retirement benefits including Social Security

When you click the Click Here link on the Retirement Benefits screen, a Retirement Benefits window pops up, telling you that you are indeed going to receive Social Security benefits (what a relief!). Based on the age when you expect the benefits to begin (assume age 65 for this example) and the amount of money you earned or will earn in your working life, Quicken tells you what you can expect in the way of benefits (Figure 1-12).

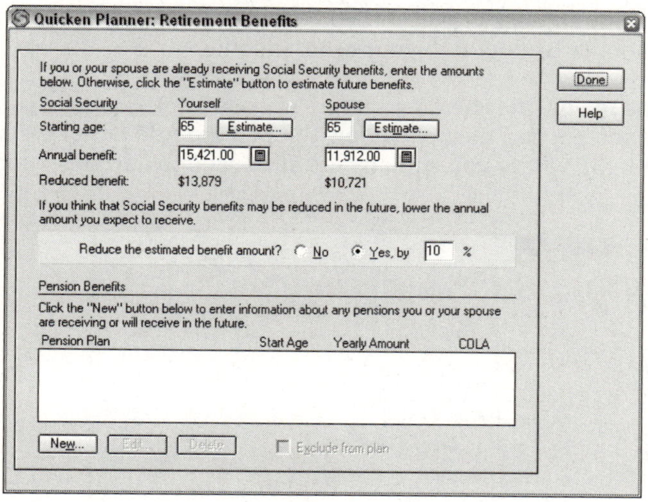

Figure 1-12: Wow! It looks like I'm going to get some Social Security benefits after all!

Click the little Estimate button to call up another box where you choose what range your average income falls in. You have to pick the range that covers the highest amount of annual salary you expect to earn in any 10-year period of your life.

If you don't have much faith in the federal government being able to make good on its promises of Social Security benefits, you can ask Quicken to reduce the projected benefit amount by whatever percent you want. I've chosen to reduce the benefit by 10 percent in Figure 1-12. This is a pure guessing game here.

If you work for a union or a company that pays pensions, click the little New button in the Retirement Benefits window to enter any pension benefit you expect to receive.

Enter miscellaneous income that doesn't fit anywhere else

The Other income line is a catchall for income you receive that doesn't fit into the salary and wages, retirement income, business income, investment income, or income from real estate categories. Suggested income items that can be reported on the Other income line include child support and alimony, inheritance money, cash gifts, royalties, and trust fund distributions.

The term income is used a bit loosely here, and what Quicken really wants to see is any odd amount of money you expect to receive. For example, if you loaned your brother $1,000 and you expect him to pay it back next year, that $1,000 should be added to your other income.

From the main Other Income screen, choose Click Here to open a little Other Income screen, and then click New to open the Add Other Income screen (Figure 1-13), where you actually are supposed to add this stuff.

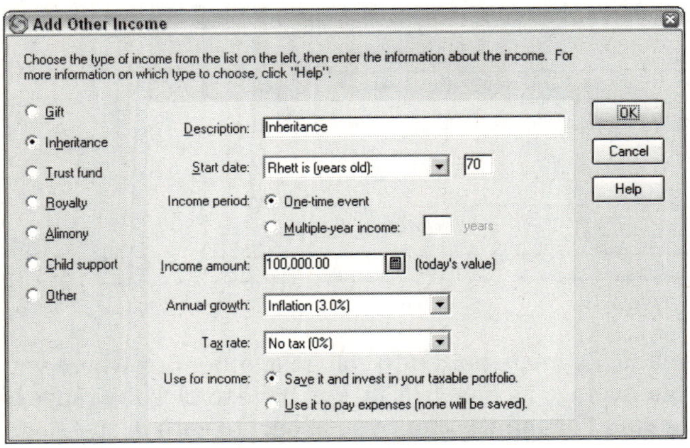

Figure 1-13: Choose a category at the left, and then describe your miscellaneous income.

Indicate the type of income by clicking one of the options at the left of the window, and then enter particulars about the income, including how much, when, and how often you expect to receive it, and your guess at what inflation is going to be in future years.

There's a field where you are to show the expected tax rate on the income you entered. This is here for a couple of reasons:

- ✦ The income might not be taxed. If the income is a gift, an inheritance, or a repayment of a loan, there won't be any income tax.

✦ The tax rate might be different from your regular income tax rate. For example, if the amount of income exceeds the amount you're used to reporting on your income tax return, the extra income might cause you to be bumped up to a higher marginal tax rate. Under today's tax laws, marginal tax rates go from 10 percent to 35 percent.

TIP: You're also expected to indicate how you expect to use this money, either for current expenses or as an investment. Quicken gives you an all-or-nothing choice for the usage of the money. If you expect to use part for current expenses and part for investment, you can split the money into two parts and enter each part separately.

Enter your estimated average tax rate

Estimating your average tax rate is a toughie: No one knows what the tax rates will be even a few years from now due to Congress's constant tinkering with the tax laws. Nevertheless, in order to get this Planner working, Quicken wants you to enter your estimated marginal tax rate (see Figure 1-14). That's easy enough to do today because you can look at your most recent tax return. As for future planning, well, you have to assume for now that tax rates aren't expected to change all that much.

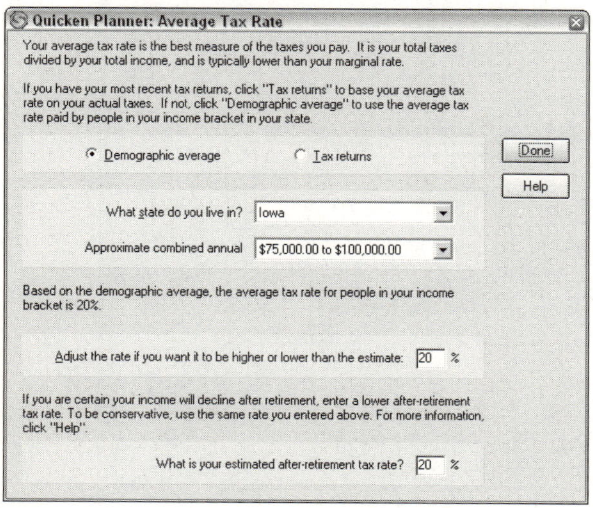

Figure 1-14: Take a stab at guessing your tax rate.

You can figure the tax rate the easy way by choosing the demographic average. Enter your state, enter your income range (combined income, if you're married), and Quicken returns an estimated average income tax rate. After you see what Quicken has come up with, you can change the amount if you like, but using the demographic average is a quick and easy way to at least get a close estimate of your income tax.

More guesses: This time, inflation

Excuse me, but Quicken would like you to voice your opinion on how you expect the nation's economy to hold up in the years to come. Without even consulting you, Quicken has assumed that we can expect inflation of 3 percent. If you think that's reasonable, you're done with the inflation screen.

Otherwise, click the Click Here link and enter your own percent.

Mary, Mary, quite contrary, how will your savings grow?

Quicken gathers up all of your bank accounts and shows you today's balance (Figure 1-15). You are to indicate whether you intend to use the money in this account (or these accounts) as part of your retirement plan or if you want to exclude the amount from the plan because you plan on spending the money NOW!

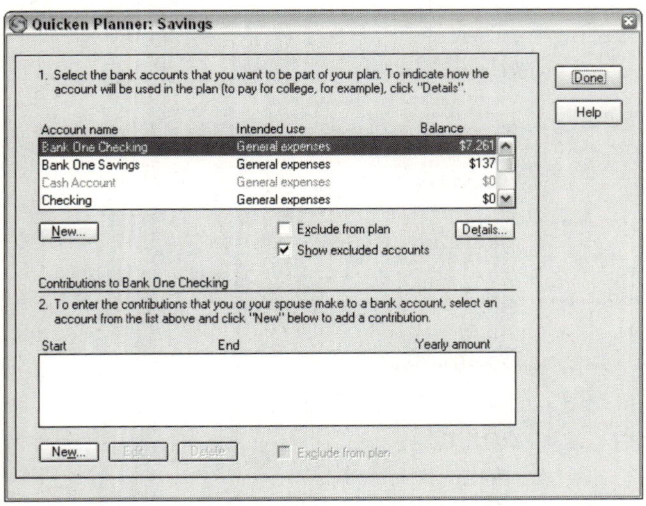

Figure 1-15: How do you expect to use your savings in the future?

Click New in the top half of the Savings window if there are accounts not included here that need to be added. Click New in the bottom half of the Savings window if you plan to make regular contributions to any of your accounts.

It's time for investments: How do you plan to use this money?

Similar to the Savings screen shown in Figure 1-15, the Investments screen (Figure 1-16) lists all of the financial investments that you own that have been recorded in Quicken.

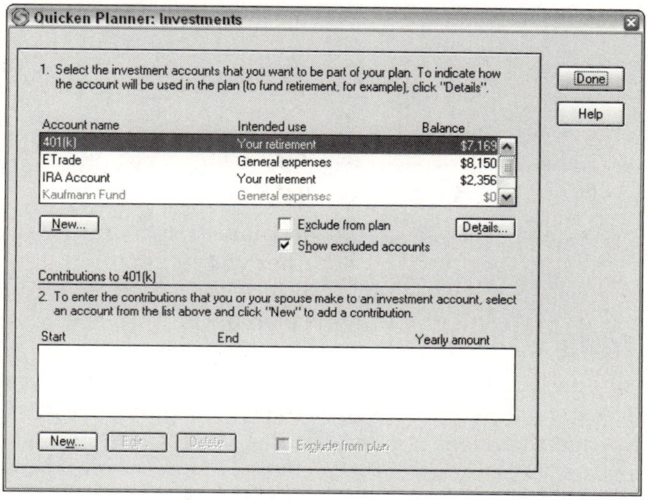

Figure 1-16: Tracking your investments.

You can show which of the investments you plan on excluding from your financial plan and which ones you want to keep in the plan.

Click the New button at the bottom of the window to add additional investments that have not yet been entered in Quicken or that you haven't received yet, but expect to in the future. If you add a new investment that has an existing balance, you have to go into the regular Quicken program to enter the information about the value of the investment.

Estimating your rate of return

Here's a really interesting part of the Financial Planner — the Rate of Return estimator (Figure 1-17). Quicken wants you to say how much, on the average, you expect to earn each year on your investments.

Guess away, and hope for the best. Check back from time to time and enter updated information based on the way the economy looks.

If some of your money is invested in tax-free funds or bonds, change the percent at the bottom of the screen to something less than 100 percent.

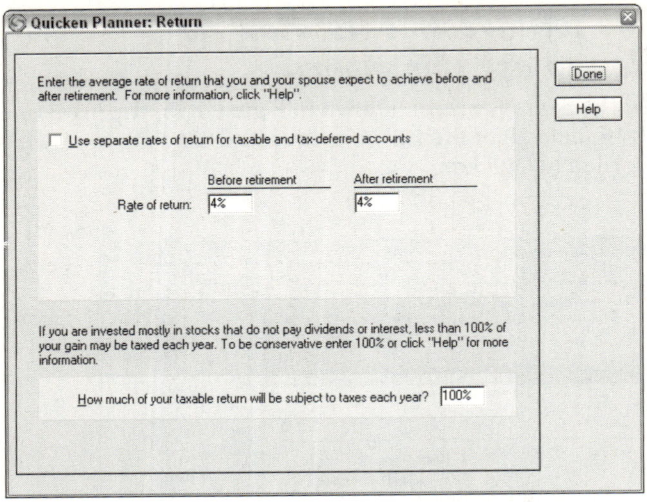

Figure 1-17: Guessing your investments' rate of return.

Asset time

Quicken scrounged around and found your assets from amongst the information you already entered. Check over the list (a sample list appears in Figure 1-18) — make changes where necessary. Add anything that didn't make it onto the list.

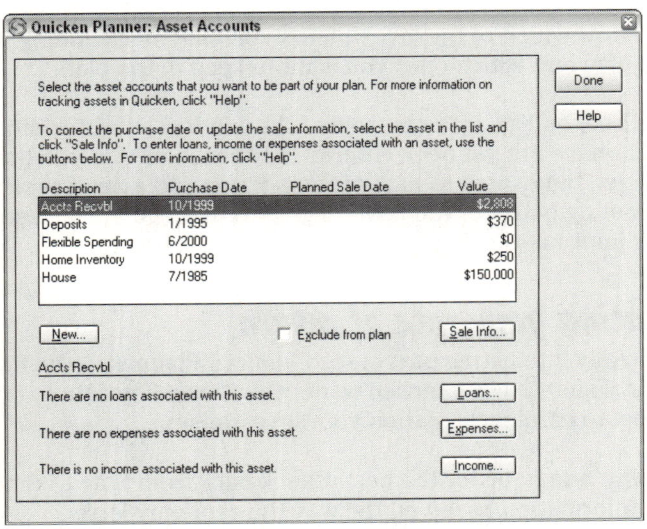

Figure 1-18: Recording your assets.

Go ahead and open the asset detail window — there's some interesting stuff here. Quicken gives you an opportunity to tie any debts you might have to their associated assets. Click on any asset on the top of the window, and then click buttons at the bottom of the window to enter or update information related to the selected asset.

You can associate a loan, expenses, and income with an asset; you can click the Sale Info button to record an estimate of when and for how much you expect to sell the asset; and you can click the Exclude from Plan check box if this asset is not going to be with you for the long haul.

Are there more homes to come? If you plan on adding a home or other sizeable asset to your stable, the next screen (Figure 1-19) is the place for you.

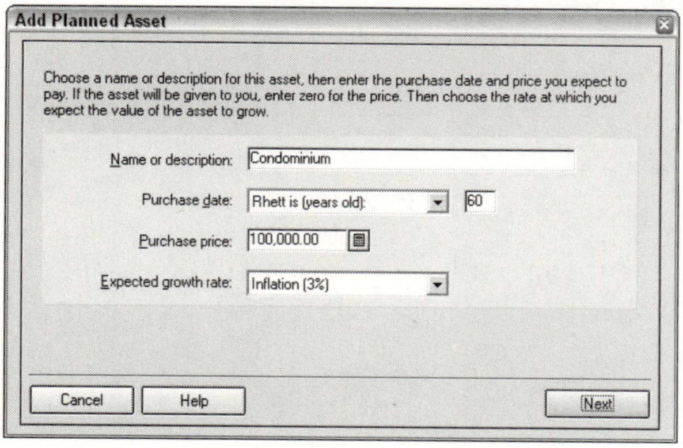

Figure 1-19: Record your dream home at the future homes and assets place.

Maybe you plan on movin' on up, or maybe you'll be ready to downsize in a decade or so. A second car might be in the cards, or maybe that Harley that's been calling out to you will finally come home to Papa. Whatever plans you have for future sizeable purchases, you can click away on the little New button and add everything you need to make your Financial Plan more accurate and personal.

But wait! You're not finished! If you plan on adding a loan to offset the cost of the future home or other assets, use the Loan button to describe that loan you think you'll need.

Loan time

Now we've gone over to the flip side of the financial planning equation — debt to offset all of those assets.

Click on over to Current Loans. Quicken displays a list of any loans you've already entered in your registers, including the start date, the duration, and the amount of the loan. Not only that, but click once on any loan and at the bottom of the Loan Accounts window (Figure 1-20), you can see the original loan amount, your current payment, the interest rate you agreed to, and how many payments are left.

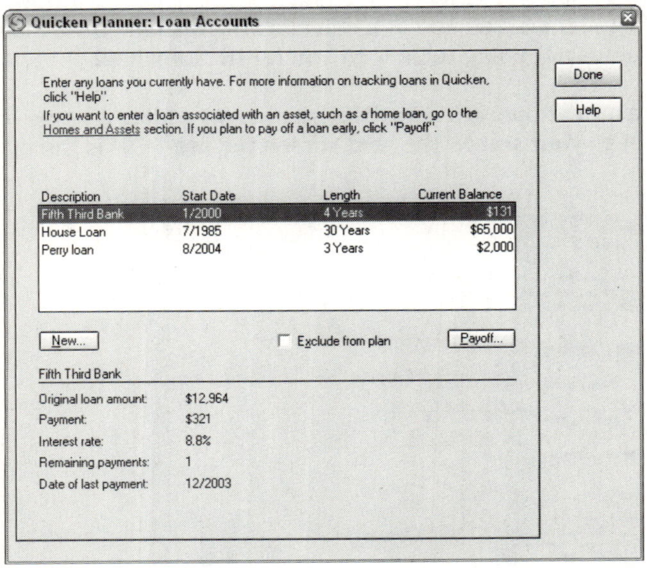

Figure 1-20: Don't forget your loans.

Click New if you need to add any new loans to your planner. Remember, these windows don't just refer to the financial situations you face currently. If you plan on adding loans in the future (or, as in the last section of this chapter, a sizeable asset), this is the time to enter a general idea of what and how much you think you'll add.

REMEMBER: You can always return to the scene of the crime to edit, remove, and add information so that your planner will be as close to absolutely accurate as possible.

Don't forget your debt reduction plan

If you set up a debt reduction plan back in Book II, like I did, Quicken is going to offer you a chance to incorporate that monthly expense into your financial plan (Figure 1-21). Jump at the chance, because your plan just isn't complete unless you include everything.

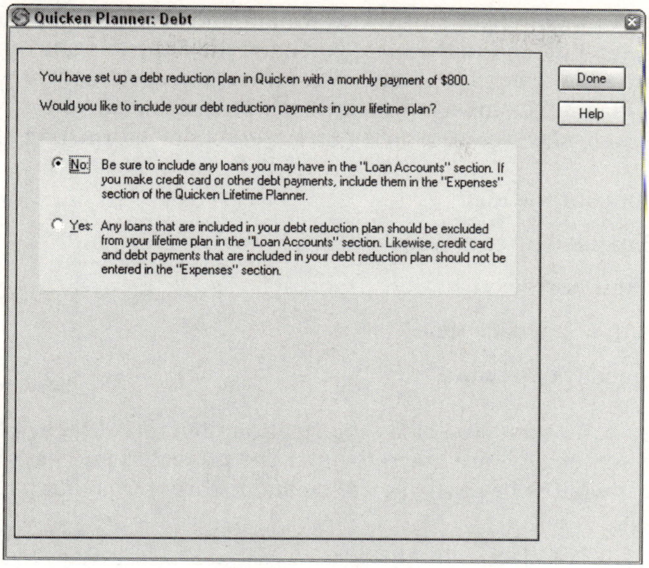

Figure 1-21: Don't forget that monthly debt payment!

There is a reminder not to duplicate loans in your financial plan. If you've already entered your loans in the Current Loans section of the plan, or if you've introduced the loans in conjunction with the assets that secure the loans, you need to remove those loans from the debt section, or not include the monthly debt reduction plan payment in your financial plan.

Likewise, if you have credit card expenses or other expenses that are part of your debt reduction plan, be sure not to duplicate those expenses later on here in the Expenses section of your financial plan.

Only one iteration of a loan per customer, please!

TECHNICAL STUFF: Quicken doesn't let you alter the debt reduction plan payment when you're working in the Financial Planner — it's a case of all or nothing. Or is it? If you wanted to, you could take the time to set up your debt reduction plan as a loan, or a current and ongoing expense, and then enter whatever payment amount you want, making sure you don't duplicate loan payments already recorded in the Planner.

Planning on borrowing some money?

If you're planning on adding a large asset that will have a loan associated with it, that loan should be added to the Planner when you add the asset, back in the Homes and Assets section.

But if you're planning on borrowing for another reason and won't have a secured asset affixed to the loan, you need the Future Loans option that appears on the menu at the left side of the planner. When you click the Here link, the Planned Loans window appears. There you can enter your future loan(s) by clicking New and giving up the essential information about the loan:

- ✦ A name for the loan
- ✦ Estimated date of origin
- ✦ Amount borrowed
- ✦ Length of payback time
- ✦ Frequency of payment

After you enter your basic loan information (Figure 1-22), click Next. On the next screen, you are asked to enter the projected interest rate. Quicken calculates what your payment will be and incorporates that payment into your plan.

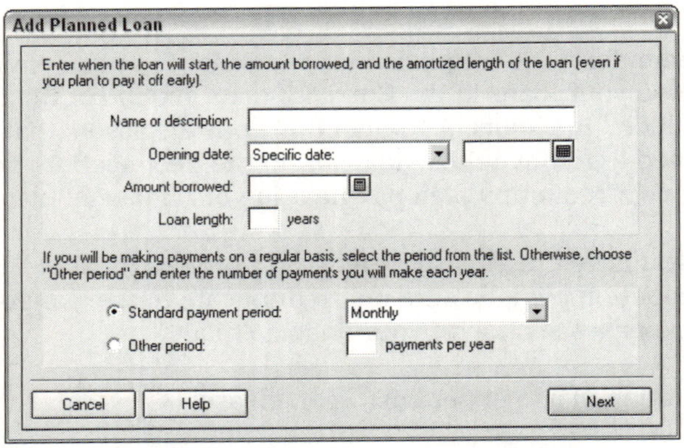

Figure 1-22: Entering future loans.

Onward to living expenses

You're nearly finished now — are you closing in on that estimated half an hour yet? When you get to the Living Expenses portion of your financial plan, you can go one of two ways. Choose Rough Estimate, and you can then enter a single amount of how much you expect to spent in general, annually, on living expenses.

Or, you can choose Category Detail, and Quicken takes you over to a Category Detail window (Figure 1-23), where you can enter exact amounts in each category to reflect what you expect your annual spending is going to be.

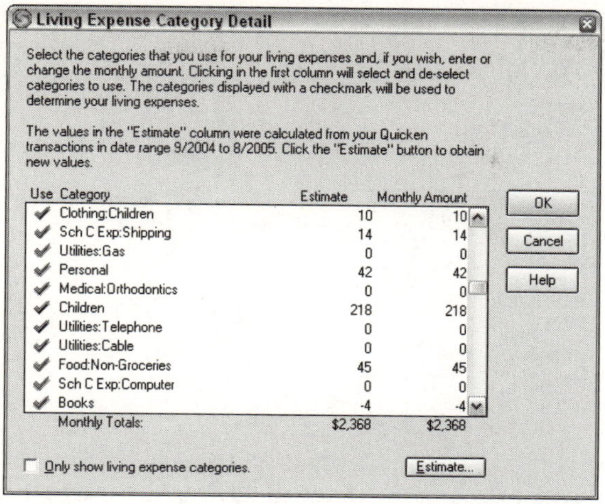

Figure 1-23: Calculating your living expenses, one by one.

REMEMBER

When you close the Category Detail window, notice the field at the bottom of the Living Expenses window where you can enter the percentage of your cash surplus that you plan to shift to savings each year.

In the Category Detail window, you can enter a monthly amount for each category of expense.

WARNING!

If you choose to use the Category Detail method, you must use this method for all of your expenses. You can't enter a rough estimate amount for some of your expenses and a category detail amount for others.

Planning for life adjustments

Some major factors can play a large part in your financial plan. In the example illustrated in Figure 1-24, the couple's son grows up and moves away from home. The parents anticipate their living expenses will decrease by 50 percent when that happens.

Try to think of events that could impact your lifestyle in a significant way, and adjust your financial plan accordingly. You can add as many of these lifestyle adjustments as you need. When entering the information for the change, you are asked to enter a date that the change is expected to occur. That date can be a function of the age of one of the family members, the retirement date or the death of a family member, or it can be a specific date.

You also need to indicate a date when the adjustment is expected to end. If the adjustment is expected to be permanent, the ending date should be "Plan End."

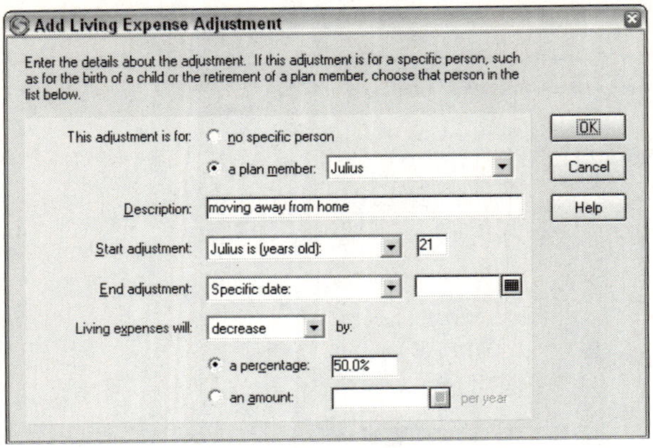

Figure 1-24: Living with change.

You can choose to increase or decrease living expenses by a specific amount or by a percentage.

Heading for college

If a family member plans on attending college, and you plan on paying for that college, you'd better plan on incorporating the costs into your financial plan. I've added a four-year college plan for the son in this sample family.

You can use the College Planner (described in the next chapter of this book) to get a handle on what your college costs are actually going to be, and then plug the numbers into the Add College Expense window in the financial planner (see Figure 1-25).

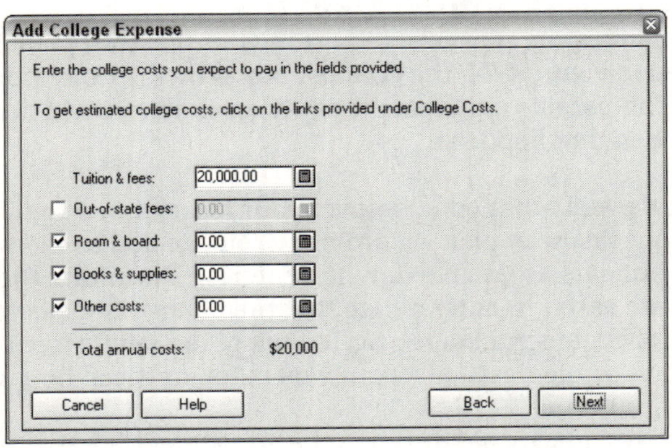

Figure 1-25: College-bound.

I estimated $20,000 per year for college costs for my imaginary child. Enter just one year of cost in the Add College Expense window — Quicken then calculates the full four-year college plan based on that annual amount.

On the next screen, you have an opportunity to enter anticipated scholarship, loan, and gift money as well as any portion that the student is expected to contribute (assuming the student is not you).

Then you have a chance to estimate the natural increase in costs that occurs with colleges each year. By default, Quicken has estimated a 3 percent increase each year. You can adjust that if you have a better idea of the rate at which your college expenses are going to increase (it seems the costs *never* decrease . . .).

Special expenses: Last but not least

There's one last category where you can enter other expenses that you didn't add in any of the other categories. Examples that are suggested in the financial planner include wedding expenses (or any big party like a 50th anniversary, for example) and vacation expenses.

Anything you can think of that is a measurable expense and that wasn't covered in the other categories should be added here, with the date the expense is supposed to begin, the duration of the expense, and the amount of the expense.

The plan, unveiled

The next step in your financial plan is to look at the plan results. Quicken starts by giving you a red or green light to indicate if your plan succeeds or fails. If the plan fails, it's time for you to get back into the various screens, and start making some adjustments that you can live with.

Before you get all excited (either positively or negatively), continue to the next plan screen to check for problems. A list of issues appears, describing areas of concern, flat-out mistakes like dates that don't make sense, hints, and reminders about areas you might want to examine more closely.

Take some time with the problems list, correcting any errors, fine-tuning the plan information, and making sure the numbers you are working with are truly legitimate. If your plan still fails, obviously you need another plan. Maybe more frugal living is necessary, a second job, retiring later, or continuing with a part-time job into retirement. Whatever the cure, isn't it great that you have some time to plan and figure out how to solve the problems now?

When you examine your plan, you'll see an Explore What If's button (see Figure 1-26). There's also a What If menu choice on the left side of your screen, and another button out on the main Planning Center screen.

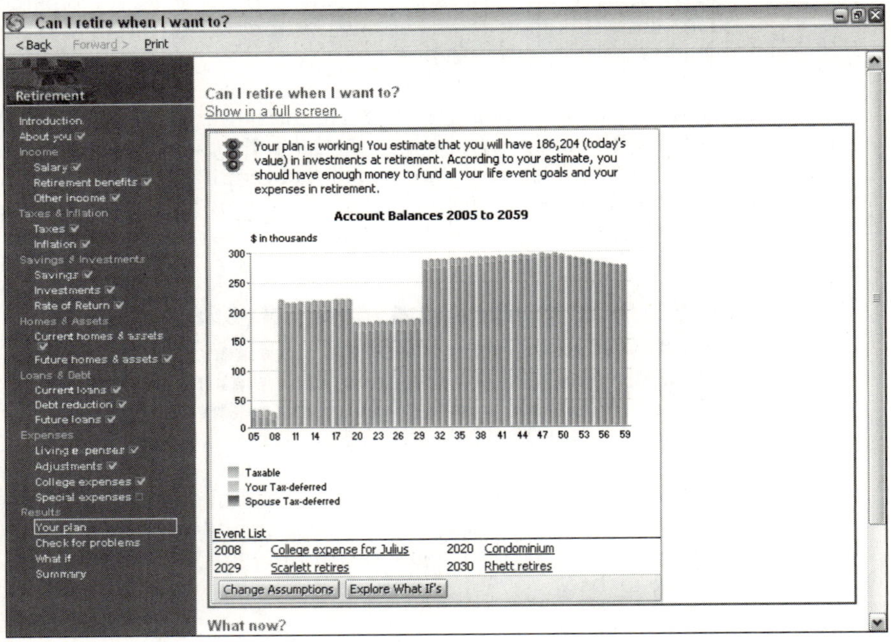

Figure 1-26: Wheee! My plan succeeds!

Choosing What If gives you a view of your plan along with several What-If questions you can consider to help bring your plan into line, such as what if you change your retirement age, what if you sell your home, what if you live longer, and so on.

Clicking any one of the what-if questions takes you immediately to the window where you can alter the entries associated with that what if.

The other alternative for dealing with a financial planning dilemma is to go down the list of assumptions (visible when you open the What If window, or visible on the main page of the Planning Center). Click any assumption to get back into the Financial Plan screens where that assumption's entries were made. You can see what you entered and also consider other options you might not have considered the first time around.

Living with your plan

Keep your financial plan by your side and refer to it often — it's easy to do with Quicken because from now on you'll be confronted with the plan each time you open the Planning Center in Quicken. When a major event (or even a minor event) in your life changes, or when the stock market improves, or you get a raise, you change your living arrangements, or whatever, get back into the Financial Planner and enter the change.

Then take a few minutes to examine the plan itself, the chart, and the Check for Problems list to see how your changes affect the rest of your planning ideas. If there are problems, try to figure out what is causing the problems and how they can be solved. A financial plan problem doesn't have to be solved overnight. But developing a workable plan for solving the problem keeps you in control of your finances.

Making a lifelong financial plan a part of your frequent financial activities can only make you more savvy when it comes to earning, saving, and spending your money.

Chapter 2: Tracking Your Retirement Savings in Quicken

In This Chapter

- **Tracking 401(k) savings**
- **Tracking IRA savings**
- **Tracking retirement savings for the self-employed**
- **Keeping tabs on your Social Security**

You know as well as I do that you don't really *need* to keep track of your retirement savings. All this nonsense about 401(k) plans and IRA accounts and other methods of using numbers and letters to signify savings accounts is part of a great plot to keep accountants and IRS agents employed and off the streets at night. If we *really* needed to save money for retirement, the government or our parents or our school teachers or our bosses would have told us to start saving, right? Oh wait a minute. I think they *did* tell us to do that . . .

Watching Over Your 401(k)

The most popular retirement plan around, after Social Security, is the 401(k) plan. Most employers offer a 401(k) plan to their employees. Those plans sometimes include attractive matching programs whereby employees are rewarded for saving money in their 401(k) plans by having their employer make additional plan contributions.

You can choose not to keep an eye on your 401(k) plan, arguing that (a) your employer already prepares reports for you and tracks your investments so you don't have to, (b) it's too much trouble because the amounts are invested in different securities and with every paycheck the investment totals change, or (c) you'll get around to it someday but not today, thank you. And that's fine if that's the way you feel.

But this is *your* retirement I'm talking about: It's the money that's going to get you through the long years of sleeping late, watching *Seinfeld* reruns, and playing Sudoku. Don't you want to at least have an idea of how much money is going to be available for all that fun?

You can be a zealot about monitoring your 401(k) in Quicken, entering every paycheck's contribution into the appropriate funds, or you can let the plan administrator do that work for you and take on more of an observer's role. But no matter which approach you like, I strongly recommend you keep at least one eye on your money. It might seem like this is your employer's investment and your only involvement is filing the reports in a drawer each quarter, but that attitude is completely wrong. This is *your* investment, and you should be completely aware of how much is invested on your behalf, how much those investments are earning, and what kind of return you can expect when you start withdrawing money from the fund.

Basic rules for 401(k) plans

Each company has its own rules and stipulations about the 401(k) plan that is offered to employees, so one company's 401(k) plan is not the same as another plan. The rules set out here are general guidelines, but you should speak with the plan administrator at your company if you want to fully understand the characteristics of your company's plan.

That said, the 401(k) plan is a tax-deferred retirement plan in which you can contribute money that is excluded from your income tax in the year of the contribution. This gives you the double benefit of being able to save for your retirement and cut taxes at the same time. Your employer might offer a matching contribution plan, which means that the more you contribute, the more the company adds to the plan.

There's a limit to how much you can contribute to the plan, and that limit is a function of the whims of Congress combined with how much money you earn, and is subject to additional limits imposed by your employer. For 2006, the most you can contribute to a 401(k) plan is $15,000, but your employer might have other rules that lower that amount. Your employer can advise you how much you can actually contribute.

Contribute means that you agree to have a certain amount of money taken out of your pay and deposited in one or more investments that your company makes available to you for your 401(k) fund. Unlike the old-fashioned company pension plan, the 401(k) is *your* money, and it's there for you no matter what, unless of course you worked for Enron, but that's another story.

WARNING!

Actually Enron's *not* another story, and we should at least address that situation here. The problem with Enron's 401(k) plan was that employees were required to invest part of their 401(k) money into Enron company stock (all employer matching contributions were made only in company stock), and when the company went belly-up, well, so did the value of the stock and thus the 401(k) investments. The moral of this story is that a little diversification can save the day.

Back to the basic rules:

- ✦ Money you put in your 401(k) reduces your taxable income in the year of the contribution and thus reduces your income tax in that year as well.
- ✦ Earnings in the plan accumulate, without being taxed, until you remove the money from the plan. When you start withdrawing money, that is when the tax begins.
- ✦ As long as you work for the employer who administers the 401(k) plan, you can't withdraw the 401(k) money, except in the case of an emergency or by taking out a loan — these situations are described in the next sections.
- ✦ There is an annual limit of how much you can contribute to the plan. In addition to the statutory limit, there is an additional amount that taxpayers over age 50 can contribute. Contribution limits are a function of the statutory limit, an allowable percentage of your salary, and additional limits set by your employer.
- ✦ When you leave your job, the 401(k) plan is yours to take if you want it. In some circumstances, you can leave the money with your employer, roll it over to a new 401(k) plan with a different employer, or roll it over to an IRA that you control yourself.
- ✦ At any time, if you withdraw money from your 401(k) plan, the money is subject to federal income tax. Depending on where you live, the money might also be subject to state income tax. The exception to this rule is for money that is borrowed from the 401(k) plan.

401(k) and the IRS

The whole point of a 401(k) plan is to save money for retirement, so digging into the money before you retire kind of defeats the purpose of the plan. To discourage people from taking the money, the IRS imposes the hefty 10 percent penalty in addition to charging income tax on the total amount withdrawn.

- ✦ **When you turn age 59½**, the 401(k) money is yours to take without penalty. You can roll the money into an IRA and let the money continue to grow while deferring the tax on the earnings, or you can leave the money where it is and withdraw funds as you need them.
- ✦ **When you turn age 70½**, it's time to get serious about taking money out of your 401(k). The IRS, after all, has been waiting patiently to collect income tax on all of that money sitting in tax-deferred retirement funds. When you hit the magic age of 70½, you are required to begin withdrawing (and paying tax on) a minimum amount each year. The minimum withdrawal amount is determined based on your life expectancy, and your life expectancy is determined by the tables produced by the IRS (scary thought that the IRS is making bets on my life expectancy).

✦ **When you die,** any amounts remaining in your 401(k) plan are turned over to whomever you named as your beneficiary. That person can choose to leave the money in the plan for a certain number of years (there are more IRS tables to tell the beneficiary how long the plan can remain intact). Eventually, whenever the beneficiary takes the money out of the plan, taxes will be due.

REMEMBER

When you set up your 401(k) plan, you were probably required to name a beneficiary. You might have that 401(k) plan for 40 years or more — during that time period it's possible that you might change your mind about who is to inherit your money when you die. If you do have a change of heart, you need to contact the 401(k) plan administrator and change that beneficiary.

Taking money out of your 401(k) before retirement

The money in your 401(k) is your money, but the IRS attempts to discourage the temptation to withdraw this money by allowing you to defer the income tax on your investment.

Technically, as long as you are employed, you are not allowed to take the money out of your 401(k) plan. However, there are some exceptions to this rule. The IRS defines four hardship situations that justify withdrawing money from the 401(k). Note that if you take money from the plan, you are required to report that money as income on your tax return and pay income tax on the money. In addition, you are probably going to be liable for a 10 percent penalty on the early withdrawal of the money. But see "Skipping out on the 401(k) penalty" sidebar later for suggestions for how you can avoid this penalty.

The IRS defines these four circumstances as hardships worthy of a withdrawal from your 401(k) plan:

✦ **College tuition:** College costs, including tuition, fees, and room and board paid for yourself, your spouse, or your dependents qualifies as a hardship. You must provide documentation of the college fees in order to take the money out of your 401(k), and the fees must be due and payable to the college within 12 months of the date on which you withdraw the money.

✦ **Down payment on purchase of primary residence:** You can withdraw 401(k) money to use as a down payment on the purchase of a home that is to be your primary residence. You have to provide copies of the settlement papers showing the down payment amount, and you have to provide evidence of your inability to obtain financing elsewhere.

✦ **Medical expenses:** The expenses must be for yourself, your spouse, or your dependents, and they must be expenses that are not reimbursable by insurance. You must provide copies of the medical bills and evidence of the fact that they are not covered by insurance.

Skipping out on the 401(k) penalty

You can avoid the 10 percent penalty for early withdrawal from your 401(k) if one of these circumstances exists:

- You are paying medical bills that exceed 7.5 percent of your income.
- You are disabled (see your plan's definition of disabled before assuming you qualify).
- You are at least 56 years old.
- You are the spouse of the employee that owns the plan and you are getting a divorce.

- **Preventing foreclosure:** If your primary residence is under a threat of foreclosure or you are being threatened with eviction, you can take money from your 401(k) to keep the lien-holder at bay. You must provide evidence of the foreclosure or eviction proceedings.

You are not allowed to exercise the hardship options for taking money from your 401(k) if you are eligible to take a loan from the plan — instead, you must borrow from the plan. You also must have exhausted all other reasonable resources for borrowing or obtaining money before you can take the money from your 401(k). You also must sign a document attesting to your hardship need and your efforts to obtain financing elsewhere.

Borrowing from your 401(k): Danger, Will Robinson! Danger!

As the owner of a 401(k) plan, you might have the right to borrow money from the plan. The terms of the plan dictate the rights to borrowing, so read the material that you received when you signed up for the plan to find out if you can borrow money. If your plan does permit borrowing, there might be restrictions that you need to consider. Some plans only allow borrowing for the hardship scenarios listed in the previous section.

TIP

If you can't find the documentation that came with your 401(k) plan, you can always ask the plan administrator at your company what the borrowing options are.

There are positive and negative elements to borrowing from your 401(k) plan. Because the money is supposed to be protected and saved for your retirement, there are long-term planning issues to consider before taking money from the plan. Here's a quick look at both the upside and the downside of 401(k) borrowing.

Potential problems and other reasons not to borrow from your 401(k):

- ✦ You temporarily lose the earning power and the compounding power of the money that is removed from the fund.
- ✦ Depending on employer rules, you might lose the ability to continue making contributions while the loan is outstanding, and thus also lose any matching contributions that the employer would have made, and of course you lose the interest and compounding from those monies.
- ✦ If you miss a payment, if you're fired or decide to quit your job, or if the company shuts down, the plan administrator has the right to recall your loan in total, immediately and without warning.
- ✦ If you fail to repay loan, the money is subject to income tax and 10 percent penalty.
- ✦ The loan must be repaid within five years (there is an exception to this rule if the money is used for a home loan).

Advantages to borrowing from your 401(k):

- ✦ It's easy. There's no loan application, no waiting for approval. It's your money and you have the right to take it. If your plan permits loans, you can borrow up to 50 percent of your vested balance (up to a maximum of $50,000).
- ✦ Did I mention that 401(k) borrowing is easy? I mean *really* easy. You can probably request the money online, and then whammo! The check's in the mail.
- ✦ The interest rate is low. At least on the surface. When you figure in the loss of earning power and the loss of compounding power that you're giving up while the money is out of the 401(k) fund, the low interest rate might not be such a good deal.
- ✦ You've got up to five years to repay the loan (as long as you keep making timely monthly or quarterly payments), and longer if the money is used for a down payment on a home purchase.

Taking money out of your 401(k) is a costly decision. Just look at Table 2-1 below to see how a withdrawal or a loan from your 401(k) affects you in the long run.

Example: You're 40 years old. You have $40,000 saved in your 401(k). You're in the 25 percent marginal tax bracket. You decide you want to withdraw $15,000 to pay for your son's college costs. If you borrow the money, you will pay it back over five years. If you withdraw the money, you also withdraw enough to pay for the tax and penalty so that you still have $15,000 to pay for college. The monthly payments of $290 represent the minimum payment necessary for repayment of the loan, assuming a 6 percent interest rate. In the loan example, the first five years of payments go toward repaying the loan, and then monthly contributions of $290 continue after five years. In the withdraw and leave alone examples, the monthly payment amount of $290 continues for 10 years.

Table 2-1 The Hidden Cost of Withdrawing Money from Your 401(k)

	Borrow $15,000	*Withdraw $15,000*	*Leave the money in your 401(k)*
Original amount in 401(k)	$40,000	$40,000	$40,000
10 percent penalty for early withdrawal	$0	$2,308	$0
25 percent income tax paid on withdrawal	$0	$5,769	$0
Total amount withdrawn	$15,000	$23,077	$0
Remaining balance	$25,000	$16,923	$40,000
Monthly payments (loan repayments or plan contributions)	$290	$290	$290
Total savings after 10 years	$72,913	$52,531	$120,301
Total cost of choice after 10 years	$47,388	$67,770	$0

As you can see in the above table, borrowing $15,000 from your 401(k) cost you $47,300 over a period of 10 years; withdrawing $15,000 cost you $67,770. This is expensive money!

Leaving your job

When you leave your job, you need to think seriously about what you plan to do with your 401(k) plan. The temptation might be to cash out; indeed, if you're leaving your job without another job waiting in the wings, that temptation might be pretty irresistible.

Cashing out of your 401(k) plan before you reach the retirement age is an expensive venture, considering the income tax and the 10 percent penalty. Make sure you are fully informed of your 401(k) options when you leave your job before simply taking the money out of the plan. Here are some options to consider (your company might have additional options as well):

- Leave the money in the plan. Check with your employer to see if you can leave your money in the company plan. If your balance is high enough, the employer is required to let you continue to participate in the plan, even if you are no longer employed at that company.
- Roll over the entire balance of your 401(k) into an IRA that you manage yourself.
- Roll over the entire balance of your 401(k) into a 401(k) sponsored by your next employer.

- Take a portion of the 401(k) account balance out in cash, and roll over the remaining balance into an IRA or another employer-sponsored plan.
- Take the entire 401(k) balance in cash and pay the tax and penalty.

When you leave the job, you are given some paperwork and forms to fill out regarding the treatment of your 401(k) plan balance. Read the paperwork carefully, and discuss your options with the plan administrator to make sure you understand what the ramifications are.

Keeping track of your 401(k)

Typically, your 401(k) plan is arranged with a collection of mutual funds from which you can choose your investment mix. How you make that choice is totally up to you, but the more informed you are about the funds, by reading stock reports and keeping up on analyst comments, the easier it will be to choose. Also, the longer you are a participant in the funds, the more first-hand experience you will have and the more intelligently you should be able to judge the performance of your investments.

As I mentioned earlier, you can go the extra mile, as it were, and enter each of your paycheck 401(k) contributions in the funds that you track in Quicken, monitoring how each investment is split among the different funds and tracking how these funds are performing. But chances are, your 401(k) plan advisor is already doing this for you. Most 401(k) plans are accessible over the Internet, so you can go to the Web site as frequently as you like, log in, and see how your funds are doing.

You still need to account for the money somehow in Quicken, setting up a place where your 401(k) contributions are recorded. Here's how the initial setup of a 401(k) plan works:

1. **Start a new account in Quicken.**

   Press Ctrl+A to open the Account List, and then click Add Account to open the Quicken Account Setup window.

2. **Enter the name of the bank or brokerage or 401(k) plan administrator in the first field, and then click Next.**

   As soon as you begin typing, Quicken displays a list of all of the banks that have set up partner relationships to provide online access with Quicken. Choose from the list, or enter the name of your financial institution even if it does not appear on the list. If you want to take advantage of online updates to your 401(k) account, you must place your investments with a Quicken partner.

3. **Choose whether you want online or manual setup.**

If your financial institution does not provide automatic transfer of data to Quicken, you won't see this question. If automatic transfer is an option and you want Quicken to set up your account automatically by going online and transferring data from the financial institution you indicated in step 2, choose the online option. If you prefer to enter information about your 401(k) investments manually, choose the Manual option.

4. **Indicate that the plan is a 401(k) plan (see Figure 2-1).**

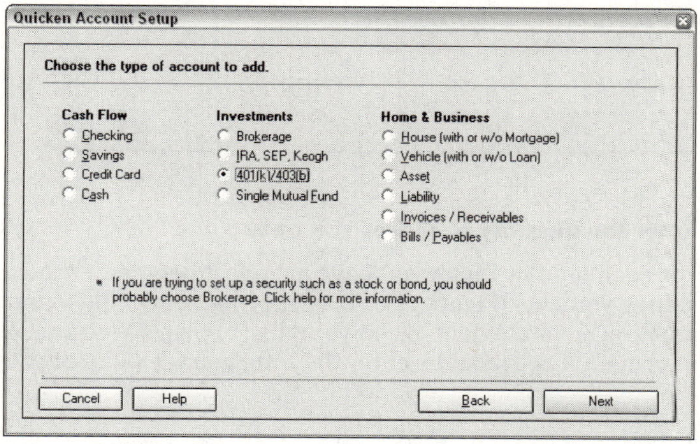

Figure 2-1: Choosing 401(k).

5. **Give the account a name to distinguish this account from any other account you've set up in Quicken, and then click Next.**
6. **Enter some more information about the account, such as the date of your last statement, the name of your employer, whether you are still employed by this employer, and whether your statement shows the number of shares of each fund you own (Figure 2-2), and then click Next.**
7. **If you have any loans against the account, enter Yes when asked, and then you will be asked to enter the original loan amount and the remaining balance. Click Next after filling in the loan fields.**
8. **Enter the name and the ticker symbol for each fund you have invested in.**

   If you don't know the ticker symbol, you can click the little Ticker Symbol Lookup button at the bottom of the list and enter the fund name. Quicken lets you know the ticker symbol. Information about the funds you've chosen for your investment is available on your 401(k) statement. Click Next after you've entered all your ticker symbols and Quicken accesses the Internet and determines the exact names of the funds that match those symbols.

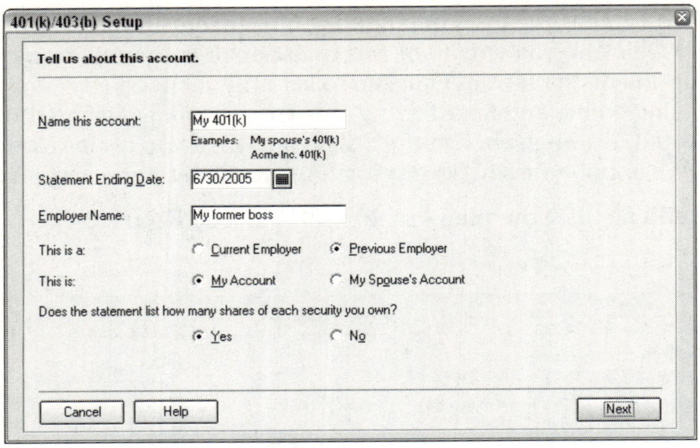

Figure 2-2: Questions, questions, questions!

9. **Enter the quantity of shares you own.**

   For each fund in which you have an investment, enter the number of shares you own (Figure 2-3). This information can be found on your most recent statement, or on your 401(k) plan's Web site. Also, if the information is available, enter the total market value of your investment.

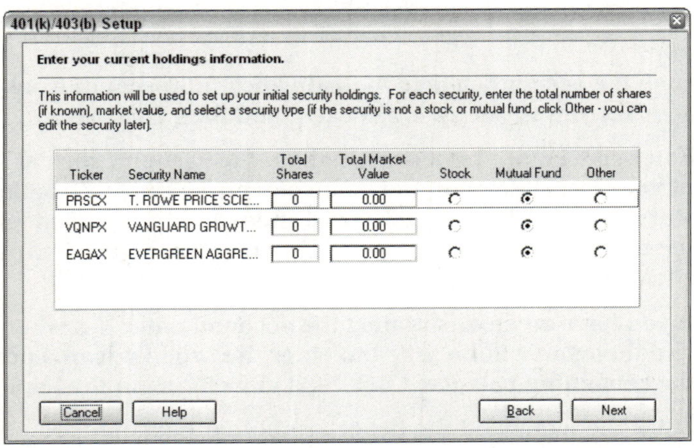

Figure 2-3: Enter your share holdings and their value.

10. **When you click Next, your account is included with your Quicken file and now becomes a part of your net worth.**

Updating your 401(k) information

You can set up your 401(k) account for automatic downloads if the financial institution or broker allows this type of transaction. See Book II, Chapter 5 for more information about setting up an account for online services. After you have established the online relationship, the 401(k) becomes part of your regular online update procedure.

If you don't have your 401(k) set up for online services within Quicken, you can easily update your Quicken account at any time by referring to your 401(k) account statement. In addition to providing paper statements, many 401(k) plans let you obtain account information from their Web site. Check with your plan administrator for access to Internet updates on your account.

To update your 401(k) account information by hand, follow these steps:

1. **Display your 401(k) account in Quicken.**

   Click on the account name over on the Account Bar at the left side of your screen, or press Ctrl+A and then double-click on the account name to display the screens that relate to this account.

2. **Display either the Summary or the Transactions tab for your 401(k) account, and then click the Update 401(k) Holdings button that appears at the top of the account screen.**

3. **Enter the date of your most recent statement, or the most recent viewing of your accounts online.**

4. **Answer the questions regarding the display of the number of shares on your statement and whether you took out a loan since your last statement.**

5. **Enter the amount of your own contributions, your employer matching contributions, and any other contributions made since your last statement, including loan repayments, or rollover amounts from another account (see Figure 2-4).**

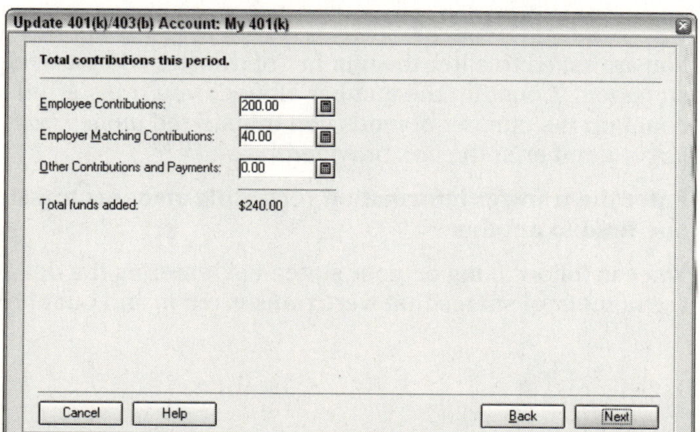

Figure 2-4: Enter your activity since your last statement.

6. **Enter withdrawals that have been made since your last statement, if any.**

7. **Enter any new securities that you've added since your last statement.**

   Quicken displays a list of the securities currently held in your 401(k) account (Figure 2-5). Click the Add New Security button to add additional securities to the list.

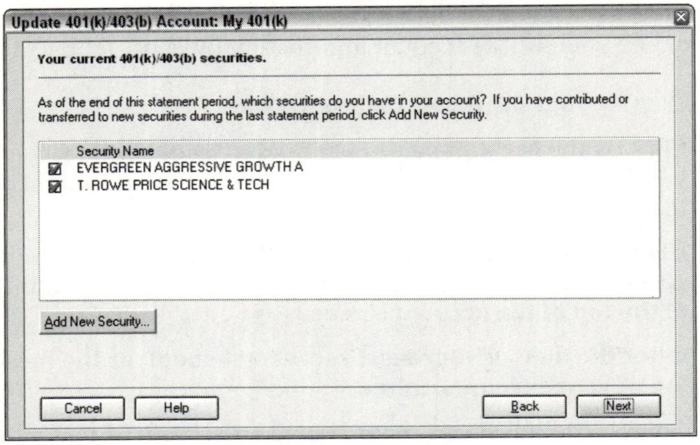

Figure 2-5: Click Add New Security if you added new securities since your last statement.

8. **Click Yes if you transferred money from one security to another (Figure 2-6).**

   A prudent 401(k) investor keeps tabs on the performance of the securities in the plan and moves money around when necessary. If your 401(k) has online access, it can be a simple matter to go to the plan administrator's Web site, see how the various funds are performing, and move money from one to another.

   You are asked to enter the number of transfers that are reflected on your statement. Count up the number of funds you transferred money *to*, and count up the number of funds you transferred money *from*, and enter the larger number in the box provided.

9. **Enter the transfer information regarding amounts transferred from one fund to another.**

   You can follow along on your statement, entering the dollar amount and the number of shares that were transferred in and out of the funds.

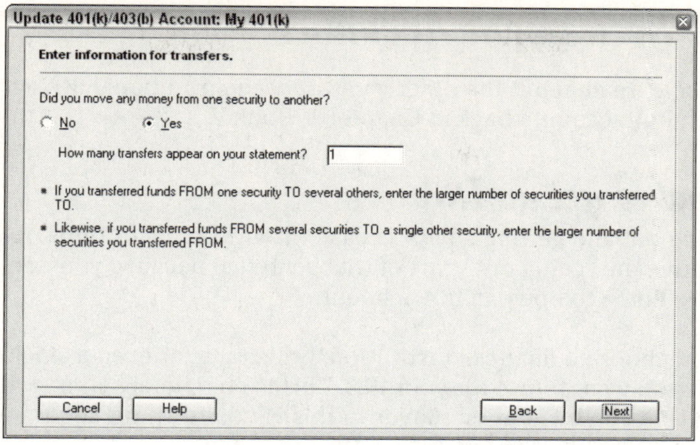

Figure 2-6: Say Yes if you changed your fund holdings since the last statement.

10. **Update your holdings.**

    Using your statement as a guide, enter the updated number of shares you own and the dollar amount of the market value of those shares (see Figure 2-7). Note that most mutual funds report share holdings out to the third decimal place. You should enter this detail in your Quicken account as well.

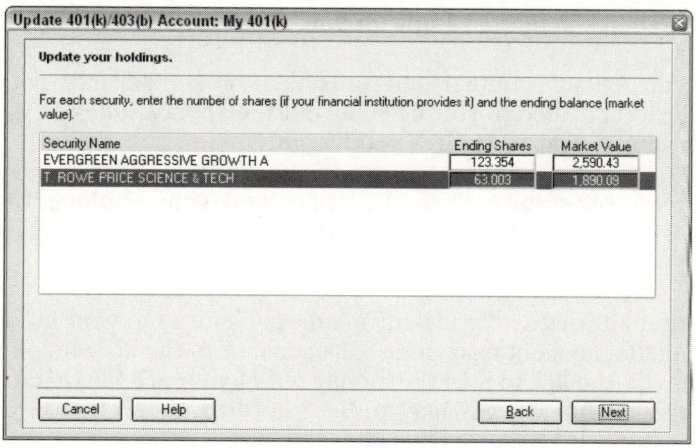

Figure 2-7: Enter your share holdings, out to the thousandth place.

11. **Verify that the information you entered agrees with your statement (click Back if you need to go back and make some changes), and then click Done to record the information in Quicken.**

Individual Retirement Accounts

You can read about the differences between traditional IRA accounts and Roth IRA accounts back in Chapter 1, Book V.

How to get an IRA

Going out and getting an IRA is easier than you might think. In fact, you can remove the "going out" part of that sentence because you don't even have to leave home to open an IRA account.

First, choose a financial institution, brokerage, or even a single mutual fund that you want to use for your IRA. This is completely your own choice. The IRA isn't run by your employer — this is your own personal savings account that just happens to get special tax treatment.

You can research mutual funds on the Internet at `www.morningstar.com` to read about the funds and get ratings. (Morningstar has a 5-star rating service that it applies to mutual funds, judging not only fund performance but such factors as diversification, qualifications of the management team, and more.)

If you want to manage your own account, mutual funds let you open an IRA by contacting the fund directly so you don't have to go through a broker. Many banks and brokerage houses also offer their own IRA funds, or will purchase shares in mutual funds for you.

You can contact a mutual fund (or bank or brokerage) and ask to have an IRA application mailed to you. Then fill out the application, sign it, and send it in with your check, and you're good to go.

TIP

After you've established an IRA, you can ask your employer to set up a direct deposit to your IRA, sending a portion of your paycheck directly to your IRA each pay period.

Another alternative for making mindless deposits to your IRA is to set up an automatic payment from your bank account to the IRA. In doing this, you authorize the IRA to take the money out of your account each month (or however frequently you like).

TIP

Or, instead of letting your employer or your IRA fund take the money, you can set up automatic payments in Quicken! That way, if you have an emergency and can't make the IRA deposit on a particular date, you can circumvent the automatic payment in your Quicken account.

Setting up your IRA in Quicken

Set your IRA account in Quicken so that you can monitor the growth and easily transfer money into your account. Here are the easy steps for setting up your IRA:

1. **Open the Account Setup window.**

   Press Ctrl+A to open the Account List, and then click the Add Account option at the top of the list. The Account Setup window appears.

2. **Enter the name of the bank or brokerage firm you use for your IRA, and then on the next screen, enter the information about that bank or broker.**

   If you have set up your IRA directly with a mutual fund, click the option indicating that the account is not held at a financial institution.

3. **Choose IRA, SEP, Keogh for the type of account (see Figure 2-8).**

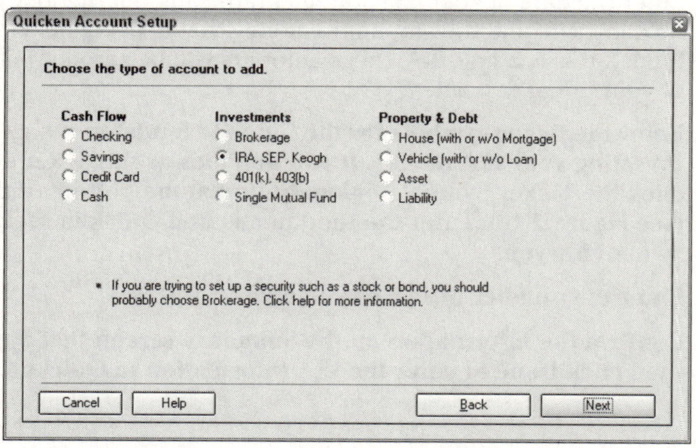

Figure 2-8: Indicate the type of account.

4. **Give the IRA a name.**

   Fluffy or Spot come to mind. Or you could call your IRA something sensible, like Gail's IRA, or Fidelity IRA. Just humor Quicken on this and give the account a name.

5. **Indicate who owns this IRA, and then choose the IRA type.**

   Click the drop-down list, as shown in Figure 2-9, and pick out which type of IRA you own. Most IRAs are traditional, meaning they qualify for deferred tax treatment and there is the possibility of making tax-deductible contributions. But maybe you have a Roth, or an Education IRA, or one of the others. Pick your IRA and move on.

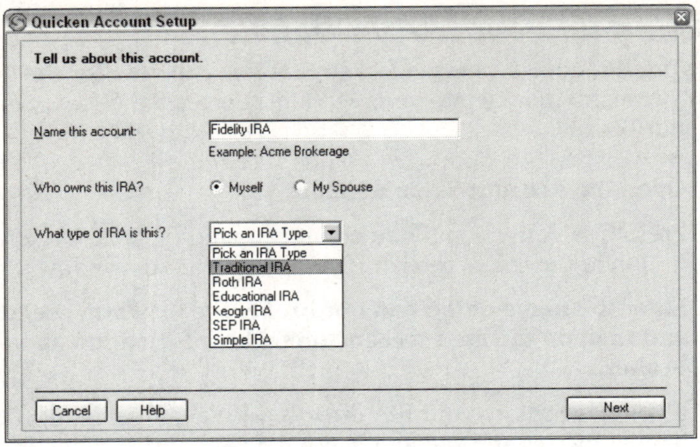

Figure 2-9: Pick the type of IRA from the drop-down list.

6. **Enter the statement information.**

   Enter the date of your last statement, the amount of money that is being held in cash, and the amount of money that is being held in a mutual fund. If this is a new IRA, these amounts will be zero, or just the amount of your initial deposit.

7. **Enter the ticker symbols for the fund (or funds) in which you're investing your IRA money. If you don't know the ticker symbol, click the Ticker Symbol Lookup button at the bottom of the screen (see Figure 2-10), enter the fund name, and Quicken seeks out the symbol for you.**

8. **Enter the number of shares you own.**

9. **Confirm the information on the Summary screen that appears, and then click Done to enter the IRA information in Quicken.**

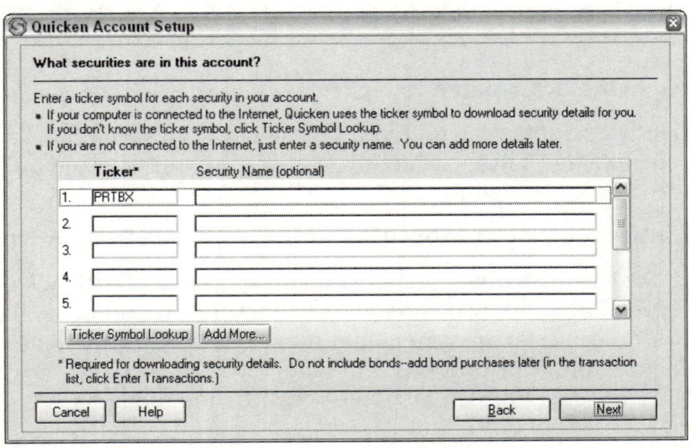

Figure 2-10: You can click the Ticker Symbol Lookup button, and Quicken searches for your fund's ticker symbol.

Making IRA contributions

When you make contributions to your IRA, enter the contribution in your bank account register, just as you would enter a bill payment. The Payee is the name of the fund that is receiving the cash, and the category is your IRA account. When you use your IRA account as the category, Quicken automatically enters a corresponding transaction in the register for your IRA account.

Timing your IRA contributions

Should you make your IRA contributions at the beginning of the year, or at the end of the year? The answer you get depends on what results you want to achieve. If you want to have your IRA money busy working for you, increasing as much as possible and taking advantage of that tax-deferral on the earnings, by all means, get your money into the IRA as early as possible. It just makes sense. The longer your money is in the account, the longer it has to increase in value.

TIP

Personally, I like to make IRA contributions monthly, a little at a time, instead of waiting until one point in the year and making the entire annual contribution all at once. The little-at-a-time method is easier on the budget, even it if does mean you relinquish use of some of your cash throughout the year.

On the other hand, if you need the use of that money during the year and want to wait until the end of the year to make your IRA contribution (or even until next spring — see the Remember below), it makes sense to hang on to the cash and use it as you need to during the year.

It's your call — determine your priorities for the money, either more earning power or more useful cash-on-hand — and then make your IRA deposits accordingly.

REMEMBER

You have until April 15 of the year after the tax year to make your IRA contributions and still get a deduction on your tax return. But waiting until next April 15 means you've lost more than a year of earning power on the money you could have contributed last year.

Taking money out of your IRA before you retire

The IRA is your money, so why can't you just take the money out and use it whenever you like? Technically, you can do just that. Unlike the 401(k), which has some pretty stringent restrictions on getting money out of the account, the IRA is your account, administered by you, and thus you make the rules, at least in terms of when you can take money out.

Just make sure you understand the consequences of pulling money out of your IRA before you write that check or request a withdrawal from your broker or from the mutual fund administrator.

- Any money withdrawn from your IRA is subject to income tax, to the extent that the money has not previously been taxed. All of the fund's earnings are in the category of having not been previously taxed. As for money you contributed to the fund, if you took a tax deduction for the contributions, that money has not yet been taxed and will be taxed when you withdraw it. If you didn't take a tax deduction when you contributed the money to the IRA, you don't have to pay tax on the money when it is withdrawn.
- Any money withdrawn from your IRA before you reach age 59½ is subject to a 10 percent early withdrawal penalty, in addition to the income tax, unless the money is used for one of the emergency situations listed below.

If you withdraw IRA money and you use that money specifically for one of these situations, you can avoid the 10 percent penalty for early withdrawal:

- Return of your IRA contribution in the same year you made the contribution.
- Medical expenditures that exceed 7.5 percent of your adjusted gross income.
- Medical insurance, if you are out of work and receiving unemployment compensation for at least 12 consecutive weeks.
- Higher education expenses, including tuition, books, fees, supplies, and equipment for you, your spouse, your child, or your grandchild attending post-secondary (that is, after high school) school.
- Costs associated with the purchase of a home, for first-time homebuyers only. These costs can include acquisition costs, settlement charges, and closing costs.

I don't know what planet the Congress was on when it made up the definition for "first-time homebuyers": In order to be considered a first-time homebuyer, you have to have not owned a principal residence for the past two years.

You can also take money out of your IRA for non-emergency use — you don't even have to have a reason. Just keep in mind that you pay federal income tax, maybe state income tax (depends on what state you live in), 10 percent early withdrawal penalty, plus you lose the earnings that that money would have accumulated in your IRA fund.

Taking money out of your IRA after you retire

This is what the IRA is really all about: Instead of dipping into the IRA whenever you get tight on cash, you're supposed to leave the money alone until you reach age 59½, when you can take the money out without having to pay that pesky penalty.

In fact, you can even leave the money in your IRA longer, until you reach age 70½, before you are actually required to start making withdrawals.

The first mandatory withdrawal from your IRA actually comes in the year after you turn 70½. Specifically, you are required to take your first withdrawal by April 1 of the year after the year in which you turn 70½. So if your 70th birthday is on August 1, 2006, you'll turn 70½ in 2007; therefore, your first mandatory IRA withdrawal must be made by April 1, 2008.

When you begin withdrawing from your IRA, you can choose between withdrawing the entire balance or receiving periodic distributions. You make this choice on the date on which your distributions begin. You do, however, still have the option of withdrawing your entire balance even after making periodic distributions.

The IRA mandatory withdrawal rules apply to traditional IRAs, not Roth IRAs. You are not required to ever withdraw the money from your Roth IRA.

As for figuring out your life expectancy, you might think you're going to live until you reach 110, but the IRS has different plans for you. The IRS publishes its life expectancy tables in Publication 590, Individual Retirement Arrangements. You can find this publication on the Internet at the IRS Web site, `www.irs.gov`, and the life expectancy tables are found in the back of the publication, under "It's about time we got our hands on the tax for all of this IRA money," or some similar title.

Here's the way the tables work: You find your age today, and then the IRS tells you how many years you have left to live (consider having a stiff drink or two before opening up these tables). You take the amount in your IRA account (or accounts — add them all together if you have more than one account), and divide by the number of years you have left to live, and that's the minimum amount of how much money you are supposed to withdraw each year from your IRA. Feel free to take more than the minimum — the more you withdraw, the more tax the IRS gets, and that makes the IRS very happy.

Calculating the minimum IRA distribution

Typically, an annual distribution from your IRA is determined by dividing the entire balance in all of your IRA accounts as of December 31 of the preceding year, by your remaining life expectancy.

Your required IRA distribution can be made in one annual withdrawal, or you can set up regular quarterly or monthly installments.

Social Security

Social Security, the nation's government-provided retirement welfare program, is available to anyone who worked for at least 10 years in his or her life. Depending on when you were born, you have to be somewhere from 65 years old to 67 years old before you are eligible to start receiving benefits.

You can actually start receiving benefits at age 62, but then you don't receive as much money as you do if you can hold on for a few more years until you get to 65–67 age bracket.

The amount you receive is not arbitrary — there are official tables where you can calculate your retirement benefit, or you can write to the Social Security Administration and ask for a statement of how much you've earned over the years and how much you can anticipate for your monthly benefit.

Go to the Social Security Administration's Web site to find the benefits calculators, at `www.ssa.gov/planners/calculators.htm`. Or you can fill out Form SSA-7004, Request for Social Security Statement, and mail the form to this address:

Social Security Administration
Wilkes-Barre Data Operations Center
P.O. Box 7004
Wilkes-Barre, PA 18767-7004

Download a copy of Form SSA-7004 at `www.ssa.gov/online/ssa-7004.html`.

What to do when it's time to start receiving benefits

When you think you're old, wise, or cantankerous enough to start receiving Social Security benefits, you can go to the Social Security Administration's Web site and access the application information online. Go to `www.socialsecurity.gov/applytoretire` to apply for benefits online.

Alternatively, you can call the SSA at 800-772-1213 and tell them that you're ready to apply for benefits.

Special rules for self-employed

Self-employed people have all the luck. Not only do they get to pay Social Security benefits like most of the rest of the nation's employees (except certain government workers and members of the clergy), but they also get to pay that much again because they don't have an employer to pay the extra share for them.

Employees who work at a job pay half of their Social Security, and the federal government requires their employers to pay the other half. It make sense, then, that if you're self-employed, there's no employer to pick up the slack with the other half of Social Security, so you get to pay the full amount yourself.

This is one of the great surprises that greet newly self-employed people who didn't do their tax research before going off on their own to launch a new business.

There is a silver lining (or at least a partially silver-tinted lining) for those self-employed individuals who have to fork over twice the Social Security tax. The IRS lets them take a deduction on their income tax return for one half of the Social Security tax paid. Just like a normal employer who gets to deduct his employees' Social Security tax on his business tax return, the self-employed person gets essentially the same treatment. It's not a great reduction in income tax, but it's a start.

Depending on your income level, your Social Security benefits might be taxable. It might not make sense at first, when you consider the fact that you pay tax on the Social Security money when the money gets withheld from your paycheck. But that's only half the story. Your employer pays for half of your Social Security benefits, and that money has not yet been taxed; therefore, the IRS wants you to pay tax on up to half of the benefits you receive.

There's a worksheet in the tax return instructions that you can use for figuring out how much of your Social Security income is going to be taxed. Here's a link to a copy of the instructions containing that worksheet:

`www.irs.gov/pub/irs-pdf/i1040.pdf`

TECHNICAL STUFF

The Social Security benefits you receive are based on the average monthly earnings during the 35 years in which you earned the most. Then a secret formula is applied to the average in order to come up with your actual earnings.

TECHNICAL STUFF

This Social Security information is all about you and the retirement benefits that you are eligible to receive based on your lifetime earnings. Other types of Social Security benefits such as survivor benefits and disability benefits are not addressed here.

Chapter 3: Savings Goals

In This Chapter

- Letting Quicken help you purchase that special something
- Setting a concrete savings goal
- Setting aside money
- Changing the goal
- Checking your progress and making that big withdrawal
- Removing the goal after you've reached it
- Using the Special Purchase Planner

Although some routine expenses come out of your monthly budget like clockwork and other large expenses like retirement seem miles away in the distance, another type of expense falls somewhere in between in terms of time and size. (Think of saving to buy a car or pay for a wedding.) Such special events — or special purpose expenses in Quicken's worldview — require dedicated savings, perhaps over a specified time frame. You could modify your overall budget for special savings goals, but Quicken offers other tools that help you more effectively zero in on and plan for a particular special savings goal. You can set up a savings goal and contribute toward that goal in the Savings Goals Planner, or you can use the Special Purchase Planner. This chapter shows you how either of these tools can help you set aside the dollars you need to make a major purchase or fund a major event.

Savings Goals and Why You Want Them

It may be true that you can't always get what you want, but you can get a heckuva lot closer to having the cash you need to pay for a car, a vacation, a computer, or anything else you want if you set aside money for the purchase on a routine basis.

Quicken includes the Savings Goals Planner to help you save a particular amount of money by a particular date. You create a savings goal in the Savings Goals Planner to specify the goal amount and date. You then make contributions to the goal using the Savings Goal Planner.

Although setting a goal may still seem like an abstract exercise, the Savings Goals Planner can help you punch up your savings performance in a few different ways:

- ✦ Financial and life coaches say that recording a goal is a powerful psychological tool in helping you target your actions to meet that goal. Setting up a savings goal in Quicken creates a real target that you can aim for.
- ✦ Quicken actually sets up a special asset account called a *savings goal account* to track your progress in reaching the savings goal. Although the savings goal account doesn't represent a real-life bank account, it does represent an area in Quicken where the funds you've contributed towards your savings goal are set aside.
- ✦ The ability to go back and track your progress towards a savings goal also motivates you to continue. When you see how far you've come, getting the rest of the way to your goal seems a whole lot easier.
- ✦ Based on the amount of time until the savings goal is to be reached, Quicken calculates how large your current monthly contribution needs to be if you want to get there in time. This specific guidance helps you contribute enough, or ramp up your contributions if you've fallen short earlier in your savings progress.
- ✦ Finally — and this is the big one — the Savings Goals Planner basically tricks you into reaching your savings goal. Each contribution you make towards the savings goal is recorded in the register as a transfer out of the cash flow (bank) account into the savings goal account. The money that was "transferred" really remains in the cash flow account, but the balance for the account factors in the transfers for the savings goal and is therefore lower. This helps you avoid spending dollars you've otherwise set aside for the savings goal.

TIP

You can still view the actual balance in the cash flow account as described in the later section called "Making Payments to Your Savings Goal."

Setting Up a Savings Goal

Like many of the other tools you've used so far in Quicken, the Savings Goals Planner appears in its own window. You can use the Savings Goals Planner to set up, contribute to, and view your progress toward as many savings goals as you need to pursue in your life. To create a savings goal, you need to know the amount you want to save and the date by which you need to save it.

In some cases, you may need to do a little research to come up with the target amount for the savings goal. For example, if you're saving to buy a car (hopefully a used car, if you're a prudent spender), you should do some research about how much the particular make/model/condition of the car you want costs. Similarly, if you're saving for a wedding or vacation, you have to price out the actual costs to have a realistic target rather than just picking a number out of the air.

Chapter 1 of this book discusses Quicken's various planners and how they can be used to help you determine how much something costs.

To open the Savings Goal Planner, choose Planning➪Savings Goals from the menu bar in the main Quicken window. The Savings Goals window opens onscreen as shown in Figure 3-1. Any previously created savings goals appear in the Goal Name list that fills up much of the window.

To set up a new savings goal, follow these steps:

1. **Open the Create New Savings Goal dialog box.**

   You've already opened the Savings Goals window. Now click the New choice at the top of the window, and the Create New Savings Goal dialog box appears.

2. **Enter a name for the savings goal in the Goal Name text box.**
3. **Enter the savings goal amount in the Goal Amount text box.**

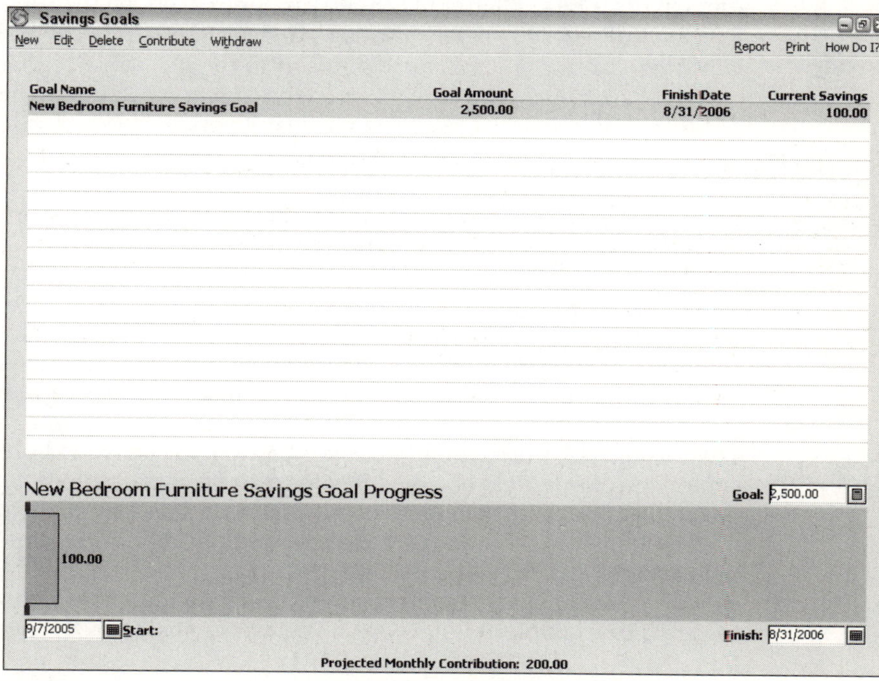

Figure 3-1: Create and manage multiple savings goals in the Savings Goals window.

4. **Enter the target date in the Finish Date text box.**

   Figure 3-2 shows example settings for a new savings goal.

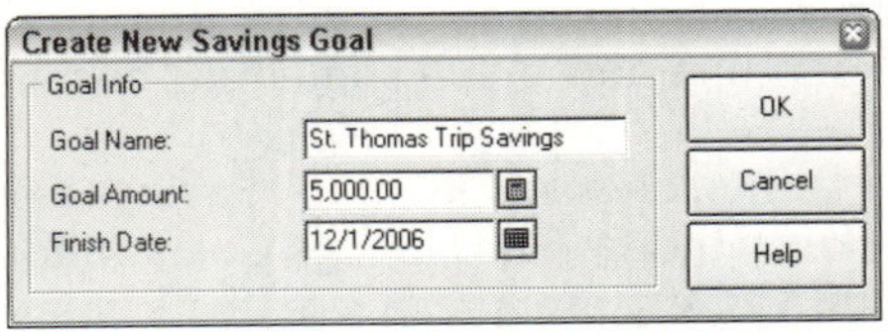

Figure 3-2: Specify a name, amount, and target date for your goal.

5. **When you've entered the goal information, click OK to add the goal to the Goal Name list in the Savings Goal Planner.**

   That's all there is to it!

REMEMBER: You can use the calculator button beside the Goal Amount text box or the calendar button beside the Finish Date text box to help you calculate or select your entry for either of those text boxes, respectively.

REMEMBER: As with in any Quicken window, to close the Savings Goals window, click the X in the upper-right corner of the window. To reopen the window at any later time, choose Planning⇨Savings Goals from the main Quicken window menu bar.

Making Payments to Your Savings Goal

When you want to set aside money towards a savings goal, you make a contribution to the savings goal in the Savings Goals Planner.

The schedule for allocating money towards your savings goal remains completely up to you. For purposes of helping you get to your goal on time, Quicken assumes that you will be making monthly contributions. But you can make contributions as infrequently or frequently as you want.

That being said, the savings goals work best if you strive to hold yourself to some type of schedule or frequency for making contributions. For example, if you like to set aside smaller contributions on a weekly basis to keep the motivational juices flowing, set aside some time every weekend to open the Savings Goal Planner and make your contribution. In other cases, your contributions might tie together more disciplined financial behavior to some reward. For example, if you've set up a savings goal to treat yourself to a spa visit as a reward for cutting back on pricey lattes, you could contribute $10 to your savings goal for every five lattes you skip.

TIP

Perhaps the easiest way to schedule contributions to your savings goal is to coordinate your contributions with the days on which you receive your paychecks.

When you're ready to make a contribution to your savings goal, all you need to know is the name of the savings goal and the account that holds the funds you want to apply to the goal. Then take these steps to make the contribution:

1. **Open the Savings Goals Planner window by choosing Planning⇨Savings Goals from the Quicken menu.**
2. **Click the savings goal towards which you want to make a contribution in the Goal Name list.**
3. **Click the Contribute choice near the top of the Savings Goals Planner window.**

   The Contribute To Goal dialog box appears, as shown in Figure 3-3.

Figure 3-3: Use this dialog box to set aside money towards a savings goal.

4. **Choose the account that has the funds to contribute (set aside) from the From Account drop-down list.**

   This is called the source account.
5. **Specify the contribution date in the Date text box.**
6. **If needed, edit the amount to contribute in the Amount text box.**

   TIP

   The value that automatically appears in the Amount text box represents the monthly contribution you need to make to reach your savings goal by the goal date.

   TIP

   Check the balance for the account you selected in step 4 at the bottom of the Contribute to Goal dialog box to ensure the account has enough funds to cover the contribution.

You can use the buttons beside the Date and Amount text boxes to calculate or find the desired amount or date entry.

7. **Click OK.**

   The Savings Goals Planner applies the contribution to the goal amount, creating a *transfer from* transaction in the source account that you specified in step 4. Jump ahead to the section called "Checking Out Your Progress" to see how to find out how you're doing in reaching your goal.

   If the Savings Goals window doesn't update automatically to reflect a contribution you just made, close and reopen the window.

   You can't undo savings goal contribution transactions. You have to go to the account register for the account from which the contribution funds were transferred and delete the transaction there manually.

Changing Savings Goals

As much as we would like life to be cut and dried, priorities and goals often shift or change entirely. For example, you might have to delay a vacation that you're saving for because of a change to a new job. Or, you might have to postpone a car purchase because your car insurance rate increased, even though there is the slight relief that the car you want to buy might cost a bit less if you wait a little longer.

The Savings Goals Planner enables you to change the amount and finish date for your savings goal. Working in the Savings Goals window, click the savings goal that you want to update in the list of goals, and then click Edit near the top of the window. Make the changes you want in the Edit Savings Goal dialog box (see Figure 3-4), and then click OK. The Goal Amount listed for the goal immediately changes in the list of goals.

Note: You can't rename a savings goal.

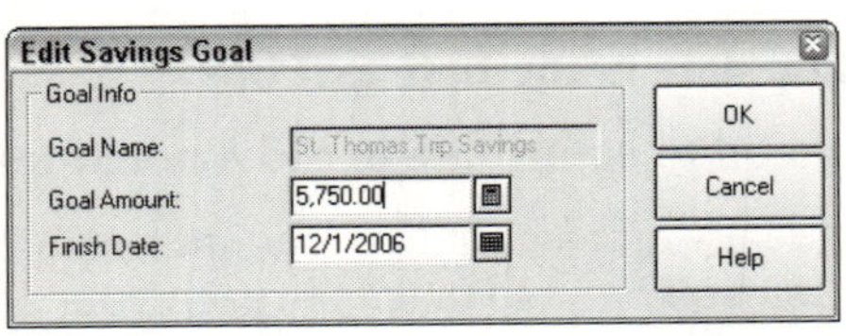

Figure 3-4: You can change the goal date and/or amount.

Checking Out Your Progress

After you've established any type of goal in life, you can step back and break out the manageable steps you must take to meet the goal. As you work toward the goal, you can check off each step you finish to document your progress and illustrate that you're moving toward success. Nothing motivates people like a strong sense of accomplishment.

If you need encouragement in meeting your savings goal, you can view your progress in the Savings Goals window. Click on the goal that you want to view in the list of goals, and the savings goal progress bar at the bottom of the window (Figure 3-5) illustrates how you're doing.

- ✦ The vertical red arrows mark the amount that you should have contributed as of the current date.
- ✦ The horizontal bar illustrates your actual contributions toward the goal to date, as follows:
  - If the bar is yellow and it stops before the red arrows, the Savings Goal Planner is telling you that you're behind schedule with your contributions, and you need to step it up to meet your goal.

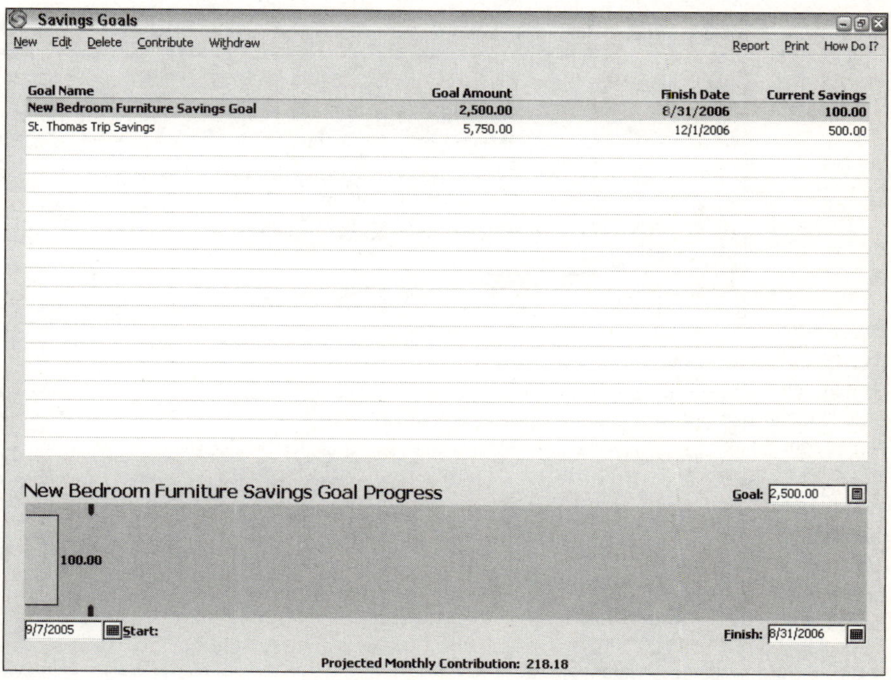

Figure 3-5: The savings goal progress bar illustrates whether you're meeting your goal.

- A green bar that extends beyond the red arrows tells you that you're ahead of schedule and should meet your goal as long as you continue to make at least the monthly contribution amount listed as the Projected Monthly Contribution at the bottom of the window.

If you want to look at the actual contribution transfers from the source (transfer from) account, open that account in the register. As illustrated in Figure 3-6, the savings goal name appears as the category name for the transfer transactions. If you want to change or delete the transfer transaction, you have to do so here in the parent (source) account for the transfer transaction. Edit or delete the transaction just as you would any other transaction, as described in the sidebar elsewhere in this chapter, "Deleting register transactions."

To see the full value of the account that you used to fund your contributions (rather than its value less the contribution amounts), you have to hide the savings goal contribution transactions. To hide those transactions, click the View button above the register, and click Hide Savings Goals, as shown in Figure 3-7. Quicken hides the transfer transactions and updates the Ending Balance amount so that it now includes the dollar values of the hidden transactions. Choose View⇨Hide Savings Goals again to redisplay the transfer transactions and ratchet the Ending Balance back downward to reflect the dollars you've set aside.

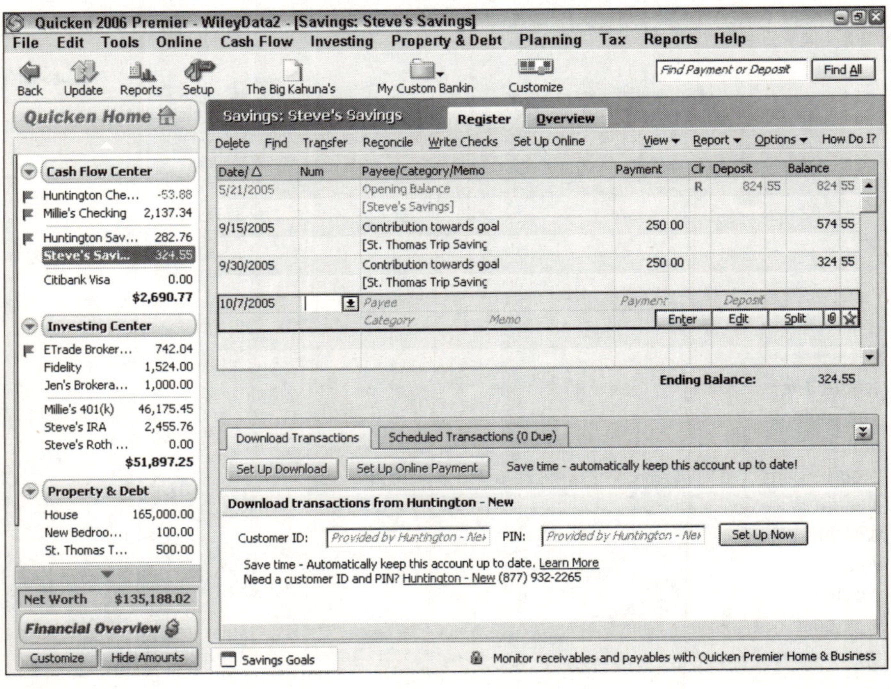

Figure 3-6: The account from which you made your contribution holds a transfer transaction for each contribution.

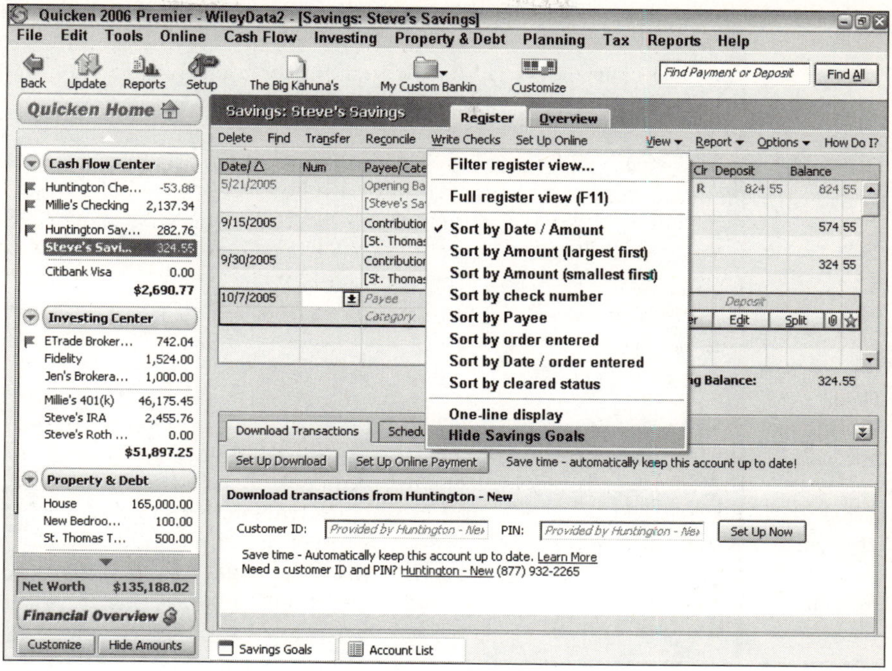

Figure 3-7: View and hide savings goal transactions via the View menu for the Register tab.

If you want, you can view the register for the savings goal (asset) account to see all of the transactions (although you can't edit them there). To view the register, choose Tools➪Account List or press Ctrl+A. Scroll down to the Account List section titled Asset Accounts (under Property & Debt Accounts). As show in Figure 3-8, the Description column identifies each savings goal account in effect. You can double-click a listed account to open its related register.

Deleting register transactions

If you need to delete a transaction from your register, click on the transaction in the register and press Ctrl+D. A small window appears asking if you are sure you want to delete the current transaction. Click Yes, and the transaction is gone.

Voiding transactions is often preferable to deleting. If you void the transaction, evidence of the transaction remains in the register. So when reconciling a bank account, for example, a voided check number (without the amount) still appears and can be cleared in the reconciliation. With a deletion, the transaction disappears completely from the register, useful for transactions that are simply mistakes, but frustrating for transactions that ought to be recorded as voids.

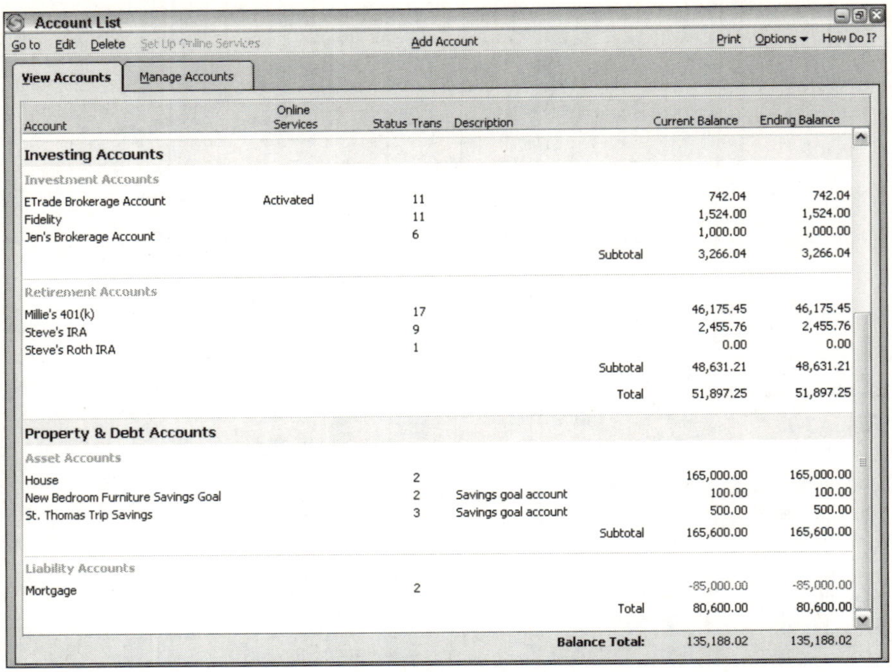

Figure 3-8: Savings goal accounts appear as asset accounts in the Account List.

TIP

You also can double-click a savings goal in the Savings Goals window to view a QuickZoom report of the contribution transactions. Chapter 2 of Book VII explains the type of report that appears, called a QuickZoom report, and gives details about how to work with reports.

Making a Withdrawal from a Savings Goal

Making a withdrawal from your savings goal basically works as the reverse of making a contribution. When you enter the withdrawal, the Savings Goal Planner transfers money from the savings goal asset account back to the account from which you made contributions. This “frees up” those dollars, so that you can enter expense transactions in the register as you spend the money on your goal trip/event/purchase/and so on in real life.

Ideally, you won’t make withdrawal transactions until you’ve met your goal. However, the Savings Goal Planner enables you to maintain the control you need to manage your overall financial picture. If you unexpectedly have to fork out money for a car repair, the Savings Goal Planner has to help you work around the reality of that unexpected expense. If you make a withdrawal from a savings goal, the Savings Goal Planner simply recalculates your progress and the monthly contributions you need to make to achieve your goal.

When you need to make a withdrawal from a savings goal, open the Savings Goals window (choose Planning➪Savings Goals from the Quicken menu) and click the goal in the list. Click the Withdraw choice at the top of the window. Make sure a source account (an account from which you made a contribution) is selected from the Put Funds Back into Account drop-down list, and then specify the withdrawal Date and Amount (Figure 3-9) in those fields. Click OK to finish the withdrawal. Quicken records the withdrawal transfer transaction in both the savings goal account and source cash flow account registers.

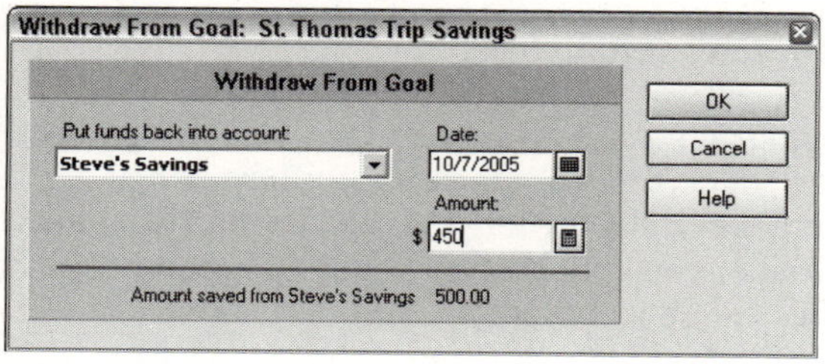

Figure 3-9: Withdraw amounts as needed from the savings goal.

As you might imagine, Quicken won't let you withdraw more money than you've contributed to the savings goal, and won't let you apply a withdrawal that's larger than an amount you've contributed from a particular account.

To undo the withdrawal, go to the register for the contribution account to which you "redeposited" (transferred) the withdrawn dollars, and delete the withdrawal (transfer) transaction.

Removing a Savings Goal

You can delete a savings goal from the Savings Goal Planner whether you've actually met the goal or not. If you've reached a goal and have withdrawn all the money or you've decided to allocate the dollars toward another financial purpose, you also can remove the goal. You can even delete a savings goal if you just decide you're not interested in funding that goal any more.

To delete a goal, follow these steps:

1. **Open the Savings Goals Planner window by choosing Planning➪Savings Goals.**
2. **Click the goal to delete in the Goal Name list.**
3. **Click Delete at the top of the window.**

   The Delete Savings Goal dialog box shown in Figure 3-10 appears.

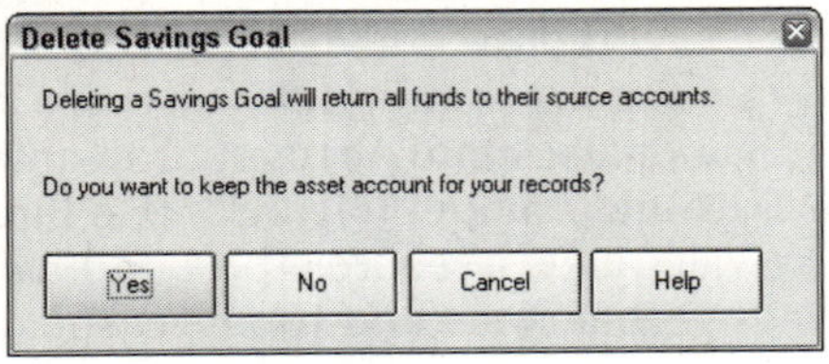

Figure 3-10: Confirm whether you want to keep the savings goal asset account.

4. Choose what you want to delete.

To remove the savings goal and keep the asset account and its transactions for the savings goal, click Yes. To remove both the savings goal and its transactions and account, click No. Either way, the Savings Goal Planner no longer lists the savings goal. If you change your mind altogether, you can stop the deletion by clicking the Cancel button.

Using the Special Purchase Planner

Although a savings goal might work well for you if you have a fair amount of discipline to review and contribute toward the goal on a regular basis, the Special Purchase Planner might be better if you need more of a kick in the pants to stick with a savings goal. Also, because the Special Purchase Planner works in conjunction with the Quicken Planning Center, you can see how your special savings goal fits in with your overall financial picture and other planning goals. This section gives the basics for working with the Special Purchase Planner. For more on working with other planners, see Chapter 1 of Book VI to get started, and then refer to Chapters 2 and 4 for more on working with other specific planners.

TIP

Specifically, the Special Purchase Planner pulls in information about any assumptions that you've entered in the Planning Center.

As when creating a regular savings goal, the Special Purchase Planner enables you to name the goal, specify how much you want to save, and set a target date for reaching the savings goal. The Special Purchase Planner goes a step further, however, enabling you to set up a recurring transaction to help you meet your goal.

You can set up a scheduled transaction to prompt you to follow through with your savings plan or even handle the savings for you. For example, you can set up a scheduled transaction to prompt you to transfer funds from a checking account to a savings account. Then, when Quicken reminds you of the transfer transaction, you can head on over to the ATM to get it done, or you can execute the transfer online with online banking or Quicken Bill Pay.

If your savings goal is particularly large ($50,000 for a home remodeling project, for example), the Special Purchase Planner's ability to help you automate your savings might make it the better choice for your planning needs.

To open the Special Purchase Planner window, follow these steps:

1. **Choose Planning⇨Special Purchase Planner, or click the Special Purchase Planner link in the Planners section of the Planning Center.**

   The Special Purchase Planner window (Figure 3-11) appears.

2. **To create the special purchase, click the Enter link in the description in the right pane of the Special Purchase Planner window.**

   The Add Special Purchase dialog box opens.

3. **Click one of the This Expense Is For option buttons to specify who the purchase is for.**

   If you click a plan member, you can use the accompanying drop-down list to choose or add a dependent.

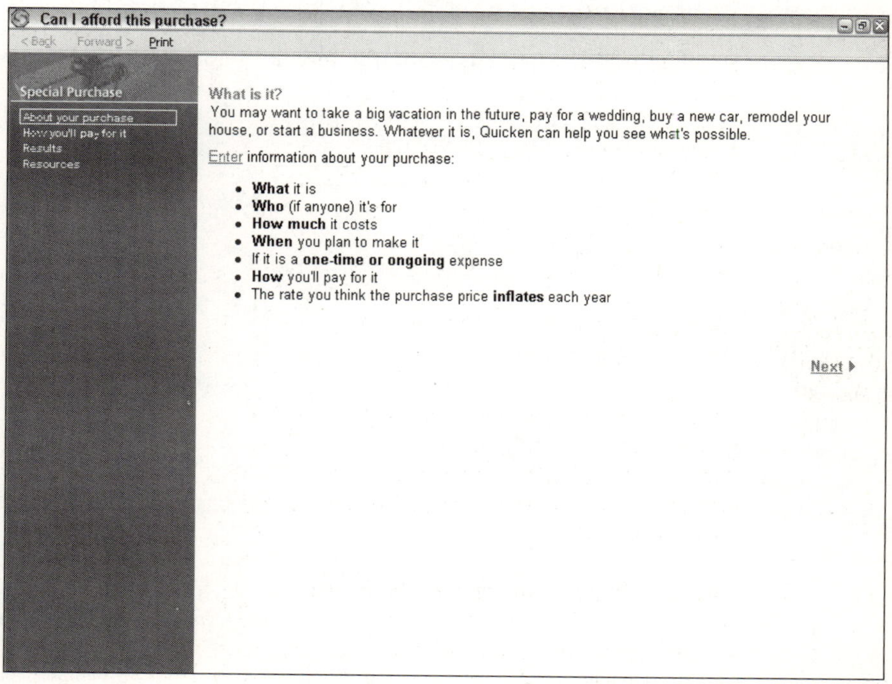

Figure 3-11: Meet the Special Purchase Planner.

4. **Enter a label for the special purchase in the Name or Description text box (Figure 3-12).**

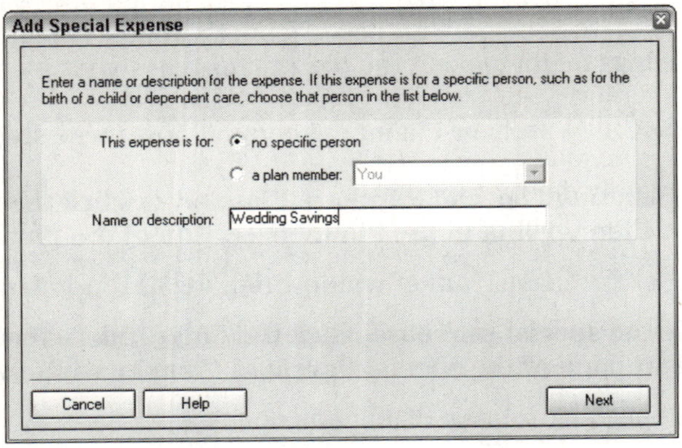

Figure 3-12: Entering a name for the special purchase.

5. **After you enter the basic information, click Next.**
6. **In the Add Special Expense dialog box that appears, specify the Start of Expense, Duration of Expense (whether it's a one-time thing like a wedding or a multiple-year thing paying off an expensive item, like furniture), and the Expense Amount. Click Next.**

   Figure 3-13 shows an example of what your entries might look like.

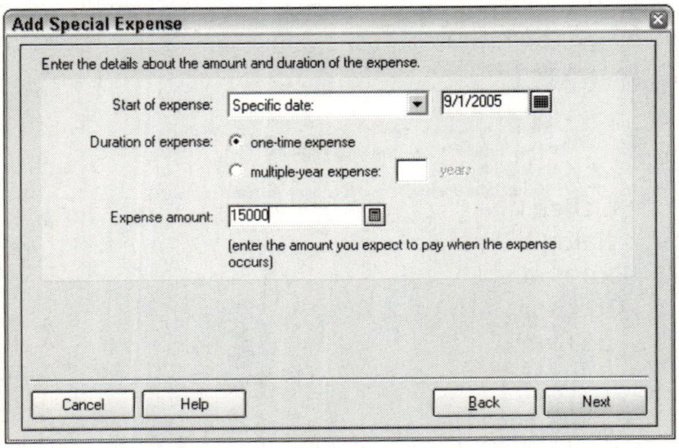

Figure 3-13: Specify when and by how much the special purchase will hit your pocketbook.

7. **Specify the source for the funding.**

The next Add Special Expense dialog box enables you to specify various sources to fund the savings. If you want to choose specific cash flow accounts to fund the savings or if you've already set aside some money, click the Choose Accounts button. Then click the Specific accounts option button in the Choose Funding Accounts dialog box that appears, and click the accounts to use in the list that appears. Or, leave the General expenses option button selected, and then enter a value in the Amount Saved Towards Expense text box. If you plan to borrow money to get to your goal, enter the loan amount in the Amount from Loans text box. If you have a monthly amount to save in mind, enter it in the Monthly Savings Target text box (Figure 3-14).

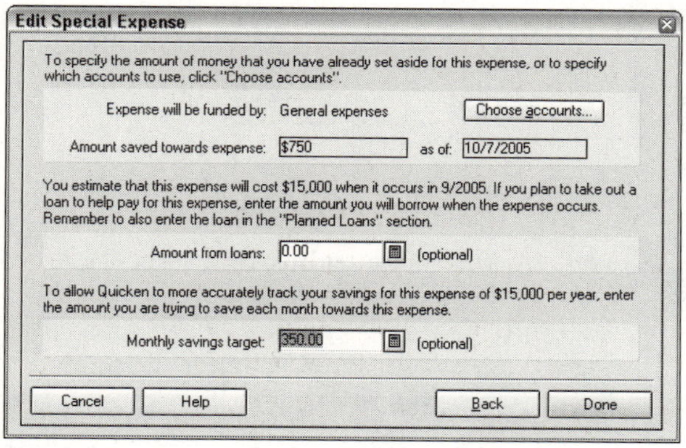

Figure 3-14: The Special Purchase Planner expects you to specify funding sources to help you meet your savings goal.

8. **Click Done, and the savings goal appears in the Special Expense list (Figure 3-15) in the Special Purchase Planner.**

9. **Click Next, and the Special Purchase Planner asks how you will pay for it.**

   In this screen, click the Schedule link to open the Create Scheduled Transaction dialog box so that you can create one or more scheduled transactions for contributing toward your goal. (See Chapter 2 of Book II to learn how to create scheduled transactions.) Or, click the Future Loan link to open the Quicken Planner: Planned Loans window, where you can click the New button to enter information about a new planned loan.

10. **After you've added any scheduled transactions or loans, clicking Next in the Special Purchase Planner or clicking Results in the list at the left displays a screen for working with Quicken Planner assumptions (Figure 3-16).**

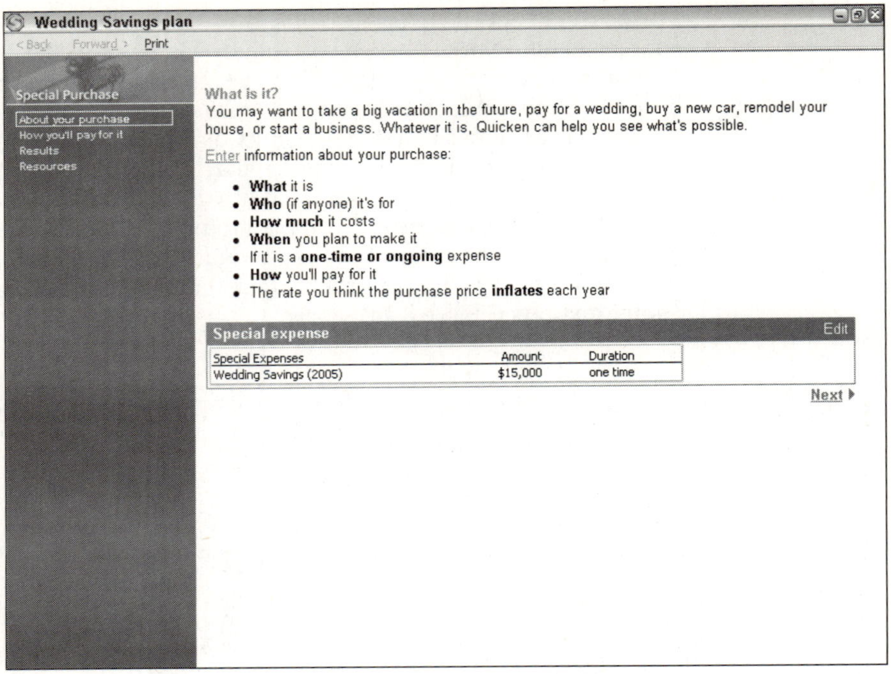

Figure 3-15: The Special Purchase Planner lists the special expense savings goals that you create.

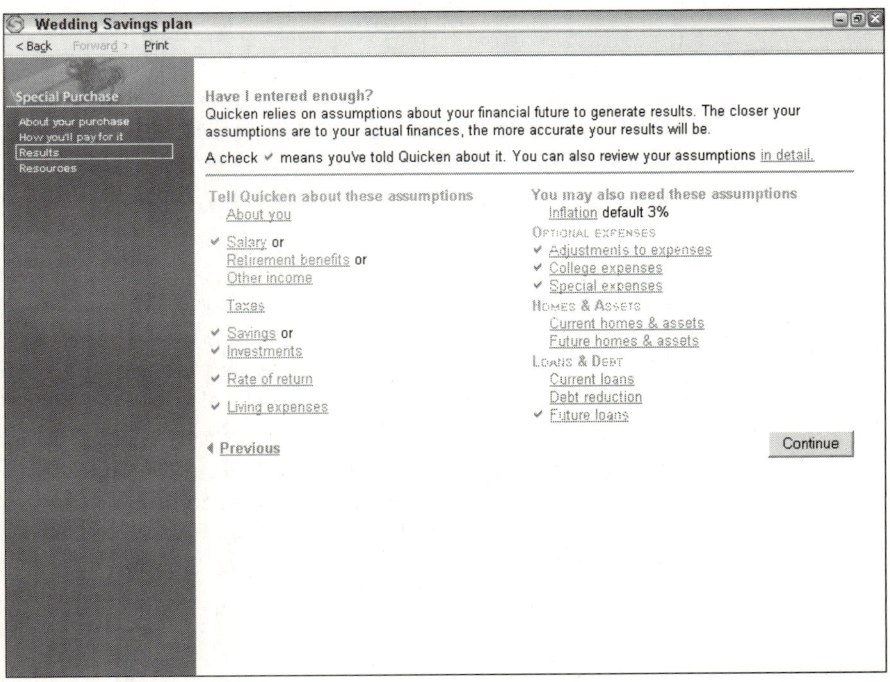

Figure 3-16: Click around here to view information about planning assumptions and special expenses that you've entered.

A checkmark appears beside the Special Expenses link under Optional Expenses, indicating that you have indeed created one or more special expenses and can click that link to open a dialog box listing those special expenses. (Edit, create, or delete special expenses in that dialog box.) Other links with a checkmark represent assumptions for which you've already entered information. To enter information about any other assumption, click its link.

TIP

Click the Resource link in the pane at the left to view links to online planning resources.

11. **When you've finished working in the Special Purchase Planner, click its X button to close the window.**

TIP

After you've added a special purchase plan, you can choose Planning➪Special Purchase Plans, and then click the plan name to start working with it in the Special Purchase Planner.

Chapter 4: Saving for College

In This Chapter

- Using the College Planner
- Making investment choices for college savings
- Tracking your 529 plan in Quicken
- Tracking your education IRA(s) in Quicken

Each family handles the cost of college education differently. Some families rely on loans and other forms of school-provided financial aid. Some are lucky enough to receive scholarship money. Others put away money here and there over a period of several years, and still others just write checks. No matter how you choose to pay for college, you can account for the savings and the costs in your Quicken program.

How Much Does College Cost?

Before you decide how much to save for college, you must answer the bigger question: How much will it cost? You'll probably be surprised to find that the answer to that question is, "Not as much as you might think." But don't jump ahead quite yet. First, take a look at this breakdown of expenses you can anticipate.

- **Tuition:** This is the basic cost of going to school. Tuition pays for the classes that the school offers.
- **Books and fees:** Most classes require students to acquire books, and some classes also require added costs like lab fees and supplies.
- **Room and board:** If the student is leaving home to go to school, you will face the cost of dormitory room or apartment rent and food. If your student is moving to an apartment, you might also have to pay the cost of utilities and renter's insurance.
- **Transportation:** Don't forget the cost of getting to and from school at the beginning and end of the semester, and maybe in between for holidays and vacation time.

Estimating tuition

It's easy to determine the cost of these pieces in today's dollars. The estimating part comes in the form of guessing what everything is going to cost when today's infant heads out the door for college, 17 or 18 years from now. Here are a couple of ways you can try to zero in on the amount you need to save for college.

- **Using statistics:** According to FinAid, "The SmartStudent Guide to Financial Aid," located at `www.finaid.org` (Figure 4-1), you can expect tuition to increase approximately 8 percent per year. This percentage is based on research on college costs over the past 45 years. But that projection really doesn't matter. If you want to track college costs yourself, start with the tables shown on the FinAid Web site, and add your own information, over the next decade or so, to determine your own best estimate of college costs. Use published information that you can obtain from the Bureau of Labor Statistics, just like FinAid did, or better yet, keep checking back with FinAid and other college sites, for updates to college cost projections.

  TIP

  Using the 8 percent annual increase as a guide, one can expect college costs to double approximately every 9 years. Although that certainly has been the case over the past half a century, it's really difficult to believe that the cost of college for today's infants is going to be four times today's costs.

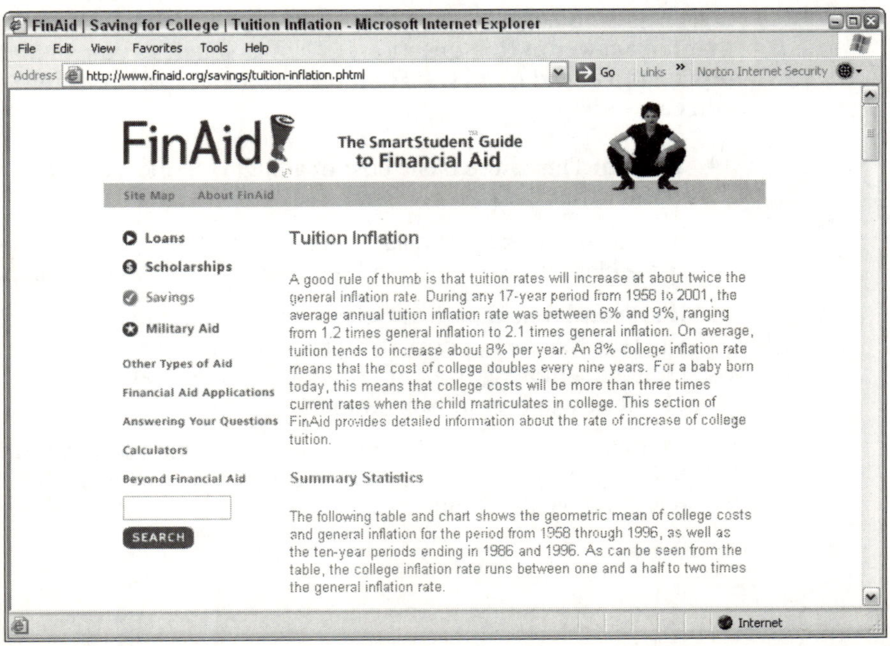

Figure 4-1: You can find college cost statistics on the Internet.

✦ **Using actual costs:** It's not difficult to find out how much college costs. Most colleges post their annual costs on their Web sites, and there are several books on the market that compare colleges and costs. If you have an idea where you think you want to send your child to college (or where you want to go yourself, if you're the student), check out the cost information for the specific schools that interest you. Dig a little deeper by calling some schools and asking for historical tuition and room/board information so you can draw your own chart of how much that school's costs increase each year.

Estimating room and board

When I went to college, I paid $100 per month to live in the dorm, and that included my food and limited maid service (vacuuming and laundering of bed sheets). Granted, that was a few years ago. But wow! What a significant change has occurred since I was a student! Last year, I paid $1,100 a month for my daughter's dorm (double room) and meal costs at a private college. The year before, I paid $800 a month for the same thing at a state university.

Once again, you can examine statistics for rising costs of room and board over a period of several years, and you can monitor the actual room and board costs at the various colleges that you think are possible choices for your child.

Estimating transportation costs

Transportation costs vary on a per student basis. Factors to consider include the distance between school and home, the frequency with which the student wants to come home, and the type of transportation necessary to get the student back and forth between home and school.

After you determine those factors, keep tabs on the cost of fuel and public transportation costs and consider car-pooling options.

For some families, transportation is a significant cost. For students who attend school close to home, transportation costs are negligible.

Estimating the cost of books and supplies

Book fees are usually a relatively small cost compared to the other costs of higher education, but this is definitely not a cost to overlook. Books can run from $500 to $1,000 per semester, and even more, depending on the type and quantity of courses the student is taking, and the availability of used books and book rentals.

College Web sites often provide an estimate of the typical cost of books for their students, and this is a good guide for planning purposes.

Great resource for college planning

You can take a lot of the headache, not to mention the debate, out of estimating the cost of a college education. Visit Salary.com's College Tuition Planner (see the following figure) where you can enter your child's age and the college of your choice to get a really cool estimate of how much the school will cost when your child is of college age. You'll also get another perspective on how much you should sock away for college.

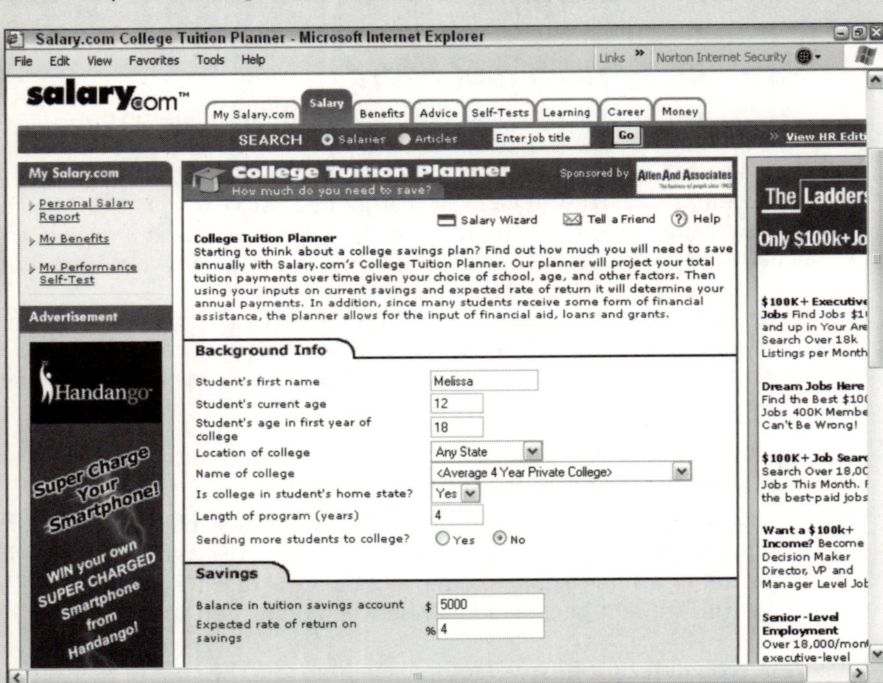

Consider incidental school supply costs as well, such as paper, pens and pencils, stapler, tape, paper clips, a planner or assignment book, folders, and so on.

College requires an investment in many other items as well. If you have more than one child, you'll learn to anticipate all of the college costs by the time you've sent two or three children to school. For the first child, incidental costs can be an eye-opener.

In addition to last-minute clothing items, your student may need (or want) larger items as well, including bedding, television, refrigerator, microwave, telephone, computer, printer, and so on. You might not need to acquire all of these things, and a roommate might help out by bringing some items. However, don't discount the possibility that these items might need to be added to your school planning list.

Using the College Planner

Quicken's College Planner provides you with a place where you can summarize everything you know about the projected cost and funding possibilities for the college education you are planning on purchasing. It only takes about five minutes to go through the planner, at least with some rough estimates — you can always come back later and fine-tune your entries with more accurate data.

Imagine the following sample scenario:

- ✦ Your child is 12 years old and you have not saved any money specifically for college.
- ✦ You intend to pay for your child to attend the state university in your home state. Should the child want to go to a different, more expensive school, you intend to have the child work and take out loans if necessary to pay for the difference.
- ✦ Based on information provided on the Web site of the state university, you know that, if your child were to go to college today, the tuition and fees for one year (two semesters) would break down as follows:
  - **Tuition:** $6,290 per semester
  - **Room and board:** $6,390
  - **Books:** $700
  - **Other mandatory campus fees:** $410
- ✦ You are willing to start saving now, and want Quicken to tell you how much you should save each month so that by the time your child finishes the fourth year of college, your payments will cover all of the costs.

Step-by-step through the College Planner

Using the information above, here's how to make your way through the College Planner:

1. **Open the College Planner.**

   Indeed — that will help a lot with this exercise! If your Planning Center screen is displayed in Quicken, you'll see the link to the College Planner over in the Planners section. Otherwise, click Planning on the Quicken menu and choose College Planner.

   If you've already played around with the College Planner, the menu option is a little different. Instead of choosing College Planner, you'll click on College Plans. From there, a side menu appears, showing you any plans you created previously, along with a choice to create a New College Plan. Pick the New College Plan and then we can continue.

   You can only plan for one child at a time with the planner. However, if you expect to have two family members in college at the same time, you can create separate plans for each family member, or just increase the amounts you enter in one college plan to accommodate two students.

2. **Click Next to move past the Welcome screen.**

   You should see the Welcome screen when you open the College Planner. If you don't, just click on Welcome over on the menu at the left, and then click Next to move on into the meat of the planner.

3. **Enter student data.**

   In a new college plan, no information is yet recorded about the student. Don't click Next yet — instead, click the Here link to open a data entry window. In the Personal Information window that appears (see Figure 4-2), enter the name of the student (click the This Expense Is For drop-down menu and choose a name from among those family members you've already introduced to Quicken, or pick <add dependent> to enter the name and birth date of another family member).

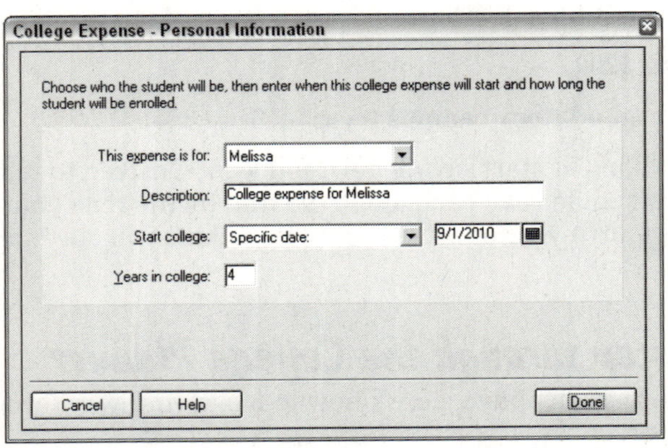

Figure 4-2: Enter personal information about the college student in your family.

You can use Quicken's description or enter whatever description you like, and then enter the date when you expect college payments to begin. In my example, I've indicated that I plan to begin paying for college in the fall of 2010. Also, be sure to indicate how many years you expect college to last. Some degree programs take five years. Some students graduate from high school with enough college credits to finish in three years. You must enter a whole number for the number of years in college. Click Done to complete the personal information window, and then Next to move ahead in the planner.

When entering information about when you expect the student to begin college, you might see a choice like, *Student name is (years old),* and then you can enter how old the child will be when college begins. If you've created a financial plan for your family, as described in Chapter 1 of this book, the creation of that plan triggers options like this one in the College Planner. If you haven't experimented with the financial plan yet, just enter the actual date when you expect college to begin.

4. **Enter college cost information.**

   Click the Here link when you're ready to enter the college cost information that you've gathered. The College Cost window appears (Figure 4-3). Remember, it's OK to estimate this information and come back later with updated amounts. Enter tuition, room and board, estimated book costs, and other expenses. Check the Out-of-State Fees box if your student is attending an out-of-state school. Other expenses can include transportation costs and the additional accoutrements of college living. As you can see when you click the Done button, Quicken multiplies the amount you entered by four (or however many years you said college would last) to come up with a preliminary cost for all the years of college.

   REMEMBER

   Be sure to enter just the costs for *one* year of college. Quicken can do the math to determine the cost of multiple years.

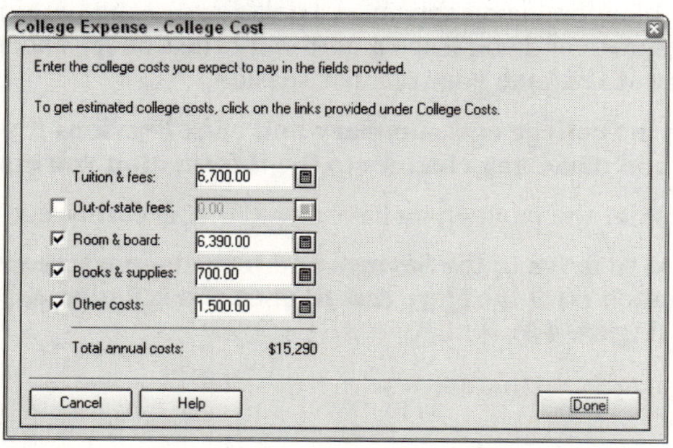

Figure 4-3: Enter your best estimate of what college costs today.

On any of the planner screens, you can click the Edit option to go back and make changes to your information.

5. **Enter student funding information.**

   On this screen, shown at Figure 4-4, you need to estimate how much money you expect to receive from grants and scholarships (financial aid), student loans, gifts, and how much you expect the student to contribute. Remember, these are per-year amounts as opposed to per-four-year amounts.

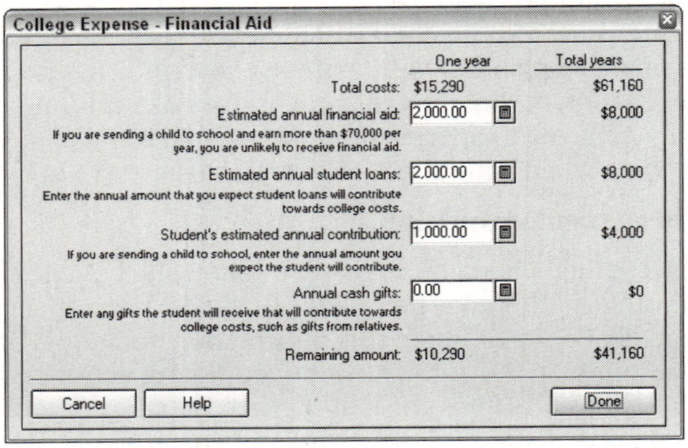

Figure 4-4: Estimate how much you expect to or hope to receive each year in funding.

Note that on the main College Planner screen, Quicken includes links to several different Internet pages that provide information about and resources for scholarships, grants, and student loans. Click any of these links to read more about these areas.

If you click out of the College Planner to explore the links provided by Quicken, and then close the Internet window you were viewing, it looks like your planner has disappeared. Look down at the bottom of the Quicken screen and you'll see a button for the College expenses. Click that button to resume your planner session.

6. **Examine the college cost summary and click Previous if you need to go back and make any changes to the information you entered.**

   Now consider the money you have saved that is earmarked for college.

7. **Click Next to move to the Savings and Investments screen of the planner, and then click the Here link to open the Inflation & Funding window (Figure 4-5).**

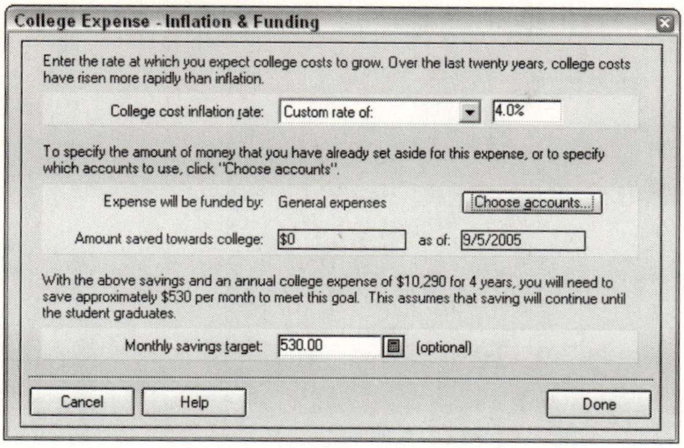

Figure 4-5: Enter your guess at college cost inflation, and then click Choose Accounts to proceed.

You are asked to enter an estimate of the rate at which you think inflation will affect college costs. This is clearly an estimate, but you don't have to pick a number out of thin air. Look at the Web sites for the college(s) you are considering. You might find some information there setting out the historical tuition and fees increases at that institution. That is how I chose the custom rate of 4 percent for my college cost inflation figure. Tuition and fees at the state university in my state have increased at an average annual rate of approximately 4 percent for the past several years.

The estimated inflation rate is an annual rate, not the total rate of increase you expect to see between now and the time your student goes to college.

8. **Click Choose Accounts to indicate where your share of the money is going to come from.**

   When you click the Choose Accounts button, the Choose Funding Accounts window appears (Figure 4-6). At the bottom of the window, enter the amount you've already put aside for college expenses. This can include amounts that you have sitting in an IRA or equity in your home, as well as savings and money market accounts. The amount you enter here should be cash you can readily access and that you fully intend to use for college. The remainder of the college expenses are going to be furnished from either your general expenses, meaning any account where you have money, or from specific accounts. Choose Specific Accounts if you want to only include certain accounts, or if you want to exclude certain accounts as sources for college funding. A list of all your accounts appears, and you can check off only the accounts that you plan to use for paying for college.

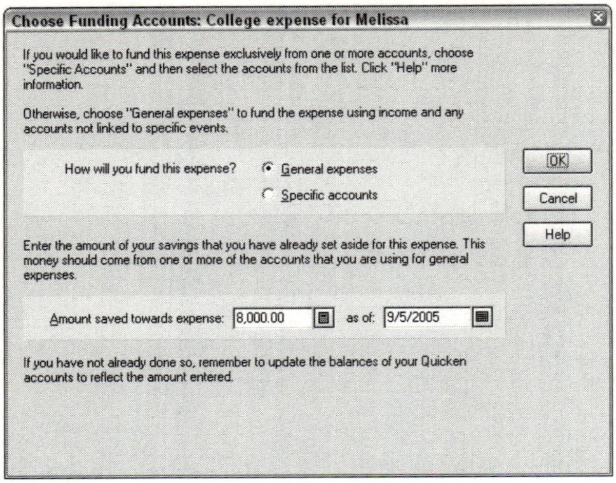

Figure 4-6: Time to let Quicken in on where you expect to get the money for college.

9. **Examine the bottom line.**

   After you enter the account information from step 8, Quicken presents you with its calculation of how much you need to put aside each month, starting now and going through all the years while your student is in college, so that you'll have enough money for college.

   On the Results screen, the college savings plan is incorporated into your larger personal financial plan in the form of an Account Balances chart. If you haven't created a personal financial plan yet, you see a list of financial subject areas where you can click to add more information. This is optional and only necessary if you want to incorporate the college expenses into a bigger all-encompassing financial picture.

10. **Click Summary on the menu at the left to see a final summary of all of the information you've entered, or click Internet Resources to find links to a variety of interesting info.**

    Using the Internet Resources links, you can find information about financial aid, scholarships, college loans, and college planning in general.

Saving (and finding) your projections

There's no need to take special steps to save your work in the College Planner. All of the information you entered is automatically saved. But the information is not where you might expect it to be. The next time you return to the College Planner, it will look like you've never been there before. Each time you start the College Planner, it returns to an empty shell. So where did your projection go?

Removing a college planning scenario

If you experiment with the College Planner and want to remove the scenario that you created, you can do so from the Results page in the College Planner in either of the following ways:

- If an Account Balances chart appears, click the Change Assumptions button that appears at the bottom of the page. Then click College Expenses from the menu at the left side of the screen. Click the Edit button that appears at the top of the page.
- If you don't have a financial plan chart, you can click College Expenses on the list of assumptions that appears.

With either method, the Quicken Planner: College Expenses window appears (see the following figure). Click on the description that you want to remove, and then click the Delete button. Click Yes when asked to confirm the deletion, and then Done to close the window.

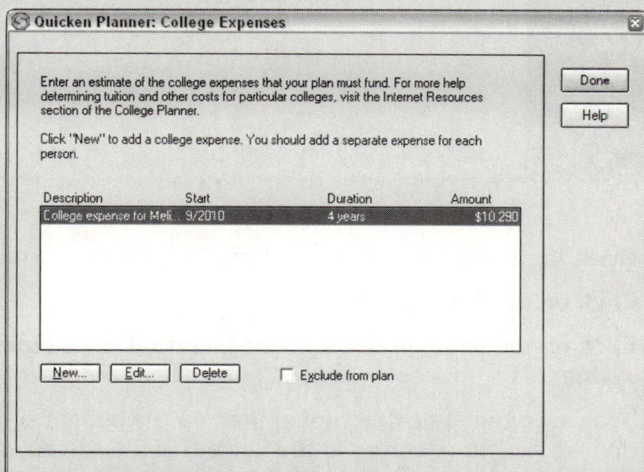

Open the Planning Center (Planning⇨Go to Planning Center), and you see your college expense plan waiting for you in the Plan: Results section, just a hyperlink away. Or, when you're in the College Planner, you can click on Results and see either a direct link to your college plan, or a link to College Expenses, which leads you to your plan (Figure 4-7).

Incorporating your college plan into your budget

After you've set up your budget, it's easy to incorporate expenses, including your college savings plan, into your budget. Here's how:

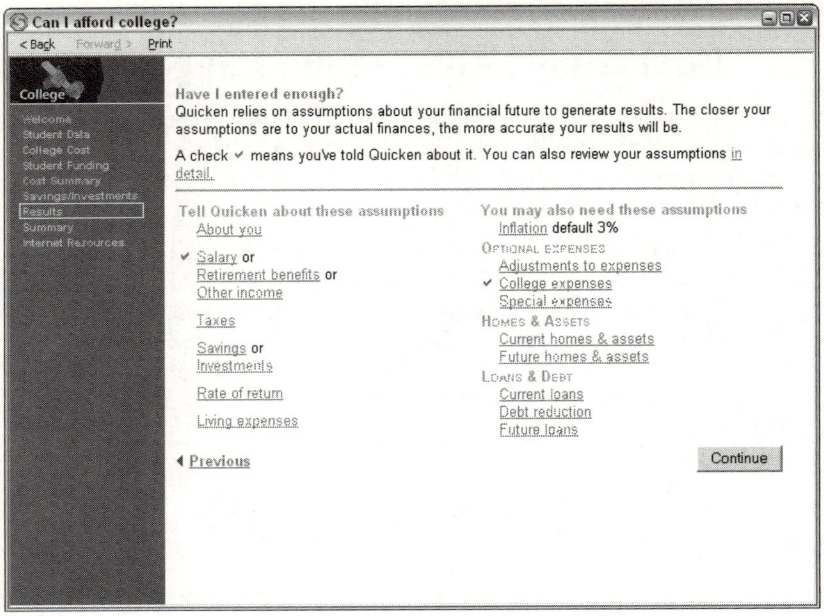

Figure 4-7: Click the College Expenses link in the right column to return to your college plan.

1. **Open the budget by choosing Planning⇨Budget from the menu.**
2. **Click on the Savings tab.**
3. **Click on the name of the account you want to use for your college savings.**

   If the account name does not appear on the budget screen, click the Choose Accounts button at the bottom of the screen, and then click on the account you want to use for your college savings. This might be a 529 account, a money market, or a savings account.
4. **On the right side of the budget screen, enter the amount you want to transfer each month (or quarter, or week, or whatever) to the college account, and indicate the frequency with which you want to make this transfer (see Figure 4-8).**
5. **Click the Apply button; otherwise, your amount won't be saved.**

   TIP: You can set up automatic transfers to your college savings account to ensure that the proper amount gets deposited.

   TIP: You'll find more information about setting up savings goals and automating your saving in Chapters 3 and 5 of this book.

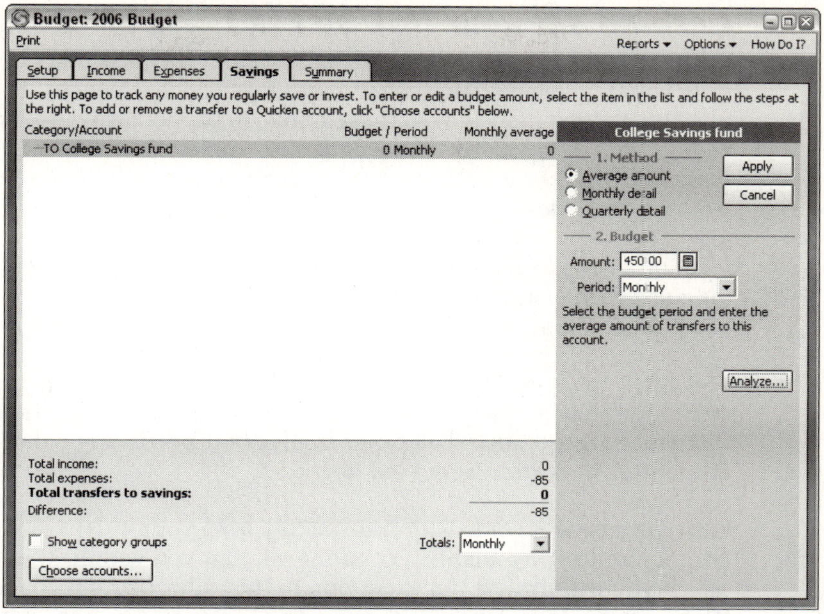

Figure 4-8: Setting up your budget for your college savings deposit.

Sources of Capital

No matter how young (or old) your child is, *now* is the time to start talking to school authorities about how to finance your child's education. Even if your child isn't in high school, you can schedule a session with the high school's college counselor. Go to college planning meetings in your community and start a dialog with financial aid people at the college where you think your child might want to attend.

Seek out information about scholarships and start thinking now about how your child can position himself to receive scholarship money — maybe by joining an organization, participating in athletics or arts, or working with community service organizations. Check with your employer and ask people you know who already have kids in college.

The high school counselor is a good source for scholarship information and can tell you what your child should do when he gets to high school to ensure the most money from colleges that offer merit scholarships. For example, the counselor might suggest that you explain to the student the importance of establishing a rapport with influential teachers because teacher recommendations are an important part of the application process. Also, your child should participate in some kind of school-sponsored or extra-curricular activity so that information can be included on the college application.

Cashing out your IRA/401(k)

Back in Chapter 2 of this book, we talked about the possibility of using money from your tax-deferred retirement funds for college expenses. The IRS makes it possible to take money from these funds, in particular your IRA, to pay for college. And although the money might be subject to income tax when you remove it from the fund, you can avoid paying a penalty on the money if it is used expressly for college costs.

You don't have to get anyone's permission to take the money out of your IRA for college expenses (except perhaps that little voice inside you that reminds you you're dipping into the money you were supposed to save for retirement).

The 401(k) plan is a different story. Remember, to take money out of your 401(k) for college, the cost has to be a bona fide hardship. You have to prove that you have exhausted all other avenues for borrowing money, including attempting to *borrow* from your 401(k).

WARNING! In situations where you withdraw money from your 401(k) or your IRA, you are required to pay income tax on the amount you withdraw, in the year in which you withdraw it. An exception to this rule occurs if you are withdrawing non-tax-deferred money from your IRA, meaning you are withdrawing money that you didn't take as a tax deduction when you contributed it to the IRA. The portion of the money you withdraw from your IRA that represents earnings on your investment will always be subject to income tax.

WARNING! If you decide to borrow money from your 401(k) account, remember the hidden costs associated with borrowing. Sometimes these costs are overshadowed by the ease of the loan and the low interest rate. See Table 2-1 in Chapter 2 of this book for an analysis of those hidden costs.

REMEMBER You cannot take a loan against your IRA money.

Home equity loan/line of credit

If you own a home, borrowing money against the equity in that home is one way to pay for college. If this is your long-range plan, be sure to monitor the value of your home over the years to make sure that the money will be there. Home values rise and fall with the marketplace, and that can affect your borrowing power. In addition, make sure you keep your credit rating up so that you can borrow without any problem.

Paying for a College Education with a 529 Plan

You can flip back to Chapter 5 of Book I for a complete description of 529 plans, what they are, how they work, and where you can go for more information. This is becoming one of the most popular methods of saving for college, particularly with families with young children. If your child is older and you only have a few years to save, the tax savings from the 529 might not be very significant.

Some states allow you to take a deduction on your state income tax return for the amount of money contributed to a 529 plan.

WARNING!

Some states don't let you create a 529 plan if your child is age 15 or older. And, some states are particularly nasty about taking money out of the plan for non-educational uses and assess an extra 10 percent penalty.

Hey, don't let one state's rules keep you from getting in on the 529 gold rush. You can participate in a 529 plan in any state: It doesn't matter if you live in that state or not, and it doesn't matter if the plan beneficiary goes to school in that state or not. So there!

TIP

If you're going to invest in a 529 plan, don't feel you have to pay the fee of a broker or financial advisor who can invest your money for you. You can go directly to the state plan to avoid fees and invest directly without a middleman.

WARNING!

Money earned in a 529 plan counts against you when it's time to calculate your eligibility for financial aid. This is one argument that financial advisors have against the 529 plans. For this reason, if you have substantial money available to invest long-term for college, it makes sense to seek the advice of a financial professional who can point you in the best direction for maximizing your earnings and keeping your financial aid options open.

Gifting stock: Not the bargain you might think

If you come from a stock-holding family, you might be planning on cashing in some of the stock you own to pay for your child's education. Although the stock might be an excellent source of ready cash, particularly if it's stock you are ready to sell anyway, don't think you're going to pull one over on the IRS by gifting the stock to your child so the child can sell the stock and use the proceeds for college.

If you gift stock that has appreciated in value, the cost basis (purchase price) of the stock transfers over to the recipient of the gift, meaning when the child sells that stock you bought for $20 a share that is now worth $150 a share, the child is going to have to pay tax on $130 per share, just like you would if you sold the stock yourself.

And it gets worse. If you gift stock on which you lost money (for example, that stock you bought for $50 a share that is now only worth $30 a share), the child's basis is the fair market value of the stock on the day of the gift, meaning the child won't get the tax benefit of that $20 a share loss. In this case, be sure you sell the stock yourself, take the tax loss on your own tax return, and then give the cash proceeds to the child.

Setting up 529 in Quicken

To set up a new 529 plan in Quicken, Intuit recommends that you use the Roth IRA structure for the account. Therefore, when setting up a new 529 plan, follow these steps:

1. **Open the Account Setup screen by pressing Ctrl+A, and then clicking Add Account.**
2. **Enter the name of the financial institution, or click the option for No Financial Institution if this is the case.**
3. **Choose IRA as the type of account (see Figure 4-9).**

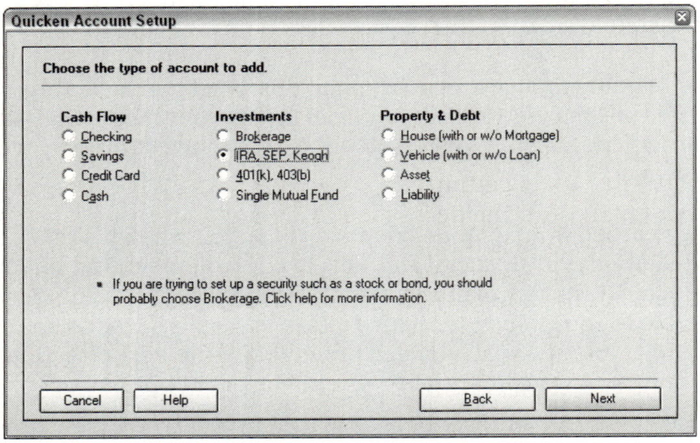

Figure 4-9: Choose the IRA option.

4. **Give the account a name that distinguishes it from your other accounts.**
5. **Indicate that this is a Roth IRA.**

   I know it's not, and you know it's not, but Quicken doesn't seem to know about 529 accounts, so we'll play along and call this a Roth IRA (Figure 4-10). That's not a far cry from the actual account type — these types of savings accounts are very similar. Click Next.
6. **Enter the particulars from your last statement.**

   If you've got a statement for this account, enter the statement date and the amount of any cash or money market money in the account. If this is a brand new account and there's nothing going on yet, just enter today's date and leave the amounts at zero. Click Next to continue.

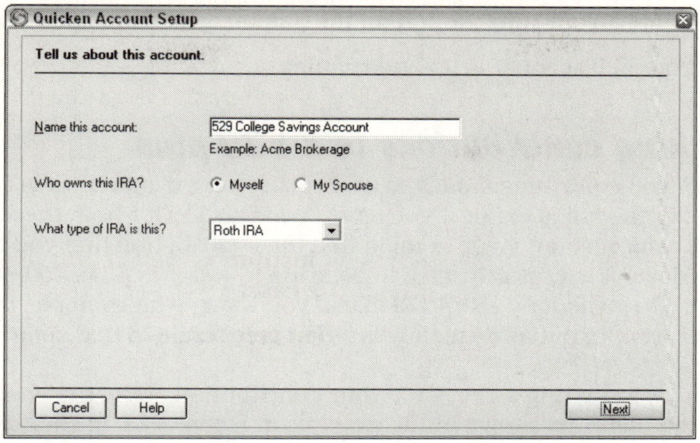

Figure 4-10: It's a 529, but we'll pretend it's a Roth.

7. **Enter the ticker symbol for each of the investments in this account.**

   If you've set up any other types of stock or mutual fund accounts in Quicken, this is getting to be routine. If you're new to this type of setup, you need to get the ticker symbol for each fund that you plan to hold in the account. Click the Lookup button at the bottom if you need help figuring out the ticker symbols. You don't have to enter the names of the funds — Quicken is going to look up your ticker symbols and enter the names. Click Next when you've finished entering all the ticker symbols.

8. **Enter your share holdings (see Figure 4-11).**

   If you haven't actually bought any shares yet, you can leave the share information at zero. If you have shares, copy the quantity, including all the decimal places, from your most recent statement.

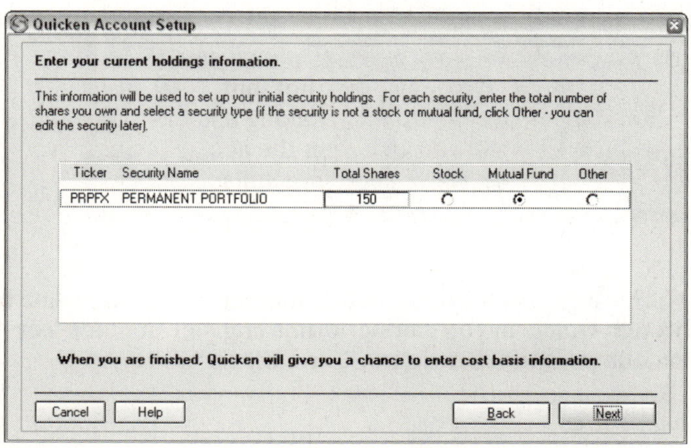

Figure 4-11: Enter the number of shares you own, or zero if you're just getting started.

9. Review your information on the Summary screen, and then click Done.

Your 529 account is up and running.

Making contributions to a 529 plan

When you contribute money to a 529 plan, you can either issue a check, or transfer the funds online if you have online access for both the 529 plan and your bank account. Keep in mind that the contribution that you make to a 529 plan doesn't necessarily have to be made to *your* 529 plan. You can contribute money to somebody else's 529 plan if you want — for example, grandparents might want to put aside money for their grandchild in that child's 529 plan.

If you're preparing a check for your contribution, write the check to the plan or fund name, as shown in the example at Figure 4-12. In Quicken, you can assign the check to a category such as 529 Plan or a Gift category. The 529 contribution is considered by the IRS to be a gift to the plan's beneficiary.

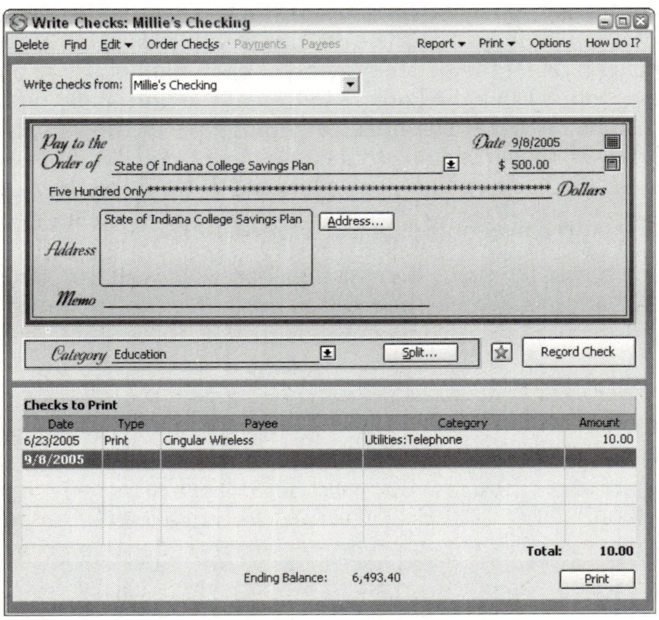

Figure 4-12: Writing a check to transfer funds into 529 plan.

If your 529 is at your own bank, and you've signed up for online banking services through Quicken, you can perform a transfer of funds from your regular bank account to the 529 account.

TIP

If your 529 is at another financial institution or brokerage, and you use Quicken Bill Pay, you can set up that account for automatic transfer as well.

Monitoring your 529 plan

Most 529 plans come with an assortment of investment choices, ranging from somewhat risky and growth-oriented to barely risky at all with lower return on investment. The idea is that when your child is young, you can afford to speculate a little with the money and try a riskier path of investing, hopeful that you'll get a little better return on your money than you would in a simple money market fund.

As the child gets closer to the time when college payments will begin, realign your 529 investments so that there is little risk and the money is safe and ready to be withdrawn and used for college payments.

Financial advisors warn investors that of all the investments you maintain, the 529 plan probably warrants the closest ongoing scrutiny. This is money that you can't afford to put at risk. So if your plan is diversified over a few different accounts and one account starts losing in value, you need to act quickly to assess the reasons for the movement and consider switching your money to a different fund option.

WARNING!

Many 529 plans charge an administrative fee; sometimes, it's an annual fee. Depending on how much you plan to contribute and how much tax savings you anticipate, the fee could essentially wipe out the benefit from having the 529 plan. It's worthwhile to carefully compare plans across the states (`www.savingforcollege.com` offers a comparative chart) before deciding which plan to use or whether the 529 is for you.

Taking money out of the 529 plan

In January, the owner of a 529 plan receives Form 1099-Q (Payments from Qualified Education Programs) indicating how much money was withdrawn from the account in the previous year. The form shows how much of the withdrawn money is made up of the fund's principal and how much is earnings. This is important if the money was not used for its intended (educational) purpose.

The plan owner can withdraw money from a 529 plan at any time. Here are some key points to keep in mind regarding withdrawals from a 529 plan:

✦ It's possible that some money was taken from the fund and rolled over into the 529 fund for another family member. This is perfectly legal and appropriate if the rollover deposit is made within 60 days of the withdrawal. In this case, there is no tax effect on the removal of money from the 529.

- Money taken from the plan and used for college-level education and related expenses (such as room and board), for the intended beneficiary, is not subject to taxation.
- Money taken from the account for any other reason is subject to a 10 percent penalty and income taxation. The *earnings* from the fund are reported on the tax return of the person who actually received the money, no matter who contributed the money to the fund. The principal portion of the money withdrawn from the fund is not subject to income tax.

Setting Up a Coverdell Education Savings Account in Quicken

The Coverdell Education Savings Account (formerly known as the Education IRA) is a tax-deferred account available as yet another option for saving for college.

Unlike the 529 plan, in which anyone can participate, income restrictions keep some people from participating in a Coverdell ESA plan.

Unlike the 529 plan, you are limited as to how much you can contribute each year to a Coverdell ESA plan. The maximum contribution is $2,000 per beneficiary. You can set up plans for multiple beneficiaries, but only $2,000 per beneficiary is allowed each year, and that includes combining contributions for that beneficiary from various sources.

More rules: The Coverdell child must be under age 18 to receive a contribution in his name.

This investment and savings account is established solely for the purpose of paying higher education expenses. Contributions are not deductible from current income taxes. Earnings grow tax-deferred and distributions are tax-free if used to pay qualified educational expenses.

You can read more information about the Coverdell ESA in Chapter 5, Book I. Briefly, here are the requirements for operating a Coverdell ESA in Quicken:

- Setting up the account is just like setting up the 529 account, except instead of describing this account as a Roth IRA, you can pick Educational IRA during the account setup phase.
- Transferring money into the account is done exactly like I described these transfers in the 529 account section. You can write a check and deposit that check, or, if you have online banking and the account is at

the same bank as your regular bank account, you can execute a funds transfer from within Quicken. If you use Bill Pay, you can transfer funds between your bank and the IRA even if they are not located at the same financial institution.

- ✦ When it's time to take money out to pay for school costs, money is distributed from the account and transferred into a bank account for purposes of using the money for tuition, fees, books, supplies, equipment, room and board.
- ✦ At tax time, the owner of the Educational IRA receives Form 1099-Q showing the total amount of money withdrawn from the account during the previous year.

WARNING!

The Coverdell plan is considered an asset of the child's and counts against her during calculations for financial aid. In the case of the 529 plan, only the plan's earnings are considered an asset of the child's for purposes of financial aid calculations.

What happens if the child doesn't go to college?

Education funds such as the 529 and Coverdell Education Savings Account are typically created with the best of intentions. But they are also sometimes created before it can be determined if the child beneficiary will actually attend college, or how much that college will cost.

If it turns out that one of these situations exist, the earnings that accumulated in the fund can be subject to both income tax and a penalty.

- The student isn't ready for college, but you need the money, so you take the money out of the plan and use it for something other than college costs.
- The beneficiary dies or becomes disabled (no penalty here).
- In the event of the Coverdell fund, the beneficiary turns age 30 without having used the money.
- The beneficiary does not go to college.
- The beneficiary goes to college but receives enough scholarship money to cover costs or doesn't incur costs in excess of the amount in the plan, and thus doesn't need all of the tax-protected money in the education fund.

To make matters more confusing, each state has its own rules about what gets taxed, to whom, and when. Basically, you should expect that if you take money out of the plan and don't use it for education, the person who gets the money pays income tax and a 10 percent penalty on the amount of the proceeds that represents earnings.

Chapter 5: Automating Your Savings Program

In This Chapter

- **Putting savings on the schedule**
- **Telling Quicken to nag you more**
- **Changing the savings schedule**
- **Managing regular investment contributions**

It's not uncommon to read stories about millionaires and how they amassed their money. Often, these people didn't launch their own businesses or succeed through some type of get-rich-quick scheme. Instead, they worked modest jobs, chose a low-key (some might say cheap) lifestyle, and saved money regularly. Although there's no guarantee that using Quicken to help you manage and save your money will make *you* a millionaire, Quicken does include some tools to remind you when to save and how much to save. Find out now how to use scheduled transactions, reminders, and transactions groups to set up and manage your savings program.

Setting Up Scheduled Savings Transactions

If you've ever listened to financial advisors give their tips for saving, you've no doubt heard the chant, "Pay yourself first." If you take this sage advice, you'll regularly place money in a savings or investing vehicle of some type rather than leaving it in a checking account where you might be tempted to spend it. The "pay yourself first" theory dictates a process of diverting money from your paycheck directly to savings, without passing Go, without collecting $200, and without first paying your bills. When you save first and live on what's left, you see that you really can cover your current needs while building an emergency fund or a long-term savings account.

I like to look at "Pay yourself first" like this. Pretend your boss calls you into the office and explains that times are tough and the company needs to cut back. Don't worry, he says, your job is safe. But . . . (you've gotta love it when they start a sentence with "But . . .") as a result of the cut backs, effective immediately, you have to suffer a 10 percent decrease in pay.

Maybe you'd start looking for a new job as soon as you leave the boss's office. In the short run, however, you're going to have to learn to live on 10 percent less income. Now — back to reality. Try turning that imaginary scenario into a forced 10 percent diversion into savings. Pretend you simply don't have that extra 10 percent. Before you know it, you just might get used to living with a little less pocket change. Then you can watch your savings grow!

How much you save is up to you. Experts say you should always have an emergency fund with at least enough savings to cover four to six months' of expenses (this is *necessary* expenses, not luxury items). So, if you need about $3,000 per month to pay for the essentials in your household (mortgage or rent, utilities, food, insurance, and transportation), you should have an emergency fund of at least $12,000 to $18,000. After you've built that base, you should save even more for long-term purposes.

TIP

Not to go on a rant, but we U.S. citizens aren't known for saving very much of our income. For the last year of reported data, the typical average savings rate was about 0 percent. Although you might hate to trade lunches out of the office for brown-bagging it, you will appreciate having the funds you need when an unexpected event hits or when there's some change in your income level.

TIP

Trying to save money? Grab a copy of my book, *Surviving Financial Downsizing: A Practical Guide to Living Well on Less Income*, for plenty of tips on cutting back your expenses without sacrificing your lifestyle.

Motivated to save yet? Good. Quicken can help you begin to make regular investments into your savings or investment accounts. Use the Scheduled Transaction List to create scheduled savings transactions.

Adding the scheduled transaction

As you learned in Chapter 2 of Book II, you can set up a scheduled transaction to remind you of any bill or deposit that happens on a regular basis. For example, you might set up a scheduled transaction to remind you to pay a monthly phone bill or to record a paycheck received.

In Quicken, you also can create a scheduled transaction to remind you to make a regular deposit to a savings or investment account (or both). For example, if you decide that you want to transfer $150 per month from your checking account to your savings account, you can set up a scheduled transaction to prompt you a few days in advance to make the transfer.

If you're banking manually in Quicken, you should create a scheduled transaction to record that $150 per month. If you're banking online with Quicken, the withdrawal transactions will download into Quicken automatically, so you don't need to create the scheduled transaction.

When you open the Scheduled Transaction List, you see commands that enable you to create your scheduled transactions, including scheduled transactions to prompt you to save your money. Follow these steps to set up the scheduled transaction:

1. **Choose Cash Flow⇨Scheduled Transaction List or press Ctrl+J from any Quicken window.**

   The Scheduled Transaction List window (Figure 5-1) appears.

2. **Click Create New⇨Scheduled Transaction.**

   The Create Scheduled Transaction dialog box opens.

3. **Choose the settings for the scheduled savings transaction.**

   Refer to Chapter 2 of Book II to learn more about the ins and outs of using the Create Scheduled Transaction dialog box. For example, the entries shown in Figure 5-2 create a scheduled transaction that reminds you to transfer $250 per month from the Huntington Checking account to the Huntington Savings account. The transaction repeats on the first of each month, with a reminder three days in advance.

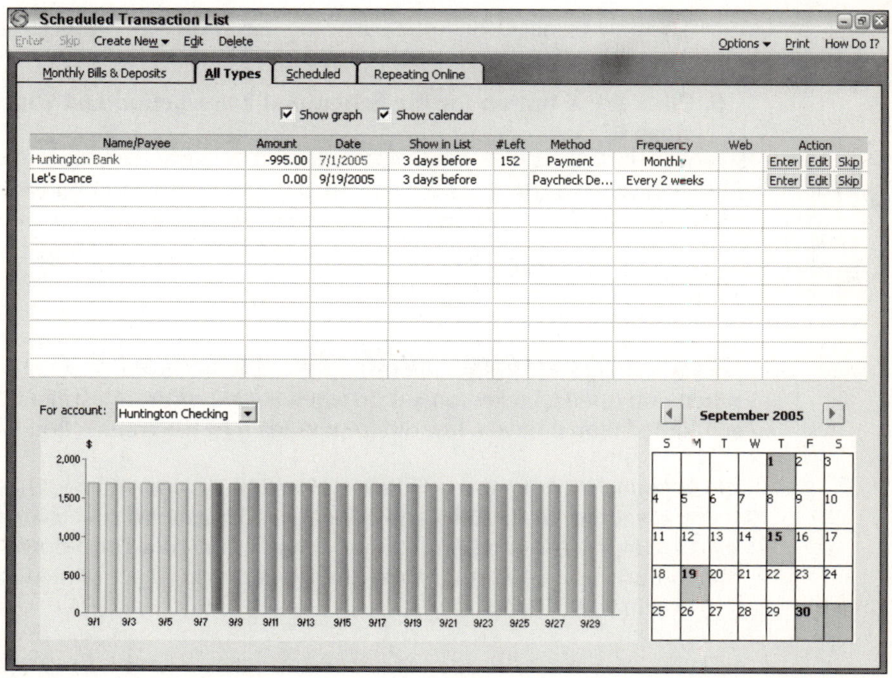

Figure 5-1: Use the Scheduled Transaction List to have Quicken remind you to set aside money in a savings or investment account.

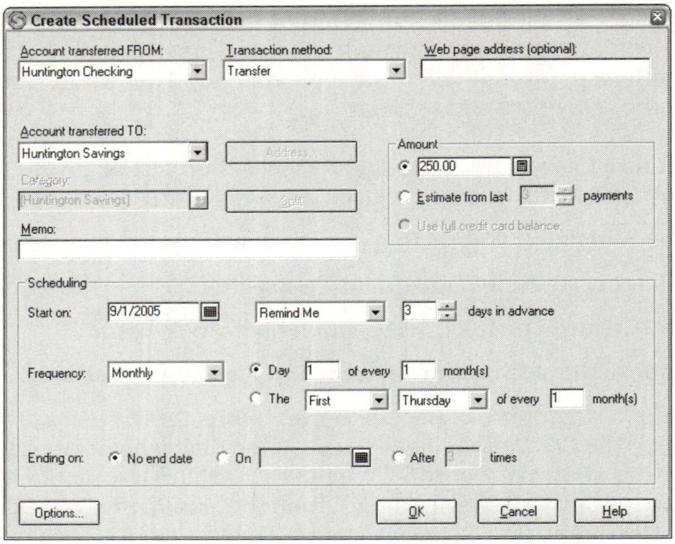

Figure 5-2: These settings create a monthly scheduled transaction for a $250 transfer from a checking account to a savings account.

4. **Click OK to finish creating the scheduled transaction.**

   The new transaction appears in the list in the All Types tab of the Scheduled Transaction List window.

5. **Click the X button for the Scheduled Transaction List window to close it.**

Shortcut alert! If the transaction you want to schedule already appears in your register, you can right-click on the transaction and choose Schedule Transaction to open the Create Scheduled Transaction dialog box. Then continue with step 3 above.

Following through with the transaction

When you open Quicken on a date when a savings or investment transaction is scheduled, you'll have a few different clues that the transaction is coming due:

✦ If you're looking at the Quicken Home page, you will see the scheduled transaction in the Bills and Scheduled Transactions section of the page (Figure 5-3). You might need to change the Show drop-down list setting to Current – by Status to see the reminder for a scheduled savings transaction that's due soon.

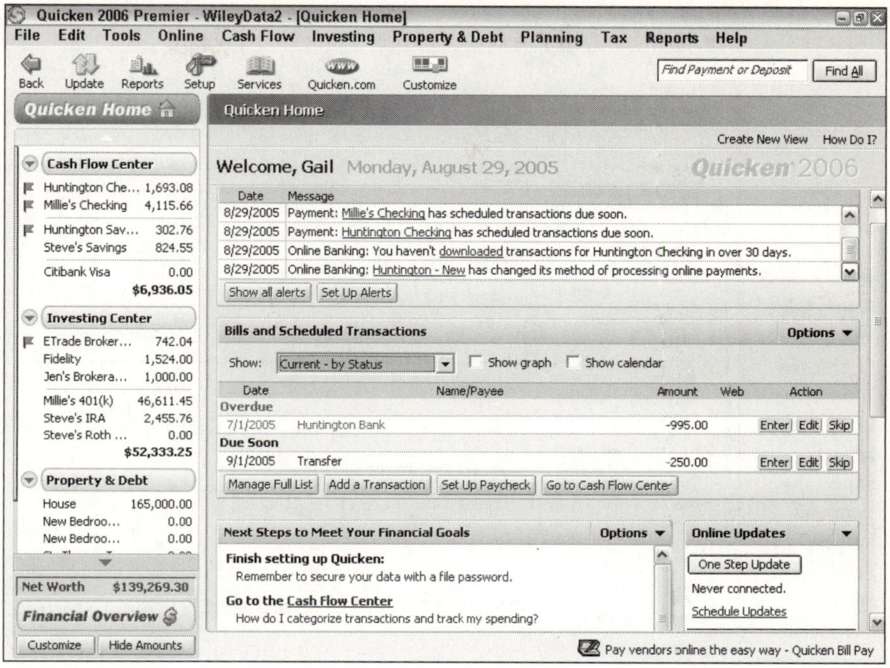

Figure 5-3: The Quicken Home page shows you overdue and due scheduled trans-actions, such as any savings transaction you've created.

- ✦ If you use Quicken's Billminder (see Book IV, Chapter 4), the scheduled transaction appears on the Billminder screen as soon as you boot up your computer.
- ✦ If the account from which the scheduled savings transaction funds will be transferred or withdrawn is visible in the Account Bar at the left side of the Quicken window, a flag appears beside the account name, signifying a scheduled transaction is pending.
- ✦ Finally, if you're working in the register for the account from which the savings funds will be transferred or withdrawn, the Scheduled Transactions tab near the bottom of the register displays something other than *(0)*, such as *(1 Due)*. Click the tab, like the one shown in Figure 5-4, to see the scheduled savings transaction.

You have to use the register and its Scheduled Transactions tab to enter the actual scheduled savings transaction, like this:

1. **Click the Enter button at the right end of the line holding the scheduled savings transaction (refer to Figure 5-4) in the Scheduled Transactions tab.**

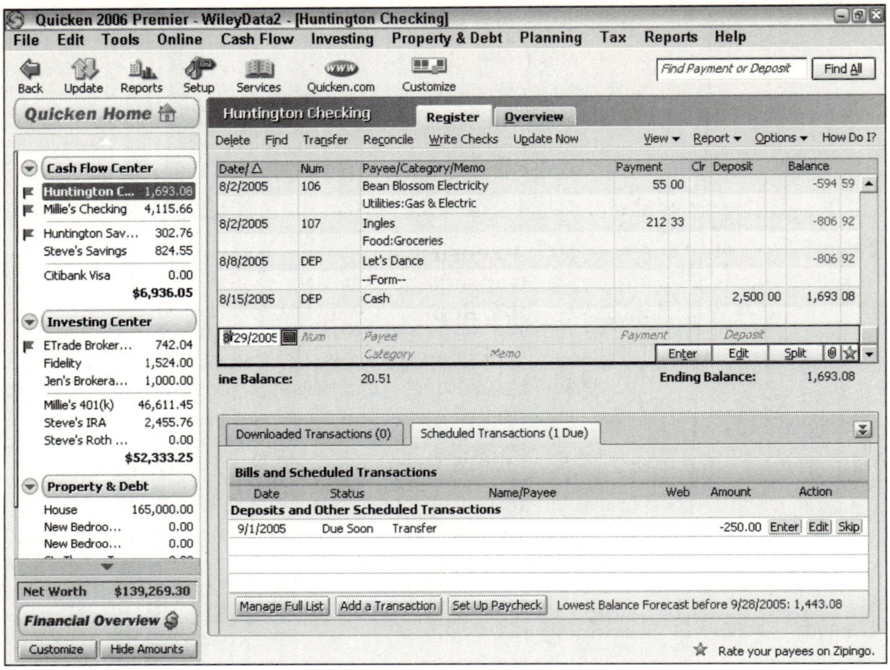

Figure 5-4: The Scheduled Transactions tab in the register shows the reminder for your scheduled savings transaction.

The Edit Current Transaction and Enter into Register dialog box (Figure 5-5) appears.

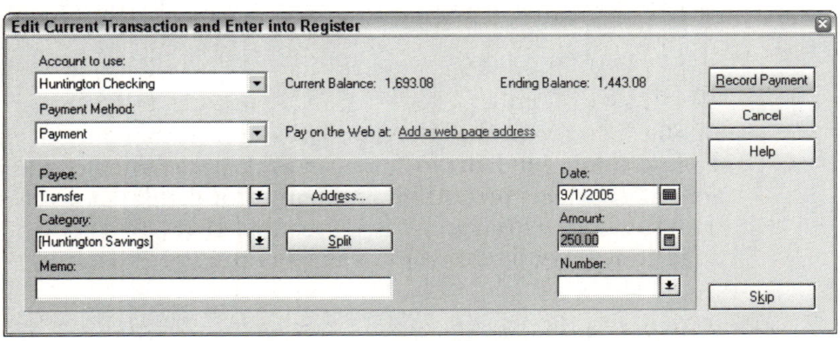

Figure 5-5: If you want to increase the amount you're going to save for the month, Quicken gives you the chance.

2. **Make any necessary changes before recording the transaction.**

   For example, if you need to delay your savings transaction, change the Date entry. If you want to save more (don't let yourself down by saving less!), increase the Amount entry.

3. **Click the Record Payment button.**

   Quicken records the transaction in the register.

4. **Now you have to ensure that the withdrawal/deposit or transfer represented by the transaction happens in the real world. Take one of the following actions, depending on the situation:**

   * If the transaction represents a transfer from a checking and savings account at the same bank, visit your bank's ATM or teller window to make the transfer.

     TIP

     Some banks allow telephone transfers of funds between accounts.

   * If the transaction represents a withdrawal from an account at one bank and a deposit to an account at another bank, visit the two banks to make each transaction.

   * If the transaction represents a withdrawal of money from a checking account to make a deposit in an investment account (and you haven't set up automatic withdrawals), send a check in the applicable amount to your investment company, using the appropriate deposit slip and account number. Similarly, if you're setting aside money for a certificate of deposit, purchase it at your bank or from an online bank.

   * If the checking and savings accounts involved are at the same bank, and your bank allows online transfers between those accounts, and both accounts are set up for online banking, you can convert the register transaction to an online instruction to make the transfer electronically. To do this, click the Num field (which would typically hold the check number) for the transaction in the register, click the drop-down list arrow that appears beside the field, and then choose Online Transfer, as shown in Figure 5-6. Update the date for the transaction to match the current date, and then click or press Enter. From there, go to the Online Center to send the transfer instruction. See Chapter 5 of Book II to learn how to send the transfer instruction to your bank.

   * If you use Quicken Bill Pay, and both accounts are set up in Bill Pay (see Book IV, Chapter 4), you can transfer the funds online at the Bill Pay window. Go to `www.quicken.com`, click My Quicken, and then click Quicken Bill Pay Log In.

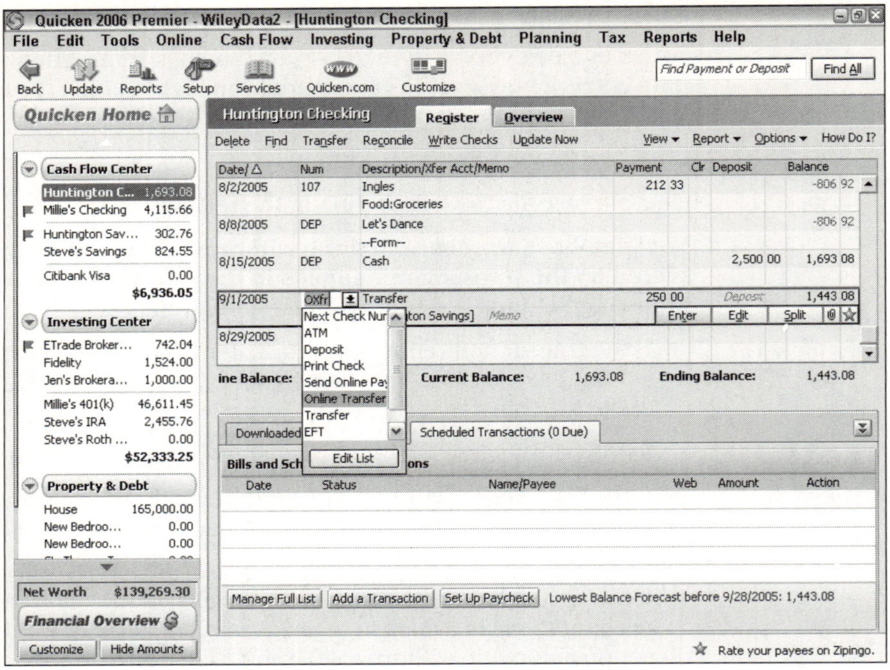

Figure 5-6: To transfer funds online for enabled accounts, convert the savings transaction to an online transfer.

Using Reminders to Increase Your Savings

You can use a couple of other tricks in Quicken to remind you to stick with your schedule of regular savings: the Calendar and alerts. As you get more familiar with Quicken, you'll decide which of the features you like best. Some people use the Calendar daily, and others never open their Calendar. Some people are conscientious about checking alerts regularly; others ignore the alerts. These descriptions provide you with some alternatives for getting notifications of your scheduled transactions. It's up to you to decide which of the features you want to use.

Scheduled transactions and Quicken's Calendar

Quicken automatically adds a notation about any scheduled transaction you set up to the Calendar. To open the Calendar in its own window, choose Tools➪Calendar or press Ctrl+K. As shown in Figure 5-7, the Calendar looks like a traditional monthly paper calendar with a square representing each day.

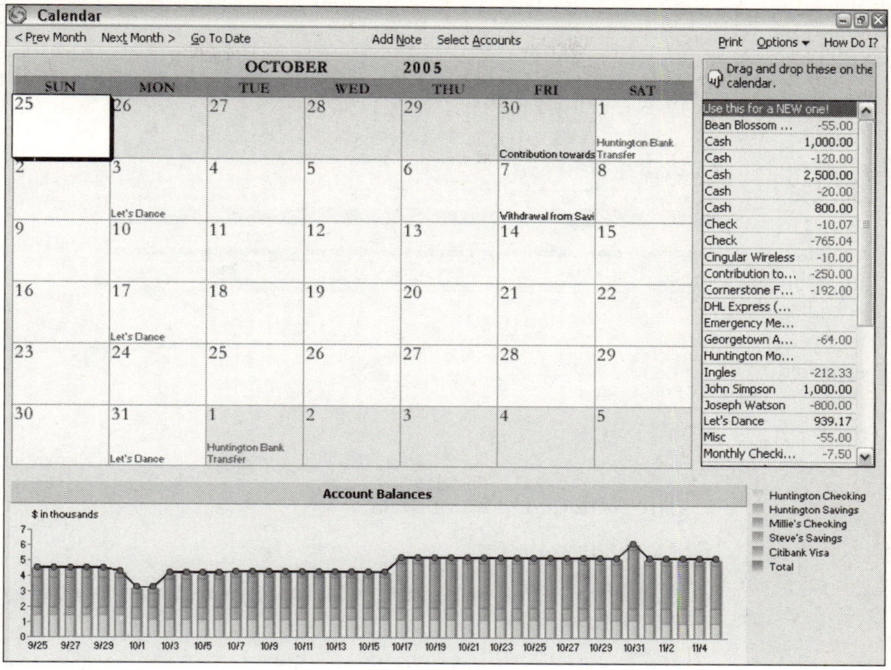

Figure 5-7: Quicken's Calendar provides a visual reminder of each scheduled savings transaction.

Click the Prev Month and Next Month buttons as needed to view the Calendar for various months. If you want to see more detail about the transactions scheduled on a particular date, double-click the box for the day. In the Transactions Due window that appears (Figure 5-8), you can click a transaction and then click the Edit button to view and change details about the scheduled transaction and all future instances of that scheduled transactions. Click the Transaction Due window X button when you've finished viewing the transactions.

TIP

If you want to schedule an instance of a memorized or scheduled transaction, you can drag the desired transaction from the list at the right and drop it onto the desired date on the calendar.

TIP

Savings goal contributions (see Chapter 3 of Book VI) that you've scheduled also appear on the applicable dates in the Calendar.

If you think a scheduled transaction is overkill, you can add a calendar note to remind you to save money without setting up a scheduled transaction. To create a calendar note for a particular date:

1. **Click the date on the Calendar.**
2. **Click the Add Note choice at the top of the window.**

Figure 5-8: When you click a day (date) square, Quicken shows you the transactions scheduled for the specified date.

The Note dialog box opens.

3. **Type the note text.**
4. **(Optional) Choose an alternate color for the note from the Note Color drop-down list.**

   Your note might look like Figure 5-9.

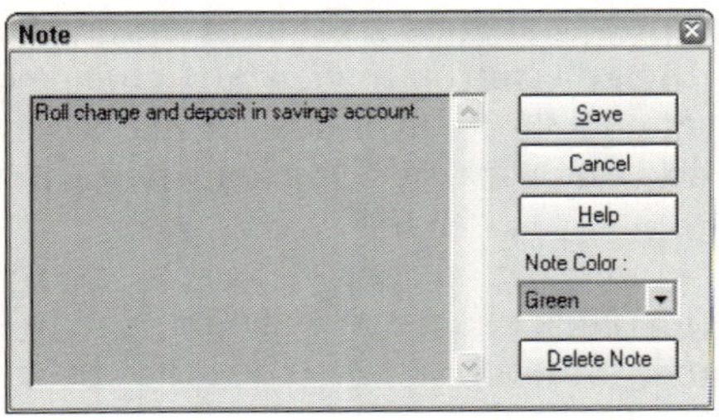

Figure 5-9: You can add a custom note — with any luck, one that reminds you to save more money — to any date on the Calendar.

5. **Click OK.**

   A small note box in the specified color appears in the upper-right corner of the date box you clicked in step 1.
6. **To view the calendar note text, move the mouse pointer over it until the note text appears in a pop up, as shown in Figure 5-10.**

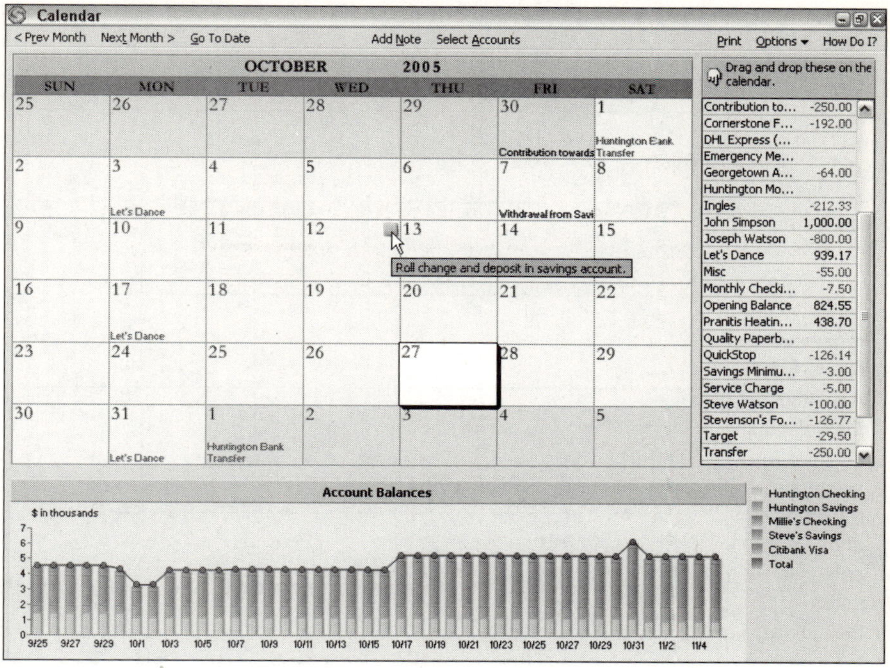

Figure 5-10: Point to the calendar note to see what it says.

TIP

To delete a note, click the note box within the date box, and then click the Delete Note button in the Note dialog box.

If you want, you can print the calendar for the currently displayed month. To start the process, click the Print button in the Calendar window, change the settings in the Print dialog box if desired, and then click OK. As the example Print Preview of a Calendar in Figure 5-11 shows, the printout also lists scheduled transactions and notes below the calendar itself.

When you've finished working with the Calendar, click the Calendar window's X button to send the Calendar into hiding.

Alerts to alert you!

Here's one last way to ensure that Quicken shows you when you have scheduled savings transactions coming . . . If you aren't seeing reminders about your scheduled transactions in the Quicken Home Page, you need to check to ensure that alerts for scheduled transactions have been enabled in the Alerts Center. Choose Tools⇨Set Up Alerts. Click the plus button beside the General category to expand that category, and then click the plus button beside Reminder. Make sure a green check box appears to the right of the Scheduled Transactions Due item, as shown in Figure 5-12. If you don't see a check, click the check box to make it appear. Click OK when you've finished enabling the alerts.

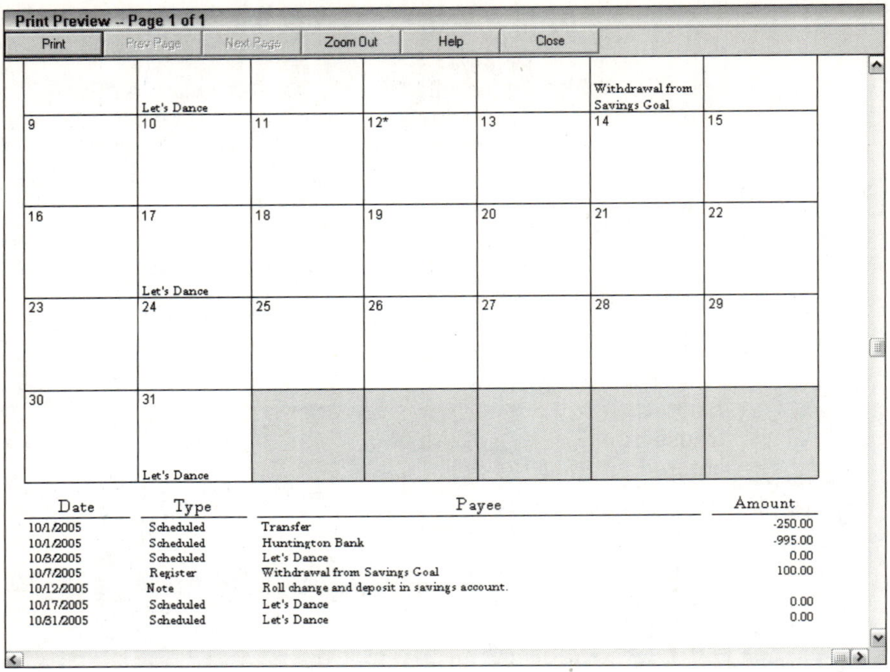

Figure 5-11: A printout of the Calendar includes the scheduled transactions and calendar notes for the month.

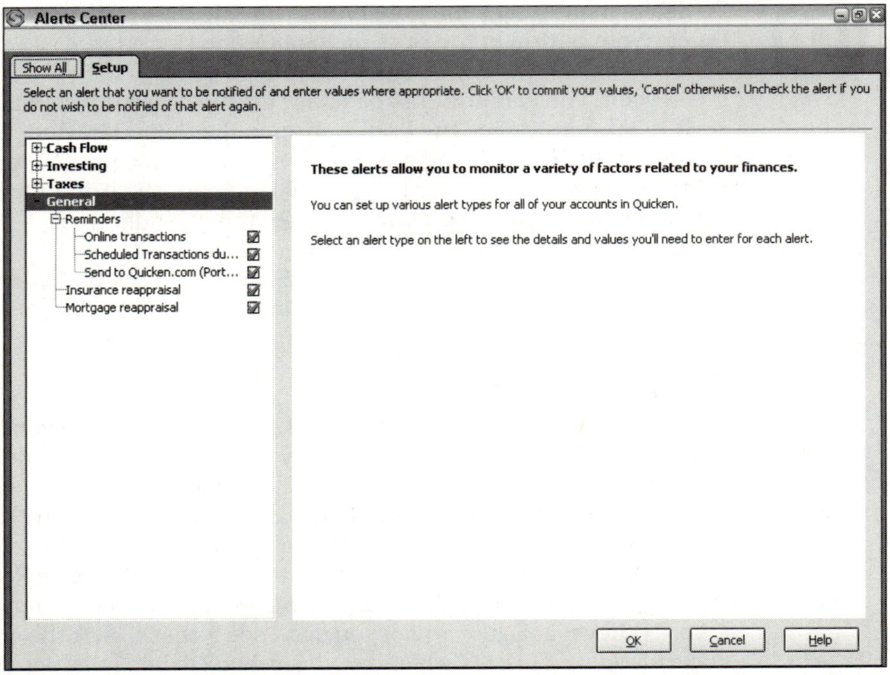

Figure 5-12: Make sure you see the green checkmark beside Scheduled Transactions Due.

Adjusting Your Scheduled Transactions

If you're being diligent with your savings efforts and are continuing to explore more ways to trim the fat out of your spending (no excuses!), you soon might need to edit the scheduled transaction you've created for your savings plan so that you can increase the amount for the transaction.

As noted briefly above, if you open a scheduled transaction from the Calendar, you can make changes to that and any future instances of the scheduled transaction. The Scheduled Transaction List also enables you make a change to any scheduled transaction, including one that you've set up to prompt you to make a regular savings contribution.

Changing a scheduled transaction changes only *future* recurrences of the transaction, not any past instances of the transaction that you've already entered into the register.

To make a change to a scheduled transaction:

1. **Choose Cash Flow⇨Scheduled Transaction List or press Ctrl+J from any Quicken window.**

   The Scheduled Transaction List window appears.

2. **Click the Scheduled tab.**
3. **In the list of transactions on the tab, click the Edit button at the right end of the line for the scheduled transaction.**

   The transaction information appears in the Edit All Future Transactions dialog box (Figure 5-13).

4. **Change settings as needed, such as increasing the transaction (savings) amount.**
5. **Click the OK button.**

   Quicken updates the scheduled transaction so that all future instances will reflect your increased savings.

6. **Close the Scheduled Transaction List window.**

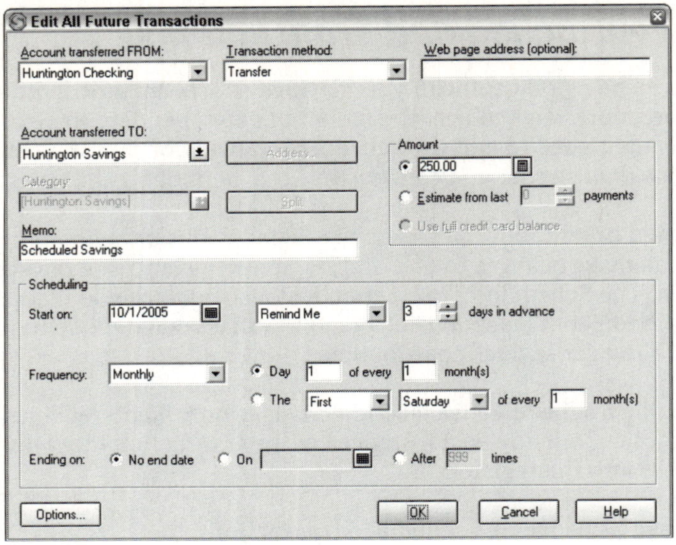

Figure 5-13: Update your scheduled transaction here.

Setting Up Investment Transaction Groups

If you make a regular contribution to an investment account to purchase more shares of a single security or fund, you can set up that transaction as a regular recurring transaction.

TIP

This type of scheduled investment, where you invest the same amount with each transaction, no matter how many shares that money purchases, has a name. You might think of it as Investing the Same Amount No Matter How Many Shares I Get. Others call this process Dollar Cost Averaging. No matter how plain or fancy the name, the process is the same.

However, if you make a monthly contribution into an investment account but then invest the money in multiple securities, you have to set up an investment transaction group to account for how you divide the full monthly sum you deposit between the various securities you subsequently purchase using the deposited funds.

The process for setting up an investment transaction group works somewhat like setting up a scheduled transaction, with a few curveballs thrown in:

1. **Assuming you just made a monthly investment into the investment account, look at the paper statement for your account, and use the**

register for the investment account to add a transaction representing each security you bought from the monthly lump sum you deposited.

Remember, click the Enter Transaction button on the Transactions tab of the investment account register to enter those transactions. Find more examples of entering investment transactions in Book III, Chapter 1.

2. **Click each of the newly added transactions on the Transactions tab of the investment account register, and then choose Edit⇨Transaction⇨Memorize Payee (Ctrl+M) to add the transaction to the Memorized Investment Txn List.**

   You can't memorize a deposit transaction, so you have to handle the actual deposit or transfer as a regular scheduled transaction.

3. **Choose Tools⇨Scheduled Transaction List or press Ctrl+J to open the Scheduled Transaction List window.**
4. **Choose Create New⇨Scheduled Transaction.**

   The Create Scheduled Transaction dialog box appears.
5. **Choose the name of the investment account in which you created and memorized transactions in steps 1 and 2 from the Account to Use drop-down list. Leave Payment selected as the Transaction method.**

   If needed, you can edit the transaction frequency settings, but there's no need to enter a transaction amount.
6. **Click the Options button in the lower-left corner of the Create Scheduled Transaction dialog box.**

   The Create Scheduled Transaction Options dialog box opens.
7. **Click the Group button near the lower-left corner of the dialog box.**

   The Edit Transaction Group dialog box opens.
8. **Type a name for the investment transaction group in the Group text box.**
9. **Click the Investment option button in the Choose Transactions section of the dialog box.**

   The transactions you memorized in step 2 should appear in the list.

   If you don't see a memorized transaction, you either memorized it in the wrong investment account, or you've already saved the transaction in another investment transaction group.
10. **Click to check the Group check box on the right side of the window for each transaction to include in the group, as shown in Figure 5-14.**

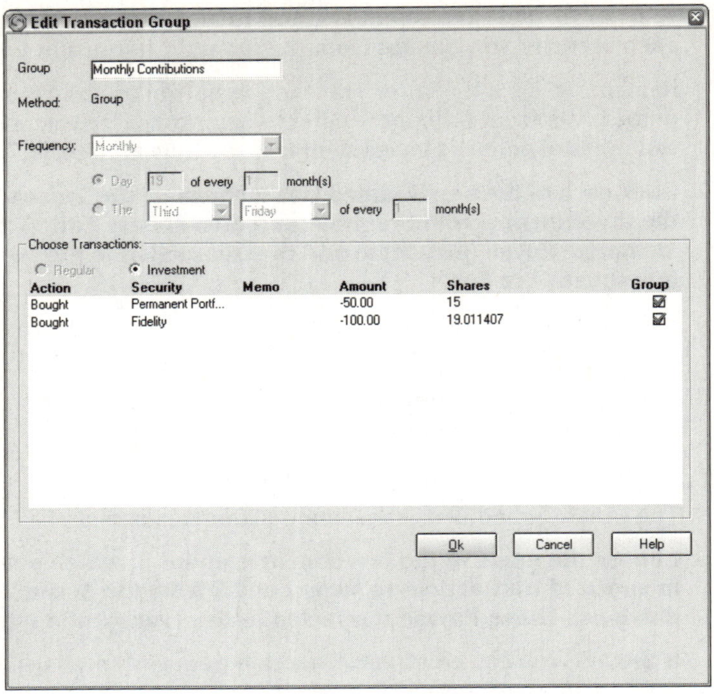

Figure 5-14: Enter a name for the investment transaction group and check off the memorized transactions to include in the group.

11. **Click OK.**

    The Scheduled Transaction List window reappears. As shown in Figure 5-15, the transaction group appears in the Scheduled Transaction window. The group name includes (Group X) to identify it as a group. The amount reflects the total of all the transactions you included in the group.

    From there, the investment transaction group behaves just like an individual scheduled transaction. You see a reminder when the transaction is coming due. You can enter the transaction group when needed using the Enter button in the Scheduled Transaction List, or the Enter button beside the group on the Scheduled Transactions tab of the investment account Transactions tab (Figure 5-16). In the Record Transaction Group dialog box, click the Record button to record the transactions.

You can use the Edit choice in the Scheduled Transaction List to change the transactions included in a selected group, or you can use the Delete choice to delete the group.

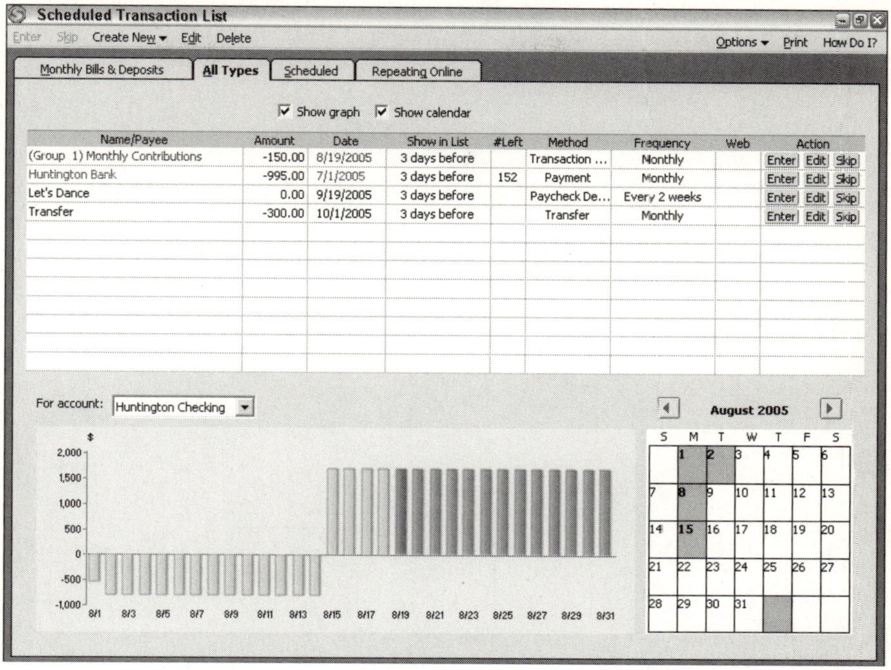

Figure 5-15: A transaction group will be identified with *(Group X)* in its name.

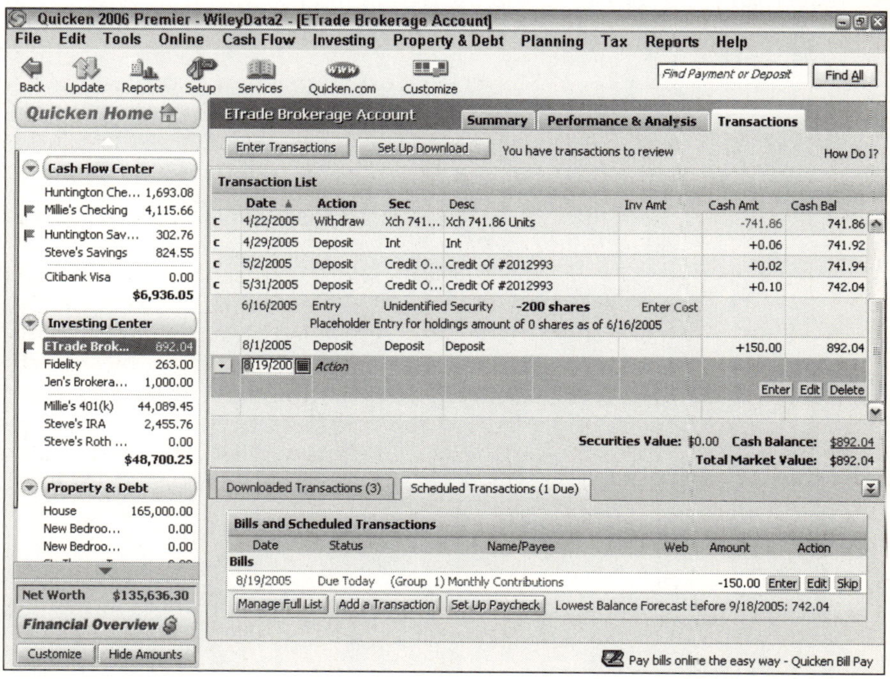

Figure 5-16: Click the Enter button to start recording the transactions included in the investment transaction group.

Book VII

Quicken Reports

Contents at a Glance

Chapter 1: Creating QuickReports

In This Chapter

- Displaying a minireport
- Using QuickReports
- Using Write QuickReports
- Customizing QuickReports
- Graphing register data

Getting a handle on how you spend your money enables you to better prioritize your expenses and savings. By applying categories to Quicken transactions, you can look back to see what type of expense or income a particular transaction represented, for example. For a look at the overview of how you're spending and making money in various categories, however, you have to turn to Quicken's graphs and reports. After you master the techniques for viewing basic graphs and reports presented in this chapter, you have the basic tools you need to become a more discriminating spender and saver.

Displaying Activity for a Category or Payee

The 2006 version of Quicken adds a great new feature that enables you to view transactions in a category or made to a particular payee directly from a register transaction. So, for example, if you want to see how much money you've spent recently for medical bills or a particular utility, you can display that information in the little report with just a couple of mouse clicks.

Quicken calls these reports *minireports*. The data that a minireport displays differs depending on whether you're viewing category or payee information:

- **Category:** Quicken can display all deposits and payments for the most recent 30-day, 60-day, 90-day, 6-month, 1-year, or 3-year period. When you choose a minireport covering 90 days or less, Quicken subtotals the data by payee. When you choose a longer time period, Quicken subtotals the information by date.
- **Payee:** Quicken also can display transactions using a particular payee in the most recent 30-day, 60-day, 90-day, 6-month, 1-year, or 3-year period. By default, Quicken selects the shortest reporting period that contains six transactions, although you can choose to display a longer time period.

You have to be working in a cash flow account to display a minireport.

A minireport may not help you solve a big financial problem, but it's a terrific tool for answering a specific question, such as whether you've made a mortgage payment in the last month (view a minireport for a transaction where your lender is the payee) or whether you've spent too many dollars on entertainment recently (view a minireport for the Entertainment Expense category).

Viewing a category minireport

When you want to see how much you've spent in a particular category, you can create a minireport that displays the transactions in that category. Create the minireport for a category by following these steps:

1. **In your register, scroll to display a transaction to which you've assigned the category in question in the register.**
2. **Click in the Category field for the transaction.**

   A drop-down list arrow and a minireport button (which has a sheet of paper on it) appears at the right end of the field, as shown in Figure 1-1.
3. **Click the minireport button.**

   The minireport appears in a pop-up box below the transaction, which you also can see in Figure 1-1. (Note that you also can right-click the Category field for the transaction and then click Launch Mini-Report for Category *Category Name* to open the minireport.)

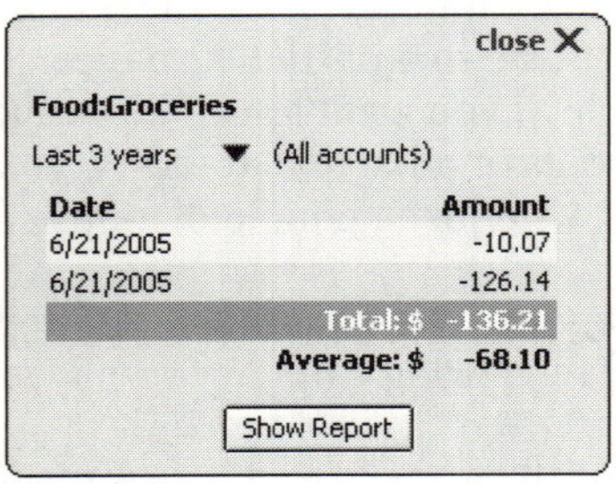

Figure 1-1: Click and click, and the minireport appears!

4. **Adjust the dates.**

   If you're not happy with the time period shown in the minireport, click the drop-down list arrow (the big black triangle) to the right of the time period shown in the minireport box, and then click another time frame (see Figure 1-2).

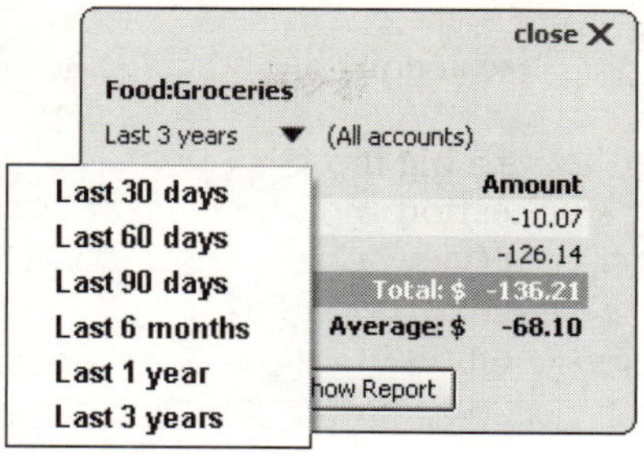

Figure 1-2: Zero in on the time frame you want for the minireport data.

5. **To close the minireport, click the X button in the upper-right corner of the report box.**

Viewing a payee minireport

As you might guess, viewing a minireport of payee data works much like viewing a minireport for a category. Simply click the Payee field in a register transaction that uses the desired payee, and then click the minireport button that appears to the right of the field drop-down list button. Figure 1-3 shows an example of a payee minireport, in this case, showing recent payments to a health care provider.

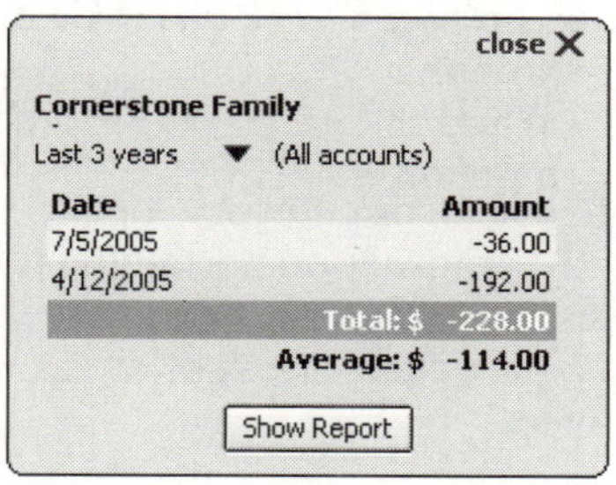

Figure 1-3: A payee minireport looks just like a category minireport.

Viewing an expanded minireport in its own window

Although a minireport looks great onscreen, you might want to work with the data further. You can show the minireport data as a full-blown transaction report by clicking the Show Report button in the minireport box. After you click that button, the report data appears in its own window, like the example in Figure 1-4. Book VII, Chapter 2 explains how to work with a full report, including how to customize, print, and save the report data. A section called "Customizing QuickReports" later in this chapter shows you the key techniques for slicing and dicing your report data. For now, you can just click the report window X button to close the report.

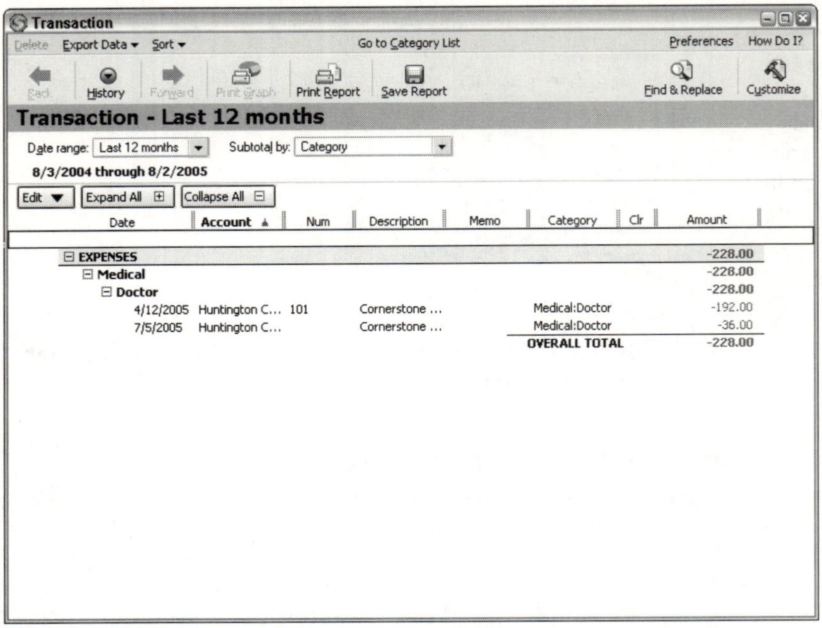

Figure 1-4: The mini-report from Figure 1-3, expanded into its own report window.

Using QuickReports Available in the Registers

You can skip the minireport and go directly to a basic report window. When you're working in the register for a bank or cash flow account, you can display a QuickReport about either the payee or category for the current transaction. A QuickReport simply lists the transaction pertaining to the payee or category, without any fancy analysis. A QuickReport can save you a lot of time if you're trying to track down a particular check or check number, or verify a payment to a particular payee.

Displaying a QuickReport takes no more effort than displaying a minireport. Here's how to display a QuickReport.

1. **Click on a transaction that uses the payee or category to show in the QuickReport.**
2. **Click on the Report option at the top of the Register tab.**
3. **Click the desired QuickReport choice (Amount Spent On or Payments Made To) at the top of the menu.**

   As you can see in Figure 1-5, the menu choices display the category and payee entries in the selected transaction.

Quicken's Help system says that you need to click in the Payee or Category field to display a QuickReport, but that doesn't appear to be the case. However, just to be sure, you can click in one of those fields before opening the report.

If the QuickReport choices do not appear at the top of the Report menu, it means you haven't selected a transaction with payee and/or category data. Click a field in the applicable transaction to make the QuickReport choices appear on the Report menu.

The QuickReport opens in its own window (Figure 1-6) and is titled Category Report or Payee Report. By default, a QuickReport displays transactions for the current year to date (YTD), but you can customize the QuickReport from there as described in Chapter 3 of this book.

QuickReports are everywhere! You also can create a QuickReport from one of the Category, Class, Memorized Payee, Online Payee and Security lists, as well as the Portfolio and Savings Goals windows, and the Security Detail view.

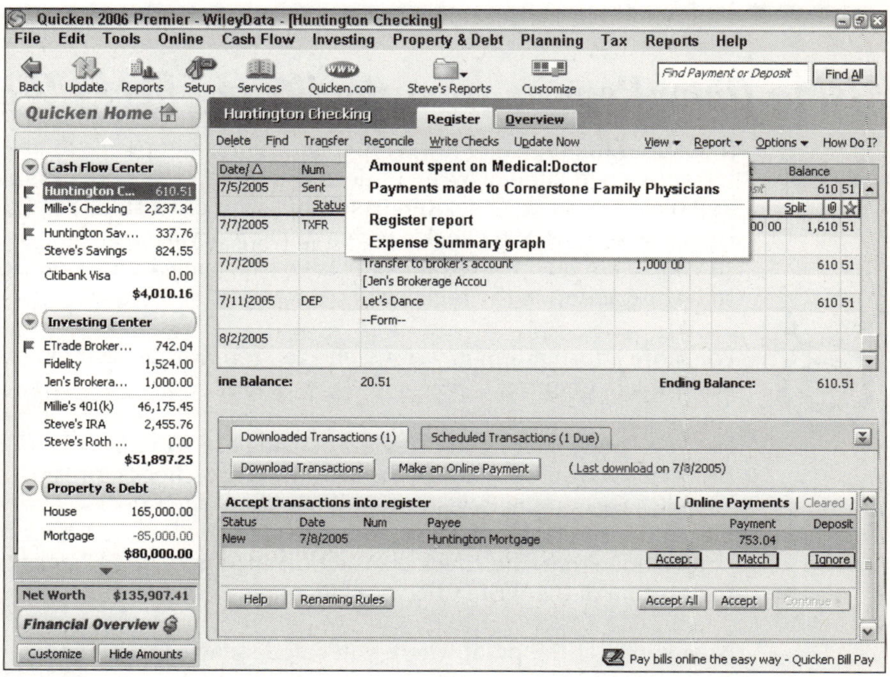

Figure 1-5: The top two choices on the Report menu in the Register tab open QuickReports.

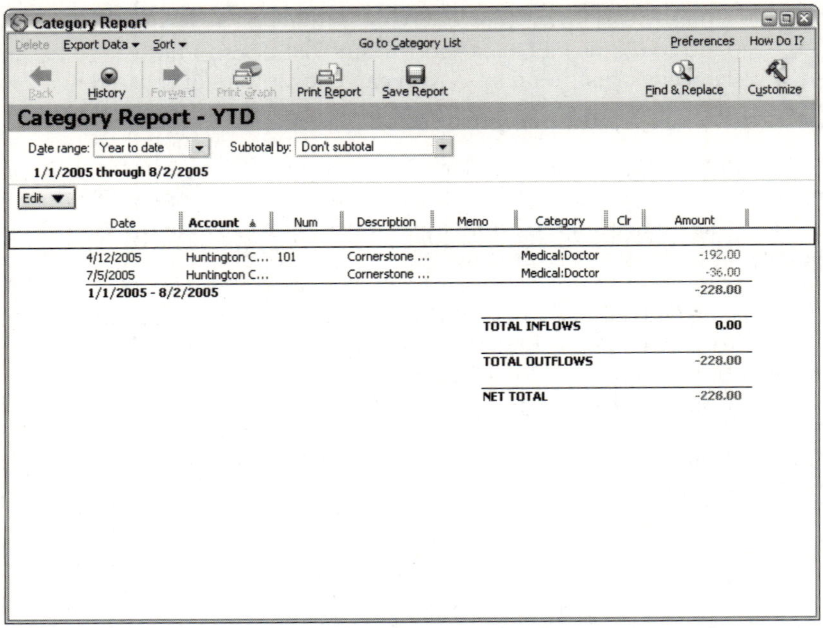

Figure 1-6: A QuickReport can show transactions for a particular category, as in this example, or for a particular payee.

Using QuickReports from the Write Checks Window

If you find the register view a bit constraining and prefer to use the more attractive and familiar Write Checks window to enter checks in Quicken, you still have access to QuickReports — but with one catch. You have to view the QuickReport of a check's payee or category *before* you print the check. (If you've already printed the check, you can only open a QuickReport for that transaction in the register.)

For more information on writing checks from within your Quicken program, see Book II, Chapter 2.

Here's a "once over lightly" review of using the Write Checks window. To open the window, you can choose Cash Flow⇨Write Checks, press Ctrl+W, or click Write Checks on the Register tab. When the Write Checks window appears, fill out the check information, and then click the Record Check button. After you've done that, the check transaction appears in the Checks to Print list at the bottom of the Write Checks window (as well as in the register).

Now you're at the point where you can display a QuickReport. With the Write Checks window still displayed, click on the transaction that uses the payee or category to report on in the Checks to Print list. Click the Report choice in the menu bar at the top of the Write Checks window, and then click the command for the type of QuickReport to create, as shown in Figure 1-7: payee (Payments Made To) or category (Amount Spent On).

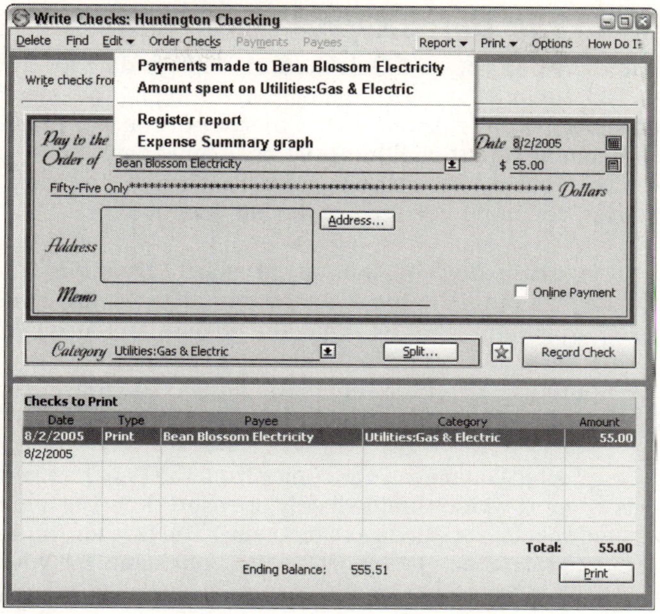

Figure 1-7: The Write Checks window features the same QuickReport choices as the Report menu on the Register tab.

Customizing QuickReports

If you take a peek back to Figure 1-6, you can see that the QuickReport provides a simple, chronological list of transactions with the specified payee or category. If you want a report that's less of a yawner and presents information the way you want to see it, you can tweak the QuickReport's appearance.

For example, say you've displayed a Category Report QuickReport that has hundreds of transactions. Rather than sort through all the transactions to find ones that are most relevant, you could sort the list by transaction amount. Or, you could change the date range, to view transactions from a shorter period such as the current or prior month.

While working with a QuickReport, you can change the date range for the data included in the report, include subtotals to add summary amounts, or change the sort order for the data. The QuickReport window includes the controls for making these report changes. These sorting methods are described below.

TIP

For the "unabridged" version of report customization, jump ahead to Book VII, Chapter 3.

Changing the QuickReport date range

When it initially pops open, a QuickReport displays data for the current year to date (YTD). In most cases, that might give you just the information you need. However, if you're displaying a QuickReport on January 2, the report won't contain much pertinent information, if any at all! On the other hand, if it's December 31 and you're looking for a transaction that took place in the prior quarter, you don't need to see the full year of data.

The Date Range drop-down list above the report data offers choices for changing the date range for the reported data. Most of the choices (Figure 1-8) are self-explanatory. For example, the Include All Dates choice expands the report to show all transactions using the specified category or payee, while the Month to Date choice limits the report data to transactions in the current month only.

In most cases, after you make your choice from the Date Range drop-down list, a new QuickReport window immediately opens to show the applicable data. (I discuss some special variations in a moment.) The title for the new report will reflect the date range that the report covers. For example, if you choose the Month to Date range, the report title changes from Payee Report — YTD or Category Report — YTD, to Payee Report — MTD or Category Report — MTD.

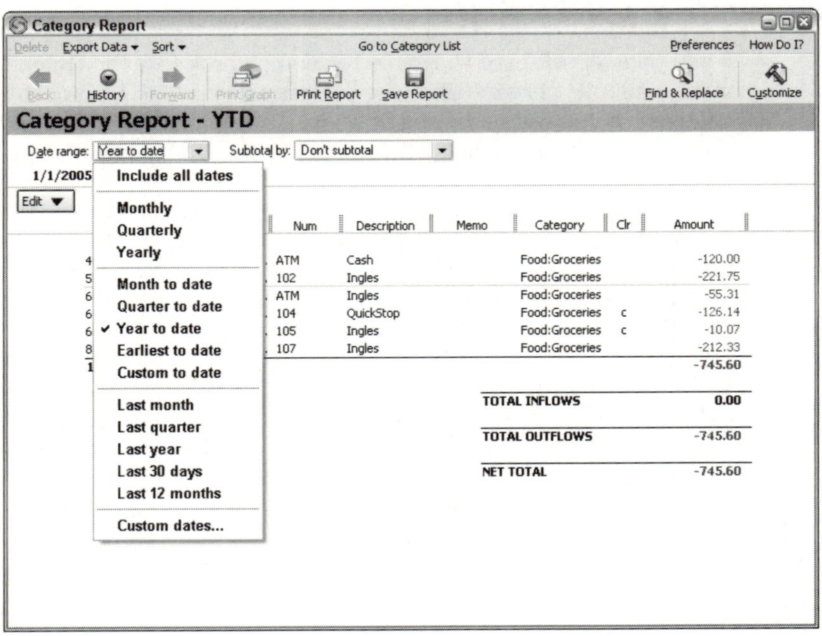

Figure 1-8: Your Date Range choice controls how much or little data the QuickReport includes.

You can double-click on a transaction in a report to jump to that transaction in the register. You also can click a transaction in the report and then click the Edit button in the report window to change the transaction from within the report window rather than jumping back to the register.

Reporting a particular month, quarter, or year

A few of the commands on the Date Range drop-down list enable you to set up the report to show info from a specific month, quarter, or year. To set up the report in this way, you must first select Monthly, Quarterly, or Yearly from the Date Range drop-down list to establish the overall reporting time frame.

After you select one of these time frames, an additional drop-down list appears so that you can select a specific reporting period, as shown in Figure 1-9. Open the drop-down list, and then click the actual month, quarter, or year for which you want to see data.

Reporting from a specified date

You may have situations where you want to report from a particular date to the present. For example, say you've opened a category QuickReport to show the transactions in the Gifts Given category. You want to see how much you've spent on gifts since your son's last birthday — September 15 of the prior year.

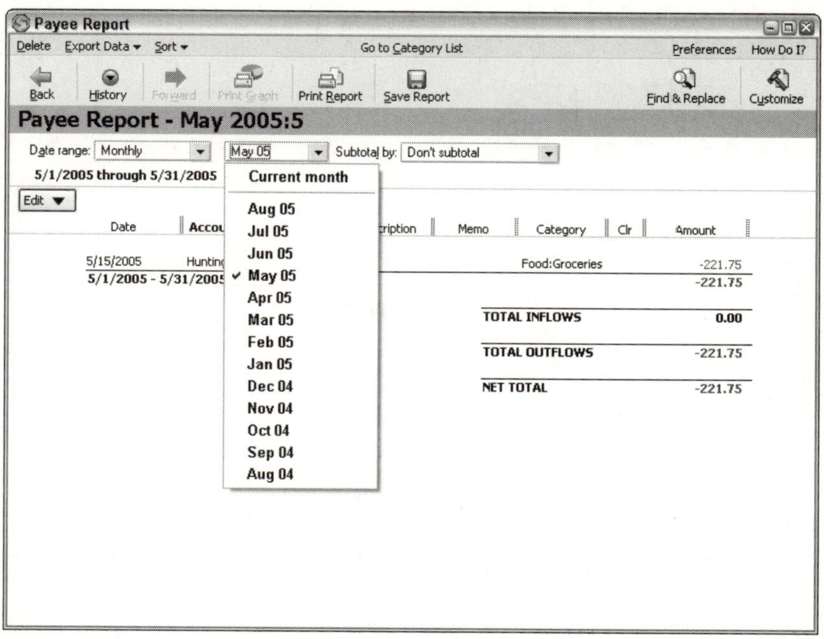

Figure 1-9: When you choose a Monthly, Quarterly, or Yearly reporting time frame, an extra drop-down appears and enables you to select the reporting period.

In such a case, you would first need to click the Custom to Date choice in the Date Range drop-down list in the QuickReport window. The Custom to Date dialog box (Figure 1-10) would open. Enter the desired date, such as 9/15/2004, in the From text box. Click OK, and presto! The report now lists transactions from 9/15/2004 to the present.

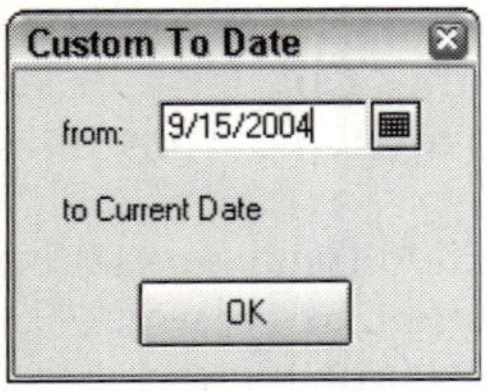

Figure 1-10: You can have the report include data starting from a specific date.

Reporting on custom dates

If *that's* not good enough, you can change the report to display transactions falling on or between specific starting and ending dates. Choose Custom Dates from the Date Range drop-down list. In the Custom Date (Figure 1-11) dialog box that appears, enter the desired starting (from) and ending (to) dates, and then click OK.

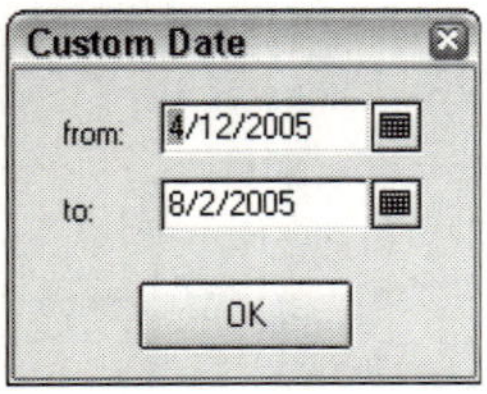

Figure 1-11: You can report transactions falling on and between particular dates.

Saving the report with custom dates

When you choose a date range other than Year to Date in a QuickReport, Quicken generates a separate new report in its own report window. Report windows work like other windows. You can minimize, maximize, and close them at will. Minimized reports appear as buttons (Figure 1-12) at the bottom of the Quicken window. To switch to another report, click its button in the Quicken window.

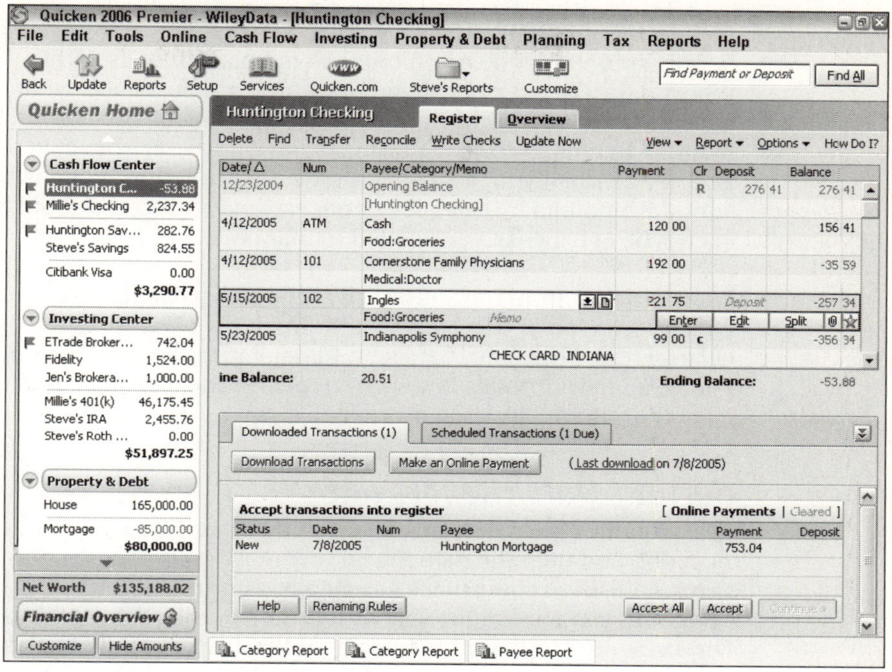

Figure 1-12: Report buttons in the Quicken window.

If you don't want Quicken to track a report variation that you've created, click the Delete button in the Report window.

When you click the window's X button for a report for which you've changed the date range, Quicken prompts you to save the report (Figure 1-13). You can click Don't Save to close the report without saving it, or Cancel to keep the report open. If you click the Save button, the Save Report dialog box appears, so that you can name the report and specify the save location. Book VII, Chapter 4 gives you the details on saving reports and using your saved reports.

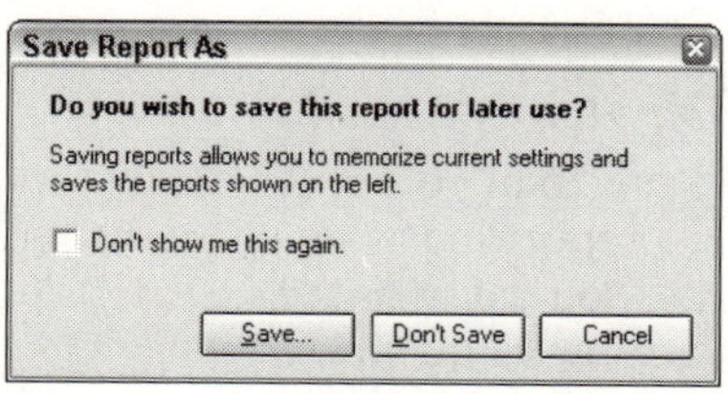

Figure 1-13: You can save a QuickReport if you've customized its date range.

Adding QuickReport subtotals

Report subtotals enable you to break out partial totals within the overall report data. For example, if you're viewing a report about your grocery expenditures, you might want to add monthly subtotals so you'll have monthly figures to compare against your budget, as shown in the example in Figure 1-14. Or, if you're viewing a payee QuickReport, you might want to subtotal amounts by category to understand the details about how much of each type of expense you've paid to that payee.

Make a choice from the Subtotal By drop-down list above the report data to choose the type of subtotals to add: Week, Two Weeks, Half Month, Month, Quarter, Half Year, Year, Category, Class, Payee, Account, or Tax Schedule. If you've added subtotals but want to remove them, choose Don't Subtotal from the Subtotal By drop-down list.

Sorting QuickReport data

QuickReports use a default sort order that lists transactions based on the Account, and then the date. Given that most reports cover a single account, this results in a report that's essentially a chronological listing of transactions. You can change the sort order to help make the report easier to use. For example, if you wanted to compare the report to the bank statement for your checking account, it would be useful to sort the report by check number (Account/Check #).

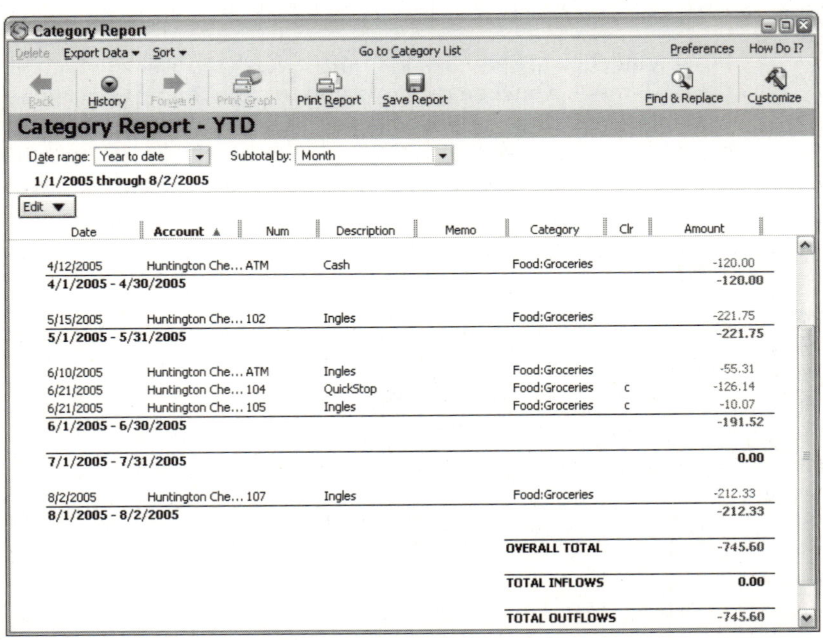

Figure 1-14: Subtotals in this report show monthly grocery expenses.

The Sort menu at the top of the report window offers several sorting choices: Sort by Account/Date (the default), Sort by Date/Account, Sort by Account/Check #, Sort by Amount, Sort by Payee, and Sort by Category. Open the menu and click a sort order to reorganize your report data instantly.

The column headings above the list of transactions in the report give you a visual cue about how the report has been sorted. The column heading for the field by which the data has been sorted appears in bold. For example, Figure 1-15 shows that the report transactions have been sorted by Amount.

TIP

You also can sort the report data by clicking the column heading for the field to sort by.

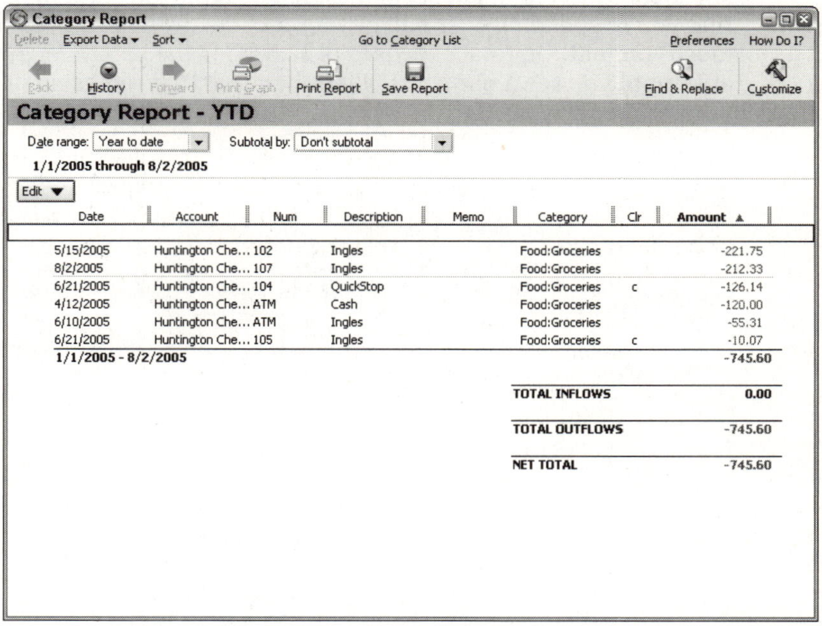

Figure 1-15: Find the bold column heading to see how data's been sorted.

TIP

Of course, you can change all three parameters—date range, subtotals, and sort order—to create a truly custom QuickReport.

Checking Out Graphs from the Register

I often joke that I don't do math on weekends because I'm giving my brain a break. The truth of the matter is that I'm often using my quality weekend time to pay bills or check my investments. My personal experience aside, it's often true that people avoid getting a handle on their finances because they "don't do numbers" or don't find a document like a bank statement to be a meaningful tool for decision-making.

If the raw data in a minireport or QuickReport report doesn't seem meaningful to you, maybe it's because you're more of a visual person, in which case you can turn to Quicken's graphs. (Note: I use the terms Chart and Graph interchangeably, like Kleenex and Tissue, or Indianapolis and My Home Town.)

As the example in Figure 1-16 illustrates, a graph presents financial information in a visual format for more meaning and impact. Seeing that you've spent $500 on rent might seem reasonable, until you see a pie chart showing that you're spending over half of your income (in other words, way too much) on rent. Or, total expenses of $2,500 for the month might see reasonable, until you see a bar chart illustrating that that represents twice your normal spending levels.

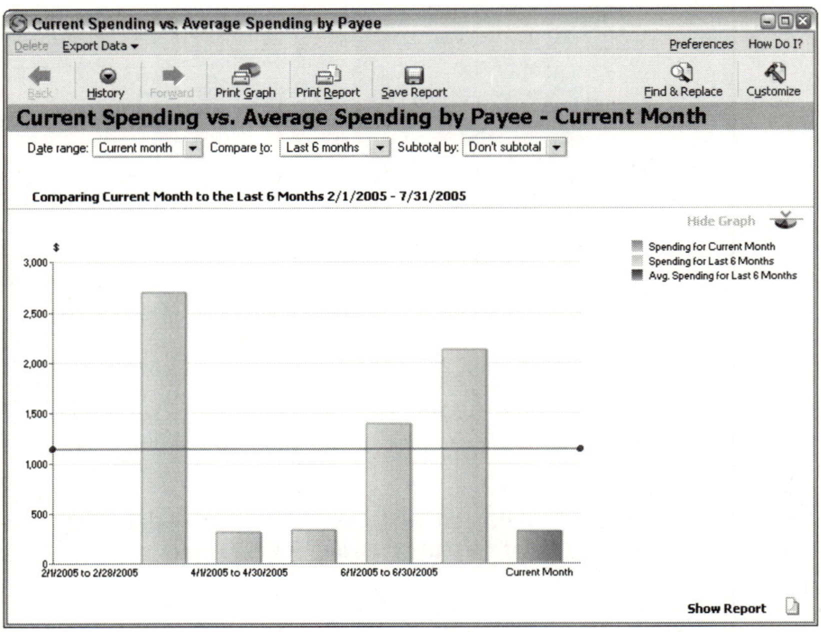

Figure 1-16: Quicken graphs like this one that analyzes spending serve as great decision-making tools.

To display a graph, choose the appropriate graph command from the Reports➪Graphs submenu. Quicken offers 14 graphs that cover cash flows, investments, and your overall financial picture. Here's a look at each of the graphs:

- ✦ **Spending by Category** displays a pie chart of total expenses entered for each category actually assigned in the register (Figure 1-17). Use this graph to try to identify where you might be over- or underspending.
- ✦ **Spending by Payee** displays a pie chart of amounts you've paid to each active payee. You might want to use this chart to zero in on overspending and to make choices about which businesses to patronize. For example, you might be buying clothing, groceries, and hardware from a single retailer, so you'd need to look at spending by payee rather than category to get a sense of how much you're spending at that retailer.
- ✦ **Current Spending versus Average Spending by Category** presents a bar chart of average spending by category for the current month and the six prior months. If you have the sense that you've overspending across the board for the month, compare the current month to the horizontal line that charts average spending.
- ✦ **Current Spending versus Average Spending by Payee** also presents a bar chart of average spending for recent months, but calculates the average by payee rather than category.

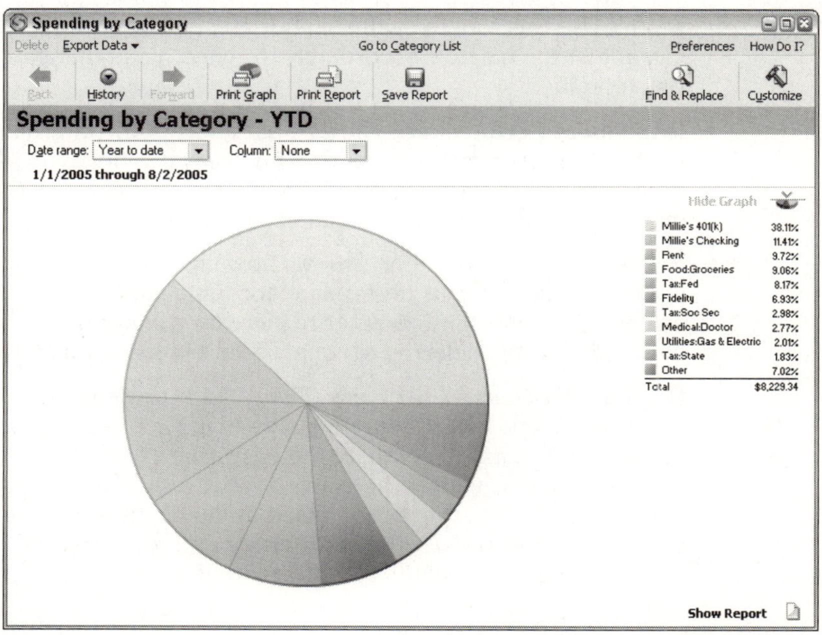

Figure 1-17: Check your spending in various categories, as well as looking at other graphs, to help you evaluate your financial choices.

TIP

Remember, if you have a month with an unusual emergency expense, your average figures might be distorted. If you experience such an event, don't give that month's data as much consideration as you otherwise would, or adjust the graph date range to try to eliminate the skewing data.

✦ **Income and Expense by Category** presents a bar chart with paired bars — one showing income and the other expenses — for each time interval charted. This graph can reveal how consistent your income is, an important issue for people who are self-employed or living from investment income. The graph shows total monthly values by default, but you can view more detailed data by payee, as explained in the later section called "Viewing data amounts."

✦ **Income and Expense by Payee** presents another graph with paired bars that presents detailed data by payee rather than by category.

✦ **Budget** graphically illustrates budget information you've set up in Quicken, using paired bars to compare budget versus actual income and expenses. (Book IV, Chapter 5 explains how to enter budget information in Quicken.)

✦ **Monthly Budget** charts the difference between expenses and income, showing graphically whether you've had a favorable or unfavorable (spent too much or earned too little) month financially.

✦ **Investment Asset Allocation** is a pie chart that illustrates how you have your money invested, by type of investment (large cap stocks, cash, and so on). Use this tool to evaluate your mix of investments, so that you can adjust the balance accordingly to reflect your changing needs and risk tolerance.

✦ **Investment Performance** shows a bar chart of the internal rate of return (IRR) for investments, by month. This chart can help you identify up or down periods or trends in the current year, so you can sell and buy investments for better performance, if needed.

✦ **Portfolio Value**, a pie chart, shows how much money you have invested in each of your various investment accounts. You can use this tool, for example, to determine whether to increase savings in taxable accounts because your tax-deferred accounts aren't growing quickly enough.

✦ **Portfolio Value and Cost Basis** (Figure 1-18) presents a stacked column chart that totals investment dollars held in each account, and uses line graphs (with dots) to compare the cost basis (how much you paid for the investments) versus the current value. Use this graph to evaluate your investment performance based on dollar amounts rather than percentages. In Figure 1-18, the chart date range and intervals have been changed from the defaults to chart more data.

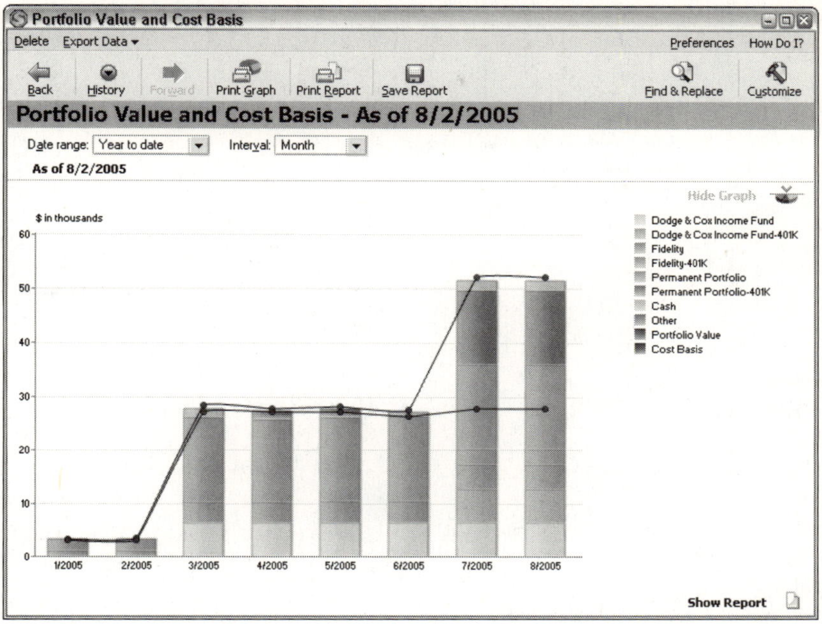

Figure 1-18: Watch your investments grow compared with what you paid for them with this Portfolio Value and Cost Basis Graph.

For some of the bar charts, the default Interval is set to None, resulting in a chart that shows a single bar of data. See the later section called "Customizing a graph" to find out how to adjust this setting to make your graph more meaningful.

- **Account Balances** charts liability and debt (credit card) accounts versus investment and bank account holdings, also charting the balance between them. Review this graph to get a handle on whether your savings are growing faster than your debts.
- **Net Worth** clarifies your overall bottom line. It uses a bar to compare your assets versus your liabilities, and uses a dot (or line when charting data over time) to identify your actual net worth. The higher the net worth value, the more real wealth you have.

Viewing data amounts

Charts do a terrific job of summarizing and presenting data, but at times, you may want to view the detail behind a pie slice, bar, or data point. You can use the mouse pointer with the legend (the graph key at the upper-right corner) and the chart elements to get more information about specific chart data.

For example, if a legend doesn't include dollar values or percentages, move the mouse pointer over a legend entry to display a pop-up box with the data for that chart (legend) item. Figure 1-19 shows an example.

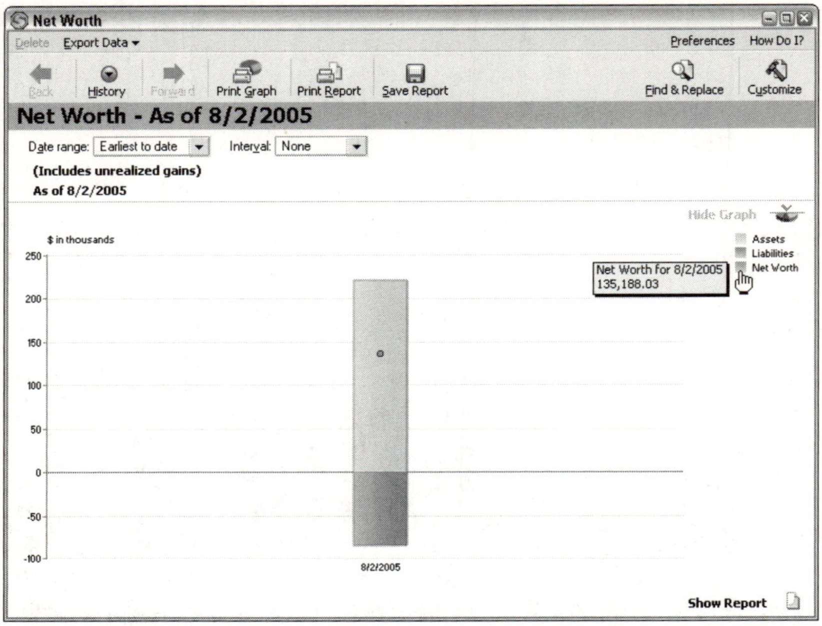

Figure 1-19: Point to a legend entry to display data for that chart element.

Similarly, you can point to a bar, slice, or point on the chart itself for a pop-up display of the data (Figure 1-20).

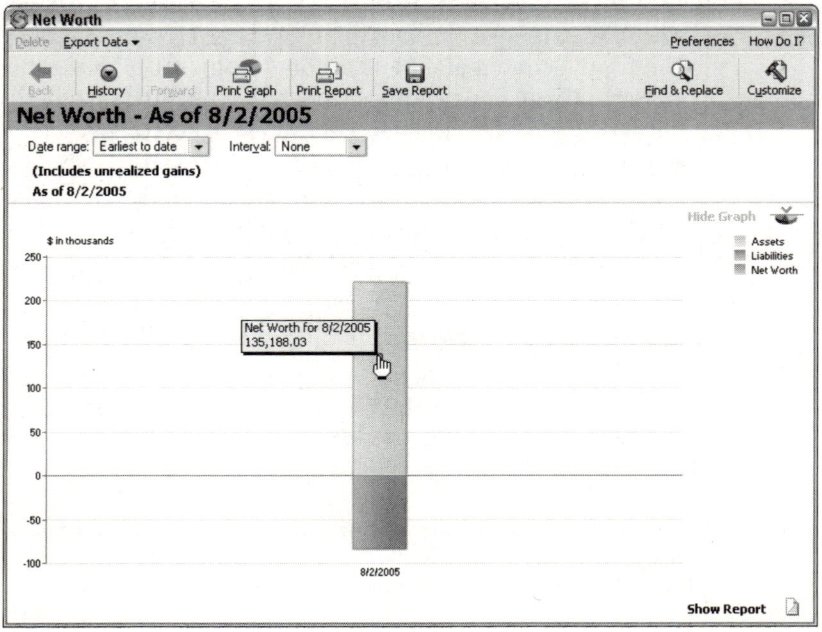

Figure 1-20: Pointing to a chart element also displays the charted value.

If the mouse pointer changes to a magnifying glass when over a chart element, double-click to open a window with the full listing of the data summarized by that bar, slice, or point. For example, Figure 1-21 shows the assets charted in the positive (above the 0 line) portion of the graph bar to the left of the window.

In some cases, double-clicking a charted element displays another chart or a report with the needed details. In such a case, you can click the Back button on the Graph window toolbar to return to the original graph.

The Graph window also includes a Show Report button in the lower-right corner. Click that button to include report data along with the graph (Figure 1-22), and then click the Hide Report button that appears to remove the report detail from the Graph window.

Customizing a graph

The process for customizing a graph works just like changing the date range and adding subtotals to a report, as described earlier in the chapter. You make choices from drop-down lists above the data, and then choose whether to save the customized graph at the prompt that appears when you close the Graph window.

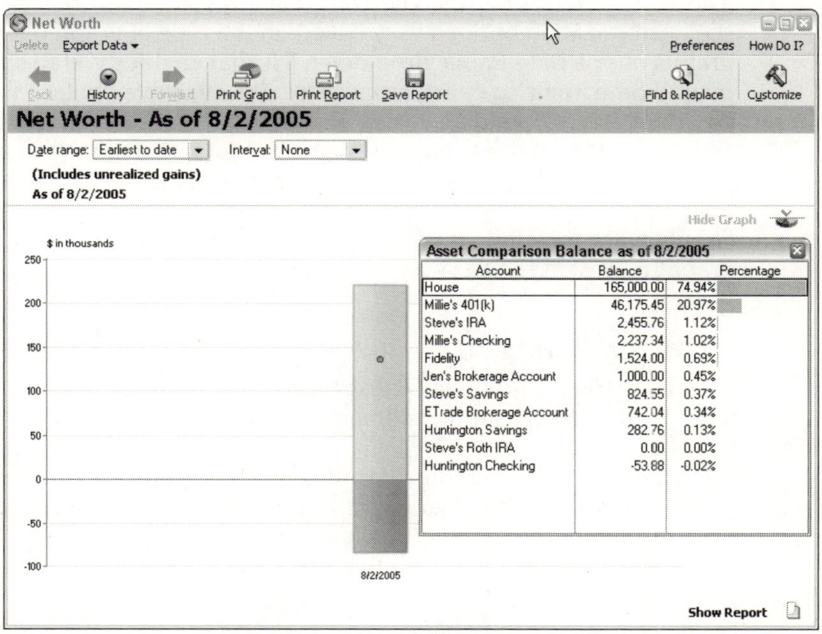

Figure 1-21: You can open a window showing detailed data about a charted summary value.

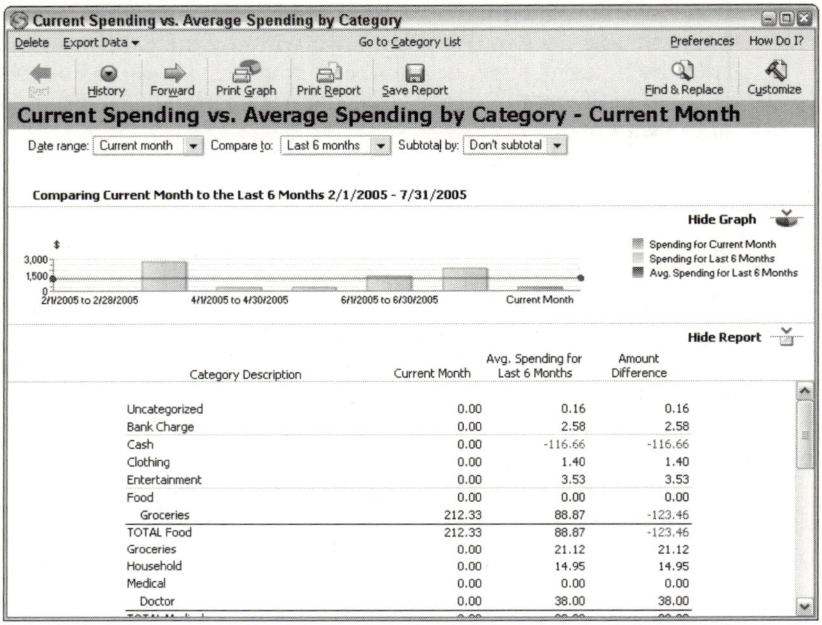

Figure 1-22: You can show or hide underlying report data along with a graph.

The key difference between customizing a graph rather than a report is that the customization options vary based on the type of graph displayed. All graphs offer a Date Range drop-down list that enables you to specify what overall time frame to chart. From there, the available choices vary. For example, the Current Spending versus Average Spending by Category graph (Figure 1-23) includes Compare To and Subtotal By controls in addition to the Date Range drop-down list below the graph title.

Simply make the choices you want from the available controls to alter the graph to present the data you need.

Printing a graph

When you open a graph in Quicken, the Print Graph button (refer to Figure 1-23) in the Graph window toolbar becomes active.

Click the button to open the Print dialog box. Chapter 4 of this book describes printing in more detail. If you want to simply print with the default settings, click the OK button in the Print dialog box.

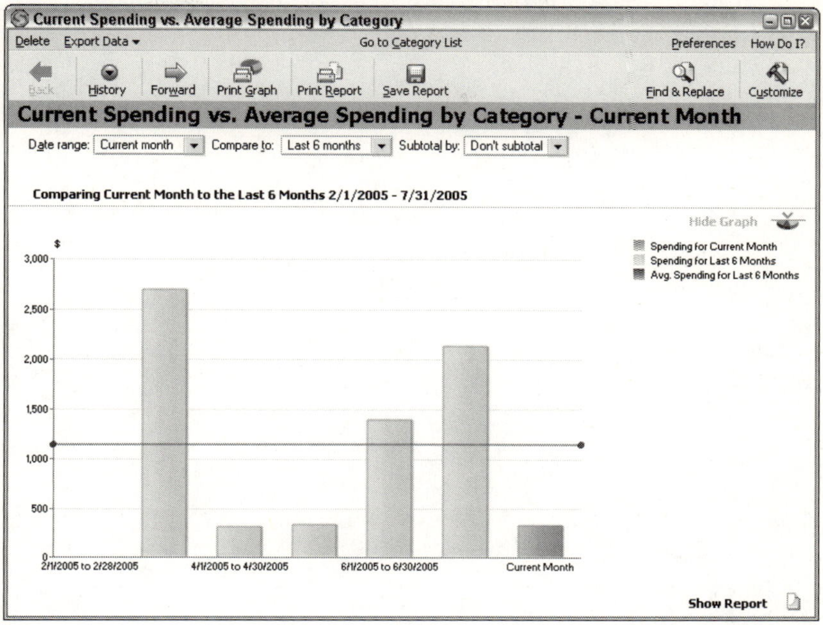

Figure 1-23: The graph window choices for customization vary depending on the chart type.

Chapter 2: Quicken's Standard Reports

In This Chapter

- Checking out the Reports & Graphs Center
- Viewing and changing a report
- Managing your transactions from within a report
- Stating your preferences for reports
- Getting easy answers

With typical screen settings, the register can only show a dozen or fewer transactions onscreen at a time. Such limited data is of limited use in terms of being a tool for planning and decision-making. And even if you sort the transactions, the register can't do things like tell you how much you spent in a particular category or over a particular time period. Quicken's comprehensive reports (and graphs) enable you to summarize and analyze all your Quicken information, freeing you from the time-consuming and mind-numbing work of finding and totaling transactions. In this chapter, see how you can use Quicken's Reports & Graphs Center to view reports that give you financial insight, to work with transactions, and to get quick answers to specific questions about your finances.

Familiarizing Yourself with the Reports & Graphs Center

Personal financial reporting used to fall squarely in the domain of well-paid financial advisors. After all, they were the ones who had the software and the time to collate reams of information. Once the more meticulous among us got our hands on basic spreadsheet software, we could — if so inclined — spend our precious free time entering information from bank and investment statements to do a little sorting and subtotaling. What fun. Why not go get a root canal while we're at it?

You can count on the inexpensive Quicken program to save you a heap o' work when it comes to analyzing your income and investments. Quicken not only offers dozens of reports and graphs, but it also organizes the reports and graphs into an easy-to-access location called the Reports & Graphs

Center. Figure 2-1 shows the Reports & Graphs Center, which you can open by choosing Reports & Graphs from the Reports menu or by clicking the Reports button on the Quicken tool bar.

TIP: The first time you display the Reports & Graphs Center or a report in Quicken 2006, the What's New in Quicken 2006 window might appear. Review the information in the window, which covers new report features. If you want to see more of what's new, click the Show Full List of What's New link in the lower-left corner. When you finish working in the window, click the Exit button in the upper-right corner.

TIP: To discontinue seeing What's New windows, click the Don't Show Me This Again check box.

The left side of the Reports & Graphs Center displays the Quicken Standard Reports list of the report (and graph) categories offered by Quicken. The My Saved Reports list at the right organizes any custom reports that you save. You can create custom folders to organize your reports in the My Save Reports list (see the next chapter for a comprehensive discussion on customizing reports).

By the way, the Reports & Graphs Center essentially treats a graph as a report, so I'll stick with just referring to "reports" to simplify descriptions in the chapter.

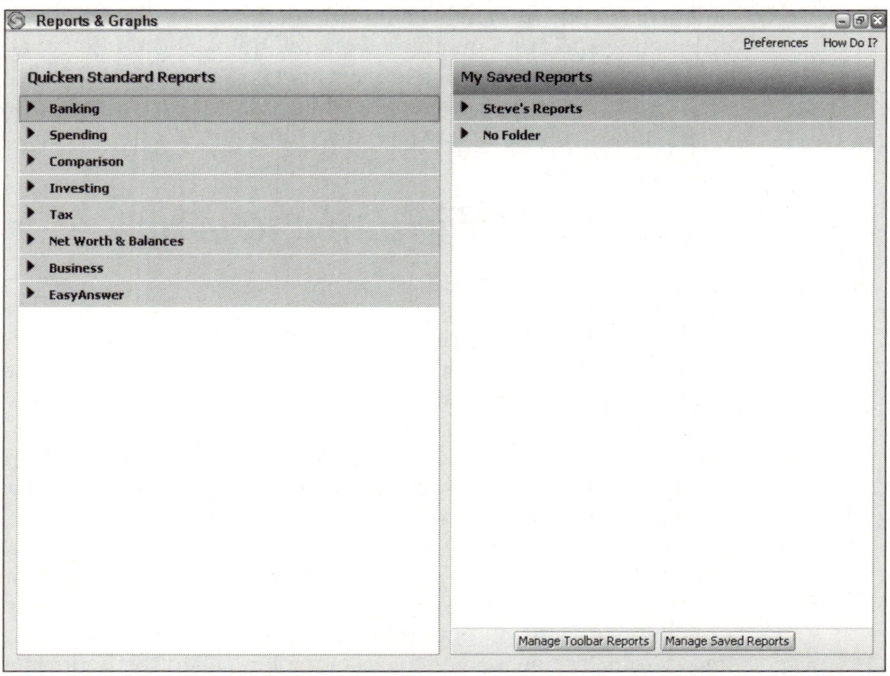

Figure 2-1: Find reports aplenty in the Reports & Graphs Center.

To see the reports in a particular category in the Quicken Standard Reports list or in a folder in the My Saved Reports list, click the category or folder name. As shown in Figure 2-2, the reports available in the category appear below the category name. Click the triangle again to hide the reports in the category. The next few sections explain how to display and work with reports from the Reports & Graphs Center.

You can use the Reports & Graphs Center to view a single report at a time, or you can leave the center open to work with multiple reports. You can click the Minimize button (it's the one that looks like a minus sign) in the upper-right corner of the Reports & Graphs Center window to "park" the Reports & Graphs Center as a button at the bottom of the Quicken window. Click the Reports & Graphs button (Figure 2-3) to restore the Reports & Graphs Center window. Any report you minimize also appears as a button at the bottom of Quicken, as Figure 2-3 illustrates. Click the button to restore the report window.

To close the Reports & Graphs Center window, click the X button in the upper-right corner of the window.

Quicken's reporting and graphing capabilities rely on the categories you assign to transactions. Reports cannot include uncategorized transactions. If you need to review what's involved with creating and using categories, jump back to Chapter 1 of Book II.

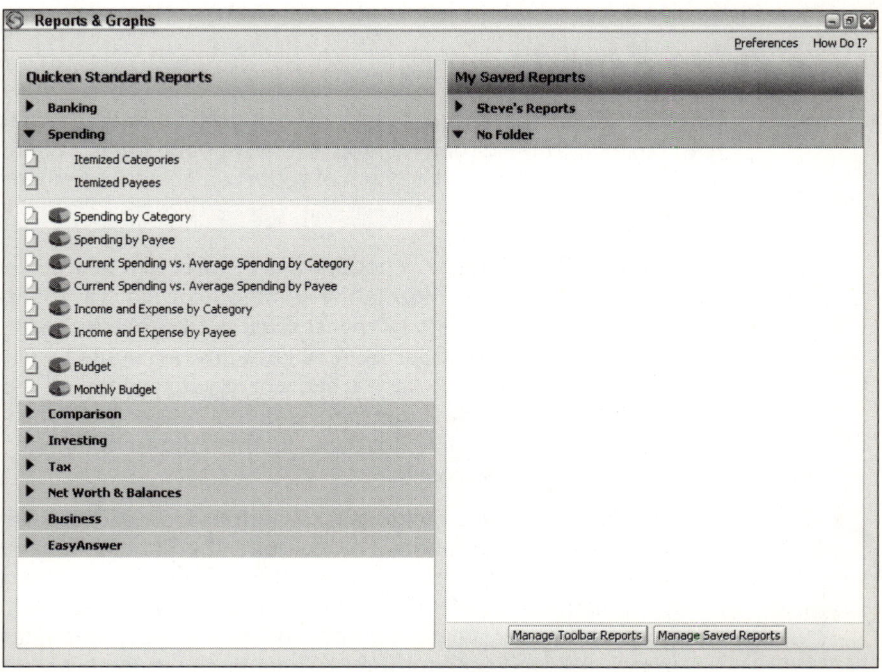

Figure 2-2: Open the category or folder to see its reports.

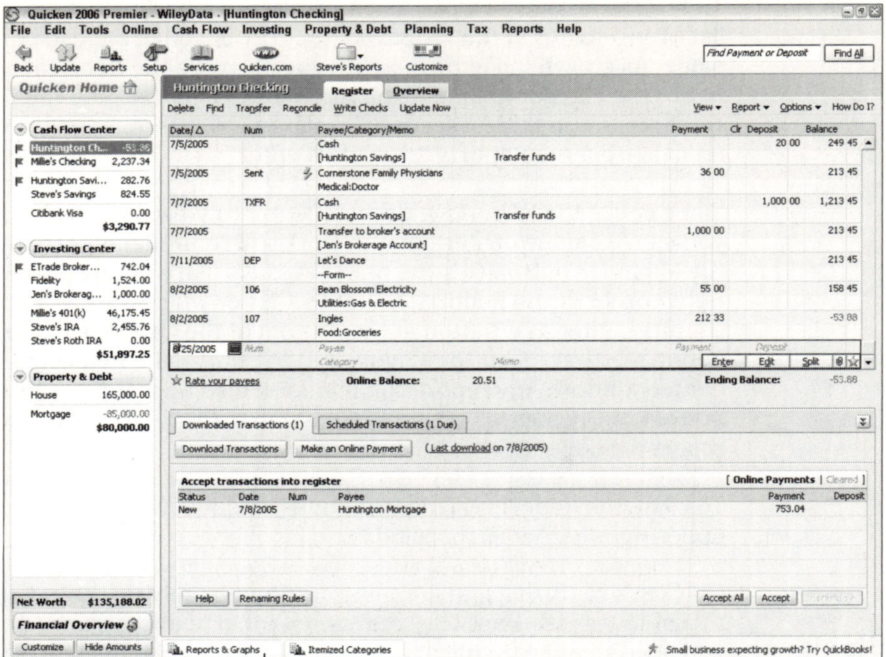

Figure 2-3: Click the button to restore the minimized Reports & Graphs Center window or a minimized report.

Click to restore the full window.

Displaying Reports

Using the Reports & Graphs Center looks pretty simple, because it *is*. Before you move on to the equally *un*-tough task of opening an actual report, pause for a moment to review the types of reports available to you in the report categories:

- **Banking:** This category contains five reports that enable you to review basic, yet essential, information about one or more accounts. For example, the Banking Summary report (Figure 2-4) groups the income, expense, and transfer transactions from all cash flow accounts by category. This report definitely can help you see where your money's coming from and where it's going. The other reports in this category are the Cash Flow, Missing Checks (which also lists all other transactions), Reconciliation, and Transactions reports.

  By default, Quicken includes transactions from all applicable accounts when it displays a report. For example, the Transactions report in the Banking category includes transactions from all cash flow and investing accounts, whereas the Banking Summary report includes transactions from all the cash flow accounts. To limit a report to display information from a selected account only, to change the reporting period from the default of Year to Date (YTD), and so on, you must customize the report as described in the next chapter.

TIP: To see a description of any report in the Reports & Graphs Center, display the reports in the category, and then move the mouse pointer over the report. A yellow pop-up tip appears to describe the report, as shown in the example in Figure 2-5.

✦ **Spending:** The Spending category includes two reports and several choices with a graph icon beside them. When a graph icon appears beside a listing in a report category, you can display either a report or a graph, as shown in Figure 2-6. The Itemized Categories and Itemized Payees group transactions from cash flow accounts by category or payee, respectively. Several more reports analyze spending and income: Spending by Category, Spending by Payee, Current Spending versus Average Spending by Category, Current Spending versus Average Spending by Payee, Income and Expense by Category, and Income and Expense by Payee. Rather than showing you all transactions, these reports help you zero in more precisely on how you're either making or spending your money. For example, the Spending by Payee report (Figure 2-7) by default shows you how much you've paid to each payee over the course of the current year to date (YTD). The Budget report compares planned versus actual income and spending by category, whereas the Monthly Budge report breaks out budgeted and actual income and spending by both category and month.

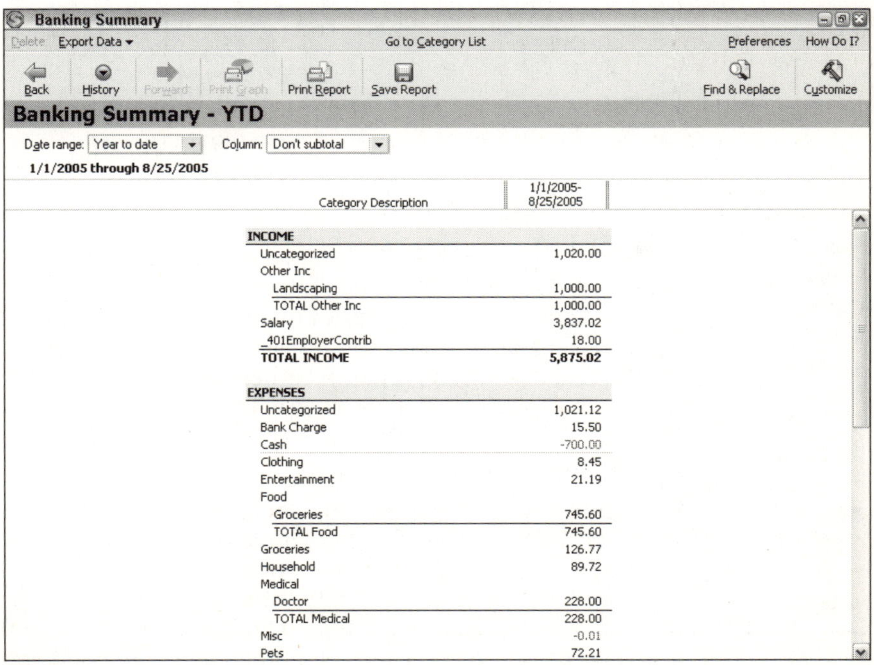

Figure 2-4: See income, expenses, and transfers by category — from all cash flow accounts — in the Banking Summary report.

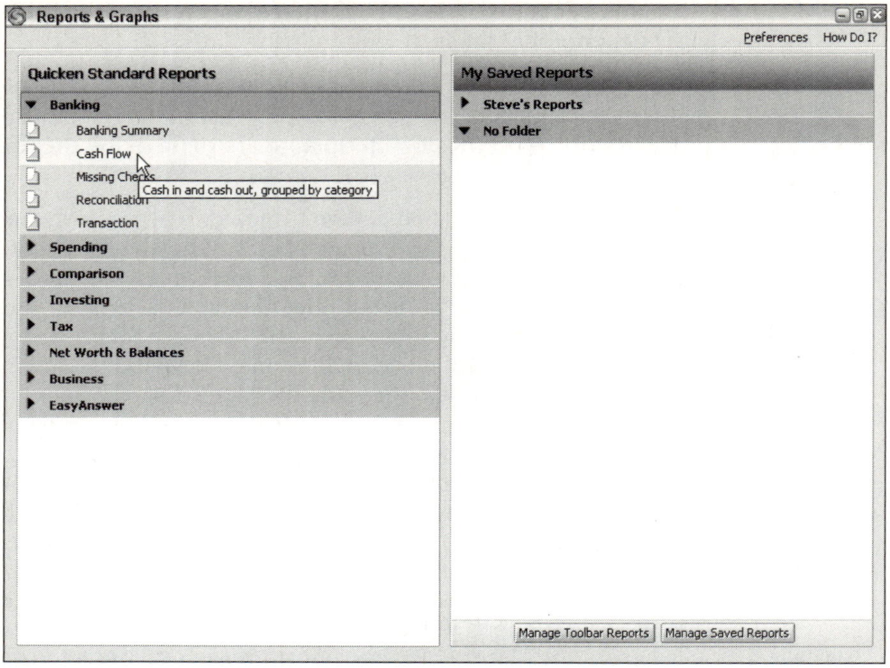

Figure 2-5: Point to a report in the Reports & Graphs Center to see a pop-up tip describing the report.

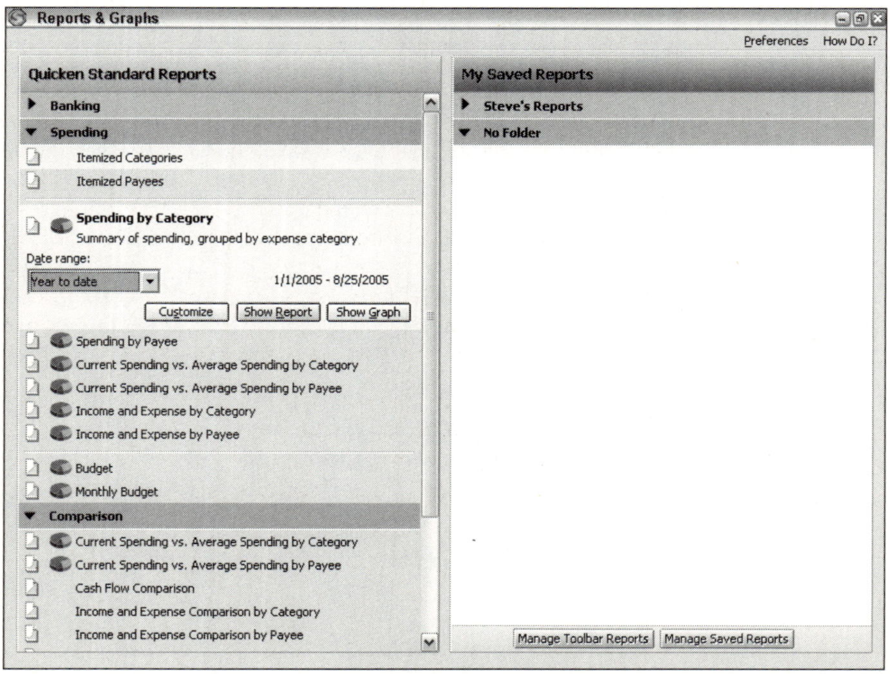

Figure 2-6: When you choose a report with a graph icon beside it, you have the option of going with a straight report or a graph, instead.

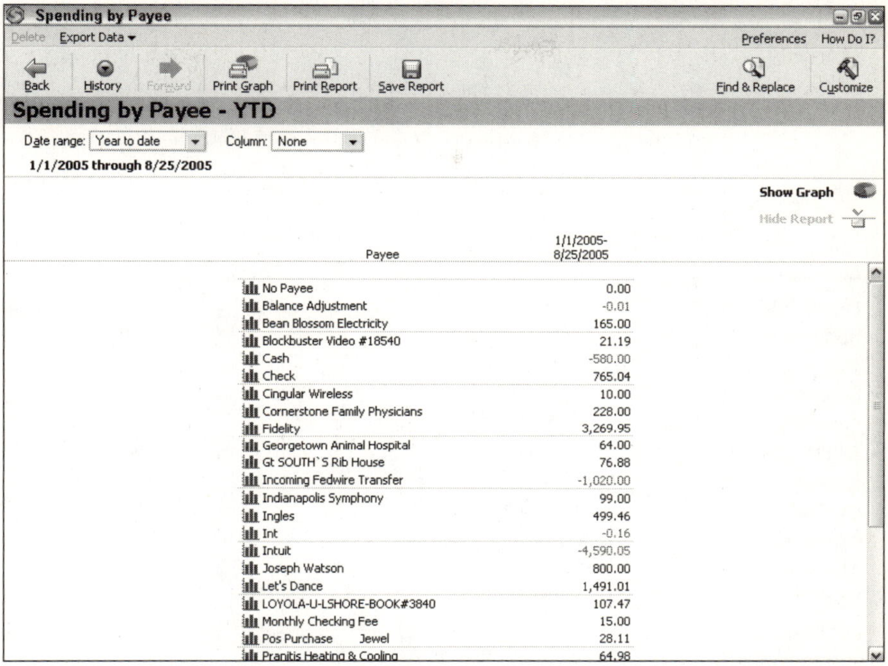

Figure 2-7: See how much you've paid to each payee in the current YTD using the Spending by Payee report.

The graphs available via the Reports & Graphs Center are for the most part the same as the graphs described in the previous chapter.

✦ **Comparison:** Most of the reports in this category basically compare financial inflows and/or outflows over a particular time period. The first two reports, Current Spending versus Average Spending by Category and Current Spending versus Average Spending by Payee (Figure 2-8), can help you determine if you're exceeding your normal spending in a particular category or to a particular payee. The Cash Flow Comparison report compares money inflows and outflows during two time periods (by default, the current YTD and the prior year). Similarly, the Income and Expense Comparison by Category and Income and Expense Comparison by Payee reports compare income and expenses during two time periods.

The Profit and Loss Comparison report as well as some reports in the Business category are part of the broader Quicken Home & Business version and must be purchased to be unlocked (more on this version in Chapter 1 of Book VIII). Click the Unlock Report button to purchase the report for use.

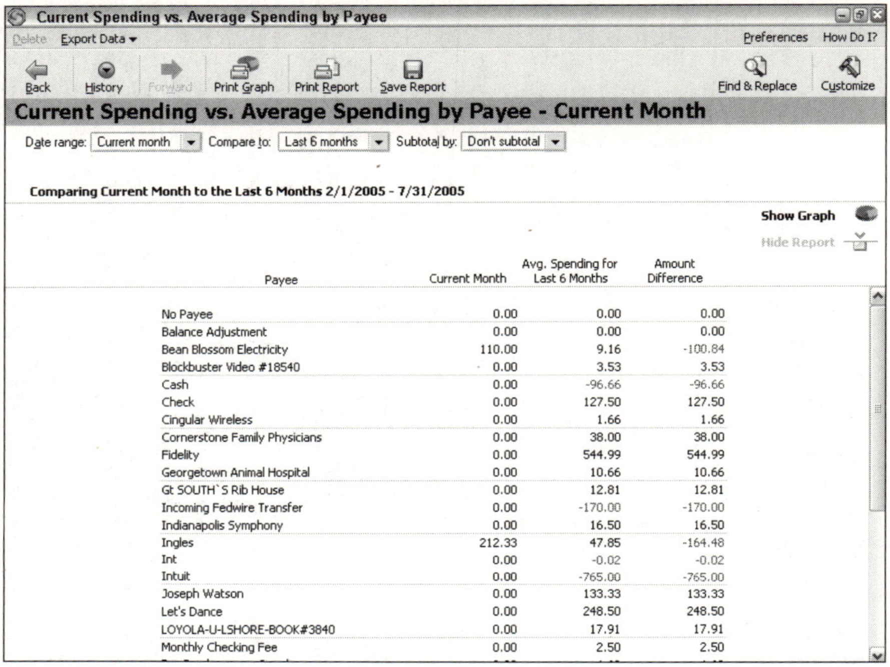

Figure 2-8: Reports in the Comparison category enable you to compare income or expenses from two time periods.

- **Investing:** The investing reports here enable you to check on the performance of the investments you're tracking with investment accounts in Quicken. These reports provide information for decision-making, as well as information that helps at tax time. For example, the Capital Gains report calculates how much you've made on securities that you've sold in the current YTD, so you can more easily report that gain. The Investing Activity report (Figure 2-9) shows quarterly investment activity and income, as well as investment performance helpful in calculating quarterly estimated tax payments. The Investment Asset Allocation report shows you how much you've invested in various *asset classes*, so that you can adjust your portfolio to reflect your risk tolerance, time until retirement, and other needs. Other investment reports cover Investment Income, Investment Performance, Investment Transactions, Portfolio Value, and Portfolio Value and Cost Basis.
- **Net Worth and Balances:** When you need to see the big picture, check out the Account Balances and Net Worth reports. The former shows you the total value of each account you've set up in Quicken. The Net Worth report (Figure 2-10) totals your assets and liabilities from various accounts and presents the bottom line. The Overall Total (defined as your total assets less your total liabilities) calculated in this report is a key measure of your overall financial health. Focus on growing this number — by increasing your assets and reducing your liabilities — to increase your wealth and security.

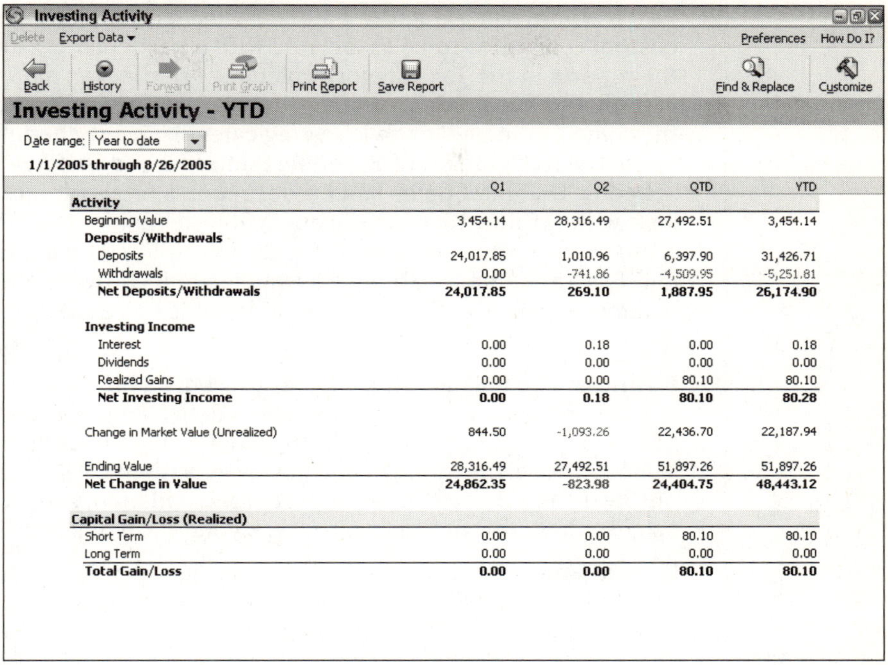

Figure 2-9: Investment reports like this Investment Activity report give you the insight you need to help build your wealth.

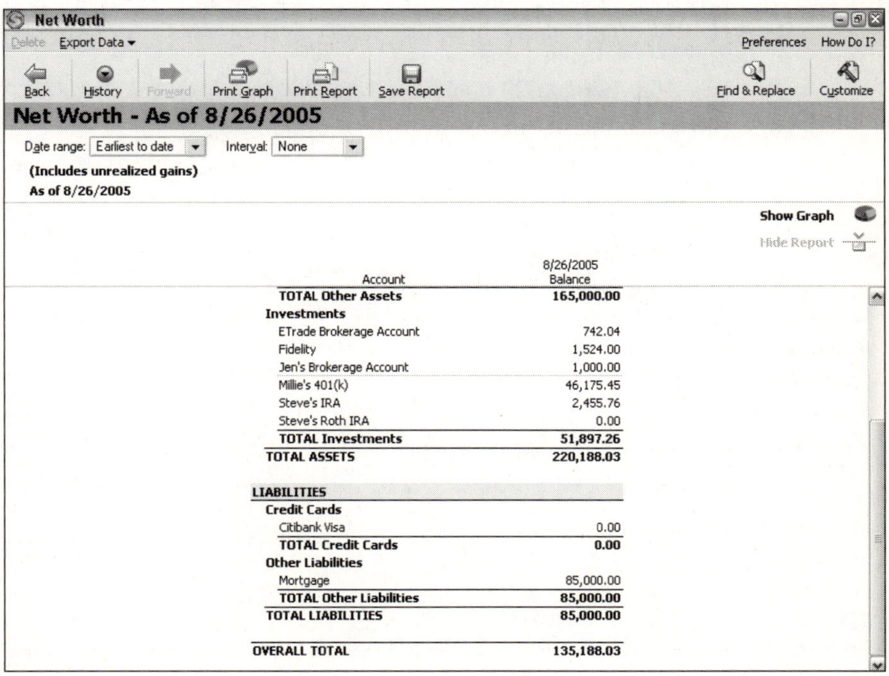

Figure 2-10: The Net Worth report presents the total of your assets less your liabilities.

- **Tax:** If you're using Quicken's standard categories and have set up any custom categories to be associated with a particular tax form line item, the reports in the Tax category calculate relevant tax data to help you with the dreaded ordeal of doing your taxes. The Capital Gains report is the same as the one in the Investing category. The Schedule A-Itemized Deductions (Figure 2-11), Schedule B-Interest and Dividends, and Schedule D-Capital Gains and Losses reports total transactions associated with tax line items on the applicable schedule. The Tax Schedule report shows all tax-related transactions, grouped by tax form or schedule. The Tax Summary Report groups tax-related transactions by income, expense, and transfer. BTW, there is quite a bit more detail on these tax repots in Book V.
- **Business:** The Balance Sheet report presents a business-style evaluation of your finances, showing your assets versus liabilities and equity. The Cash Flow, Cash Flow Comparison, and Missing Checks reports are the same as those appearing in categories described earlier. The remaining business-only reports must be purchased and unlocked. From there, you can use them within Quicken to track your small business finances.
- **EasyAnswer:** The reports here help you answer plain English questions about your finances. See the section later in this chapter called "Checking Out an EasyAnswer Report" to discover more.

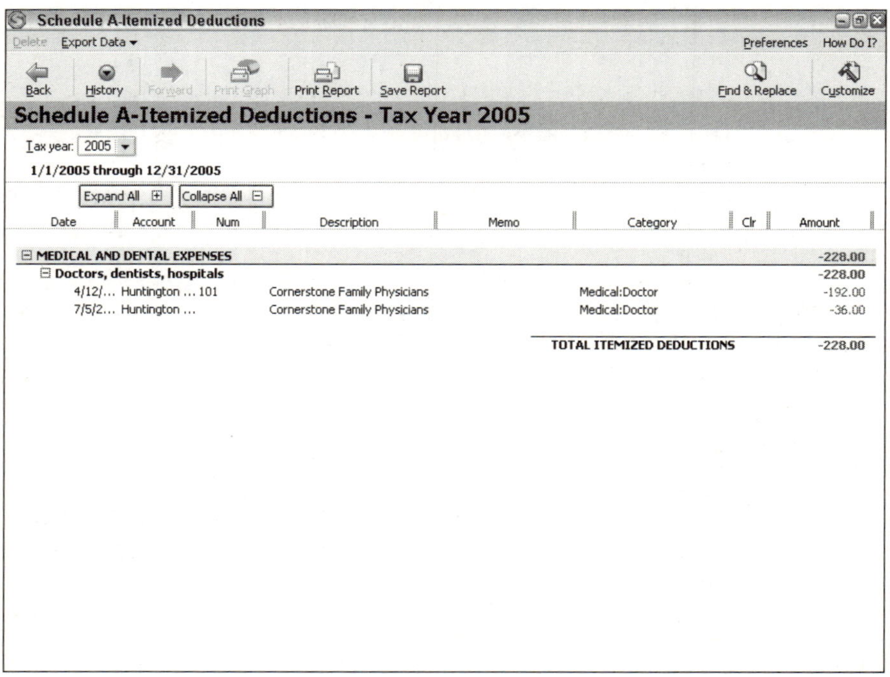

Figure 2-11: Quicken can total transactions for reporting on schedules A, B, and D of your federal tax returns.

Methods for displaying a report

Quicken 2006 actually offers a number of different ways to start displaying a report when you need it. You can work from the Reports & Graphs Center, use the Reports menu, or even use the Quicken tool bar. Whichever method you choose, you can display a powerful report in a matter of moments.

If you want to display a report from the Reports & Graphs Center, follow these steps:

1. **Choose Reports⇨Reports & Graphs Center or click the Reports button on the Quicken tool bar.**

   The Reports & Graphs Center window appears.

2. **Click a category in the Quicken Standard Reports list or a folder in the My Saved Reports list.**

   The reports in the category or folder appear in a list.

3. **Click the report name.**

   The basic choices for setting up the report appear below the report name, like the example in Figure 2-12. The options presented vary depending on the report, but generally consist of drop-down lists for choosing a Date Range, Payee, or Compare To (time period to compare to).

4. **Choose the desired report settings from the drop-down lists below the report name.**

5. **Click Show Report or Show Graph (refer to Figure 2-12) to open the report.**

   The report appears in its own window onscreen, and from there, you can change it and print it as described later in this chapter and in the next two chapters.

TIP

When you choose the Reconciliation report from the Banking category, Quicken immediately prompts you to print the report because this report does not display onscreen. Click the Show Report button, enter a Report Title in the Reconciliation Report Setup dialog box that appears, and then click Print to send the report to the printer.

The Reports menu lists the same categories as in the Reports & Graphs Center. To open a report, click the Reports menu, move the mouse pointer over the category name, and then click the report in the submenu that appears. For example, you would choose Reports⇨Spending⇨Spending by Payee to open the Spending by Payee report. Note that when you use this method, Quicken displays the report using default report settings rather than prompting you to make choices as the Reports & Graphs Center does.

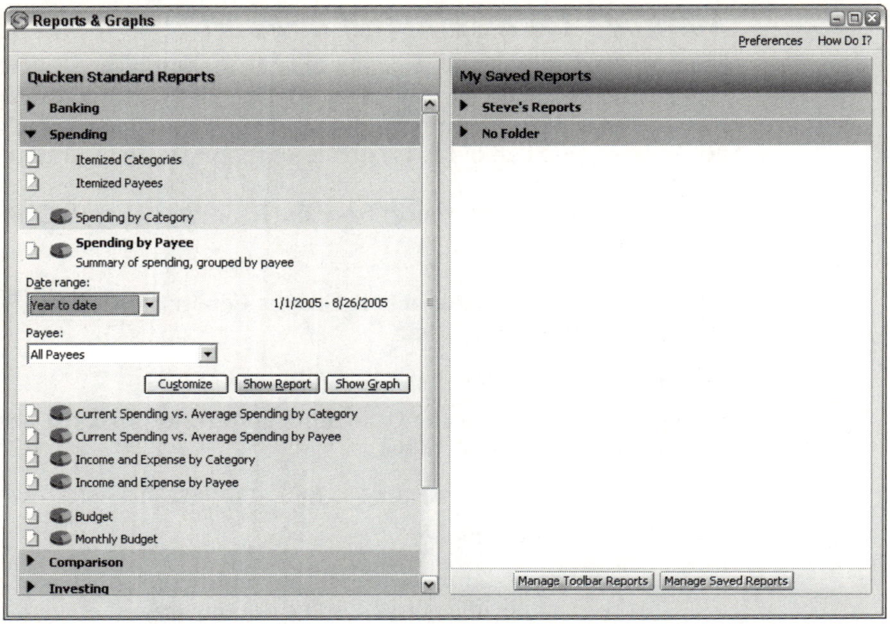

Figure 2-12: The Reports & Graphs Center offers basic options for setting up the report you've chosen.

In some cases, the Register and Overview tabs for some accounts offer a Reports menu. Click Reports to open a menu of reports (Figure 2-13) available for that account. Click the report you want to display using default settings.

If you save a custom report, you can add a button for displaying that report to the Quicken tool bar. To get the lowdown on this trick, see Chapter 4 of Book VII.

Changing report contents

To make sure that you can review the information you need, Quicken enables you to change some report settings within the report window onscreen. The available choices appear at the top of the report window and vary depending on the report you're viewing. (These are the quick and dirty settings. If you want to really dig into wrangling report information, skip on to the next chapter in Book VII.)

In many cases, you might want to change the time period the report covers. You can make this change by choosing a Date Range from the drop-down list like the one shown in Figure 2-14. A few of the commands on the Date Range drop-down list enable you to set up the report to show info from a specific month, quarter, or year, or from other specific time periods. To get more specifics about specifying the report Date Range, and so I don't have to repeat myself, see Chapter 1 of Book VII. That section also tells you how to save a report with custom dates when Quicken prompts you.

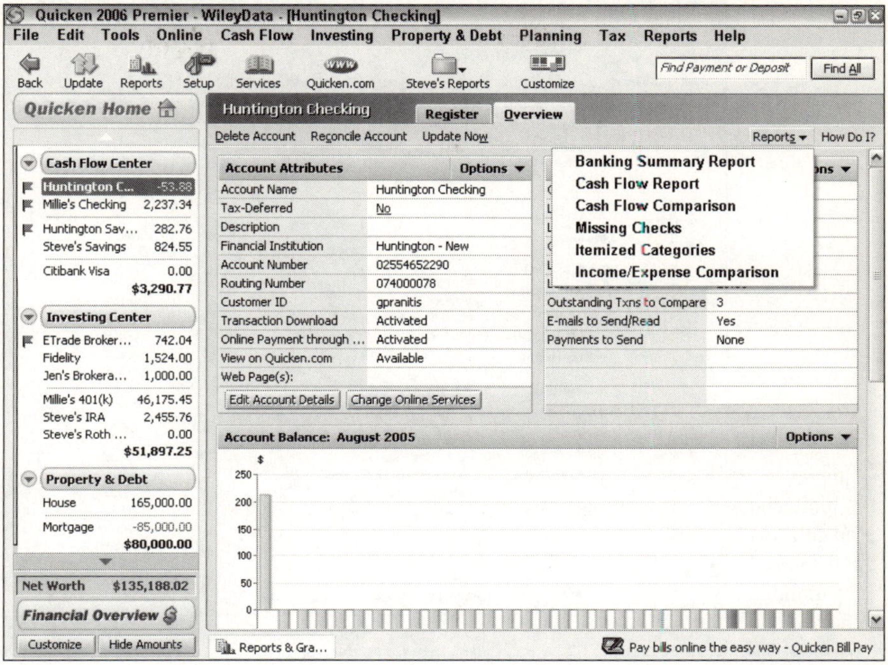

Figure 2-13: You also can display a report from the Register or Overview tabs for some accounts.

Some reports might include other settings, such as an Interval setting. The choices on the Interval drop-down list (Figure 2-15) tell Quicken how to total information for the columns in the report. For example, if you choose Quarter, the report totals a quarter's worth of transactions for each column, rather than totaling a month's worth of transaction.

TIP

You can click the Show Graph button near the upper-right corner of the report data, when it appears, to display a graph of the report information above the data itself. If you decide you don't need the graph, click the Hide Graph button that subsequently appears to remove the graph.

Some reports also work in an outline fashion to present the information from various accounts. When that's the case, Expand All and Collapse All buttons appear above the report data, and small minus sign buttons appear to the left of each account name (Figure 2-16). Click the minus button beside an account to collapse or hide its transaction, showing only the account name and subtotal on a single line. Click the plus sign button beside a collapsed entry to expand (redisplay) its transactions. To expand or collapse all the transactions in the report, use the Expand All or Collapse All buttons at the top. Collapsing data enables you to hide irrelevant stuff without having to customize the report. Nifty!

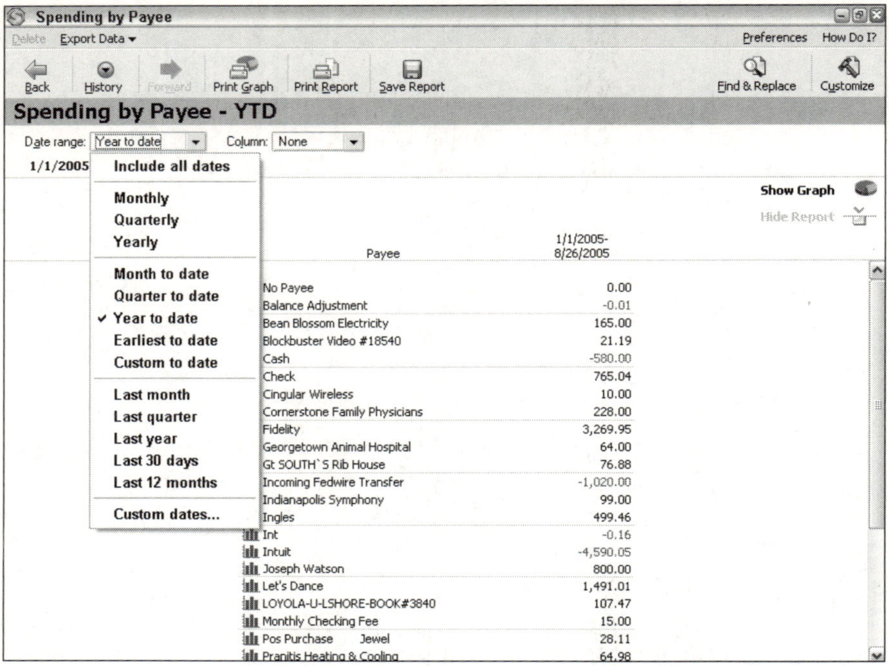

Figure 2-14: Change a report using the controls at the top of the report window.

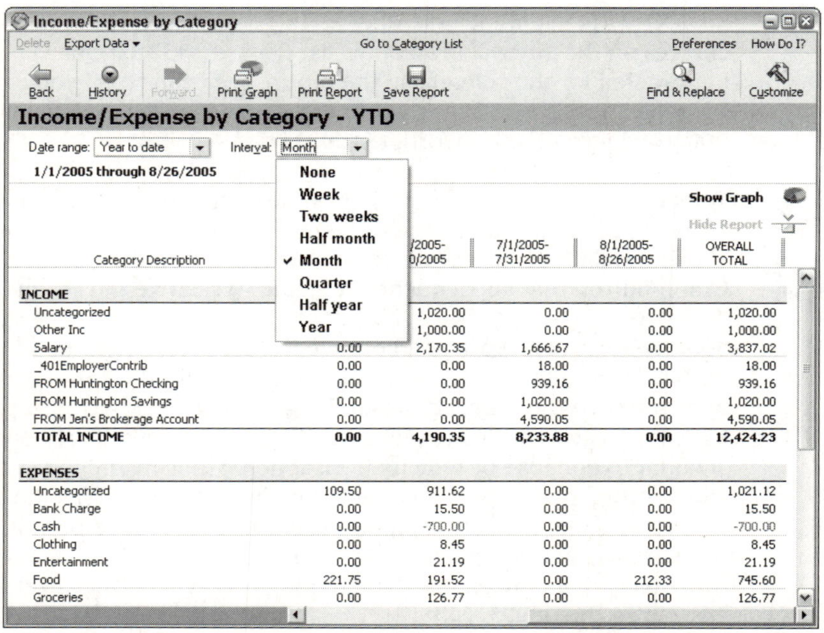

Figure 2-15: The Interval choice controls the columns shown in the report.

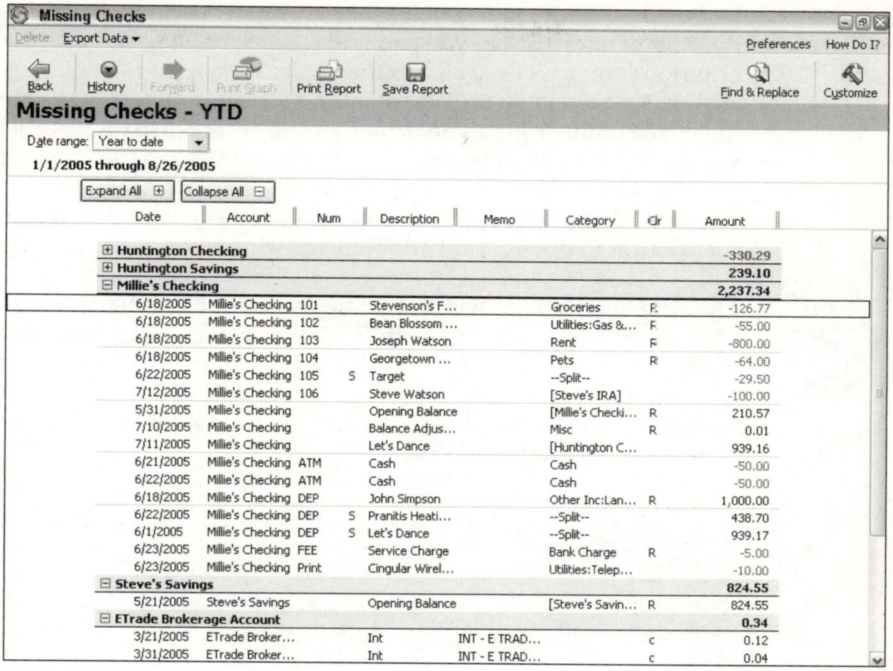

Figure 2-16: Expand and collapse transactions to streamline a long report.

Working with Report Transactions

Some programs are — pardon this rant — Dumb with a capital D when it comes to reports. In such a program, the report might appear in its own window and you might get to change a few print settings like margins, but that's it. You can't really work with the data itself in any meaningful way.

Quicken reports, in contrast, remain flexible so that you can really *use* the information, and even fix information. This section covers how to find and change transactions in a report. Finding a transaction might be important if you have a question about the transaction. And fixing a transaction that's wrong, well, the point of that is obvious.

Searching for information in a report

If you've ever used the Find and Replace capabilities in your word processing program, this will be familiar. If you've read Chapter 2 of Book II, you've probably been there and done this. In any case, it'll still be a snap for you to learn.

Rather than scrolling through a lengthy report to find a transaction with the right bit of information, you can find a transaction based on information (a criterion) you specify. Quicken then spits back a list of matching transactions, so you can zero in on the one of interest. For example, if you can't remember the check number for a check that you wrote to Cash on a particular date, you can search for all transactions that have *Cash* in the Payee field.

The tool bar for every report window includes a Find & Replace button. Click that button to open a Find and Replace window.

TIP

The Find and Replace window is the same Find and Replace window that appears when you choose Edit⇨Find & Replace⇨Find/Replace from the main menu.

Figure 2-17 shows the choices to make at the top of the window to find transactions with Cash in the Payee field.

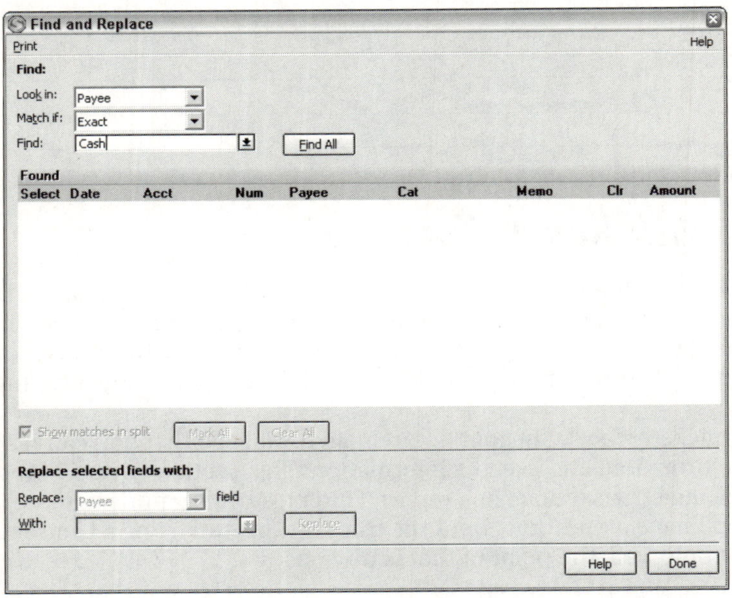

Figure 2-17: These settings tell Quicken to find all transactions with Cash entered as the Payee.

Here's how to use each of these controls:

- **Look In:** To specify what field Quicken should search, choose the field from the Look In drop-down list, or leave All Fields selected to search all fields.
- **Match If:** Make a choice from the Match If drop-down list to make the search more or less precise. For example, Exact tells Quicken to identify only transactions that match exactly, whereas Contains returns any

transaction that has a version of the word or phrase to find. Likewise, Starts With and Ends With return partial matches. If you're searching based on a field that holds values (such as the Amount field), you can use the Greater, Greater or Equal, Less, or Less or Equal choices to control how many matches Quicken returns.

✦ **Find:** Type the word, phrase, or amount to match. If a drop-down list arrow appears beside this text box, you can click it to see a list of existing Quicken entries for the field, so that you can click the one to match.

After you choose or enter the needed Look In, Match If, and Find information, click the Find All button. The Found section of the Find and Replace window lists all transactions that match the criterion you set up. Figure 2-18 show the transactions resulting from the Find entries shown in Figure 2-17.

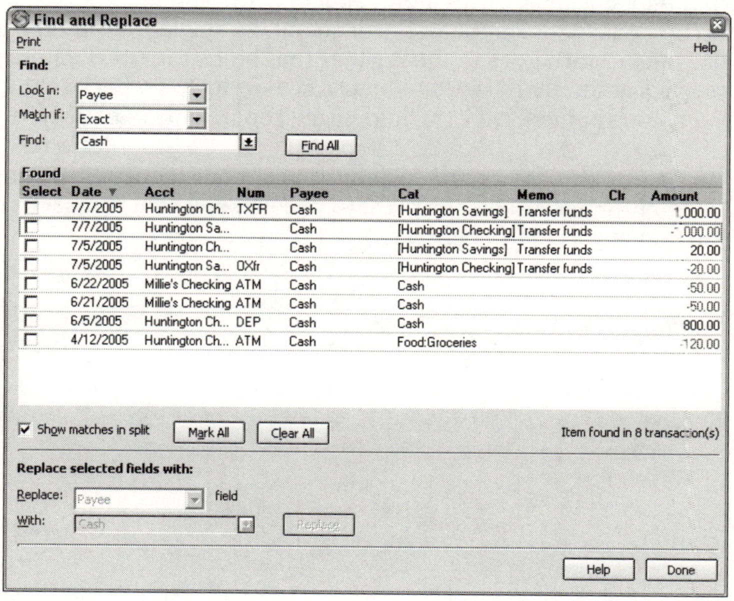

Figure 2-18: Quicken has fetched the transactions matching the criterion set up in Figure 2-17.

From there, you can do a couple of things with the found transactions. You can click the Print choice near the top of the window to open the Print dialog box and send the list of matching transactions to the printer. If you're feeling really crazy, you can replace information in a transaction. Click the check box for the transaction(s) to change in the Found list, so that a check mark appears. Near the bottom of the window, specify the field holding the data to replace using the Replace drop-down list. Then enter the replacement information for the field in the With text box. Click the Replace button to change the field information.

Done with the find and/or replace? Then click Done. Well done.

Jumping to a transaction in the register

Sometimes a report may include a transaction or total (depending on the type of report you've displayed) that might look unfamiliar or downright wrong. If you need to review a suspicious transaction in the register or want to see the detail about the values Quicken added to create a particular total for a category or payee, you can zoom in on the data.

When you're working in the report, first click on the item or entry to zoom. If you click on an actual transaction, in most cases, the transaction is highlighted. If you instead click a calculated total for a category or payee, a black outline appears around the item amount (Figure 2-19). In either case, move the mouse over the transaction or item, so that the mouse pointer turns into a magnifying glass. Then, double-click.

What happens next varies a bit depending on whether you zoomed a transaction or a calculated amount. If you zoomed a single transaction, Quicken minimizes the report, goes to the register that holds the transaction, and selects the transaction there so that you can review it. To go back to the report from which you zoomed, click the minimized report button below the register.

Note: When you're working in some investment reports, zooming a transaction might open a dialog box where you can edit that transaction, rather than taking you to the register.

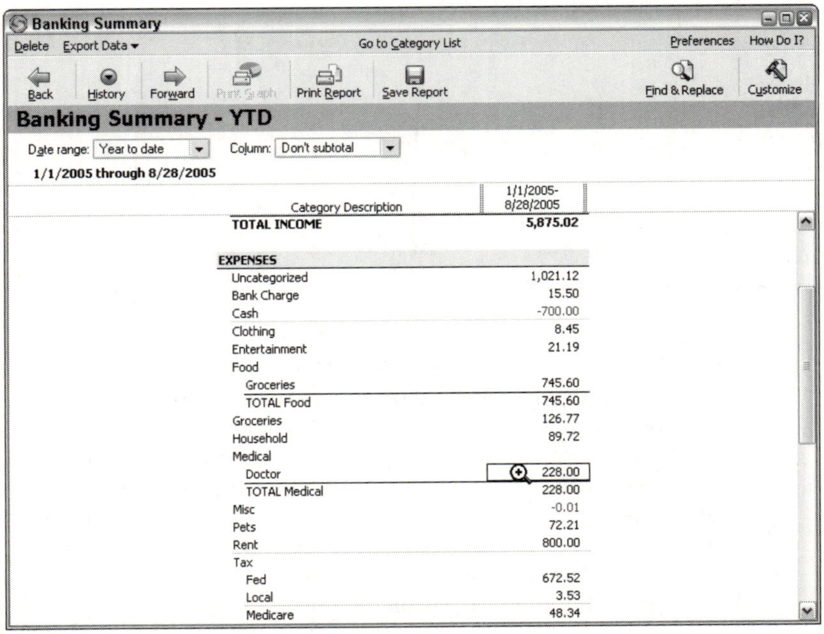

Figure 2-19: When you see the magnifying glass pointer, you can double-click the selected item to zoom it.

If you double-clicked a report value that Quicken calculated, Quicken instead displays a QuickZoom report. This report lists the transactions that Quicken totaled to yield the report value. For example, Figure 2-20 shows the QuickZoom report resulting from double-clicking the report value shown in Figure 2-19. The QuickZoom report works like the other reports described in this chapter. You can change the basic report settings using the controls at the top.

If you want to return to the report from which you zoomed, click the Back button on the QuickZoom report window's tool bar. Click the Forward button from the original report to go back to the QuickZoom report. When you close the QuickZoom report window, Quicken asks whether you want to save the report, a topic covered in Chapter 4 of Book VII.

TIP

See Book VII, Chapter 1 to find out more about zooming from a graph. Note that if you Shift+click a bar or slice, Quicken hides it, so you must then re-create the graph to redisplay the hidden bar or slice.

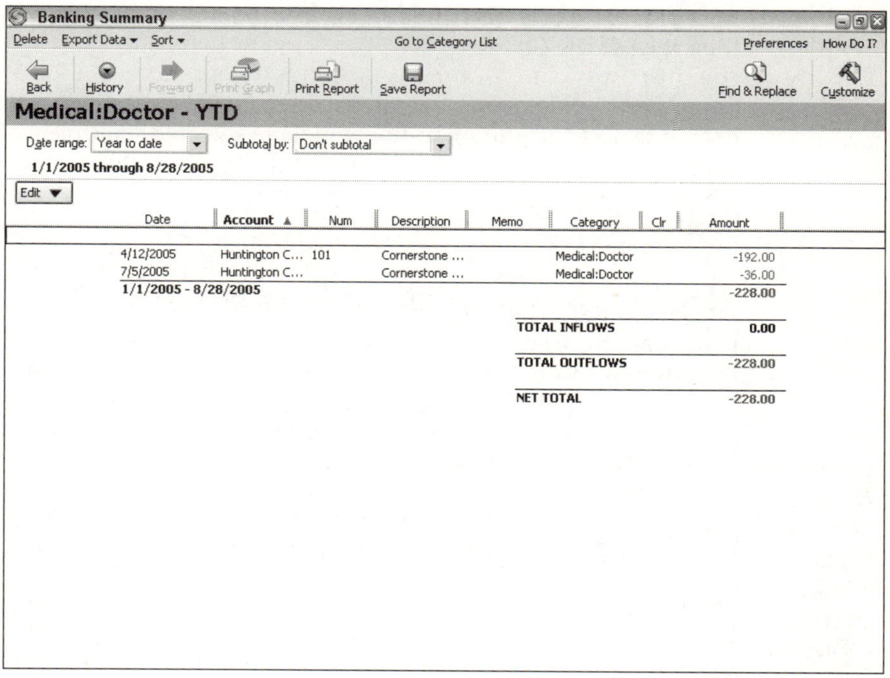

Figure 2-20: The QuickZoom report that resulted from double-clicking the report item shown in Figure 2-19.

Selecting report items

Quicken 2006 introduces a great new feature for those who might be a bit lazy. (Naw, not *you*!) In some reports, Quicken saves you the trouble of needing to zoom to make a correction. In those types of reports (reports listing transactions, as well as QuickZoom reports that itemize transactions for a particular payee or category), you can select and make basic changes to a transaction.

But just as you have to select text or values to change in a word processing or spreadsheet program, you have to select one or more transactions in a report to be able to edit the transaction.

To select a single transaction to edit, click it in the report window. Quicken displays a selection highlight across the full transaction.

If you want to select multiple transactions (Figure 2-21, top) that appear sequentially, click the topmost transaction, press and hold the Shift key, then click the bottommost transaction, and release the Shift key. To select multiple non-sequential transactions (Figure 2-21, bottom), click the first transaction, press and hold the Ctrl key, click additional transactions to select, and then release the Ctrl key.

From there, you're ready to edit the selected transaction(s) — or not. If you decide to skip the edit operation and have selected multiple transactions, simply click away from the selection, either on a single transaction or on a blank area within the report window, and the transaction or group is deselected.

Modifying transactions from a report

Inaccurate transaction in a report got you down? Then change it! You may have already noticed that in most reports that list transactions, especially QuickZoom reports that break down category or payee information, a new Edit button appears above the report column headings. If you click the Edit button, the menu that appears gives you choices for editing any transaction(s) you've selected in the report using the methods described above. Figure 2-22 shows the Edit button menu choices in a QuickZoom report that breaks out the transactions in an expense category.

REMEMBER

The Edit button menu choices change depending on the nature of the selected transaction.

Changes you make using the Edit button menu choices apply in both the report and the register, so be careful. For most transactions, you can click one of the following menu choices to make a change:

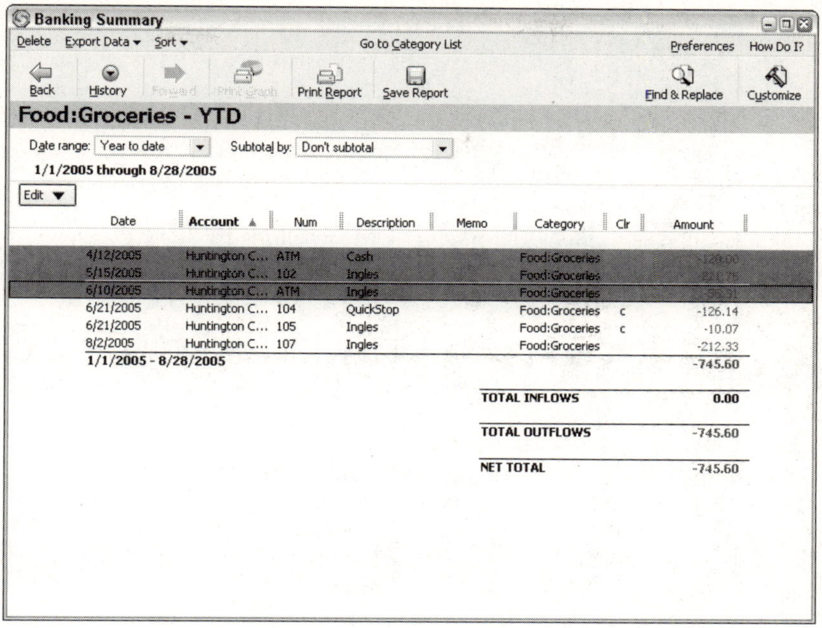

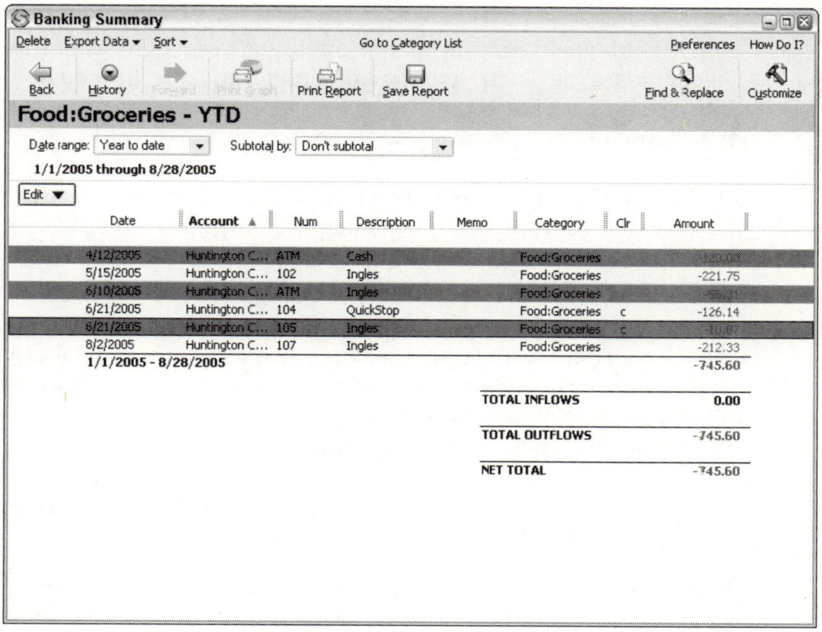

Figure 2-21: Shift+click to select sequential transactions (top), or Ctrl+click around to select transactions at will (bottom).

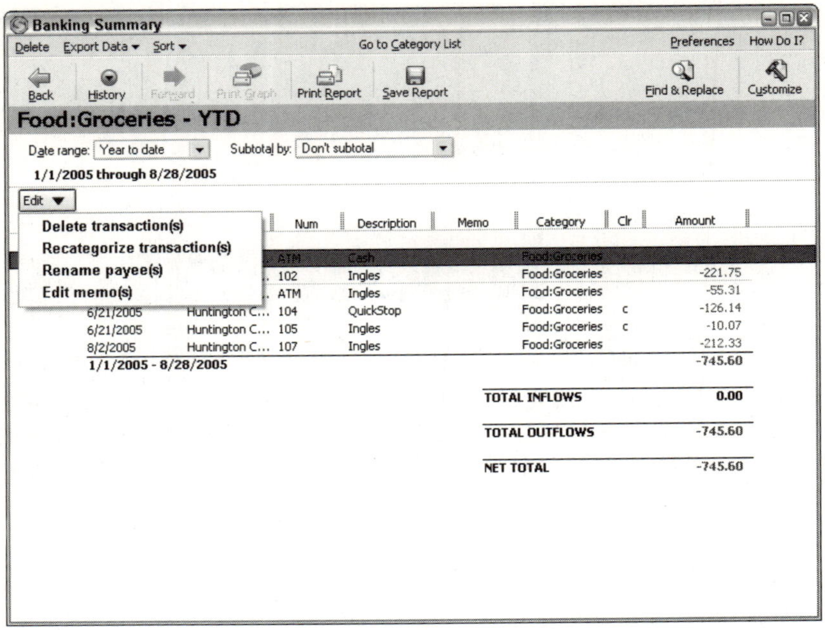

Figure 2-22: Use the Edit button menu to change up the selected transaction.

Stop! Before you delete or change anything, you might want to back up your Quicken data file. Jump over to Appendix A to learn how to do that deed. With a solid data backup, you always can restore your prior data file if you blew it and nuked a transaction or goofed up a change.

- **Delete Transaction(s):** Click this choice in the menu to delete the selected transaction(s). Quicken 2006 displays a message box prompting you to confirm the deletion. Click OK, but only if you *really* want to delete the selected transaction(s). You can't undo a deletion.
- **Recategorize Transaction(s):** Click this choice on the menu when you want to change the Category field entry assigned to the selected transaction(s). Quicken displays the Recategorize transactions dialog box. Click the Category drop-down list arrow, click the new category to assign (Figure 2-23), and then click OK. (Rather than choosing a category from the drop-down list, you also can type a new category, and then Quicken asks you to click Yes to add the new category after you click OK in the Recategorize Transactions dialog box.)

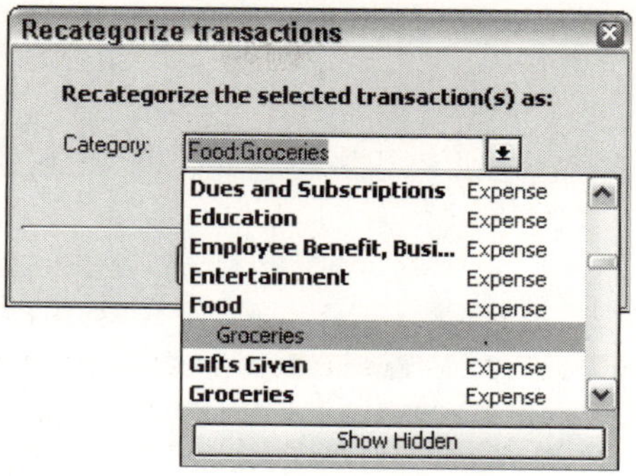

Figure 2-23: Choose the new category to apply to the selected transaction(s).

- **Rename Payee(s):** If you entered or assigned the wrong payee name to the selected transaction(s), or if the payee entity's name has changed, click this command to fix the situation. In the Rename Payee dialog box that appears, click the Payee drop-down list arrow and click the desired payee, or simply type a new payee in the Payee text box. Then click OK.
- **Edit Memo(s):** This last Edit button menu choice enables you to add or update the Memo field entry for the selected transaction(s). After you click Edit memo(s), the Edit Memo dialog box appears. Type the new memo text you want into the Memo text box, and then click OK.

If you've got a real eagle eye, you might have taken note of the fact that when you're dealing with a report that breaks out the transactions in a particular category, the report window menu includes a Go to Category List choice so that you can jump to the Category List window to make changes or additions.

Resolving a placeholder transaction

When it encounters a discrepancy, Quicken might insert a Placeholder Entry (placeholder transaction) to resolve the account information. This typically happens in investment accounts, where you specified a total number of shares owned that doesn't match up with the total number of shares from share purchase transactions. Or, Quicken might add a placeholder transaction to provide an estimated cost for securities purchased.

In a report window, Quicken identifies a Placeholder Entry by placing an asterisk (*) next to the placeholder value. In addition, a message near the bottom of the report window alerts you to the Placeholder Entries. Figure 2-24 illustrates both of these cues.

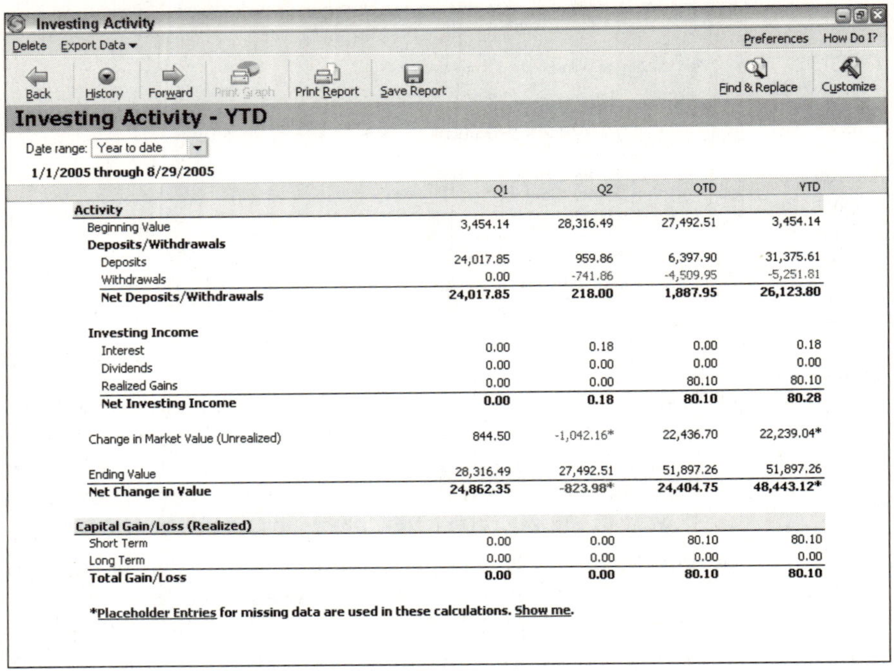

Figure 2-24: When a report includes placeholder values, Quicken identifies them for you.

If you want to resolve a Placeholder Entry to ensure that your Quicken data is as accurate as possible (a plus if you're relying on Quicken for tax reporting), you can work directly from the report window, like this:

1. **Click the Show Me link at the right end of the message about the Placeholder Entries.**

   The Resolve Placeholder Entries window appears, listing the securities for which Quicken has entered placeholder transactions.

2. **Click the plus button to the left of a security name to expand its transactions.**

   As shown in Figure 2-25, a link identifies the Placeholder Entry.

   If you click the link for a security name in the Resolve Placeholder Entries window, the Security Detail View window opens with more information about the security.

3. **Click the Placeholder link.**

   The Enter Missing Transactions dialog box shown in Figure 2-26 opens.

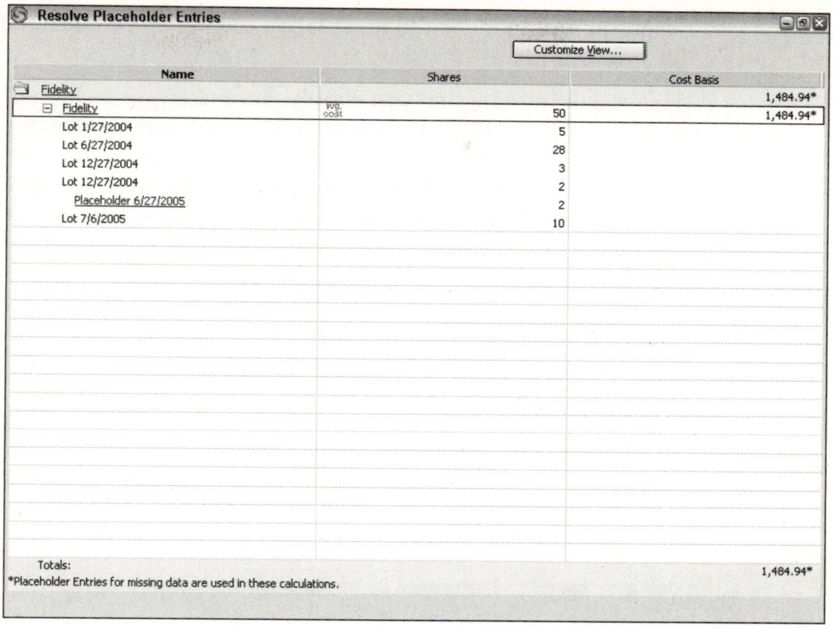

Figure 2-25: A link identifies the Placeholder Entry.

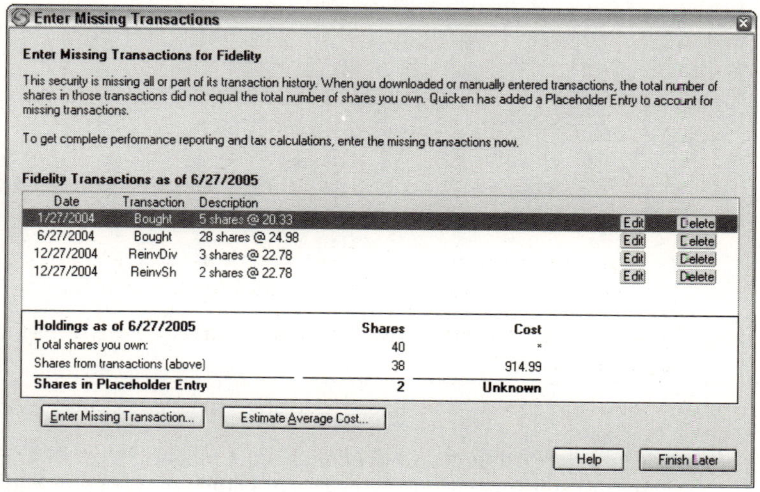

Figure 2-26: Use the Enter Missing Transactions dialog box to resolve a Placeholder Entry.

4. **Take a look at the information listed near the bottom of the dialog box to determine what to do to resolve the transaction.**

   For example, the example shown in Figure 2-26 indicates that the Placeholder Entry added two more shares of the security to account for a discrepancy between the number of shares currently owned and the share purchase transactions entered in Quicken.

5. Based on what you see in step 4, use one of three methods to resolve the transaction:

- If you determine that you simply entered the wrong number of shares or cost information for a transaction, click the transaction in the transactions list, and then click the Edit button beside it. An Edit dialog box like the one shown in Figure 2-27 opens. (Its specific name changes depending on the selected transaction.) Make the changes needed to correct the transaction and resolve the Placeholder Entry, and then click Enter/Done. For example, to resolve the discrepancy shown in Figure 2-26, you could change the Number of Shares entry for the transaction shown in Figure 2-27 from *28* to *30* (to account for the two shares added by the Placeholder Entry), change the Total Cost entry, if applicable, and then click Enter/Done. If the Recalculate Investment Transaction dialog box appears, click an option button to specify whether Quicken should adjust the Price, Shares, Total Amount, or Commission/Fee for the transaction to make the math work, and then click OK to finish editing the transaction.

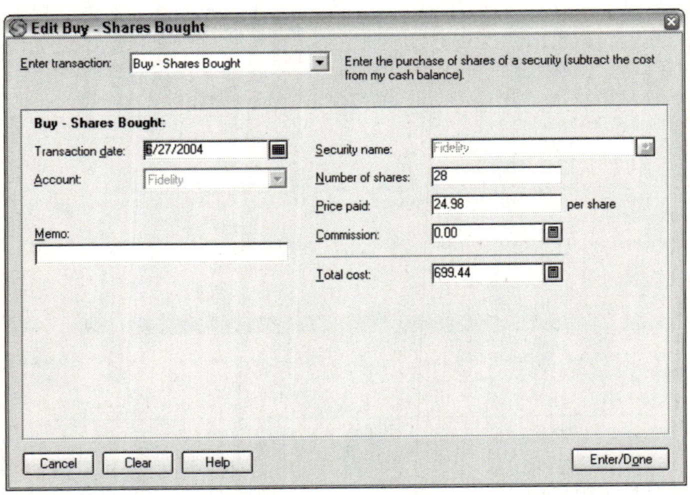

Figure 2-27: Editing a transaction can resolve the placeholder.

- If you determine that a transaction is missing overall and you have accurate information about the missing transaction, click the Enter Missing Transaction button near the bottom of the Enter Missing Transactions dialog box. A Buy–Shares Bought dialog box, which resembles the dialog box shown in Figure 2-27, appears. Enter the transaction information, and then click Enter/Done. A message window indicates that your new entry will not affect the share balance because the new transaction will replace the Placeholder Entry. Click Yes to confirm your entry.

- If you determine that a transaction is missing but you don't have accurate cost or other information about it, click the Estimate Average Cost button near the bottom of the dialog box. Quicken opens the Enter Missing Transactions dialog box shown in Figure 2-28. Make sure that the As Of drop-down list shows the date for the Placeholder Entry. Then enter the approximate Cost and Price/Share information in those text boxes and click OK. Quicken assigns the estimated cost information to the Placeholder Entry.

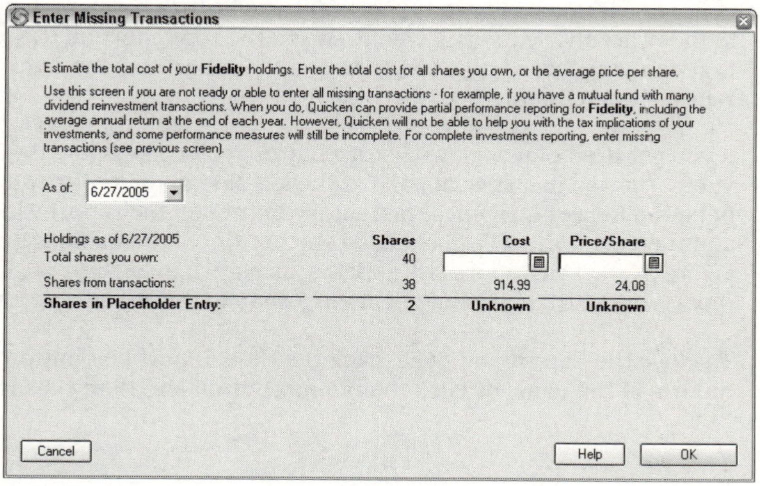

Figure 2-28: Estimate cost information for the placeholder transaction.

If you use the third method above to resolve the transaction, don't rely on Quicken alone to report tax information about the security involved. That's because you've just entered *estimated* information, not *accurate* information, so Quicken's calculations are affected accordingly.

6. **Back at the main Enter Missing Transactions dialog box, the area below the transactions list should (if you edited or added a transaction) tell you that the Placeholder Entry now has 0 shares. Click the Done button.**

   Quicken returns you to the Resolve Placeholder Entries window.

7. **Repeat steps 2 through 6 to resolve any other placeholder entries listed.**
8. **Click the X button to close the Resolve Placeholder Entries window.**
9. **Back in the main Quicken window, click the minimized button for the report that previously held the Placeholder Entries to redisplay the report.**

   It should now be free of asterisks and the message about Placeholder Entries.

Using the History and Report List

If you've displayed a QuickZoom report or have made changes to create numerous versions of a report (see the next chapter), the report window that you're working in tracks the history of your actions. That Report History enables you to back up to any previous report or version of a report that you've viewed in the current report window.

When you've viewed more than one report in the current report window, the History button on the tool bar becomes active. Click that button to open a menu of previously viewed reports (Figure 2-29). This menu lists the reports in the order that you displayed them, so the top report on the menu was the first one you viewed. Click the name of the report to jump back to, which redisplays the report.

If you get tired of using the History button, you can display the list of reports you've viewed in a special pane at the left side of the report window. To open the Report List, click the History button on the report window tool bar, and then click Show Report List at the bottom of the menu (refer back to Figure 2-29). The Report List appears, as shown in Figure 2-30. Click any report in the list, and it reappears in a snap in the report window.

To close the Report List pane, click the Hide Report List button below the reports in the pane, or click the History button and then click Hide Report List.

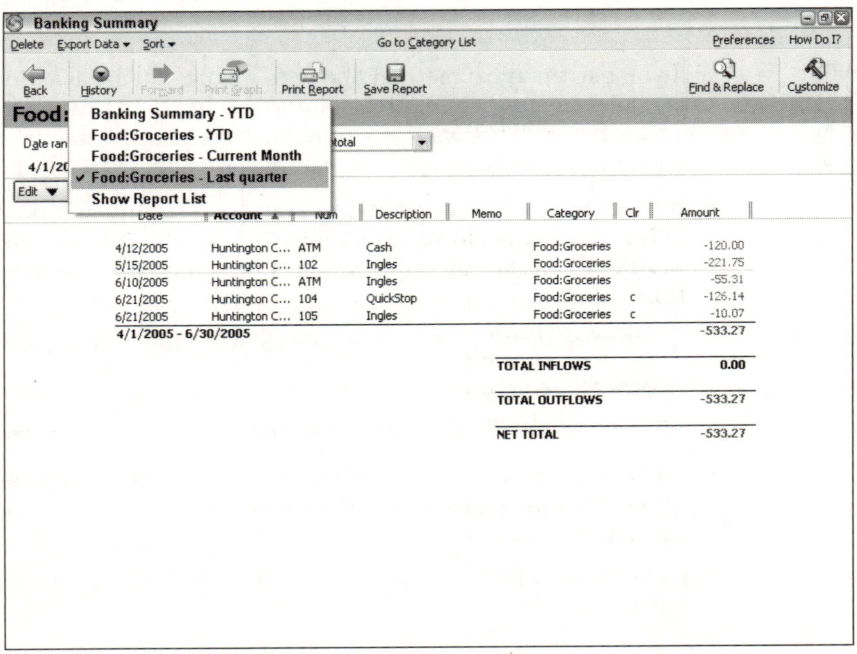

Figure 2-29: Use the History button to go back to another report.

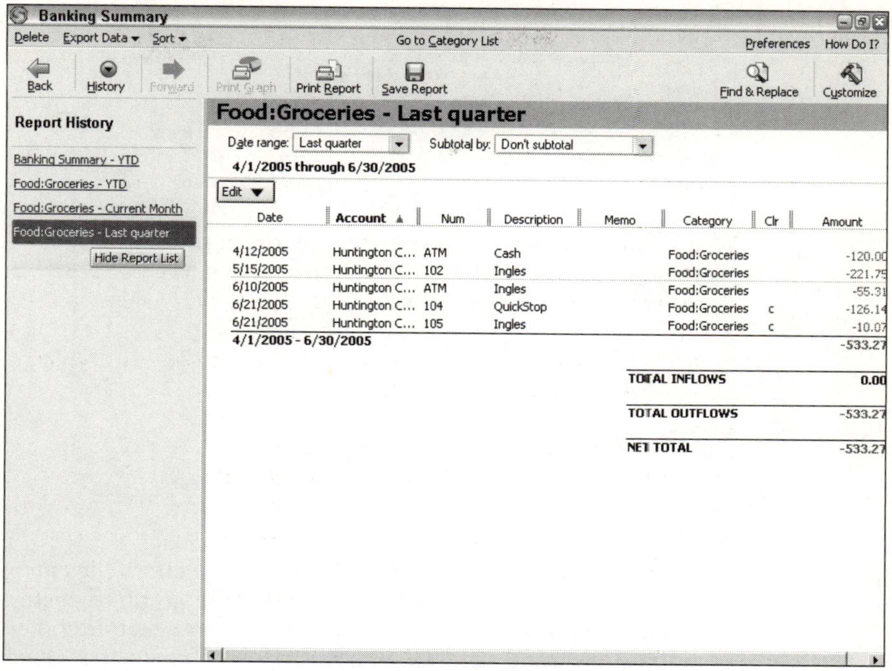

Figure 2-30: Use the Report List at the left to redisplay a previously viewed report.

Setting Defaults: Report Preferences

You've probably displayed quite a few reports while checking out the information in this chapter, so you may have already noticed a similarity. By default, each report uses a default Date Range of the year to date (the current YTD). The Quicken program enables you to change this default setting, as well as a few others, to cut down on your work in setting up reports and graphs the way you want them to be.

Change report defaults in the Quicken Preferences dialog box. To start changing preferences for both reports and graphs, choose Edit⇨Preferences⇨Quicken Program, and then click Reports and Graphs in the Select preference type list at the left side of the Quicken Preferences dialog box. If you're already working in a report window, simply click the Preferences choice on the window menu bar. Either way, you get to the overall preferences for Reports and Graphs, shown in Figure 2-31.

The Select Preferences area at the right side of the Quicken Preferences dialog box enables you to change five overall settings for reports and graphs. If you're not happy with the date ranges used for reporting and comparison, make alternate choices from the Default date range and/or Default comparison date range drop-down lists. If either of your choices require you to supply custom dates, additional drop-down lists appear.

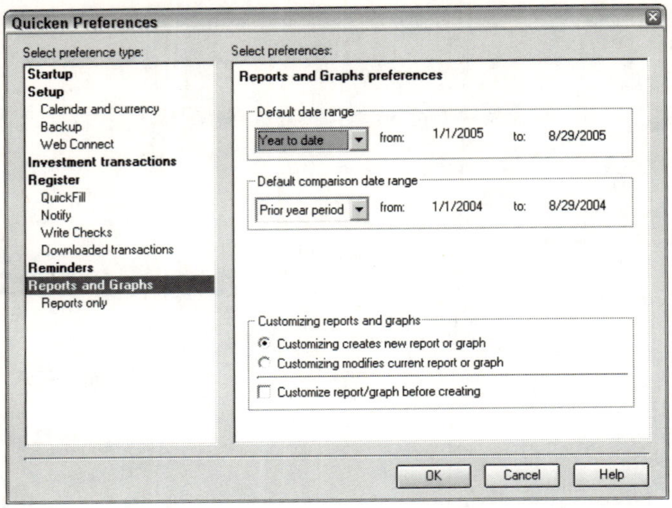

Figure 2-31: Change some "mile high" preferences for reports and graphs here.

Down in the Customizing Reports and Graphs section, click an option to specify whether customizing creates a new report or graph or customizing modifies a current report or graph. Note that making the latter choice doesn't turn off the history tracking in the report window. It means that Quicken only prompts you to save the report you're currently viewing in the report window. In such a case, if you've created multiple reports that you want to save, use the History button or the Report List to display each one, and then use the Save Report button to save each one. Find out more about saving reports in Chapter 4 of Book VII.

If you want to specify more detail for each report you create via the Reports menu or Reports & Graphs Center, check the Customize Report/Graph Before Creating check box. When that option is checked, Quicken automatically opens the Customize dialog box when you create a new report so that you can specify more detailed report settings.

If you want to drill down further in working with report defaults, click the Reports Only choice in the Select Preference Type list at the left side of the Quicken Preferences dialog box. The Select Preferences choices at the right change as shown in Figure 2-32.

Click either the Description, Name, or Both option button under Account Display to control what account information appears in reports. Ditto for the Category Displays options, which controls the category information each report shows.

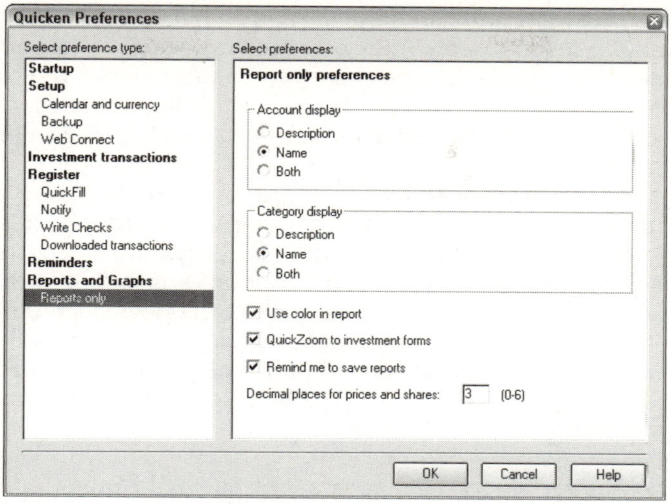

Figure 2-32: These preferences apply to reports only.

If you've got only a black-and-white printer, clear the Use Color in Report check box to eliminate color use, so the onscreen reports more realistically matches the printouts you'll get. Clear QuickZoom to Investment Forms to turn off the QuickZoom capability for investment transactions such as buy and sell transactions. You might want to do this to prevent yourself or another user in your house from monkeying with investment transactions and thus introducing errors.

If you don't want Quicken to prompt you to save a report when you've changed the Date range or another setting, clear the Remind Me to Save Reports check box.

Finally, if you want Quicken to use more or fewer than three decimal places for security prices and share amounts, edit the Decimal Places for Prices and Shares entry accordingly.

When you think you've got it in terms of preference settings for reports and graphs, click the OK button to close the Quicken Preferences dialog box and apply the new preferences.

Checking Out an EasyAnswer Report

If you think some of the report names Quicken uses sound a little too esoteric, Intuit has felt your pain and has adjusted Quicken accordingly. You can get answers to some key questions about your financial health with EasyAnswer reports.

Each EasyAnswer report uses a plain English question as its report name. For example, if you're wondering how much you spent on a particular type of expense like auto fuel (a growing expense these days), you could use the How Much Did I Spend On ? EasyAnswer report. If the term *net worth* stumps you every time, just use the What Am I Worth? EasyAnswer report, instead.

To open an Easy Answer report, choose Reports➪EasyAnswer or click EasyAnswer in the Quicken Standard Reports list at the left side of the Reports & Graphs Center. The ten available EasyAnswer reports appear in the list. Click the report to use, and its options appear below the report name, as shown in Figure 2-33. In the case of the How Much Did I Spend On? report shown in the figure, choose an expense category from the Show Spending On drop-down list and a report time frame from the For the Period drop-down list. From there, click the Show Report (or Show Graph) button, and Quicken presents the EasyAnswer!

TIP: The EasyAnswer report that appears uses one of the other report names because each EasyAnswer report is essentially a customized version of one of the other reports, minus the propeller-head name. You can work with the EasyAnswer report just as you would any other report.

REMEMBER: If no transactions relate to a category, payee, or reporting period that you specify for a report, the report window informs you that there are no matching transactions. You can close the report window and return to the Reports & Graphs Center to try the report using alternate settings.

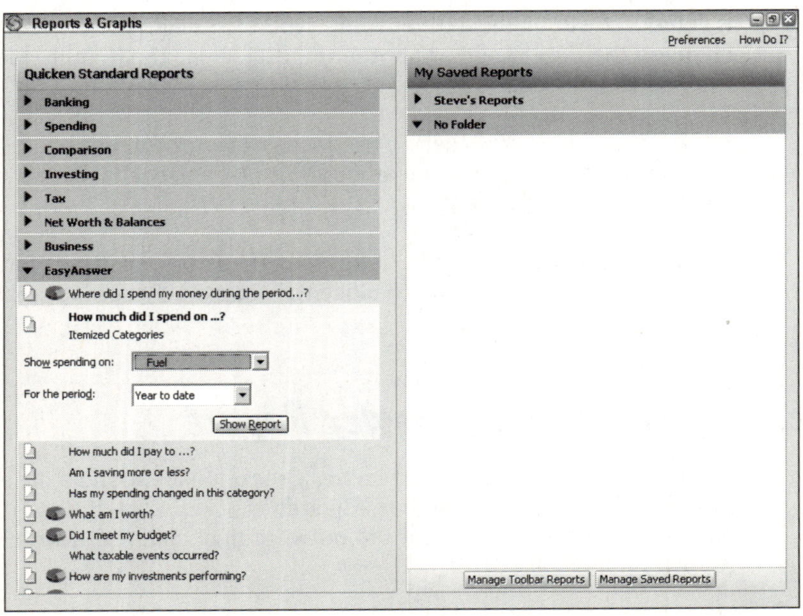

Figure 2-33: Each EasyAnswer report asks you to choose one or more settings to make your question more specific.

Chapter 3: Customizing Reports

In This Chapter

- **Choosing your own report title**
- **Setting the date range to change the amount of data reported**
- **Telling Quicken how to sort and subtotal the report**
- **Controlling accounts used for the report**
- **Getting the right categories or payees**
- **Pumping up your report one last time**

As great as Quicken's reports are, they aren't perfect for every occasion. For example, Quicken by default includes the data from every account in every report. That's hunky-dory, except if you want a report covering only a single bank (cash flow) account. You know you can get an EasyAnswer report about a single payee or category and that the regular reports cover all payees and categories, but what if you need something in between? Well, I have good news for you, my friend. Quicken enables you to customize reports in a variety of ways. Using the Customize *Report Title* dialog box, you can change such settings as the report title, what columns a report shows, what bank accounts it reports on, what categories and payees it covers, and even more. Does that sound more like it? Good. In this chapter, I take a look at how to make a report that covers what you want it to.

Opening the Customize Dialog Box

The Customize *Report Title* dialog box holds all the settings you can use to change the information and layout used by the report. To open the Customize *Report Title* dialog box, you can click the Customize button rather than the Show Report or Show Graph button (Figure 3-1) when creating the report in the Reports & Graphs Center. Or, if you created the report directly from the Reports menu or decide after the fact to make a few changes, click the Customize button on the report window tool bar. No matter how you got there, the Customize *Report Title* dialog box appears.

TIP

This chapter is calling it the Customize *Report Title* dialog box because the full name of the dialog box changes to reflect the title assigned to the report you're customizing.

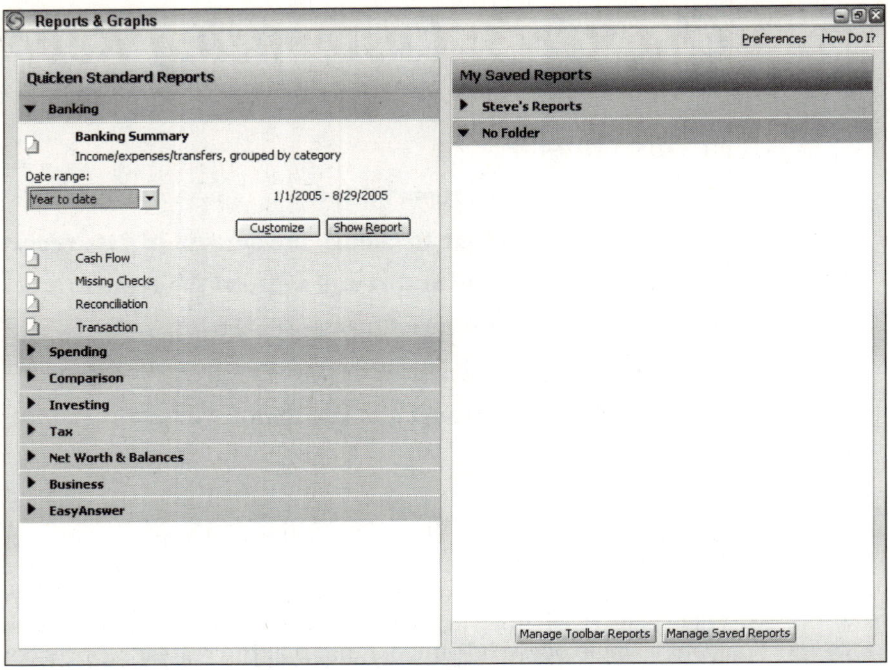

Figure 3-1: The Reports & Graphs Center gives you the option of customizing the report before it opens.

The Customize *Report Title* dialog box offers several tabs of settings for changing the report. You can change the settings on a single tab and then click OK. Or, if you want to change a variety of report settings, you can leave the Customize *Report Title* dialog box open and work on as many tabs as needed before clicking OK. The rest of this chapter explains the settings on each tab, so you know exactly where to go if you only want to change a setting or two.

TIP

If the Customize *Report Title* dialog box doesn't include an OK button, it includes Show Report and/or Show Graph buttons. Click one of those to display the customized report.

One last heads-up. The settings offered by the Customize *Report Title* dialog box change slightly depending on the report type and sometimes depending on other customization settings, as well. For example, the dialog box only offers the settings for working with columns and sorting the report when you're working with a transaction report. So, if you can't find a setting, chances are it isn't available for that type of report.

Changing a Report Title

A report title like *Banking Summary — YTD* may not inspire you to be a better saver and a wiser spender, and *Itemized Categories — YTD* doesn't work too well if you've customized a report to cover only a single category. You can customize any report title to use the text you want. Prefer *John's Power Banking* to *Banking Summary — YTD*? Change the report title. Does *Petrol Spending* sound a whole lot more James Bond than *Itemized Categories — YTD*? Change the report title.

The process for changing a report's title starts just like the process for customizing other report features. First, open the Customize *Report Title* dialog box.

The control for changing the report title appears right on the first tab of the dialog box, the Display tab. Make the desired title change in the Title text box (Figure 3-2). You can either drag over the text box contents and type a brand new title, or you can click in the text box and edit the existing entry using the keyboard.

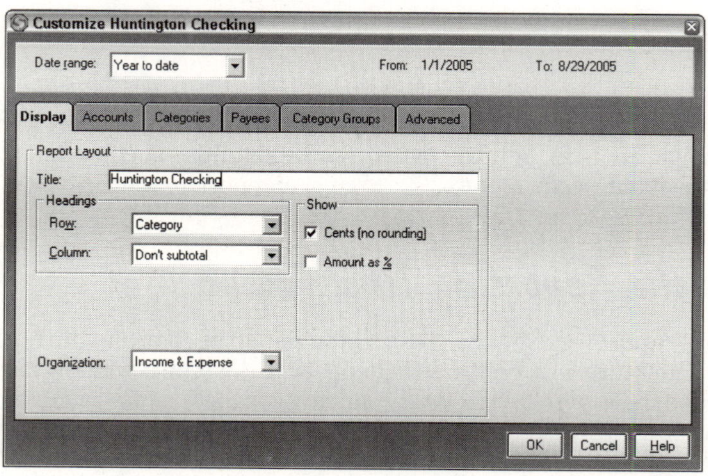

Figure 3-2: Enter a new report title in the Title text box of the Display tab.

If you're content with changing the report title alone, click OK to open the new report or turn to the report window. As the example in Figure 3-3 shows, the new title appears below the window tool bar, and it also appears when you print the report. (Check out the final chapter in this Book VII, Chapter 4, to bone up on printing reports.)

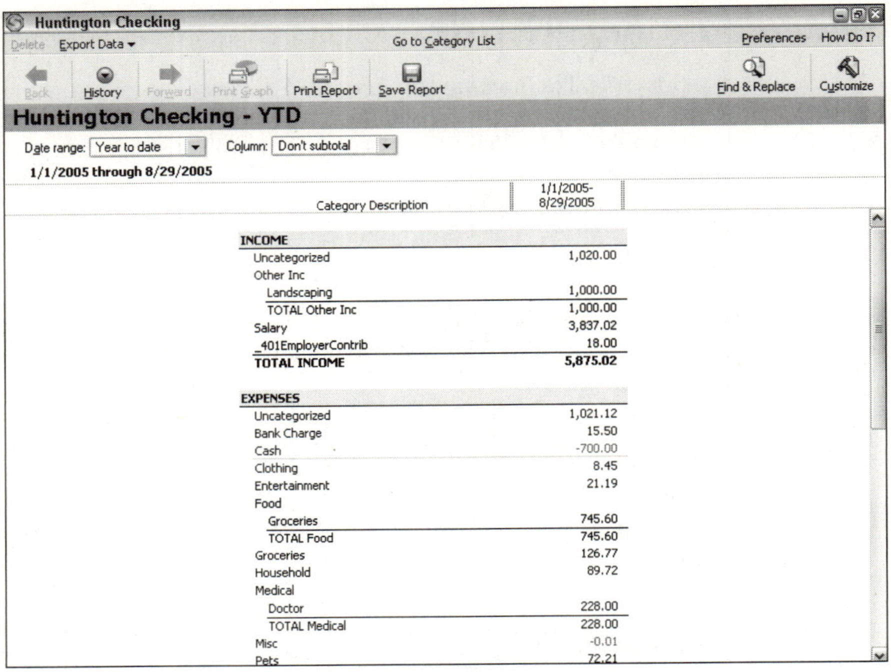

Figure 3-3: A custom report title in action.

In this example, the report title was customized for a report that is based on a single account. You can make your report titles specific like this or more fun as your needs dictate.

Changing the Reporting Time Frame

Most reports and graphs give you the option of changing the reporting period or date range with controls that appear in the report window itself, right above the report data. If you've already got the Customize *Report Title* dialog box open, you can change the date range for the report right in there, too.

The Date Range drop-down list appears at the top of the Customize *Report Title* dialog box and is visible no matter what tab in the dialog box you've selected. Open the Date Range dialog box, and click on the overall setting to use. If other controls appear to enable you to specify more detail, make entries and choices as needed. For example, Figure 3-4 shows the settings that restrict the reporting period to the month of June, 2005.

So that this book doesn't become a broken record, you can jump back to Chapter 1 of Book VII to review how to use each of the Date Range settings Quicken offers for reports.

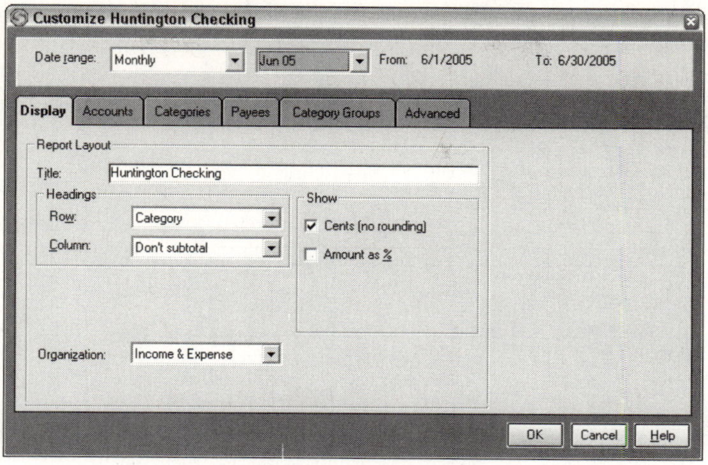

Figure 3-4: To show a report for June of 2005 only, choose a Monthly Date Range and then select Jun 05 from the second drop-down list that appears.

Note: For comparison reports, the Customize *Report Title* dialog box includes controls for you to specify two time periods to compare for the report.

Sorting Report Information

By default, Quicken sorts the information in a transaction report by Account/Date. That means that Quicken first groups the transaction by account, and then sorts the transactions by date within each account group. That'll work on a bad day.

When you're really looking at the nitty-gritty of how you manage your money, however, it might be useful to arrange your transactions in another way. For example, it might be more constructive to sort by the Amount field if you want to see what transactions you spent the most money on.

Quicken actually gives you two different ways to change the sort method on the report. You can click a column heading in the report itself to sort by that column. A triangle appears beside the column heading for the column currently used to control the sort, as shown in Figure 3-5. Some columns just aren't sort-friendly (Memo columns, for example), so if you click and nothing happens, Quicken doesn't offer sorting for that column.

TECHNICAL STUFF

Unlike some other programs where you can sort by column heading and then click the column heading a second time to reverse the sort order, Quicken only enables you to sort in one direction.

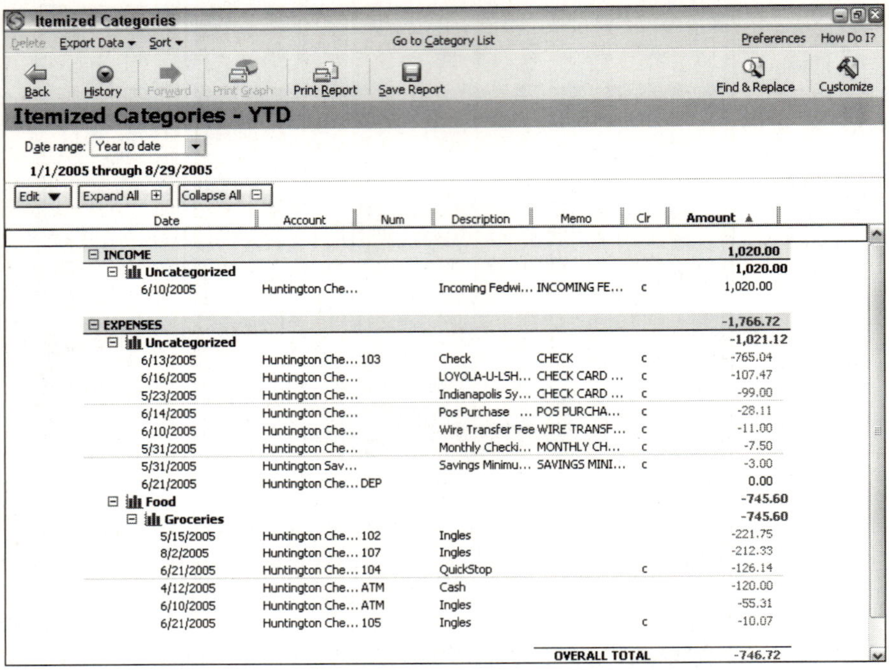

Figure 3-5: The triangle at the top of the Amount column shows I've sorted the account by Amount, from smallest to largest.

The other way to sort, of course, is via the Customize *Report Title* dialog box. When you're working with a report with transactions that can be sorted, the Display tab of the dialog box includes a Sort By drop-down list. Open that drop-down list and click one of these sort orders:

- **Account/Date (the default):** Groups transactions alphabetically by account, and then sorts from least recent to most recent by date within each group. Also groups first by account type if the report covers information from different types of accounts.
- **Date/Account:** Groups transactions first by date (least recent to most recent), and then by account type, and lastly alphabetically by account name.

  TIP: When you sort by a field that includes words and phrases, like an Account name, Payee, Category, or Description field, Quicken always sorts in ascending alphabetical order; that is, from A to Z rather than from Z to A.

- **Account/Check #:** Groups accounts first by type and then by name, and then sorts by check number within each group. Transactions without a check number or with an entry like *ATM* in the Num field are listed as a group either before or after the numbered items.

- **Amount:** Sorts based on the entries in the Amount field, listing transactions from lowest to highest in terms of the amounts.

  Keep in mind the fact that the larger a negative number is, the lower that number appears on that great number line in the sky. Thus, when you're sorting a report by amount and that report includes expenses, it's going to look like your sort is working from the largest number to the smallest, when actually it's working from the smallest number (which is to say the largest *negative* number) to the largest positive number. If that doesn't make sense, don't complain to me — write a letter to your third-grade math teacher and ask for a refresher course.

- **Payee:** Sorts based on the entries in the Payee field.
- **Category:** Sorts based on the entries in the Category field.

Controlling Subtotal Options

The settings for "subtotaling" report information get a little hairy because they differ quite a bit for different report types. And in some cases, a setting you choose doesn't exactly subtotal the data, but instead rearranges it. That being said, take a look at the settings for subtotaling and organizing the report information that appears on the Display tab of the Customize *Report Title* dialog box.

For most transaction reports, you can work with the Organization drop-down list and the Show section settings to control report information. The default choice from the Organization drop-down list is Income & Expense, which divides transactions into distinct Income, Expenses, and Transfer sections in the report. In contrast, the Cash Flow Basis choice divides transactions into Inflows and Outflows sections (refer to Figure 3-6), with transfers out of the account (such as transfers into a related asset account) included in the Outflows section. For budget, comparison, and summary reports, the Organization drop-down list may include a Category Group choice that subtotals by category group rather than one of the other two methods just described.

Because some of these subtotal/organization settings might have a subtle or unexpected impact in a report, you might try changing one at a time and then clicking the OK button to see the results in the report. That way, if you don't like the result of a change, you can go back to the Customize *Report Title* dialog box to reverse it immediately.

If you've created multiple budgets, use the Budget drop-down list that appears on the Display tab in the Customize *Report Title* dialog box to choose the budget to use for the report.

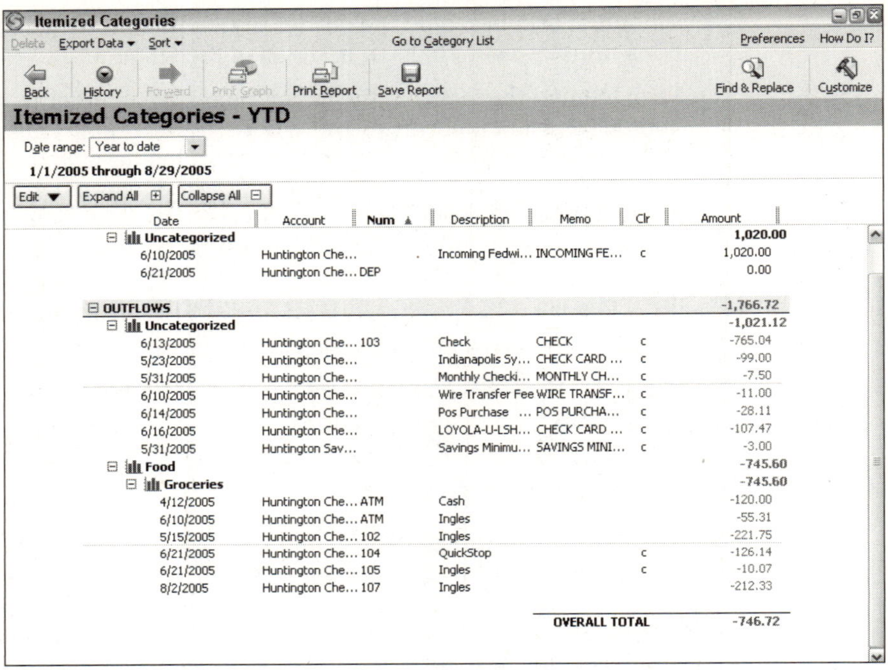

Figure 3-6: This report has been subtotaled based on cash flow (Inflows and Outflows) rather than by Income, Expenses, and Transfers.

When you've turned on multicurrency support in Quicken's Preferences (Chapter 1 of Book III includes a look at using the multicurrency feature in Quicken), the Display tab of the Customize *Report Title* dialog box includes a Currency drop-down list. You can open the drop-down list (Figure 3-7) and click another currency to have Quicken recalculate all the report values and present them in the newly specified currency. You might need to make such a change if you have a second home overseas and want to track expenditures on that location in both currencies, or if you have some income from a source other than the United States.

In the Show section of the Display tab (also in Figure 3-7), clear the Cents (No Rounding) check box to round dollar values to whole numbers in the report. Check the Totals Only check box to eliminate the display of individual transactions and instead display only totals and subtotals in the report.

If some of the transactions in the report have been split between categories, a Breakdown of Split Trans. check box also appears in the Show section. Check that check box to have the report display the full breakdown of the transaction by category, rather than simply displaying a single line item with *-Split-* in the Category field. Figure 3-8 shows an example of a split transaction breakdown.

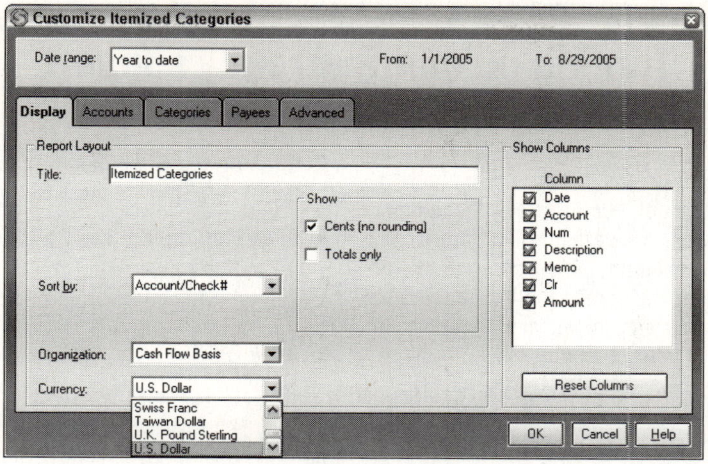

Figure 3-7: Quicken can convert report information from one currency to another with multi-currency support enabled.

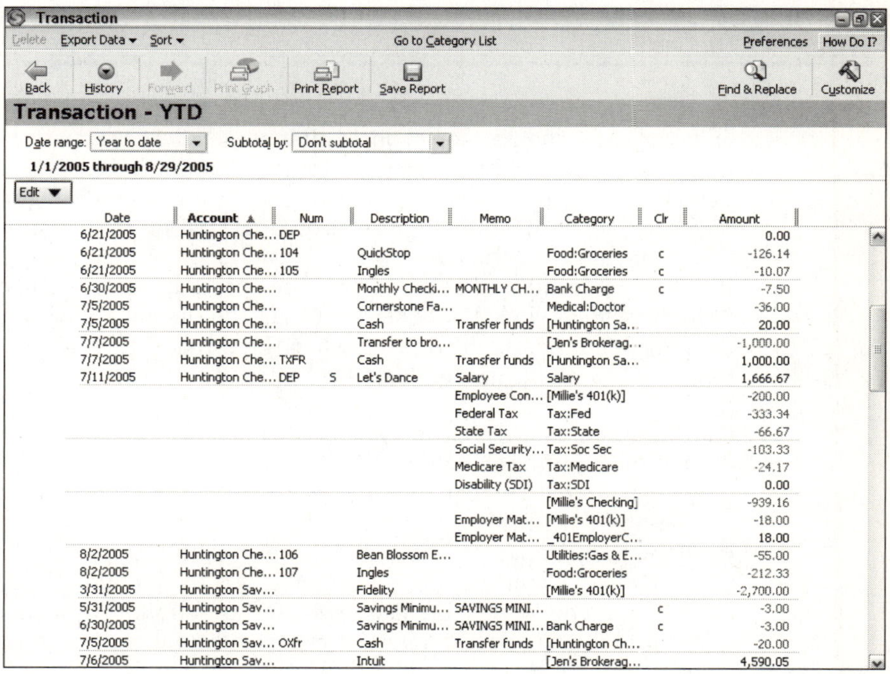

Figure 3-8: A report can display all the assigned categories for a split transaction.

Turning on multicurrency support

If you need to track your accounts and investments in foreign currencies, you can turn on Quicken's multicurrency feature. This feature enables you to track accounts and investment purchases, sales, and earnings in different currencies; transfer money between accounts of differing currencies; update the exchange rate in your Quicken program; and create reports in the currency of your choice.

Turn on the multicurrency feature by following these steps:

1. **Click Edit⇨Preferences from the Quicken menu, and then choose Quicken Program from the side menu.**

   The Quicken Preferences window appears.

2. **Click on the Setup heading to display the list of headings beneath Setup.**
3. **Click on Calendar and Currency.**
4. **Select the Multicurrency Support check box.**
5. **Click OK.**

If you ever want to turn off Multicurrency Support, just follow the steps above, and then uncheck the Multicurrency Support check box.

Summary and comparison reports offer some alternate customization settings. For example, the Display tab for the Customize Banking Summary dialog box includes a Headings section. Make a choice (Category, Class, Payee, or Account) from the Row drop-down list there to control how to select and subtotal the information on each row in the report. To break out the report information over multiple time periods, make a choice from the Column drop-down list. The settings from the Display tab of the Customize Banking Summary dialog box shown in the top of Figure 3-9 result in the report subtotaling and organization shown at the bottom.

For other summary reports, such as the Portfolio Value and Cost Basis report, the Headings section of the Display tab includes an Intervals drop-down list, so that you can choose the intervals (and therefore the number of columns) for the report data. Or, the Headings area for a report like the Portfolio Value report might include a Subtotal By drop-down list, so that you can choose whether the report subtotals by Account, Security Type, Asset Class, and so on. You also might see an Amount As % check box. Select it to display percentages for report subtotals rather than dollar values.

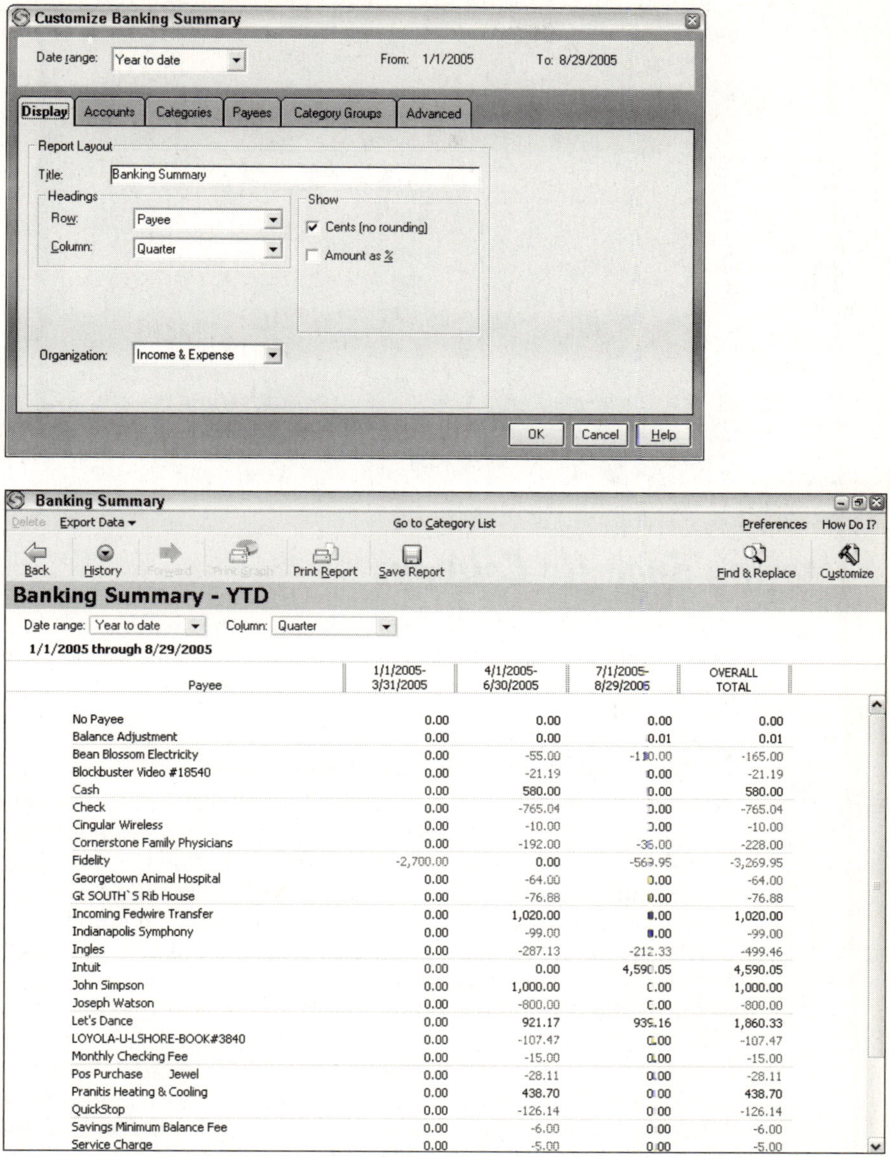

Figure 3-9: Headings settings (top) resulting in a customized Banking Summary report (bottom).

Book VII Chapter 3

Customizing Reports

Finally, the comparison report settings throw a couple of last curve balls at you. As shown in Figure 3-10, the Show section of the Display tab in the Customize *Report Title* dialog box for these reports includes Difference as % and Difference in $ check boxes. Check these check boxes as needed to show the differences in percentages, dollars, or both.

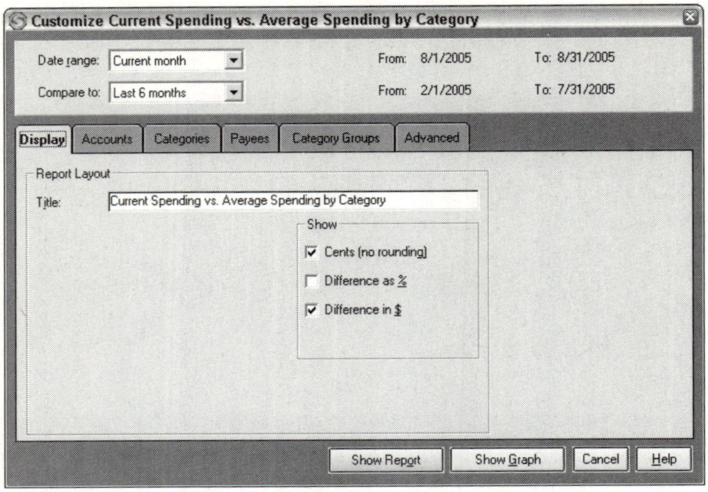

Figure 3-10: A comparison report can show differences in percentages, dollars, or both.

Selecting Specific Columns

You might think you've had your fill of hearing so much about report customization by now, but the worst really is over. This section breezes through how to control the field columns that appear for a transaction report.

Selecting and resetting columns

When you're working with a transaction report such as the Itemized Categories report, the Display tab of the Customize *Report Title* dialog box includes a Show Columns section at the right. Each of the columns listed in the Column list in that section corresponds with a field from the register. By default, all columns are selected on many reports. If you don't need to see a particular bit of information on your transactions report, click the check box for that column (field) in the Column list to clear the check box, and this removes the column from the report.

For example, in Figure 3-11 the Memo and Clr column check boxes have been unchecked. That means the information from those fields will not be shown in the report when you close the Customize *Report Title* dialog box.

TIP

The contents of the Description column change depending on the types of transactions being reported. For example, for transaction reports about cash flow accounts, the Description column shows the Payee information.

After you play with this capability, you'll see that hiding a column cuts down on extra white space in a report and makes the report more readable. So, for example, if you don't typically add a Memo field entry for your transactions, you should definitely hide the Memo column in your report. Figure 3-12 shows the Itemized Categories report with the Memo and Clr fields hidden (the settings from Figure 3-11) to give you some idea of the difference that controlling columns can make.

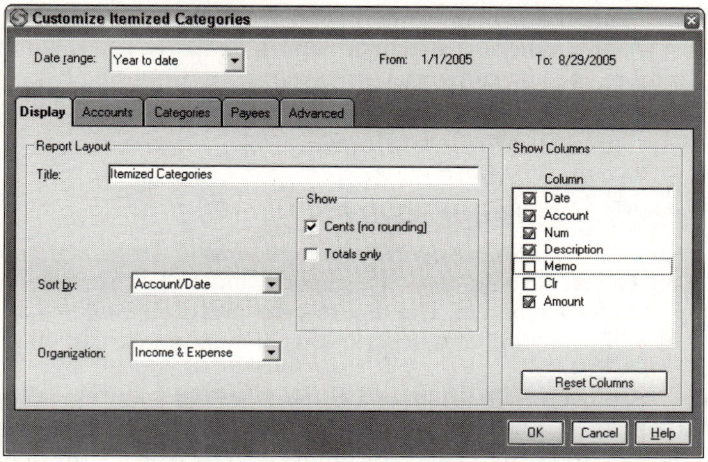

Figure 3-11: In the Column list at the right, clear the check beside any column to hide that column in the report.

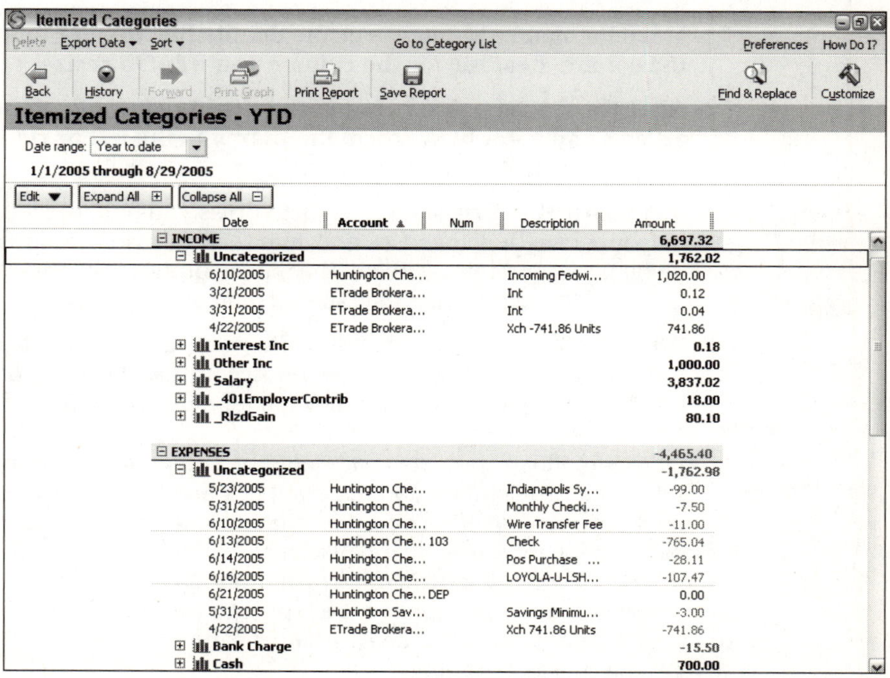

Figure 3-12: The Itemized Categories report with the Memo and Clr columns hidden by clearing check boxes as shown in Figure 3-11.

If you want to show all the columns again, reopen the Customize *Report Title* dialog box from the report window. You can either recheck all the check boxes in the Column list, or simply click the Reset Columns button.

If you've already set up a report to show only transactions from a particular account as described later under "Selecting Specific Accounts," it makes sense to hide the Account column and simply add the account name to the report title for a more streamlined report. Similarly, if you limit the report to cover more specific categories or payees (see "Choosing Report Categories or Payees"), hide the Description or Category columns and let the title reflect what the transactions show.

Changing column width

You have a little bit more control over columns in a transaction report. You actually can resize columns in the report window. For example, refer back to Figure 3-12 for a moment. The report looks pretty streamlined, but most of the entries in the Account and Description columns appear cut off at the right.

The . . . (ellipsis) to the right of a column or field entry clues you in to the fact that Quicken has had to cut off the information because the column is too narrow. You can fix this type of problem by resizing the column to make it wider. Use this technique to change the column width:

1. **Move the mouse pointer over the double-line divider to the right of the column heading for the column you want to resize.**
2. **After the mouse pointer changes to a split pointer (with horizontal arrows and a double-vertical line), drag to the left or right to adjust the column size, as illustrated in Figure 3-13.**

   Remember that "dragging" means to press and hold the left mouse button, move the mouse around, and then release the mouse button. If you press and release (click the mouse button), that won't change anything if you're trying to resize a column.
3. **When the column reaches the width you want, release the mouse button. Figure 3-14 shows how the Account and Description column entries look once those columns have been widened.**

As Figure 3-14 illustrates, even widening the columns may not make for a perfect report. You still may want to go back and hide some additional columns. Also, you need to be aware that making the columns wider (or smaller) also changes the overall width at which the report will print. You should therefore preview the report printout after you've made changes to the report columns, and change the report to use the Landscape (wide page) print orientation, if needed. If you jump ahead to the next chapter, you're covered on these operations.

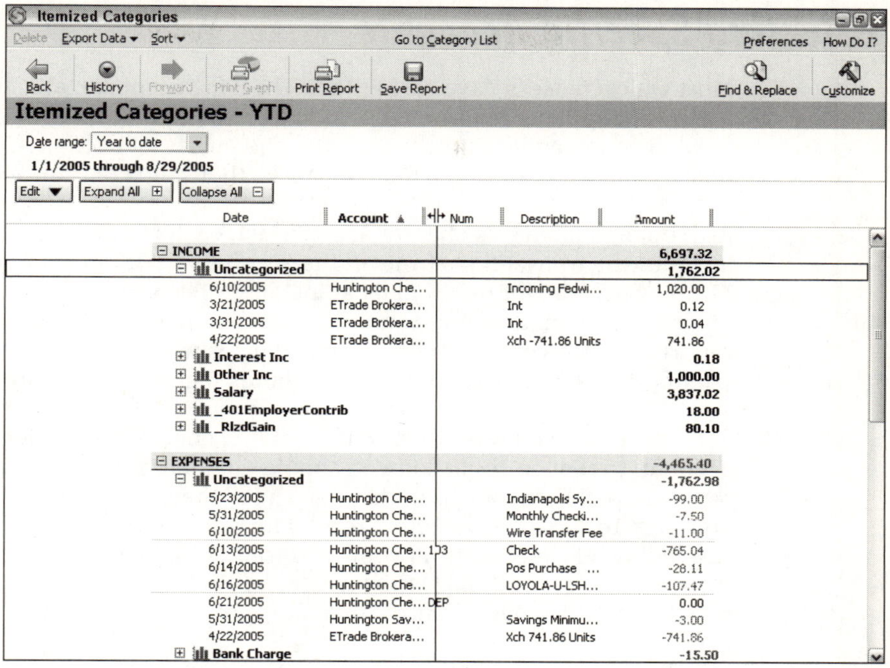

Figure 3-13: Drag the right column heading divider in the report window to resize the column.

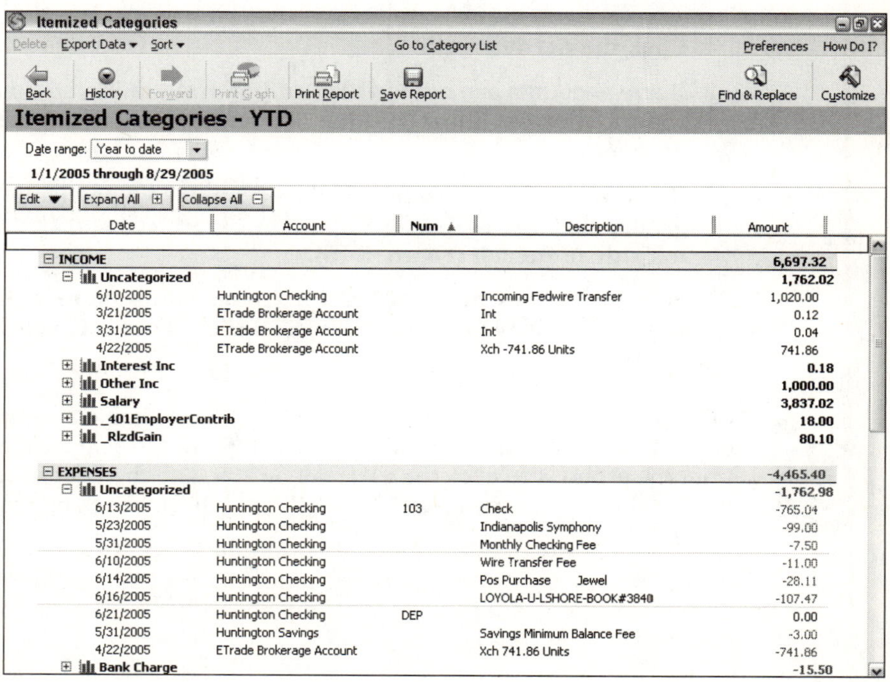

Figure 3-14: You can now see the full account names and descriptions because the Account and Description columns are wider.

Selecting Specific Accounts

Most Quicken users have savings and checking accounts, at a minimum, that they track in their Quicken file. Add in a credit card account or two, a retirement account, an investment account, and any asset accounts, and you quickly can wind up with a file that tracks thousands of transactions.

As I touched on in this chapter and the last, each Quicken report by default includes the transactions from *all* the accounts set up in your Quicken file. Although that might be OK in most instances because Quicken itself disregards investment account transactions when creating a banking (cash flow) report and vice versa, there may be instances where you want to exercise your option to limit the number of accounts included in a report.

For example, if you want to view the missing checks from a single checking account, to reduce confusion you should customize the Missing Checks report to pull data only from that particular checking account. Similarly, if you want to see the investment results for your mutual fund account only (excluding information from your brokerage, 401(k), IRA, and other investment accounts), customize the Investment Performance account to show only the data from your mutual fund account.

Use these steps to select the accounts to include in the report from within the Customize *Report Title* dialog box:

1. **Click the Accounts tab.**
2. **If any accounts are not visible and you want to include them in your report, click the Show (Hidden Accounts) check box to display the accounts.**
3. **If you want to work with only the accounts in a particular account group, click the desired group in the Select Account Group area at the left side of the tab (Figure 3-15).**
4. **Select the check boxes of those accounts you want to include in the report, and leave the check boxes of those accounts you want to omit blank.**

TIP: Click the Mark All button to check (include) all available accounts from the current group. On the other hand, the fastest way to select a single account from the group is to click the Clear All button, and then click the check box for the single account to include in the report, checking that account alone.

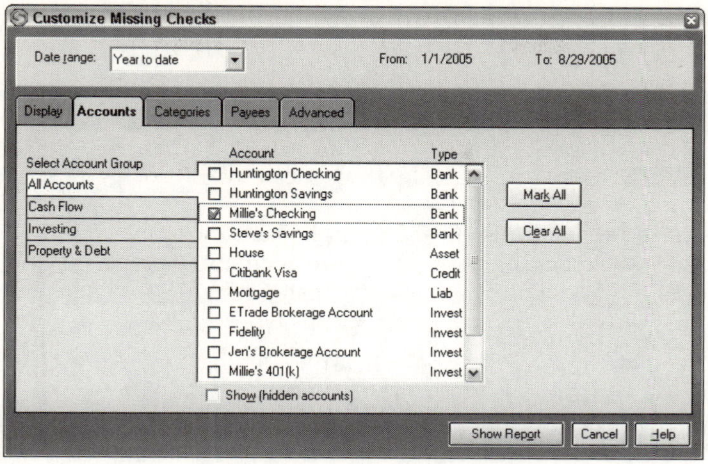

Figure 3-15: Use the Accounts tab to choose the accounts holding data to include in the report.

Choosing Report Categories or Payees

The Categories and Payees tabs in the Customize *Report Title* dialog box enable you to control a report's scope by indicating which categories or payees the report should cover. Because both these tabs work in an identical fashion, you can find out about this once and only once here.

On each tab, you have the option of limiting the report information via selecting categories or matching specific information.

The left side of the tabs include the selection section: Select Categories on the Categories tab and Select Payees on the Payees tab. As Figure 3-16 shows, you can include or exclude report categories or payees by checking and unchecking items in the list. (The Payees tab lists payees rather than categories.) Use the Expand All and Collapse All buttons to expand and collapse the list as needed. Of course, the Mark All button checks all the list items, and the Clear All button unchecks everything. To scroll quickly to a category or payee in the list, start typing its name in the Type *Category/ Payee* Name to Search List text box. The list immediately scrolls to show that category or payee.

If you don't want to mess with clearing the check boxes for all the categories or payees, and you know what category (or subcategory) or payee you want to cover in the report, you can leave all the categories or payees checked and instead use the Matching section at the right.

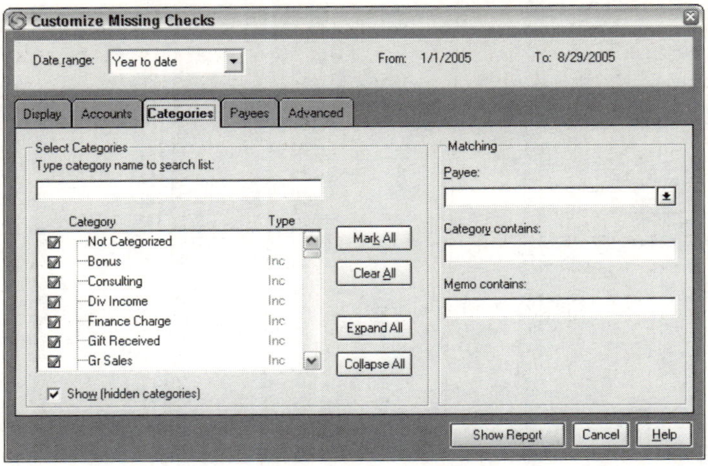

Figure 3-16: Check and uncheck categories or payees as desired, to control their appearance in the report.

When you're working on the Categories tab, select a payee from the Payee drop-down list to shown only transactions using a particular payee. To limit the report to a particular category or subcategory, type the category or subcategory name in the Category Contains text box. To limit the report to show only transactions with a particular Memo field entry, type the applicable entry in the Memo Contains text box. Using Matching, the entries shown in Figure 3-17 would limit the report to list only transactions with *Ingles* as the Payee and *Food:Groceries* as the specified Category (subcategory).

To specify a subcategory, type the category name, a colon, and then the subcategory name, as in **Utilities:Cable TV**. No spaces immediately before or after the colon!

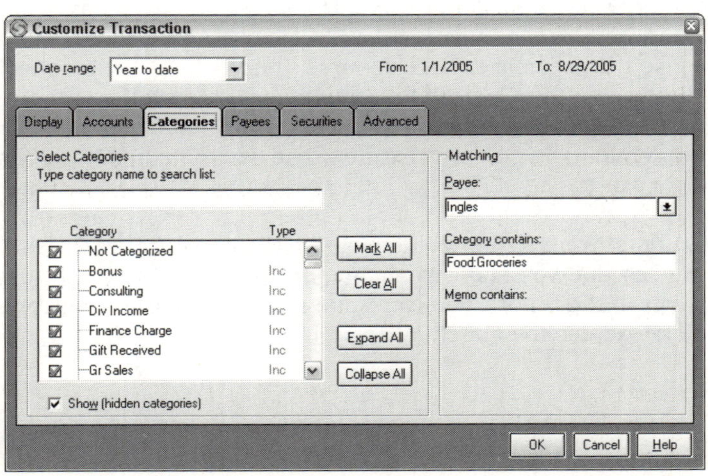

Figure 3-17: Only transactions matching these Payee and Category Contains choices will appear in the report.

The Matching settings on the Payees tab work almost identically. Choose a category from the Category drop-down list and type match entries into the Payee Contains and Memo Contains text boxes. Figure 3-18 shows an example of matching on the Payees tab. Matching transactions have *Pets* specified as the Category and *Target* specified as the Payee.

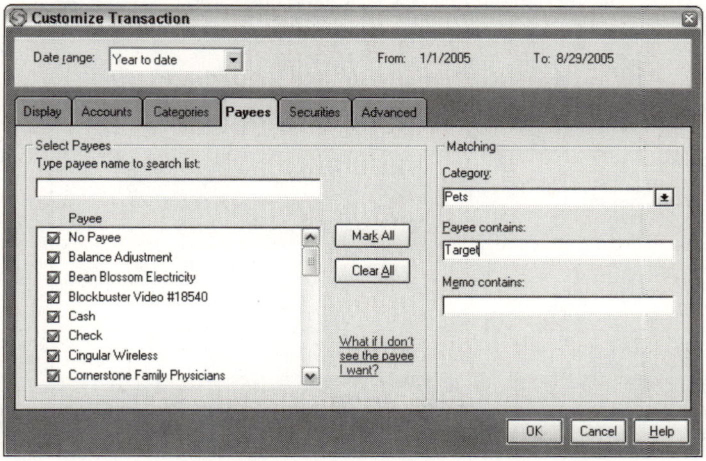

Figure 3-18: Once again, only transactions matching these Payee Contains and Category choices will appear in the report.

TIP

The Category, Payee Contains, and Memo Contains text boxes also will make a match if you enter only a partial name or phrase. For example, you could enter **Tar** rather than *Target* in Figure 3-18, and the report would still include all transactions with *Target* as the Payee. However, if you enter such a partial term, the report includes other matching transactions, too. Quicken also would return transactions using *Tarheel*, *Tarpon*, *Mortar*, or any other variation of "tar" in the Payee field.

Other Customization Settings

The publishers of Quicken want you to be able to customize a report as needed; they really do. But it might seem like you actually have too many choices when you discover that certain other tabs can appear in the Customize *Report Title* dialog box, depending on the type of report you're working with. With any luck, this streamlined presentation helps you work with the additional tabs that can appear in the Customize *Report Title* dialog box:

- **Classes:** If you've created classes in Quicken, you can use this tab to control which classes the report displays. Clear a check box to hide that class in the report.

- **Category Groups:** Budget, comparison, and summary reports include this tab, shown in Figure 3-19. To exclude the transactions falling within a particular category group from the report, clear that category group's check box in the Category Group list.

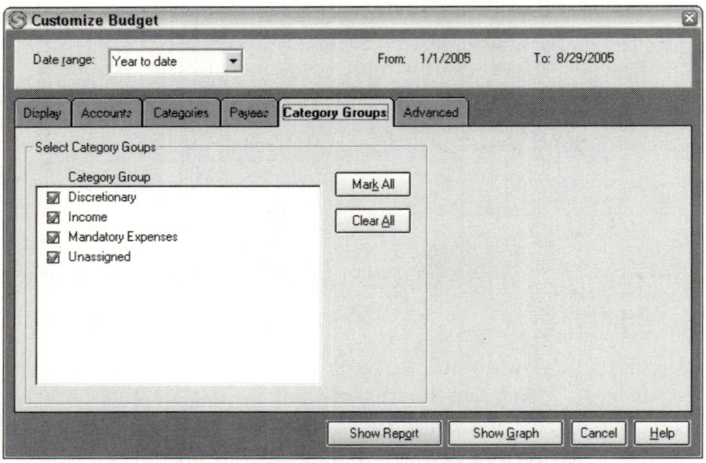

Figure 3-19: If a report uses category groups, you can specify whether to include them in the report you're customizing.

- **Actions:** For some investment accounts, such as the Investment Transactions report, you may see an Actions tab for customization. The Action list here identifies the different kinds of actions represented by account transactions, including such entries as Bought (buying shares of a security), Div (a dividend received), IntInc (interest income), and so on. Click the check box for an action in the list to clear its check box (excluding those transactions from the report) or select its check box (including its transactions in the report).

  TIP: Clicking the Mark All or Clear All buttons always marks (check) or clears (uncheck) all the items in a list of customization choices.

- **Securities:** This tab (Figure 3-20) appears for investment reports and some business reports, enabling you to exclude or include transactions about a particular security in the report. As with the similar customization settings, click to clear and check the check box for any security to exclude or include, respectively, in the Security list. If you want to limit the list to only a matching security, type the security's name in the Security Contains text box in the Matching section of the tab. Even better, if you want to exclude everything but securities with similar names (such as the securities in a particular mutual fund family), enter a partial name in the Security Contains text box.

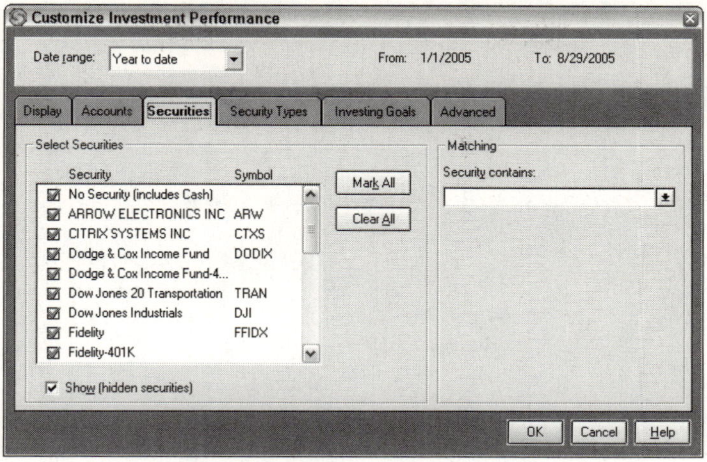

Figure 3-20: You can limit investment and business reports by security when the Securities tab is available.

- **Security Types:** If you're interested in having an investment or business report show only particular types of securities, use the Security Types tab. You know the drill: Clear and select check boxes in the Type list to control what types of securities appear in the report.
- **Investment Goals:** The last way to slice and dice investment data is by investing goals on the Investing Goals tab. Check and uncheck items in the Goal list as needed to control report contents.

Quicken may include even more report customization settings if you buy, unlock, and download more of the business reports. Click the Unlock Report button that appears after you click the desired report to start the process for purchasing it.

Using Advanced Settings

The final tab that appears in the Customize *Report Title* dialog box for most report types is the Advanced tab. The settings on this tab (Figure 3-21) vary widely, and weirdly enough, the tab appears for some report types — but includes no settings or controls.

Figure 3-21 specifically shows the settings you get for many transaction reports. In the Transactions section, you can make a choice from the Amounts drop-down list to tell the report to show transactions with only certain dollar amounts. For example, if you choose Greater Than from the Amounts drop-down list and then enter 100 in the text box that appears, the report displays transactions only with an entry of more than $100 in the Amount field.

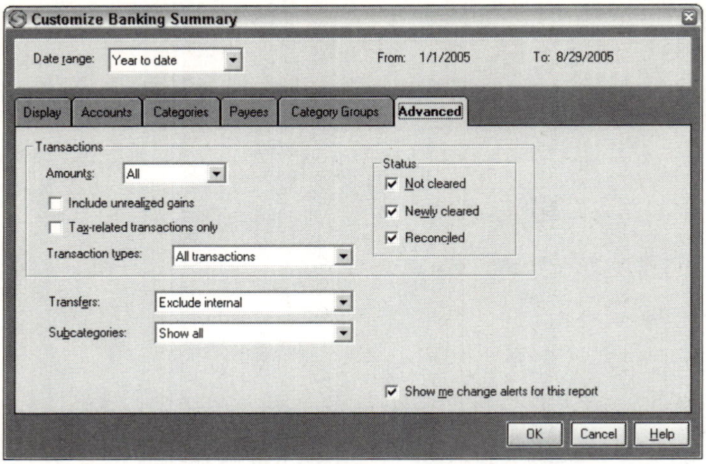

Figure 3-21: Getting advanced with customization.

Still in the Transactions section, check the Include Unrealized Gains check box to include "paper" gains from securities not yet sold in a report showing investment gains. Check Tax-Related Transactions Only to limit the report to transactions with a tax-line-linked category or subcategory assigned. Or, limit the report to show only Payments, Deposits, or Unprinted checks by making the appropriate choice from the Transaction Types drop-down list.

The Status box on the tab lists check boxes representing various transaction status entries. To exclude transactions marked with a particular status from the report, clear the check box beside the status: Not Cleared, Newly Cleared, or Reconciled.

At the bottom of the tab, make a choice from the Transfers drop-down list to control whether all or some transfer transactions should be excluded from the report. Determine whether to include or exclude transactions with a subcategory assigned by making the desired choice from the Subcategories drop-down list. Check the Show Me Change Alerts for This Report check box at the bottom, and Quicken alerts you if you're opening a saved report and have added new categories, classes, or securities that you may need to add to the report manually by changing customization settings.

Budget reports include one last option, a Categories drop-down list. To limit the categories reported, choosing Non-Zero Actual/Budgeted throws out any category that's not used in the register or the budget you've set up, whereas choosing Budgeted Only includes only categories used in the budget you set up in the Budget dialog box.

Note: Quicken Premier Home & Business includes some additional Advanced customization settings. Refer to the Help system for more information if you upgrade to that version of Quicken.

Chapter 4: Printing and Saving Reports

In This Chapter

- Keeping a custom report for later use
- Using the Quicken tool bar to view custom reports
- Putting report data into another format
- Setting up, checking out, and printing a report

The last chapter gave you quite a taste of the dozens of choices you can make to customize a report or graph. Got them all memorized yet? I didn't think so. Fortunately, you don't have to remember all the settings you used to create the perfect custom report. After you've set up the report and it looks good to you, you can save the custom report so that you can open it again in the future as the information in your Quicken file changes. In this chapter, you see how Quicken enables you to manage and access your saved reports using folders and the Quicken tool bar. You also find out how to convert report data to another format for use in another program, and how to make perfect printouts of your report information.

Saving and Organizing Reports

When you first learned about Quicken's Reports & Graphs Center in Chapter 2 of Book VII, you saw that it features a special area at the right called My Saved Reports. Not surprisingly, that's the location in Quicken where you can store and organize your saved custom reports for easy access at a later time. You can create custom folders to hold different types of reports, save and open reports, and manage the reports that you've saved by moving them to another folder or deleting them if they're no longer needed.

When you open the Reports & Graphs Center for the first time, the My Saved Reports list is completely empty, as shown in Figure 4-1. Read on to find out how you can fill it up!

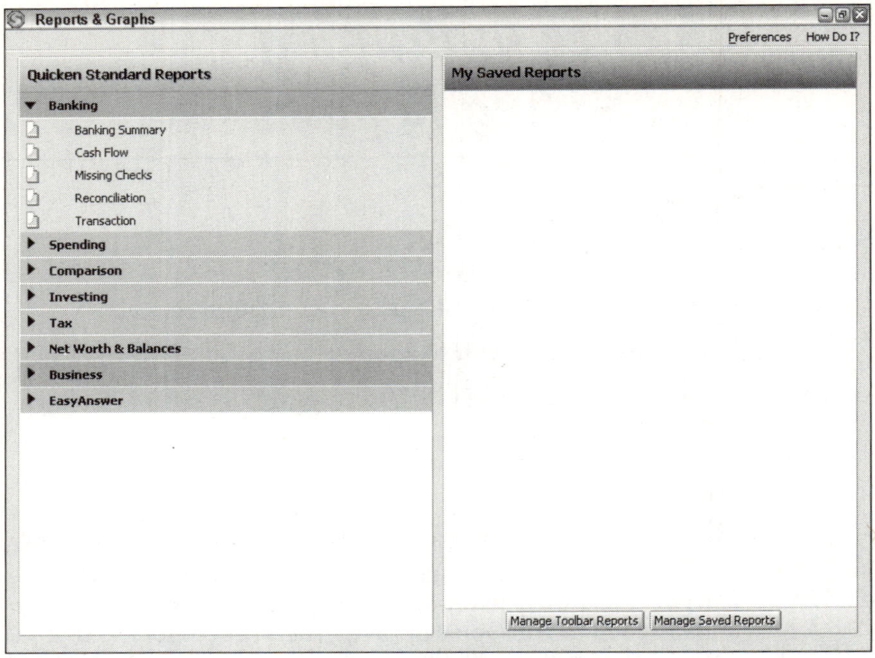

Figure 4-1: Take a peek at the My Saved Reports list in the Reports & Graphs Center.

Creating a report folder

Most users accumulate quite a few custom saved reports over time. Just as the Quicken Standard Reports list in the Reports & Graphs Center groups reports by category so that you can jump to the report you want much more quickly, organizing your many custom reports in the My Saved Reports list into logical groups keeps each report within easy reach.

To accommodate both meticulous pre-planners and people who fly by the seat of their pants, Quicken provides two ways to create folders to hold reports. If you fall into the meticulous category, you might want to plan out what folders you need and add them in advance. For example, if you know you plan to use Quicken to manage both bank accounts and investments, you could create folders named My Custom Banking Reports and My Custom Investing Reports before even creating any reports. If you want to create custom report folders in advance, from the My Saved Reports list, follow these steps:

1. **Open the Reports & Graphs Center.**

   The fastest way to open the Reports & Graphs Center is to click the Reports button on the Quicken tool bar.

2. **Click on the Manage Saved Reports button at the bottom of the My Saved Reports list.**

   The Manage Saved Reports dialog box (Figure 4-2) appears.

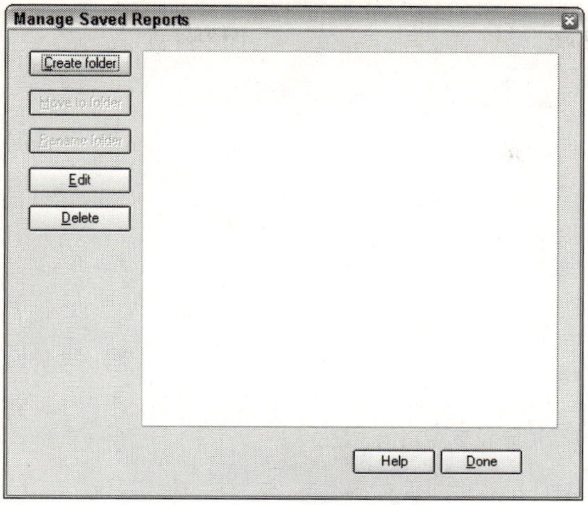

Figure 4-2: Create report folders and manage custom reports right in here.

3. **Click the Create folder button near the upper-left corner of the dialog box.**

   The Create New Report Folder dialog box appears.

4. **Type a name for the new folder in the Name text box of the Create New Report Folder dialog box.**

   Figure 4-3 shows an example.

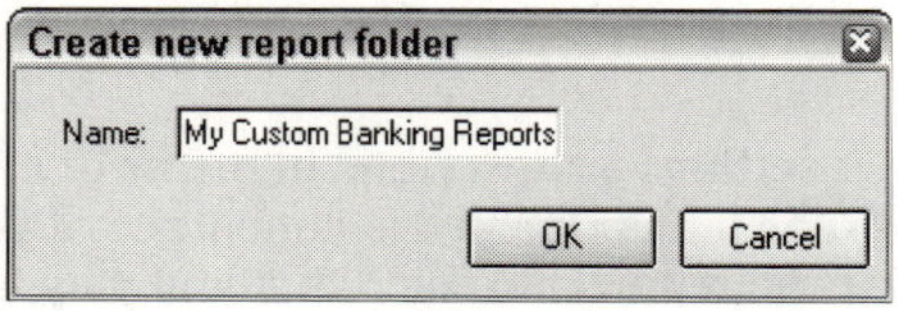

Figure 4-3: Give a descriptive name to each report folder you create.

TECHNICAL STUFF

Your report folder name can have up to 39 characters, including spaces. This challenges you to stick with snappy but descriptive folder names.

5. **Click OK.**

   The new folder appears in the Manage Saved Reports dialog box. And, if it's the first folder that you've added, Quicken also adds the No Folder area (Figure 4-4), which holds any custom reports that you don't store in a specific folder.

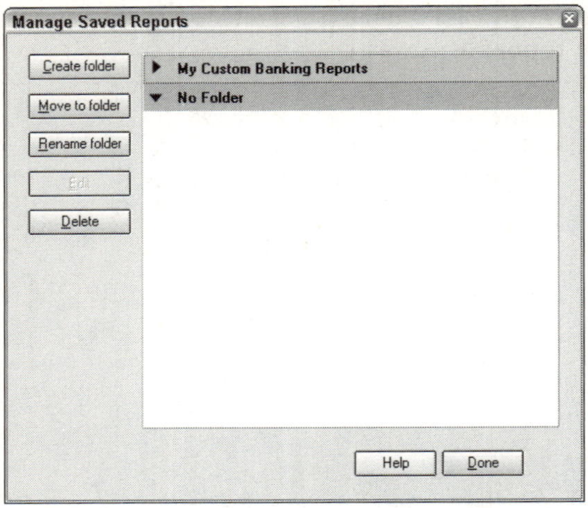

Figure 4-4: Quicken adds the No Folder area below any custom folders you create.

6. **Repeat steps 3 through 5 to add other folders, as needed.**
7. **Click Done to close the Manage Saved Reports dialog box.**

If you're not big on pre-planning, that's fine, too. You can create a folder during the process of saving a custom report. Without digging too deep into that process (because that discussion is coming up next), you can click the Create Folder button in the Save Report dialog box to open the Create New Report Folder dialog box shown in Figure 4-3. As described in steps 4 and 5 above, type the folder name and click OK. From there, you can finish saving your custom report.

Saving a report

Any time you change report settings as described in the prior chapter, you are creating a custom report as far as Quicken is concerned. If you've changed a lot of settings for the report and think that you may want to use that report again, you should save the custom report to add it to the My Saved Reports list in the Reports & Graphs Center. That way, you can redisplay the report any time you need it rather than having to remodify one of Quicken's standard reports.

TIP: You also can save and manage custom graphs using the same steps as described from here on in the chapter.

Chapters 2 and 3 of Book VII both touched on the fact that when you change report settings such as the reporting time frame (Date Range) and then close the report window, a Save Report As dialog box asks whether you want to save the customized report. You can either wait until Quicken prompts you to decide to save, or you can initiate the save on your own. The following steps for saving a report cover both methods of saving:

1a. **In the report window for the customized report, click the Save Report button on the report window tool bar (Figure 4-5).**

OR

1b. **When you close the report window and the Save Report As dialog box appears (also in Figure 4-5), click the Save button.**

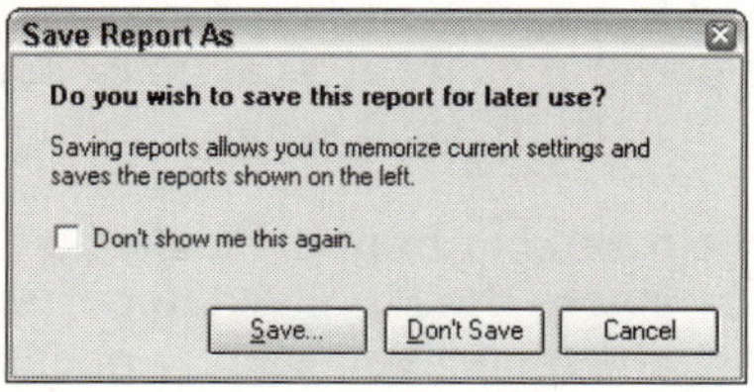

Figure 4-5: Start saving a report from the report window tool bar or the Save Report As dialog box.

If you prefer not to save the report and still want to close the report window, click the Don't Save button in the Save Report As dialog box. To leave the report window open without saving, click the Cancel button.

2. **In the Save Report dialog box that appears (Figure 4-6), edit the entry in the Report Name text box, replacing the default name of the report.**
3. **Enter an optional description for the report in the Description text box.**

   Quicken forces you to keep the Description text box entry short and sweet — you're limited to 21 characters.

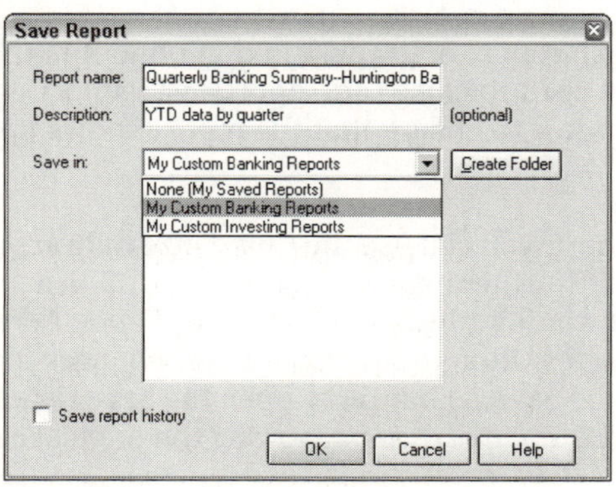

Figure 4-6: Use the settings in the Save Report dialog box to control where to save the report and how to name it.

4. **If you want to save the report in a custom folder that you've created previously, open the Save In drop-down list, and then click the name of the folder to use.**
5. **Click OK.**

   Quicken saves the report in the Reports & Graphs center. If you started the save while in the process of closing the report window, Quicken then closes the report window.

Opening a custom report

Quicken offers multiple ways to perform many of its actions, including displaying a custom report when you need to use it again.

- **Method #1** involves using the menu bar from the main Quicken window. Open the Reports menu and point to the My Saved Reports & Graphs choice. A submenu appears. If the report you want to open appears on the submenu (because you didn't save it in a particular folder), click the report name. If you put the report in a folder that you created earlier, point to the folder name (Figure 4-7), and then click the report. It opens directly in its own window.

  TECHNICAL STUFF: "Pointing" to something onscreen means that you should move your mouse pointer over the item. In Method #1, for example, you don't have to click on the My Saved Reports & Graphs menu choice — just placing your mouse pointer over the choice causes the side menu to appear.

- **Method #2** applies if you're already working in the Reports & Graphs Center. You can open the custom report from the My Saved Reports list there. If you saved the report in a particular folder, click the folder name to expand the list of reports stored in that folder. Click the name of report to open (Figure 4-8), adjust the Date range (or any other setting presented by Quicken), and then click Show Report. The report appears onscreen in its own window.

TIP: If you just saved a custom report or graph and don't find it in the Reports & Graphs Center, you may need to close the Reports & Graphs Center window and then reopen the window to ensure that the report shows up in the My Saved Reports list.

TIP: If you open a custom report, you can use the Customize button on the report window's tool bar to make further changes to the report. When you subsequently close the report window, the Save Changes to *Report Name* dialog box appears. Click the Save button to save your latest changes to the existing custom report, or click the Save As button to open the Save Report so you can save the report under a new name, thus preserving the original custom report.

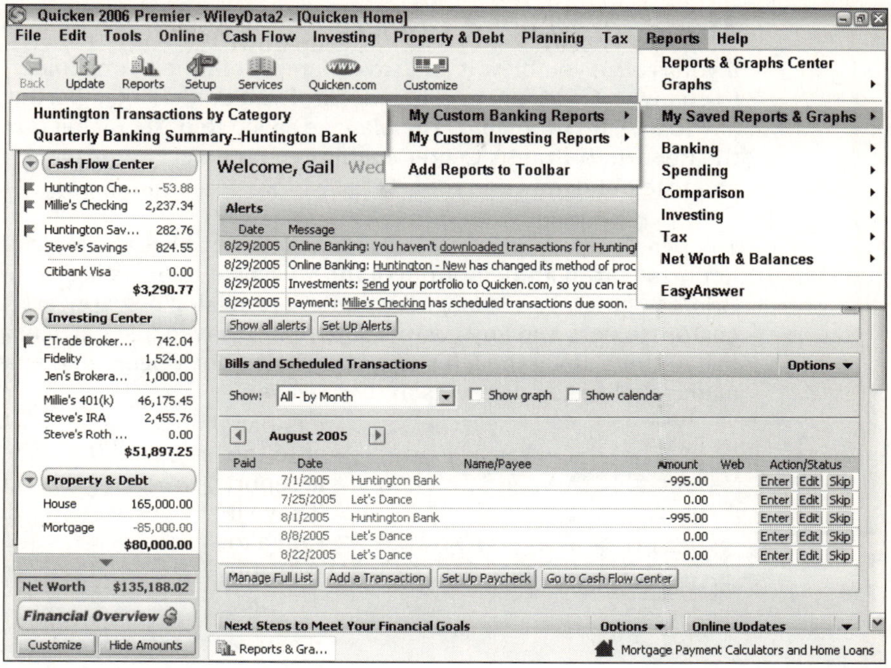

Figure 4-7: The Reports menu adds a command for each saved report, as well as a submenu for each custom report folder.

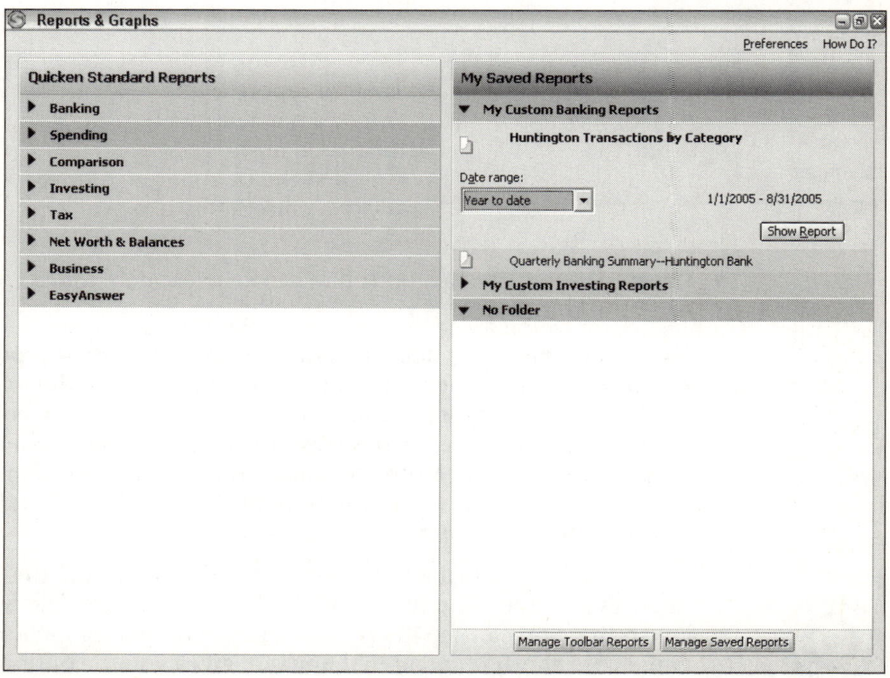

Figure 4-8: The My Saved Reports list enables you to open a saved custom report.

Managing saved reports

If you realize you blew it and saved a report in the wrong folder, if you want to change a folder or report name, or if you don't need a particular report any longer, no problemo. The Manage Saved Reports dialog box available via the Reports & Graphs Center enables you to tweak report and folder names and trim out deadwood reports.

To open the Manage Saved Reports dialog box, click the Managed Saved Reports button at the bottom of the My Saved Reports list in the Reports & Graphs Center. The Manage Saved Reports dialog box appears, listing your custom folders and any custom reports not saved in a particular folder. The five buttons along the left side of the dialog box (Figure 4-9) enable you to manage folders and reports in these ways:

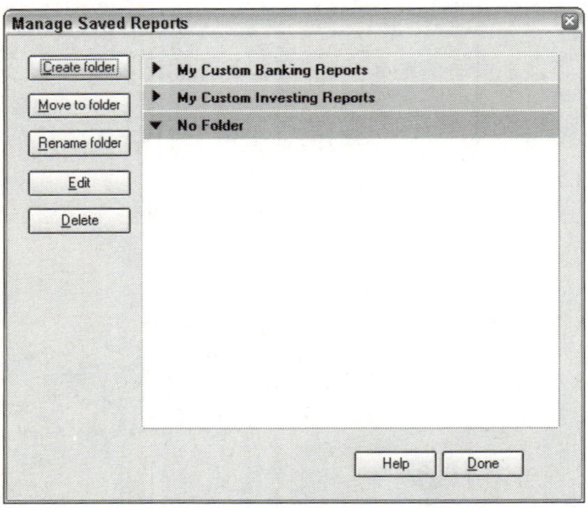

Figure 4-9: The Manage Saved Reports dialog box serves as the nerve center for folder and report changes.

- **Create Folder:** Use this button to create even more folders, as described earlier in the chapter.
- **Move to Folder:** This button lets you move a particular report out of one folder and into another. To make the move, first click the folder that currently holds the report so that you can see the report to move. Click on the report, and then click the Move to Folder button. Open the Name drop-down list in the Move to Report Folder dialog box that appears, click the name of the folder that will be the "new home" of the custom report (Figure 4-10), and then click OK.

TIP: You also can initiate a few report changes directly from the My Saved Reports list in the Reports & Graphs Center. Click the folder name in the list so that you can see the report name, and then right-click the report name. The shortcut menu that appears gives you the option to Delete,

Edit, or Move to (move the report to) another folder. Similarly, right-click a folder name to see a shortcut menu offering New, Delete, and Rename commands.

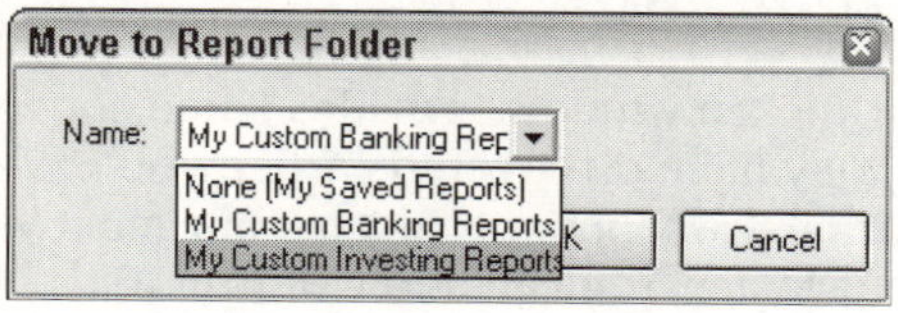

Figure 4-10: Choose a new folder for the report in this dialog box.

- **Rename Folder:** If you botched naming a folder, click the folder in the list in the dialog box, and then click the Rename Folder button. Type a new name or edit the existing name in the Name text box of the Rename Report Folder dialog box that appears, and then click OK.
- **Edit:** Rather than actually enabling you to recustomize a custom report, this choice enables you to change a custom report's name and description. Click the folder that holds the report to change, click the report name itself, and then click the Edit button. In the Edit Saved Report dialog box that appears, change the entries in the Report name and Description text boxes, and then click OK.
- **Delete:** You can delete both reports and folders using the Delete button. To delete a folder or report, select the deletable item in the Manage Saved Reports dialog box, and then click the Delete button. Click OK in the warning message box (Figure 4-11) that appears to continue with the deletion.

WARNING! Be really sure before you click OK because you can't retrieve a deleted report or file. Also, if you try to delete a folder that has reports in it, Quicken won't continue with the deletion. You need to move or delete all the reports in the folder before you can delete that folder.

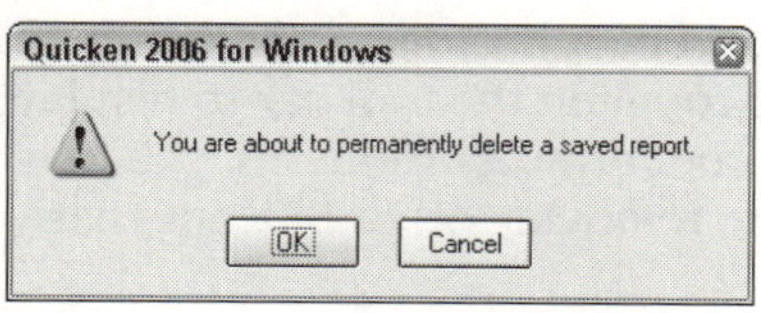

Figure 4-11: Quicken forces you to confirm that you want to delete a report or folder because the deletion is permanent.

After you've finished making the changes you want, click the Done button at the bottom of the Manage Saved Reports dialog box to close the dialog box and return to the Reports & Graphs Center.

Adding Reports to the Tool Bar

The tool bar in the main Quicken window provides some convenient shortcuts. Even better, as you may have discovered earlier, you have some control over what buttons appear on the tool bar to make your most vital Quicken operations even faster and easier. You can add a button to the Quicken tool bar for your favorite custom report, or for a custom folder holding one or more custom reports. This technique gives you quick and direct access to your reports.

Adding the report

You can initiate the process of adding a custom report (or folder with multiple reports) to the tool bar from three different directions:

- ✦ Choose Edit⇨Customize Tool Bar. Next click the Manage Tool Bar Reports button in the lower-left corner of the Customize Tool Bar dialog box that appears.
- ✦ Choose Reports⇨My Saved Reports & Graphs⇨Add Reports to tool bar.
- ✦ Click the Manage Tool Bar Reports button at the bottom of the My Saved Reports list in the Reports & Graphs Center.

Any of those three routes opens the Manage Tool Bar Reports dialog box, which lists the custom folders and reports that you created earlier. As Figure 4-12 shows, you can add either individual reports or entire folders to the tool bar. To add the folder and all the reports in it to the tool bar, click the check box beside the folder name to check it. To add an individual report directly to the tool bar (without a folder), click the folder name (not the check box) so that you can see the reports in the folder, and then click the check box beside the report to add to the tool bar so that a check appears. Click OK. The next time you're working in the Quicken window, a button for each folder and/or report should appear on the Quicken tool bar.

Note: If you don't see the folder/report buttons immediately or see a single button named More, there's no room on the tool bar to display all the report buttons, report folder buttons, and other buttons. So, you may want to customize the tool bar a bit further, removing other buttons that you use less often.

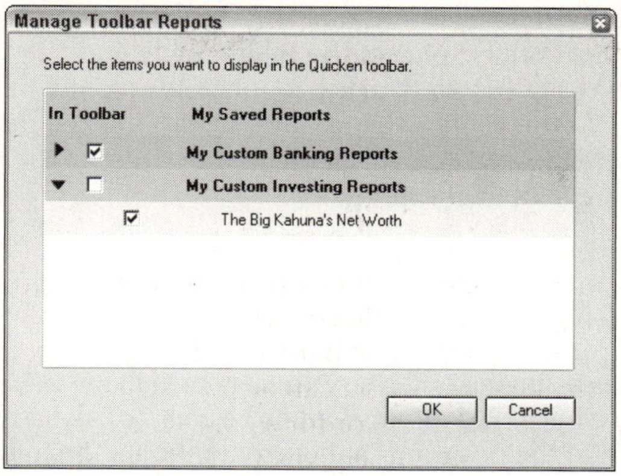

Figure 4-12: Check a folder or report to add it to the main Quicken tool bar.

Viewing the report from the tool bar

A quick glance at the Quicken tool bar tells you whether you can access a tool bar report with a single click or if you have to work extra hard and use (gasp!) two clicks.

If you added a single report to the tool bar, its button looks like a sheet of paper and includes the first several characters of the report's name. The Big Kahuna's report in Figure 4-13 is a single report button. You can click the tool bar button to open the report immediately.

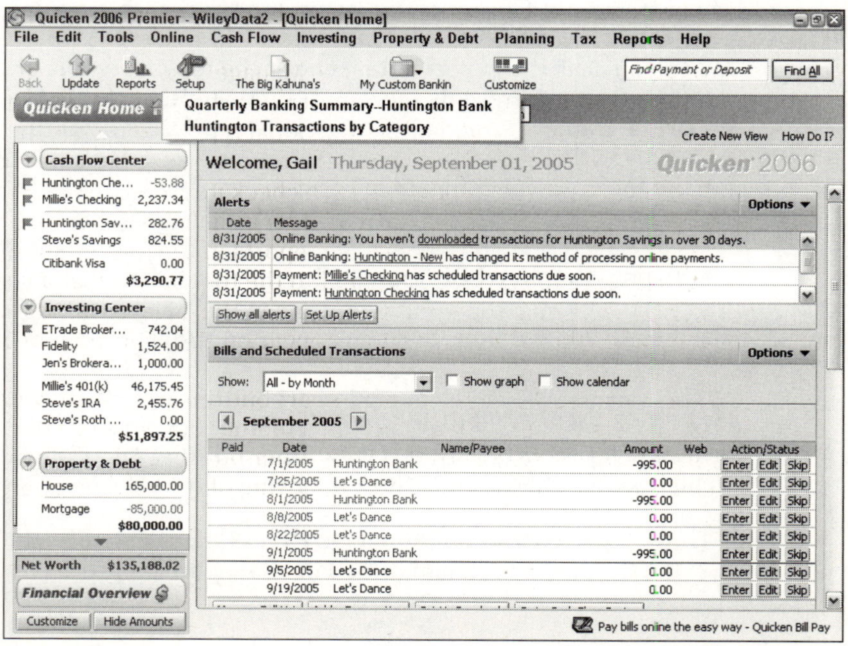

Figure 4-13: The tool bar enables you to open a report in one click (or two, if a folder appears on the tool bar).

If you added a folder of reports to the tool bar, the tool bar button has a folder on it and also includes the first part of the folder name and a down-pointing arrow. I've added the My Custom Banking report folder to my tool bar. As you can see in Figure 4-13, when I click the folder button, Quicken displays a menu with the reports in that folder. I can click the name of one of the reports and the report pops open in its own window.

Exporting Report Data

Virtually no one uses a single computer program as if living in a vacuum. Most people need to move information between programs, to take advantage of a feature not available in the program that currently holds the information, to share information with others, or to keep records. Although Quicken's reports provide a good deal of flexibility, you might find instances when you want that data in an alternate format for planning and other purposes.

That's why you can *export* the data from any report or an image of any report or graph that appears in the report window. Exporting converts the report data or graph picture into another file format that certain other programs can use. For example, if you want to play with some "what if" scenarios with regard to the future performance of your investments, you could export the Portfolio Value report to a format that your spreadsheet program can use. If you want a record of how your finances looked on a particular date, you could save an image file of a graph. Or, if you need to e-mail some financial information to your tax preparer but don't want to send the entire Quicken file, you could create a PDF image of the report and e-mail that image instead.

When you click the Export Data menu at the top of a report or graph window, Quicken presents the export format options available for that report or graph:

- Report to Excel Compatible Format
- Copy report to Clipboard
- Report/Graph to PDF format

Read on to find out how these three choices work.

Report to Excel compatible format

Available for reports only, this command enables you to export data as a tab-delimited .TXT (plain text) file. Follow these steps to export the file:

1. **After you choose the Report to Excel Compatible Format command, the Create Excel Compatible File dialog box appears (Figure 4-14).**

This dialog box works just like any other file saving dialog box. Use the Look In list and folder icons to select the folder in which you want to save the file.

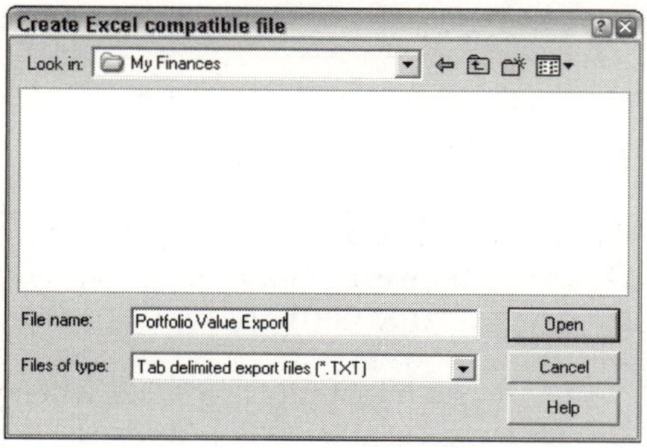

Figure 4-14: Exporting a plain text version of a report.

2. **Type a name for the exported file in the File Name text box.**

   If you want to include the current date in the name for the exported file so that you'll know when you saved the data, be sure to enter the date with hyphens (1-15-05 Net Worth), not slashes, as the slashes are not permitted in filenames.

3. **Make sure that Tab Delimited Export Files (*.TXT) appears in the Files of Type field.**

4. **Click Open.**

   It seems strange that you click the Open command here: Nothing opens when you click this command. To be more precise, the command should probably read Save.

   Be sure to remember the folder location where you saved the file so you can find that file when you open your Excel program.

5. **To work with the data in Excel, use that program's File⇨Open command or Open button.**

6. **Choose Text Files from the Files of Type drop-down list at the bottom of the dialog box, and then navigate to the folder that holds the file and click Open.**

   The Text Import Wizard dialog box appears.

7. **Make sure that the Delimited option button is selected in the Text Import Wizard dialog box, and then click Finish.**

   After you've opened the exported file, you may need to reformat some of the cells and resize the columns, as shown in Figure 4-15.

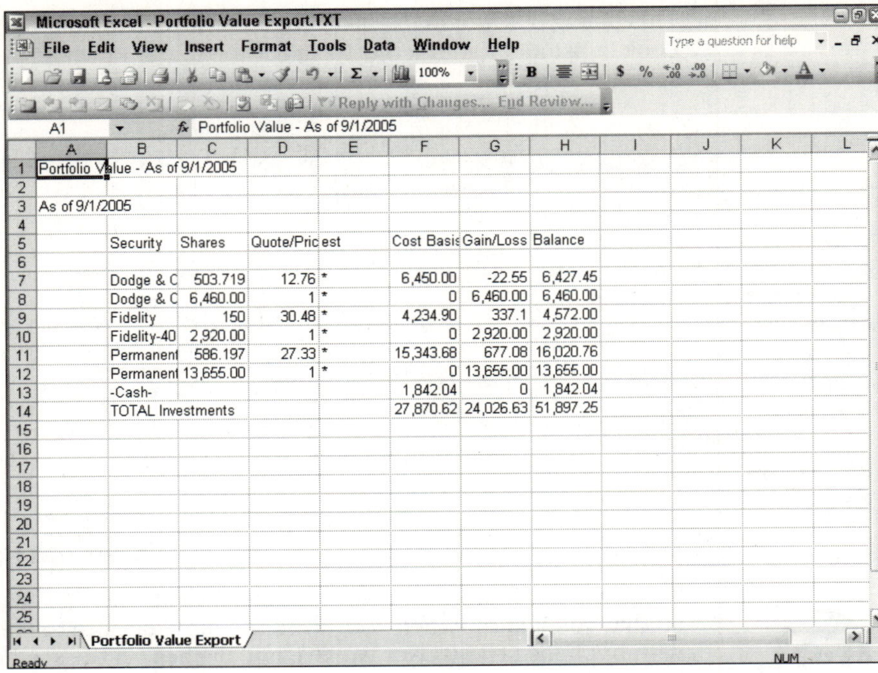

Figure 4-15: The plain text report opened in Excel.

Tab-delimited means that a tab appears between each column of data in the file. *Plain text* means that the file format uses very basic characters only, with no fancy formatting.

Even though the name of the command includes "Excel compatible," many spreadsheet, word processing, and database programs can open plain text files.

Copy Report to Clipboard

The Copy Report to Clipboard command appears for both reports and graphs. If you use this command to copy a report, Quicken copies the report data as tab-delimited plain text. If you use the command to copy a graph, Quicken *still* copies only the report data, rather than as a picture of the graph as you might expect.

To export using the Clipboard, follow these steps:

1. **Click the Export Data button at the top of your report, and then choose Copy Report to Clipboard.**
2. **Go to the destination application (typically a word processing program).**
3. **Create or open the document where you want to use the data.**

4. **Choose Edit⇨Paste or click the Paste button on the tool bar, or press Ctrl+V.**

   The report data appears in the document.

The Clipboard is a special holding area in your computer's memory. Information you copy goes to the Clipboard, from which you can paste the information into another document or program. The Clipboard holds only one copied image or set of report data at a time, so each time you export a report to the Clipboard, the exported data replaces the previous Clipboard contents.

Report/Graph to PDF format

This last export command uses a special printing driver to create a PDF file with an image of the report data or graph. Follow these steps to create your PDF file.

1. **Click the Export Data button at the top of your report, and then choose Report to PDF format.**

   Choosing this command opens the Print dialog box (Figure 4-16), which in this case uses a special printing driver to write the PDF file as a file on your hard disk.

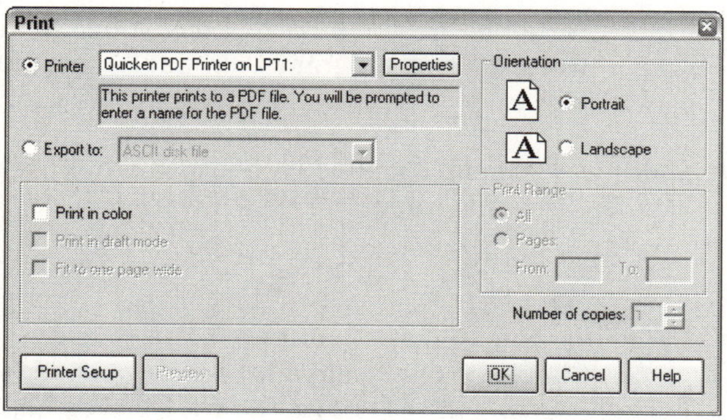

Figure 4-16: Quicken "prints" to export the PDF file.

2. **You can just leave most of the settings in the Print dialog box as is, with the exception of checking the Print in Color check box if you want a color image, or changing the Orientation (Portrait versus Landscape) choice.**
3. **Click OK, and Quicken opens the Save to PDF File dialog box.**
4. **Specify a save location and filename, and then click Save to create the PDF file.**

   You can open the PDF file in any program that supports that format, like the one shown in Figure 4-17.

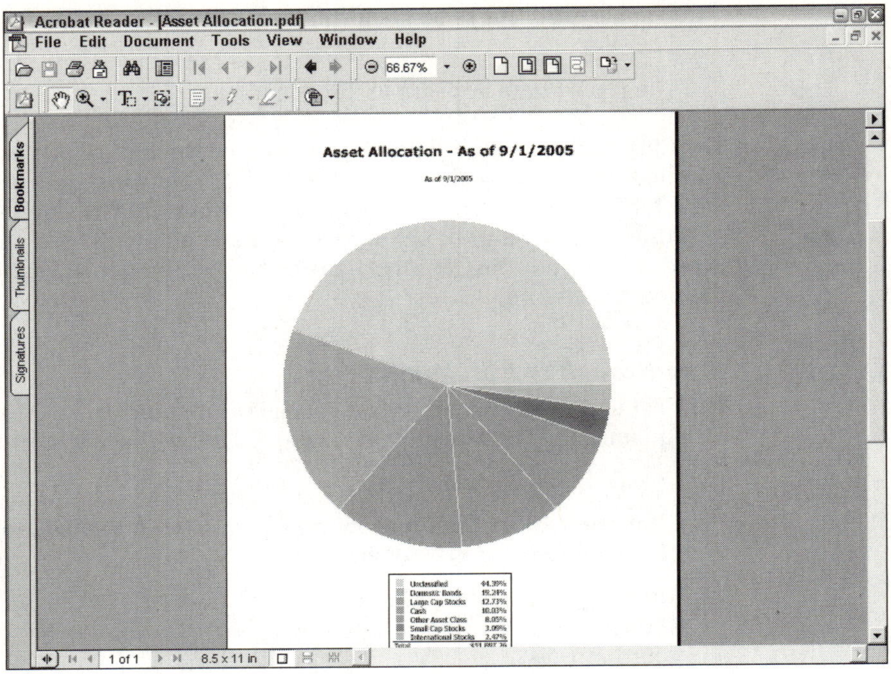

Figure 4-17: A PDF file of a Quicken graph.

PDF is short for the Portable Document Format developed by Adobe Systems. You can download a free program (Acrobat Reader) for opening PDF files from `www.adobe.com/products/acrobat/readermain.html`.

PDF files are a nice way to send secure data because other users can't change the file unless they have special PDF software.

Printing Your Report

Sooner or later, you'll need to get some of your Quicken reports off the screen and onto paper. For example, you might have a meeting with an investment advisor or tax planner, and want to provide that expert with some information about your current financial picture. Printing Quicken reports and graphs works much like printing in other applications, so if this information is a yawner to you, skip it for now and only come back to it if you need to.

Customizing print features

To print a report or graph, you have to be working in the window for that report or graph. Click the Print Report or Print Graph button on the window tool bar to open Quicken's Print dialog box.

As shown in Figure 4-18, the Print dialog box offers only a few basic settings.

- Make sure that you have the right printer selected from the Printer drop-down list (beside the option button of the same name).
- Choose the Portrait (tall) or Landscape (wide) page orientation.
- Specify which report pages to print and how many printout copies to make using the Print Range and Number of Copies settings.
- When active, click the Print in Color, Print in Draft Mode, and Fit to One Page Wide options, as needed. (Those first two options may or may not be active, depending on the printer you selected.)

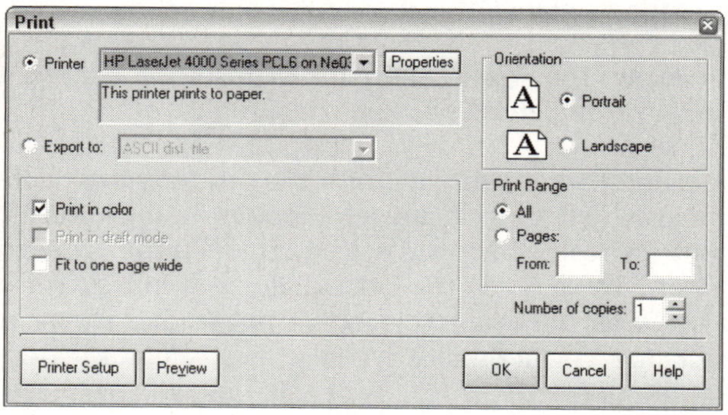

Figure 4-18: Use Quicken's Print dialog box to cover the basics for your print job.

If you just exported a PDF file of a report or graph, be sure that you choose the correct printer from the Printer drop-down list. Your printer setting might still point to PDF.

You also can click the Export To option button that appears in the Print dialog box, and then choose a file format to export the report or graph data to an ASCII, tab-delimited text, or .PRN (for Lotus 1-2-3) file.

Quicken lets you change a few layout settings via the Print dialog box. Click the Printer Setup button at the bottom left of the Print dialog box to open the Printer Setup for Reports and Graphs dialog box shown in Figure 4-19, and then choose from these options:

- You can enter larger or smaller margin sizes in the Left, Right, Top, and Bottom text boxes. Just be aware that you can't specify a margin that's smaller than your printer can handle. Most printers require minimum margins of .25 inches all around, although some printers may require even larger margins. Consult your printer documentation to learn its minimum margin settings.

✦ If you want to change the font (letter type) for the report headings or body, click either the Heading Font or Body Font buttons in the Fonts area, choose the alternate font in the dialog box that appears, and then click OK.

When you've finished making your printer setup choices, click OK to return to the Print dialog box.

The heading and body fonts you select become the defaults for all reports and for future Quicken work sessions.

If you choose a font that you don't like and want to return to the original, remember that the font Quicken originally specified for both headings and body text was the Arial font.

You can also access the Printer Setup for Reports and Graphs dialog box by choosing File➪Printer Setup➪For Reports/Graphs.

After you've made your style selections, the printer you selected from the Printer drop-down list controls any additional printing choices. Click the Properties button beside the printer name to open the Properties dialog box for your printer. The sample Properties dialog box in Figure 4-20 offers basic settings on two tabs, plus an Advanced button to click for even more settings like choosing a print quality. If you're using a color inkjet printer, you should see additional settings for ink density and so on. After you've selected the property settings you prefer, click OK to apply them and return to the Print dialog box.

Getting a preview

If you've changed a lot of print settings or have created a custom report that you've never printed, it's a good practice to preview the printout to identify any problems that might exist or to see how many pages the report contains. To preview the printout, click the Preview button in the Print dialog box. Quicken displays the Print Preview. To get a close-up of what's going on with the report, click with the mouse anywhere on the report. (The mouse pointer changes to a magnifying glass automatically in Print Preview.)

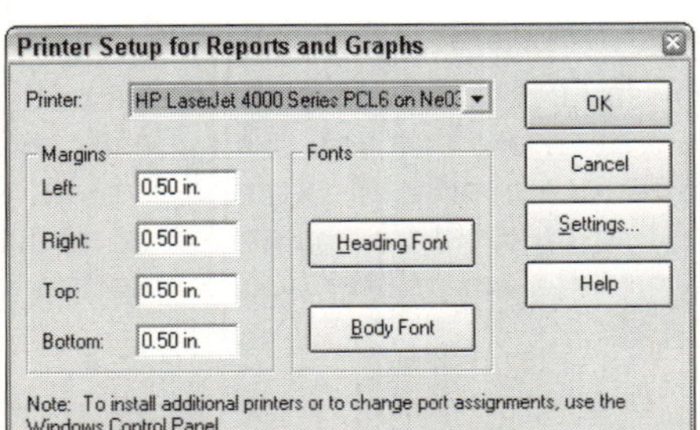

Figure 4-19: You can adjust basic report layout settings.

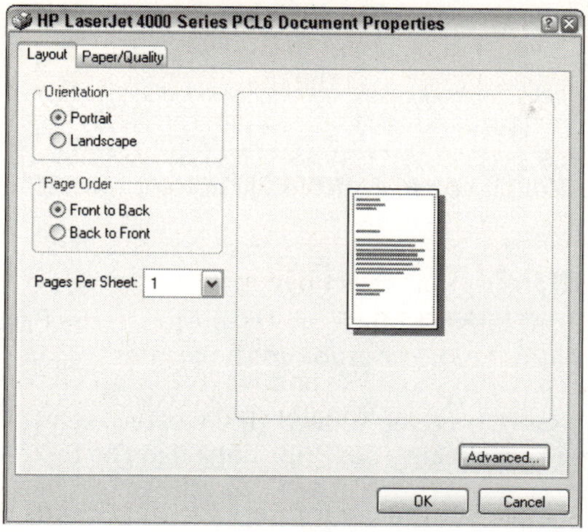

Figure 4-20: Each printer has its own unique properties.

As you can see in the example in Figure 4-21, this particular report looks fine with new heading and body fonts applied, but some of the columns appear cut off at the right. To fix this problem, you would need to redesign the report back in the report window. To cancel the report printout and return to the report window, click the Close button at the top of the Print Preview. You have to reopen the Print dialog box to make your changes.

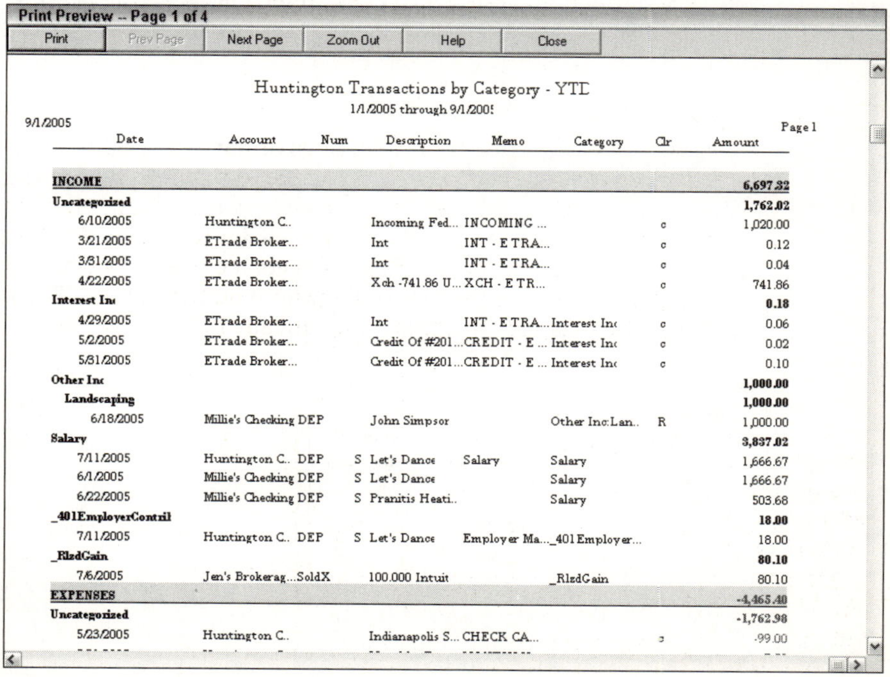

Figure 4-21: Preview a report printout for appearance, readability, and length.

Unlike in some other programs, closing the Print Preview in Quicken cancels the whole print job.

While in the Print Preview window, you can use the Next Page and Prev Page buttons to check each page in the printout, and the Zoom Out/Zoom In button to get the overall picture of each page in the printout.

Print, baby, print!

If you skipped the Print Preview, click the OK button in the Print dialog box (Figure 4-18) to send the report or graph to the printer.

If you took the road more traveled to the Print Preview, send the print job to the printer from there by clicking the Print button at the top of the preview window.

Give your report printout pages one last read to make sure there weren't any discrepancies between what you saw onscreen and how it printed. Then you're good to go!

Book VIII

Small Business Finances

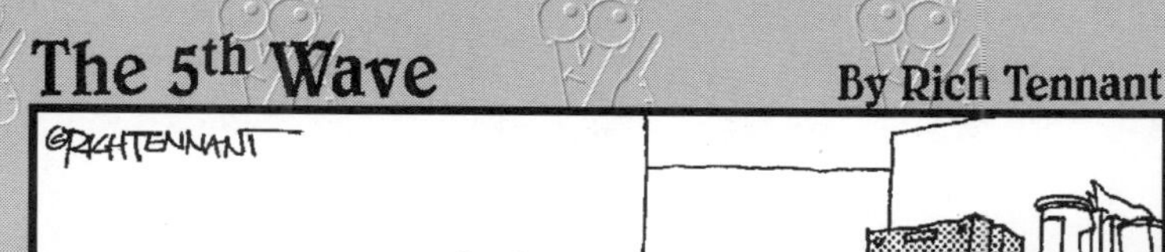

"This is your personal finance software?! This is what you're running?! Well, Heck – I think this could be your problem!"

Contents at a Glance

Chapter 1: Quicken Premier Home & Business

In This Chapter

- **Exploring features of the Home & Business Program**
- **Advantages to using Home & Business**
- **Upgrading to Home & Business**

You might think you need QuickBooks or a more sophisticated accounting program if you have a small business, but the truth is that Quicken has everything most small businesses need. You can track your business income and expenses, receivables and payables, produce payroll, and keep track of your business assets with Quicken.

What You Get with Quicken Home & Business

Poke around in Quicken and you find all sorts of features guaranteed to make your small business record-keeping task easier. Here's a sample of what you find in the latest version of Quicken Home & Business. (Note: This list describes the features from the 2006 version of Quicken Home & Business. In addition, all of the features of the regular Quicken program are also included in the Home & Business version.)

- With the Business Center, a business overview including list of receivables and current payables.
- A special report that shows how your business activity fits into your Schedule C tax form.
- Ability to store and attach copies of electronic receipts and tax forms right in your Quicken program.
- Tracking capability to monitor tax-deductible mileage.
- The ability to track multiple jobs and prepare estimates.
- Features to produce invoices, monthly statements, and related accounts receivable reports.
- Ability to track accounts payable and produce related reports.

- Option for customizing business forms including the capability of placing your company logo on the forms.
- Free access to live customer support.
- 60-day money-back guarantee.

Is Quicken Home & Business for you?

You might be wondering if you have the type of business that can take advantage of the features offered by Quicken Home & Business. Here are some points to consider when making the choice between Quicken and other software programs:

- Quicken is not a network-friendly program. Although different people can take turns using the program, the program cannot be used by multiple users simultaneously.
- Quicken does not offer the specialized password-protection features of the full-bodied accounting programs. You can password-protect your entire Quicken data file, but not specific features of the file.
- Quicken does not offer *customized* versions for particular industries such as construction or manufacturing or retail.
- Quicken does not offer point-of-sale features.
- Quicken does not have the ability to track inventory.
- Quicken does not offer the audit features that more sophisticated accounting programs include.
- Perhaps the most significant difference between Quicken and other accounting programs is that Quicken is not a traditional double-entry accounting program. In true accounting programs, one transaction has a double effect, just as in real accounting. With Quicken, you can make entries that only affect one account.

These all appear to be shortcomings of the Quicken program, and warnings for the skeptical business-owner. But don't forget all the great features of Quicken, many of which you can't find in a business accounting program:

- Stellar investment tracking, including the ability to download current investment values.
- Personal finance features that let you operate both your personal financial life and your business from the same program.
- Integration with TurboTax for seamless tax return preparation.

✦ Economical online banking functions — many banks coordinate their online services with Quicken for free or for a very small charge. With QuickBooks, you might find you have to pay more and be more selective when coordinating with online banking features.

So the bottom line is this: You have to decide what your business needs, and then find the program that fits your business. Quicken offers a 60-day money-back guarantee of the Home & Business program, so if you want to experiment, you can do so without risk. Note also that an upgrade from Quicken Premier to Quicken Home & Business is only $10.

Some business enterprises require an accounting program that has complete double-entry accounting features and the more sophisticated accounts receivable and accounts payable features that accrual-based businesses use. But plenty of businesses don't need the extra bells and whistles. See if your business sounds like one of these — if it does, you should be just fine using Quicken, and might not even need the Home & Business version:

✦ Schedule C and Schedule E businesses. You know who you are. You report your business activity on a Schedule C or Schedule E tax form that accompanies your personal income tax return. The Schedule E is for reporting rental activity. Other businesses go on the Schedule C.

✦ Hobbies turned into businesses. If you're already a Quicken user and find that your hobby is generating income, or expect that your hobby might turn into a viable business in the future, it's time to start tracking your business as an entity within Quicken.

✦ If you own a business and comingle your business and personal bank accounts, you're going to love using Quicken to separate the two entities and produce reports that show just how your business is faring.

✦ Does your child operate a business? Odd jobs that start out small can escalate into actual business ventures. Babysitting can become daycare, tutoring can become classroom teaching, lawn mowing can become a lawn service, and so on. When the odd job becomes a viable business, it's time to keep track of income and expenses.

✦ If you're planning a business venture in the future and right now are just accumulating information, acquiring some assets, and incurring start-up expenses, be sure to track all of those cash outlays in your Quicken program.

✦ Even small corporations that have a minimal number of employees can use Quicken as their accounting program. As the business grows, a transition to a more complete accounting program such as QuickBooks is a simple export command away.

Creating a separate data file for your business

You can combine your business information with your personal information in Quicken, and if you are a sole proprietor who uses your personal bank accounts to handle your business income and expenses, the combination of the two makes a certain amount of sense. On the other hand, if it's possible to separate your business and your personal financial transactions, you might want to consider keeping a completely separate Quicken file for your business. You can keep the file on the same computer as your personal file, but the two would not interact with each other. Here are some advantages to keeping your business transactions in a separate file.

- You can password-protect your Quicken files. If you're not the only person using your Quicken program, you might want password-protection on either your business or your personal file or both.
- If you combine business and personal financial activity in one file, you might find that you use subcategories and classes to separate your business transactions from your personal transactions. You can avoid this extra work and use top-level categories for your business activity if you keep the business in a separate file.
- If you use an outside accountant or an off-site bookkeeper to help with your business finances, you might want to give that person a separate data file that doesn't include your personal financial information.
- You can quickly produce business-only reports, including tax reports, in your separate business file without having to customize reports to segregate personal information from business information.
- With two separate files, you remove the risk of mingling your personal and business activities, classifying a business activity as personal or vice versa.

Advantages to using Quicken for a small business

If you've read this entire book up to this point, you're already familiar with many of the advantages Quicken has to offer its users. But if you're a small business owner and you hopped right to this chapter, thinking this is all you need to learn, you might be interested in this list of cool things that you can do with Quicken. These features are particularly nice for business owners:

- You can use your Quicken data to prepare your tax returns. By entering tax line assignments that cross-reference your income and expenses to the proper lines on your tax return, you can produce reports that enable you to quickly determine what amounts to put on your tax return. And if you use TurboTax tax preparation software, you can export your Quicken information directly into your tax return. See Book V for more information on how the tax features work.
- Use Quicken to create all the reports you need to see how your business is doing, analyze cash flow, compare actual activity to your budget, track receivables and payables, and determine your net worth. Customize the

report within the Quicken program and save your customized reports for future use, or export your reports to your spreadsheet program for more advanced customization.

✦ It's not enough to know if you have enough money in the bank to pay this week's bills. As a business owner, it's imperative that you have a sense of the value of your business. On any day, you must be able to produce a net worth report for your business. And if you want to determine your overall net worth, net worth reports can include your personal accounts too.

✦ In addition to seeing your net worth report, potential lenders and investors need to know whether your business is making money. Produce cash flow reports and profit and loss statements that show how your business operates.

Structuring Your Categories for a Small Business

Whether you use a separate business file or combine your business and personal finances in one file, you need to set up the categories that are going to be most useful to you in your business.

Typical business categories

Quicken Home & Business provides a category list replete with business-related categories that you might encounter. You can use the list as is, but hardly anyone is going to want every category chosen by Quicken and only those categories. It's more likely that you'll take Quicken up on its offer to let you hide categories you don't need, or even delete categories you're certain you'll never need, and then add your own categories.

If you already have a chart of accounts for your business, you can use that as a guide for creating your Quicken categories. If you're new to the whole business of choosing and creating categories, here are some guidelines that can help point you in the right direction.

A chart of accounts is divided into five groups of accounts, and you should follow this same grouping when deciding what categories you need to set up in Quicken for your business. Consider each account group, determine what is appropriate for your business from each type of account, and create your main categories from these selections.

TIP

After you've set up your main categories, you can add additional top-level categories at any time. Also, you can add subcategories and sub-subcategories, as many levels as you need, to create the kind of organization scheme that works best for you.

- **Assets:** Assets are the things you own. This group includes the following types of categories:
  - Bank accounts
  - Investment accounts
  - Accounts receivable
  - Inventory
  - Fixed assets, such as land, buildings, furniture, equipment, vehicles, and computers
  - Deposits that you make on utilities or other services
- **Liabilities:** Liabilities are the amounts you owe. Typical Quicken liability categories include
  - Accounts payable
  - Credit cards
  - Deposits that you receive from customers
  - Taxes that you've collected from customers and employees and owe to the government
  - Loans
- **Equity:** Equity is another word for net worth. In Quicken, your equity is computed on your net worth statement. However, you might have some equity categories that include the following:
  - Owner's draw
  - Contributed capital
  - Capital stock
  - Dividends
- **Income:** The categories for the income you earn depend heavily on the type of business you run and the sources for your income. Here are some sample categories that you might see in this group. Remember that these categories are in addition to any personal income you record in your Quicken file:
  - Sales
  - Personal service income
  - Interest income
  - Dividend income
- **Expenses:** The way in which you spend your money in order to run your business results in a plethora of categories that you can use to track your spending. Remember that the more detailed you get with your categories,

the easier it is to budget and monitor your spending. If your expense category list gets too long, consider grouping subcategories under main category headings. Here are some sample categories you might have in your business:

- Rent
- Salaries and wages
- Advertising
- Insurance, including auto, liability, health, life, workmen's comp, disability, property
- Office supplies
- Travel
- Taxes, including payroll, property, sales, income
- Utilities
- Leased equipment
- Repairs
- Computer supplies
- Trash removal
- Manufacturing costs
- Packaging
- Shipping
- Automobile expense
- Bank fees
- Legal and other professional services
- Dues, licenses, subscriptions
- Interest expense
- Meals and entertainment
- Telephone, cell phone
- Internet service
- Copying, faxing

Creative use of subcategories

Subcategories in Quicken give you the ability to record your financial transactions with detailed precision, and at the same time produce reports that are not cluttered with tons of categories. Here's an example. You want to get a handle on your shipping costs by creating a category called Shipping. For more detail, you break that category into two subcategories called Packaging and Mailing. By assigning your shipping costs to the proper category, you can see how much you spend on the packaging part of your shipments as opposed to the amount spent on the actual mailing costs.

Want more detail? Create sub-subcategories under Packaging for Boxes, Tape, Wrapping Paper, Labels, Bubble Wrap, Packing Filler. Create sub-subcategories under Mailing for Priority Mail, Ground Transport, Air Transport, Overnight Mail, or whatever specific services your company uses.

After you get the subcategories and the sub-subcategories set up (and you don't have to stop there — Quicken actually lets you create 16 levels of subcategories (sub-sub-sub-sub-sub- and so on). So feel free to go nuts with your categories if that will give you the information you need to more effectively run your business.

Using multiple levels of subcategories

Although Quicken provides the capability of layering up to 16 levels of subcategories, you probably don't need to go that in-depth with your category assignments. On the other hand, here are some examples of how you might use multiple levels of subcategories effectively.

- Previously in this chapter I discussed setting up subcategories for shipping. You might want to track detailed shipping costs for each type of item that you ship. In this case, your parent category could be Shipping, and then you would break out the various types of items you ship in the next level of subcategory. Under each item type, you would have the sub-subcategory breakdown for Packaging and Mail, and then you would go to a fourth level of sub-sub-subcategories for the detail of types of package and mail services that you use.
- Another example of how to use the various levels of subcategories is to consider tracking your vehicle expenses. Say you have two cars and you use each car for both business and personal travel. You need to report the cost of operating each car on your tax return, and then allocate expenses between business and personal based on the percent that your business mileage is of the total. Your overall expense category might be called Automobile. The first subcategory can separate each vehicle, so you'd have a subcategory for Car 1 and another subcategory for Car 2. On the sub-subcategory level, you can break out detailed expenses for each car's fuel costs, repairs, insurance, registration, oil changes and other maintenance, and so on.

Don't be afraid to get creative with your subcategories. The goal is to get the best information you can out of your Quicken program, and if multiple layers of subcategories achieve that goal, go for it!

Setting up subcategories

The trick to successfully setting up subcategories is to start with the top-level category. If you haven't got the parent, you can't create the kids. Actually, that's not quite true: You can create a parent category and then later turn that parent into a kid. (We've all been there, right?!) Let me just show you how it's done:

1. **Open the Category list.**

   Choose Tools➪Category List, or press Ctrl+C (or Shift+Ctrl+C).

   Ctrl+C is the standard Quicken command for opening the category list. Sometimes, this command morphs into Shift+Ctrl+C. I've placed the second option as an alternative throughout the book. You can tell which command your program responds to by either trying both commands to see which command works, or by looking at the keyboard shortcut that is listed on your Tools menu across from Category List.

2. **Open the Set Up Category window.**

   Click the New button at the bottom of the Category List to open the setup window.

3. **Enter the name and a description for your new category.**

   Enter your information in the Set Up Category window, as shown in Figure 1-1.

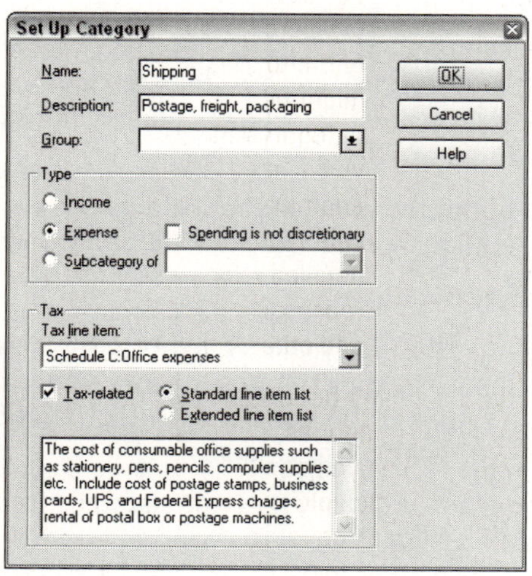

Figure 1-1: Setting up a new category

Make sure your category name is unique and that you haven't already created another category for the same type of transactions. Occasionally I create a new category, forgetting that I already have another category doing the same job, like Phone and Telephone, or Postage and Mailing.

4. **Select a group name if you're using category groups, or you can leave the group blank.**

   Category groups are used for budgeting purposes; for example, in situations where you want to budget an amount for a group of expenses without having to provide a detailed expense breakdown in the budget. You could set up a group for entertainment expenses that would include movies, theatre, sporting events, amusement parks, and so on, and budget just one amount for all entertainment.

5. **Choose whether this category is for income or expenses.**

   In Quicken, all categories are either income or expense. It's income if money is coming into your accounts from this category. It's an expense if money is going out.

6. **Indicate subcategory information.**

   If this is a top-level category, do not mark the subcategory option. If you've already set up the top-level category and this is to be a subcategory, click the subcategory of option and choose the higher category from the drop-down list.

7. **Enter optional tax information.**

   If you choose to produce tax-related reports through Quicken, check the Tax-Related check box and select the appropriate tax line from the Tax Line Item drop-down list. You must select a tax line if you want the amount to appear in your Tax Summary Report.

   For more information about tax lines, tax reports, and creating tax returns from the information in your Quicken file, see Book V.

8. **Click OK to save your new category.**

   You can come back at any time and make changes in the category information. Open the category list, click on the category you want to change, and then click the Edit button at the bottom of the list. An Edit Category window appears where you can make changes.

   You don't have to open each category individually for editing in order to assign tax lines. You can assign tax lines to your categories efficiently by using the Tax Line Item Assignments window in the Category List.

Subcategories in Quicken reports

Most Quicken reports display both top-level categories and subcategories. The top-level category name appears, and then the subcategories associated with that category appear indented, beneath the top-level category, like children assembled beneath the parent. You can drill down to see the detail of any subcategory amount by double-clicking on the amount.

Top-level category amounts cannot be drilled if subcategories are present.

If you want to hide the display of the subcategories and only show the top-level category amounts on your report, follow these quick steps:

1. **Open the Customize window.**

   With the report displayed, click the Customize button that appears in the top-right corner, or press Alt+U. A Customize window appears.

2. **Click the Advanced tab.**

   Several tabs appear in the Customize window. The Advanced tab is the right-most tab (see Figure 1-2).

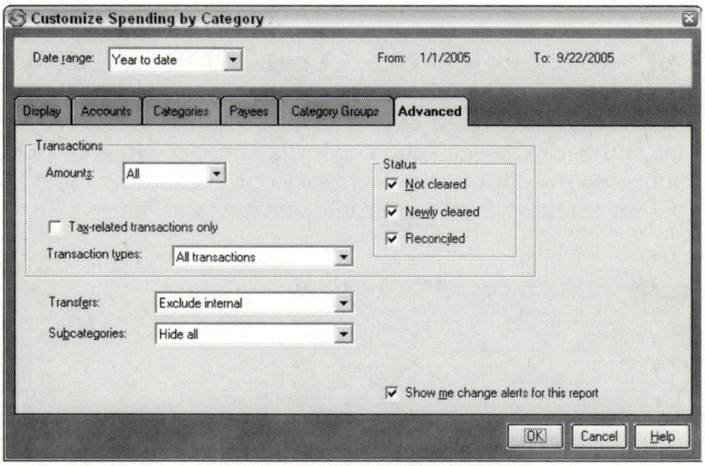

Figure 1-2: Click the Advanced tab to hide subcategories.

3. **Hide subcategories by clicking the Subcategories drop-down list and choosing Hide All.**

4. **Click OK.**

   Your report reappears, this time with only the top-level categories.

   Although it appears that you can drill down on the amounts that appear on your report, drilling on top-level categories provides you with an empty report, even when no subcategories are present on the report. The actual transactions still reside in the subcategories, thus there is no detail associated with the top-level category.

Changing the level of a subcategory

There might come a time when you want to reorganize your categories. Perhaps you want to make Telephone a subcategory under Utilities instead of the top-level category status you originally assigned. Or maybe you want to pull Internet Service out from under the category heading of Computer and let it have a top-level category all its own.

You can change the hierarchy of a category easily by editing the category. Just follow these steps:

1. **Open the Category List.**

   Choose Tools⇨Category List from the menu, or press Ctrl+L.

2. **Edit a category.**

   Click on the category whose hierarchy you want to change, and then click the Edit button. The Edit Category window appears.

3. **Change the subcategory status.**

   If you're moving a category from a lowly subcategory level to a top-level, you need to choose Income or Expense as the category type. As you can see, you can't uncheck the subcategory option. But choosing Income or Expense has the effect of unchecking the subcategory. If you want to make this category a subcategory of another category or even another subcategory, click the subcategory option, and then find the appropriate parent category from the drop-down list (see Figure 1-3).

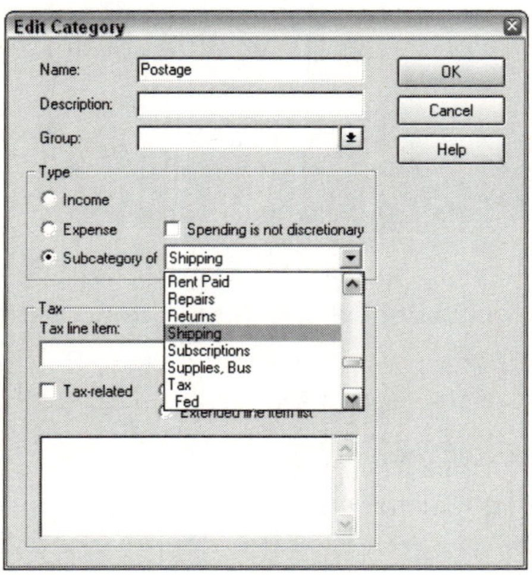

Figure 1-3: Click the drop-down list to pick a parent category.

4. **Click OK.**

   Clicking OK implements the category level change.

Changing the level of a category has an immediate ripple effect throughout your Quicken program. Don't worry — no transactions are harmed when you change the category to a different level. But all transactions associated with that category are revised and are now part of the new level.

WARNING!

Some of your reports might change when you change the level of a category. If you are relying on printed reports that include the category you are changing, you might want to reprint those reports.

Using classes

The Quicken Class feature provides another way for you to organize your transactions and pinpoint transactions of a certain type. With classes, you assign a transaction to a category, and then tag the transaction with a class.

For example, in the previous section, we talked about creating subcategories under your top-level shipping category for packaging supplies and mailing costs. What if you want to track the shipping costs for different types of items that you ship? Say you ship personal items as well as items that relate to your business. You don't want to have to set up two sets of the same categories and subcategories. Instead, you can set up a class for personal and another class for business, and then with each shipping expense you record, you put it in the proper subcategory and assign a class, either personal or business.

Here's another good use of classes. Perhaps you own rental property and you have the same types of income and expenses for each property. Instead of creating separate categories and subcategories for each piece of rental property, which can result in a lot of duplicated effort, just set up a class for each piece of rental property, and tag your transaction to the proper class.

TIP

You can split transactions among different classes. So if you pay for repairs on two different rental units, you can enter one transaction when you pay for the repairs, and then enter the transaction as a split transaction and assign the proper expense to each rental unit.

Setting up some classes

Creating classes in Quicken is easy. First, decide what kinds of classes you want. The decision is all yours — there are no restrictions on the type of classes you create — it's simply a matter of how you want to track your Quicken transactions and what will be most useful for you. The classes you create stay with Quicken and you can use them, or not, on any of your transactions.

TIP

If you upgrade to a new version of Quicken at some point in the future, your class descriptions move forward into the upgraded version.

When you're ready to set up your classes in Quicken, you can follow these steps, or you can wait until you are ready to record transactions and set up new classes on-the-fly, as you need them.

1. **Open the Class List.**

   Choose Tools⇨Class List from the menu, or press Ctrl+L. The Class List appears. There are no default classes that come with your Quicken program, so the first time you open the Class List, the list is empty, as shown in Figure 1-4.

Figure 1-4: At first, your Class List window is empty.

2. **Open the Set Up Class window.**

   Click New in the Class List window and the Set Up Class window appears.

3. **Enter the name for your class.**

   The name is required; the description is optional. Enter a name for your class (see Figure 1-5). You are limited to 40 characters, including spaces. Enter a description if you like.

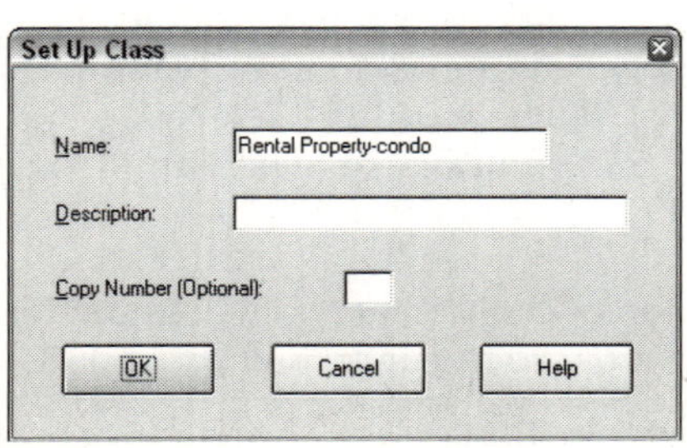

Figure 1-5: Enter a meaningful name for your class.

4. **Enter a copy number, if you dare.**

   The copy number basically lets you use the same class name for different types of transactions. Going with the rental property example I gave earlier, rather than naming your classes with the address of each rental property, you could just use Rental Property as the class name, and then assign a separate copy number to each property. I'm not sure how you'd remember which number goes with which property, but I guess that's a problem for a different day. Personally, I prefer to skip the copy numbers and give more meaningful and separate class names to each class.

5. **Click OK.**

   Your Set Up Class window closes and the new class is added to your Class List.

6. **Repeat steps 1-5. Over and out.**

Keep going — you're on a roll! Continue setting up all the classes you think you will want to use. Just close the Class List window by clicking the X in the corner when you've finished entering your classes.

WARNING!

There's no reminder system in Quicken to tell you that you need to assign a class to a transaction. It's up to you to remember about the classes and include the class when entering your transaction.

You can edit the name of a class if you made a misspelling or decide to change a class name. Just open the Class List, click on a class, and then click the Edit button, make your changes and click OK. If you decide you don't want to use a class, click the class name and click Delete. But beware — see the following Warning.

WARNING!

If you delete a class that has been used in some transactions, that class name is removed from the transactions you assigned to it. Those transactions are no longer part of any class.

Assigning classes to transactions

Now that you've got these classes, what are you going to do with them? Going forward, you can assign transactions to classes as you enter the transactions. If you want to get some historical information into your classes, you can go back to existing transactions and assign classes too. To assign a class to a transaction, follow these steps:

1. **Start entering the transaction or click on a transaction that needs a class assignment.**

2. **Open the Class List.**

   Either choose Tools⇨Class List from the menu, or press Ctrl+L. Either way, the Class List appears (or not — see the upcoming Warning).

3. **Choose your class.**

   There are three ways to pick a class — you can click on the class, you can arrow down to the class, or you can start typing the name of the class. One way or another, you get that class selected. In Figure 1-6, I've chosen my rental townhouse as the class for this particular transaction.

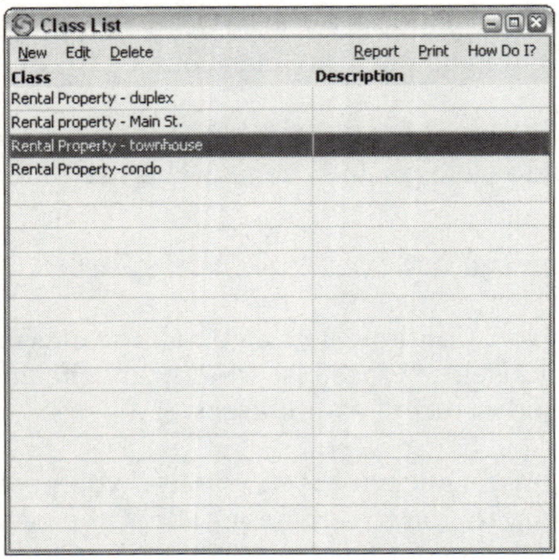

Figure 1-6: Double-click a class, or arrow down and press Enter.

4. **Accept the class.**

   Either double-click on the class or press Enter when the class has been selected. Either action has the effect of closing the class window and assigning the class to the current register transaction.

   You don't have to have your cursor in the Category field when entering a class. As long as you've clicked somewhere on the transaction, you can open the Class List and select a class at any time.

   You don't lose your chance to assign a class if you forget to do so when entering a transaction. You can go back to previously entered transactions and assign classes at any time.

   The Class List cannot be opened from the Write Checks window in Quicken. You can manually enter a class by placing a slash (/) after the category name and entering a class, or you can wait until you record the check and it appears in your register, and then assign the class in the register transaction as described above.

OK, class, time for some reports

After you set up classes, you can see the results of your labors by producing reports that include class groupings, or by producing reports that only reflect the transactions in a particular class.

If the Quicken report you are working with provides the opportunity to display additional columns, you can select Class as your column option, and your report opens up to display a column for each class (see Figure 1-7).

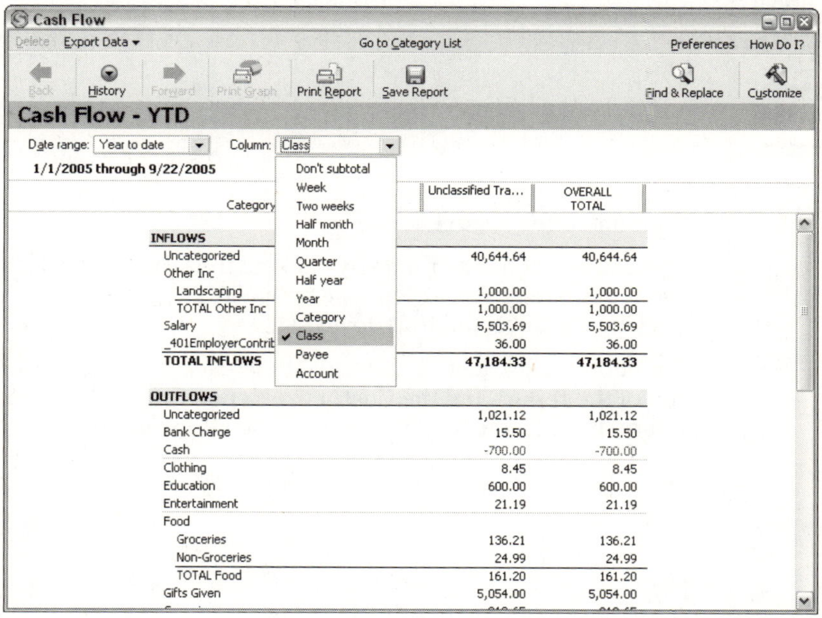

Figure 1-7: Click the drop-down list at the top of your report, and then choose Class.

You can easily access class reports that show you the transactions that have been tagged with a particular class. Here's how:

1. **Open the Class List.**

   Choose Tools⇨Class List from the menu or press Ctrl+L.

2. **Choose a class.**

   Click on the class that you want to see represented in the report.

3. **Open the Class Report.**

   Click the Report button at the top of the Class List window (see Figure 1-8). The Class List slides down to the bottom of your Quicken window, appearing as a button, and the Class Report appears, displaying all transactions that have been assigned to the class you chose.

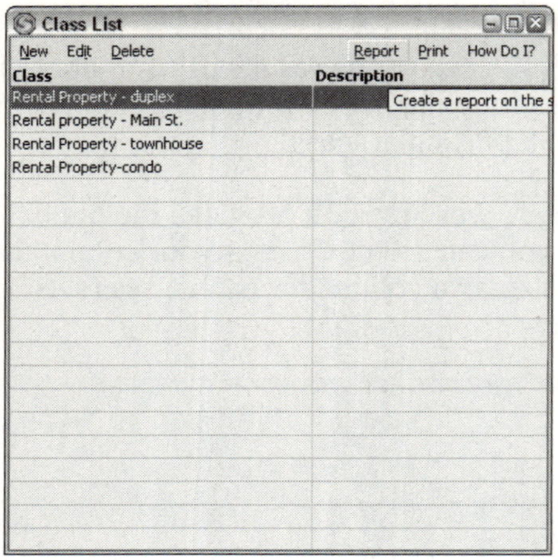

Figure 1-8: Open the Class Report by clicking Report in the upper-right corner.

4. **Customize the report.**

   You can select a date range by clicking the Date Range drop-down list at the top of the report, or choose how you want the report subtotaled by clicking the Subtotal drop-down list.

   For more sophisticated customization, click the Customize button at the top of the report and the Customize Report window appears. For more information on customizing reports, see Book VII.

Chapter 2: Tracking Accounts Payable and Accounts Receivable

In This Chapter

- **Introducing cash versus accrual basis bookkeeping**
- **Using Quicken to track receivables**
- **Producing invoices**
- **Using Quicken to track payables**
- **Recording bills**

When you work at a job, you earn money that is paid to you on a regular basis: weekly, biweekly, semimonthly, or perhaps monthly. In most cases, you do the work, and then you receive your pay. In other words, at any given time, your employer probably owes you money for some work you have done. You have an *account receivable*. And when you charge a purchase on your credit card, you've made the purchase, but you haven't yet paid for it. Until you actually pay your credit card bill, you have an *account payable*.

Welcome to the World of Accrual Basis Bookkeeping

If you prepare financial reports that show your Accounts Receivable and your Accounts Payable, you are said to have prepared *accrual basis reports*. If instead, you only report on income that you have actually received and you only report on expenses that you have actually paid for, you are said to have prepared *cash basis reports*. Businesses are required to pick whether they want to report their income and expenses on an accrual basis or a cash basis, and then they are expected to stick with that choice.

But the truth is, most individuals and their small businesses use a hybrid of cash and accrual when making reports and preparing tax returns. Here are some examples of income and expenses that get mixed up in the cash versus accrual presentation:

- It's December 31, 2006. Your paycheck that covers the period from December 16 through December 31 won't be issued until January 15, 2007. When you assemble your tax information for 2006, chances are good that you're not going to include that January 15, 2007 paycheck in with your taxable income for 2006. So your tax return is prepared on a cash basis, right?

- You broke your leg in December, 2006 and decided to purchase crutches and a ramp for your front door steps. You have enough medical expenses in 2006 to take advantage of the itemized deductions and you want to include as many expenses as you can as 2006 deductions. You are allowed to include the December purchases of crutches and a ramp as part of your 2006 tax deductions, even though you won't actually pay the credit card bill until 2007. So, your tax return is now partially prepared on an accrual basis.
- It's July and you're preparing financial statements for your banker because you want to borrow some money to remodel your home. You owe $10,000 in credit card debt. You anticipate earning a bonus of $5,000 from your job in December. You can bet your banker wants to see that $10,000 in debt on your financial statements. Accrual basis. But the December bonus — well, a lot can happen between now and December, including you might not have your job or your employer might change his mind about that bonus. So no bonus goes on the financials. Cash basis.

As you can see, the presentation might get muddled. But you know what you owe and you know what is owed to you. No matter how you ultimately present this information on tax returns and financial statements, you can keep track of all of your receivables and payables in Quicken.

Quicken Home & Business offers separate receivables and payables features, but you can keep track of these amounts just fine even in regular versions of Quicken, simply by setting up the accounts you need and making the proper entries.

If you enter receivables and payables in Quicken Home & Business and then receive or pay the amounts, the receivables and payables accounts are automatically cleared. This process is described later in this chapter. In other versions of Quicken, clearing the receivable is a two-step process. You need to clear the receivables and payables accounts manually as well as enter the receipts and the payments in your bank account register.

TIP: If you've entered a receivable in an Accounts Receivables account, here's a quick method for entering the deposit in your bank account register. First, open the receivables account register. Find the receivable for which you have received payment and click on it. Cut the transaction, and then open the bank account register and Paste the transaction, saving yourself having to actually enter the transaction twice. The same process works for payables.

Using Quicken's Accounts Receivable and Invoicing Features

Because we can probably all agree that entering your paychecks when you earn them instead of when you receive them is impractical, here's an example of accounts receivable that actually occurs in real life.

Say that you own a little catering business. You meet with your customers, determine their needs, receive an order, arrange a date for delivery, purchase the ingredients and supplies that you need, prepare the food, deliver the food, send an invoice, and, ta-da! get paid!

One of the issues you're going to discuss with your customer is, "When does a receivable exist?" Is the customer committed to pay you when the order is made? When you've purchased the food? What if you purchase the food and the customer changes his mind and cancels the order? Who is responsible for paying for the food? Perhaps you arrange to take a deposit when the delivery date is determined. Or maybe you make the customer commit in writing to pay your costs if the order is cancelled after a certain date. These are issues to consider when establishing your business and dealing with customers. These are also issues to consider when entering your income in Quicken.

Say you agree to fill an order that costs the customer $500. When you sign an agreement with the customer, you receive a down payment of $250. If you fail to fulfill your end of the bargain, you are responsible for returning the deposit. If the customer cancels the order, the deposit is yours to keep. The balance of the remaining $250 is to be invoiced when the food is delivered, and the payment is due 30 days thereafter.

In Quicken, you need to record the $250 when you receive it, and then the receivable of the additional $250 when you invoice that amount. Finally, you record the final payment when you receive it.

- I recommend that you set up a separate account called Escrow or Customer Deposit or a similar name. When you receive deposits, like the initial $250 that your customer paid you, those amounts get entered into the Escrow account register, to remain there until you actually earn the money. In that way, you can keep track of amounts that technically aren't yours yet.
- If you're tracking the individual job, you need to keep track of the costs as you purchase food and other items specifically for that job. You can use the Class feature to assign the purchases to a class that represents that job, or you can track the actual job if you use Quicken Home & Business. Each time you make a purchase for that job, tag the amount so it is associated with the job.

- ✦ When the job is complete, you can transfer the escrow money into your regular bank account, clearing the amount from your escrow account.
- ✦ Issue an invoice for the remaining $250. At this time, you record the account receivable.
- ✦ When you get your money, the receivable account is relieved of the $250 and the money is deposited in your bank account.

Setting Up Accounts Receivable

Setting up Accounts Receivable is much like setting up a bank account in Quicken; however, the account isn't actually a cash account and there is no bank associated with the account. Instead, the account is used to keep a record of the amount owed to you. Follow these steps to create your Accounts Receivable account:

1. **Open the Account List.**

   Choose Tools➪Account List from the menu or Press Ctrl+A. The Account List appears, showing all your existing accounts and their current balances, as well as some general information such as which accounts are activated for online services.

2. **Open the Quicken Account Setup window.**

   Click the Add Account option to open the Setup window. You are asked to enter basic information about your account.

3. **Check the option to indicate that this account is not held at a financial institution, and then click Next.**

   Remember, this is not an actual cash account. The Accounts Receivable account is merely a place to keep a record of how much money is owed to you.

4. **Choose the account type.**

   Unless you're using the Home & Business version of Quicken, you won't see a choice for Accounts Receivable. However, you do want the Accounts Receivable to appear with your other assets on your financial statements, so choose Asset as the account type (see Figure 2-1), and then click Next.

5. **Name the account Accounts Receivable.**

   You can call the account whatever name seems appropriate to you, but Accounts Receivable, A/R, or Receivables are the most appropriate.

6. **Skip the next questions.**

   There is no bank statement for this account, so you don't need to change the statement date. The date automatically defaults to today's date, and that's fine. Leave the ending balance at zero (see Figure 2-2). Even if you have some existing receivables that you want to list in this account, you need to list them individually or else how will you know what they are? Therefore, you'll enter those receivables later. For now, just stick with a zero balance.

7. **Click Done.**

   The new Accounts Receivable account is ready to be used. The register for the account opens when you click the Done button. The account itself can be found over on the Account Bar, under Property & Debt.

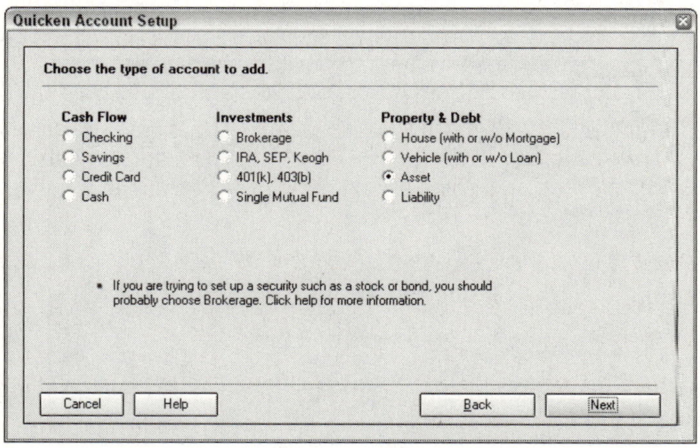

Figure 2-1: Select Asset as the account type.

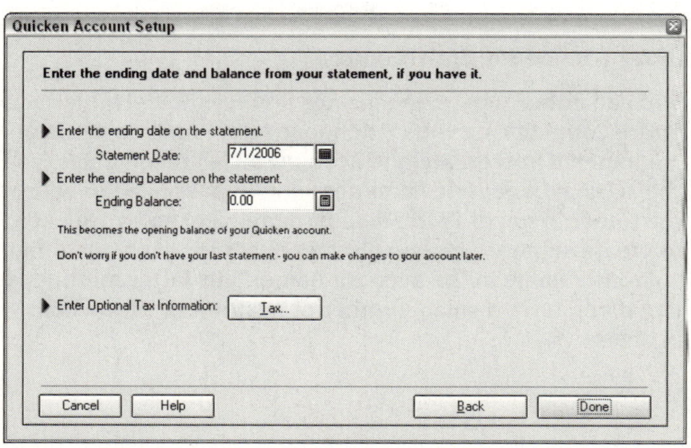

Figure 2-2: Leave this information as it is without entering any changes.

In Quicken Home & Business, you can create an Invoices/Receivables account by following these steps:

1. **Open the Business Center by clicking the Business Center option on the Account Bar at the left of your screen, or choosing Business Center from the Business menu.**
2. **Open the Account Setup window.**

   With the My Data tab selected in the Business Center, click the Add Account button. There are a couple of Add Account buttons in the Business Center — it doesn't matter which one you click.
3. **Select the account type.**

   Choose Invoices/Receivables as the account type, as shown in Figure 2-3, and then click the Next button.

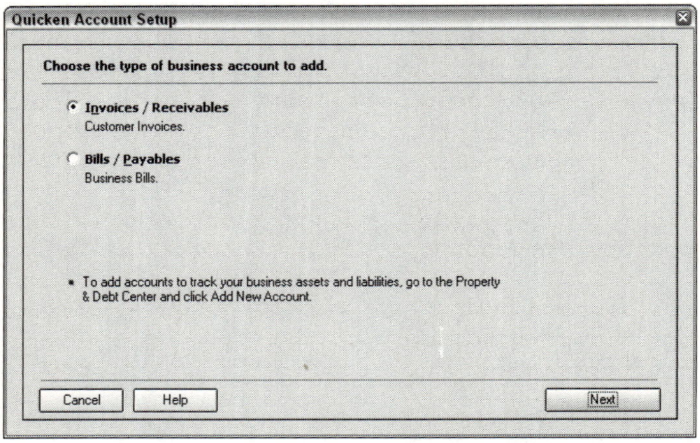

Figure 2-3: Choose Invoices/ Receivables to set up your receivables account in Quicken.

4. **Enter a name for the account.**

   You can either create one master Invoices/Receivables account for your entire company, or you can choose to set up a separate account for each customer. If you create one account for all receivables, you want to give the account a generic name that encompasses all of your receivables. Customer Invoices is the default name chosen by Quicken. If you choose to create separate receivables accounts for each customer, include the customer name in the account name. This latter method is more effective if you have a small number of customers with whom you do a lot of business.

TIP

You can't name the Invoices/Receivables account Accounts Receivable because that name is already used by Quicken. However, the name you choose is going to appear on your financial statements, so be sure to pick a professional-sounding name, such as *Outstanding Invoices* or simply, *Receivables*.

When you finish setting up the Invoices/Receivables account, the register for that account appears. See "Setting up invoices" below for information on how to enter transactions into this register.

Accounts Receivable and Your Reports

When you create invoices, the invoices are recorded in your receivables account and become a part of your recorded earnings at the time they are recorded.

When you have an Accounts Receivable account, the information in that account is available to be included in your reports. For example, when you produce a report of your earnings, you can include your receivables in those earnings to see how much money you've really made, even though you haven't yet received all of the money. On your net worth statement, the receivables appear as an asset, increasing your net worth.

WARNING!

If you need to prepare a cash basis report, make sure your receivables are *not* included in the report totals.

In Quicken Home & Business, the invoices/receivables account that you create appears on your Net Worth statement in a section called Other Assets.

Setting up invoices

You must have the Quicken Home & Business program to actually take advantage of Quicken's invoices feature, but that doesn't mean you can't create invoices and enter them in Quicken. Whether you use Home & Business or not, you still need to invoice your customers and keep track of those invoices.

In Home & Business, here is the process for creating an invoice.

1. **Open the Invoice form.**

   In the Business Center, on the My Data tab, click the Create an Invoice button. A separate window that looks like an actual invoice form appears. You can also choose Business➪Invoices and Estimates➪Create Invoice from the menu. Or, if the Invoices register is visible, click the Create New button at the top, and then choose Invoice.

TIP

If the standard invoice form that comes with your Quicken program does not provide the fields you need, or if it contains fields that you don't need, you can create your own style of invoice. See Chapter 5 of Book VIII for an example of how you can customize your invoice form so that it provides exactly the columns and fields that you need for your business.

2. **Enter customer name.**

   At the top of your invoice, you need to enter the name of the customer in the Customer field (see Figure 2-4). After you enter the name, Quicken saves that name and makes it available on a drop-down list for future use.

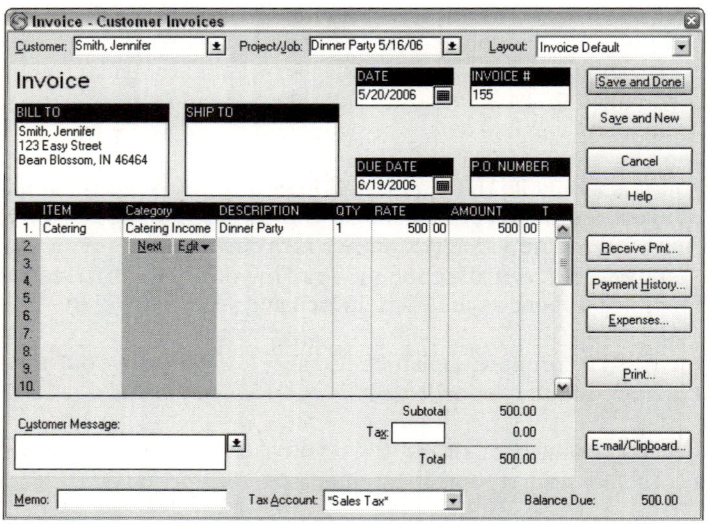

Figure 2-4: Fill out the invoice form just as you would fill out a paper invoice.

TIP

You can enter your customers by last name first, or first name first. I typically enter the customer's last name first, and then the first name. It's easier to search by last name through an alphabetical list. On the other hand, if you only have a few customers, your list will be quite short, so searching might not be a problem.

3. **Enter the type of project or job.**

   At the top of the invoice form, you need to enter the job or project type. This is a name of your choosing. When you enter a name for the first time, a window appears asking if you want to create a new project/job with the name you entered. You have to choose Yes or you can't enter the project name. When you click Yes, the New Project/Job window appears (Figure 2-5), where you can enter as much or as little information about the project as you like. The minimum information you can enter is the project name, which is what I've done in Figure 2-5. Click OK to return to the Invoice form.

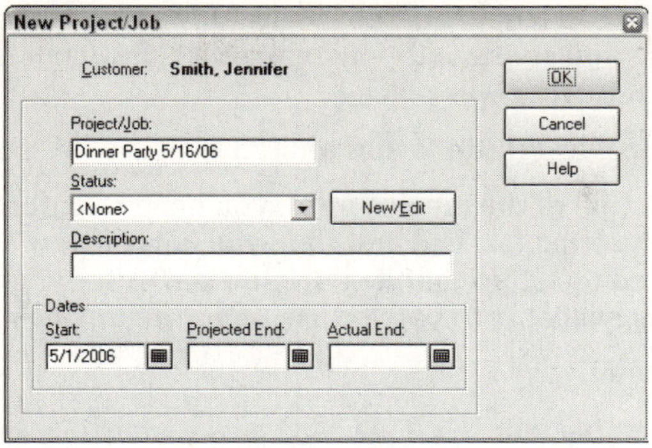

Figure 2-5: Enter information about the project or job for which you are creating an invoice.

Project/job names are associated with each customer. For each customer, you need to set up a new project/job name, even if it is the same project/job name you use with other customers.

4. **Enter your customer's address.**

   If you plan to mail this invoice, enter a mailing address on the invoice in the Bill To section. The address is optional, especially if you intend to e-mail the invoice. If the Ship To address is appropriate for this customer, enter information in that field as well.

   You only need to enter a customer's mailing address once. Quicken remembers the address and displays it the next time you create an invoice for this customer.

5. **Enter the invoice date.**

   Quicken automatically places today's date in the Date field. You can accept that date or change to whatever date you need. Quicken automatically enters a Due Date 30 days after whatever date you enter in the Date field.

6. **Enter an invoice number.**

   After you've created one invoice in Quicken and assigned a number to that invoice, Quicken automatically increments the invoices and enters the next available number in the Invoice # field. You can accept this number or overwrite it with another number if necessary.

7. **Confirm the due date.**

   The Due Date field gets filled in automatically. You can change the due date to whatever date you want.

8. **Enter a P.O. number.**

   If your customer provides you with a Purchase Order number, enter that number in the field provided. This is a number your customer generates, not a number you create yourself. If your customer hasn't given you a

P.O. number, you can leave this field blank, or perhaps enter the name of the contact who you spoke with, or some other pertinent information regarding how the order was placed.

9. **Enter the invoice descriptions and amounts.**

   In the lower portion of the invoice form, you need to enter the details of what you are invoicing for. The first time you enter a new item, you are going to be asked to set up that item in Quicken. After you've set up an item, the item is available to you for use on future invoices.

10. **Set up a new item.**

    An item is something you sell. This can be a service, like catering (in the example shown in Figure 2-6) or legal services, or a tangible item like handmade pottery or quilts, or even an intangible item like computer software. Enter a name for the item, and then enter the category where income from sales of this item should be recorded (see next step). Enter an optional description. If you charge the same fee over and over again for this item, you can enter the fee in the Per Item Rate field. If the fee is not fixed, leave this field blank. Click OK to save the item.

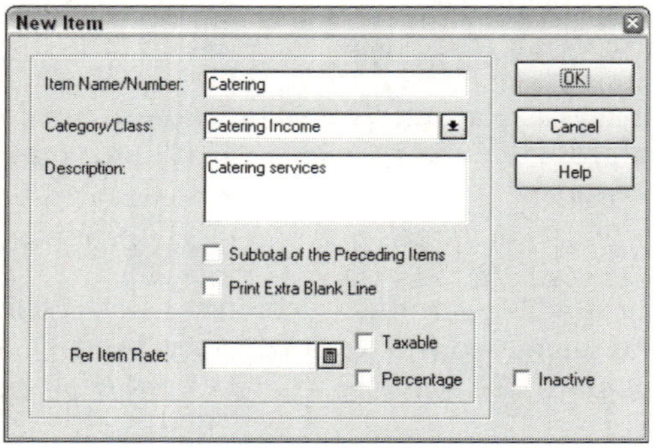

Figure 2-6: Enter information about the item you sell on your invoices.

11. **Set up a new category.**

    When you set up your new item, you had to indicate the category where income from this item should be recorded. If this if the first time for recording income from this item, you might need to set up a new category. When you enter a category name that has not been set up previously, the Set Up Category window automatically appears (Figure 2-7). Give the category a name, keeping in mind that this name is going to appear on your financial statements. Confirm that the Income option is selected. You can assign the category to a tax line at this time if you like (see Book V for more on tax lines), or you can take care of that at a later time.

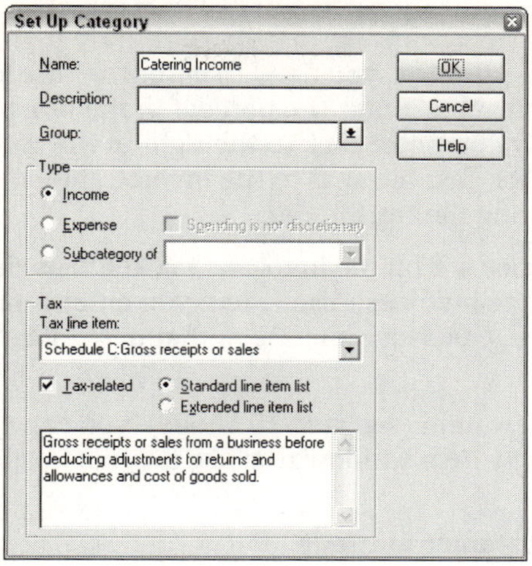

Figure 2-7: Enter pertinent information about your new income category.

12. **Enter or revise the description.**

    Back to the invoice after all those side trips to set up categories and items. After you start using invoices regularly, most of the information you need is already set up and available to you on drop-down lists. Now it's time to enter an optional description in the Description field of the invoice. If you entered a description when you set up the new item, that descriptive information already appears on the invoice. You can accept that description or override it if there is something more appropriate you want to enter on the invoice for this customer. For example, I offer tax services to my clients. When I prepare a tax return for a client, I enter Tax Return Preparation as my service. Because I prepare different types of tax returns and the returns are for different years, no one description fits all of the tax return preparation services I perform, so I left the description area blank when I set up my item, and I enter the appropriate description in the description field on the invoice.

13. **Enter the quantity and rate or amount.**

    Quantity and Rate are optional fields on your invoice, but useful fields as well. If you sell multiple quantities of an item, you can enter the quantity on the invoice, and then enter the per-item rate. Quicken takes care of the multiplication for you and enters a total in the Amount column. Alternatively, if you are offering services, the Quantity and Rate fields might not be useful to you. In that case, you can leave those fields blank (or remove them altogether — see Chapter 5 for more of a discussion on customizing your invoice forms), and just enter the total amount in the Amount column.

14. **Verify sales tax.**

    If you have to charge sales tax, you need to enter the rate in the Tax box at the bottom of the invoice. Enter the percent in the box provided. If tax doesn't automatically compute, click to the right of the amount in the T column to place a T for Taxable next to the invoice amount. Quicken takes care of calculating the tax for you.

    When you click to place a T on the invoice, Quicken tags that item as being taxable for future invoices. Also, when you enter a sales tax percentage on an invoice, Quicken remembers that percentage for future taxable sales.

    When you set up a new item (see step 10 above), you can check the Taxable box in the New Item window to make an item taxable every time you sell it.

15. **Enter an optional customer message.**

    The Customer Message box is for a brief message that prints on the bottom of the customer's invoice. Quicken comes already loaded with a few Chatty-Cathy-type phrases, such as "All work is complete!" and "We accept credit cards." You can enter your own glib (or otherwise) phrases, and they are saved, along with Quicken's phrases, on the drop-down list, ready for future use.

16. **Enter an optional memo.**

    At the very bottom of the invoice form is the Memo field. The information you enter here *does not* print on the invoice, so you can be as casual and as direct as you want. This information is for your eyes only.

17. **Send your invoice!**

    You've come this far — don't stop yet! You can click the Print button to print a paper copy of the invoice, or you can click the E-mail/Clipboard button to send your invoice by e-mail. Click Print and the Print Invoice window appears. Click OK to print your invoice. Click E-mail/Clipboard and the Send Invoice by E-mail window appears (Figure 2-8). Verify the e-mail information, enter the customer's e-mail address if necessary, and then click OK. You are asked to provide some information about your own e-mail address and server if this is the first time you've emailed anything from Quicken. After all the information is entered, an e-mail message appears (Figure 2-9). You can enter any personal comments that you want to include, and then click the Send button to e-mail the invoice.

18. **Done at last!**

    Save the invoice by clicking Save and Done or Save and New. The first option closes the invoice window; the second opens a new invoice window. In both cases, the invoice is saved and entered in your Invoices register.

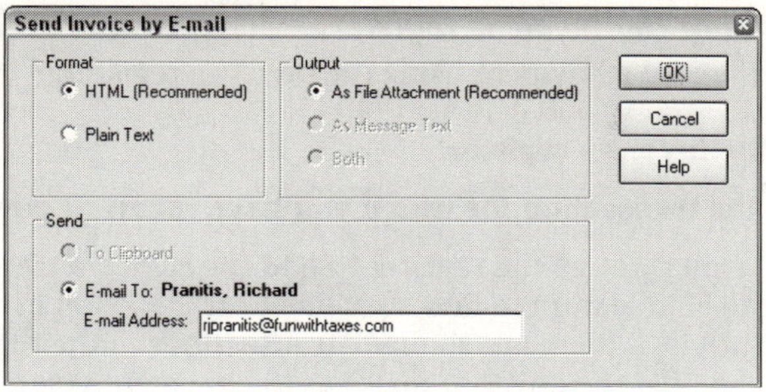

Figure 2-8: Enter the e-mail address to which your invoice should be sent.

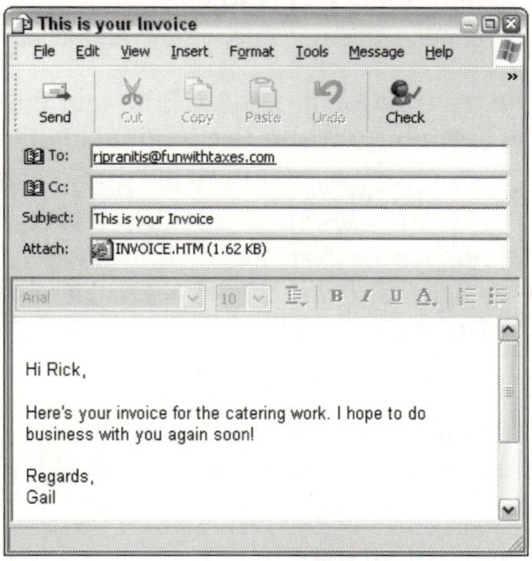

Figure 2-9: Enter a personal message if you want, and then click Send to dispatch your invoice.

TIP

By using the Invoices account, you can see at a glance which invoices haven't been paid and send notices to the customers with outstanding invoices.

Receiving a payment

When you receive a payment, you need to deposit the money and record the deposit in Quicken. You know all about how to record deposits, but what about the deposit of an amount you have recorded as a receivable? Not only do you need to deposit the money, but you need to clear the receivable so you no longer show the customer as owing money to you. If you're recording your invoices as accounts receivable in Quicken Home & Business, here's how to record the payment of an invoice.

You can record the payment of an invoice in Quicken Home & Business in one of three ways. I describe each method here, and you can pick the one you like best or the one that seems most appropriate at the time you receive a payment.

Method 1: Using the Invoices register

Here's how to record a payment using the Invoices register:

1. **Display the Invoices register.**
2. **Click on the transaction for which you have received payment.**

   You can scroll through the register to find the right transaction, or you can use the Find feature to find a particular transaction in the register. But the truth is, if there are so many transactions in the register that you can't quickly find the one that matches the payment you received, try one of the other two methods presented here. They work more quickly when you have many outstanding receivables.
3. **Click the Form button.**

   On the right side of the transaction are Enter, Edit, and Form buttons (Figure 2-10). Click the Form button and the original invoice appears.

   If the Form button doesn't appear, you've turned off the Transaction toolbar in Quicken's Preferences window. No matter. When you click on a transaction in the receivables register, a little green checkmark appears in the Category field. Clicking this checkmark has the same effect as clicking the Form button.
4. **Open the Customer Payment window.**

   On the original invoice that appears, click the Receive Pmt button. The invoice disappears from your screen and the Customer Payment window appears (Figure 2-11).
5. **Verify the payment amount and date.**

   The customer payment window opens, showing today's date and the full amount of the invoice in the Payment column. If this information is correct, there are no changes to make. If the customer made a partial payment instead of the full amount, change the payment amount. If the payment was received on a date other than today, enter the actual payment date. If you like, you can enter a check number in the field provided.

   If more than one invoice is outstanding for this customer, all of the outstanding invoices are listed at the bottom of the Customer Payment window. The payment has been applied to the invoice you had open in step 3 above. See the section, "Method 3: Using the Record a Payment button" later in this chapter for more information on how to change the invoice to which the payment is applied.
6. **Verify the bank account information.**

   The account listed in the Deposit To field is the account to which this deposit will be recorded. Make sure this is the account where you actually plan to deposit the money!

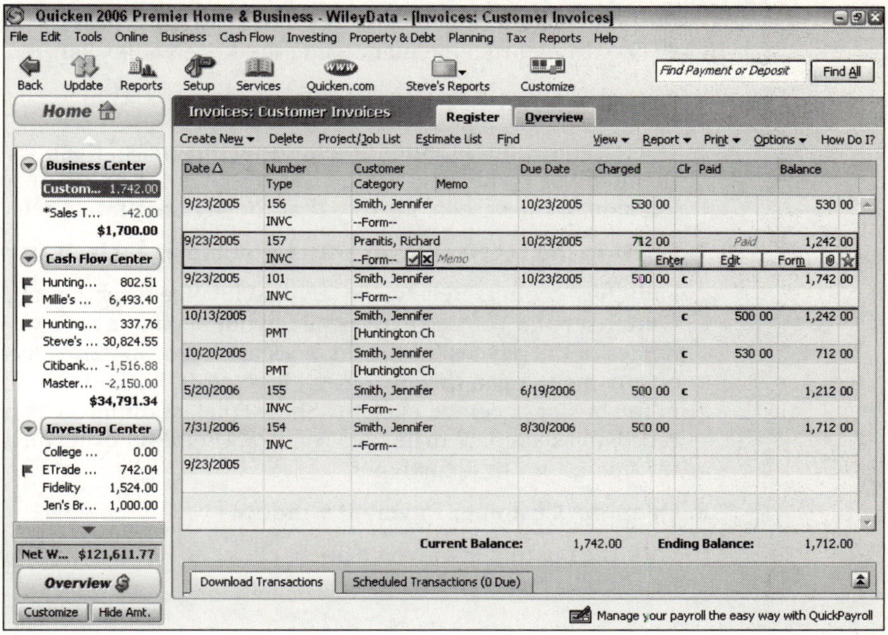

Figure 2-10: Click the Form button to display the original invoice.

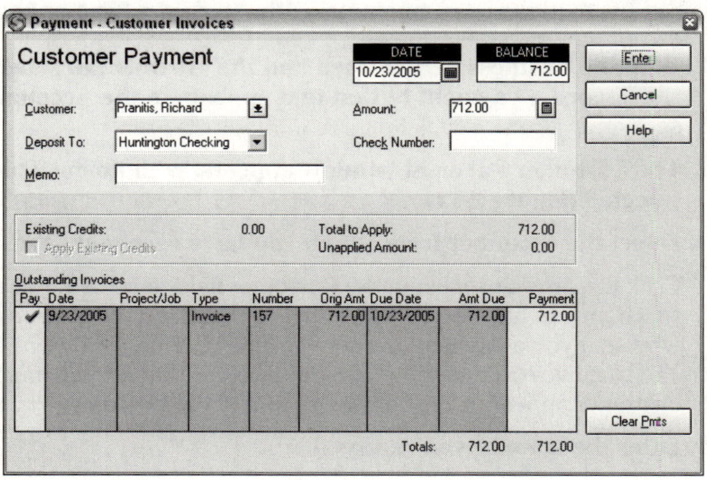

Figure 2-11: Record your customer's payment.

7. Complete the transaction.

Click OK. The Customer Payment window closes. The receivable is marked as Cleared in your Invoices register.

The payment you received has been recorded as a deposit in your bank account. However, you still need to take or send the money to the bank for an actual deposit in your account.

Method 2: Using the Receivables list in the Business Center

Here's how to record a payment using the Receivables list:

1. **Display the Business Center.**

   Open the Business Center by choosing Business➪Business Center from the menu or by clicking on the Business Center in the Account Bar at the left side of the screen. Be sure that the My Data tab is selected.

2. **Click on the receivable for which you have received payment.**

   Find the Accounts Receivable (Unpaid Invoices) section of the Business Center screen. You see a list of all of your accounts receivables. The names of the payees for the invoices are hyperlinked. You can click right on a name to open the customer's invoice. If the list is too long to display in the business center, click the Show Full List option. The complete list of receivables appears in its own window. Double-clicking on a name opens the invoice for that customer.

3. **Open the Customer Payment window.**

   With the customer's invoice open, click the Receive Pmt button. From here, go to step 5 in Method 1 and continue.

Method 3: Using the Record a Payment button

Here's how to record a payment using the Record a Payment button.

1. **With the Business Center open and the My Data tab selected, click the Record a Payment button that appears in the Accounts Receivable section.**

2. **The Customer Payment window appears, with no customer or invoice selected (Figure 2-12).**

3. **Select the customer from whom you have received payment.**

   Click the drop-down list in the Customer field to see a list of all customers to whom you have ever issued invoices. Click on the name of the customer who sent you a payment. As soon as you click on a different field, or press Tab to move to a different field, the invoices that are outstanding from this customer appear in a list at the bottom of the Customer Payment window.

4. **Enter the amount you received.**

   Enter the amount in the Amount field. Quicken automatically assigns this amount to outstanding invoices, the oldest invoice first and then the next oldest, and so on, as you can see in Figure 2-13.

5. **Verify the application of the money.**

   If for some reason you want to apply the amount you received to an invoice other than the one(s) selected by Quicken, you can change the amounts in the Payment column, applying the correct amount to each invoice.

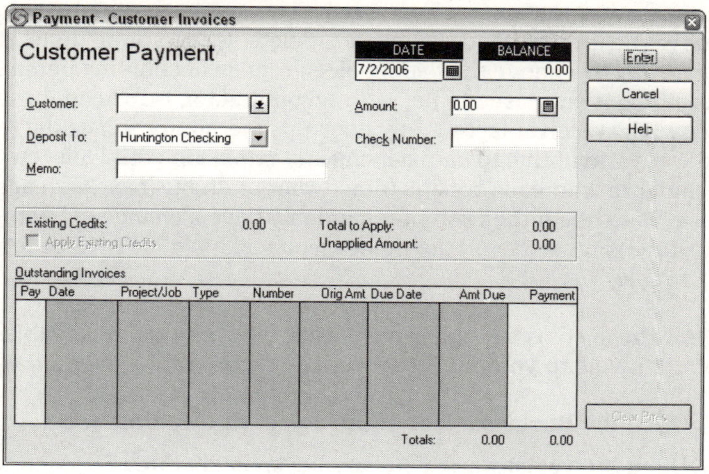

Figure 2-12: Select a customer to see all outstanding invoices and record a payment.

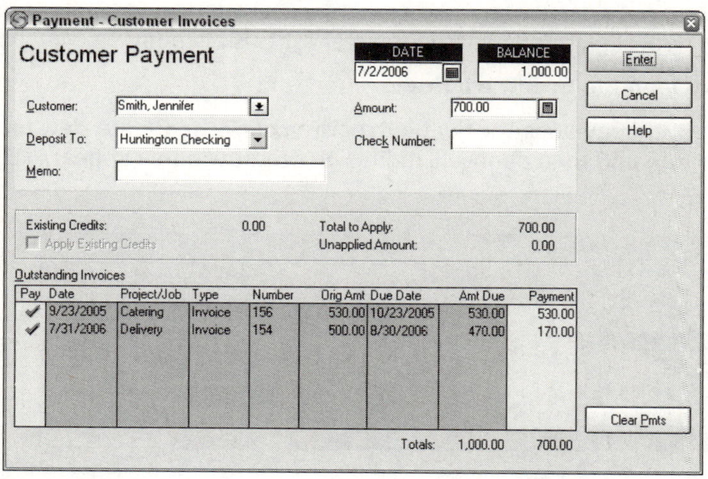

Figure 2-13: Make sure the money you received is applied to the appropriate invoices.

6. **Complete the entry of payment information.**

   Pick up with step 5 from Method 1, verifying the date and bank account and then recording the deposit.

Dealing with bad debts

When customers don't pay you, you have what is known in the accounting world as a *bad debt.* If you've issued an invoice in Quicken for an amount that has gone bad, you need to clear your system of the invoice; otherwise, your income is going to reflect an amount that you know you're not going to receive.

The quick and easy way to remove the bad invoice is simply to do that — remove the invoice. Find the invoice, delete it, and you're done. Fini. But the *proper* way to remove the bad invoice, from an accounting perspective, where everything is supposed to be, well, accounted for, is to keep the invoice but remove the receivable. Not only does this method preserve the record of how you were attempting to earn a living and remain in your Quicken file as a reminder of who you probably don't want to do business with again in the future, but should the customer suddenly have a change of heart (or a change of fortune) and send you the money, you still have the invoice intact and retrievable.

Follow these steps to issue a *credit* that relieves your receivables of the amount owing to you but preserves the record of the event in your file:

1. **Open the Business Center and select the My Data tab.**
2. **Open the register for your invoices/receivables.**

   In the Business Center, under the heading Business Accounts, you see your Customer Invoices (or whatever you named it) account. Click the hyperlink to display the register for this account.
3. **Open the Credit window.**

   In the invoices/receivables register, click the Create New menu at the top, and then choose Credit. The Credit window appears (Figure 2-14).

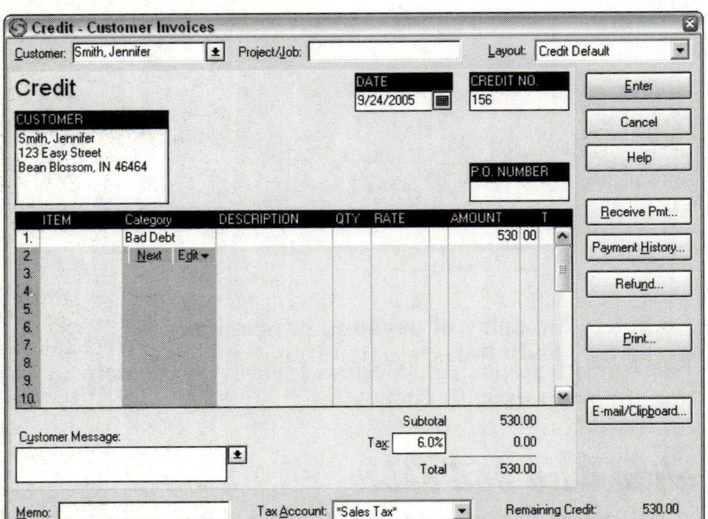

Figure 2-14: Enter the original invoice number and the amount of the bad debt.

4. **Select the customer name.**

   Choose from the drop-down list to enter the customer name in the Customer field.

5. **Enter the original invoice number and the amount of the bad debt.**

   Here's one place where you're going to wish Quicken were more of an advanced accounting program. It would be really nice if Quicken displayed for you all of the outstanding invoices for this customer. Instead, you need to know the invoice number from the amount you are writing off. If you don't have the number handy, you can close this window, find the invoice back in the register, and then reopen the window and start over again.

6. **Enter the bad debt information.**

   Down in the Category field of the Credit form, choose Bad Debt as the category for this transaction. Enter the amount you are writing off in the Amount field, as shown in Figure 2-14. Enter the amount without a minus sign. Quicken knows this is a credit instead of an income amount.

7. **Open the Customer Payment window.**

   Click the Receive Pmt button and you should see a little box warning you that you have entered a duplicate number (Figure 2-15). This is because your Credit Memo number is the same as the Invoice number you entered previously. Go ahead and click OK, and the Customer Payment window appears.

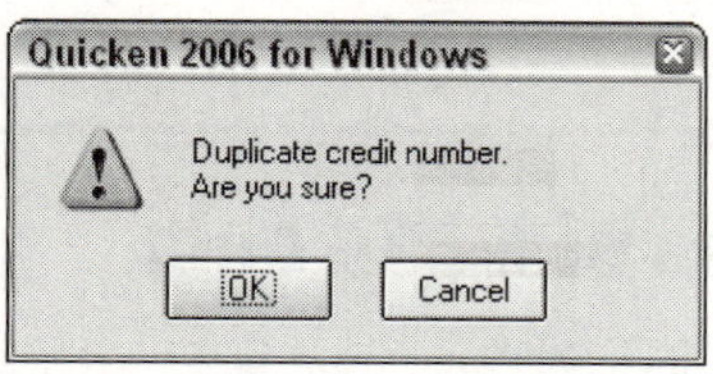

Figure 2-15: Click OK to move on to the next step.

8. **Apply the credit to the outstanding invoices.**

   See the credit amount in the middle of the window? Check the box to Apply Existing Credits to the outstanding invoices (see Figure 2-16). The amount of the bad debt (or credit, as Quicken is calling it here) is instantly applied to the customer's oldest invoice first, and then any remainder is applied to the next oldest invoice, and so on.

9. **Record the bad debt.**

   Click Enter to record the bad debt. The invoice(s) remains in your Invoices/Receivables register, but it is marked as cleared.

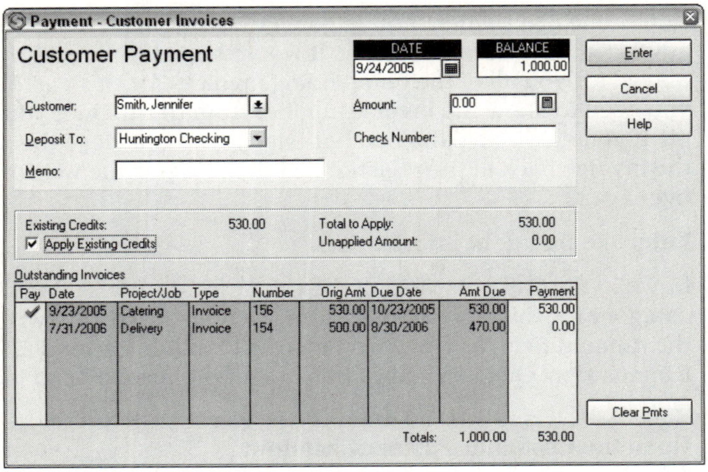

Figure 2-16: Check the box to apply the bad debt amount against the earliest invoice.

Sample Quicken reports throughout the receivables process

Tracking your receivables is easy when you can produce reports showing all of the amounts owing to you. Produce a receivables report in Quicken Home & Business by opening the Reports & Graphs Center, and then clicking Accounts Receivable, found in the Business category.

Tax ramifications of a bad debt

If you are a cash basis taxpayer and you record a bad debt in your Quicken records, that event has no effect on your tax return. Because you are a cash basis taxpayer, you don't record income on your tax return until you actually receive the income. Recording the bad debt has the effect of clearing the invoice in your Quicken file, but because the income wasn't recorded on your tax return, you get no tax benefit from recording the bad debt.

If you are an accrual basis taxpayer, and a bad debt occurs, the bad debt is recorded as an expense for tax purposes. This is because the invoice amount has been recorded with your income for tax purposes. You certainly don't want to pay income tax on the income from a bill you'll never collect, thus the income is offset by the bad debt and there is no tax effect.

The only report available to you in Quicken's Accounts Receivable section of the report list is the Payments Due by Customer report (see Figure 2-17). Enter a date range, and then click Show Report to display the A/R by Customer report that lists each customer and the amount of receivables for the designated date range.

By default, the A/R by Customer report displays each customer with a receivables column for each month. You can change the column display to something other than month by clicking the Column drop-down list at the top of the report and making a different choice. I prefer the Don't Subtotal option. That provides me with a total amount due for each customer. I can click on the amount due to see a detailed report showing what makes up that total amount for each customer.

Another A/R report I like is the Customer Invoices report. Not found on the standard reports menu, the Customer Invoices report appears when you display your Net Worth report (located in the Net Worth & Balances group on the standard reports list), and then double-click on the Customer Invoices amount on that report. The Customer Invoices report appears (see Figure 2-18), showing all outstanding invoices as of the date of your Net Worth report. Double-click on any invoice listed in the report to view the actual invoice.

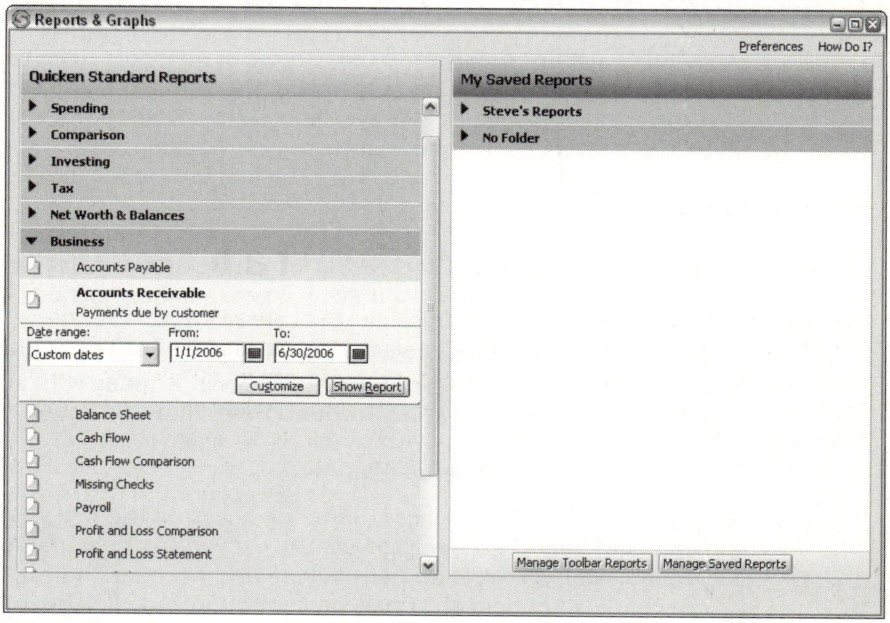

Figure 2-17: Enter the date range for your A/R report.

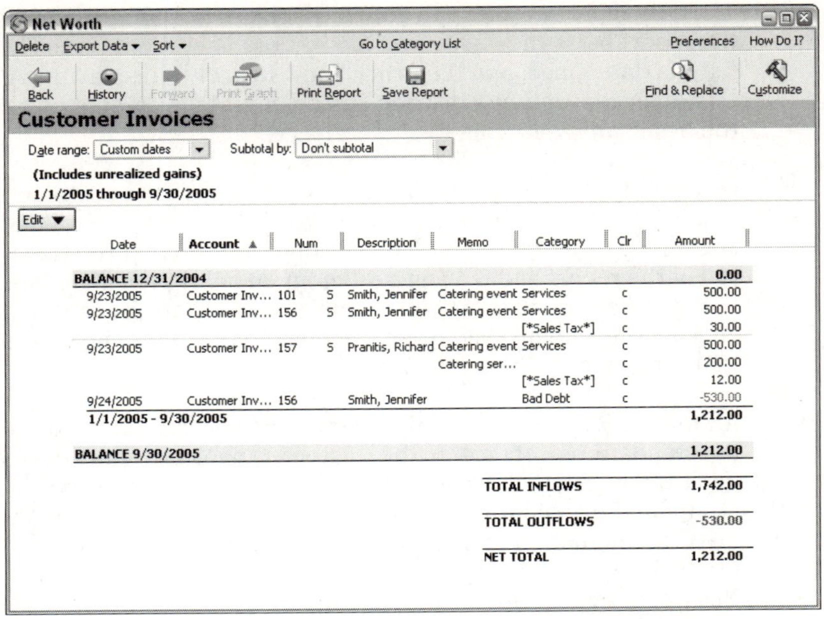

Figure 2-18: The Customer Invoices report gives me the detail of all outstanding invoices.

Using Quicken's Accounts Payable Feature

Accounts Payable are basically the reverse of Accounts Receivable — instead of someone owing money to you, you owe money to someone else. If you are an accrual basis taxpayer, you are required to track receivables. Even if you aren't an accrual basis taxpayer, tracking payables in Quicken provides you with a nice way to keep track of how much money you owe, to whom, and when the payments are due.

Payables appear in your Quicken Net Worth reports as a liability, and, in the Business Center, you can always see your outstanding payables.

Quicken Home & Business provides the tools you need to record and track accounts payable. The first order of business in working with accounts payable is to create a payables account. Here's how it's done:

1. **Open the Account Setup window.**

   You can go to the Business Center and click on the Add a Business Bills Account hyperlink (see Figure 2-19). Or, you can open the Account List by pressing Ctrl+A, and then clicking Add Account. Indicate that this account is not held at a financial institution and click Next. When the list appears showing all the types of accounts, choose Bills/Payables.

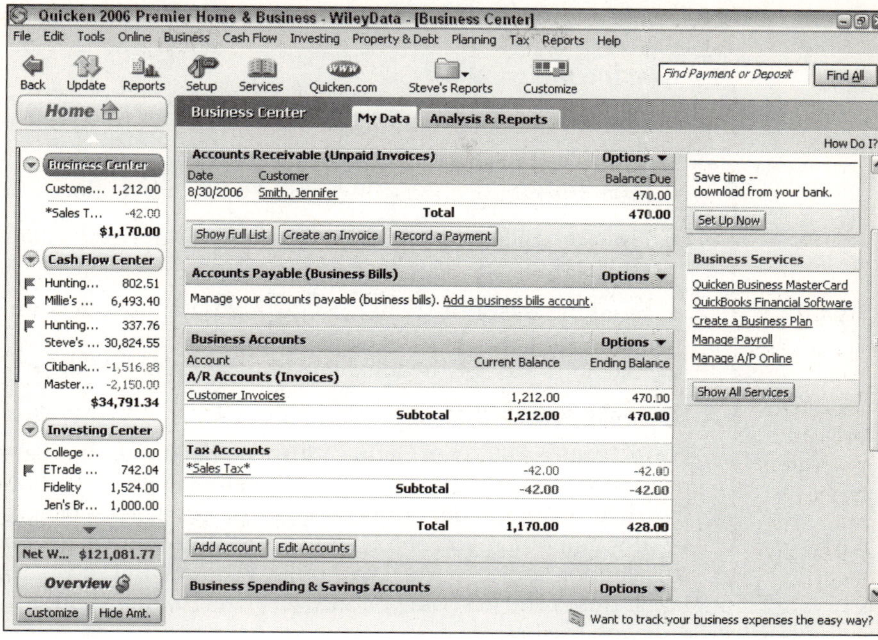

Figure 2-19: Click the hyperlink to set up your bills/payables account.

2. **Give the account a name.**

   Quicken has pre-selected Business Bills as your account name. You can use this, or choose another name if you prefer.

   TIP: You might want to set up two bills accounts — one for business bills and one for personal bills.

3. **Wrap it up.**

   Click Next and you're finished. Wow! That was incredibly easy!

Receiving a bill

Say you've got your bills/payables account all set up and ready to use. Now you just have to go to the mailbox to see if you've got any bills to enter. This is probably the only time in your life you're going to look forward to getting bills in the mailbox!

The idea behind using the bills/payables account is that when you receive a bill, the amount gets entered immediately in Quicken. Not only does this ensure that you'll get a reminder telling you to pay your bill on time, but by entering the amount you owe in your Quicken file, your financial statements show a truer picture of your finances. Now not only do you see what you spent on your finances, but you also see what you have committed to pay for.

Here's how to proceed when you receive a bill:

1. **Open the Bill window.**

   Take your pick — there are (at least) three ways to open a new bill window.

   - From the menu: choose Business⇨Bills and Vendors⇨Create Bill.
   - From the Bills register: Click the Create New drop-down menu and choose Bill.
   - From the Business Center, on the My Data tab: Click the Create a Bill button, or, click the Options drop-down menu across from the Accounts Payable heading and choose Create a Bill.

2. **Enter the vendor name.**

   In the Vendor field (see Figure 2-20), you need to enter the name of the person or company that sent you the bill. You can't continue entering information on the bill until you make an entry here. Quicken saves the vendor name that you enter, so the next time you create a bill, you'll see this vendor added to the list of other vendors on the Vendor drop-down list. If this is the first bill you've ever entered, this vendor is the only entry on the list.

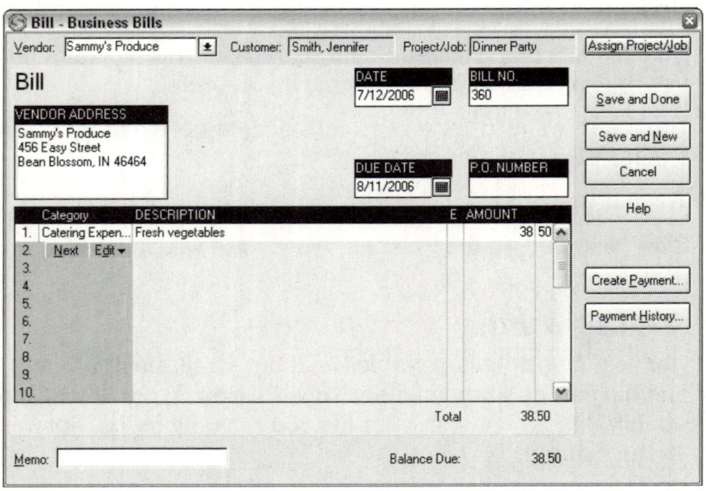

Figure 2-20: Enter information directly from the bill you receive in the mail to the bill on the screen.

3. **Enter the vendor address.**

   In the Vendor Address field, enter the mailing address where the payment is to be sent. Quicken remembers this address as you enter it, so the next time you enter a bill from this vendor, the address appears automatically.

4. **Verify the date.**

   Quicken automatically enters today's date in the date field. You should decide what date you want to use when you enter bills. You can either use today's date, the date the bill was received in the mail, or the actual date on the bill. Entering the date on the actual bill in most cases gives you the greatest assurance of having the correct due date entered on the bill.

5. **Verify the due date.**

   Like I said before, if you used the actual bill date as the date in step 4, Quicken automatically calculates 30 days from that date as the due date. Check the due date on the bill and make sure 30 days is correct, or change the due date if necessary. This is the date Quicken uses for reminders, so you want to make sure this date is correct. That way, you are reminded to pay the bill on time and can avoid potential late charges.

6. **Enter the bill number.**

   The bill number is the number on the vendor's bill — this is not a number generated by Quicken. Each vendor has its own bill numbering system, so these numbers are not chronological like your invoice numbers are.

7. **Enter the P.O. number.**

   This step is optional. If you use purchase orders and your purchase orders have numbers, you can enter the P.O. number here for your own reference. This field is purely for your own information and doesn't tie into any other forms in Quicken.

8. **Enter the category.**

   In the Category field, you need to pick the category where this expense should be recorded. Click the drop-down arrow to see your company's complete category list. If you need to set up a new category, just enter the category name here, and you get to add the category to your list.

9. **Enter a description.**

   Enter the description of the item(s) you purchased. You can use the description that appears on the actual bill you received, or embellish it to explain in more detail what you actually purchased.

   REMEMBER: The bill is for your use only, so you can enter any description that you want.

10. **Enter the amount.**

    Enter the total amount of the bill in the Amount column. This is the amount you plan to pay.

    TIP: If you plan to pay less than the amount shown on the bill (for example, due to a dispute over the price or a discount for early payment), I recommend you enter the full amount of the bill first, and then on the next line, enter the reduction and a description of why the amount is reduced. The reduction amount gets entered as a negative number in the amount column.

11. **Enter an optional memo.**

    At the bottom of the bill is a Memo field. You can place any information you want in this field — it is for your use only.

12. **Save the bill.**

    Click Save and Done to close the bill window. Click Save and New if you have another bill to enter. In either case, the bill is saved and entered in your Bills register.

Paying your bills

Wouldn't it be nice if we could just enter bills and not have to worry about paying them too? Fat chance. Bills need to be paid, and here's how to execute that task fairly painlessly. Just like with the methods we discussed earlier for recording the receipt of payments, there are three ways to record the payment of a bill.

Method 1: Using the Bills register

Here's how to record payment using the Bills register:

1. **Display the Bills register.**

   From the menu, choose Business⇨Business Accounts⇨Business Bills (or whatever you named your bills account). Or, open the Business Center, display the My Data tab, and under Business Accounts, click on the hyperlink to the Business Bills account. Or, over on the Account Bar at the left side of the screen, under the Business Center heading, click on the Business Bills account.

2. **Click on the transaction for which you want send a payment.**

   You can scroll through the register to find the right transaction, or you can use the Find feature to find a particular transaction in the register. Or, try one of the other two methods presented here if your list of payables is long and unwieldy.

3. **Click the Form button.**

   Enter, Edit, and Form buttons are in the register on the right side of the transaction. Click the Form button or the little green checkmark, and the original bill appears.

4. **Open the Payment to Vendor window.**

   On the original bill that appears, click the Create Payment button. The bill disappears from your screen and the Payment to Vendor window appears (Figure 2-21).

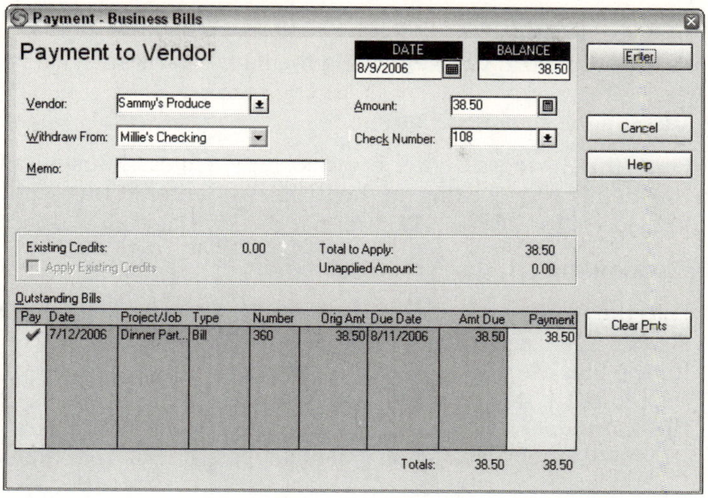

Figure 2-21: Record your payment.

5. **Verify the payment amount and date.**

   Today's date appears in the date field, and the full amount of the bill appears in the payment field. Verify that today is the date on which the payment is to be made, or change the date if necessary. If you plan to pay some amount other than the full amount, enter the actual amount you want to pay.

6. **Enter bank account information.**

   In the Withdraw From field, choose the account from which the payment is to be made.

7. **Fill in the Check Number field.**

   When you click the drop-down list in the Check Number field, you see there are options for selecting the next available check number, electronic payment, and so on. Pick the option that applies to how you want to make this payment.

8. **Complete the transaction.**

   Click Enter. The Payment to Vendor window closes. The bill is marked as Cleared in your Bills register. The amount is recorded in the bank account you selected, with the payment method you selected.

   The payment still needs to be dispatched. Depending on the method you chose, you must initiate the electronic transfer or print a check. Look back at Book IV, Chapter 4 for more information on payment of bills.

Method 2: Using the Payables list in the Business Center

Here's how to record payment using the Payables list:

1. **Display the Business Center.**

   Open the Business Center by choosing Business⇨Business Center from the menu or by clicking on the Business Center in the Account Bar at the left side of the screen. Be sure that the My Data tab is selected.

2. **Click on the bill that you want to pay.**

   Find the Accounts Payable (Business Bills) section of the Business Center screen. You'll see a list of all of your payables. The names of the vendors for the bills are hyperlinked. You can click right on a name to open the related bill. If the list is too long to display in the Business Center, click the Show Full List option. The complete list of bills appears in its own window. Double-clicking on a name opens the bill from that vendor.

3. **Open the Payment to Vendor window.**

   With the bill open, click the Create Payment button. From here, go to step 4 in Method 1 and continue.

Method 3: Using the Make Payment button

Here's how to record payment using the Make Payment button:

1. **With the Business Center open and the My Data tab selected, click the Make Payment button that appears in the Accounts Payable section.**

2. **The Payment to Vendor window appears, with no bill selected (Figure 2-22).**

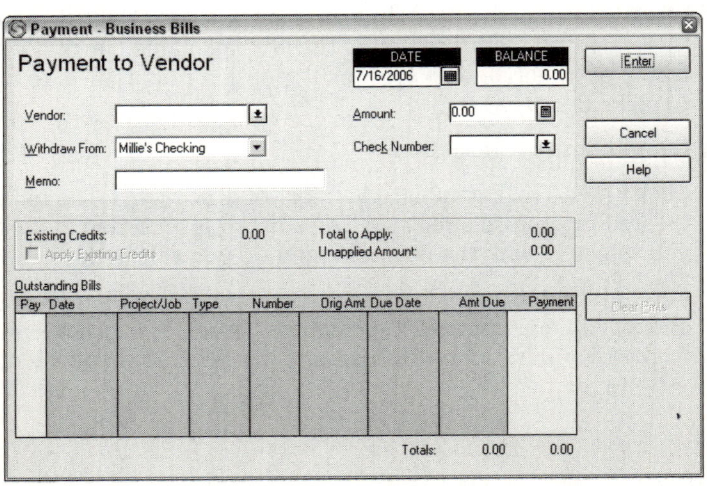

Figure 2-22: Select a vendor to see all outstanding bills and record your payment.

3. **Select the vendor from whom you have received a bill.**

   Click the drop-down list in the Vendor field to see a list of all vendors from whom you have ever entered bills. Click on the name of the vendor who sent you the bill. As soon as you click on a different field, or press Tab to move to a different field, the bills that are outstanding from this vendor appear in a list at the bottom of the Payment to Vendor window.

4. **Enter the amount you want to pay.**

   Enter the amount you plan to pay in the Amount field. Quicken automatically assigns this amount to outstanding bills, the oldest bill first and then the next oldest, and so on, as you can see in Figure 2-23.

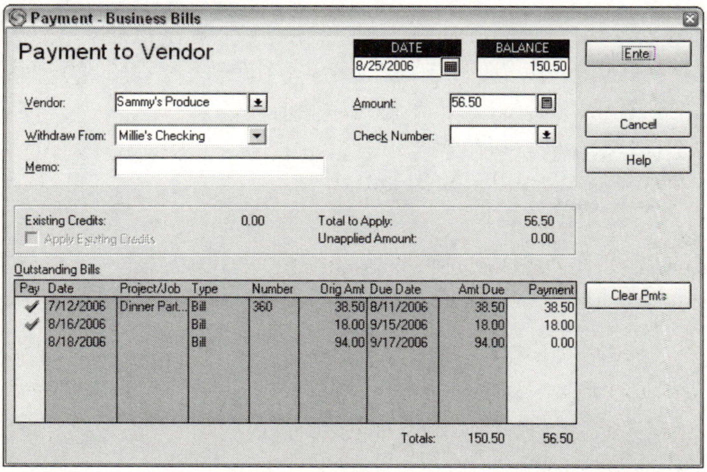

Figure 2-23: Quicken distributes the payment to the bills, oldest bill first.

5. **Verify the application of the money.**

   If, for some reason, you want to apply the payment to a bill other than the one(s) selected by Quicken, you can change the amounts in the Payment column, applying the correct amount to each bill.

6. **Complete the entry of payment information.**

   Pick up with step 5 from Method 1, verifying the date and bank account and then recording the payment.

Producing a payables report

If you're using Quicken Home & Business, you can display a report showing all of your accounts payable as of any particular date. Open the Reports & Graphs Center, and click on Business to see a list of all the business-related reports available. Click Accounts Payable and choose the date range you want to use for the report (see Figure 2-24).

Click the Show Report button to display your Accounts Receivable report. For more on business reports, see Chapter 5 of Book V.

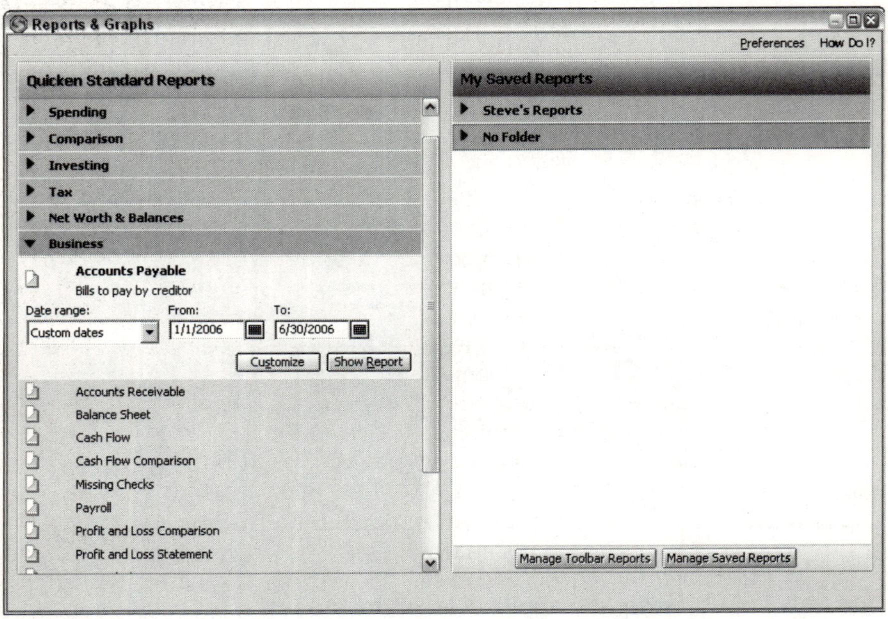

Figure 2-24: Choose the date or date range for your Accounts Payable report.

Chapter 3: Tracking Jobs and Payroll

In This Chapter

- **Keeping track of your various projects**
- **Issuing estimates**
- **Setting up payroll**
- **Issuing paychecks**
- **Recording and paying payroll taxes**

Businesses can take advantage of special Quicken features to keep track of individual projects and also to compute payroll. Project-oriented businesses include businesses that perform work on a per-client basis, such as legal and accounting and other professional services, construction companies, Web-design companies, and many, many more. As for payroll, if your payroll is just a few people, you might not need an actual payroll program like the one Quicken offers. But if you have more than a few employees, or if you're not entirely familiar with payroll tax requirements and want the assurance provided by using a program instead of figuring out payroll yourself, Quicken's payroll program might be just the ticket for you. You can track both jobs and payroll without the add-ons of Quicken Home & Business and QuickPayroll. In this chapter, I show you how to track these facets of your business both ways; you can decide which method is the most useful for your business.

Keeping Track of Your Projects

Some work naturally separates itself into individual projects. Other work is viewed as a whole. In the last chapter, I used the example of a catering company. A caterer who works for one client at a time, one event at a time, can gain a better understanding of the business profitability by tracking all of the expenses and related income from each project, separately. An artist who paints for a living, on the other hand, might purchase art supplies that are used on many different projects — trying to track the expenses for each individual work of art would be nearly impossible.

If your business lends itself to organization by jobs, you might want to take a look at Quicken Home & Business for its job-tracking capabilities. If you only have a small number of jobs, consider using separate categories for each job's expenses, or assign a separate class to each job.

Here are some advantages to tracking your income and expenses on a per-job basis:

- You can assess the profitability of each job individually, thus helping you decide if certain jobs are worth the time and money you invest.
- You can produce work-in-progress reports on a per-job basis to determine how your expenses compare to your income while the job is still in progress.
- You can produce a report showing all the expenses on a particular job to show to the customer or client who needs to know your costs.
- You can compare your costs on a job to your preliminary estimate to see how close you came to your estimate and determine if your estimating procedures are accurate.

Setting up your Project/Job list

In the Home & Business program, Quicken uses the terms *project* and *job* interchangeably, and I do too. You can use whichever name you prefer, or you might even call your jobs something completely different, like pieces, or cases, or tasks, or activities. It doesn't matter what name you use — the process for working with these projects is the same. Here I show you how to set up a project in Quicken Home & Business.

1. **Open the Business Center.**

   Either choose Business➪Go to Business Center from the menu, or click on the Business Center on the Account Bar at the left side of your screen.

2. **Click the Analysis and Reports tab.**

3. **Open the Project/Job List link.**

   Click the hyperlink to Project/Job List on the right side of the screen. The Project/Job list appears, and any projects you already have entered in Quicken appear on the list.

   Instead of going through the Business Center, you could choose Business➪Business Lists➪Project/Job List from the menu.

4. **Open the New Project/Job window.**

   Click the New button at the top of the Project/Job List window. The New Project/Job window appears, ready for you to enter information (see Figure 3-1).

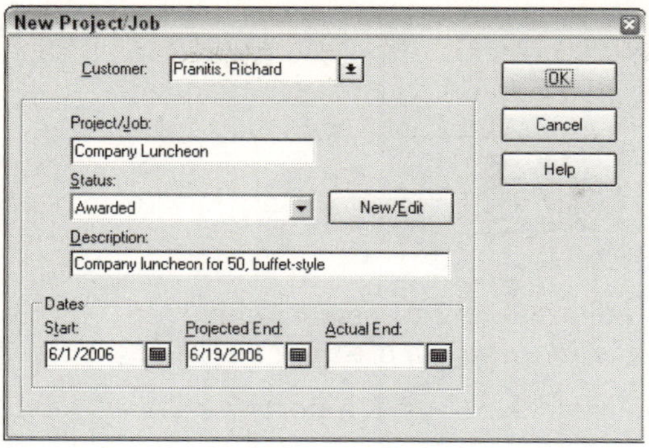

Figure 3-1: Enter information about your project.

5. **Enter the customer name.**

   You can click the drop-down arrow to see the existing customer list. Click on one of the customer names to select that customer. If the customer for whom you are doing this job doesn't appear on the list, you can enter the name of a new customer. Quicken automatically adds the new customer to the list for future use.

6. **Enter the job name in the Project/Job box.**

   Enter the name you want to use for this job. The name might be a case number, or a descriptive name.

7. **Enter the job status.**

   Quicken provides you with a Status drop-down list of five possible statuses: Awarded, Closed, In Progress, Not Awarded, Pending. You can pick from these job statuses, or you can enter a different job status. If you want to add to the job status list, click the New/Edit button. The Project/Job Status window appears (see Figure 3-2). Click on a status you want to change, and then enter the new status name in the Status to Add/Replace field. Click either the Replace button to replace the original status with your new name or the Add button to add your new status to the others on the list. Click OK when you're finished making your changes.

   Job status is an optional choice. If you don't want to use a job status, just select <None> as your Job Status.

8. **Enter a description.**

   The description is optional, but entering a narrative description gives you an opportunity to elaborate a little about the particular project.

9. **Enter appropriate dates in the three date-related fields.**

   The Start date is the date on which you started or expect to start the project. The Projected End date is the date when you expect the project will be completed. If you are entering information about a job you've already completed, you can enter the Actual End date as well.

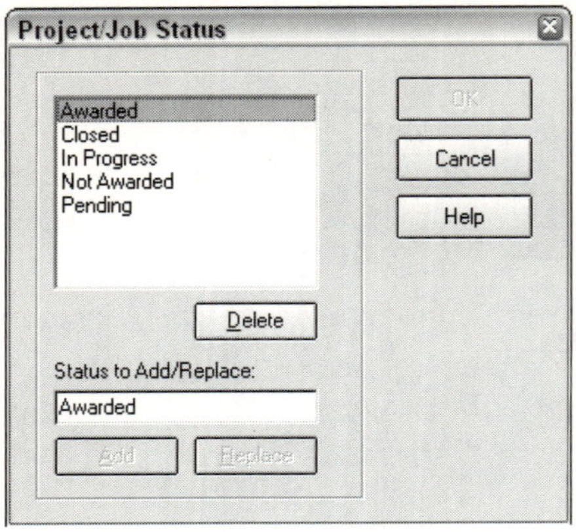

Figure 3-2: Edit or add to the Project/Job Status list.

You can choose to Edit a job on the Project/Job list by clicking on a job and then clicking the Edit button at the top of the list. The Edit Project/Job window appears. When you've completed a job, you can edit the job to enter the actual ending date and to change the status to show the job is finished.

10. **Close the New Project/Job window.**

    Click the OK button and the window closes, the project is added to your Project/Job list, and you are now ready to start assigning income and expenses to this job.

    If you don't have Quicken Home & Business, you can use Quicken's Classes feature to track individual projects. Classes are available with all versions of Quicken.

Factors to consider when tracking job information

Tracking jobs is more than just keeping good records. Here are some points to consider when examining the progress on your jobs:

- Based on your original estimate of the job cost and amount of time needed to complete the job, you can use job tracking to determine what percent of the job is completed, and how much money and time is left to expend.
- If you plan on billing your customer as the job progresses instead of all at once, a progress report created from the transactions that relate to a particular job can be quite useful.
- You can track your accounts receivable by job and see at a glance on the Project/Job list which expenses you've been reimbursed for and where you've spent money with no reimbursement.

Working with jobs

After you've set up some jobs (if you haven't, no matter, you can create your jobs as you need to use them), it's time to see how to apply a transaction to a particular job. Say you own a catering company. Your company is preparing to cater a business luncheon for 50 people and is purchasing some of the food necessary for that function. Here's a sample transaction:

1. **Go to the store, call your supplier, send an order form by mail or fax, or make an Internet order.**

   Ah — I think you can figure out that step without my help!

2. **Receive the bill.**

   OK — you remember how to enter bills, right? If not, check back to the previous chapter, and then report back here. Enter the bill as you normally would, but before you close the window, go on to the next step.

3. **Enter the Project name.**

   Click the Assign Project/Job button at the top of the Bill window. The Select Project/Job window appears (Figure 3-3). Click on the project name, and then click the OK button. If the project hasn't been set up yet in Quicken, click the New button, set up the project, and then come back here.

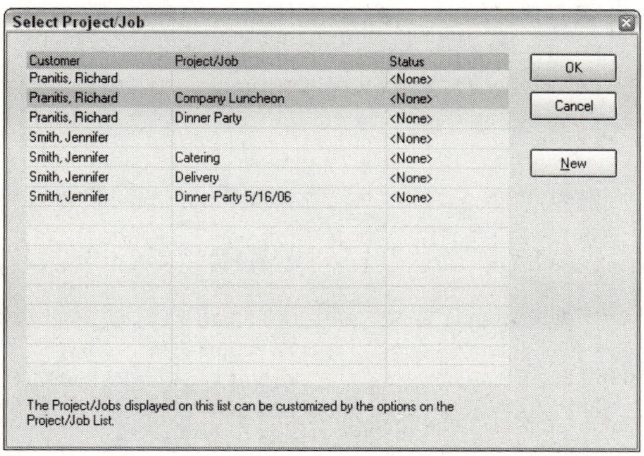

Figure 3-3: Pick a project.

4. **Save your bill.**

   When you close the Select Project/Job window, the customer name and the project name appear at the top of your bill (Figure 3-4). Go ahead and click one of the Save options to close the Bill window and save the bill.

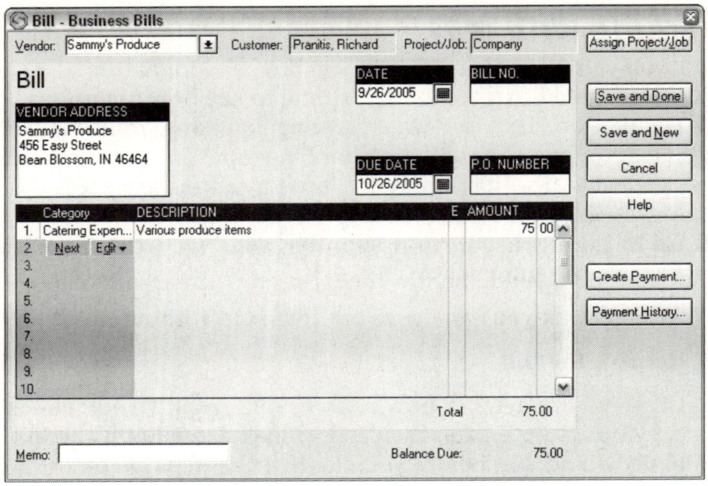

Figure 3-4: See the customer and project name at the top of the bill?

5. Check out the results.

Display the Project/Job list (remember you can find this on the Analysis & Reports tab of the Business Center). The bill you just entered has been added to the expenses for the particular job, as shown in Figure 3-5.

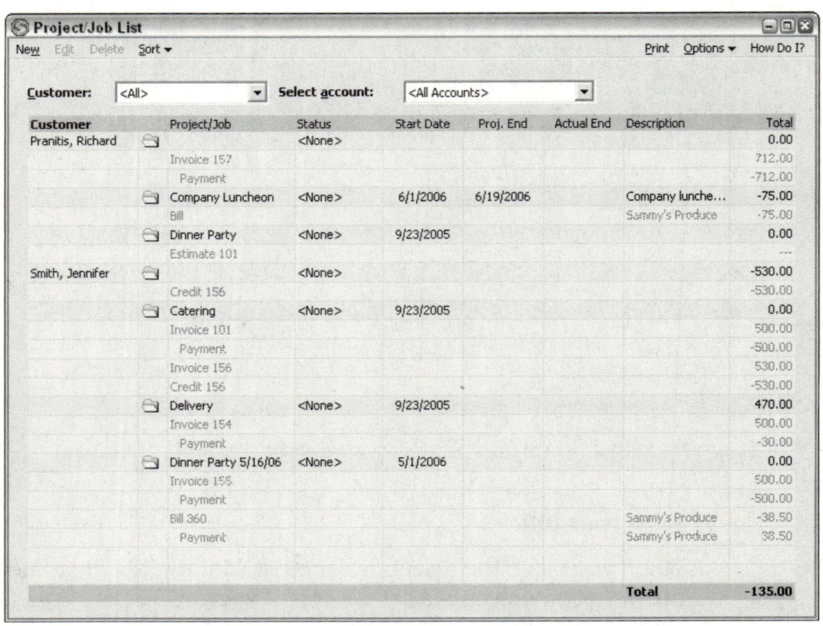

Figure 3-5: The $75 bill from Sammy's Produce has been entered under the Company Luncheon job.

TIP: When you enter expenses that relate to multiple jobs, be sure to take the time to split the transaction and assign the appropriate amounts to each job. In the long run, this provides you with much more accurate and useful information, even if it takes a little extra time up front to record the transaction.

Recording income on projects

The process of recording income on a project is nearly identical to recording a bill. When you open the invoice form, the first thing you do is choose a customer name. As soon as you pick a customer, a drop-down arrow appears in the Project/Job field, and the accompanying list shows all projects assigned to that customer (see Figure 3-6).

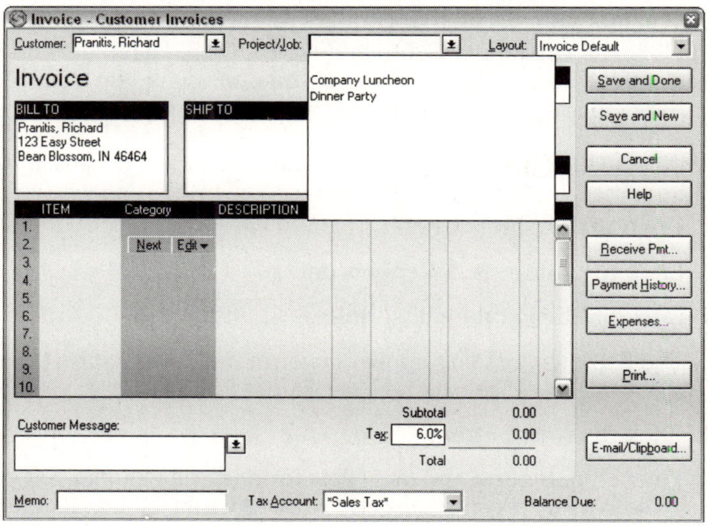

Figure 3-6: The list of projects for the customer you enter appears when you click the drop-down arrow.

As with entering bills, when you enter an invoice that is tied to a particular project, you can see the results immediately in the Project/Job list. The income from the invoice has been added to that particular job.

Seeing how a project is progressing

Quicken Home & Business comes with some built-in project reports so you can track the progress of your projects as you incur expenses and send invoices that relate to particular projects.

Choose Business from the Reports menu, and you'll see there are two Project/Job reports available. The first, Project/Job, shows your income and expenses organized by class, with a separate column for each class. The second report, Project/Job by Project, shows your income and expenses with a separate column for each project. Whether you use classes or projects to define your jobs, there is a standard report for you.

You can customize the project reports by clicking the Customize button, and then identifying what information you want to see. For example, if you only want to see income and expenses from particular categories that relate to your projects, click the Categories tab in the Customize window and select the categories you want to see displayed on the report.

Creating job estimates

An estimate is an approximation of how much you expect to charge a customer for a particular project. You can prepare an actual estimate form in Quicken that you can give to your customers. As the job progresses, the estimate form can be converted to an invoice. Once again, the estimate is a feature of Quicken Home & Business. If you don't have the Home & Business version, you are stuck with creating your estimates on paper.

Here's a step-by-step introduction to setting up an estimate form:

1. **Open the Business Center.**
2. **Click the Analysis & Reports tab.**
3. **Click on the Estimate List link.**

   The Estimate List link appears over in the Tools list on the right side of the Analysis & Reports tab (see Figure 3-7).
4. **Click the New button.**

   The Estimate form appears. This form is quite similar to Quicken's Invoice form. If you've already worked with Quicken invoices, you may have noticed that the steps in creating an estimate are familiar.

   There are a few differences between the estimate and the invoice forms. The estimate form doesn't include a shipping address, a due date field, or a P.O. number field, which are all fields you'll find on the invoice form. Also, the invoice form includes buttons to record the receipt of payment, a payment history summary, and an opportunity to apply expenses.
5. **Enter the customer name.**

   There is a drop-down list in the Customer field at the top of the Estimate form. If you've already entered this customer's name on another Quicken form, the name appears on the drop-down list. For new customers, enter the name and Quicken automatically remembers it for the next time you want to use it.

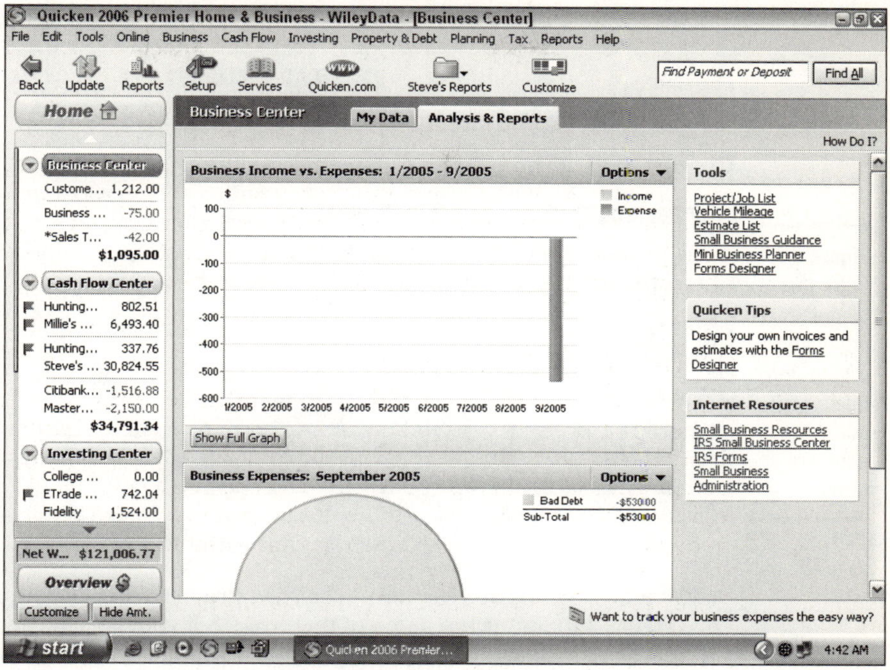

Figure 3-7: Click Estimate List to open a list of your active estimates. From there, click New to open a new estimate form.

Consider whether you want to enter your customer names by last name first or first name first, and then use the same method for entering all of your customer names. That consistency makes it easier to search lists and reports to find particular customers.

6. **Enter a project or job name.**

   If you have entered other project names for this customer, the drop-down list in the Project/Job field is populated with these names. If this is the first time you've worked on a project for this customer, the drop-down list is empty. You can choose from any existing project names on the drop-down list, or enter a new name. In Figure 3-8, for example, I've entered a new project name, Dinner Party, for my sample catering company. If you enter a new name, you are prompted to set up the new project/job, as described in step 7.

7. **Click Yes to create the new project/job.**

   This step only appears if you are entering a new project/job for this customer. You are asked if you want to create the new project/job. Clicking Yes allows you to proceed to the setup screen explained in step 8. You must set up the project if you want to use that project name on your estimate.

8. **Enter information about your project/job.**

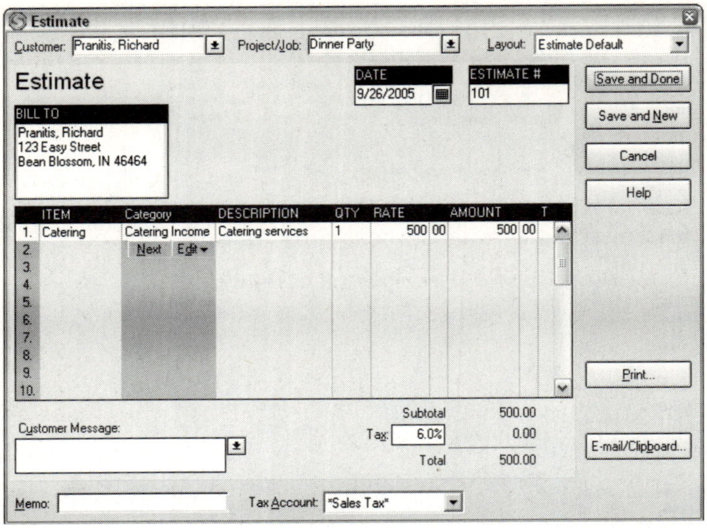

Figure 3-8: Enter the customer name and project/job name at the top of the estimate form.

When you click Yes in step 7, the New Project/Job window appears (Figure 3-9). Enter the name of the project. If you use Quicken's job status feature (described in "Setting up your Project/Job list," earlier in this chapter), you can enter a status. Because this is an estimate and not yet an actual job, you'll probably use the Pending status. Any other entries, such as job description and date information, are optional. Click OK to complete the setup process.

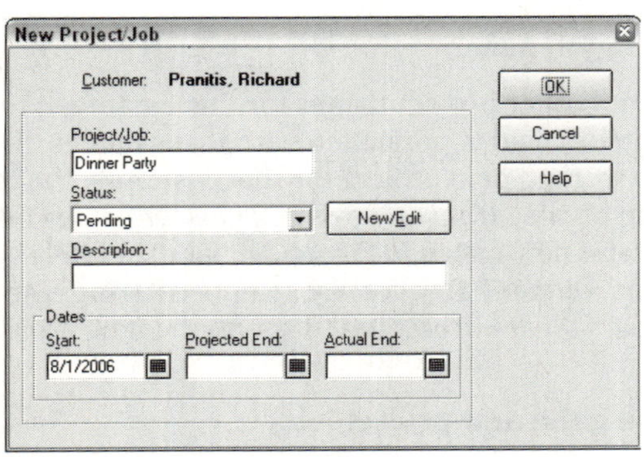

Figure 3-9: Enter information about the project or job for which you are creating an estimate.

9. **Enter your customer's address.**

   The address is optional but useful if you plan to mail this estimate. Also, after you enter the address, Quicken remembers that address and automatically places it on future forms created for this customer.

10. **Verify the date.**

    Quicken automatically places today's date on the estimate form. You can change the date if you want.

11. **Verify the estimate number.**

    After you've created your first estimate in Quicken and assigned a number to that estimate, Quicken automatically fills in the Estimate # field on future estimates with the next chronological number.

12. **Enter the estimate descriptions and amounts.**

    In the lower portion of the estimate form, enter the details of what you expect to charge the customer for this job. Each item you enter must be set up in Quicken (see Chapter 2, Book VIII for more information about using and setting up items). The completed estimate shown in Figure 3-8 includes one item for Catering.

13. **Verify quantity, rate, and amount.**

    If you are estimating the cost of multiple quantities of an item, enter the quantity in the Qty field on the estimate form. If you have already entered a rate for this item when you created the item in Quicken, the rate automatically appears on the estimate form and the amount is calculated based on the quantity that you enter. You can change the rate that appears on the form, or enter a rate if the rate field is blank.

14. **Verify sales tax.**

    If you charge sales tax and want to include that charge on your estimate, verify that the correct rate appears in the Tax field at the bottom of the estimate form. Also, verify that the items that qualify for sales tax are marked with a T in the T column to the right of the Amount column on the estimate. Quicken calculates the sales tax based on the tax rate and the taxable items shown on the form.

15. **Enter an optional customer message.**

    When creating estimates, the customer message area is a necessary field. Make sure you indicate in this field the expiration date for your estimate, or use a standard phrase that describes the life expectancy of the estimate. Phrases such as "Prices good for 60 days from the date on this form" and "Estimate will expire on 10/31/06" provide you with some protection from having a customer come back two years later trying to get the job done for outdated prices.

WARNING!

I strongly recommend that you use the message section of the estimate to enter a termination date for the estimate. Rather than leaving the estimate open-ended, you should let the customer how long you expect to honor the price information provided in the estimate.

16. Send the estimate.

You can click the Print button to print a copy of the estimate for delivery, or you can click the E-mail/Clipboard option and the Send Estimate by E-mail window appears (Figure 3-10). Verify the e-mail information, enter the customer's e-mail address if necessary, and then click OK. You are asked to provide some information about your own e-mail address and server if this is the first time you've e-mailed anything from Quicken. After all the information is entered, an e-mail message appears allowing you the option for entering personal comments. Click the Send button on this message and your estimate is dispatched!

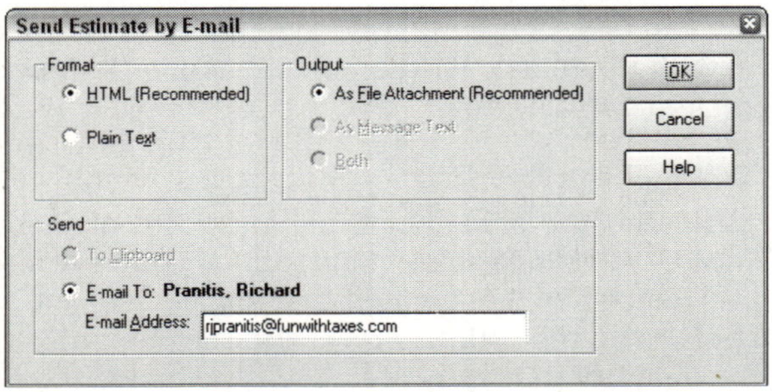

Figure 3-10: Go high-tech and send your estimate by e-mail!

17. Save the estimate.

Click Save and Done or Save and New to save the estimate. The first option closes the estimate window; the second option opens a new estimate window and you can start all over again with a new estimate. In both cases, the estimate is saved and appears on your Estimate List (see step 3).

You might be thinking, "Whoa! This estimate looks like an invoice! Have I just increased my reported income by the amount on the estimate?" Well, no, silly. That's why it's an estimate. It's just a formalized document that shows what you've been thinking. No financial transaction is associated with an estimate, and therefore no financial transaction is carried out in Quicken when you create an estimate. The estimate is purely for your information, for your customer's information, and for you to use going forward as a guide to your performance on a task.

REMEMBER

At any time you can view your outstanding estimates by clicking the Estimate List link in the Business Center.

Tracking Payroll in Quicken

If you have employees, you need to prepare and keep track of payroll information. It's imperative that you get this right — your employees are relying on you to file the correct forms, pay the correct amounts of taxes on their behalf, and prepare year-end forms for them so they can prepare their income tax returns.

You can use an outside payroll service to perform payroll duties, or you can do the work yourself. If you prepare your own payroll, you can either create the computations yourself or you can use Quicken's QuickPayroll to make your payroll chore easier.

QuickPayroll isn't cheap, at least not in comparison to what you paid for your Quicken software. When this book went to press, the price of QuickPayroll was $129 per year. If you only have a few employees, you might not be able to justify the price of this payroll service. If you want to give the service a try, Quicken lets you subscribe for 30 days at no charge. If you don't cancel before the 30 days expire, you are charged the $129. See for yourself if you like the service well enough to pay for it.

Quicken's QuickPayroll: What's in the box?

If you're curious about QuickPayroll, you can go to the Web site and find out more about the program: `www.payroll.com/quickpayroll`. QuickPayroll offers the following features:

- The program doesn't need to be used with Quicken — it is a standalone program. You can use a different computer for payroll than you do for your Quicken program if you want.
- Information from QuickPayroll can be seamlessly incorporated into your Quicken program so your Quicken accounts will be up to date.
- All federal and state taxes are automatically calculated with the QuickPayroll program.
- You can print paychecks from the QuickPayroll program.
- QuickPayroll provides you with payroll reports summarizing your payroll and payroll tax activity.
- Any changes in either federal or state tax rates that occur at any time during the year can be downloaded into your QuickPayroll program at no additional charge.
- Security is available in the form of password protection for your QuickPayroll data.

Contact the IRS and your state government to find out filing requirements

- You must apply for a Federal ID number if you plan to withhold and pay payroll taxes. To do so, you need to fill out federal form SS-4, Application for Employer Identification Number, and submit the form to the IRS. Shortly thereafter, the IRS sends you a packet of information about how and when to remit income taxes withheld from your employees as well as Social Security tax, Medicare tax, and federal unemployment tax.
- Your state expects you to report employee earnings information to the state government as well. You should check with your state government to find out how to collect and remit income and unemployment taxes in your state.

Setting up payroll in Quicken

If you've decided to go it alone and calculate and enter your own payroll information, I can help you get everything set up in Quicken. You need to create some new categories and accounts, and you'll want to set up some reminders so that you don't lose track of how much tax you have to pay, what forms you need to prepare, to whom, and when.

I'm going to discuss federal income taxes here. It would take a whole book and time that I don't have to discuss all of the state regulations because each state has its own distinct rules. In addition, many cities assess income taxes. And that doesn't even begin to address foreign considerations if you have international employees. The more complex your tax situation is, the more necessary an outside tax professional is. But I'll bet you already know that.

New accounts you need

You need to keep track of and pay four federal taxes throughout the year. Some of these taxes you're going to withhold from your employee's pay, and some of them you're going to pay yourself. Here's the rundown:

- **Federal income tax withholding:** This is the income tax that you withhold from your employees. The IRS and Congress have gotten together to create a great little booklet called Circular E, which is filled with page after page of tax tables guaranteed to put you to sleep at night, as well as other useful information about all the taxes you need to pay and withhold. You can download a copy of Circular E at `www.irs.gov/pub/irs-pdf/p15.pdf`.

✦ **Social Security tax:** Otherwise known as FICA, half of this tax is withheld at a flat 6.2 percent of your employee's wages. The other half, another 6.2 percent of the wages of each of your employees, is paid by you because you're kind and generous and, oh yeah, you like to obey the law.

✦ **Medicare tax:** You withhold 1.45 percent of your employee's wages to pay for half of the Medicare tax. The other half, another 1.45 percent of the wages of each employee, is paid by you.

✦ **Federal unemployment tax:** No withholding for this one. You as the employer pay the federal share, and oh, by the way, don't forget to check with your state to find out how much unemployment tax you have to pay at the state level. Some states let you withhold the state unemployment tax from your employees; others make you pay it yourself. It's all the same, right? One assumes that employees' wages are slightly lower in states where the employer pays the tax, and higher if the employees pay the tax themselves.

You need to set up liability accounts to handle these taxes — here's how:

1. **Open the Account List.**

   Choose Account List from the Tools menu or press Ctrl+A. The Account List appears, ready for you to take some action.

2. **Open the Account Setup window.**

   From the Account List window, click the Add Account option at the top, or press Alt+A. The Account Setup window appears.

3. **Indicate that this is not a bank account.**

   Choose door number 2, This Account Is Not Held at a Financial Institution. Click Next to continue.

4. **Choose Liability.**

   That's right — these are liability accounts we're setting up. Liability, if you recall, means you owe money. You're going to use these accounts to keep track of the tax money you owe to Uncle Sam. Click Next to continue.

5. **Give the account a name.**

   You've got four of these to take care of, one at a time. Table 3-1 provides some sample names you can use, or you can make up your own. Just make sure you use names that make sense so you can find your way back to these accounts without any trouble.

Table 3-1 Sample Liability Account Names

Tax	*Account Name*
Federal income tax withholding	Payroll FIT Withholding
Social Security tax	Payroll FICA Payable
Medicare tax	Payroll MCARE Payable
Federal unemployment tax	Payroll FUTA Payable

If you want to go ahead and set up liability accounts for your state taxes at this time as well, feel free.

TIP: Quicken searches through your account names when preparing its Payroll report and includes all accounts with the word Payroll contained in the name; therefore, I use the word *Payroll* in all of my payroll-related account names.

7. **Enter a date and the amount you owe.**

   You can't leave the date field blank, so enter today's date, or the date when the most recent tax payment period ended. Enter whatever the current amount is that you owe for this particular payroll tax (see Figure 3-11). Are your payments all caught up? Then enter zero.

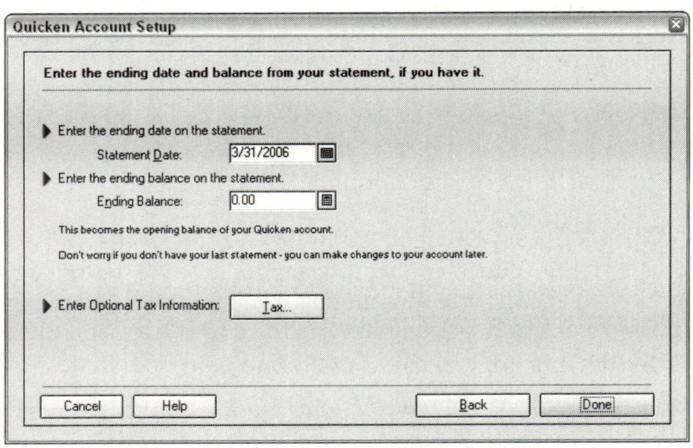

Figure 3-11: Enter the account statement information for your liability accounts.

8. **Finish the setup.**

   Click the Done button to complete the setup. You'll be asked if you want to create an amortized loan for the amount owing. This is a standard question whenever you set up a liability account, but this doesn't have anything to do with your payroll tax liabilities, so click No.

9. Start over again.

Go back to square one and start the process over again until you've set up all of your payroll liability accounts.

TIP

If you use Quicken Home & Business, you can set these liability accounts up as business payables accounts.

Setting up payroll expense categories

In addition to the payroll liability accounts, you have some payroll expense categories that need to be created. These are the categories you use to keep track of your share of the payroll taxes — the amounts you have to pay beyond what you can withhold from your employees. You should set up the following categories:

- ✦ Social Security tax expense
- ✦ Medicare tax expense
- ✦ Federal unemployment tax expense

Depending on the rules of your state, you might also have to set up a state unemployment tax expense category if you pay SUTA to your state.

Set up your payroll expense categories by doing this:

1. Open the Category List.

Choose Tools➪Category List, or press Ctrl+C (or Shift+Ctrl+C). The Category List appears, showing every category you've created thus far. The accounts you've set up appear in brackets at the very bottom of the list.

2. Open the Set Up Category window.

Click the New button, found at the bottom of the list, and the Set Up Category window appears, as shown in Figure 3-12.

3. Enter the category name in the Name field.

Now for the fooler — you thought you were going to enter a type of tax for the category name. Not so fast. First start with a top-level category called Payroll, and then you can group all the payroll stuff under that parent heading. So Payroll it is.

4. Enter the Type.

Choose Expense as the type for this category. Income would be for payroll that you receive as an employee. Expense is for the payroll and related expenses you give to others.

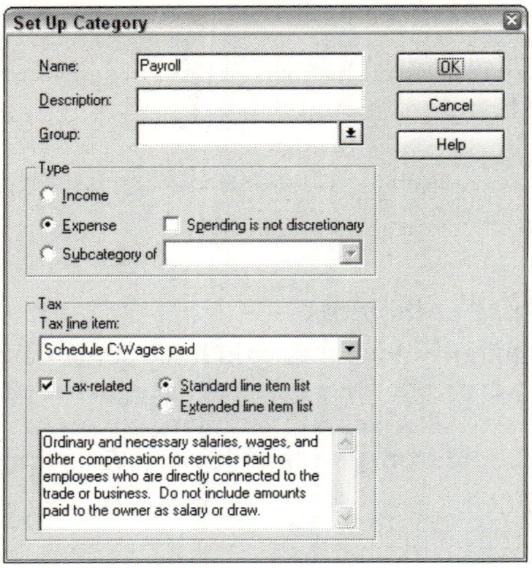

Figure 3-12: Set up all the categories you need to track your payroll costs.

5. **Enter a tax line.**

   Are you going to use Quicken to help with your tax return? I certainly hope so. In that case, you need to pick an appropriate tax line for summarizing your payroll information. For more information on tax lines and tax returns, see Book V.

6. **Finish the job.**

   Click OK and the new parent category is added to your category list, ready for you to populate it with baby categories.

7. **Repeat the above steps for all of the following categories that need to be entered as subcategories of the Payroll category:**

   - Gross wages
   - FICA employer's share
   - Medicare employer's share
   - FUTA
   - SUTA employer's share (only use this if you, as the employer, pay the state unemployment tax yourself)

More payroll setup stuff

You're almost there! You've filed your SS-4 and received your federal identification number and information about paying and withholding income taxes. You probably received a copy of the Circular E in the mail as well (but you know where to download it even if you don't have a hard copy). You've contacted your state government (and by the way, if you have employees who live in more than one state, you need to get in touch with the governments for all of those states to make sure you've got all the tax rules straight).

You need to take care of just one more thing: You need to get information from your employees. You can't just start withholding arbitrary amounts of income tax from your employees. The amount of federal and state income tax you withhold is based on a number of criteria:

- ✦ The marital status of your employees
- ✦ The number of allowances the employees claim on their W-4 forms
- ✦ The frequency with which you pay your employees

Wait a minute — go back to that second item. The one about the W-4 forms. If you think way back to Book I, Chapter 1, I discussed W-4 forms from the perspective of you being the employee. Well, now you're the employer and, instead of worrying about your own W-4 form, you need to pester your employees to make sure they fill out those forms and give them to you.

The W-4 form shows you the total number of allowances each employee is claiming. These allowances play a part in determining how much income tax to withhold from each paycheck.

TIP

You can download your very own copy of Form W-4 from the IRS Web site. Go to `www.irs.gov/pub/irs-pdf/fw4.pdf`. You can even fill out the W-4 online, and then print a paper copy of the form.

Paying your employees

Now that you've got all the information you need, it's time to try your hand at actually paying your employees. So here we go — it's payday!

More federal paperwork

While you're at it, in addition to the W-4 form, you need to collect an I-9 form from each of your employees. This form doesn't have anything to do with the monetary part of hiring, but the I-9 usually gets distributed to employees at the same time they are asked to fill out their W-4 form, so we might as well talk about the form here.

The I-9, otherwise known as Employment Eligibility Verification Form, is issued by the U.S. Citizenship and Immigration Services department. The purpose of the form is to provide a document attesting that your employees are U.S. citizens and have the right to work in this country.

Don't bother sending these forms anywhere. You as the employer are required to keep the I-9 and the W-4 in a file somewhere at your place of business.

The starting point for determining your payroll amount and the taxes that are owed is to calculate the gross wages. *Gross wages* is the term used to describe how much an employee earned, based on the salary or wage that was promised when the employee was hired. A little basic math makes this task much easier.

- **Salary:** If your employee receives a fixed annual salary, divide that salary by the number of pay periods in the year, and that is the amount of the gross wages for one paycheck. In other words, if Jimmy is hired at a base salary of $30,000 per year and you write checks twice a month, that translates into 24 paychecks per year, so $30,000 divided by 24 = $1,250 per paycheck. Jimmy, of course, isn't going to take home anywhere near $1,250 on his paycheck, but that's the number you start with.
- **Wages:** If your employee earns a certain wage per hour, the wage amount is multiplied by the number of hours worked in the pay period in order to determine the gross wages. So, if Georgie worked 40 hours per week, for half of a month, that works out to about 86.67 hours for one pay period. If her hourly rate is $10 per hour, her gross wages for the pay period are $866.67.

The next step is to determine the tax withholding for each employee. You can use the tax tables in Circular E to figure this out. Also, you can search for free withholding calculators on the Internet.

Even if you use the Circular E to calculate your taxes, it can't hurt to verify your calculations with an online calculator. The IRS has a withholding calculator on its Web site at `www.irs.gov/individuals/article/0,,id=96196,00.html`. Click the Continue to the Withholding Calculator link at the bottom of the page, and then fill in the blanks as you work through the calculator.

Using the online calculator at the IRS Web site, I've calculated the following withholding amounts for Jimmy and Georgie. The results appear in Table 3-2.

Table 3-2 Payroll Calculations

Item	*Jimmy*	*Georgie*	*Explanation*
Gross wages	$1,250.00	$866.67	Total amount earned for current pay period
Federal income tax withholding	$67.00	$27.00	Based on each employee being married and claiming two allowances
Social Security tax (FICA)	$77.50	$53.73	6.2 percent of total wages
Medicare tax	$18.12	$12.57	1.45 percent of total wages
Take-home pay	$1,087.38	$773.37	Gross wages less the various withholding amounts

Note: I've used 2005 tax withholding rates to calculate the federal income tax. Withholding percentages change slightly each year. Be sure you are using up-to-date withholding tables (a current year Circular E or a withholding calculator that has been kept current) when calculating withholding amounts for your employees.

The table above shows the amounts that an employer would withhold for these two employees, based on the circumstances described on these employees' W-4 forms, the amount of salary and wages they earn, and the frequency with which the payments are made.

State income tax, and perhaps local income tax, as well as other types of deductions might also apply to these employees.

Entering a paycheck in Quicken

When you've made all the calculations, and you're ready to create the check, here's how to make the entry in Quicken.

Although you know you're going to pay an amount to each employee that is less than the total wages earned, you still need to account for all of the wages and all of the taxes in Quicken. Don't just write a check for the net amount and not record the tax withholding. You need to enter the tax information in addition to the salary and wages so that you can properly report and pay your taxes.

Here are the steps to entering a check for payroll:

1. **Open the register for the account from which you are paying the payroll.**

   Click the account name on the Account Bar at the left side of the screen. The register appears with your cursor in position to enter a new transaction.

2. **Enter the date of the paycheck.**

   Quicken automatically starts with today's date. If necessary, change the date to the actual payday.

3. **Enter the check number.**

   If you know the number, enter it now. Or, you can choose Print Check if you plan to print the check from within Quicken, or enter EFT if this is to be an electronic payment.

4. **Enter the employee name.**

   The employee name goes in the Payee field. Remember that if you have QuickFill turned on, the name fills in as soon as you begin typing it.

5. **Enter the amount of the check.**

   In the Payment field, enter the *net* amount of the check — the actual amount you intend to write the check for.

6. **Open the Split Transaction window.**

   Press Ctrl+S to open the Split Transaction window.

7. **Enter the gross wages.**

   Start with the whole enchilada — enter Payroll: Gross Wages as the first split item, and enter the actual amount of gross wages before deductions ($1,250 in the case of Jimmy in Table 3-2).

8. **Enter the taxes withheld.**

   Enter the federal withholding, the FICA withholding, and the Medicare withholding. These amounts get entered as negative numbers, reducing the gross wages to the point where the check detail amount equals the actual check amount. You can confirm the calculation at the bottom of the Split Transaction window — your goal is to get the Remainder amount down to zero. You can see what I've done in Figure 3-13.

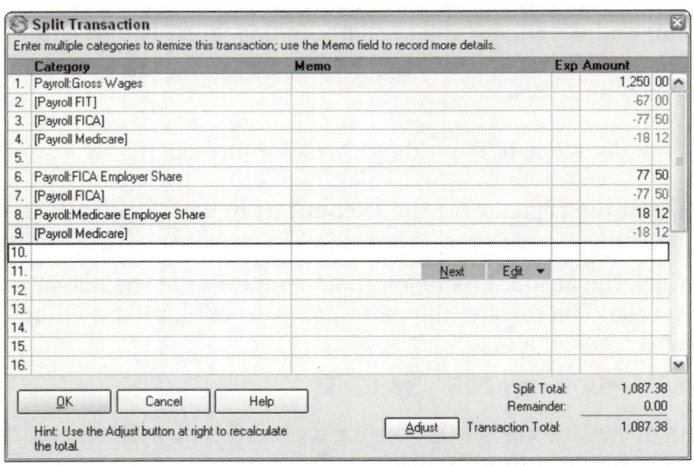

Figure 3-13: Enter the detailed information about the employee's gross wages and withholdings.

9. **Enter employer taxes.**

   If you like, you can take this one step further and enter your employer taxes at this time. You have to enter these amounts sometime and it makes sense to take care of these entries all at once, in the same transaction. In Figure 3-13, I entered the employer share of FICA and Medicare. The expense amount equals the amount withheld from the employee's pay and is entered as a positive number. The liability amount equals the expense amount and offsets this amount as a negative number. Thus the remainder balance at the bottom stays at zero, and I've taken care of entering my employer payroll tax expense and liability for this transaction.

10. **Enter state taxes.**

    Before closing up the split transaction window, enter any state taxes that you withheld from this employee's pay as well. That lowers the net check and increases your liability account for state taxes withheld.

11. **Save the check.**

    Click OK to save the information you entered and to enter the check in the register.

12. **One last step — pass out the paychecks!**

    Whether you write checks by hand, print checks in Quicken, or electronically transfer the funds, this task must be performed regularly and on time!

Chapter 4: Recording Fixed Assets

In This Chapter

- **Setting up fixed assets in Quicken**
- **Calculating depreciation**
- **Recording depreciation**
- **Selling a fixed asset**

I bet you've acquired plenty of items over the years that you intend to keep. And I'm not talking about that comfy flannel shirt you "borrowed" from a former boyfriend, or that turntable that's buried under an inch of dust in the garage. I mean real tangible items of value that you could sell for cash and that increase your value to lenders and investors. I'm talking about items like cars and houses and computers and furniture — these are items that have a measurable value, and these are items that you need to take the time to account for in your Quicken program.

Recording Your Business's Fixed Assets

Several types of fixed assets should be recorded in Quicken. For example, personal fixed assets that are associated with a loan, such as a car or a house, should be recorded along with the loan so you can monitor the balance of the loan and stay on top of your monthly payments. You'll find specific information about entering cars and homes in Book IV. Other assets, such as your household furniture and personal possessions, can be recorded in Quicken so that you have a permanent record for insurance purposes. See Chapter 3, Book IV for details about entering your personal assets in Quicken.

The assets you purchase for your business should also be recorded in Quicken. It's particularly important to record business assets, including computers, machinery, and other equipment. Here are some reasons why you need to keep track of these possessions:

- The IRS requires you to report the cost of your business assets and depreciate that cost a period of years. You find out more about depreciation later in this chapter.

Excuse me? What's all this I hear about depreciation?

Depreciation expense is a fancy way of saying that over time your assets deteriorate and lose value, so you have to account for that loss in value by reducing the reported value of the assets.

The U.S. Congress and the Internal Revenue Service have gone to great lengths to make the process of calculating depreciation about as confusing as it can possibly be, but hey, that's what we taxpayers pay those folks for. Here, I'm going to leave the really confusing stuff to the pros and just cover some easy examples that you can follow as a guide.

Typically, on business financial statements, fixed assets are reported at their original cost, and then a separate line on the financial statement shows the amount of value that has been whittled away by depreciation. The accumulated depreciation amounts are deducted from the asset cost, leaving you with a net fixed asset value on the financial statements.

Quicken is not quite so accommodating as more high-powered accounting programs, so you should skip the accumulated depreciation account and enter your depreciation reduction in value right in the asset accounts.

So, for a really simple example, say you purchased a computer that is expected to last for five years (did I also mention that the IRS has a very unrealistic view of how long certain assets really last?). The computer cost $1,000. Each year we record depreciation of ⅕ of the computer's value or $200. The $200 is reported as an expense on our profit and loss statement and the computer appears on the net worth statement at a reduced amount. At the end of the first year, the computer would be reported at $800 on the net worth statement, at the end of the second year, $600, and so on. By the end of the fifth year, the computer has no value according to your financial statements.

By the way, one of the more oddball vagaries of the tax laws is that *all* fixed assets are expected to depreciate in value according to the IRS, even personal residences and classic cars, which historically have risen in value each year. Go figure.

- ✦ Any lender or investor will want to see information about all of the assets that add to the value of your business.
- ✦ To determine the value of your own business, you need to have a record of the assets you own.

I focus on the business assets in this chapter because the personal assets have been covered earlier in this volume. Recording fixed assets in Quicken requires entering the cost of the asset, and recording related depreciation expense. Sounds like a piece of cake, right? Quicken doesn't really get into the whole depreciation picture, so setting up your assets won't be quite as easy as you might think. But never fear. You can get the job done!

Looks like we need some more categories

Now, set up a category for recording depreciation expense. Keep in mind that no money is going to pass through this category. Depreciation expense is strictly a transaction that is reported on paper. No matter. You need the category in order to include the amount on your financial statements. Set up your depreciation expense category by following these steps:

1. **Open the Category List.**

   You can probably do this in your sleep by now, but for the record, choose Category List from the Tools menu, or press Ctrl+C (or Shift+Ctrl+C).

2. **Open the Set Up Category window.**

   Click the New button that's hanging around down at the bottom of the Category List. The set up window appears, front and center.

3. **Enter the category name.**

   Depreciation Expense is the standard name to go with here. Other names might come to mind, such as Asset Write-Off, Something My Accountant Knows What to Do With, and so on. But remember, this category is going to show up on some of your financial reports, so just stick with the familiar name, as I've done in Figure 4-1.

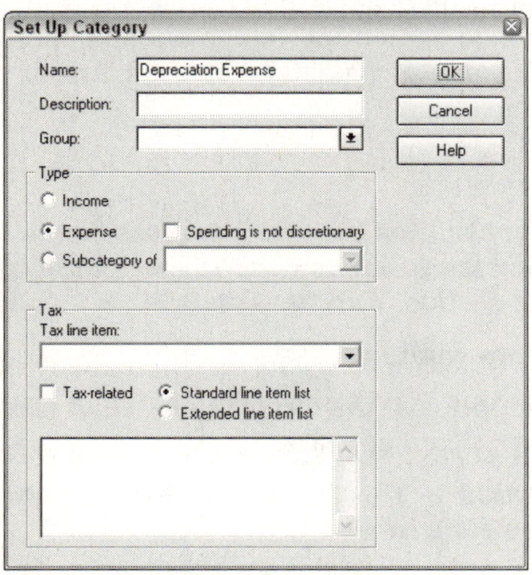

Figure 4-1: Enter **Depreciation Expense** as the category name.

4. **Enter a description.**

   Or not. The description field is optional; however, feel free to use the Description field to wax eloquent about what you think of the depreciation category.

5. **Choose your category type.**

   The type is Expense. This is the main depreciation expense category — the parent category, if you will. If you have lots of different types of assets and would like to create little baby subcategories to keep track of the depreciation expense for each asset or each type of asset separately, feel free to come back later and create more categories, using this one as the top-level category.

6. **Indicate that this is a tax-related category.**

   You can skip the tax line field. If you scroll through the list of available tax lines, you see that Quicken doesn't even bother including a line for depreciation expense. This is one amount you're going to have to enter yourself on your tax return, even if you use the automatic export feature to send your tax data to TurboTax. Checking the tax-related box, however, has some value. Quicken includes the depreciation expense on your tax reports if you check this box.

7. **Save the category.**

   Don't forget to click OK so your entries can be saved.

Time to go computer shopping!

Now that we've got our depreciation expense account created, we can go ahead and record the acquisition of an asset. I'll stick with the example of the computer that I mentioned earlier. Say you go out and purchase a computer for $1,000, and that computer is going to be used in your business. Here's how to record the purchase:

1. **Open the Account List.**

   Choose Tools⇨Account List from the menu, or press Ctrl+A. The Account List appears. Just so you know, our new account is going to appear down in the Property & Debt section, with the Assets.

2. **Open the Account Setup window.**

   Click the Add Account option at the top of the Account List. The Quicken Account Setup wizard appears.

3. **Choose the second option — This Account Is Not Held at a Financial Institution — and then click Next.**

4. **Choose the account Type.**

   Select Asset as the account type (see Figure 4-2). Asset is found in either the Home & Business group or the Property & Debt group, depending on which version of Quicken you use.

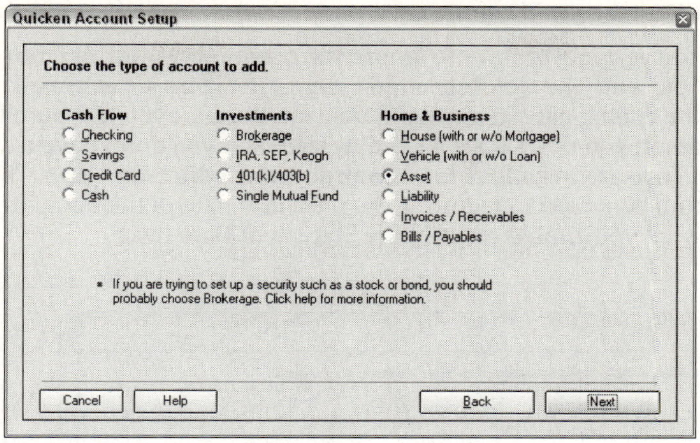

Figure 4-2: Our new computer is classified as an asset.

5. **Enter a name for the asset.**

   Each asset must have a unique name (see Figure 4-3). So if you have three computers, each one is going to have to go by a different name. You can use serial numbers, computer models, include the name of the person whose desk the computer sits on (for example, Katherine's computer), or maybe tell where the computer is located (Warehouse computer). Whatever name you choose, just make sure you can remember which computer is which. And this goes for all assets, not just computers. Each asset account you create must have a name different from all other accounts.

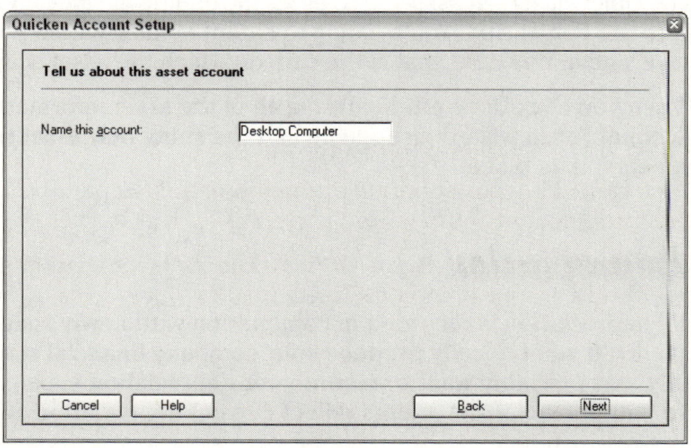

Figure 4-3: Enter a unique name for this asset.

6. **Enter the purchase date.**

   You're going to have to ignore the questions in Quicken now and go with your gut. The Quicken screen shown in Figure 4-4 asks you to indicate the ending date from your statement. Because you just purchased a fixed asset, you don't have an ending date and you don't have a statement. Those are questions for a bank account, which this isn't. The information you need to record is the purchase date of the computer, so that's what you should enter in the Statement Date field.

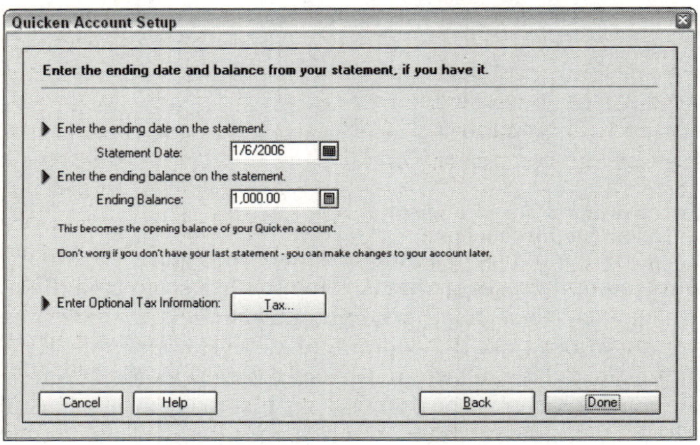

Figure 4-4: Enter the purchase date and the original cost of your asset.

7. **Enter the asset cost.**

   The Quicken screen asks you to enter the ending balance on your bank account. Forget that. You're going to enter the information you want to save, and in this case, that is the date on which the asset was purchased.

   When you click Done after entering all of the asset information, the Account Setup wizard disappears and the shiny new asset register appears in its place.

Recording Depreciation

Usually depreciation is recorded in conjunction with newly issued financial statements. If you typically produce your company financial statements monthly, you probably want to record your depreciation expense monthly as well so your financial statements reflect current depreciation adjustments.

To depreciate or not to depreciate

Depreciation is a means of deducting the cost of assets from your tax return. Assets purchased for a business represent a business expense. But often, the expense doesn't really relate to just one year of our business activity, so the IRS expects us to spread the cost over the years when the asset is to be used in the business. This cost spreading is called *depreciation*.

Each business must make its own decisions regarding which purchases represent ordinary business costs that get expensed currently and which expenses represent long-term purchases that need to be depreciated.

Generally, items that add value to your business and that are expected to last and be useful in your business for more than one year should be depreciated. Often the costlier items you purchase are the items you depreciate. But this isn't always the case. I used to own a movie theatre and I purchased light bulbs for my movie projector. The bulbs cost close to $1,000 apiece — sounds like a depreciable expense, right? Wrong! Each bulb only lasted about six months. These were regular costs of doing business instead of depreciable costs.

Look more toward how long an asset is going to last, and then consider the cost. A waste basket might last 20 years or more, but if it only costs $10, you don't have to depreciate it. When advising my clients, I usually use about $250 as a cutoff for depreciating items instead of expensing them. If an item costs less than $250, I generally recommend expensing the item instead of recording it as an asset. If the cost exceeds $250, I advise the client to look at the expected longevity of the asset and whether it adds value to the business to decide if it needs to be depreciated.

Here's how to record the depreciation expense for your business asset:

1. **Open the register for the asset to be depreciated.**

   You can find the asset listed on the Account List (Ctrl+A) — just double-click on the asset name to open the related register.

2. **Enter the date.**

   Determine when you will produce your financial statements, be it monthly, quarterly, or annually. The date of the depreciation transaction should coincide with whatever time frame you choose for reporting your business activity. So if you produce your financial statements every quarter as of the last day of the quarter, your depreciation transactions should be dated March 31, June 30, September 30, and December 31. In the Asset register, enter the date for this depreciation transaction. In Figure 4-5, I've entered March 31.

3. **Enter a description.**

   I've used Quarterly Depreciation Expense as my description.

How much depreciation should I report?

The depreciation guide published by the Internal Revenue Service is 112 pages long. Reducing all of the material in that guide into a few paragraphs here is obviously impossible. So let me instead give you an overview of how depreciation is calculated. You can then either use the guide, talk with an accountant, talk with an IRS representative, or use an online depreciation calculator to determine how much depreciation expense to enter in your program.

The first part of calculating depreciation expense is determining the *useful life* of the asset. The number of years of useful life assigned to an asset often has little to do with how long the asset is actually expected to last. Buildings last hundreds of years, but the IRS says that a building should be depreciated over anywhere from 10 years to 39 years, depending on the type of building. Automobiles are to be depreciated over 5 years, as are computers and cows. Furniture gets a 7-year life expectancy, whereas fruit trees are expected to last 10 years.

To demonstrate how meaningless these rules are, back in the 1980s, automobiles were depreciated over 3 years, furniture was in the 5-year bracket, and buildings, remarkably, were depreciated over only 15 years. The actual life expectancy of these items hasn't changed — just the way in which they are treated for tax purposes is different. The 1980s tax rules allowed for much quicker write-offs of asset purchases, with an eye toward stimulating economic development.

Anyway, back to the present. There are tables in the depreciation guide for figuring out how much to depreciate each year because the calculations are not as straightforward as you might expect. In fact, they're pretty darn confusing. An easy way to calculate depreciation is to use what is known as a *straight-line* method, whereby you divide the cost of the asset over the life of the asset, using the life expectancy designated by the IRS.

So for a computer that cost $1,000, using the straight-line method, I'm going to calculate that the computer has a 5-year life, so I'll depreciate $1,000 per year, or $16.67 per month, or $50 per quarter.

For detailed information on alternatives for determining depreciation amounts, see IRS Publication 946, How to Depreciate Property, at `www.irs.gov/pub/irs-pdf/p946.pdf`.

4. **Enter the amount.**

   In the Decrease column, enter the amount of depreciation. In this example, I've entered $50 as my quarterly depreciation expense.

5. **Enter the category.**

   You set up a depreciation expense category earlier. That is the category to use for recording this transaction.

6. **Record the transaction.**

   Click the Enter button or press Enter to record your transaction. You'll see that the balance of the asset in the far right column has been reduced by the amount of depreciation expense.

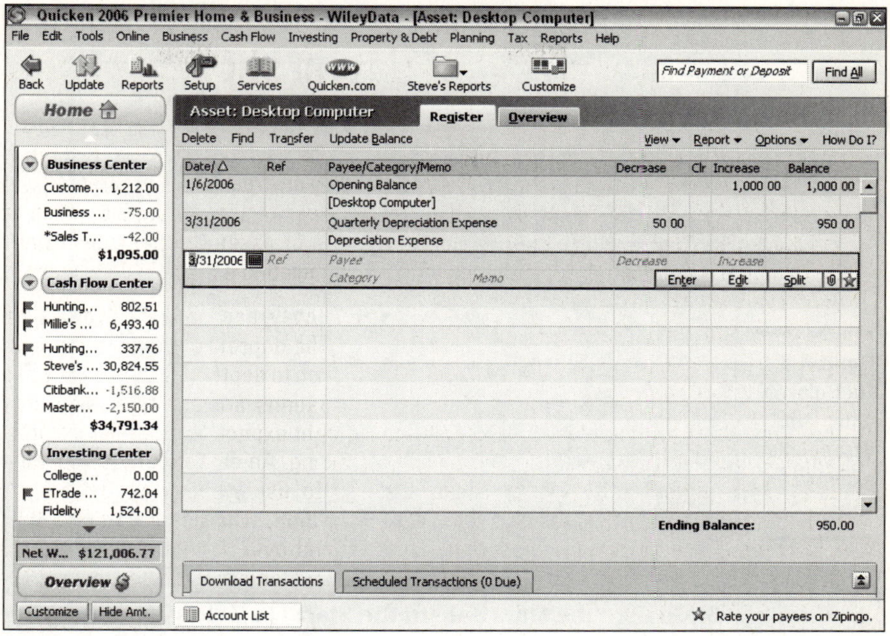

Figure 4-5: Record a depreciation expense entry.

Only business assets need to be depreciated. No tax deduction is allowed for depreciation of personal assets.

Automating Depreciation

Recording depreciation can get pretty tedious. After you calculate the amount, the entries are the same, month after month, or quarter after quarter. Automating these entries is easy, so turn the task of recording depreciation over to Quicken. Follow these steps to schedule an automatic entry of depreciation expense:

1. **Open the Asset register.**

   If you closed the register after entering your depreciation expense, press Ctrl+A and double-click on the Asset register.

2. **Open the Create Scheduled Transaction window.**

   Right-click on the depreciation transaction that you entered in the Asset register, and then pick Schedule Transaction from the pop-up menu. The Create Scheduled Transaction window appears (Figure 4-6). Many of the fields have already been completed, using information from the register transaction.

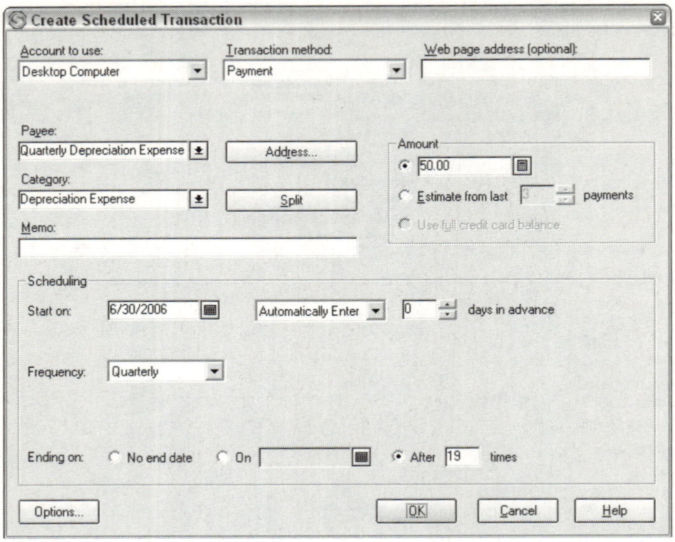

Figure 4-6: Let Quicken enter your depreciation expense for you.

3. **Change the start date in the Start On field if necessary.**

   Quicken automatically entered the date one month after the date of your depreciation transaction. If you're going to enter depreciation monthly, go ahead and keep that date. I'm going to enter depreciation quarterly, so I've changed the date from April 30 to June 30.

What's this I hear about a Section 179 deduction?

The Section 179 deduction (named for the section of the Internal Revenue Code that defines the deduction) is the IRS's way of letting you deduct the full cost of your depreciable assets in the year of acquisition, instead of trying to figure out all the rules for calculating depreciation costs. The amount of Section 179 depreciation you can take has a limit, and this limit seems to change depending on how generous or stingy our Congressmen feel. For 2005, eligible taxpayers are allowed to deduct the full purchase price of assets up to $105,000.

For 2006 and 2007, the annual Section 179 deduction limitation is supposed to increase based on an adjustment for inflation. As of this printing, the Section 179 deduction limitation is scheduled to revert to $25,000 in 2008 with no annual adjustment for inflation.

There are many rules and restrictions regarding the use of Section 179, so it's possible you or your asset won't qualify for the deduction. It's best to check with a tax advisor before choosing to expense your assets. Take a look at the "Whoa! Not so fast with that Section 179 deduction!" sidebar before you start adding up how much of your asset costs you can deduct.

Whoa! Not so fast with that Section 179 deduction!

You've probably heard the saying that a little knowledge can be a dangerous thing. That statement definitely applies to the Section 179 deduction, the tax deduction that allows you to avoid calculating depreciation on fixed assets and take an expense deduction for the entire purchase price instead. I can't say strongly enough how important it is that you discuss the depreciation treatment of your assets with a tax professional. Here are just a few reasons why the Section 179 deduction might not be for you:

- Some assets don't qualify for the deduction. For example, a home office must be depreciated, not expensed. Heating and air conditioning units and property used in rental lodging, such as appliances or furniture, don't qualify for the deduction either.
- If you own property that qualified for a Section 179 deduction at one time but is no longer used more than 50 percent for business (such as a vehicle used partly for business and partly for personal purposes), you are subject to recapture rules that might require you to pay tax on some of the Section 179 amount previously deducted.
- If you sell an asset prior to the end of the asset's recovery period and you took a Section 179 deduction on that asset, you might face an unfavorable tax treatment on the profit from the sale of the asset.
- Depending on how much income your business reports, you might not get a tax benefit from claiming the Section 179 deduction.
- Even if your asset qualifies for the Section 179 deduction, if you expect to pay tax in a higher tax bracket in the future, you might be better off depreciating the asset and getting a greater benefit from deducting the depreciation in later years at a higher tax rate.

These are only some of the many considerations to keep in mind when thinking about taking a Section 179 deduction. Claiming the deduction is not a slam-dunk by any means. Talk to a tax pro and make sure you're following the law and, at the same time, giving yourself the best possible tax treatment for your depreciable assets.

4. **Select automatic entry.**

   In the Scheduling area of the Create Scheduled Transaction window, change the Remind Me choice to Automatically Enter. This way your transaction can be entered by Quicken in your register without your having to give any approval.

5. **Choose how many days of advance notice you want to receive.**

   I don't care to have advance notice of the depreciation transaction because it's not like I have to have money available to make a payment, so I've set my days in advance field to zero days. However, you can enter as many days notice as you want in this field.

6. **Choose the frequency you want Quicken to use for entering depreciation in your asset account.**

   I've selected Quarterly in the Frequency drop-down list for the frequency of my depreciation entries.

7. **Indicate last depreciation entry.**

   You need to let Quicken know when to stop entering depreciation amounts in your register. Calculate how many total depreciation entries there should be (five years of monthly entries would be 60 entries, five years of quarterly entries would be 20 entries, and so on), subtract the number of entries you've already made (one, if you're setting up this automation after making your first depreciation entry), and the remainder is the number you want to enter in the After xx Times field. I've entered 19 in my schedule.

8. **Complete the scheduled transaction.**

   Click OK to save the transaction and to put Quicken to work on entering your depreciation.

   Repeat these steps for each asset whose depreciation you want to automate.

Selling, Losing, Throwing Away, or Otherwise Getting Rid of Your Asset

Whether you keep your depreciable asset for the full term of the depreciation period or remove it from the premises before the depreciation period is up, at some point, you probably are going to want to remove the asset from your active accounts so it no longer shows up on your financial statements. Here are the alternatives for taking care of this task under a variety of circumstances.

- **You sell the asset.** In the case of a sale, you need to remove the asset from your accounts and also record the profit or loss on the sale. Say you sell the sample computer for $200 after using it for one year. After one year of depreciation at $50 per quarter, the computer value has been reduced by $200 to a total of $800. In the bank account register where you record the deposit for the money you received on the sale, enter your deposit as a split transaction. As you can see in Figure 4-7, I've entered the remaining value of the computer, $800, as a reduction in the computer account, and I've entered the $600 loss on the sale in a category called Loss from Sale of Asset. The net effect of subtracting the $600 loss from the $800 remaining undepreciated cost is my $200 deposit. In Figure 4-8, you can see that the computer's register now displays a zero balance. If you sell the asset for a profit instead of a loss, you still need to enter a transaction that reduces the asset balance to zero. The additional category in the split transaction will be a profit category instead of a loss category.

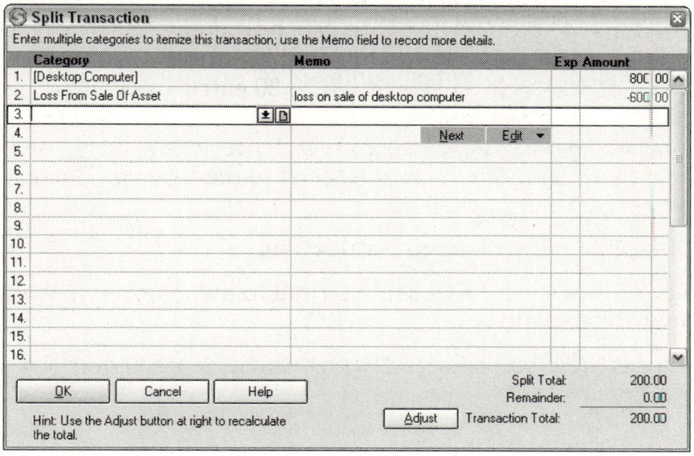

Figure 4-7: Enter the deposit from the asset sale in your cash account.

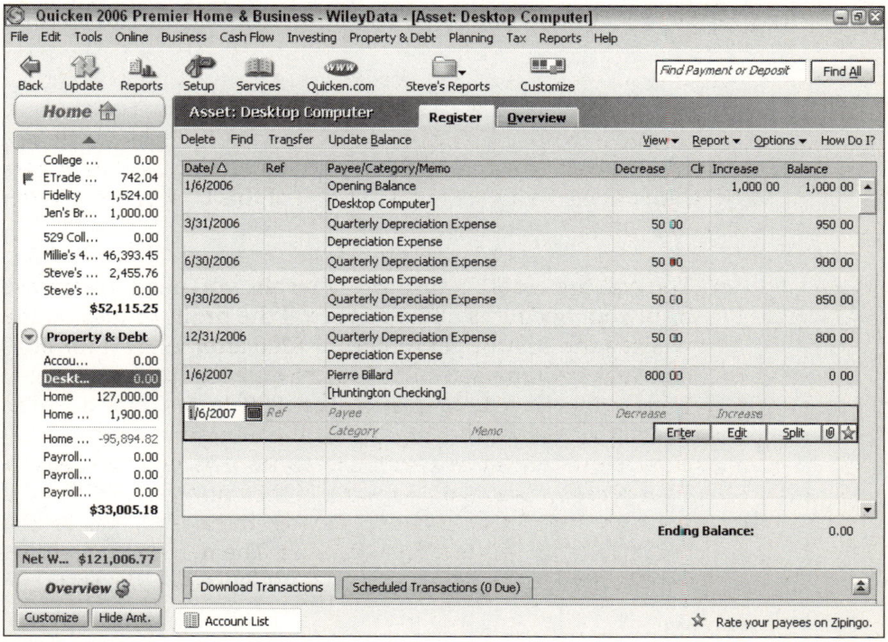

Figure 4-8: The split transaction from the cash account flows through to the account for the asset you sold.

✦ **You stop using the asset.** If the asset is no longer of use to you, and you discard or otherwise retire the asset, you need to make an entry in the Asset register itself, zeroing out the balance in the register and charging the remaining amount to an expense category. In this case, if I stopped using the asset after one year, I would charge the $800 remaining in the Asset register to computer expense and cease quarterly depreciation.

If you remove an asset or stop using an asset before the depreciation period is ended, be sure to change the rules of your scheduled transaction so that no additional depreciation amounts are recorded.

Chapter 5: Business Forms and Reports

In This Chapter

- Getting to know business forms
- Customizing business forms
- Reports to show how your business is doing

Plenty of visionaries foresee a world of offices completely devoid of paper. Personally, I probably produce enough paper to fill a couple of dozen offices all by myself. But that's me, and I'm way behind the times when it comes to saving and filing forms and reports electronically. Don't let me be a bad example for you. The firms that walked away intact from the 2005 Hurricane Katrina disaster in New Orleans are thanking their lucky stars they had the foresight to use a variety of online and offsite storage techniques for saving their data. Many companies returned to business in the days after Katrina, in a new location, but without missing a record-keeping beat. You'll be happy too when you see how easy it is to create and keep your documents with Quicken. Add a little creative back-up planning (see Appendix A) and you can go paperless too!

Getting to Know Common Business Forms

Several forms are found in the typical business office. Although these forms come in many different shapes and sizes and colors and scents (scents?), the basic form types remain the same. Here is a rundown of the categories into which most business forms fall:

- **Invoice:** The mighty invoice is the form you send someone who owes you money. We call the outgoing forms *invoices* and the incoming forms *bills* just to keep track of which is which, but the terms are actually interchangeable.
- **Statement:** A statement is a reminder that you send to a customer that hasn't gotten around to paying your invoice yet. The statement can be a copy of the original invoice with a friendly pay-up-or-else note attached, or it can be a completely separate form. In particular, if your customer hasn't paid several different invoices, you can use the statement to

summarize all of the outstanding invoices. Statements often act as little invoices themselves because a business often tacks on a late payment charge when they send a statement.

- **Estimate:** Another breed of invoice, the estimate is like a demo invoice, showing the customers what they can expect to see on an invoice if they order your products or services. Customers aren't expected to pay you when you give them an estimate.
- **Bill:** The bill is the flipside of an invoice, only this time, you're on the receiving end. Get a bill, and you can be sure someone across town is tapping a toe, drumming fingers on a desk, or performing some other act of impatience while waiting to receive your moolah.
- **Order, or purchase order:** Some companies like to have a formal record of what they ordered. The order form or purchase order provides that record, setting out exactly what the customer wants to buy.
- **Receipt for payment:** For those companies that really like to generate paperwork, there are the receipts, basically a thank-you note to the customer who paid the bill. The receipt also serves as evidence that the bill has been paid, so if the seller inadvertently sends out a statement demanding payment, the buyer can wave the receipt around, thumbing his nose and chanting, "Na-na-na-na-na!"
- **Check stub:** I'll throw this one out here with the others, just because I once worked in an office where we saved all of the check stubs from each check we wrote. The stub would be attached to the bill that was being paid, and then filed away in the proper file. (That was before we had computers where we could easily look online to see which check number was used to pay a bill.)

I'll bet if you looked around your office at all the different types of paperwork filling up your nooks and crannies, you could classify nearly every type of paper into one of the above categories.

Standard forms available from Intuit

So where do all these forms come from? Somebody has to be in the business of actually making forms so that all the other businesses have forms to send to each other. It's a vicious circle of some sort, no doubt conceived by some alien culture that's floating in space, just waiting for us to bury ourselves alive in an insurmountable heap of paperwork.

Many office forms have gone purely electronic. For example, every time I order a book online, for example, I see a screen showing me what the book is going to cost (bill), and after I dispatch my payment, I receive an e-mail message thanking me for my order (receipt). But forms of the paper variety are still the standard for many businesses. If you need to produce paper forms, you have a few choices. You can create your own paper forms, you can create forms right in Quicken or in other programs that you might own, or you can purchase preprinted forms.

TIP

If you want duplicate copies of your forms, the preprinted forms are probably your best bet — they come with duplicates built in. Or you can sit at your computer all day, pressing Ctrl+P to print the same forms over and over again.

You don't have to go far from the mothership to get standard, preprinted forms for use in your office and for use with your Quicken program. Take a quick trip to the Internet, as I demonstrate in the steps below, and you'll see what I mean:

1. **Open the Quicken home page, at `www.quicken.com`.**
2. **Click the Products & Services button at the top of the Quicken home page.**
3. **Open the Checks & Supplies page.**

   On the left side of the Products & Services page, in the Other Quicken Products section (Figure 5-1), click Quicken Checks & Supplies. Choose from a variety of products (Figure 5-2) offered by the kind folks at Quicken/Intuit.

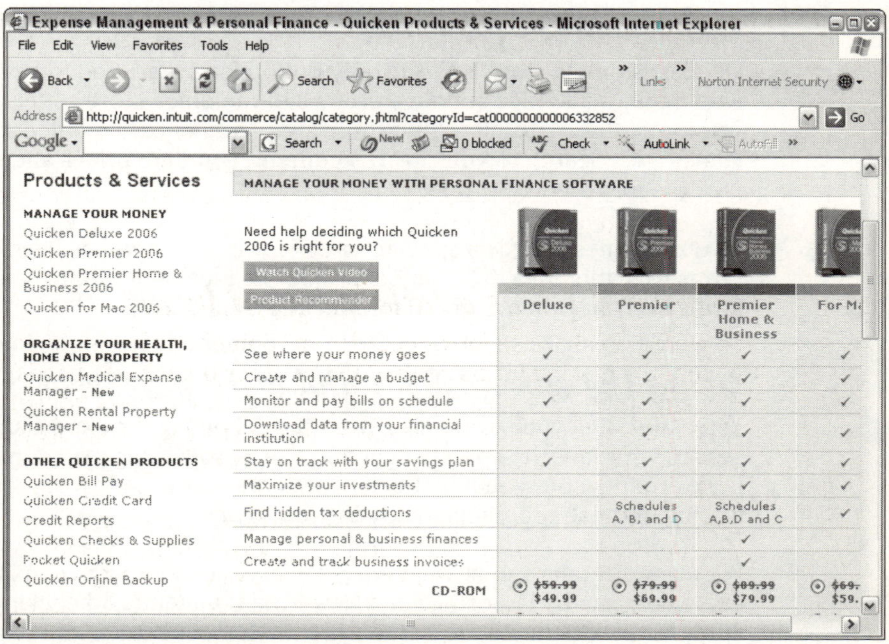

Figure 5-1: Click on Quicken Checks & Supplies to see the office products Intuit has to offer.

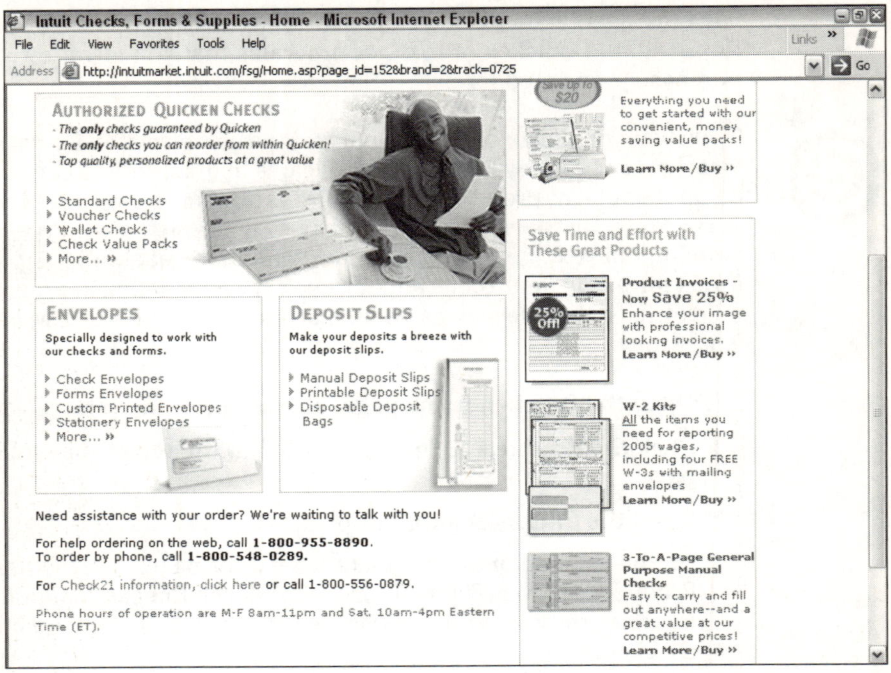

Figure 5-2: Quicken offers a variety of business forms that you can order online.

Other sources for forms

Quicken's online store isn't the only option for preprinted forms. Have you ever been to an office supply store? All of the office stores offer their own version of these products, and there are plenty of online office supply outlets as well. Search to your heart's content, compare prices and styles, and pick the forms you want.

If your business needs a special type of form, and if you use enough of the forms to justify the cost, don't overlook the idea of designing your own forms and have them printed for you at a print shop.

Using the spreadsheet and word processor

You can design your own forms from scratch using the expertise you possess in your favorite spreadsheet and word processing programs. And if you poke around a bit, you might discover some ready-made form templates lurking in those programs, ready for you to use.

For example, take a look at Figure 5-3. I found this invoice template in my Excel program by choosing File⇨New from the menu and clicking the Spreadsheet Solutions tab in the window that appeared. Other standard forms are available in Excel, and other programs offer similar model forms that you can put to use in your business.

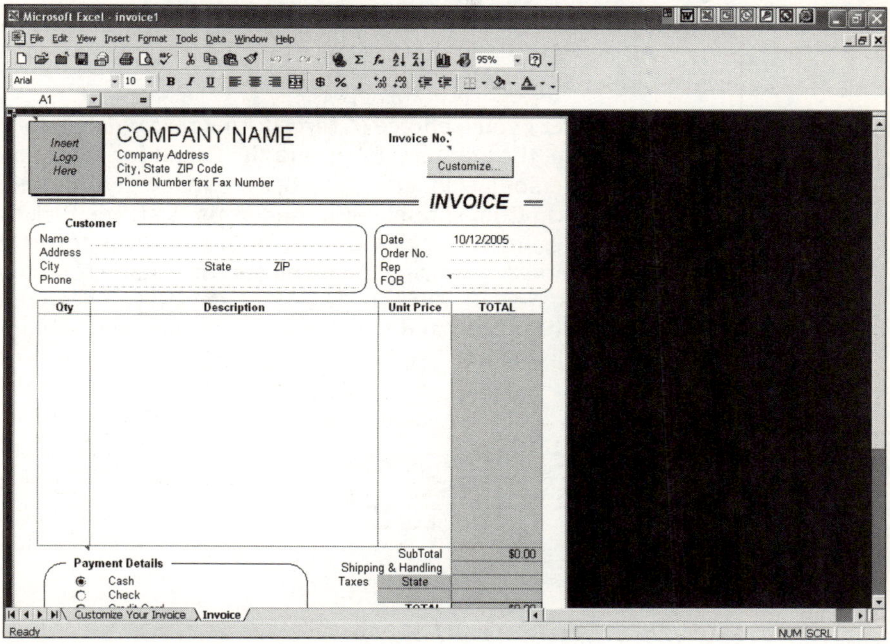

Figure 5-3: Look what I found in Excel!

Customizing forms in Quicken

As I discuss in Chapter 2 of this book, you can create invoices and other forms right in your Quicken program. If you don't like what you see onscreen, change it! It's not hard to take an existing Quicken form and customize the layout and the fields that appear on the form so that the form is more useful for your business. Here's an example of how you can create your own form right in Quicken:

1. **Display the Business Center.**

   Click the Business Center heading in the Account Bar at the left side of the screen. Make sure the Analysis & Reports tab is selected in the Business Center.

2. **On the right side of the Business Center window, in the Tools area, click the <u>Forms Designer</u> link (Figure 5-4) to open the Forms Designer.**

   The Forms Designer window appears, with an Invoice form displayed.

3. **Choose the form you want to design.**

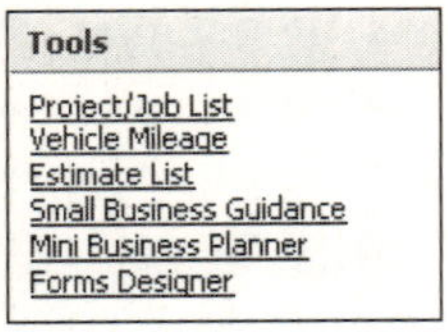

Figure 5-4: Click over to the Forms Designer.

Quicken offers you a choice of three forms that you can futz with: the Invoice form, the Estimate form, and the Credit form. You can create your own personalized, customized, systematic, hydromatic, greased-lightning form from scratch with the Forms Designer. Pick the form you want to redesign by clicking the Layout menu at the top of the Forms Designer. Choose New from the menu and the Create New Layout window appears (Figure 5-5). Click the Select a Layout Type drop-down menu to display your choices, and then choose from Invoice, Estimate, or Credit. I've picked Invoice to use for this example.

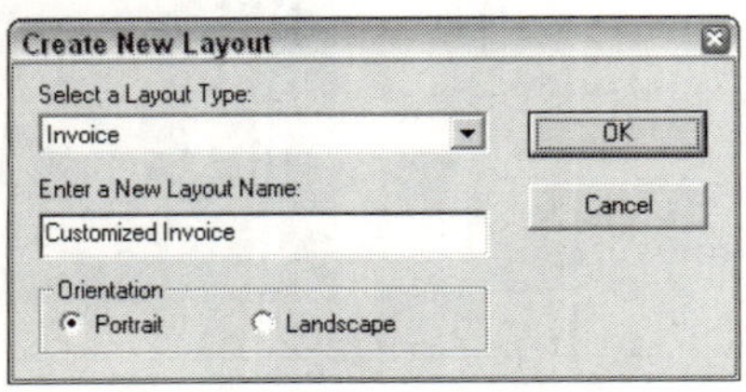

Figure 5-5: Pick which form you want to use as your starting point.

4. **Give your new form a name.**

   With the Create New Layout window still open, enter a name for this form in the Enter a New Layout Name field. If you need a variety of forms to use for different types of transactions, be sure to give this form a name that distinguishes it from the other forms you plan to create.

5. **Choose Portrait or Landscape.**

   Do you like your forms sideways? You can have the form tall (portrait) or wide (landscape) — make your choice. Then click OK and you're ready to begin designing.

6. **Choose the fields that should appear on your form.**

   On the left side of the Forms Designer, you see a list of all of the fields that are eligible to appear on the form. If you look closely at the list, you can see that each item that actually appears on the form is checked off in the little check box that appears next to the name of the field (see Figure 5-6). Your first order of business is to decide which fields you want to have on your customized form. Uncheck any fields you want to remove; leave checkmarks in the fields that should stay.

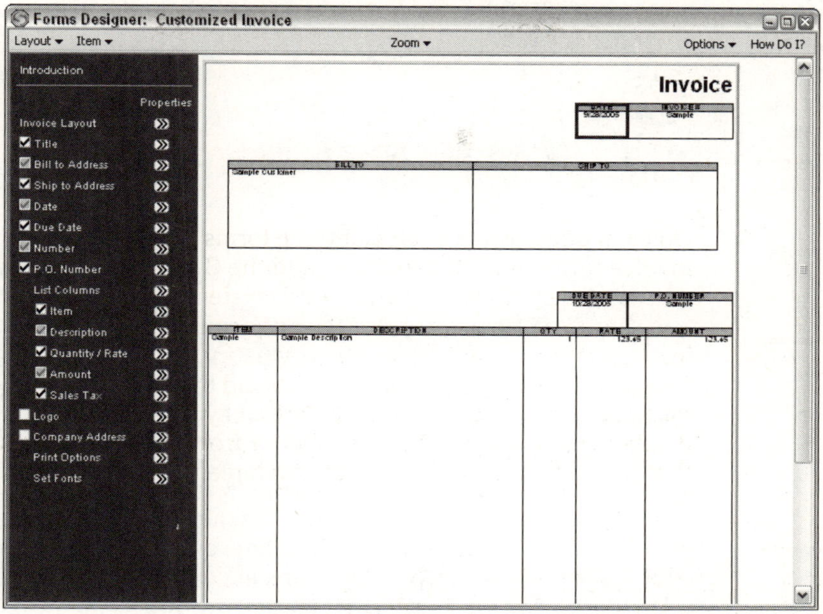

Figure 5-6: Pick which form you want to use as your starting point.

Some fields are required, and Quicken won't let you remove those fields in the Forms Designer. For example, on the Invoice form, you have to have a bill to address, a date, an invoice number, a description, and an amount. Quicken has dimmed the check boxes for these fields so you can't remove them. But you find out how you can get around this sticky rule in step 7.

7. **Change the names of fields!**

   Ha! So what if you can't take away the invoice number field? If you don't use invoice numbers, you can change the name of the field as it appears on the form, so that the field is called something more appropriate to your business. In this example, you make some changes to the actual fields that appear on this invoice. For this example, I'm going to create an invoice for an accountant who offers tax preparation services. First, instead of calling this form *Invoice*, I'm going to change the title that appears on the form to *Tax Preparation Services*. Click the Properties double-arrow that appears to the right of the Title field over in the left column, and a window called Title of Layout appears (Figure 5-7). Replace *Invoice* with *Tax Preparation Services* and click OK. The new title appears in place of the word *Invoice* on the form. Using the same technique, I'm also going to replace the name of the *Number* field with *Tax Return Year*. Finally, I'm going to keep the field for Bill To, but completely remove the name by just leaving the name field blank.

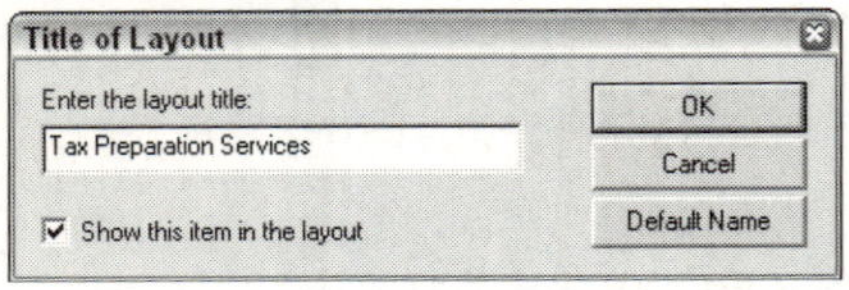

Figure 5-7: Change the name of any title on the report to a name that's more appropriate to your business.

8. Resize the field.

Uh-oh. I changed the name of the title to *Tax Preparation Services* but it appears that that title doesn't fit on my form (Figure 5-8). That problem can be remedied by changing the size of the field. Click on the form, right on the field you want to resize, and a blue outline appears around that field. Place your mouse pointer on the edge of the outline and drag to stretch or shrink the field. After I resized my Title field, the entire title fits (Figure 5-9).

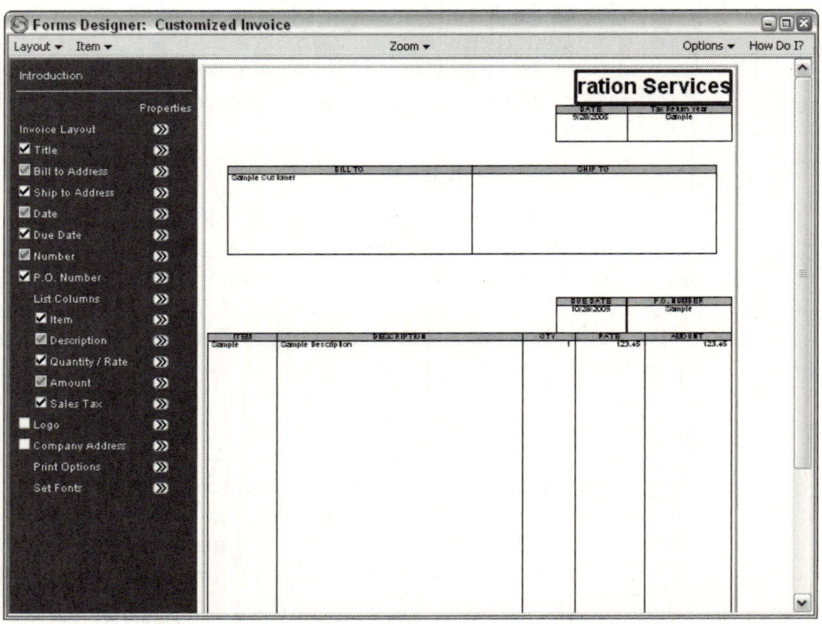

Figure 5-8: Sometimes the fields provided aren't the right size for the text you want to enter.

9. **Move the field by dragging.**

   You can drag fields around on the report if you want to place them in a different location. For example, I'm going to drag my title over so it appears in the center of the form instead of on the right side. Click any field to drag it to a new location. If you want to align the field with another field that appears on the report, use the Align option on the Item menu. The next step shows how Align works.

10. **Resize the field based on an existing field.**

    You can drag a field to get to the size you want, or you can let Quicken resize the field to match an existing field so that you make sure you get exactly the size you want. I want my Date field to be exactly the same size as my Number field (which I renamed to *Tax Return Year*, using the method in step 7). So I click on the field I want to resize (the Date field) and choose Item➪Size Item. When the Size Layout Item window appears, I click the Number field (still called Number, as you can see on the list at the left, even though I've changed the heading of the field to T*ax Return Year*) because that's the field I want to match to. I want both the height and the width of the fields to be identical, so I pick Both in the Size Settings (Figure 5-9), and then click OK. My two fields are now of identical size.

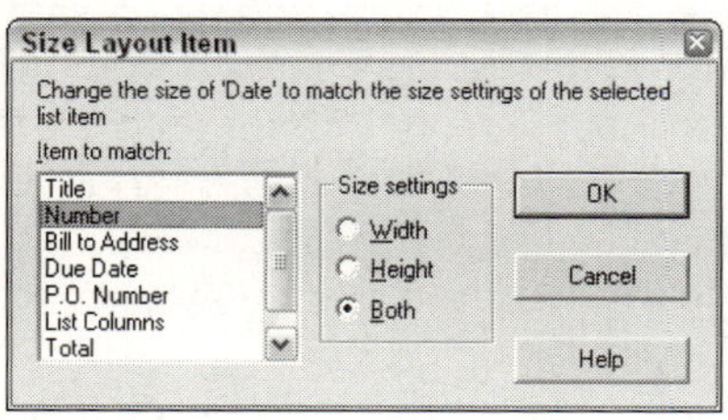

Figure 5-9: Resize fields with precision using the Size Layout Item window.

11. **Align one field with another.**

    For a precise placement of a field and a more professional look, you can align one field with another. Click on the field you want to align, and then choose Item➪Align Item from the menu to open the Align Layout Item window. In Figure 5-10, you can see that I've moved my Date field beneath the Number field. I want the right and left edges of these two fields to line up with one another. I click on the Date field, and then choose Align Item from the Item menu. In the window that appears, I choose Right Border and Right Border for the two sides I want to match up, making sure that Number is selected as the field to align with in the drop-down list provided. I've already sized these two fields so they are the same size, so I only have to line up one edge for them to be aligned on both sides. The final result is that the right and left margins of the two fields are in precise alignment with one another.

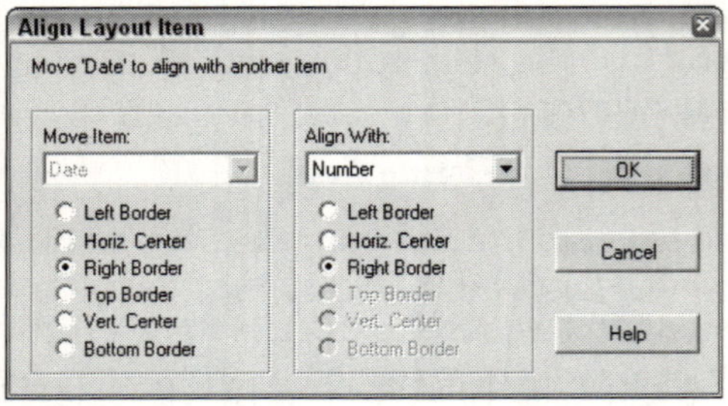

Figure 5-10: Use Align to match the placement of fields precisely.

12. **If you decide you're not content with dragging my title to the center of the form and eyeballing it, you can ensure that the title is *exactly* in the center of the form.**

    I click on the Title field, and then choose Position from the Item menu. In the Position Item in Page window that appears (Figure 5-11), I choose Horiz. Center and click OK. The title moves to the dead center between the two horizontal margins.

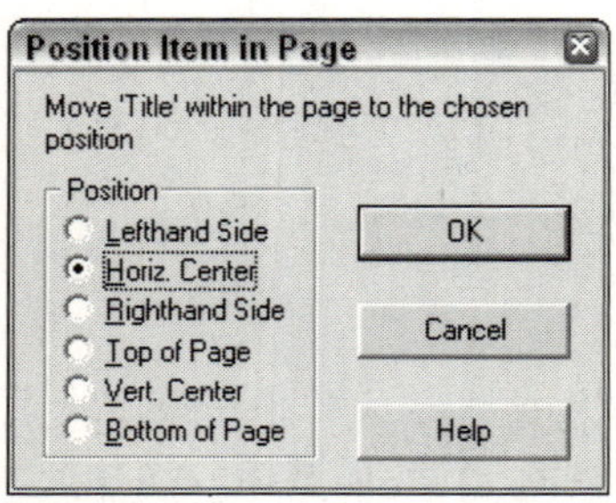

Figure 5-11: Position a field exactly where you want it.

13. **Make other changes until you're satisfied with the layout of the form.**

    Continue working with the form until you get it just the way you want it to look. For my form, I did away with the Item, Ship To Address, P.O. Number, Quantity, Rate, and Sales Tax fields.

14. **Change type styles.**

    You can customize the font choice on your forms as well. I think the form title is too stark, so I'm going to change the font to something more soothing. Click the double arrow next to the Set Fonts option on the left side of the Forms Designer. The Set Layout Fonts window appears (Figure 5-12). From the Select Layout Font to Set drop-down list, pick the item for which you want to change a font. You can change the font for any or all of the items on list, but only one item can be changed at a time. I've chosen Title Text Font for my first change.

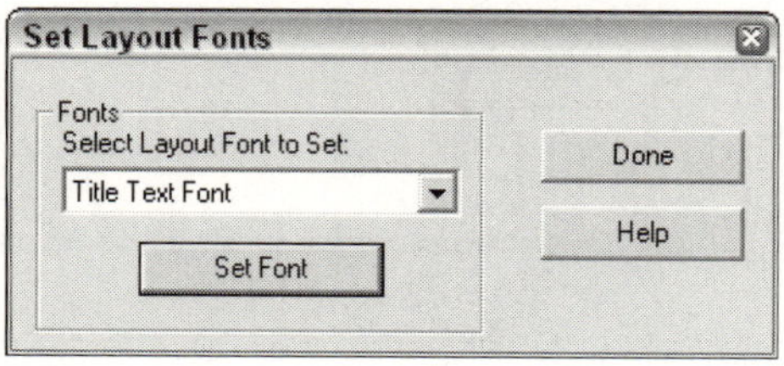

Figure 5-12: Change the fonts on your form.

15. **Open the Fonts window.**

    Having selected the area of the form that needs a new font, click the Set Font button and the Font window appears. Choose the font, the style, and the size you want to use, and then click OK. Your change is incorporated into the report.

    WARNING! Changing the size of the fonts can cause some fields to move around a bit. You might have to relocate some of the fields after you're finished changing the fonts.

16. **Enter company information.**

    You can enter your company name and address, and you can also place a logo on the form if you have one. Click the Logo option on the left side of the designer window to open the Print Logo dialog box to print your company name or click the Browse button to upload the file containing your logo.

    Click the Company Address option on the left side of the designer window to open a field on the form window where you can enter your company name and address. Then you can use the Font option as described in step 14 above to change the font for your company address information if you like.

17. **Save your finished form.**

    All that work — don't forget to save! Take a look at your finished project and pat yourself on the back (you can see my finished project in Figure 5-13). Then, click the Layout menu at the top of the Forms Designer window and choose Save. The form is saved using the name you entered way back in step 4. (Actually, it appears that Quicken automatically saves the form, but the Save option appears on the menu, so just for good measure, it makes sense to use this option. It can't hurt . . . .)

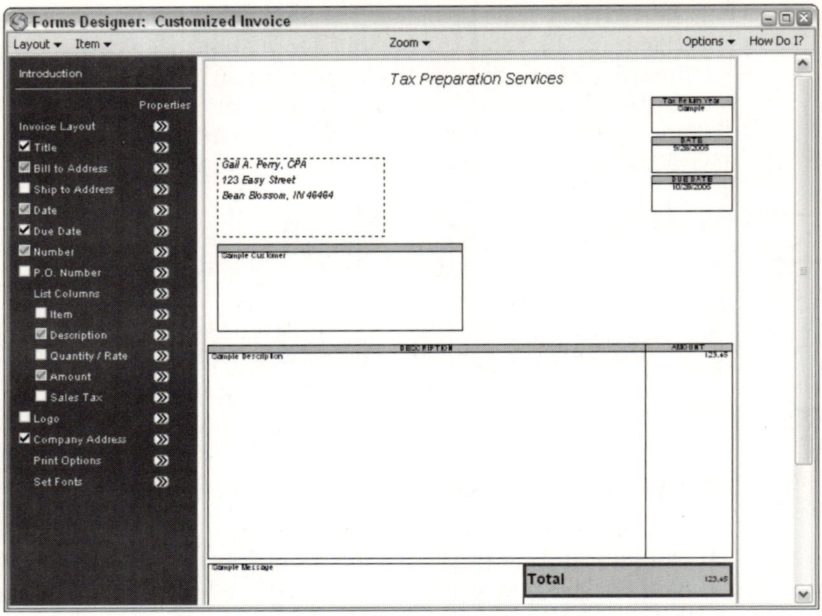

Figure 5-13: Don't forget to save your finished form!

18. **Click the X in the upper-right corner to close the designer window.**

    Rather than starting all over again, if you want to design another form that is similar to the one you just finished, click the Layout menu and choose Copy while your new form is still on display. You'll be asked to give the copy a name. Now you have two customized forms of the same type, and you can start designing a new form with all of the features of your other customized form.

Creating Business Reports in Quicken

Reports are a necessary part of running a business. You have to know how your business is doing, whether you're making money, how much your customers owe you, how much you owe, where your money comes from and where it goes, and so on. Many of the reports you need are standard in Quicken and have been covered in Book VII. But a few reports are unique to the Home & Business version of Quicken, and you should be familiar with them. Choose Reports⇨Business from your Quicken menu, or open the Reports & Graphs Center and click on Business. You'll see the business reports that Quicken considers to be standard (see Figure 5-14).

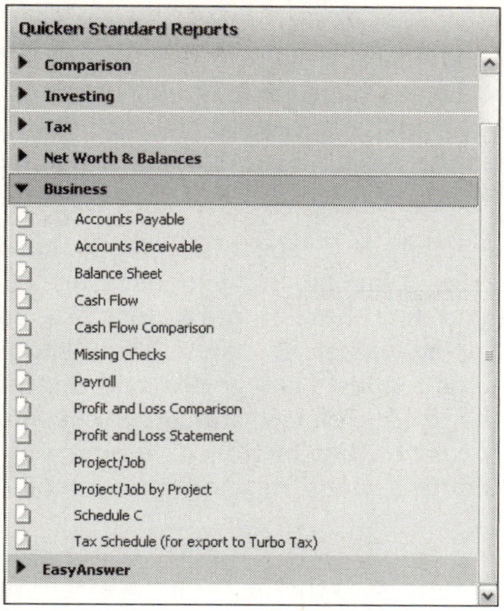

Figure 5-14: These are the standard business reports that come with your Quicken program.

Click on a report name, and you'll immediately see a little notice if the report is available only in Home & Business. Only a few reports are available only in Home & Business, and of those, some are available with a different name in other versions of Quicken.

Herewith, a quick rundown of some of the more important business reports you'll find only in Home & Business:

✦ **Payroll:** The payroll report shows a list of all your payroll accounts and categories, both income and expense, along with a separate column for each of your employees. If you recall, in Chapter 4 of this book, I set up some payroll accounts and categories. I was careful to place the word *Payroll* in the name of each account or category. Quicken seeks out these accounts and categories containing the word *Payroll*, and that is what is assembled on the payroll report.

✦ **Profit and loss statement and profit and loss comparison:** Much like their cousins, the income and expense reports, the P&L reports show your income, your expenses, and the difference between the two. The P&L comparison report lets you specify two different periods of time to compare performance. For example, you might want to know how you did during the same quarter last year and this year. The P&L comparison report tells you. Notice that the P&L reports in the Business section of the Reports & Graphs list indicate they are only available in Home & Business. However, there are income and expense comparison and cash flow comparison reports available in other versions of Quicken. These reports can get you to information like the business P&L reports.

- **Project/job reports:** These reports are unique to Home & Business. They display the income and expenses for your projects, grouped by project or class. You don't have access to projects in non-Home & Business versions of Quicken, but you do have access to classes, and you can create a report pretty similar to the project/job reports by organizing your reports by classes.
- **Schedule C report:** The Schedule C report in Home & Business summarizes the Schedule C business income and expenses according to the Schedule C tax lines. If you don't have Home & Business, you can do what I've done. I've set up a Quicken file where I use Schedule C Income and Schedule C Expense as top-level categories, and then all of the Schedule C transactions are entered into subcategories under these two top-level categories. It's easy to then customize a report to show just the transactions in the Schedule C categories, and this can be done in any version of Quicken.

The bottom line on business reports is that, although certain reports are set up for you in Quicken Home & Business and are extremely handy, you can get the information you need out of any version of Quicken by choosing and customizing the reports that display transactions from the categories you want to analyze.

Whenever you customize a business report that you find is useful, take the extra time to memorize the report so that you can access the report again in the future without having to re-create the report from scratch.

Quicken's standard reports appear on the left side of the Reports & Graphs window. Over on the right side of the window is the list of reports you have created and saved. If you're frantically searching for a report you customized in the past, check out the list on the right side of the Reports & Graphs window.

Index

Numerics

A

B

C

D

E

F

G

H

M

N

O

P

Q

R

S

T

U

V

W

Y

Notes

Notes